LEGALITY AND LOCALITY

*The Role of Law in Central–Local
Government Relations*

Legality and Locality

*The Role of Law in Central–Local
Government Relations*

MARTIN LOUGHLIN

CLARENDON PRESS · OXFORD
1996

Oxford University Press, Walton Street, Oxford OX2 6DP

Oxford New York
Athens Auckland Bangkok Bombay
Calcutta Cape Town Dar es Salaam Delhi
Florence Hong Kong Istanbul Karachi
Kuala Lumpur Madras Madrid Melbourne
Mexico City Nairobi Paris Singapore
Taipei Tokyo Toronto
and associated companies in
Berlin Ibadan

Oxford is a trade mark of Oxford University Press

Published in the United States
by Oxford University Press Inc., New York

British Library Cataloguing in Publication Data
Data available

Library of Congress Cataloging in Publication Data
Loughlin, Martin.
Legality and locality : the role of law in central-local
government relations / Martin Loughlin.
p. cm.
Includes bibliographical references and index.
1. Central-local government relations—Great Britain. 2. Local
government—Law and legislation—Great Britain. I. Title.
KD4765.L68 1996
342.41'09—dc20 [344.1029] 96–13511
ISBN 0–19–826015–6

1 3 5 7 9 10 8 6 4 2

Typeset by Graphicraft Typesetters Ltd., Hong Kong
Printed in Great Britain
on acid-free paper by
Bookcraft Ltd., Midsomer Norton, Avon

For Nancy

CONTENTS

ACKNOWLEDGEMENTS

This book has had such a long gestation period that I find it almost impossible properly to acknowledge the help that I have received. My filing cabinets, which are stuffed full of unpublished papers, reports, notes and opinions, attest to the generosity of so many people not only in local and central government but also from other public agencies, the world of finance and the legal and accounting professions. Since a number of these people prefer to remain anonymous, I feel that the best course would simply be to express in rather general terms my profound thanks to them all. So far as my academic colleagues are concerned, I trust that my debts to them are properly acknowledged in the notes to the text. There is, however, a small group for whom that recognition would be altogether inadequate. Malcolm Grant, Jeffrey Jowell and Patrick McAuslan have provided a constant source of encouragement, especially in those early years when the fog seemed thickest. They have read and commented on many of the papers in which the views I express in this book have been shaped. More recently, I am specifically indebted to Colin Crawford, Neil Duxbury, John Evans and Anthony Ogus for the care, precision and skill with which they have commented on particular chapters in draft form. If the reader thinks that the thesis of the book remains obscure or lies too deeply buried under detailed exposition, it will not be for the want of this group trying to get me to express my argument more clearly or concisely.

Most of my writing on this subject over the last decade or so has, in one form or another, been commissioned. Given the pace of change in the field this is not altogether surprising; otherwise, much academic commentary without a previously identified outlet would have been overtaken by events by the time it was published. I should therefore like to thank those who, during this period, have invited me to write or present papers on particular topics within this field. Not only did they provide me with the opportunity to have a first stab at the issue, but they also helped me to stick with the subject when other avenues were beginning to look more enticing (and certainly more straightforward). I am particularly obliged to the Commission for Local Democracy and to the editor of *Public Law* for permission to draw directly on material which was first published by them and which forms the basis for chapters 2 and 6 respectively. Finally, I should like to thank Richard Hart at OUP for his patience and encouragement throughout.

Martin Loughlin

TABLE OF CASES

UK CASES

EC CASES

US CASE

TABLE OF LEGISLATION

STATUTES

STATUTORY INSTRUMENTS

EC DIRECTIVE

INTRODUCTION

This book seeks to trace the main dimensions of recent conflicts between central departments and local authorities and to reveal something of their significance. It does so by focusing on the role of law in shaping the central–local relationship. This is an aspect of central–local government relations which is neglected in many contemporary studies and yet is of vital importance in identifying the character of that relationship. Precisely why this should be so is not self-evident. The main objective of this introduction is therefore to highlight the importance of this legal dimension to the study of central–local relations and then to explain the way in which the key themes of the study are to be addressed.

Most contemporary studies of central–local government relations adopt a politico–economic approach. Since the recent conflicts between central departments and local authorities have provided the main institutional forum through which many of the ideological struggles of late twentieth century British politics have been fought out, this is readily understandable. In retrospect, it seems clear that the election of a Conservative government in 1979, after a period of Labour dominance during the 1960s and 1970s, marked a decisive shift in both politics and policy. Since then, the Conservatives have been granted four consecutive terms in office and have pursued a radical social and economic programme which has had a major impact on virtually all aspects of government. For various reasons, however, the institution of local government has been a key target for fundamental reform. Since most of these reforms have been vigorously opposed by many local authorities, this has generated a serious crisis in central–local government relations, not least because the Conservatives, during this period, have seen their power base in local government almost entirely destroyed.[1]

These recent conflicts in central–local government relations provide the main subject of this book. However, while the various economic, social and political changes are undoubtedly of the first importance in understanding the dynamic of central–local government relations, the legal dimension comprises an indispensable aspect of any attempt to assess the impact which these developments have had on our system of government. Law certainly has been a critical factor

---

[1] This process of decline has been occurring ever since the early 1980s. It is not without significance, e.g., that none of the metropolitan authorities abolished by the Local Government Act 1985 was Conservative-controlled. The cumulative effect of this progressive deterioration may be gauged by the fact that, after May 1995, the Conservatives controlled not one council in either Scotland or Wales and no councils in the metropolitan areas of England. Of around 500 local councils in Great Britain, there was in mid-1995 a Conservative administration in only 13 English authorities: 8 district councils, 1 county council and 4 London borough councils.

within the contemporary period. Indeed, one of the most important manifestations of the contemporary transformation in central–local government relations has been the utilization of law as a primary instrument for regulating the relationship. In recent years we have seen not only a tremendous growth in the volume of new legislation affecting local government but also the unprecedented phenomenon of the courts regularly being prevailed upon to act as an umpire in disputes between central departments and local authorities.

This book focuses on the legal dimension to these recent developments. Certainly, a great number of novel legal issues has arisen during this period, ranging from rather arcane matters of statutory interpretation to politically-charged disputes in which it seemed almost inevitable that the judiciary would find themselves bound up in controversy. From this perspective, the contemporary period constitutes an important chapter in the development of administrative law. Seen in this light, an important objective is to provide a documentary account of this episode and to place it in an appropriate context.

The book also has another, altogether more ambitious, objective, one which equally concerns public lawyers and those social scientists interested in the question of governance. It is tempting to suggest that this second objective is to address the constitutional issues raised by these developments but I hesitate to do so simply on the ground that, whenever such terminology is invoked in this country, academics tend to lose the capacity to talk about the issues in a balanced manner. Whatever label is placed upon this second objective, however, it is clear that some sort of framework is necessary for assessing the significance of recent trends. Questions about the character of this framework revolve around two basic themes. First, there is the theme of *locality*: what role has the idea of local government played in the shaping of our governing arrangements? What constitutional issues (if any) are raised once the central State ceases to recognize the need within our governing arrangements for a robust system of local government? The second theme is that of *legality*: what role has law performed in shaping our arrangements of government? And how effective can law be in regulating the relationship between central departments and local authorities?

Each of these themes contains both historic and contemporary dimensions. The former focuses on the question of whether a tradition of local government may be identified within the system of government which has evolved and also seeks to locate the traditional role of law in regulating government. The contemporary formulation raises a set of issues concerning the legitimacy and effectiveness of recent developments, two facets which, within our constitutional tradition, have often been entwined with one another. These two dimensions are closely linked since the existence of particular traditions of government can provide useful benchmarks against which to assess the significance of recent developments. But throughout this century the issues raised by the themes of locality and legality have remained largely hidden from view. Consequently, it is not easy even to present an adequate formulation of the issues.

These themes of locality and legality have been submerged primarily because of the existence of a political consensus over the character of the modern administrative State. As the tasks of government increased, local government was allocated a major set of responsibilities and became responsible for consuming around one quarter of total public expenditure. Since the importance of local government seemed self-evident, political scientists tended generally to focus on the issue of the functional effectiveness of the system rather than the intrinsic virtues of local institutions. Another facet of this general political consensus has been the fact that inter-governmental disputes have tended to be resolved by way of negotiation and bargaining through administrative channels. The efficacy of such networks has meant that lawyers have been insulated from the need to address some basic questions concerning the character of law in the modern administrative State. What has been particularly important about the developments since 1979, then, is that these difficult questions concerning our traditions of locality and legality have been exposed for examination.

I have tried to draw out the various aspects of this study in the form of a series of linked essays. Each chapter is relatively self-contained and is designed so that it may be read independently of the others. Each examines a particular theme concerning the role of law in central–local government relations. Nevertheless, the essays are so arranged that they may be seen as building on one another to form an integrated view of the subject. They are designed cumulatively both to provide a documentary account of the legal aspects of recent developments and to present an explication of the general themes of legality and locality.

Given the book's general themes, the identification of a tradition of local government, and a traditional role for law within that tradition, is of crucial importance. This issue is examined in Chapter 1, 'The Question of Local Government'. What are the main characteristics of the tradition of local government within the British system of government? What significance does this tradition have within the modern arrangements of government? What role has law played in underpinning this tradition of local government? In Chapter 1, I try to show that the tradition of local government does have a particular meaning. Notwithstanding the claim that England is 'pre-eminently the country of local government',[2] however, this tradition is today better understood as a modern rather than an ancient tradition, one which derives its strength not from any formal division of power between the centre and the localities but instead (somewhat paradoxically) from the acknowledged sovereign authority of the centre. Rather than viewing local government as an autonomous sphere of responsibility, it should actually be seen as an arena in which the centre is bound up in the affairs of the localities. Nonetheless, it is a tradition in which local authorities have been accorded a broad discretionary authority within an interdependent network of government to administer within their areas. Our tradition of local government

[2] E. Jenks, *An Outline of English Local Government* (London, 5th edn., 1921), 9.

rests primarily on modern practices which are sustained by a set of political understandings.

This tradition of local government has important implications for thinking about law. Modernization, having been accomplished without a fundamental constitutional break, has been essentially a political achievement. One consequence of this is that the modern reformation of local government is not always fully reflected in the legal framework which underpins the institution. Institutional continuity has meant that there can be no clear separation between what Maitland called 'folk-law' and 'jurist-law'[3] and the ramifications of this have not often been properly acknowledged. The issue may perhaps be more clearly expressed by transposing Maitland's terminology into a contemporary idiom. Thus, a distinction might be drawn between the idea of law as an expression of the normative ordering of society and law as a juridical nexus of rights and duties enforceable in the courts. Today, most lawyers have become accustomed to thinking about law only in the latter sense. In so doing, however, they are thereby unable to give expression to the position of local government within our system of government, since that status is not simply a product of positive law. Further, it is not simply the case that positive law needs to be supplemented by conventional understandings. Rather, it is necessary to understand the general political culture within which the legal framework is embedded even to make sense of that structure of positive law. If we aim to understand the role of law within government, we are obliged to embrace the broader idea of law as the institutionalization of social life.

It is only by adopting this broader conception of law that we can understand the link between locality and legality. And it is only once these traditions have been assimilated that the significance of contemporary developments may be grasped. What in essence has occurred is that the political consensus which sustained the tradition of local government and which conferred meaning on the juridical structure of the central–local government relationship began to disintegrate. Though the roots of the difficulties lie deeply buried in structures of the modern reformation, the strains became manifest as the Government acted radically to alter the role of local government in social life. The general implications of these recent developments on the status of local government are examined in Chapter 2, 'Contemporary Trends', which touches on the constitutional question of the continuing importance of the institution of local government in the contemporary framework of government.

One critical aspect of the changes which are outlined in Chapter 2 is that of the role undertaken by law in the process of reform. What in effect has happened is that, as the networks sustained by conventional understandings have been challenged, affected interests have turned to positive law as an authority structure governing the central–local government relationship. This has resulted in

---

[3] F.W. Maitland, *Township and Borough* (Cambridge, 1898), 14.

what may be termed the 'juridification' of central–local government relations. The concept of juridification here has a relatively precise meaning; it refers to a process through which 'folk-law' is being supplanted by 'jurist-law' as the determinant of that relationship. This general process of juridification of central–local government relations is of fundamental importance. It involves a basic shift in legal consciousness, causing us to turn immediately to positive law in seeking to discern the nature of the relationship and to search for meaning in a particular legal text rather than first seeking to understand custom and practice in order to cast light on the significance of that text within the general regulatory framework. Juridification involves nothing less than a shift in the conception of legality incorporated within the structure of governance of this country.

Juridification of the central–local government relationship has not only been a major undertaking; it has also been a highly complex, ambiguous, confusing and frustrating exercise. In so far as it may be assumed to be a deliberate policy of the centre, the Government seems both to have over-estimated the complexity of law and under-estimated the complexity of the environment it was supposed to regulate. Many of the practices associated with juridification have been the subject of widespread disapproval throughout the system and have often been associated with policy failure. The process highlights many of the issues which have been raised concerning the legitimacy and effectiveness of recent developments; it also seems to be directly linked to the issue of locality. Certainly the thrust of recent legislation has been to treat local government more as an instrument of central government policy than as an institution of community governance. But even in the areas of ambiguity, the judiciary seems incapable of giving expression to any alternative image of local government. In part, this has been because, within the modern framework of central–local relations an informal (non-juridified) structure of administrative law has emerged, the effect of which has been for most of the century to conceal many of the critical questions from the attention of the judiciary. The traditionalists on the bench thus tend either to defer to the wisdom of public authorities or (if they suspect that something is wrong) simply to assert jurisdiction without any adequate justification, while those modernizers who identify the need to develop a new jurisprudence invariably seek to construct one on a platform of individualistic rights and duties. None of these approaches seems able satisfactorily to accommodate the idea of local authorities as institutions of governance.

The general significance of this process of juridification is only gradually becoming clear. This is hardly surprising since not only has the pace of recent change been frenetic but also it seems evident that the implications of the process are many-faceted. I have therefore tried to simplify the exercise by using each chapter to follow through the issues from a particular perspective. In Chapter 3, I examine 'The Challenge of Municipal Socialism'. During the 1980s, many Labour-controlled local authorities sought to rekindle a tradition of 'municipal socialism', an exercise which resulted in these councils developing collectivistic policies which were in direct antagonism to those being promoted by central government. Their abililty to develop such initiatives in a hostile governmental environment in itself provides a useful index of the degree of autonomy which remained vested in local institutions. From our perspective, however, what is especially interesting is that their attempt to do so resulted in the local councils themselves being obliged to engage in a systematic examination of the legal capacity of local government shorn of conventional restraints. The resulting central–local conflict thus highlights in a particularly acute fashion the flexibility and ambiguity of the legal framework governing that relationship. Furthermore, since many of the more interventionist and controversial powers acquired by central government have been drafted with the activities of this group of local authorities in mind, the study also provides some insight into the difficulties which the Government faced in seeking to use law as a primary instrument for regulating the system.

The nature of the modern framework of local government is one in which what the Webbs called the 'cash nexus'[4] comes to occupy a central role both in the design of local government and in the form of the central–local relationship. This idea of the 'cash nexus' reflects the potentially conflicting financial interests of three key groups: those who vote for local services, those who pay for them, and those who consume or benefit from them. With the emergence in the twentieth century, first, of a democratic foundation for local government and then later the assumption by central government of a responsibility both for the management of the economy and the welfare of society, the form which the cash nexus has taken has become highly complex. And it has been partly the complexity and fluidity of this nexus that has resulted in the courts being displaced and coming to play a marginal role in regulating the system.

Perhaps the most important mechanism through which the centre has exerted its influence over the cash nexus has been through the use of grants in aid of local expenditure. As the proportion of local expenditure met by central grants increased, distribution arrangements of ever greater intricacy have been devised in an attempt to ensure that greater financial dependency did not serve to transform local authorities simply into agents of the centre. As a result, during the second half of this century, most central support has taken the form of a general grant which has been unhypothecated to specific services and whose general shape has been determined as a result of discussions between affected parties within administrative networks. It is certainly an aspect of the governmental process in which the courts have been almost totally uninvolved. In recent years, however, this has changed. As central government has increasingly sought to use the grant mechanism as an instrument of expenditure restraint, conflicts have been generated and this has resulted in local authorities turning to the courts to act as umpires of the central–local financial relationship. This fascinating, though

---

[4] S. & B. Webb, *English Local Government* (London, 1922), vol. 4, 435.

rather disconcerting, episode is examined in Chapter 5, 'On Tapers, Targets and Caps'. In this chapter, the complexities of the system and the challenges presented to the courts are analysed. In general, the episode highlights not only the limitations in the use of courts as regulators of the financial relationship but also the problems associated with the exercise of seeking to transform such a complex relationship into a rule-based game.

Though the courts have not generally been involved in policing the cash nexus in local government, there has nevertheless been one aspect of this nexus which the courts have been prepared to express in the form of a relatively precise juridical relationship. During the twentieth century, the judiciary have occasionally articulated a specific legal duty which a local authority is said to owe to its ratepayers. In Chapter 4, 'Fiduciary Duty in Public Law', the origins and status of this judicially-developed concept are examined. This duty has assumed a particular importance in recent times. In part this has been because of the ramifications of the decision of the House of Lords in *Bromley LBC* v. *Greater London Council*.[5] Another influential factor, however, has been the nature of the reforms promoted by the Government. Many of the recent reforms may be understood as attempts to refashion the cash nexus in local government in a form designed to give much greater influence to those who pay for local services. The concept of fiduciary duty thus seemed to be one which the Government might actually be able to harness for the purpose of using the courts as a powerful enforcement agency for this general political programme. In Chapter 4 this experience is analysed. Though the judiciary resisted the opportunity to transform their role into one of ensuring that local authorities were not thriftless in their use of ratepayers' money, the resurrection of the fiduciary concept in *Bromley* did create a great deal of uncertainty during the early years of the decade and certainly contributed to the destabilization of the traditional framework of central–local government relations at a critical moment of transition.

Chapter 6 on 'Innovative Financing in Local Government' explores one specific response within local government to the breakdown of conventional practices. When the Government began to use the system of local government finance as an instrument of expenditure restraint, it appeared not to recognize fully that accounting practices in local government had traditionally been the product of administrative guidance or professional norms rather than precise legal prescription. Consequently, when the financial squeeze was applied through the establishment of centrally-imposed expenditure targets or caps on rate levels, many local authorities simply responded to this rule-game by examining various methods of optimizing their financial position. The result was the proliferation of various schemes, some of great complexity, which were devised primarily to circumvent central controls. These various schemes not only frustrated the Government's expenditure objectives but also considerably enhanced both the financial and

---

[5] [1983] 1 AC 768.

legal risks at stake as a result of local authority involvement in capital markets. When a number of these risks materialized in circumstances of great controversy, their effect was felt throughout the system of local government. In Chapter 6, these various practices are examined and the legal problems associated with them are analysed. In general, the essay highlights some of the problems that arise when a highly complex system which functions through self-regulation based on professional standards is both politicized and legalized.

Finally, in Chapter 7, 'The Juridification of Central–Local Government Relations', the impact of these recent developments on the institutions of government is examined and evaluated. One effect of the Government's local government programme has been to ensure that both Parliament and the courts have become more actively involved in local government affairs. In neither respect has this been a particularly gratifying experience. Though Parliament has over the last sixteen years been responsible for approving a local government legislative programme of unprecedented scale, the contemporary experience reveals little of the historic role of Parliament as an institution for airing local grievances. Rather, the episode seems simply to illustrate the extent to which Parliament has now been transformed into an instrument of Government policy. The general effect of this legislative programme has been to reinforce the basic thrust of recent trends which has resulted in law becoming utilized as a primary tool for regulating the central–local relationship. And this instrumentalization of law has inevitably affected the role of the courts within the system. This has also been a rather unsettling experience which largely highlights the institutional and cultural limitations on the judiciary's ability to police the system. If the basic message to be read from the Government's programme is that locality is no longer an important touchstone within modern government, the phenomenon of juridification must essentially be viewed as a symptom of the constitutional problems which that programme has exposed.

Ultimately, what the book seeks to demonstrate is that the issues raised by this study do not simply concern the institution of local government. Our tradition of local government is directly linked to our system of parliamentary democracy. Further, the manner in which the system of central–local government relations has evolved reveals a great deal about our tradition of public law. An examination of these issues through an explication of the themes of legality and locality therefore requires us to address some basic questions about the nature of contemporary British government.

1

THE QUESTION OF LOCAL GOVERNMENT

The recent conflicts in central–local government relations have left many commentators struggling to find a vocabulary through which to provide a satisfactory explanation of changes which have been taking place. The endeavour has not been wholly successful. The language of constitutional discourse, for example, is today riddled with ambiguities. It is not even clear whether this is a descriptive or normative language; and certainly when used normatively it is manifestly incapable of commanding anything like universal endorsement.[1] Then there are those who draw on recent trends to proclaim 'the death of local government'.[2] What remains unexplained in such analyses is the fact that there has scarcely been a time when local government has not been viewed by some as languishing in a critical condition;[3] and, indeed, that it may be from the existence of such tensions that local government is actually sustained.[4] Furthermore, even if such prognostications were well-founded, we remain unsure whether we should mourn the loss or put out the flags to welcome in a new era of lean, task-orientated,

[1] See, e.g., M. Elliott, *The Role of Law in Central–Local Relations* (London, 1981) which seeks to identify the basic propositions underpinning the constitutional framework of central–local government relations. Cf. M. Grant, 'The role of the courts in central–local relations' in M. Goldsmith (ed.), *New Research in Central–Local Relations* (Aldershot, 1986), 191, at 195: 'Elliott ... offers no criteria for moving from description of certain widespread practices ... to asserting that they have a prescriptive effect, save that his propositions are based on constitutional assumptions that are shared by both commentators and citizens'.

[2] See, e.g., A. Alexander, *The Politics of Local Government in the United Kingdom* (London, 1982), 2: 'Local government is an essential part of Britain's democracy, but unless conscious steps are taken to revive it, the end of local government may be in sight.'; T. Burgess and T. Travers, *Ten Billion Pounds. Whitehall's Takeover of the Town Halls* (London, 1980), 188: 'The [effect of the] Local Government, Planning and Land Bill 1980 ... will be within a very short time to replace genuine local government by the dependent outposts of a large central bureaucracy. It marks the beginnings of the wholly centralized state'.

[3] See, e.g., W.A. Robson, *Local Government in Crisis* (London, 1966), 150: 'there is a strong tendency [today] to concentrate power at the centre to an excessive degree and ... [a]s a consequence we are in danger of becoming a managerial society, with the levers of power in the hands of an elite ...'; E. Cannan, *The History of Local Rates in England* (London, 2nd edn., 1912), viii–ix: the growing use of central grants-in-aid amounts to a 'transfer of expense from the localities to the State' which will undermine our traditions of local self-government and will lead to 'the citizen deliver[ing] himself bound hand and foot into the custody of the official expert'; J.T. Smith, *Government by Commissions Illegal and Pernicious* (London, 1849), 53: 'Local self-government is [being] systematically attacked' by central government 'which is straining to make every fundamental law and institution of the country bend beneath the yoke of irresponsible centralized commissions'.

[4] See J.A.G. Griffith, 'Foreword' in M. Loughlin, D. Gelfand & K. Young (eds.), *Half A Century of Municipal Decline 1935–1985* (London, 1985), xi–xii.

responsive governance.[5] Nor can lawyers avoid these issues by retreating to some narrow conception of legal analysis. Cultural contextualization remains a critical aspect of legal analysis.[6] The real problem is that so much of that context has been taken for granted for so long that we are no longer able to identify the framework which might help us to assess the significance of contemporary developments.

One reason why lawyers have been unable to engage in evaluation is because of the poverty of what might, for want of a better term, be called politico–legal discourse. In particular, we have never managed to cultivate the facility of articulating, in a juristic language, the institutional framework of governance which commonly has been termed 'the State'.[7] The idea of the State has generally been shunned by English jurists, who have either hidden behind such ancient forms as 'the Crown' or have obscured the matter by focusing on the majestic concept of sovereignty. Sir Ernest Barker was certainly right in pointing out in 1914 both that '[t]he idea of the State is one which is little grasped in England' and that 'legally there is no such thing as the State'.[8] His underlying message, i.e., that there are reasons why, in the twentieth century, these questions might need to be addressed, seems to have been largely ignored.

In order to understand the significance of developments in central–local government relations, and in particular to assess the role of law in that process, the issues which Barker touches on must certainly be considered. This type of inquiry takes us into the peculiarities of our constitutional history and to the importance of a tradition of local government within that history. Local government is certainly not part of what Maitland called 'the showy side of the constitution'.[9] Yet, especially for those who believe that to know the city (let alone the empire) is to know its streets, it may be neglected only at the price of forming a highly distorted view of our constitutional arrangements. England has, for good reasons, been referred to as a 'stateless society', a society which lacks a state tradition.[10] In seeking to understand why a conception of the State was not forged in the evolving relation between government and society in England,[11]

[5] The case for change is presented and examined in: N. Ridley, *The Local Right: Enabling not Providing* (London, 1988); G. Mather, 'Thatcherism and Local Government: an evaluation' in J. Stewart and G. Stoker (eds.), *The Future of Local Government* (London, 1989); I. Holliday, 'The new suburban right in British local government – Conservative views of the local' (1991), vol. 17, no. 6, *Local Government Studies*, 45.
[6] See C. Geertz, *Local Knowledge. Further Essays on Interpretive Anthropology* (New York, 1983), 181.
[7] For an examination of the historical emergence of the idea of the State see: Q. Skinner, 'The State' in T. Ball, J. Farr & R.L. Hanson (eds.), *Political Innovation and Conceptual Change* (Cambridge, 1989), ch. 5.
[8] E. Barker, 'The Rule of Law' (1914) 2 *Pol. Q.* 117, at 139, 118.
[9] F.W. Maitland, 'The materials for English legal history' in *Collected Papers* (Cambridge, H.A.L. Fisher ed., 1911), vol. II, 1 at 7.
[10] K.H.F. Dyson, *The State Tradition in Western Europe* (Oxford, 1980), viii, 36–44.
[11] This book examines law and government in England and Wales only. Wales has been absorbed into the English system since at least 1535, when the Statute of Wales completed the organization of Welsh lands into English shires. The book thus refers to 'the English State'. On the general difficulties of conceptualizing the British State see: J.G.A. Pocock, 'The Limits and Divisions of British History: In Search of the Unknown Subject' (1982) 87 *American Hist. Rev.* 311.

particular attention must be paid to the institution of local government. This, then, is the critical question of local government. It is through a consideration of this question that the significance of recent developments in the central–local relationship might best be assessed.

The Tradition of Local Self-Government

In their classic analysis of local government, Redlich and Hirst acknowledged that a 'fundamental antithesis between centralisation and "autonomous" decentralisation runs through the whole history of English government and its organisation'.[12] Though this is a tension which exists in all States, it has assumed a particular importance in England. Our tradition of local government has been accurately, though rather ambiguously, summed up by W.J.M. Mackenzie as 'an ethical commitment to an extremely vague notion of local self-government'.[13] What is this notion of 'local self-government'? What relevance does it have for seeking to understand the constitution?

The origins of the idea seem to be founded in the claim that 'England is preeminently the country of local government'.[14] This claim is based on the fact that the main outlines of local government in England, i.e., the township, the hundred and the shire, were drawn long before central government (as distinct from simple political overlordship) came into existence. Central administration, Jenks argues, was the creation of the Normans, and local administration, which 'was probably the unconscious adaptation of primeval Teutonic custom to the conditions of new settlement', was at least five hundred years older.[15] Consequently, whenever the centre has vested new tasks in local government, or even when it sought to establish new units of local government, it has tended to work with the existing fabric. Thus, although the hundred has disappeared, the township (which became known by its ecclesiastical name of parish) and the shire (better known by its Norman name of county) provided the basic institutional framework of local government through centuries of unbroken political development.

Alongside the parish and the county, there emerged the borough. Though apparently forming no part of the original Teutonic settlement, it has been suggested that, if local government in Middle England had been surveyed at the time of the Norman Conquest, a remarkable pattern would have been evident: Oxfordshire, capital Oxford; Bedfordshire, capital Bedford; Hertfordshire, capital Hertford; Staffordshire, capital Stafford; Herefordshire, capital Hereford. Each shire had a burh or borough and the two seemed to form an integral unit: 'The shire maintains the burh; the burh defends the shire.'[16] 'One might think that

[12] J. Redlich and F.W. Hirst, *Local Government in England* (London, 1903), vol. I, 10 (hereafter, Redlich and Hirst).
[13] W.J.M. Mackenzie, *Theories of Local Government* (London, 1961), 7.
[14] E. Jenks, *An Outline of English Local Government* (London, 5th edn., 1921), 9.
[15] Ibid.　　　[16] F.W. Maitland, *Township and Borough* (Cambridge, 1898), 37.

godless French republicans had been here already', commented Maitland, 'so mechanical, so rationalistic, so utilitarian is the allotment.'[17] Thus, even in the eleventh century there existed a distinctive pattern of local government, which acknowledged the differences between town and country, and which is recognizable today as providing the foundations of contemporary local government arrangements.

Remarkable though it may be, this degree of institutional continuity does not, of itself, add up to a tradition of local self-government. The existence of basic contradictions between form and reality has been a major theme in the development of our governing institutions; indeed, many regard the ability to retain ancestral forms while recasting their meaning and significance as constituting the peculiar political genius of the British.[18] In order to assess the significance of this practice, the pattern of continuity must be understood in the context of traditions of constitutional thought.

The doctrine of the ancient constitution

The English are unusual, not so much in the extent to which they strive to understand their system of government by turning to the past, but rather in their apparent need to demonstrate that progress is rooted in antiquity. This method is manifest in the views of those seventeenth-century common lawyers who were concerned with the immemorial nature of the constitution. Their views were gradually shaped into the doctrine of the ancient constitution; a doctrine based on the claim that the ancient customs of the Anglo-Saxon constitution not only provide the democratic foundations for liberty but also constitute a body of fundamental law to which all are bound. The doctrine emerged in the seventeenth century debates primarily to assert the privileges of Parliament and the common law courts against the prerogative claims of the Crown.[19] The ideas lingered on, only to re-emerge within a grand tradition of constitutional history which flourished in the nineteenth century[20] and which has become known as the 'Whig interpretation of history'.[21] It is through the claims of the Whig

[17] F.W. Maitland, 'The Origin of the Borough' in *Collected Papers*, vol. III, 31 at 37. Maitland's argument that the borough constituted a unit in a system of military defence has, however, been the subject of criticism. See H.E. Bell, *Maitland. A Critical Examination and Assessment* (London, 1965), ch. III.

[18] See, e.g., J. Millar, *An Historical View of the English Government* [1787] (Glasgow, 1803), vol. IV, Essay VII (arguing that the practice of accommodating traditions serves to bolster respect for power); W. Bagehot, *The English Constitution* [1867] (London, R.H.S. Crossman ed., 1963), 61 (the dignified parts of the constitution are those 'which excite and preserve the reverence of the population' whereas the efficient parts are 'those by which it, in fact, rules').

[19] See J.G.A. Pocock, *The Ancient Constitution and the Feudal Law* (Cambridge, 1957) esp. ch. II.

[20] The leading figures were Stubbs, Freeman, Macaulay and Hallam. See J.W. Burrow, *A Liberal Descent. Victorian Historians and the English Past* (Cambridge, 1981).

[21] See H. Butterfield, *The Whig Interpretation of History* (London, 1931); id., *The Englishman and His History* (Cambridge, 1944).

constitutional historians that the importance of local self-government has been accentuated.

Within this tradition of constitutional thought, local self-government lies at the centre of the historic constitution and provides the source of our liberties. This tradition of local self-government was based on the belief that exclusive responsibility for the management of local affairs under the ancient constitution, including that of taxation, rested with the *gemote* (moot or meeting) of all the freemen of the township. The gemote, it was claimed, constituted the foundation of the entire political structure, since it was the heads of the gemotes (the *reeves*) who met collectively in the *witenagemote* (great council) from which the modern Parliament emerged. The structure of political authority thus rested on the will of the people expressed through their local communities. Neither the king nor his government had the power to make law or levy taxes without first obtaining the consent of the nation in Parliament. 'There was a time', declared Freeman, 'when every freeman of England . . . could claim a direct voice in the councils of his country . . . when he could boast that the laws which he obeyed were laws of his own making, and the men who bore rule over him were rulers of his own choosing.'[22]

From this perspective, English constitutional history is seen as the history of the struggle to ensure that these ancient local liberties, the fundamental laws, are not usurped by the central authority; that is, by what we might now call the State. The traditional Whig view was that the Norman Conquest was simply a disturbance, rather than a breach, in constitutional continuity. The historic outcomes of post-Conquest struggles may be seen reflected in such documents as the Magna Carta, the Petition of Right and the Bill of Rights. These, the Whigs argued, assert no new political principles. They simply require the better observance of the ancient fundamental laws and seek the redress of grievances which have arisen as a consequence of their neglect.

This doctrine of the ancient constitution thus provides an important source of the historic appeal to a tradition of local self-government. It was this doctrine on which Joshua Toulmin Smith rested his nineteenth-century defence of the tradition. 'Local self-government', argued Smith, 'lies at the very basis of free institutions, and is the only effectual guarantee for the responsibility of those in authority.'[23] Local self-government, in essence, immunizes the system from the claims of the central State.

Attractive though it may be, the idea that the local institutions of the Anglo-

---

[22] E.A. Freeman, *The Growth of the English Constitution* (London, 1876), 54.

[23] J.T. Smith, *Government by Commissions* (above, n. 3), 51. See also, id., *Local Self-Government and Centralization* (London, 1851); id., *Local Self-Government Unmystified* (London, 1857). Cf. A. de Tocqueville, *Democracy in America* [1835] (New York, D.J. Boorstin ed., 1990), vol. 1, 61: '[M]unicipal institutions constitute the strength of free nations. Town meetings are to liberty what primary schools are to science; they bring it within the people's reach, they teach men how to use and how to enjoy it. A nation may establish a free government, but without municipal institutions it cannot have a spirit of liberty.'

Saxons were the cradle of English liberties contains a number of basic difficulties. By endeavouring to interpret the past in the light of the present, the doctrine seems to rest on historical anachronism.[24] In seeking to confer on certain ancient practices the status of 'fundamental law', for example, the Whigs evoke an idea of 'constitutional practice' which connotes, not simply a traditional way of doing things, but a modern sense of adhering to recognized procedure, the deviation from which must be denounced. While we do find a certain fixity of forms within Anglo-Saxon society, with regard, for example, to judicial procedure, it must be doubted whether they existed in relation to the practices of government.[25] There is, however, a more rudimentary difficulty with the doctrine of the ancient constitution; viz, that it would appear to be based on myth. The Whig idea that an immemorial constitution had descended, largely unchanged, to the seventeenth century, when attempts were made to subvert it by the Stuart Kings, has been found to be contradicted by historical evidence.[26]

Constitutional rights and administrative duties

The emergence of the concept of sovereignty had, by the eighteenth century, all but eroded the belief in the idea of law as ancient custom to which all were bound. In seeking a reconciliation between sovereignty and liberty, however, English commentators tended to fix on certain practical questions rather than to turn to theory. Such theorizing, it seems, was mainly left to outsiders who were anxious to discover the mainspring of the English system.

Foremost amongst such foreign commentators was Montesquieu, who had feared that the monarchical traditions of Europe, which seemed to be foundering, might come to be replaced by various forms of despotic rule. In searching for a model to protect against this possibility, Montesquieu claimed to have discovered the answer in an English version of constitutionalism, founded on the basic principles of constitutional monarchy, bicameral legislature, independent judiciary, trial by jury, and the lack of a standing army.[27] Montesquieu claimed that the English system, being based on the mechanism of the separation of powers, enabled a reconciliation to be effected between royal integrity, aristocratic wisdom and popular sentiment. This idea of a balancing mechanism within constitutional

---

[24] See P.B.M. Blaas, *Continuity and Anachronism. Parliamentary and Constitutional Development in Whig Historiography and in the Anti-Whig Reaction between 1890 and 1930* (The Hague, 1978).

[25] See, e.g., G.B. Adams, *Constitutional History of England* (London, 1920), 9.

[26] See Pocock, *The Ancient Constitution and the Feudal Law* (above, n. 19); Blaas, *Continuity and Anachronism* (above, n. 24), chs. 2, 3; Burrow, *A Liberal Descent* (above, n. 20), 19–21; Q. Skinner, 'History and ideology in the English revolution' (1965) 8 *Historical Journal* 151. As to the more rarified claim that there existed some ideal lost constitution which had either been usurped by the Normans or been overlain by feudalism, Burrow (ibid., 20) commented that it 'was more or less invulnerable to historical criticism', but only 'provided it remained unperturbed by the mere lack of evidence'.

[27] Montesquieu, *The Spirit of the Laws* [1748] (New York, T. Nugent trans., 1949).

arrangements which operated to preserve liberty in the face of change became the dominant imagery of the period.[28] However erroneous his characterization may have been, his interpretation was one which was happily adopted by the leading legal scholars.[29]

There was, however, one basic question which Montesquieu had failed to broach. How, in actuality, was the country governed? This issue had not troubled his English followers and it was left to be addressed by another foreigner during the nineteenth century. The revolutionary crises of 1848 had shaken all the constitutions of Western Europe, leaving only the British constitution unaffected. How had this been achieved? Surely it was because of the liberalism of our institutions, which had ensured harmony between the monarchical, aristocratic and democratic elements? Rudolf Gneist was not convinced. If the constitution was, in reality, founded on the separation of powers, then Britain might have been especially prone to conflict. Gneist investigated beyond the façade of the central governmental structure and discovered that the real basis of English government was to be found not in separation but in unity. England, Gneist contended, was governed from top to bottom by a class of wealthy landowners, who performed unpaid personal service not only as members of the Lords and Commons but also as Justices of the Peace who administered the counties. Beneath the apparent divisions there existed a deep unity, which Gneist referred to as 'self-government'.[30]

The 'real practical basis' of the English constitution was to be found not in a system of rights but in a network of duties: 'It is not the rights of Parliament and the forms of parliamentary government that have founded England's greatness, but . . . the personal co-operation of all, from the lower classes in the social scale upwards in the daily duties of the State'.[31] Within this network, the Justices of the Peace, who were appointed by the King on the recommendation of the Lord Lieutenant of the county, performed a critical role. Being entrusted with the combined tasks of administration and justice free from active control by the central authority, the Justices constituted the principal organs of self-government. These 'simple, sober and earnest' institutions, though they are 'far removed from the fantastic pictures once disseminated . . . by the author of the *Esprit des Lois*', are 'firm and durable, and in the hour of danger and trial . . . they display the energy and greatness of character of a proud free nation'.[32] Gneist believed that 'it is

[28] See M.J.C. Vile, *Constitutionalism and the Separation of Powers* (Oxford, 1967), ch. III.

[29] See, e.g., J.N. Shklar, *Montesquieu* (Oxford, 1987), 112: 'Montesquieu in effect wrote out the English constitution, and Blackstone in copying it gave that version a semi-official standing.'

[30] Gneist's writings on this subject, which are primarily contained in *Self-Government: Communalverfassung und Verwaltungsgerichte im England* (Berlin, 1871) and *Englische Verfassungsgeschichte* (Berlin, 1882), have not been translated. An extensive critical discussion of his work is to be found in Redlich & Hirst, Vol. II, Bk. III.

[31] R. Gneist, *The History of the English Constitution* (London, P.A. Ashworth trans., 1886), vol. II, 428, 438.

[32] Ibid., 438–9. See also at 436: 'The real origin of the English constitution and its social bases were unknown to Montesquieu.'

only the transformation and moderation which class contrasts receive from this local self-government, that produces those moderate political parties, which are capable of conducting a parliamentary government after the English fashion'.[33]

Gneist's portrayal of the system of self-government was rather complex. It was based not only on personal service and an aristocratic principle, but also on a sense of cohesion between sovereign rights and local government. Gneist did not root his scheme in some romantic-historical idea of Teutonic folk-freedom with political authority being constructed from the locality upwards. He argued that the English state was highly centralized and that 'England has to thank the Norman kings for an absolute government which enabled her to develop a consciousness of unity and strength at a time when all the great nations of the Continent were disintegrated by feudalism.'[34] It was precisely because England had centralized early and that no serious challengers existed to the sovereign authority of the central State that it was able to concede so much liberty to the organs of local government. But the autonomy of the Justices of the Peace was purely administrative and it was strictly limited by the legislative power of Parliament and policed by the common law courts.

If Montesquieu's account was built on a foundation of Enlightenment liberalism, Gneist's analysis was coloured by Prussian Hegelianism. For Gneist, 'Society' meant the entire sphere of social and economic relations and formed an arena of social conflict; the State, by contrast, embodied the idea of self-rule and freedom. The critical issue was whether the antithesis between Society and the State was capable of being reconciled. Gneist's answer was that the 'historical self-government of England establishes the organic connection of State and Society' which constitutes the essential feature of a *Rechts-Staat*.[35] Self-government is a form of class government in which the landowners earn the right to the preponderant voice in government by virtue of the additional duties and financial burdens cast upon them and, through this process, 'the people were impressed with a consciousness of duties to the State, were filled with a sense of the unity of the State, and were made capable of organising and managing their own affairs'.[36]

Though Gneist certainly identified a major weakness in Montesquieu's constitutionalist edifice, his own interpretation of the tradition of local self-government is scarcely immune from criticism. Josef Redlich accurately identified the most important limitations. Redlich's argument was that the tradition of local self-government personified by the Justice of the Peace is better expressed as representing a workable compromise between the centralizing tendencies of the Crown and the desire to keep alive its local institutions.[37] After the Conquest, the policies of the Crown were directed both to preventing the build up of

---

[33] R. Gneist, *The History of the English Constitution* (London, P.A. Ashworth trans., 1886), vol. II, 387.

[34] Redlich and Hirst, vol. II, 395.

[35] Gneist, *Self-Government* (above, n. 30), 879; quoted in Redlich & Hirst, vol. II, 381.

[36] Gneist, *Verfassungsgeschichte* (above, n. 30), 285; quoted in Redlich and Hirst, vol. II, 396.

[37] Redlich and Hirst, vol. II, 395–400.

political feudalism and to acquiring the entire power of the State and it was discovered that the former policy could be realized only by maintaining the old local communities as units of jurisdiction and administration. Thereafter, the true history of the development of local government is to be found 'in the slow transformation of the relationship between the Judicature and the Crown',[38] since it is only after the independence of the judicature was established that the Crown became unable to control and direct local administration.

Redlich further argues that at the end of the seventeenth century, after the turmoils in which the Stuart kings had 'played for a part in internal administration and lost', the old organic system of local administration was retained 'because it was well-suited to the ruling classes who triumphed at the Revolution'.[39] Consequently, the structure of eighteenth century government which Gneist had designated as self-government 'was in truth a form of government in which all authority was monopolized by certain social and economic interests, and employed by them to their own advantage'.[40] And not even Gneist's 'empty abstractions' could mask the fact that '[o]ne of the principal features of aristocratic "self-government" was its subordination of efficiency to the maintenance of class rule'.[41]

Characteristics of local self-government

The historical evidence suggests that any attempt to locate the tradition of local self-government in some ancient constitution which interposes local institutions as the key institutions of government seems highly implausible. In large measure, the durability of local institutions is explained by the fact that the post-Conquest State was highly centralized and, to the extent that these institutions flourished, they did so because they were of benefit to the central State. The continuity of these institutions is certainly an important consideration. Being based on the territorial divisions of ancient communities, being, in Gomme's apt phrase, 'localities properly so called'[42] rather than centrally constructed prefectures, they were more likely not only to represent the interests, but also to claim the allegiance, of their areas. Nevertheless, it would appear that they have always been, albeit in complex ways, bound up in the policies of the State.

If there is a highpoint to be identified in the tradition of local self-government, it is to be found not in ancient times but during the eighteenth century. At that time, the central State had specific but limited concerns which related mainly to foreign policy[43] and, for reasons which have been well expressed by Redlich, during the eighteenth century both the Crown and Parliament left local governing

---

[38] Ibid., 399.   [39] Ibid., 401, 402.   [40] Ibid., 402.   [41] Ibid., 403, 409.

[42] G.L. Gomme, *Lectures on the Principles of Local Government* (London, 1897), 15–18.

[43] See, J. Brewer, *The Sinews of Power* (London, 1989). Brewer examines the growth in power of central government during the eighteenth century and argues that the accretion of powers was not aimed at 'domestic regulation' but at 'enhancing the government's ability to wage war'.

authorities to deal with matters of internal government. There were few subjects of an administrative character which were beyond their remit[44] and there were few restraints on the manner in which they were exercised.

The structure of local government at that time, however, was a complex mosaic of parochial, manorial, borough and county institutions, originating in a jumble of local customs, common law, royal charters and Acts of Parliament and inextricably entangled with one another in accordance with local needs and circumstances.[45] There was certainly no recognizable system of local government. The justices of the peace viewed themselves as deputies of the King, charged with the duty of holding the King's courts and maintaining the King's peace, and were granted a general commission to govern the counties as they thought fit. The idea that 'there existed any kind of lawful autonomy in the fifteen thousand Parishes and Townships would have seemed to the country gentleman . . . an absurd and a dangerous contention'.[46] Furthermore, the municipal corporations, which generally thought themselves exclusive bodies existing independently of the communities in which they were found, viewed their remarkable privileges with great complacency.

Notwithstanding this great jumble of authorities and powers, the Webbs, in the course of their monumental examination of the history of local government, did manage to distil the main characteristics of the eighteenth-century system of local self-government.[47] Six primary features were identified as shaping the contours of the system. At the basis of local self-government lay the principle of *personal obligation*; a duty on 'every respectable male resident . . . to undertake, without salary or other remuneration, one or other of the customary or statutory offices of Manor, Parish or County', whether 'as an incident of tenure or status . . . or for a brief term in rotation with his neighbours'.[48] This principle helps to explain the lack of a conception of local administration by permanent, salaried officials and thus reflects the idea of self-government. A second feature was that of *freehold tenure* of certain local offices, such as Parish Clerk or the Clerk of the Peace, which led to local offices being held as sinecures. Thirdly, there was the principle of *self-election or co-option*: 'by far the most widely approved constitution for local institutions, right down to the early decades of the nineteenth century, was the distinctively oligarchical structure of a close body recruiting itself by co-option'.[49] Only in the parish Vestry was there anything like a democratic principle at work, and this practice varied across the country. The principle of self-election was allied with *vocational organization* as a basis for local government, a principle which reflected the influence of

---

[44] See W.S. Holdsworth, *History of English Law* (London, 1938), vol. x, 160–2 for an inventory of powers and duties of the Justices.
[45] See B. Keith-Lucas, *The Unreformed Local Government System* (London, 1980).
[46] S. & B. Webb, *English Local Government. Vol. 4. Statutory Authorities for Special Purposes, with a Summary of the Development of Local Government Structure* (London, 1922), 354.
[47] Ibid., ch. v.   [48] Ibid., 356.   [49] Ibid., 371.

producer groups, such as the Church, the universities and merchant and craft guilds, in local governance. Running through all these practices was that of the *property qualification*, 'the assumption that the ownership of property . . . carried with it, not only a necessary qualification for, but even a positive right to carry on, the work of government'.[50] Finally, the structure of local administration depended on *local custom and common law* and thus to an almost unchecked local autonomy since the Justices were, as judges, to enforce their own decisions and they and the Municipal Corporations 'could only be questioned by suit in the Courts of Westminster, a very expensive and uncertain method of redress'.[51]

The features identified by the Webbs thus capture the essence of the English tradition of local self-government. In order to assess its contemporary significance, the critical question to examine is whether this eighteenth-century structure of local self-government was equipped to respond to the challenges presented by the economic and social changes of the Industrial Revolution. Before dealing with this matter, however, the constitutional aspects of this tradition of local self-government should more directly be examined.

The Constitutional Heritage

Men are drilled and regimented into communities in order that the state may be strong and the land at peace. Much of the communal life that we see is not spontaneous. The community is a community, not because it is a self-sufficient organism, but because it is a subordinate member of a greater community, of a nation. The nation is not a system of federated communities; the king is above all and has a direct hold on every individual. The communities are far more often the bearers of duties than of rights; they appear before the courts chiefly as punishable units; the proudest city will lose its liberties if it exceeds or abuses those powers that are given to it from above. But above the king himself – thus even a royal justice may think – is the greatest of all communities, 'the university of the realm'. The England that saw the birth of English law, the England of Magna Carta and the first parliaments, was a much governed and a little England.[52]

In the above passage, Maitland touches on all the major issues which must be considered when seeking to understand the traditional constitutional position of local government. Four general themes may be extricated. The first concerns the question of how the local community is to be signified in legal discourse. How are these 'regimented' units vested with legal personality? This first question has direct implications for the remaining themes, since these all touch on the relationship between the local community and the central authorities (the position

---

[50] Ibid., 386.   [51] Ibid., 393.
[52] F. Pollock and F.W. Maitland, *The History of English Law before the time of Edward I* (Cambridge, 2nd edn., 1898), vol. 1, 688.

of the local community as 'a subordinate member of greater community'). The second issue to address is that of the relationship between the units of local government and the central State ('the king [who] is above all'). Thirdly, we might specifically consider the manner of association between localities and Parliament. Finally, what is the role of the courts in dealing with local authorities as 'punishable units'?

Within each of these themes aspects of the basic tension of constitutional discourse between sovereignty and law may be discerned. This tension has created particular problems for English lawyers, mainly because of the degree of institutional continuity in our system of government. This lack of a distinct break between what Maitland called 'folk-law' and 'jurist-law' has, in effect, resulted in lawyers being unable to venture too far into the realm of 'legal metaphysics'.[53] Such difficulties are never far from the surface when we examine these questions. Nevertheless, by examining each of these four themes, we might come closer to understanding the relationship between local government, the central State and 'the university of the realm'.

The legal foundations of local government

'Time was', commented Maitland, 'when we in England had a respectably neat system of legal geography'.[54] The whole country, in theory at least, was divided into towns: Cambridge was a town and the community of Cambridge a township. But how was that community signified in law? The question is complicated by the fact that these issues first arise when the idea of government is intertwined with our system of land law and when certainly there was no clear division between private law and public law. Every acre of land was assumed by law to lie in some town or other, but the question, 'to whom does this parcel of land belong?' blended the idea of ownership (private law) with that of lordship or rulership (public law) in a vague medieval idea of *dominium*. Similarly, when we inquire whether the township was an association of co-owners, or had a distinct legal personality, the issue was clouded by the rather indistinct idea of *communitas*.

The sense of unity in the township did eventually present itself as a governmental power which could be distinguished from proprietary ownership. But how, in legal terminology, was this 'group unit' to be characterized? This question 'remained at a low stage of legal development' for some time, largely because of the work done behind the idea of the trust.[55] Gradually, a number of communities emerged which had reached a higher stage of organization than that of the generality of townships. These communities were the boroughs and, by the fifteenth century, the borough had been recognized in law as a corporate body with

---

[53] F.W. Maitland, *Township and Borough* (Cambridge, 1898), 14.
[54] Ibid., 7.
[55] Maitland, 'Trust and Corporation' in *Collected Papers*, vol. III, 321 at 397.

distinct rights and duties. The view was then taken that the corporation was a *persona ficta* and thus owed its personality to some act of the sovereign power:

> Thus 'the Fiction Theory' leads us into what is known . . . as 'the Concession Theory'. The corporation is, and must be, the creature of the State. Into its nostrils the State must breathe the breath of fictitious life, for otherwise it would be no animated body but individualistic dust.[56]

In consequence, it came to be recognized that incorporation must be the outcome of royal charter. Municipal incorporation by charter had become established by the fifteenth century and around this stage it also was accepted that the ancient boroughs of England had acquired their corporate character by prescription. The Romanist doctrine of corporations thus provided 'an apt lever for those forces which were transforming the medieval nation into the modern State'.[57] The 'federalistic structure' of medieval society, based on a vision of the body politic as a system of groups, was thus threatened by the idea that everything which 'stands between the State and the individual has but a derivative and precarious existence'.[58]

In addition to the suggestion that the borough was a creature of the State, the identification of the borough as a corporation also served to distinguish the borough from the community. Consequently, '[t]he "all" that is unity will not coincide with, may stand apart from, the "all" of inhabitants'.[59] This is significant precisely because, during the Middle Ages, the idea of the community interest was reflected not in a distinction between public and private affairs, but in the idea of commonality:

> Even in the boroughs the common bell calls the commons of the town from the common streets and the green commons to the common hall, and in the common hall assembled they set their common seal to a lease of their common land, for which a fine is paid into their common chest. All is common; nothing public; the English for *res publica* is commonwealth; the public house was once a common inn.[60]

With this spirited parody,[61] Maitland signalled the fact that, with the apparent transformation of the *communitas* into a *universitas*, a host of issues remained

---

[56] F.W. Maitland, 'Introduction' in O. Gierke, *Political Theories of the Middle Age* (Cambridge, 1900). Maitland suggested that the fiction theory was the work of canon lawyers: 'It [the phrase *persona ficta*] slowly stole from the ecclesiastical courts, which had much to say about the affairs of religious corporations, into our temporal courts, which, though they had long been dealing with group-units, had no home-made theory to oppose to the subtle and polished invader.' (ibid., xiv). This view has, however, been challenged: see, e.g., F. Pollock, *Essays in the Law* (Oxford, 1922), 151.

[57] Maitland, 'Moral Personality and Legal Personality' in *Collected Papers*, vol. III, 304 at 310.
[58] Ibid.   [59] Maitland, *Township and Borough* (above, n. 53), 85.
[60] Ibid., 32.   [61] Cf. S. Webb (below, n. 131).

to be resolved, not least amongst them being the question of how rights in corporate property are to be construed.[62]

It is within this convoluted history that an answer is to be found to the origins of the legal foundations of local government. As a result of an evolutionary process,[63] the vague medieval ideas of *communitas* and *dominium* became differentiated and, through the fog, a set of dualisms – between community and the State, between trust and corporation, between ownership and governance, between the common and the public, and between unanimity and majority – gradually emerged in political and legal consciousness. Furthermore, these dualities seemed, in a rather inchoate sense, to be linked with one another. In the end, what made the accomplishment of a transition to a conception of local government as a set of corporate institutions which derived their status from the State both a rather blurred process and, though long drawn, a relatively smooth one was the fact that in English law a distinct line between private law and public law had never been drawn.

Though the institutions of local government today take the form of corporate bodies, this history suggests that there is a danger in taking 'jurist-law' too literally. 'Group-personality' as Maitland recognized, 'is no purely legal phenomenon'.[64] As we shall see, the problems which emerged within the municipal corporations during the eighteenth century arose precisely because a strictly legal view of corporate property was taken, one which failed to recognize that the distinction which had been made was essentially a political achievement which carried with it certain political responsibilities.[65] Furthermore, 'if the English county never descended to the level of a governmental district, and if there was always a certain element of "self-government" in the strange system that Gneist described under that name, that was due in large measure . . . to the work of the Trust'.[66] Maitland's general point is that the group-units of local government exist to serve complex social and political needs and the legal concepts invoked,

---

[62] Maitland further suggested that this shift from community to corporation, was bound up with the emergence of the concept of the majority: 'Our habit of treating the voice of a majority as equivalent to the voice of an all is so deeply engrained that we hardly think that it has a history.' In the early Middle Ages, however, it was unanimity which was required and the transition to the view that a majority vote is as effective as a unanimous vote appears to be associated with the evolution of community into corporation. *Township and Borough* (above, n. 53), 34–5.

[63] Maitland, ibid., 22–3: 'The borough community is corporate; the village community is not. . . . Law sees differences of kind where nature has made differences of degree. . . . [I]n rough, so it seems to me, the law was right. . . . Corporateness came of urban life.'

[64] Maitland, 'Moral Personality and Legal Personality' in *Collected Papers*, vol. III, 314.

[65] Maitland, *Township and Borough* (above, n. 53), 13–14: 'Our law, if I am not mistaken, had never dictated to the boroughs what they should do with their property: it has trusted to their honour. If, observing all constitutional forms, . . . the corporators divided among themselves the income or the land of the corporation, they were, I believe, unpunishable and their acts were valid. But, whatever may have been the law, we surely feel that in William IV's reign it was scandalous that the corporators of a great town should think . . . that the property of the corporation . . . was their property.'

[66] Maitland, 'Trust and Corporation' in *Collected Papers*, vol. III, 321 at 397.

whether they are those of the trust or the corporation, should be understood primarily as instruments which have been utilized in an effort to cater for those requirements.

Local institutions and the central State

By the end of the eighteenth century, it had been recognized thoughout continental Europe that responsibility for the internal administration of the country was that of the central State. As the functions of government increased, a distinction had gradually emerged between judgment and the execution of a judgment and, from this differentiation, two discrete activities came to be identified: the rule of judicature and the rule of administration (or administrative law). Administrative law was rooted in the power of the sovereign to issue ordinances and, since administration was acknowledged to be the peculiar domain of the sovereign, these orders were treated as his law and were considered to be equivalent to the laws of the land. It was through administrative law that the central State regulated and controlled the activities of local institutions.

This continental tradition may be contrasted with the English experience. Though England has, at least since the Conquest, always been ruled from the centre, the central State has not generally sought to administer from the centre. While there have been periods during the Henrician Reformation or the Stuart dynasty when attempts were made to introduce administrative law, the idea that administration is the special preserve of the sovereign, in the sense that disputes concerning administrative issues should be resolved by separate courts in accordance with special principles, has never been accepted. This achievement has been primarily the result of efforts to ensure that the common law formed an undivided system of law. Consequently, no clear distinction has been drawn between public law and private law, the administration has remained subordinated to the ordinary law, and the principle of the rule of law comes to represent the rule of judicature.[67]

There are two particular implications of this tradition of the rule of law which may be highlighted. The first is that there has never emerged in England a hierarchical and undifferentiated concept of 'administration'. The central State exercises no inherent superior jurisdiction over local institutions. Local institutions emerge not simply as creatures of the central State, but as representations of historic communities within a structure of national laws to which both the Crown and the localities are bound. It is in this sense that we may call the English inheritance a tradition of local government rather than a system of local administration.

The second, equally important, implication of the rule of law tradition concerns

---

[67] See A.V. Dicey, *Introduction to the Study of the Law of the Constitution* (London, 8th edn., 1915), ch. IV; E. Barker, 'The Rule of Law' (1914) *Pol.Q.* 117.

the role of Parliament. The common law, as an undivided system of national laws, could not be altered by the Crown alone, but only with the consent of the people expressed in Parliament. This principle of parliamentary sovereignty is thus entwined with the idea of the unity of law. There being few significant prerogative powers in the domestic sphere, the King-in-Parliament, as a supreme legislature, came to exercise absolute authority over internal administration. The Act of Parliament thus became the form through which was framed, not only all new laws, but also all the ordinances which regulate the conduct of administrative activity. Consequently, for the exercise of their legal powers, the institutions of local government become answerable not to the central State, but rather to the courts and, ultimately, to Parliament. In the English tradition, then, the relationships between the centre and the localities were not primarily worked out through arrangements between central departments of State and the institutions of local government, but through a network of relationships between local government, Parliament and the courts.

Parliament and the localities

Within the English tradition, the Act of Parliament became the formal method by which the will of the central State was expressed to the localities. The significance of this achievement resides in the fact that the central State needed to secure the approval of a Parliament which was composed essentially of the representatives of local communities. The House of Commons, as its name implies, was a body consisting of representatives of the ancient local communities who were (and still are) referred to as such in parliamentary proceedings. Furthermore, though peers attended Parliament in their own right, they too took (and take) local titles. Parliament thus provided the localities with a forum within which their interests and grievances could be brought to the attention of the central State. Such practices caused Redlich and Hirst, with only slight exaggeration, to suggest that the House of Commons was 'almost like a House of confederated states'.[68]

Until the end of the eighteenth century, the King and Parliament had generally left local institutions free to deal with their own responsibilities. When, however, new needs made themselves felt through the demand for new services, the centre inevitably became involved. These demands took the form of petitions from local bodies seeking new powers to act. By retaining control over this process, Parliament was able to assume a jurisdiction which in continental states had become the preserve of the central authority under administrative law. This was achieved primarily through the private Bill procedure, in which Bills were generally presented on the petition of local bodies and were deliberated upon

[68] Redlich and Hirst, vol. I, 17. See also, J. Prest, *Liberty and Locality. Parliament, Permissive Legislation, and Ratepayers' Democracies in the Nineteenth Century* (Oxford, 1990), 1–2.

mainly by the representatives of the localities concerned. Thus, in the evolution of parliamentary practice it gradually came to be recognized that two different activities were being carried out under the general form of an Act: legislating both for the common interests of the country (public general legislation) and for special needs of the locality (private or local Acts). Through the development of this latter instrument,[69] Parliament became the connecting link between central and local government.

This direct control which Parliament exerted over local institutions provided a mechanism for central regulation of local government which was consonant with the spirit of the constitution. Control through a Parliament in which the localities were fully represented could be seen to reflect the tradition of local self-government. Indeed, as the Webbs commented, the Commons, in dealing with matters of internal local administration often felt itself 'to be scarcely more than a legislative "clearing house" of the several Courts of Quarter Sessions' and the 'Knights of the Shire who sat at Westminster habitually regarded themselves as the spokesmen of these Courts, from which they received instructions as to Bills to be promoted, supported, amended or opposed'.[70] Furthermore, in so far as Parliament assumed an essentially judicial mode in adopting the private Bill procedure,[71] this practice of the High Court of Parliament seems to reinforce the basic principle of the rule of law.

Local government and the courts

The principle of the rule of law is founded on the rule of judicature: that every exercise of public power must be lawful and that, having no system of administrative law, the sole judge of legality is the ordinary courts applying the ordinary (*sc.*, common) law. There have been occasions, especially under the Tudors and Stuarts, in which attempts were made to fashion a special administrative jurisdiction. Under Henry VIII, for example, proclamations and royal warrants were issued direct to the Justices of the Peace, thus bringing them directly under the authority of the Crown, and under the Stuarts the Star Chamber, a committee of the Privy Council, threatened to develop into a supreme administrative authority.[72] These measures eventually led to fundamental constitutional conflict in the seventeenth century and after the Restoration no further attempt was made to develop a separate administrative jurisdiction.

By the eighteenth century, then, the courts had emerged as the principal

---

[69] See F. Clifford, *History of Private Bill Legislation* (London, 2 vols., 1885–87); O.C. Williams, *The Historical Development of Private Bill Procedure and Standing Orders in the House of Commons* (London, 1948); S. Lambert, *Bills and Acts: Legislative Procedure in Eighteenth Century England* (Cambridge, 1971).

[70] S. & B. Webb, *English Local Government* (above, n. 46), vol. 4, 388.

[71] Redlich and Hirst, vol. II, 340: '[T]he work of Private Bill legislation is in reality largely judicial.'

[72] See, e.g., Maitland, *The Constitutional History of England* (Cambridge, 1908), 261–4.

agencies for the control of local action. This control was effected mainly through the use of the prerogative writs which enabled the actions of Justices to be brought to judicial attention. However, this principle of judicial enforcement of administrative responsibilities had the effect only of bolstering a principle of legal supremacy which was already reflected in the basic structure of local governance. The fact that most of the work of local administration was carried out by Justices of the Peace who were themselves also judicial officers served to convey the idea that governance was rooted in law and that administrative duties should be undertaken in a judicial spirit.

The idea of the State

From this sketch of the constitutional framework of local government which had taken shape by the end of the eighteenth century, some tentative views about the nature of the English State might be drawn. In one sense, there is no difficulty in identifying the State in the eighteenth century, though it was a State which had a limited number of objectives and governance of the localities was not one of them.[73] When we look more closely, however, and particularly if we focus specifically on the implications for local government, the issue becomes less clear. In law, the concept of the Crown serves as the symbol of State power and by the nineteenth century the view might even be taken that the Cabinet is the Crown in commission. But Parliament as a deliberative assembly maintains an ambivalent position within this structure[74] and, of course, the Cabinet may also be viewed as a group of senior Ministers drawn from Parliament and responsible to Parliament for their actions. Furthermore, unlike the French system in which local authorities are viewed as agencies of the State and which occupy a sub-ordinate position in a hierarchical relationship with the centre, our local government tradition is rather different.[75] Though corporate status is conferred by the sovereign, these group-units had an existence which predated State recognition and, when pressed, Maitland had been prepared to argue that in law they ought to have been acknowledged as independent legal persons.[76] We experience certain analytical difficulties over this question of the State because, in Maitland's words, 'we are not logical enough to be elementary'.[77]

---

[73] See J. Brewer, *The Sinews of Power* (above, n. 43).

[74] When considered in relation to the idea of the State, Parliament appears as a site of struggle. Although the Commons represented the ancient local communities, the House became bound up in the policy of the State. In Elizabethan times, for example, a decisive step was taken to remove the residential qualifications of members. The select body thus had power to confer the rights of a freeman on non-residents and through this practice grew up the pocket or nomination boroughs. The system of parliamentary franchises thus became bound up with the policy of the Crown and Parliament became used as a tool of the State. See Redlich and Hirst, vol. I, ch. II.

[75] We might, however, also note how the practice of the Crown, at various stages in history, of handing over town government to a narrow, select body can also be seen as an attempt to make municipal institutions the subservient instruments of the Crown. See Redlich and Hirst, vol. I, 26–8.

[76] Maitland, 'Moral Personality and Legal Personality' in *Collected Papers*, vol. III, 304.

[77] Ibid., at 311.

Our political and legal history has been such that we have no tidy arrangement of institutions and organizations which we may identify as constituting the
apparatus of the State. In the epigraph to this section, Maitland talks of there
being, above the king, 'the university of the realm'. What might this mean? It
is all too easy to translate this phrase as the supremacy of the law. The resonances
are certainly there. Though local institutions are constructed and the king is
above all, the relationship is not simply one of superior and subordinate. This
is because kingly power is subject to the law expressed by the courts and through
Parliament and, particularly as a result of the establishment of a responsible
Ministry, that kingly power is subject to Parliament's will. In delving further
into the question of the ties that bind the nation, however, we might look beyond
formalities and institutions and consider the symbolic dimensions of political
culture.

In adopting such a perspective, some assistance may be derived from the
work of Gneist. In his examination of the English system of self-government,
Gneist recognized that cohesion was achieved not because of institutional mechanisms but through the shared culture of the governing class. He recognized that
the custom of the governing families in giving their sons an education in public
schools and Oxford and Cambridge equipped them with what was necessary to
enable them subsequently to assume office as a Justice of the Peace and then
perhaps move on to Parliament: 'The justices of the peace thus qualified needed
no longer the assistance of a body of jurists learned in the law ... and thus
[made] the appointment of jurists learned in the law superfluous in the commissions of the peace.'[78] Gneist continued that these practices 'are all based on a
well-considered system, calculated so as to concentrate every element of political power in a class relatively homogeneous'.[79] This culture not only replaced
the need for institutional balancing mechanisms, but also rendered a formal body
of 'jurist-law' unnecessary. Though Redlich was critical of many aspects of
Gneist's thesis, this is one in which he seemed to acquiesce, and indeed ampli-
fied when considering the character of our higher judiciary:

> The competence of the English judge is so vast that serious embarrassments would
> beset the work of government were it not for the peculiar characteristics and qualifications
> which convention and training attach to this great office. If English judges, like so
> many of their continental brethren, were civil servants and state officials, who, from
> the outset of their career, have been removed by disciplinary rules from any free and
> open participation in the political life of the country, then the possession of such
> plenary powers would lead direct to government by the bench. But English judges, as
> is well known, have not had an official training. They are not drawn from the Civil
> Service, but from the ranks of practising barristers who have taken some part in public
> and parliamentary life. Indeed promotion is often – perhaps too often – the reward for
> political services.[80]

[78] Gneist, *The History of the English Constitution* (above, n. 31), 374.
[79] Ibid.   [80] Redlich and Hirst, vol. II, 370.

The conclusion we are moving towards is that the lack of a formal State tradition in England was the product of a high degree of cohesion within the governing class. Our Justices, Parliamentarians and judges were all educated in a common tradition of rule. And it was this shared culture of the governing class which rendered unnecessary both a distinct, logical arrangement of institutions which possessed the formal power to enforce the State interest and a formalized body of 'jurist-law'. We had no need for a concept of the State or for a system of public law.

The Reformation of Local Government

At the beginning of the nineteenth century, England was a 'much governed' nation. But the administrative apparatus of government, though extensive, was also haphazard. There existed a great array of local authorities with overlapping boundaries, varying responsibilities, diverse memberships and different rating powers. Some of these authorities were ancient, some were feudal survivals, and others were modern statutory creations. On the face of things, it seemed unpromising material on which to found a tradition of local self-government. To the extent that local institutions were able to govern communities adequately, they seemed able to do so only under particular conditions. Once these conditions disappeared, the inadequacies of the system were likely to be exposed.

With the coming of the Industrial Revolution during the late eighteenth century, the foundations of local governance were severely undermined. As a result of increased trade, growth in population and the rapid conversion of rural communities into urban centres, those social structures – based on landlord-tenant or master-servant relationships – which underpinned local government began to disintegrate. Furthermore, as the situation in Manchester exemplified, the impact of urbanization often meant that the governmental challenge was greatest in the areas in which local governmental arrangements were the most inadequate. Describing the scene of 'this noisome labyrinth' in which 'humanity attains its most complete development and its most brutish', Tocqueville commented in 1835 that '[e]verything in the exterior appearance of the city attests the individual powers of man; nothing the directing powers of society'.[81]

The transformation of the physical environment in these growing urban centres created major problems of housing, sanitation, crime and environmental pollution for which the traditional arrangements were hopelessly deficient. The principle of personal obligation, for example, made sense only in so far as the duties were of a customary nature, were restricted in extent and were unspecialized in character. The responsibility to maintain a lane did not extend to the construction of a new highway to cater for new demand. Furthermore, even if, through

---

[81] A. de Tocqueville, *Journeys to England and Ireland* (London, 1958), 108.

some action or other, a new highway were to be built, nothing could be expected of the parish by way of maintenance other than that provided by an untrained farmer who had accepted a year's service as Surveyor of the Highways.

New arrangements were required to deal with these new challenges. The initial response was the establishment, under local Acts, of special bodies, such as sewer commissions, improvement commissions and turnpike trusts and at this stage it seemed possible that the ancient local institutions might continue to represent the locality in a ceremonial sense, while these special bodies would undertake the utilitarian functions of government.[82] However, the local action of promoting private legislation had come primarily from the 'new rich', the industrialists and merchants of towns and cities such as Leeds, Liverpool and Manchester who found themselves excluded from the County Commission of the Peace and the municipal corporation. And eventually these groups began to demand the reform of these local institutions under the banner of 'equal privileges for all of equal station'.[83] What were the guiding principles of these changes?

The political philosophy of the reformation

There seems little doubt that Bentham's utilitarian philosophy played a significant role in shaping the character of the reforms affecting local government in the mid-nineteenth century.[84] Bentham had sought to devise a science of politics from immutable laws of human nature; in his formulation, the principle of utility was translated from individual self-interest to public action through the principle

[82] See J. Prest, *Liberty and Locality* (above, n. 68), 13: 'In this way many localities would come to replicate the situation in Parliament itself, where there was an obvious distinction between the more honorary position of the House of Lords and the more useful functions performed by the House of Commons.'

[83] The phrase belongs to the Liverpool merchants who, in their petition for reform, stated 'that all in equal station should enjoy equal privileges and be subjected to equal duties': *First Report of the Municipal Corporation Commission* (London, 1835), vol. iv, 2705. Quoted in S. & B. Webb, *Local Government, Vol. 3. The Manor and the Borough* (London, 1908), 701. See also: F. Vigier, *Change and Apathy: Liverpool and Manchester during the Industrial Revolution* (Cambridge, Mass., 1970); E.P. Hennock, *Fit and Proper Persons. Ideal and Reality in Nineteenth Century Urban Government* (London, 1973); D. Fraser (ed.), *Municipal Reform and the Industrial City* (Leicester, 1982).

[84] The precise influence of Benthamism on the administrative reform movement has, however, become one of the major controversies of nineteenth century history. See, A.V. Dicey, *Law and Opinion in England in the Nineteenth Century* (London, 1905), Lect. VI; H. Perkin, 'Individualism versus Collectivism in Nineteenth Century Britain: A False Antithesis' (1977) 17 *Journal of British Studies* 105; O.O.G.M. MacDonagh, 'The Nineteenth-Century Revolution in Government: A Reappraisal' (1958) 1 *Historical Journal* 52; id., *Early Victorian Government, 1830–1870* (New York, 1976); J. Hart, 'Nineteenth-Century Social Reform: A Tory Interpretation of History' (1965) 31 *Past and Present* 39; H. Parris, 'The Nineteenth-Century Revolution in Government: A Reappraisal Reappraised' (1960) 3 *Historical Journal* 17; id., *Constitutional Bureaucracy* (Clifton, New Jersey, 1969); D. Roberts, *Victorian Origins of the British Welfare State* (New Haven, 1960). For a concise introduction to the debate see: A.J. Taylor, *Laissez-faire and State Intervention in Nineteenth-Century Britain* (London, 1972).

of the greatest happiness of the greatest number.[85] Utility was the benchmark against which all laws and institutions were to be assessed; any appeal to preserve local custom and common law on the ground that it embodied traditional wisdom handed down by our ancestors, for example, was rejected as simple superstition. Bentham devised a plethora of schemes for social reform, many of which touched on local government matters including prisons, Poor Law reform, schools and the reform of the magistracy. Furthermore, these reforms all tended to follow a common organizational pattern. Bentham's philosophy can, in general, be understood as a sustained assault on the influence of the aristocratic principle in government.

Bentham based his administrative reforms on the principles of hierarchy, centralization and the establishment of a set of rewards and punishments which would ensure effective and responsible public service.[86] He planned, in effect, to subject public administration to the discipline of commercial principles by, for example, putting out to competitive tender tasks such as the execution of public works or the management of prisons and then ensuring that the work was properly undertaken by subjecting contractors to surveillance through inspection. Although he was, towards the end of his life, working on a scheme for local government reorganization in which all authorities, elected on universal suffrage, would exercise delegated legislative powers over the range of their jurisdictional competence,[87] Benthamism in general was a highly centralist philosophy. As Halevy recognized: 'The State, as conceived by Bentham, is a machine so well constructed that every individual, taken individually, cannot for one instant escape from the control of all the individuals taken collectively.'[88] Since the necessity was to secure the greatest happiness of the greatest number, no local authority, it would appear, could be given autonomous powers in respect of its locality. There could be no sphere of public administration in which the central State could not interfere.

Although the imprint of Benthamite thinking can be identified on many of the major local government reforms of the nineteenth century, the process was 'complicated, slow and entirely undramatic' and the outcome was not so much that of creating order from chaos as that of replacing one patchwork with another.[89]

---

[85] See E. Halevy, *The Growth of Philosophical Radicalism* (London, M. Morris trans., 1928); J. Plamenatz, *The English Utilitarians* (Oxford, 1966); D. Roberts, 'Jeremy Bentham and the Victorian Administrative State' (1959) 11 *Victorian Studies* 193.

[86] See N.L. Rosenblum, *Bentham's Theory of the Modern State* (Cambridge, Mass., 1978), ch. 6.

[87] See 'Constitutional Code' in *The Works of Jeremy Bentham*, vol. IX (Edinburgh, J. Bowring ed., 1843), chs. xxv–xxx.

[88] E. Halevy, *The Growth of Philosophical Radicalism* (above, n. 85), 432.

[89] E. Halevy, 'Before 1835' in H.J. Laski, W.I. Jennings and W.A. Robson (eds.), *A Century of Municipal Progress* (London, 1935), 34 at 35. Writing in the second half of the century, Maitland took the view that local government constituted 'a pretty wild confusion' (*The Constitutional History of England*, London, 1908, 499) and that: 'Taken as a whole, our local government is a weltering chaos out of which some decent order has to be got.' ('The Shallows and Silences of Real Life' in *Collected Papers*, vol. I, 472).

Nevertheless, the overall effect was to institute a new set of organizing principles underpinning local government and, through central action, to establish a
modern system of local government.

The organizational pattern which emerged through the myriad reforms of the
nineteenth century often ran directly counter to the principles which the Webbs
had identified as underpinning the traditions of local self-government. Thus, the
old principle of personal obligation was superseded and gradually replaced by
the use of contractors to undertake public tasks. We also see the salaried officer,
appointed because of technical competence, come to challenge the authority of
the holders of freehold offices. With appointed staffs and the use of contractors,
the ratepayer – the person charged with the responsibility of defraying the costs
of these services – steadily emerges as the predominant economic interest in
local government. Furthermore, though the oligarchical principle of co-option is
never fully ousted, it is gradually replaced by the principle of representative democracy in local government. Finally, we should consider the impact of central
action. As a result of parliamentary action prescribing the constitution and powers
of local authorities, common law and local custom are replaced by statute as the
foundation of local government. And, with such statutes vesting supervisory
powers in central government departments, the courts are substituted by central
government as the primary agencies of control over local affairs.[90]

The new patchwork

The English reaction to the French Revolution of 1789 appeared to have knocked
back the cause of reform for almost half a century. The breakthrough eventually
came with the Reform Act of 1832, which had the effect of reducing the power
of the aristocracy in the Commons and enabling the Whigs to maintain their
influence in government for another half century. The 1832 Act, in giving just
over five per cent of the population the franchise, was scarcely a democratic
measure. It nevertheless marked a great turning point precisely because, being
a compromise measure which was devoid of principle, it paved the way for the
gradual democratization of Parliament.

The reformed Parliament immediately turned its attention to the archaic arrangements of local government which by 1832 had, under the general pressure
of social and economic change, largely fallen into decay. The concern came to
focus primarily on the municipal corporation, which had become 'hardly better
than a Tory dining club'.[91] Since it 'had been the policy of the aristocracy to
cripple the municipal spirit and the municipal constitutions for Parliamentary
and political purposes', it thus became 'the policy of the middle classes, now
that they had obtained political power, to reform the authorities'.[92]

[90] See S. & B. Webb, *English Local Government* (above, n. 46), vol. 4, 428.
[91] Maitland, *Township and Borough* (above, n. 53), 94.
[92] Redlich & Hirst, vol. I, 113.

The first step was to appoint a Royal Commission in 1833 to inquire into the existing state of the municipal corporations. The Commission concluded that 'the general characteristic of [the charters of most corporations] is that they were calculated to take power away from the community, and to render the governing class independent of the main body of burgesses' and thus that it 'has been customary not to rely on the municipal corporations for exercising the powers incidental to good municipal government'.[93] These powers had invariably been conferred by local Acts, not on the municipal corporation, but upon trustees or Commissioners. Though the corporation had 'the nominal government of the town', the actual duties had been transferred to other hands.[94] The Commission thus suggested that 'a thorough reform must be effected before they can become . . . useful and efficient instruments of local government'.[95]

Reform soon followed. In the words of Joseph Parkes: 'Municipal Reform was the steam-engine for the mill built by Parliamentary Reform.'[96] The Municipal Corporations Act 1835 restored municipal corporations as governmental institutions by separating the functions of justice from those of administration and by establishing the corporations as representative councils elected by the local ratepayers. The Act also imposed on the corporations the duty to expend their revenues 'for the public benefit and improvement of the borough'.[97]

Many have pointed to the Municipal Corporations Act of 1835 as ushering in the modern era of local government.[98] Nevertheless, the 1835 Act affected only the 178 municipal corporations already in existence and which covered only one-seventh of the population of English and Wales.[99] Furthermore, the Webbs suggested that this limited focus was 'not inspired by any reverence for mediaeval institutions' but it was simply that the reformers 'were unconscious of the existence . . . of the greater part of the structure [of local government], intimately related though it was to the Municipal Corporations that they were attacking'.[100] The fundamental importance of the 1835 Act is to be found in two of its basic features. First, the Act was a measure of 'sweeping simplicity'[101] which, in imposing a uniform constitution on the boroughs, established the juristic

---

[93] *Report of the Royal Commission on Municipal Corporations* (London, 1835), 17.

[94] Ibid.   [95] Ibid., 49.

[96] S.J. Reid, *Life and Letters of the First Lord Durham* (London, 1906), vol. II, 72; quoted by S. & B. Webb, *English Local Government*, vol. 3 (above, n. 83), 748.

[97] Municipal Corporations Act 1835, s. 92. As Maitland emphasized: 'The public, not the common, benefit' (*Township and Borough* (above, n. 53), 32).

[98] See, e.g., Laski, Jennings and Robson (eds.), *A Century of Municipal Progress* (above, n. 89), ch. III (Jennings, 'The Municipal Revolution').

[99] S. & B. Webb, *English Local Government*, vol. 3 (above, n. 83), 693. Manchester and Birmingham, for example, not having existing municipal corporations, were not directly affected by the Act. The Act did, however, make provision for other towns to be granted similar charters by the Privy Council and under this provision both Manchester and Birmingham gained their charters in 1838. See S.D. Simon, *A Century of City Government. Manchester 1838–1938* (London, 1938), ch. III; D. Fraser, *Power and Authority in the Victorian City* (Oxford, 1979), ch. 4.

[100] S. & B. Webb (above, n. 99), 693.   [101] Ibid., 738.

concept of the municipal corporation.[102] Secondly, by imposing on the town council the general duty of 'the good rule and government of the Borough',[103] it reversed the tendency to split off function after function to special authorities. The Act thus restored the principle that a general authority should assume responsibility for the governance of the locality. 'The English idea of administrative autonomy', commented Redlich and Hirst, 'was here for the first time coupled with the democratic idea of equal rights for all active self-supporting citizens or burgesses.'[104]

This process of municipalization was gradually extended to the other institutions of local government during the course of the century.[105] The Local Government Act of 1888 created elected county councils to undertake the governmental functions previously assigned to the Justices in Quarter Sessions and established the councils as corporate bodies with a constitution and franchise almost identical to that of the municipal corporation. Further, by the Local Government Act of 1894, the ancient system of parish government by vestries was swept away and a pattern of urban and rural district councils established. It was as a result of this process that, during the twentieth century, it became possible to generalize the rules relating to the constitutions of all local authorities.[106] While the Webbs had detected 'the pure milk of Benthamism'[107] in the 1835 Act principles, Redlich and Hirst rightly pointed out that, even by the end of the century, 'the system still seems very complicated when compared with the simple and orderly plans upon which the local districts of continental administration are laid out'.[108] Furthermore, 'by its careful patching up and renovation of old areas . . . the English Parliament has created a territorial system built on history and consecrated by custom, which is far more valued, and therefore far more valuable, than those mathematical departments into which a centralised government, working from above and guided by purely rational and *a priori* principles, has cut and carved the land of France.'[109] That the historic boundaries had not been sacrificed to system was itself a reflection of the tradition of local self-government.

The Benthamite influence over local government reform seems more powerful, however, once the focus shifts from structure to functions. From this perspective, the critical moment which opened the new era was not the 1835 Act, but the

---

[102] Cf. Redlich and Hirst, vol. I, 112: '[T]he constitutions of towns differed one from another in accordance with their charters of incorporation, which had been acquired at times and under conditions so various. A cluster of privileges and customs, venerable and valid, individualised each town and clothed it in its particular garb of law and rights. No statute had ever defined a municipal corporation. In 1833 you could hardly have found two municipal corporations of the same species; and there was no genus, or none known to the Jurist.'

[103] Municipal Corporations Act 1835, s. 90.

[104] Redlich and Hirst, vol. I, 129.

[105] See B. Keith-Lucas, *The English Local Government Franchise. A Short History* (Oxford, 1952).

[106] See, Local Government Act 1933.

[107] S. & B. Webb, *English Local Government*, vol. 4 (above, n. 46), 755.

[108] Redlich and Hirst, vol. II, 7.   [109] Ibid., 7–8.

Poor Law Amendment Act enacted in 1834. Halevy, for example, suggested that it is to the 1834 Act that we should turn in seeking 'the most genuine attempt made after 1832 towards a systematic organization of English Local Government'.[110] By the 1830s, the financial burden of poor relief, which was administered by 15,000 parishes and which 'affected everybody, pleased few, and was understood by nobody',[111] was becoming unbearable. A Royal Commission, on which Bentham's disciples were heavily represented, was established and produced a report which led to the formulation of the 1834 Act. This Act marked a more distinct break with the historic traditions of local self-government.

The 1834 Act was constructed on five basic principles. First, working from 'rational and *a priori* principles' rather than areas 'consecrated by custom',[112] the administrative map was redrawn and new units were created by grouping parishes together into Unions. Secondly, rather than permitting local discretion, it was anticipated that there would be a relatively uniform system of local administration of the poor law by the elected Boards of Guardians. Thirdly, in order to realize this objective, a Central Board was established and vested with extensive powers to promulgate rules and orders to be followed by the Guardians. Fourthly, local salaried officials were appointed to assist the Guardians in administering poor relief but who, in effect, were subordinated to the Central Board. Finally, the 1834 Act worked on what might be called the *ad hoc* principle; that is, the Benthamite principle which dictated that efficient government depended on the creation of special institutions – both local and central – for each governmental task.

The tensions between the principles of the 1834 and 1835 Acts enable us to identify the stresses which shaped the process of nineteenth-century reform. The municipalization movement was based mainly on the principle of self-government, particularly as there was no effective method of directing a council to exercise its powers and even the enforcement of duties required judicial proceedings to be instigated. But the councils possessed few powers and these could be extended only by Act of Parliament. Initially this was left mainly to local initiative through the promotion of private Bills,[113] and then to the framing of permissive legislation; that is, public general legislation which left local authorities free to adopt the powers conferred.[114] However, eventually the model of public general legislation which generally empowered, or occasionally re-

[110] E. Halevy, 'Before 1835' in Laski, Jennings and Robson (eds.), *A Century of Municipal Progress* (above, n. 89), 15 at 34.

[111] S.E. Finer, *The Life and Times of Sir Edwin Chadwick* (London, 1952), 42.

[112] Redlich and Hirst, vol. II, 7.

[113] See, e.g., D. Fraser, *Power and Authority in the Victorian City* (above, n. 99) which shows the manner in which the corporations of Liverpool, Leeds and Birmingham (chs. 2–4) built up their powers through local Acts.

[114] A good example of which was the Local Government Act 1858. See, R.J. Lambert, 'Central and Local Relations in Mid-Victorian England: the Local Government Act Office, 1858–1871' (1962) 6 *Victorian Studies* 121. See also J. Prest, *Liberty and Locality. Parliament, Permissive Legislation, and Ratepayers' Democracies in the Nineteenth Century* (Oxford, 1990). Of the centre's

quired,[115] authorities to undertake particular tasks was utilized.[116] And with this development, the principles relating to poor law administration, especially that of central State supervision, came to play a more prominent role.[117]

The reforms of the 1830s thus incorporate a basic tension between self-government and centralization which reverberated throughout the nineteenth-century reformation of local government. Though the reconstitution of local government seemed designed to restore the principle of self-government, the necessity of addressing the problems impressed on the public consciousness as a consequence of demographic, social and economic change provided a critical impetus for central action. The poor law reforms thus seemed to be the harbinger of centralization and provided a model which was to be emulated in the field of public health from the 1840s[118] and education after the 1870s.[119]

This synthesis is, however, a little too neat. Halevy, for example, has argued that the acquiescence of the ruling gentry in the Benthamite poor law reforms was in fact a clever manoeuvre. Not only did the reforms relieve them of both a great financial burden and the pressures of mounting unpopularity; since the reforms were applied 'in such a way as to render any body of salaried officials hateful to the masses', the working class came to view 'the previous regime of parish overseers controlled by county magistrates as a kind of paradise lost' and, consequently, 'the gentry gained more in moral influence than they had lost in administrative power'.[120] Halevy's general point is that the manner in which the

---

attitude, Prest comments: 'Localities where it was possible to walk of an evening to a permissive public bath-house or a permissive public library along streets laid out under an adopted Act and lit by permissively installed gas-lamps would attract residents. House values would rise, and other towns would want to follow suit' (208–9). Cf. Maitland, above, 21 and Webb, below, 38–9.

[115] It should be noted here that local Acts were, more or less, entirely permissive. See H. Finer, *English Local Government* (London, 2nd edn., 1945), 183.

[116] This impetus came about mainly through the public health movement and then later through educational reform: see W.C. Lubenow, *The Politics of Government Growth. Early Victorian Attitudes Toward State Intervention 1833–1848* (Newton Abbott, 1971), ch. 3 (public health); Redlich and Hirst, vol. I, 134–73 (development of a sanitary code); vol. II, 224–36 (organization of education).

[117] See S.E. Finer, *The Life and Times of Sir Edwin Chadwick* (above, n. 111), 88: '[T]he administrative proposals of the [Poor Law] Report are worthy of the highest praise. They have proved the source of nearly all the important developments in English local government, viz. central supervision, central inspection, central audit, a professional local government service controlled by local elective bodies, and the adjustment of areas to administrative exigencies.'

[118] The link is personified in Chadwick, Bentham's former secretary, who, as Secretary to the Poor Law Commission, discovered a close connection between poverty and ill-health and between ill-health and poor sanitary conditions. His *Report on the Sanitary Condition of the Labouring Population of Great Britain* (London, 1842) had a great influence on the shaping of the first general Public Health Act of 1848.

[119] The controls of the Board of Education were, however, largely inherited from the practices of the Committee of the Privy Council which, since the mid-nineteenth century, had been providing grants to voluntary associations to provide and maintain schools and which, from the outset, had asserted that this power implied a power of inspection. See W.I. Jennings, 'Central Control' in Laski, Jennings and Robson (eds.), *A Century of Municipal Progress* (above, n. 89), 417 at 446.

[120] E. Halevy, 'Before 1835' in Laski, Jennings and Robson (eds.), *A Century of Municipal Progress* (above, n. 89), 15 at 34–5.

1834 Act was implemented served to bring ignominy on the idea of a strong centralized state. Hence the complicated, slow, and undramatic development of the reform movement and the fact that after 1834 we see 'not order arising out of chaos, but only a new patchwork taking the place of an old one'.[121]

The pursuit of efficiency

In the introduction to his masterly study of nineteenth-century English history, Halevy contrasted the reality of government in 1815 with the picture Montesquieu had presented in the mid-eighteenth century. Halevy argued that Montesquieu had got it wrong; English liberty was not founded on the separation of powers. However, *contra* Gneist, neither was it rooted in self-government. Liberty in England, Halevy suggested, was based on the inefficiency of its governing institutions. The administration was chaotic and corrupt, with many officials holding posts simply as sinecures. The country was governed without a police force and '[t]o palliate the evils of such a system men reckoned on the phlegmatic temperament of the people'.[122] But, he contended, '[t]he public was prepared, if necessary, to put up with a certain amount of disorder if it was the price of freedom'.[123] Gneist was correct on one point. The single thread holding society together in 1815 was the fact that the entire apparatus of the State – the judiciary, the legislature, central and local government, and the military – was under the control of a single class, the aristocracy.

The main question which Halevy examined – how was it that such a society survived the nineteenth century without revolution? – does not directly concern us, though we might take note of his observation that in seeking an answer we must look beyond constitutions towards the organization of economic and religious life. His general point on the relationship between inefficiency and liberty, however, is of fundamental importance. It is this relationship which shapes many of the debates about the character of the nineteenth-century reformation of local government. Do the changes mark the beginning of the end of local self-government (as Gneist and Toulmin Smith proclaimed)? Or should they be seen (in line with the argument of Chadwick and the Benthamites) as leading to the establishment of a modern system of local government freed from the incompetencies of class rule?

Gneist had been critical of the reformation, and particularly the shift to the principle of democracy, on the ground that, as a result, the State had lost the cement of self-government. The imposition of duties on the governing class, Gneist argued, enables social interests to be transcended since it 'unites and reconciles the propertied to the working classes, and accustoms them to live

---

[121] E. Halevy, 'Before 1835' in Laski, Jennings and Robson (eds.), *A Century of Municipal Progress* (above, n. 89), 15 at 34–5.
[122] E. Halevy, *A History of the English People in the Nineteenth Century, vol. I. England in 1815* (London, E.I. Watkin and D.A. Barker trans., 1924), 44.
[123] Ibid.

peaceably together'.[124] Through the removal of personal service and its replacement with the principle of election, however, self-government had been destroyed. Instead of the State being the bulwark against social interests, it became a mere grouping of those interests. Gneist also contended that voting is not sufficiently active and responsible a process to provide a sufficiently strong link to hold together classes with distinct interests. This argument was partly conceded in the nineteenth-century reformation, to the extent that it was recognized that participation in the election of councillors should be restricted to those who, as ratepayers, made a direct contribution to the council's funds. But Gneist realized that it would eventually be conceded that the only foundation left for the State was that of the natural right to equality and that 'a State built on such a foundation is meaningless, undefined, and purposeless'.[125]

One basic difficulty with Gneist's argument is that he seemed to assume that local spirit and the sense of duty disappeared as a result of the reformation on a democratic foundation, whereas, as the experience of the unreformed municipal corporations attests, the direct opposite seems closer to the truth. Under the traditional arrangements, local authorities could summon neither the resources nor the imagination to provide the administration required for a modern industrial society. In the face of such challenges, the tradition of local self-government seemed simply to stand for 'the subordination of efficiency to the maintenance of class rule'.[126] Given the apparent conflict between local liberties and efficient services, the reformers, taking the view that the appeal to local liberties had simply come to represent a haven for class-based government, came down on the side of efficiency.

What was required, the Benthamites argued, was not veneration of the ancient, complex structure of government but a simple, clear, understandable and efficient system. Under the traditional arrangements, 'the anarchy of local autonomy was heightened by the fact that there was nothing that could be regarded, either in theory or practice, as a system of Local Government'.[127] The problem which must be addressed when establishing a system, however, is that it seems to require some common framework; and this not only suggests central action which might restrain local initiative but also implies a degree of uniformity which could undermine a sense of diversity lying at the heart of the idea of local government. Gneist may have been wrong on specifics, but in principle there does seem to be a basic tension between efficiency and autonomy in the modern local government system.

This tension between efficiency and autonomy is further exacerbated by the character of the reformation. The Webbs refer to the new system as being an 'Association of Consumers' or a 'ratepayers' Democracy' in which 'membership

---

[124] R. Gneist, *Self-Government* (above, n. 30), 941; quoted in Redlich and Hirst, vol. II, 387.
[125] Ibid.
[126] Redlich and Hirst, vol. II, 409.
[127] S. & B. Webb, *English Local Government*, vol. 4 (above, n. 46), 353.

was obligatory and universal' and in which, for most of the whole of the nineteenth century, 'the only question agitating the successive generations of "reformers" seemed to be how exactly this exclusively territorial Democracy was
to be organised'.[128] Again, Gneist may have been wrong in his detailed analysis,
but in raising the question of whether voting is sufficiently active a process to
bind localities, he touched on an important issue.[129] With this reformation, the
cash nexus became a basic issue for local government, with the result that the
relationships between those who are voting for services, those who pay for them,
and those who consume them comes to underpin many of the tensions in the
system. Furthermore, once the State begins to take an interest in the health and
welfare of the people, the central authority will, especially because of the differences in the relative wealth of different local authorities, almost inevitably
become involved in the activities of local government.

Finally, though we should strip it of its Hegelian embellishment, we might
take note of Gneist's argument that, with the emergence of democracy, the clash
of social interests cannot easily be transcended. At the turn of the twentieth
century, Redlich and Hirst suggested that party politics was not a significant
factor in local government.[130] Though the forms of political organization were,
at that stage, in their infancy, political ideology was nevertheless already beginning to exert an influence on local affairs. However, as Sidney Webb highlighted
in a famous passage, these ideological issues were often still camouflaged beneath the rhetoric of technique:

> The 'practical man', oblivious or contemptuous of any theory of the Social Organism
> or general principles of social organisation, has been forced by the necessities of the
> time, into an ever deepening collectivist channel. Socialism, of course, he still rejects
> and despises. The Individualist Town Councillor will walk along the municipal pavement,
> lit by municipal gas and cleansed by municipal brooms with municipal water, and
> seeing by the municipal clock in the municipal market, that he is too early to meet his
> children coming from the municipal school hard by the county lunatic asylum and
> municipal hospital, will use the national telegraph system to tell them not to walk
> through the municipal park but to come by the municipal tramway, to meet him at the
> municipal reading room, by the municipal art gallery, museum and library, where he
> intends to consult some of the national publications in order to prepare his next speech
> in the municipal town-hall, in favour of the nationalisation of canals and the increase

---

[128] S. & B. Webb, *English Local Government*, vol. 4 (above, n. 46), 437, 444, 445.

[129] Cf. Maitland, *Township and Borough* (above, n. 53), 34–5 ('One of the great books that
remain to be written is The History of the Majority').

[130] Redlich and Hirst, vol. II, 44: 'The giant struggle between capital and labour scarcely touches
local administration. . . . In one aspect it is a private war between employers and employed, waged
with the weapons of lock-out and strike. In another it is a Parliamentary war, in which each party
struggles for the enactment of new and the amendment of old laws in its own favour. But English
administration, like justice, is simply the carrying out of the law, and consequently takes no part in
this conflict – except, it may be, indirectly, when questions arise as to the rate of wages to be paid by
a local authority.' By the 1920s, however, this had ceased to be the case. See, e.g., ch. 4, 209–12.

of the government control of the railway system. 'Socialism, sir,' he will say, 'don't waste the time of a practical man by your fantastic absurdities. Self-help, sir, individual self-help, that's what made our city what it is.[131]

The emergence of this political dimension not only brings matters to the surface in local council decision-making, but also presents issues for the centre. 'The existence of *two* representative bodies [*viz.*, Parliament and the local authority] governing any given area', Ivor Jennings recognized, 'at once raises difficulties as to their mutual relations'.[132] Political conflict within local affairs is one matter but what of political conflict between a local council and the central government?

The general point to be made is that, once we understand the nineteenth-century reformation of local government as being motivated by the pursuit of efficiency, the key issues the system faces are those which derive from the tensions between efficiency and autonomy, the tensions amongst the conflicting interests expressed in the cash nexus in local government, and the potential for conflict between local and national political mandates. The nature of each of these tensions ensures that the question of local government will thereafter be bound up with the affairs of the central State.

Central Control

Local government has traditionally exercised an authority which is independent from that of the central State. The central State was mainly concerned with foreign policy issues and possessed few inherent powers relating to internal affairs. The most important of the prerogative powers concerning local matters was that of patronage through the power to appoint Justices and judges. There was, however, no active supervision of local government: in 1815 the Home Secretary was assisted by two under secretaries and eighteen clerks,[133] and with an establishment of only twenty the Home Office simply did not possess the administrative capacity to undertake active supervision of local affairs. Certainly, there existed no power to issue general administrative orders to local government and the relationship between central and local government was not viewed as being hierarchical. The conduct of local affairs was mainly regulated by common law and by Act of Parliament and under the supervision of the judiciary.

The character of the nineteenth-century reformation of local government, however, increasingly led to the vesting of statutory powers of supervision of local action within a central authority. For the traditionalists, this trend was to

---

[131] S. Webb, *Socialism in England* (London, 1890), 116–17.
[132] W.I. Jennnings, *Local Government in the Modern Constitution* (London, 1931), 5.
[133] See Redlich and Hirst, vol. II, 238 (n. 1).

be deplored. 'We are losing sight daily ... of *principles*,' Toulmin Smith proclaimed, 'and allowing ourselves to be made the dupes of presumptuous *empiricism*.'[134] Such practices undermined the rule of law: 'we are departing more and more ... from the "golden and straight metwand of *the law*", and allowing ourselves to be drawn in bondage to the "incertain and crooked cord of *discretion*"'.[135] The Benthamites, however, saw distinct advantages in vesting a central authority with an unfettered discretion and argued in particular that the courts were ill-informed on the public policy of the law and could frustrate administration by defeating administrative regulations on 'verbal or technical grounds'.[136] But what of the practice?

Supervision by central departments

The Poor Law Commission established under the 1834 Act was the first central department of State created for the purpose of regulating and controlling local authorities in the execution of their tasks. The Commission continued after 1847 as the Poor Law Board and, in 1871, that Board was merged with the Public Health Department of the Privy Council and the Local Act Branch of the Home Office to form the Local Government Board. The Local Government Board continued in that form until, in response to functional reorganization, it was in 1919 reconstituted as the Ministry of Health. Though not having an exclusive authority – the Home Office, for example, retained responsibility for the police and in 1899 the Board of Education was established from two committees of the Privy Council – the Local Government Board became the central department with fairly general powers of supervision over local government.

Although various statutes had clearly established an administrative relationship between the central department and the local authority, this relationship was not a simple one of superior and inferior. Local authorities certainly became bound to the central department by many administrative ties but the Board's 'province is a mosaic of distinct pieces dissimilar in shape and size'.[137] The Board possessed no general right to issue administrative commands which compelled obedience; in the words of Redlich and Hirst, 'it is a Board of controls, but not a Board of control'.[138] As a recent study of the Board concluded, there was 'a noticeable underdevelopment of mechanisms for the assertion of strong incorporating leadership by the centre' and 'the Board became, not the leading edge of the instrumental state, but a by-word for compromise, pragmatism and conservatism'.[139] That is, anyone examining the late nineteenth century structure

---

[134] J.T. Smith, *Government by Commissions Illegal and Pernicious* (above, n. 3), 367 (emphasis in original).

[135] Ibid. The references are to Sir Edward Coke C.J., 4 Inst. 41.

[136] S.E. Finer, *The Life and Times of Sir Edwin Chadwick* (above, n. 111), 88.

[137] Redlich and Hirst, vol. II, 257.   [138] Ibid.

[139] C. Bellamy, *Administering Central–Local Relations 1871–1919. The Local Government Board in its Fiscal and Cultural Context* (Manchester, 1988), 237, 233.

of central controls for evidence that the centre was assuming a strategic, directive responsibility over local government could not help but be struck by the
inefficiency of the arrangements.

Furthermore, the pattern of this mosaic of controls not only exhibited a degree
of inefficiency but was one which seemed to respect the independent authority
of local government. Consider, by way of example, the development of the
principle of central supervision of police forces. This principle was established
by the County and Borough Police Act 1856 which required the Home Secretary's consent to the appointment of the chief constable or for changing the
establishment and empowered him to make orders relating to such matters as
pay, equipment and discipline. Important though these powers may be, there was
no general power of direct executive compulsion vested in the Home Secretary.
Instead, section 16 of the Act made the payment of central grants dependent on
the local force being maintained in a 'state of efficiency'. Thus, the Home
Secretary was unable to direct local forces or to interfere with the administration
of the force but he was able to set a general standard of efficiency for the
country. Further, if a force was considered to fall below those standards of good
order, the centre had no power to intervene but simply possessed the power
to inflict a fine by withholding grant. The structure of the Act thus seemed
to respect the principle of local autonomy. Through an elaborate mechanism, the
statutory framework sought to promote the national interest in developing an
efficient system of police without resorting to the creation of a police state.

In general, the statutory arrangements continued to ensure that the initiative
in promoting and developing a service lay with the local authority. Central departments were not empowered to direct local authorities as to the manner in
which their powers should be exercised. They did, however, possess power to
take action if a local authority neglected a duty, but even then the powers of the
centre were circumscribed. Consider an example from the field of public health.
If a local authority defaulted on its duty of establishing and maintaining a proper
sytem of drainage or water supply, then the Local Government Board possessed
certain powers to act to ensure compliance with the duty. Nevertheless, there
were particular safeguards: that the Board must receive complaints; that it must
undertake a local inquiry to determine whether the authority is in default; that,
if default is found, it must issue an order giving the authority time to make good
the default; that if after the expiry of the time period action has not been taken,
the Board should either proceed by seeking mandamus in the courts or undertake the work itself; and that if the latter course is adopted the authority may
appeal to the courts against an order to defray the cost of the works.[140] The
powers of central departments were usually confined to the enforcement of
duties and, even then, generally through the medium of the courts.

There were, nevertheless, various powers which central departments seemed

---

[140] Public Health Act 1875, s. 299.

to have acquired from either Parliament or the courts. The Local Government Board, for example, obtained certain powers over private Bill legislation which traditionally had been exercised by Parliament alone. Thus, as a result of the growing burden on Parliament of dealing with private Bills, the process was streamlined through the use of the technique of the provisional order. This technique required the local authority to petition the Minister rather than Parliament and this resulted in the Minister holding an inquiry rather than a Parliamentary committee being established. If ministerial approval were obtained the order was made, though it did not become valid until confirmed by Parliament.[141] While streamlining central business, the use of this technique did mark a shift in activity from the legislature to the executive.[142] As an illustration of the acquisition of powers of a judicial character, it might be noted that the Local Government Board acquired the powers of a tribunal of appeal for parties aggrieved by the auditor's decisions on surcharge or disallowance. These powers included the power to remit surcharge or disallowance, even if the decision were unlawfully made, in cases in which it was considered 'fair and equitable' so to do.[143] What the pattern of controls thus seemed to indicate was not so much the establishment of a directive control by the centre, but rather the construction of a system of administrative law.

The characteristic technique of this structure of central supervision was that of inspection: 'for bureaucratic subjection and centralised omnipotence Parliament has substituted the principle of inspectability'.[144] The Home Secretary's supervision of police was, for example, rooted in inspection; each police authority was required to produce an annual report to the inspectors who were obliged 'to visit and inquire into the state and the efficiency of the police for every

---

[141] Provisional orders could be made under many Acts, including the Tramways Act 1870, the Gas and Water Works Facilities Act 1873, the Public Health Act 1875 and the Local Government Act 1888. These statutes conferred powers to make orders in relation to such matters as the compulsory acquisition of land, the supply of gas, the alteration of local authority boundaries and the amendment of local Acts.

[142] A further example of this shift may be found in the use of Royal Commissions of Inquiry which since the beginning of the nineteenth century were used to investigate pressing problems of social and economic life and which were the source of almost all of the century's administrative reforms. Redlich and Hirst (vol. II, 320) estimated that over 150 Royal Commissions were established between 1832 and 1844 and that they provided a key vehicle through which 'Bentham's demand for the application of scientific principles to legislation and government' could be realized. Being established by Royal prerogative they were roundly condemned by Toulmin Smith as a violation of fundamental law, since they usurped the role of the High Court of Parliament as Grand Inquest of the Nation: see J.T. Smith, *Government by Commissions Illegal and Pernicious* (above, n. 3), Bk. II, ch. I. While generally approving of the technique, the Webbs did offer the following assessment of the Report of the Royal Commission on Municipal Corporations: 'Both as a summary of the facts and as an analysis of the causes, this General Report is inaccurate and misleading. The historical student must dismiss it as a bad case of a violent political pamphlet being, to serve Party ends, issued as a judicial report.' (*English Local Government*, vol. 3 (above, n. 83), 721).

[143] Poor Law Audit Act 1848, s. 4. Under the Local Authorities Expenses Act 1887 these powers were extended to permit the Board to sanction expenditure which would otherwise be unlawful. In the year 1888–89 the Poor Law authorities made 1,130 applications to the Board to sanction expenditure and approval was granted in all but 29 cases: Redlich and Hirst, vol. II, 274 (n. 2).

[144] Redlich and Hirst, vol. II, 246.

county and borough' and to 'report generally on such matters' to the Secretary of State.[145] Inspection, the technique invented and promoted by Bentham, was the foundation of central supervision not only in relation to the police, but was also applied to the poor law, public health, education and, through audit, to the system of local finance and expenditure. Inspection enabled the centre not only to keep itself informed of the work of local authorities but also directly to encroach on that work.[146] Inspection provided the channel through which the centre 'perform[ed] its functions as a guardian of public rights and interests without resorting to the imperative mood'.[147] 'It is an invention characteristically English', concluded Redlich and Hirst, 'for it is designed to obtain the advantages of efficiency without the incubus of bureaucracy.'[148]

The impact of the changes introduced in the second half of the nineteenth century certainly had the effect of formally placing the central State in a key position in relation to the reformed local government system. However, although 'the accretion of formal powers over local authorities ... was real and it was considerable' it was, as Christine Bellamy has shown, 'strategically incomplete'.[149] The centre became 'entangled in a mass of detailed procedural checks in which strategic direction was unavailable', 'lack[ed] certain key powers' and was unable 'to assert a formative role in general service development'.[150] Bellamy argues that this was much influenced both by the manner in which property interests were reflected in local government and also by 'the weakness of statist doctrines in the UK'.[151] The pattern of controls may also reinforce Halevy's general theme that a degree of inefficiency is a basic aspect of our constitutional settlement. But, perhaps most importantly for our purposes, it may indicate that the objective was not so much to provide the centre with powers of strategic direction but rather to vest it with appellate or supervisory powers which were characteristic of a nascent system of administrative law.

These points may be highlighted with respect to default powers which, in form, constitute a particularly intrusive type of central intervention. The origins of this type of power, which was first used in section 49 of the Sanitary Act 1866, owe more to the local authority's sense of dignity than to creeping *dirigisme*;[152]

---

[145] County and Borough Police Act 1856, s. 15.

[146] See, e.g., Public Health Act 1875, s. 205 which empowered inspectors of the Local Government Board to attend any meetings of the local authority.

[147] Redlich and Hirst, vol. II, 247.   [148] Ibid., 251.

[149] C. Bellamy, *Administering Central–Local Relations 1871–1919* (above, n. 139), 10–11.

[150] Ibid., 11.   [151] Ibid., 15.

[152] The general objective of this provision was to extend the common law principle permitting affected property owners to complain to local justices to secure the removal of nuisances to the case of a local authority which had failed in its duty to supply water and sewerage facilities. The proposal thus was to permit a complaint to the Justices. Many of the large authorities, however, complained of the indignity of placing elected councils under the supervision of magistrates and, in response, the Government substituted complaint to the centre which, after local inquiry, could, if default was found, appoint commissioners to undertake the work: see Bellamy, ibid., 217. It was the existence of problems with the commissioner solution (assuring the quality of the work, encouraging incompetent authorities to utilize the works properly and the like) that led to the adoption of the alternative of an order of mandamus which was introduced in the 1875 Act.

certainly the aim was to motivate local authorities to act rather than have the central authority assume their responsibilities. Bellamy has calculated that between 1875 and 1885 the centre undertook 114 inquiries under section 299 of the 1875 Act but of these only five orders for mandamus were issued by the courts.[153] The Board seemed prepared to undertake default proceedings only where a local authority showed 'wilful intransigence' and this general reluctance 'stemmed partly from the administrative and legal difficulties of successfully prosecuting a default case, and partly from a strongly articulated view that formal intervention by the central authority in more than a very few exceptional cases was both impracticable and inappropriate'.[154]

In general, the assessment of the structure of the central–local government relationship provided by Redlich and Hirst seems basically sound: 'The Local Government Board is emphatically not a motor engine; it does not supply power to set in motion the machinery of local government; and in practice the Board takes the initiative even less than the letter of the law might lead one to suppose.'[155] The reason they provided was that 'an average Englishman . . . will not tolerate a bureaucratic State within a State, or allow an official department to pose as an embodiment and personification of the State itself'.[156] The most basic reason, however, was that the panoply of central controls which were acquired were best understood as laying the foundations for a system of administrative law.[157]

Judicial supervision

It has generally been accepted that, during the eighteenth century, local institutions operated independently of central government. According to the Webbs, the Justices 'enjoyed, in their regulations, an almost complete and unshackled autonomy' and the municipal corporations 'regarded their corporate property, . . . as well as their exemptions and privileges, as outside any jurisdiction other than their own'.[158] These local bodies derived their authority from the law and could be confined and checked only by the superior courts of law. An important consequence of the nineteenth-century reformation, however, was that central government began to replace the courts as the primary agency for regulating the conduct of local institutions. One further consequence of the reformation was to bring about a greater degree of formalization in the mechanisms of judicial control.

[153] *Administering Central–Local Relations* (above, n. 139), 218.
[154] Ibid., 218. The legal difficulties in using mandamus were well described by the Royal Sanitary Commission in 1871: see H. Finer, *English Local Government* (London, 2nd edn., 1945), 308–9.
[155] Redlich and Hirst, vol. II, 300.
[156] Ibid., 300–1.
[157] See, e.g., A.V. Dicey, 'The development of administrative law in England' (1915) 31 LQR 148. The *locus classicus* which is expressive of the concerns of the traditionalists is G. Hewart, *The New Despotism* (London, 1929).
[158] S. & B. Webb, *English Local Government*, vol. 4 (above, n. 46), 352.

This formalization came about with the emergence in the nineteenth century of the *ultra vires* doctrine and its application to local authorities. The doctrine was formulated by the courts mainly in relation to disputes in the mid-nineteenth century concerning the trading powers of railway companies established under statutory powers, where it was held that 'a statutory corporation, created by Act of Parliament for a particular purpose, is limited, as to all its powers, by the purposes of its incorporation as defined in that Act'.[159] As a result of the 'statutorification'[160] of local government, this doctrine came to be applied to local authorities.[161] The courts, recognizing that an overly-strict application of the doctrine could frustate the ability of local authorities to undertake the tasks entrusted by Parliament, tried to assume a flexible approach, holding that 'whatever may fairly be regarded as incidental to or consequential upon those things which the Legislature has authorised, ought not (unless expressly prohibited) to be held to be *ultra vires*'.[162] Nevertheless, many have criticized this development. William Robson, for example, argued that the courts applied the *ultra vires* doctrine to local authorities without 'understanding . . . the fundamental difference between a joint-stock company trading for profit and a local governing authority providing public services in the common interest' and contended that the doctrine imposed a great limitation on the activities of local authorities.[163] There are a number of issues here that must be unravelled.

The primary justification provided by the courts for devising the principle was that, since these corporations were 'armed with the power of raising large sums of money', if they were not strictly confined to the purposes for which they were constituted, they 'might acquire such a preponderating influence over some particular branch of trade or commerce, as would enable them to drive the ordinary private traders out of the field, and create in their own favour a practical monopoly, whereby the interests of the public would be most seriously injured.'[164] But is there a major difference here between the railway companies and the

---

[159] *Ashbury Railway Carriage & Iron Co.Ltd* v. *Riche* (1875) L.R. 7 H.L. 653, 693 (per Lord Selborne).

[160] The term is taken from G. Calabresi, *A Common Law for the Age of Statutes* (Cambridge, Mass., 1982), ch. 1.

[161] See, e.g., *Attorney-General* v. *Newcastle-upon-Tyne* (1889) 23 QBD 492. With the nineteenth-century reformation all English local authorities, with the exception of the boroughs, became statutory corporations. The boroughs, by virtue of their creation by the Crown by charter under its common law powers, possessed the powers of an ordinary person. As a result of the statutory reforms in the Municipal Corporations Acts of 1835 and 1882, however, the use of the borough fund (as distinct from corporate property) came to be governed by the *ultra vires* principle. Since the levying of rates became a necessity for carrying out modern governmental functions, the issue was of marginal interest and in the Local Government Act 1972 the boroughs ceased to exist and were reconstructed as statutory corporations. For a contemporary argument in relation to the London boroughs, however, see: *Hazell* v. *Hammersmith LBC* [1991] 2 WLR 371.

[162] *Attorney-General* v. *Great Eastern Railway Co. Ltd* (1880) 5 App.Cas. 473, 478; *Attorney-General* v. *Manchester Corporation* [1906] 1 Ch. 643. This principle has since been codified in statute. See now Local Government Act 1972, s. 111.

[163] W.A. Robson, *The Development of Local Government* (London, 1931), 195–9.

[164] *Attorney-General* v. *Great Northern Railway Co.* (1860) 1 Dr. & Sm. 154, 159–60.

reformed local authorities? It has been mentioned that, with the establishment of ratepayers, democracies, the cash nexus became a critical question in local government and it is perhaps not surprising that the courts took the view that they should seek to ensure that an appropriate balance was maintained.[165] Also, since there was great controversy during the second half of the nineteenth century over the issue of municipal trading,[166] it was only to be expected that concern would be expressed that the corporation did not abuse its special, if not monopolistic, position.[167] Given the legal structure of the reformed authorities, the application of the *ultra vires* doctrine to their activities seems only to be expected.

Further, the specific issue concerning the *ultra vires* principle is not always identified. Before the emergence of that principle, local authorities remained bound by law. If legal constraints were not a major issue in the eighteenth century, this is probably attributable to the steadier pace of life in those days, the extensive common law powers which the Justices possessed, and the fact that the privileges of the boroughs were rooted in grant or prescription. What must be emphasized is the point that, even if the reformed corporations were recognized as ordinary persons, they would enjoy only the rights and privileges of ordinary persons; they certainly would not be regarded as autonomous governing bodies. That is, a distinction must be drawn between purpose and privilege. The *ultra vires* principle limits a corporation to the purposes for which it was incorporated: a local authority thus cannot operate a laundry service without obtaining Parliamentary sanction. The fact that the corporate body has only those privileges which are conferred by law – so that, for example, it may not without parliamentary consent tax its inhabitants, even though the objective is to promote the common good – is not essentially an aspect of the *ultra vires* principle. It is, in reality, an illustration of the requirement that parliamentary approval is required for any special privileges which may interfere with private rights, and is thus a reflection of the basic constitutional principles of parliamentary sovereignty and the rule of law.[168] What seems to lie at the root of Robson's criticism is a sense of frustration at our apparent inability to develop through law an adequate recognition of the distinctive character of governance. If so, however, it is a problem which may lie in Parliament's hands as much as those of the judiciary.

To the extent that the courts developed a general supervisory jurisdiction over local government during the latter half of the nineteenth century, it was achieved

---

[165] See further ch. 4 below.

[166] See, e.g., *Attorney-General* v. *Manchester Corporation* [1906] 1 Ch. 643 (corporation cannot incur expenditure on a general parcels delivery service as an incident of powers to run a tramways service); *Attorney-General* v. *Fulham Corporation* [1921] 1 Ch. 440 (corporation cannot justify laundry service as an incident of powers to provide washhouses). See H. Finer, *Municipal Trading. A Study in Public Administration* (London, 1941).

[167] See, e.g., *Attorney-General* v. *Sheffield Corporation* (1871) LR 6 QB 652 (no power to incur expenditure from borough fund to oppose water company's Bill in Parliament).

[168] See W.I. Jennings, *Local Government in the Modern Constitution* (above, n. 132), 8.

mainly through the development of the prerogative writs.[169] They did so by extending the use of prerogative remedies, which had been designed to control the actions of courts of inferior jurisdiction, to the quasi-judicial functions of administrative authorities. It is generally acknowledged that the courts were set on course by Brett LJ who, in 1882, stated that 'whenever the Legislature entrusts to any body of persons other than the superior Courts the power of imposing an obligation upon individuals, the Courts ought to exercise as widely as they can the power of controlling those bodies of persons, if those persons admittedly attempt to exercise powers beyond the powers given to them by Act of Parliament.'[170] Since the 1880s, the courts have adapted the writs to keep local authorities within the boundaries of their powers.

When the exercise of these powers was subject to official review in the early 1930s, it was accepted that the maintenance of the jurisdiction was essential, though the Committee also acknowledged that the existing procedures were 'too expensive and in certain respects archaic, cumbrous and too inelastic'.[171] During the early decades of the twentieth century, however, the general tendency was to amend the local government statutes so as to incorporate provision for appeal to the courts on questions of law, which thereby had the effect of marginalizing the significance of prerogative writ procedure in local government affairs.[172] Some commentators have also sought to derive more critical conclusions about the general impact of judicial supervision. As a result of his studies of judicial decisions concerning local authorities, Jennings drew as its general point 'the frequency with which the Courts manage to interpret – no doubt correctly in law – in such a way as to obstruct efficient administration'.[173] 'It is a remarkable fact', he continued, 'that so often a decision of a court acts as a spanner in the middle of delicate machinery.'[174]

It is against the background of these judicial developments that we might return to the issue of default powers. As has been noted, the default power seems to provide an administrative alternative to the judicial supervision of local authorities. The power may thus be viewed as a particular instance of the general trend away from judicial supervision by a process of making statutory provision for appeals to the central department. However, rather than treating this

---

[169] Jennings notes that *Brice on Ultra Vires*, the standard work which was written in 1877, did not even mention the jurisdiction of the prerogative writs, whereas its successor in 1930 (*Street on Ultra Vires*) discusses the question at considerable length: Jennings, 'Central Control' in Laski, Jennings and Robson (eds.), *A Century of Municipal Progress* (above, n. 89), 417 at 422.

[170] *R* v. *Local Government Board* (1882) 10 QBD 309, 321.

[171] *Report of the Committee on Ministers' Powers*, Cmd. 4060 (London, 1932), 99.

[172] See Jennings, 'Central Control' in Laski, Jennings and Robson (eds.), *A Century of Municipal Progress* (above, n. 89), 417 at 424.

[173] W.I. Jennings, *Local Government in the Modern Constitution* (above, n. 132), 3.

[174] Ibid. See also Jennings, 'Central Control' in Laski, Jennings and Robson (eds), *A Century of Municipal Progress* (above, n. 89), 417, 428: 'The judges usually have had no experience of the problem which local government have to face; they have known only that property has had to bear new burdens.'

development as constituting a shift towards administrative overlordship, in the sense of seeking to transform local authorities into agents of the central State, it might better be understood as providing a means of protecting local authorities against the uncertainties and rigidities of judicial review. A distinct jurisprudence of public law had not been developed and the common lawyers had expressed great hostility to any such possibility. One obvious method of avoiding this was strictly to limit the range of administrative issues which were presented to the courts for resolution. From this perspective, the establishment of administrative appeal to central departments was in the interests not only of local authorities but also of the judiciary.

This point may be illustrated by examining developments in audit procedure. When the powers of disallowance and surcharge were introduced in 1844, provision was made for appeal on points of law either to the Queen's Bench Division or to the Poor Law Commission.[175] In 1848, however, the Commission was given the power to remit disallowances and surcharges[176] and thereafter, since the procedure was not only cheaper and more speedy but also more flexible, administrative appeal became the standard method of challenge. The tension which thus existed between the auditor's obligation to enforce the *ultra vires* principle and the hardship which strict application of the principle might occasion was reconciled through the exercise of this administrative jurisdiction. During the 1880s one in seven surcharge determinations were appealed, about 7,500 cases a year, and the vast majority of these were confirmed and remitted.[177] The trivial character of many of the surcharges occasionally led to embarrassing publicity.[178] What such cases often indicated, however, was not so much the ignorance of local officers, but rather an inability of the centre to grasp the complex details of the system when drafting statutes and orders. In order to avoid this type of difficulty, the Board, apparently without controversy, acquired powers in 1887 to sanction unlawful expenditure.[179] Thereafter, appeals decreased (by 1914 they had steadied at under 3,000 a year) and, after peaking at 3,000 in 1897, the number of sanctions granted was running at 2,300 in 1914.[180] This powerful discretionary power was used not only to avoid technical disallowances but also to remove difficulties over apparently reasonable expenditure which was of doubtful legality.[181] What these audit developments show is the gradual emergence of a structure of administrative law in which issues of policy and

[175] Poor Law Amendment Act 1844, s. 36.

[176] Parochial Debt and Audit Act 1848, s. 4.

[177] C. Bellamy, *Administering Central–Local Relations 1871–1919* (above, n. 139), 174–5.

[178] Bellamy (ibid., 176) cites the example of a case in 1883 when the auditor disallowed expenditure of 3s. 3d. (about 16p) on toys for the Wisbech Union Workhouse.

[179] Local Authority (Expenses) Act 1887, s. 3.

[180] C. Bellamy, *Administering Central–Local Relations 1871–1919* (above, n. 139), 174, 176.

[181] Probably the most notorious example was a Board circular of 1904 which announced that the 1887 Act powers would be used to regularize payments made by London boroughs for public work projects for the unemployed: Local Government Board Circular 37 of 1904–5, 29 October 1904. See Bellamy, ibid., 178.

legality were closely intertwined. This administrative law, being a development which cut across our constitutional traditions, could not openly be recognized, regularized or juridified.

Furthermore, there is evidence to indicate that the courts, recognizing the limits of their competence and conscious of the pressures on managing their own business, readily acquiesced in the emergence of this informal and relatively closed system of administrative law. Consider, for example, the leading case of *Pasmore* v *Oswaldtwistle UDC*[182] in which the plaintiff mill-owner, having unsuccessfully petitioned the authority to bring the sewers up to standard, sought an order of mandamus requiring the authority to discharge its statutory duty under the Public Health Act 1875. In finding for the authority, the House of Lords upheld their claim that the plaintiff should have used the statutory default procedure provided for in section 299 of the 1875 Act. The House held that, where statute created the obligation and provided a remedy, the general rule is that it could not be enforced in any other manner: 'the particular jurisdiction to call upon the whole district to reform their mode of dealing with sewage and drainage should not be in the hands, and should not be open to litigation, of any particular individual, but should be committed to a Government department'.[183] In recognizing that the decision rested 'on considerations of policy and convenience'[184] their Lordships could be understood to be sanctioning an administrative resolution of the matter for precisely the reasons articulated by the Royal Sanitary Commission over 20 years earlier when it stated that:

> The remedy by *mandamus* does not appear adequate. The process is long and dilatory; and the case, when at last brought to issue, would be of a nature which a Court of Law is eminently unfitted to try. Details of sewers and sewage; quantity and quality of water supplied; character and volume of water within reach; capacity of works to be constructed, their nature and general arrangement; state of domestic offices; mode in which scavenging is done and removal of refuse carried on: these and similar questions would be the points for discussion, and the mere statement would appear to afford sufficient proof that they cannot with any satisfactory result become the subject of judicial decision.[185]

Such action seemed to acknowledge the fact that the courts simply did not possess the capacity to reach an adequate resolution of these administrative issues. The matter was better left to administrative channels and, through the establishment of these centralized checking mechanisms, a non-juridified system of administrative law emerged. The relationship between this structure of administrative

---

[182] [1898] AC 387.
[183] Ibid, 395 (per Lord Halsbury).   [184] Ibid, 397 (per Lord Macnaghten).
[185] Report of the Royal Sanitary Commission in 1871; quoted in H. Finer, *English Local Government* (London, 2nd edn., 1945), 308.

law and the jurisdiction of the superior courts remained uncertain,[186] but the courts did not appear to be zealous to assert their supervisory jurisdiction.

The characteristics of central control

Within the tradition of local self-government, Parliament maintained responsibility over local affairs through its power, on petition from the localities, to grant extensions to local powers through private Acts. Such local Acts were an archetypal expression of local governance; Parliament acted as an endorsing authority but made little attempt to introduce any system into the governance of local affairs across the country. The pressures of modern life, however, spawned a series of major challenges. The changes brought about by industrialization exacerbated the problems of poverty and pressed their concerns on the centre. The variegated response of local bodies to the tasks of providing the basic physical infrastructure of urban existence left many issues concerning the health and welfare of the population unaddressed. The initial response resulted in the creation of a multiplicity of local bodies equipped with particular powers and thus compounded the complexity of local governance. Further, Parliament was subjected to severe strains in seeking, in the traditional manner, to cope with a huge increase in the administrative business of attending to the requests of the localities. Circumstances demanded change; local government needed to be placed on a more systematic foundation and the manner in which local government business was addressed by the centre required reform.

The response – the nineteenth-century reformation of local government – also brought about a transformation in the relationship between central and local government. By the end of the century, local government had been placed on a statutory foundation, with the powers of local authorities being generally contained in public general legislation. In itself, this implied no great restriction on local autonomy, although to those who were unable to appreciate the relationship between 'folk-law' and 'jurist-law' it may have conveyed the impression that local government was a creature of the centre. The real change, however, came about mainly from the character of this legislation. First, to the extent that the legislation sought not only to vest powers but also to impose duties, the locality, at least in a formal sense, became an instrument of the centre. But more generally, the nature of this legislation, in vesting a range of administrative powers in central departments, ensured that the central State became a critical factor in local government. The practice then arose of central departments using

---

[186] See, e.g., *R* v. *Minister of Health, ex parte Dore* [1927] 1 KB 765 (Poplar borough councillors, having unsuccessfully challenged an auditor's surcharge by writ of certiorari, then successfully applied under the alternative procedure of administrative appeal to the Minister for remission. The Minister's decision was successfully challenged by writ of certiorari on the ground that, once one route had been adopted, the alternative was lost and the Minister had no right to entertain the application. For case in general see Ch. 4, 210–12)

their powers to put flesh on the skeleton of the primary legislation and thus shaping the manner in which the general powers of local authorities could actually be exercised. Further, with the growth of these general powers of supervision, petitions for extensions to local powers came to be channelled through central departments and, even in those cases ultimately coming before Parliament, central government exercised a predominant influence. Local authorities began to lose their channel of direct access to Parliament.

In one sense, Parliament became, for the first time, a true legislative body with responsibility for laying down general rules of social conduct and leaving to departments of State the task of addressing questions of administration. But, even if this development is explicable in terms of the increasing differentiation between legislative and administrative tasks under rapidly escalating workload, the important point is that it left central departments bound up in the conduct of local government. Parliament became displaced and the central Executive took over supervisory tasks. Furthermore, this shift in control over local affairs was not inevitable. After the reformation of local government, Parliament could have moved beyond its practice of sanctioning specific grants of power to local authorities and entrusted them with general powers of local government.[187] The refusal so to do must, to some degree, reflect a centralist ethos which had emerged in the course of the reformation.

The character of this centralizing tendency should not, however, be misunderstood. The central authority did not, in the nineteenth century, act as an instrumental State which sought to direct local authorities and tried to transform them into agents of the centre. Nor, however, does the language of partnership seem adequate to express the relationship between the central authority and local government. As Bellamy has shown, at least until the First World War, much of the centre's energies were directed mainly towards that of seeking to define and patrol the boundaries of the central–local divide.[188] The centre thus seemed more concerned to limit the incursions of the localities into matters of high politics – especially by limiting the demands of local authorities on the national Exchequer and the money markets – than to give strategic direction to local authorities on the manner in which their tasks should be carried out.

The system of central controls which was established was thus much more in the nature of an emerging system of administrative law than one which sought to guide and promote service development by local government.[189] This model was in many respects a reflection of the importance of the cash nexus principle in the reformed local government system and the consequent tensions which this

---

[187] Proposals to vest in local authorities a power of general competence were the subject of a number of Bills during the 1920s, albeit unsuccessfully. See W.A. Robson, *The Development of Local Government* (London, 1931), 206–11, H. Finer, *English Local Government* (above, n. 185), 196.

[188] C. Bellamy, *Administering Central–Local Relations 1871–1919* (above, n. 139), *passim*.

[189] See H.W. Arthurs, *'Without the Law'. Administrative Justice and Legal Pluralism in Nineteenth Century England* (Toronto, 1985), ch. 5.

engendered: the central authority thus saw itself as a checking agency to ensure that the interests of individuals and sectional groups were properly considered and that local majorities did not abuse their powers. This role is manifest in a number of practices including the adoption of the principle of inspectability and of the consequential reporting and accounting procedures to which local authorities were subject, in the appellate jurisdiction acquired by the central departments, and even in the way in which controls over private Bills were used as a mechanism for regularizing powers and as a way of working through in experimental fashion a range of administrative solutions to governmental challenges.[190] And, as we have seen, this nascent system of administrative law was acquiesced in by the courts which possessed neither the resources nor adequate working methods to exert effective supervision over local decisions affecting individual interests.[191]

Local Government in the Administrative State

Though the process of reforming local government had been set in train during the 1830s, it did not reach the final stages of completion until the early decades of the twentieth century. The most obvious milestones signalling the completion of the process were the enactment of the Local Government Acts of 1929 and 1933, the latter of which was consolidatory. The Acts of 1888 and 1894 had reformed the basic structure of modern local government, with single-tier county boroughs forming the urban authorities and the rest of the country being based on a two-tier, county-district division. This structure remained largely unaffected by the 1929 Act, though the 1933 Act constitutes the consummation of the general process of statutorification, in providing, for the first time, a common set of organizational rules governing all local authorities. Most importantly, however, the 1929 Act marked the culmination of the 1835 Act principle that a local council should assume responsibility for all locally-provided public services. After the structural reforms of the late nineteenth century, further progress in the realization of this principle was made, most notably with the absorption of the school boards by local councils in 1902.[192] In the 1929 Act, the major remaining *ad hoc* service, the administration of the Poor Law by the Boards of

---

[190] In 1882, for example, Parliament rationalized parliamentary procedure by establishing the Police and Sanitary Regulations Committee which considered all private Bills promoted by local authorities concerning police and sanitary powers. This Committee adopted a quasi-judicial method of working and were not in general prepared to confer new powers outside existing precedents except where there existed 'strong local reasons'. See J. Willis, 'Parliament and the Local Authorities' in Laski, Jennings and Robson (eds.), *A Century of Municipal Progress* (above, n. 89), 400 at 408–9; C. Bellamy, ibid., 203–8.

[191] For examples of such acquiescence see *Board of Education* v. *Rice* [1911] AC 179 and *Local Government Board* v. *Arlidge* [1915] AC 120. See W.J.L. Ambrose, 'The new judiciary' (1910) 26 LQR 203; A.V. Dicey, 'The development of administrative law in England' (1915) 31 LQR 148.

[192] Education Act 1902.

Guardians, was integrated into the system and 'the principle of concentrating as far as possible in one Local Authority for each area the administration of all expenditure from public funds' was realized.[193] With this achievement, the basic outline of the modern institution of local government was fashioned, though it was not in fact until 1948 that the democratic character of local government was fully established.[194]

Although the enactment of the 1929 Act marked the culmination of the process of reformation, it should not be assumed that it also signals the beginning of a new period of stability. Since 1929 the system has been continuously adjusted as part of the exercise of finding an appropriate role for local government within the modern administrative state. In seeking to identify this role, three factors – functions, structure and finance – have been of particular importance. From the 1930s, various adjustments were made to the functions of local government which cumulatively have had a significant impact on the character of the institution. Furthermore, the 1929 Act had left unresolved the problems of relating functions to local government areas and it was not until the 1960s that these issues were officially addressed. Finally, though many of the 1929 Act provisions emerged from the recommendations of various official bodies since the turn of the century, its enactment was most directly prompted by post-war economic difficulties and its consequences for the financial regime of local government. This question of local government finance has continued to pose difficulties ever since. By briefly considering each of these factors, we might more readily identify the character of the modern institution of local government.

The restructuring of local government functions

From the 1930s, the general tendency of establishing local authorities as the sole agencies of local administration was being promoted in conjunction with a trend towards removing certain services from the purview of local government by way of centralization. These adjustments were undertaken for three main reasons: that local administration of certain services was inefficient and anachronistic; that, though local control were possible in principle, the existing areas rendered the exercise administratively impractical; and, finally, because of a policy of nationalization of public utilities. Examples falling into the first category include the removal of outdoor relief for the able-bodied unemployed in 1934[195] and the

---

[193] *Report on the Transfer of Functions of Poor Law Authorities in England and Wales* (Maclean Committee), Cmd. 8917 (London, 1918).

[194] The 1835 Act principle of the ratepayer franchise had by the end of the nineteenth century been extended to all institutions of local government, but it was only in the Representation of the People Act 1948 that the most basic principle of representative democracy – vesting the right to vote in every person of full age living in the area – was permanently extended to local government. See B. Keith-Lucas, *The Local Government Franchise* (above, n. 105), 224.

[195] Unemployment Act 1934, which established the Unemployment Assistance Board to administer the new service.

assumption of responsibility for the trunk road network by the Ministry of Transport in 1936.[196] Such adjustments were relatively uncontentious and removed inappropriate burdens from local authorities.[197] The best example concerning the inappropriateness of local authority areas was that of the removal of the local authority hospital services evolved from the Poor Law institutions to the national health service which was established in 1946.[198] In promoting this reform, the Government acknowledged that the areas of local government had not been adjusted in the light of social and economic change.[199] The policy of nationalization affected local government mainly through the loss of their electricity and gas trading services with the establishment of national structures operated through regional boards.[200]

Though the loss of these responsibilities did not inevitably lead to a diminished status for local government, it did result in a significant restructuring of local government. Local authorities mainly lost production-orientated services. Furthermore, since the reforms of the early decades had brought to local councils such responsibilities as education and the poor law, this realignment gave local government a distinct social service orientation. With the establishment of the welfare state, many local government services, such as education, housing and personal social services, became of primary importance to government. Consequently, despite losing certain functions, local government continued to increase the share of total public expenditure which it consumed.

This restructuring of local government functions had a major impact on the character of the central–local government relationship. Since local government has become more heavily dependent on central government for financial support for providing services, the financial link is perhaps obvious. However, even without this financial dependency, the form of the restructuring seemed to indicate that the centre had a vital responsibility to act as a check on the actions of local government. This argument stems from economic analysis which seeks to demonstrate that there are certain limitations to a local authority's ability

---

[196] Trunk Roads Act 1936, which made the Ministry of Transport the highway authority for 4,500 miles of trunk roads. A further 3,685 miles were added to this network by the Trunk Roads Act 1946.

[197] See, e.g., the *Report of the Royal Commission on Unemployment Insurance*, Cmd. 4185 (1932), para. 192: 'The Associations of local authorities have unanimously pressed upon us the view that the cost of unemployment should be a national and not a local charge. We have much sympathy with that view. The causation of unemployment is a difficult and complex subject, but it will be agreed that widespread dislocations are likely to be due to national rather than to local conditions'

[198] National Health Service Act 1946.

[199] See, e.g., Mr Key, Parliamentary Secretary to the Minister of Health, HC Debs., vol. 422, cols. 209–10 (1 May 1946): '[I]t has been asked: "Why not take over the local authority hospitals? Why not use the local government geographical distribution, the local government managerial machine, for what, in fact would become a greatly improved local government service?" I answer: Because of existing geographical areas and functional distribution that is administratively impossible. . . . We have not made its sphere of operations grow with the character of the services we have developed, nor with the means and needs for wider areas of administration.'

[200] Electricity Act 1947; Gas Act 1948.

independently to pursue policies of income redistribution.[201] Since one consequence of the restructuring is that much of local government expenditure is
potentially redistributive, it could be argued that, within the administrative state,
central government has a legitimate role to play in supervising, regulating and
co-ordinating local authorities simply to ensure the effective implementation of
policy.

The reorganization of local government

The nineteenth-century reformation had resulted in the establishment of a local
government system which was divided along urban–rural lines. This structure
reflected the organic link between shire and borough which was rooted in tradition. However, while the relationship between shire and borough may have
formed an integral unit in earlier times, it eventually came to be identified as a
source of conflict. With continuing urban growth in the twentieth century, conflicts were created between urban and rural authorities as towns and cities grew
beyond their administrative boundaries. The tensions were heightened after the
1920s, when reforms were introduced which had the effect of making claims
by the towns to enhanced status more difficult to sustain. Thus, although it acted
'as a dam to keep back the flood of proposals for boundary extensions and new
creations of county boroughs', the Local Government (County Boroughs and
Adjustments) Act 1926 'did not affect the springs that fed that flood'.[202] Despite
the pressures resulting from social, economic and demographic change, the nature
of the system ensured that there would never be unanimity amongst the various
groups of local authorities over the need for, and certainly the form of, any
reorganization.

The problem was not simply that local authorities were engaged in a zero-sum
game for territory, taxbase and status. Transcending this political game was the
fact that, if local government areas were reconstructed as functionally effective
units unrelated to historic boundaries, they would cease to be 'localities properly
so-called',[203] would thus lose their historic claims to be independent governing
bodies and, since the link between 'folk-law' and 'jurist-law' would be broken,
would rapidly come to be viewed as being emanations of the central State.
Consequently, in Alan Alexander's words, 'the conflict that was built into the
local government system in the nineteenth century created *immobilisme* in the
twentieth'.[204] Furthermore, if central government attempted to intervene and

---

[201] See W.E. Oates, *Fiscal Federalism* (New York, 1972), ch. 1; C. Foster, R. Jackman & M.
Perlman, *Local Government Finance in a Unitary State* (London, 1980), 42–5.

[202] B. Keith-Lucas and P.G. Richards, *A History of Local Government in the Twentieth Century*
(London, 1978), 201.

[203] G.L. Gomme, *Lectures on the Principles of Local Government* (above, n. 42), 15–18.

[204] A. Alexander, 'Structure, Centralization and the Position of Local Government' in M. Loughlin,
D. Gelfand and K. Young, *Half A Century of Municipal Decline 1935–1985* (London, 1985), 50 at
52.

impose reorganization, that decisive action would itself serve to reaffirm the sense of hierarchy in the central–local relationship. As a result of these various difficulties, although the need for reorganization had been widely recognized by the 1930s, it was not until the 1960s and 1970s that local government reforms were enacted.

The reforms which eventually materialized were part of a broader techno-cratic movement which viewed institutional modernization as the key to the reversal of Britain's economic decline. During this period reports on staffing[205] and management,[206] as well as local government structures[207] were commis-sioned, all of which seemed to share the view that local government formed a vital link in the renewal of the machinery of British government.[208] Reform of local government in London in the 1960s marked the watershed,[209] since it revealed to the centre that 'it was possible to effect quite radical change without allowing the local authorities affected to take any part in the formulation of the terms of reference of the inquiry preceding change, or in the process following the inquiry but preceding Ministerial decision'.[210] The subsequent establishment of the Redcliffe-Maud Commission to examine local government in England thus implied 'the total rejection of the principle that local authorities had a right to define the scope and nature of the change themselves'.[211]

The processes of implementation were not without their difficulties.[212] In particular, the Redcliffe-Maud Commission, appreciating that the failure of the existing structure 'to recognise the interdependence of town and country' was its 'most fatal defect',[213] recommended the establishment of larger, unitary author-ities. The Local Government Act 1972, however, introduced a two-tier system which, in the view of some, simply perpetuated the antagonisms within local government and 'ensured that local government would be ill-equipped to resist

---

[205] *Report of the Committee on the Staffing of Local Government* (London, 1967) (Chmn: Sir G. Mallory).

[206] *Report of the Committee on the Management of Local Government* (London, 1967) (Chmn: Sir J. Maud); *The New Local Authorities: Management and Structure* (London, 1972) (Chmn: M. Bains).

[207] *Report of the Royal Commission on Local Government in Greater London* (Cmnd. 1164, 1960) (Chmn: Sir E. Herbert); *Report of the Royal Commission on Local Government in England* (Cmnd. 4040, 1969) (Chmn: Lord Redcliffe-Maud).

[208] See, e.g., the Bains Report, 6: 'Local government is not, in our view, limited to the narrow provision of a series of services to the local community, though we do not intend in any way to suggest that these services are not important. It has within its purview the overall economic, cultural and physical well-being of that community and, for this reason, its decisions impinge with increasing frequency upon the individual lives of its citizens.' See also, Redcliffe-Maud Report, Cmnd. 4040, para. 28 and see ch. 2, 83–4.

[209] London Government Act 1963 (establishing the Greater London Council and 32 London borough councils).

[210] L.J. Sharpe, '"Reforming" the Grass Roots: an Alternative Analysis' in D. Butler and A.H. Halsey (eds.), *Policy and Politics* (London, 1978), 82 at 103.

[211] J. Morton, *The Best Laid Schemes?* (London, 1970), 17.

[212] See B. Wood, *The Process of Local Government Reform: 1966–1974* (London, 1976).

[213] Redcliffe-Maud Report, Cmnd. 4040, vol. 1, para. 85.

the rapid increase in the pressure for centralization'.[214] While this assessment underestimates the complexities of the process, the strains were certainly evident from the outset.

There was undoubtedly a considerable degree of ambivalence over these local government reforms. Notwithstanding the claims of the official reports that the reforms were designed essentially to restore local authorities as functionally effective units and thus to reverse the trend towards centralization,[215] it has been also suggested that, particularly since effective central control and co-ordination required a significant reduction in the overall number of local authorities,[216] local government reorganization should in fact be viewed as a facet of the central-ization process.[217] The main problem was that the reformers sought to equate functional effectiveness with the enhancement of local democracy.[218] Sharpe has argued that this is erroneously to conflate system (functional) capacity with gov-ernmental (democratic) capacity and that it is this error which provides the key to appreciating why the reforms should be branded a failure.[219]

In general, Sharpe argued that the essence of local government is that it is local and that the 'number of local units must be a function of the needs and conditions of the sub-national communities whose existence justifies the crea-tion of a local government system in the first place'.[220] Consequently, '[i]f the structure of local government is ... to be determined by the needs of central government then it is difficult to see the justification for a local government system, as opposed to some form of deconcentrated central administration'.[221] Continuing this line of argument, Sharpe suggested that 'we ... need to restore the democratic criterion to a central place in the determinants of reorganization', that the result of this would be to turn 'the functionalist approach on its head',

---

[214] Alexander, in Loughlin, Gelfand and Young (eds.), *Half A Century of Municipal Decline* (above, n. 204), 50 at 64.

[215] See, e.g., Ministry of Housing and Local Government, *Reform of Local Government in Eng-land*, Cmnd. 4276 (1970), paras. 61, 62: 'Much of central government's interest ... consists of reconciling the proposals of different authorities and dividing between authorities that part of the nation's resources which is allotted to spending by local government. The extent of this intervention will automatically diminish with the reduction in the number of authorities ... Reform will thus bring greater freedom in its train. But the Government are also determined to take positive measures to reverse the trend towards centralisation.'

[216] We might note that the effect of the 1972 Act reforms was (outside London) to reduce the number of local government units in England and Wales from 1,391 to 422.

[217] Sharpe, ' "Reforming" the Grass Roots' in Butler and Halsey (eds.), *Policy and Politics* (above, n. 210), 82 at 104–5.

[218] See, e.g., Redcliffe-Maud Report, Cmnd. 4040, vol. 1 para. 272: 'If, as we have said, a minimum population of around 250,000 is necessary for the efficient administration of services it seems to us an inescapable corollary that local democracy will be ineffective unless organized in units of at least that size.'

[219] L.J. Sharpe, 'The failure of local government modernization in Britain: a critique of function-alism' (1980) *Canadian Public Administration* 92, 106–8.

[220] Sharpe, ' "Reforming" the Grass Roots' in Butler and Halsey (eds.), *Policy and Politics* (above, n. 210), 82 at 105.

[221] Ibid., 105–6.

and that we must recognize that, 'as a multifarious agency, local government should *not* be functionally appropriate as measured by the needs of any particular services or groups of services it provides'.[222] That is, within the administrative State, the single-minded pursuit of efficiency had the tendency of subverting the system of local government.

Financing local government

The nineteenth-century reformation established ratepayer democracies in local government. Though reorganized as governmental institutions which were vested with a range of new functions, the 'cash nexus' imposed significant limitations on local action. Except for a few of the older municipal corporations which possessed a substantial corporate estate,[223] local authorities were, throughout the nineteenth century, heavily dependent for their revenues on the rates. Within the frame of a restricted franchise the limits of what was politically acceptable were soon reached and this financial-political nexus 'could not but act as a check to any imaginative approach to the problems of urban life'.[224] It was not until the end of the century that these restrictions were loosened. Partly this was because of the gradual extension of the franchise, which coincided with a growing involvement of party organizations in local politics. But a particularly important factor was the alleviation of the rate burden by the introduction of Exchequer grants. During the middle of the nineteenth century, Exchequer grants accounted for only around 5 per cent of local government expenditure, a proportion which remained fairly stable until the 1870s.[225] By the turn of the century, however, it has been estimated that around 20 per cent of local government expenditure was grant-aided.[226]

This growth in grant-aid, however, also caused concern. The centre was worried at the increasing proportion of tax revenues which were being absorbed by local grants. But there was also an apprehension that the use of grant-aid, especially in conjunction with the imposition of duties on local authorities, served to transform the authorities into instruments of central policy. One solution to these concerns were the Goschen reforms of 1888 which scrapped most specific grants and replaced them with an assigned revenue system under which the grant to be distributed came from the revenue collected from certain excise taxes and probate

[222] Sharpe, ' "Reforming" the Grass Roots' in Butler and Halsey (eds.), *Policy and Politics* (above, n. 210), 114–15.

[223] Liverpool Corporation, for example, in 1853 possessed an estate valued at £4m. This estate was used not only to finance capital projects but also subsidized revenue expenditure at a rate of £60,000 a year, which was equivalent to a shilling (about 5p) in the pound on the rates: see, D. Fraser, *Power and Authority in the Victorian City* (above, n. 99), 38.

[224] E.P. Hennock, 'Finance and politics in urban local government in England, 1835–1900' (1963) VI *Historical Journal* 212, at 217.

[225] M. Schulz, 'The Development of the Grant System' in C.H. Wilson (ed.), *Essays on Local Government* (Oxford, 1948), 113 at 116, 127.

[226] Ibid. See also C.D. Foster, R.A. Jackman and M. Perlman, *Local Government Finance in a Unitary State* (London, 1980), 133.

duties.[227] These reforms thus tried to place the burden directly on the general taxpayer and to remove central government as an active player in the process. But how were these revenues to be distributed between authorities? Allocation in proportion either to rateable value or to population was rejected on the grounds that it would result in the greater proportion going to the richer authorities. Great difficulties were experienced, however, in finding an adequate measure of need. 'This problem of finding the correct or acceptable indicator of needs has', in the words of a recent authoritative study, 'bedevilled block grant distribution ever since.'[228]

During the twentieth century the financial relationship between central and local government has been transformed. Local government expenditure has continued to increase; from 4.5 per cent of gross national product (GNP) in 1890 to 18.4 per cent in 1975.[229] Furthermore, when expressed as a proportion of personal disposable income, the rate burden has remained remarkably stable and much of the growth in local expenditure has been met by central grants. By the mid-1970s over half of local expenditure was being provided for by central government grants. The method of distributing this grant has been varied. The Goschen reforms of 1888 were gradually undermined by the proliferation of specific grants linked to particular services. A major attempt at rationalization occurred in the 1929 Act with the replacement of many specific grants with a block grant, which was unhypothecated to specific services and was designed to assist poorer authorities in meeting their spending needs. This general grant did not, however, incorporate grants for the main services of education, housing and the police and it was only after 1958, when education was absorbed into the system, that this general grant has covered the allocation of the majority of grant aid to local government.

The establishment of the block grant principle has not, however, alleviated the tensions. These tensions are now buried in the complex and detailed formulae used to govern grant distribution, though they have occasionally bubbled to the surface, particularly when the Government has sought to use the system to restrain local expenditure. Further, the entrenchment of the principle of equalization in grant distribution has exposed two additional difficulties with the system. First, since it implied that standard services should be capable of being provided at standard rate poundages, it threw into relief certain difficulties and anomalies in the system of valuation of property on which local rates were based and thus exposed weaknesses in the rating system. Secondly, the equalization principle also highlights the rather difficult relationship between local government and redistribution.

---

[227] Local Government Act 1888, Pt. I.

[228] Foster, Jackman and Perlman, *Local Government Finance in a Unitary State* (above, n. 226), 175.

[229] R. Jackman, 'Local Government Finance' in Loughlin, Gelfand and Young (eds.), *Half A Century of Municipal Decline* (above, n. 204), 144 at 147.

This vexed relationship between local government and redistribution requires further elaboration. Looking back to the 1920s we see that the economic difficulties of the period caused the Government in the 1929 Act to introduce total de-rating of agriculture and 75 per cent de-rating of industry. These reforms thus had the effect of placing the bulk of the rate yield burden on households. And since the incidence of rate burden amongst households was regressive, it could be argued that, with the growth of grant-aid, the regressive nature of the rating system provided a general restraint on use of local powers for redistributive purposes. From the 1950s, however, the position began to change. Industry was re-rated in 1958 and this was followed in 1967 by the introduction of the domestic element in rate support grant, which amounted in effect to a form of super-rating of industry and commerce. The combined impact of these measures resulted in the rate burden of households being reduced from around 66 per cent before the war to 44 per cent by 1981.[230] Further, as a result of the introduction of the rate rebate scheme in 1966, the regressive nature of the system was significantly modified and by 1981 around 30 per cent of households were in receipt of rate rebates.[231] The combined effect of these measures to equalize and to alleviate the burden on the less wealthy meant that in certain authorities rating could be used as a mechanism of redistribution, particularly since the restructuring of local government functions had tended to increase the incidence of redistributive local services. Thus, in the words of Richard Jackman, '[i]t is not the grant proportion but the redistributive nature of most of the services provided by local authorities that invites, or even necessitates, intervention by central government'.[232] And this seemed further to imply that, if local autonomy was to be revived, the redistributive dimension of local services would have to be reduced.

Central–Local Government Relations

This survey of change in the structure, functions and financial arrangements of local government during the twentieth century suggests that local government has become a powerful agency of government within the administrative State, but that the price of this power is that the affairs of local government have become inextricably bound up with those of the centre. How then were arrangements between the centre and the localities co-ordinated and organized? In a major study published in 1966, John Griffith identified three basic factors which condition the central–local relationship.[233] The first is that it is the local authorities

---

[230] R. Jackman, 'Local Government Finance' in Loughlin, Gelfand and Young (eds.), *Half A Century of Municipal Decline* (above, n. 204), 156.

[231] Ibid., 157.   [232] Ibid., 167.

[233] J.A.G. Griffith, *Central Departments and Local Authorities* (London, 1966), 17–18. Cf. D.N. Chester, *Central and Local Government. Financial and Administrative Relations* (London, 1951), 39–47.

which provide the services and therefore, although the centre may encourage, forbid or frustrate, the local authority is generally both the first and last actor. Central departments can themselves take governmental action by, for example, causing motorways or new towns to be built and, if they involve local authorities in these exercises, the relationship may be expressed in terms of principal and agent. Where local authorities are exercising their own statutory powers, however, this terminology is inappropriate. Secondly, and drawing on that first principle, Griffith suggested that it is a misdescription to characterize the relationship as one of control since, although departments certainly impose controls, local authorities also make their impact on departments; the relationship is two-way. The third factor is the general acceptance of a national minimum standard for most services which central departments will insist on local authorities attaining.

These considerations help us to understand the character of the central–local relationship in the twentieth century. In particular, since one consequence of the third factor is that the rules and regulations are generally drafted with weaker authorities in mind, the legal framework of the central–local relationship tends to present a rather distortive view of actual relations. Furthermore, although the relationship is not essentially one of principal and agent, Griffith also considered that the language of partnership was 'a pleasant and comforting evasion'.[234] Though in a broad sense departments and authorities exist to promote the public welfare, in many situations their interests differ. However, the point of general importance is that, while the power relations are invariably unequal, central departments and local authorities recognize that they are locked in a network of interdependency which requires a degree of mutual understanding, co-operation and compromise.[235]

The legal framework

As a result of the nineteenth-century reformation underpinned by the principles of 'statutorification' and *ultra vires*, the most basic function of law in local government became that of establishing a structure 'enabling local authorities to experiment with the provision of new services, to keep the public-service frontier moving, and to order their priorities for themselves as they judged best for their localities'.[236] Local government law was primarily concerned with powers rather than duties and established an essentially permissive regime.[237] Thus, local housing authorities, although imposed with a duty 'to consider the housing conditions in and the needs of their district with respect to the provision of

---

[234] *Central Departments and Local Authorities* (above, n. 233), 18.

[235] See also R.A.W. Rhodes, *Control and Power in Central–Local Government Relations* (Farnborough, 1981); id., '"Power dependence". Theories of central–local relations: a critical assessment' in M. Goldsmith (ed.), *New Research in Central–Local Relations* (Aldershot, 1986).

[236] J. Prest, *Liberty and Locality* (above, n. 68), 219–20.

[237] *First Report of the Royal Commission on Local Government* Cmd. 2506 (1925), ch. II which provided a detailed inventory of local authority functions and allocated the various responsibilities into 'obligatory functions' and 'permissive functions'.

further housing accommodation' were thereafter simply empowered to provide housing accommodation.[238] And local authorities were empowered to make bye-laws 'for the good rule and government' of the county or borough and for the 'prevention and suppression of nuisances therein'.[239]

However, even the duties cast on local authorities have generally been drafted in broad, and often highly subjective, terms. Thus the basic duty of the local education authority was 'to contribute towards the spiritual, moral, mental and physical development of the community by securing that efficent education ... shall be available to meet the needs of the population of their area'.[240] This general form is quite common. In relation to public transport, for example, the authority was under a duty 'to promote the provision of a co-ordinated and effi-cient system of public passenger transport' to meet the needs of the area.[241] The basic objective of such statutory grants of power thus seems to be that of null-ifying, or at least strictly limiting, the potentially restrictive effect of the *ultra vires* doctrine.

At the same time, the law has served to vest Ministers with extensive powers which enabled them to exercise a supervisory jurisdiction over the activities of local authorities. A number of the earlier statutes appear in effect to vest a tutelary power in the central departments. Thus, the Ministry of Health was established 'for the purpose of promoting the health of the people'[242] and the Board of Education was 'charged with the superintendence of matters relating to education'.[243] Such formulations, however, have generally been of less impor-tance than the range of specific powers conferred on Ministers. These include powers: to issue rules, regulations and orders;[244] to approve the bye-laws, plans and schemes of local authorities;[245] to determine various appeals against local authority decisions;[246] to intervene in default of action by local authorities;[247] to exercise certain controls over local officers;[248] and to inspect, inquire and obtain

---

[238] See, e.g., Housing Act 1925, ss. 57–62; Housing Act 1957, ss. 91, 92.

[239] Local Government Act 1933, s. 249.   [240] Education Act 1944, s. 7.

[241] Transport Act 1978, s. 1(1); Transport Act 1968, s. 9(3).

[242] Ministry of Health Act 1919, s. 1.   [243] Board of Education Act 1899, s. 1.

[244] The Police Act 1919, s. 4, for example, stated that the Home Secretary must, from time to time, make 'regulations as to the government, mutual aid, pay, allowances, pensions, clothing, expenses, and conditions of service of the members of all police forces in England and Wales, and every police authority shall comply with the regulations so made.' For details of departments' powers of subordinate legislation see: *Report of the Committee on Ministers' Powers* (Cmd. 4060, 1932), Minutes of Evidence, vol. 1.

[245] See, e.g., Local Government Act 1933, s. 249 (bye-laws); Education Act 1944, s. 11 (school development plans); National Assistance Act 1948, s. 34 (schemes for the provision of welfare services).

[246] See, e.g., Town and Country Planning Act 1947, s. 16 (appeal against decision on application for planning permission); Education Act 1944 s. 37(4) (appeal against school attendance order).

[247] See, e.g., Public Health Act 1875, s. 299 (see, above, 41, 49); Housing Act 1957, ss. 171–7.

[248] Local Government Act 1933, s. 100 (county clerk cannot be dismissed without consent of Minister). Ministerial controls existed over, e.g., appointment of children's officer (Children Act 1948, s. 41), chief education officer (Education Act 1944, s. 88), and chief constable (Police Act 1964, s. 4).

reports.[249] In addition to these administrative controls, there existed a panoply of financial powers relating to the payment of grants and controls over local authority borrowing.[250]

The logic of this legal framework, which both conferred substantial powers of local authority action and extensive powers of central supervision, is revealed only once it is appreciated that its function was to establish a broad framework of interdependent relations within which the centre and the localities would be obliged to negotiate and bargain over the manner in which these various governmental responsibilities were exercised. The legal framework provided a skewed picture of actual relations between central and local government; conventional practices were much more important than legal formalities. Furthermore, this facilitative legal framework, in performing an essentially power-conferring role, did not establish any clear and authoritative norms for resolving disputes which might arise within the system. Disputes were to be resolved through administrative processes according to standards which emerged through practice and, to the extent that the jurisdiction of the courts was more or less ousted, a relatively closed system of administrative law was constructed.

In order to explain and justify this general characterization, various aspects of the system must be considered. The first point to note is that the courts were unwilling to acknowledge that, if the interests of citizens were detrimentally affected by the exercise of a local authority's powers to provide services, they might give rise to enforceable legal rights. Thus, since the Housing Acts gave the local authority general rights of management over their stock,[251] the courts were unwilling to confer any legal protection on tenants whom the authority proposed to evict. 'It is, to my mind,' said Lord Porter in 1948, 'one of the important duties of management that the local body should be able to pick and choose their tenants at their will.'[252] And even in the 1970s the courts, despite recognizing that the exercise of statutory powers by local authorities gave rise to 'one of the constitutional problems of our time',[253] continued to support this stance on the ground that local authorities are in the best position to manage in the light of local circumstances and the 'electors are in a far better position than this court ever could be to decide whether the powers have been exercised in a way which meets with general approval'.[254]

[249] See, e.g., Education Act 1944, s. 77 (inspection of educational establishments); Housing Act 1957, s. 181 (general Ministerial power to hold local inquiry); Local Government Act 1929, s. 51 (requiring all local authorities to 'make to the Minister such reports and returns and give him such information with respect to their functions as he may require').

[250] See, e.g., Local Government Act 1933, s. 218 (Ministerial consent required for local authority borrowing).

[251] See, e.g., Housing Act 1957, ss. 111–13, 158.

[252] *Shelley* v. *London County Council* [1949] AC 56, at 66.

[253] *Bristol DC* v. *Clark* [1975] 3 All ER 976, 980 (per Lawton LJ).

[254] Ibid., at 981. See also *Cannock Chase DC* v. *Kelly* [1978] 1 All ER 152. We might note that, in adopting this position, the courts were expressing their traditional reluctance to interfere with the decisions of elected local authorities. For the classic statement of this position see *Kruse* v. *Johnson*

Further, the courts persisted with this approach even when statutes appeared to confer certain rights. Thus, although education authorities, in exercising all powers and duties, were required to have regard 'to the general principle that, so far as is compatible with the provision of efficient instruction and training and the avoidance of unreasonable expenditure, pupils are to be educated in accordance with the wishes of their parents',[255] the courts consistently held that the provision could not found an independent head of claim.[256] The courts also refused to accept that, had breach of duty been found, mandamus could be an appropriate remedy: 'it is not a statute intended to benefit parents in the same way that the Factories Acts are intended for the protection of workmen'[257] and the central supervisory powers were held to be sufficient to indicate that Parliament intended that action for any transgression should be taken by the Minister.[258] This judicial reluctance to perform a supervisory role, even in relation to the enforcement of duties, seems rooted in a sense that it lacks the competence to make an assessment of the character of duties formulated by reference to such terms as 'efficiency', 'adequacy' and 'needs'.[259]

This system of administrative law was not, of course, entirely closed, particularly as the statutes often provided a right of appeal against local authority decisions to the courts. It remained, nevertheless, a specially constructed regime. In a survey of cases reported in the Local Government Reports for 1930, Jennings concluded that 'in not a single reported case in 1930 did the ordinary rules of law apply in proceedings taken against a public authority'.[260] In the design of this system, the services of the ordinary courts were used but the law was special: 'The hands may be the hands of Esau but the voice is that of Jacob'.[261] It was, in general, a system which was designed to keep the courts out. The Secretary of State's powers under the Education Act 1944, for example, were

(1898) 2 QB 91, 100: 'A bye-law is not unreasonable merely because particular judges may think it goes further than is prudent or necessary or convenient . . . Surely it is not too much to say that in matters which directly and mainly concern the people of the county, who have the right to choose whom they think best fitted to represent them in their local government bodies, such representatives may be trusted to understand their own requirements better than Judges'.

[255] Education Act 1944, s. 76.

[256] *Watt* v. *Kesteven CC* [1955] 1 QB 408; *Wood* v. *Ealing LBC* [1967] 1 Ch. 364; *Cumings* v. *Birkenhead Corporation* [1972] Ch. 12.

[257] [1955] 1 QB 408 at 415 (per Ormerod J).

[258] For a similar point see *Wyatt* v. *Hillingdon LBC* (1978) 76 LGR 727 in which the Court of Appeal dismissed an action in damages based on the authority's alleged failure to provide adequate home help facilities as required under the Chronically Sick and Disabled Persons Act 1970 on the ground that the default procedure under s. 36 of the National Assistance Act 1948 provided the appropriate remedy.

[259] In the context of duties under the Education Act 1944, for example, see: *R* v. *Hereford and Worcester LEA, ex parte Jones* [1981] 1 WLR 768; Second Report from the Education, Science and Arts Committee, Session 1981–82, *The Secondary School Curriculum and Examinations* HC 116, para. 9.11; Initial Government Observations on the Second Report from the Education, Science and Arts Committee, Session 1981–82 (Cmnd. 8551, 1982), 12.

[260] W.I. Jennings, *Local Government in the Modern Constitution* (above, n. 132), 31.

[261] Ibid.

clearly intended to provide not simply an alternative to judicial review but a more appropriate remedy since 'litigation is inherently vexatious and expensive, and also because many of the issues that might arise could be of a specialist and technical character'.[262] Judicial supervision of local authorities, a basic characteristic of the traditional regime, had been replaced by the administrative supervision of central departments.

On the issue of central supervision, there is a danger in adopting too literal an interpretation of the powers of central departments. Ministers, as Griffith reminds us, 'have no overall statutory duties to ensure that housing is adequate, that the road system meets national needs, that public health provisions are appropriate, that the police and fire services are efficient'.[263] Even the Education Act 1944, which contained the strongest general formulation seeking to place the Minister in the role of overlord, is highly ambiguous. Section 1 of that Act stated that the Minister's duty 'shall be to promote the education of the people . . . and to secure the effective execution by local authorities, under his control and direction, of the national policy for providing a varied and comprehensive educational service'. Griffith comments that, although 'a foreign lawyer . . . might regard section 1 . . . as an unambiguous statement of a highly centralized system . . . [b]oth in statutory provision and in practice, section 1 means less than it says'.[264] The main reason is that the centre was not provided with the specific range of powers needed to give effect to that intention. If, for example, the Department 'wished to influence the shape of secondary education in a local authority, it has had to resort to the use of powers not primarily, or even at all, intended for that purpose'.[265]

The centre's powers were generally used in a strategic sense only to enforce a basic minimum standard of provision or to protect the centre's interests relating to the management of the economy. The powers available to the centre seemed in fact to have been designed mainly for the quasi-judicial purpose of ensuring the fair treatment of the various local interests affected by the exercise of local authority powers. Certainly, these powers had not been devised for the purpose of giving an overall strategic direction to local policy development; indeed, there are doubts as to whether the centre, with its generalist civil service tradition, could actually summon the necessary resources for this purpose. The manner in which the centre's powers had been drafted seemed basically to indicate that what was intended was the construction of a system of administrative law.

This interpretation is reinforced by an examination of the manner in which

---

[262] Second Report from the Education, Science and Arts Committee, Session 1981–82, para. 9.16.

[263] Griffith, *Central Departments and Local Authorities* (above, n. 233), 52.

[264] Ibid., 98–9.

[265] Ibid., 51. See also, R. Buxton, *Local Government* (Harmondsworth, 1970) who suggested that the provisions of the 1944 Act 'well illustrate the confused coexistence between national and local government which characterizes the education service' and argued that the Act 'does not provide any effective means of coercing the local authority to do what the government requires' (196).

central powers have in practice been used. We might, for example, note the way in which audit procedure has evolved[266] or the practices of the centre in confirming local authority bye-laws.[267] Even the more coercive default-type powers tend to have much greater bark than bite, especially since they are cumbersome instruments, which involve great expense, a high degree of formality and cannot be put into effect expeditiously.[268] To take an extreme example, consider the Ministerial power under section 6 of the Local Government Act 1948 to reduce the amount of grant payable to a council if 'he is satisfied . . . that the council have failed to maintain a reasonable standard of efficiency . . . or . . . that the expenditure of the council has been excessive and unreasonable'. This apparently Draconian power was in practice unworkable. In part, this was because it required the laying of a report before Parliament and thus involved a major political commitment. However, this power could only be applied retrospectively and, after it had been exercised, the final determination of rates and expenditure levels was still left with the local authority. In such circumstances it was difficult to see what benefits could flow from the invocation of the provision.[269] Close examination of many of these central powers tended to show that they were less intrusive than they initially appeared.

One consequence of this general framework was that there was not a great deal of legal consciousness in the conduct of central–local government relations. A good example concerned the legal regime relating to the provision of further education. Although local authorities were empowered to make provision for further education, the power became operative only after schemes had been submitted to, and approved by, the Secretary of State.[270] Few schemes were drawn up and submitted. Since, as a matter of routine, local authorities nevertheless provided further education within their areas, these programmes seemed to be sustained by tacit administrative approval rather than formal legal authority. Furthermore, if the lack of legal authority imposed a constraint on local authority action, new legislation could always be promoted; and generally central government were not unresponsive.[271] And the fact that such legislative action

---

[266] See, above, 48–9.

[267] See H. Finer, *English Local Government* (above, n. 115), 303: 'The model bye-laws prepared by the central Departments are based on long experience and in relation to the proposals of hundreds of authorities. Indeed, it is not easy for a local authority to get any *original* bye-law approved; the central Department demands precedents!'

[268] See D.N Chester, *Central and Local Government* (above, n. 233), 107–23.

[269] Though these powers were only repealed in the Local Government, Planning and Land Act 1980, s. 53(11)(c); Sched.8, they were retained in the Scottish legislation. Nevertheless, the Local Government (Scotland) Act 1966, s. 5 had to be amended by the Local Government (Miscellaneous Provisions) (Scotland) Act 1981, s. 14 before the powers could be invoked as an instrument of expenditure restraint: see A. Midwinter, *The Politics of Local Spending* (Edinburgh, 1984), ch. 3.

[270] Education Act 1944, ss. 41, 42.

[271] Consider two examples. In *R* v. *Sheffield Corporation* (1871) LR 6 QB 652 the court held that borough councils had no power to charge to the borough fund the cost of opposing private Bills which they believed to be against the interests of the borough. This case, which aroused a 'storm of indignation' (Redlich and Hirst, vol. II, 365) caused Parliament to enact the Borough Funds Act

was often required because of judicial decision which upset settled understanding served only to confirm the necessity of keeping courts out of the system.

The legal framework was thus designed to provide administrative rather than judicial supervision of the exercise of the local authority's statutory powers and duties, especially in circumstances in which policy factors – requiring judgments of adequacy or efficiency – were involved. Furthermore, this was a regime in which the courts, notwithstanding one or two controversial judgments, readily acquiesced.[272] Certainly the High Court was considered to be an inappropriate institution for the resolution of policy disputes between central departments and local authorities. In general, judicial procedures were simply too slow, too expensive and overly formal, and the adversarial proceedings were felt to be unsuited to the task of addressing claims which required the weighing of a variety of conflicting interests. Judicial proceedings were also felt to be a singularly inappropriate means of resolving central–local disputes since, as is generally recognized, any externally imposed settlement of a dispute between interdependent bodies which were obliged to maintain continuing relations with one another was unlikely to provide a genuine resolution of the dispute; negotiation rather than adjudication was likely to prove a more effective means of dispute resolution. In addition to the institutional limitations of courts, some commentators argued that, given the individualistic legal culture of the judiciary, the courts were likely to frustrate policy decisions rooted in a collectivist ethos.[273]

Many of these characteristics of the legal framework of central–local government relations were thrown into relief as a result of the protracted dispute about

---

1872 which, albeit not to the entire satisfaction of the councils, rectified the situation: see Bellamy, *Administering Central–Local Relations 1871–1919* (above, n. 139), 200–1. The second example concerns the case of *Prescott* v. *Birmingham Corporation* [1955] Ch. 210 in which the Court of Appeal declared *ultra vires* the defendant's old age pensioners' concessionary fares scheme. Immediately following the judgment, a Private Member's Bill, which became the Public Service Vehicles (Travel Concessions) Act 1955, was promoted which effectively nullified the effect of the judgment: see further ch. 4, 214–17, 229.

[272] This role is perhaps best exemplified by the case of *Associated Provincial Picture Houses Ltd* v. *Wednesbury Corporation* [1948] 1 KB 223 in which Lord Greene MR, seeking to distance the courts from the criticism which they encountered as a result of the decision in *Roberts* v. *Hopwood* [1925] AC 578 (see ch. 4, 210–12), arrived at the formulation that judicial review was not exercisable on the grounds of unreasonableness but only if the decision was 'so unreasonable that no reasonable authority could ever have come to it' (234). Though the judgment was scarcely a model of clarity, Lord Greene seemed to suggest that this test meant that, before the courts could intervene, the decision must be 'so absurd that no sensible person could ever dream that it lay within the powers of the authority' (229). Griffith has suggested that it was only in the 1930s that 'the courts began to accept these powers with any grace' but that in the post-war period the judges seemed 'to be leaning over backwards almost to the point of falling off the Bench to avoid the appearance of hostility': J.A.G. Griffith, 'The law of property (land)' in M. Ginsberg (ed.), *Law and Opinion in England in the Twentieth Century* (London, 1959), 116, at 116, 120.

[273] For representative accounts of this theme see: H.J. Laski, 'Judicial Review of Social Policy in England' (1926) 39 *Harvard Law Rev* 839; W.I. Jennings, 'The Courts and Administrative Law – the experience of English housing legislation' (1936) 49 *Harvard Law Rev*. 426; J.A.G. Griffith, 'Judges in Politics' (1968) 3 *Govt. & Oppos.* 485; P. McAuslan, 'Administrative law, collective consumption and judicial policy' (1983) 46 MLR 1.

comprehensive schooling during the 1960s and 1970s. The adoption by the new Labour Government in 1964 of the policy of comprehensive education disrupted the post-1944 concord and, particularly as the Government decided to implement its programme without seeking new legal powers, it also highlighted ambiguities in the powers and duties of central and local authorities. The Government's request that local authorities draw up plans for comprehensive reorganization within a year[274] thus seemed 'to be a statement of national policy without the means to enforce it'.[275] As Buxton put it, the Minister's powers were of 'an *ad hoc* and arbitrary nature, and were certainly not developed with the intention of giving Whitehall power to impose nation-wide reorganization'.[276] Furthermore, when schemes were proposed and implemented, parents opposed to the abolition of grammar schools then sought to assert their rights. The resulting strains, best illustrated through the extended Enfield dispute,[277] demonstrated the ambiguous nature of parental rights in the system. And when, during the 1970s, central government exercised its statutory powers to require Tameside Metropolitan Borough Council to continue with an approved implementation scheme, the resulting legal action led to one of the most controversial judicial decisions of modern times.[278] In interpreting the Secretary of State's power under section 68 of the 1944 Act as sanctioning action only if the local authority were acting in a *Wednesbury* unreasonable fashion, the court seemed to confirm the interpretation of the central–local relationship as being constructed as a system of administrative law.[279] For many, however, the *Tameside* decision served only to confirm Jennings's view that judicial review 'often . . . acts as a spanner in the middle of delicate machinery' and that the courts consistently interpret powers 'in such a way as to obstruct efficient administration'.[280]

The disputes which arose over the issue of comprehensive schooling provide good illustrations of the general point that the statutory framework was not intended to establish a normative framework which would be rigorously policed by the courts. There were simply too many lacunae, irregularities and ambiguities

---

[274] Department of Education, Circular 10/65.

[275] Griffith, *Central Departments and Local Authorities* (above, n. 233), 511.

[276] Buxton, *Local Government* (above, n. 265), 198.

[277] See *Bradbury* v. *Enfield LBC* [1967] 1 WLR 1311; *Lee* v. *Enfield LBC* [1967] 66 LGR 195; *Lee* v. *Department of Education and Science* [1967] 66 LGR 211. See Buxton, *Local Government* (above, n. 265), 202–15.

[278] *Secretary of State for Education and Science* v. *Tameside MBC* [1977] AC 1014. See, e.g., P.P. Craig, *Administrative Law* (London, 3rd edn., 1994), 434–5; J.A.G. Griffith, *The Politics of the Judiciary* (London, 4th edn., 1991), 120–3; M. Loughlin, *Local Government, the Law and the Constitution* (London, 1983), 74–82; D. Bull, '*Tameside* Revisited: Prospectively "Reasonable"; Retrospectively "Maladministration"' (1987) 50 MLR 307; P. McAuslan, 'Administrative law, collective consumption and judicial policy' (1983), 46 MLR 1, 14–15.

[279] See, e.g., Second Report from the Education, Science and Arts Committee, Session 1981–82, *The Secondary School Curriculum and Examinations* (HC 116), para. 9.16: '. . . it appears to be the Department's view that sections 68 and 99 are dangerously punitive measures, difficult to enforce in the courts, and that they are measures of absolute last resort'.

[280] Jennings, *Local Government in the Modern Constitution* (above, n. 132), 3.

in the framework and the statutory language was too opaque for the judiciary to be confident of explicating it as a juridical nexus of enforceable rights and duties. 'Jurist-law' had to be understood against the background of 'folk-law'; or, to give Maitland's formulation a modern twist, sense could be made of the legal framework only by first appreciating the political culture within which it was embedded.

The conduct of central–local relations

Gneist and Halevy were agreed that cohesion in the traditional constitution was attributable to the institutionalization of an aristocratic principle (though, for Halevy, Gneist's idea of 'self-government' was treated as a synonym for class government). Throughout the nineteenth century many of the concerns expressed about the likely effect of extensions to the franchise implicitly recognized this point and the stance adopted by many public figures to reform was shaped by their assessment of the lingering power of deference.[281] At the turn of the century, it could be observed that the 'gradual substitution of a democratic for a privileged franchise has not done away with the governing classes . . . and was not found to have deprived the upper classes of political leadership'.[282]

This situation changed in the twentieth century. With the break up of the great estates after the First World War, the landowners gradually abdicated from local politics[283] and eventually the 'social leaders' came to be replaced by less exalted 'public persons'.[284] Also, after 1918 the Labour party began to gain a significant strength in local government and this often led to anti-socialist alliances between Liberals, Conservatives and ratepayer organizations.[285] After 1945, when the first local elections under universal adult suffrage were held, the party contest rapidly became institutionalized in local government. And during this post-war period, local politics was also assimilated into the national contest between the major parties. This process of 'nationalization of local politics', however, depended less on institutional mechanisms than on the shared assumptions and values of local and national politicians.[286]

---

[281] See, e.g., W. Bagehot, *The English Constitution* (London, R.H.S. Crossman ed., 1963), 274–5. Dicey believed that constitutionalist values could be protected by the British practice of 'democracy tempered by snobbishness': A.V. Dicey, *Lectures on the Relation between Law and Public Opinion in England during the Nineteenth Century* (London, 1905), 57. See also A. Briggs, *The Age of Improvement, 1783–1867* (London, 1959), ch. x.

[282] Redlich and Hirst, vol. I, 278.

[283] D. Cannadine (ed.), *Patricians, Power and Politics in the Nineteenth Century* (Leicester, 1982), esp. 2–15.

[284] J.M. Lee, *Social Leaders and Public Persons* (Oxford, 1963); G.W. Jones, *Borough Politics* (London, 1969).

[285] K. Young, *Local Politics and the Rise of Party* (Leicester, 1975).

[286] J. Gyford, 'The Politicization of Local Government' in Loughlin, Gelfand and Young (eds.), *Half A Century of Municipal Decline* (above, n. 204), 77, 87; J. Gyford and M. James, *National Parties and Local Politics* (London, 1983).

Since the legal framework of local government gave a great deal of freedom to local authorities to determine their own working arrangements, efficient decision-making structures could be devised through administrative processes to accommodate the emergence of party politics. However, in general local politics took the form of 'administrative politics' in which officers exerted great influence over the decision-making processes.[287] The claims of democratic politics certainly were acknowledged, but often this primarily required officers to exercise their managerial skills to sell policies to the political leadership. This practice of administrative politics thus went hand-in-glove with a tradition of 'managerial professionalism' which had emerged in local government, in which a highly professionalized staff delivered services through a hierarchically structured, departmentally organized local authority.[288] Although, in law, the relationship between the council and its staff was essentially that of master and servant, the reality of the working relationship between members and officers tended to be rather different.[289]

The conduct of central–local government relations may best be appreciated in the context of these traditions of local politics and managerial professionalism. Both the political and the professional networks which have emerged in the twentieth century have been built on the foundations of these traditions. Furthermore, these networks have become of vital importance to the structure of modern governance. Since, as we have seen, the legal framework does not systematically place the centre in a directive position, central co-ordination of policy development has in practice been achieved (to the extent that in practice it has been achieved) through these various networks.[290] The emergence and institutionalization of these policy communities and professional communities has led in effect to the establishment of a 'national local government system'.[291]

Policy communities have been defined as 'stable, integrated policy networks' which, though 'predicated on the asymmetrical relationship between government and other actors', have become a key method of involving affected actors in the processes of policy-making.[292] Of particular importance in the central–local context is the role of the local authority associations, of which Griffith comments that it 'is difficult to exaggerate their importance in influencing

---

[287] See M. Hill, *The Sociology of Public Administration* (London, 1972), ch. 11.

[288] J.D. Stewart, 'The Functioning and Management of Local Authorities' in Loughlin, Gelfand and Young (eds.), *Half A Century of Municipal Decline* (above, n. 204), ch. 5; Griffith, *Central Departments and Local Authorities* (above, n. 233), 534: 'The professionalism of local government officers is the greatest single force which enables local authorities to carry out, with much efficiency, the considerable tasks entrusted to them.'

[289] On the nature of conventional practices in local government see: W.J.M. Mackenzie, 'The Conventions of Local Government' (1951) 31 *Public Admin.* 345.

[290] See L.J. Sharpe, 'Central Coordination and the Policy Network' (1985) XXXIII *Political Studies* 361.

[291] P. Dunleavy, *The Politics of Mass Housing in Britain, 1945–1975* (Oxford, 1981), 123–4; R.A.W. Rhodes, *The National World of Local Government* (London, 1986).

[292] Rhodes, ibid., 23, 26.

legislation, government policies and administration and in acting as co-ordinators and channels of local authority opinion'.[293] The professional communities, of which there are numerous linkages,[294] are particularly important in facilitating two-way communication between local and central government through the development of a common technical language, the recognition of a common 'operating ideology'[295] and the shared membership of a professional association. These professional communities are of particular importance in establishing norms of conduct which are not specified by law; and, in a sense, this self-regulatory mechanism provides a partial privatization (or non-juridification) of a system of administrative law.[296]

It is through this elaborate policy network that the business of central–local government relations was conducted. Within this network, the formal legal powers and duties of the relevant parties are simply one – and invariably not the most important – of a range of factors which shape the relationship. In the course of business, certain informal 'rules of the game' or conventional understandings emerge and these tend to provide a better explanation of behaviour than the formal legal position. During the period between 1970 and the early 1980s, for example, Rhodes identified the following as being amongst the most important of these informal rules: *pragmatism*, that doctrinal disputes should not prevent basic work being undertaken; *fairness*, that parties affected by proposed policies should have the opportunity to state their case; *accommodation*, that where agreement is not possible, the loser should not be antagonized; *territoriality*, that actors do not extend their demands beyond their known remit; *secrecy*, that discussions should take place in private and be limited to affected parties; *trust*, that the effectiveness of discussions depends on assessments of reliability; *local democracy*, that local authorities have a sphere of competence within which central departments should not interfere; and *the right to govern*, that there is a sphere in which the centre has the right to intervene to protect its conception of the national interest.[297]

Clearly, such conventional rules provide only guides and, like most sets of general principles, exist in tension with one another. But such rules provide a better clue to the character of this interdependent network than the statutory

---

[293] Griffith, *Central Departments and Local Authorities* (above, n. 233), 33.

[294] M. Laffin, *Professionalism and Policy: The Role of the Professions in the Central–Local Government Relationship* (Aldershot, 1986); D. Rosenberg, *Accounting for Public Policy. Power, Professionals and Politics in Local Government* (Manchester, 1989), ch. 3.

[295] L.J. Sharpe, 'Instrumental Participation in Urban Government' in J.A.G. Griffith (ed.), *From Policy to Administration* (London, 1976), ch. 6. Cf. the discussion of 'assumptive worlds' in K. Young, 'Values in the Policy Process' (1977) 5 *Policy and Politics* 1.

[296] On the importance of professions in transforming a conception of rights into functions, and thus socializing legal rights without having to address these complexities in a juridical sense see: T.L. Haskell, 'Professionalism *versus* Capitalism: R.H. Tawney, Emile Durkheim, and C.S. Peirce on the Disinterestedness of Professional Communities' in T.L. Haskell (ed.), *The Authority of Experts. Studies in History and Theory* (Bloomington, Ind., 1984), 180 at 188–9.

[297] Rhodes, *The National World of Local Government* (above, n. 291), 391–2.

framework. As Griffith acknowledged, the 'antagonism which from time to time arises between the groups [viz., central departments and local authorities] is an indulgence which each can afford because both recognize this necessary inter-dependence'.[298] But what are the general conditions which sustain this network of interdependency? We have seen in relation to the issue of comprehensive schooling that severe strains were placed on the network as a result of an issue of education policy being identified as a party political question. Could the system survive more extensive strains which might arise from the re-emergence of ideological politics? To what extent, that is, did this network rest on a basic congruence of political values?

The Triumph of Benthamism?

The chronicle which has unfolded in examining the question of local government has been that of the gradual absorption of the institutions of local government into the apparatus of the central State. The ideal of local self-government consists of the belief that local communities should be able to express their collective identity, sustain a degree of civic consciousness and maintain an existence independent of the central State. These local institutions, which are thus sustained by their close association with the traditional patterns of social life, have often been acknowledged as constituting the strength of free nations. This view has been closely associated with Tocqueville, who commented that 'it is man who makes monarchies and establishes republics, but the township seems to come directly from the hand of God'.[299] But Tocqueville also recognized that '[t]he difficulty of establishing its independence rather augments than diminishes with the increasing intelligence of the people', that '[a] highly civilized community can hardly tolerate a local independence', and that local institutions 'cannot defend themselves with success [against a strong and enterprising government] unless they are identified with the customs of the nation and supported by public opinion'.[300]

However the traditional arrangements of English local government are to be characterized (and it is stretching credulity to its limits to view the aristocratic arrangements of class rule as being analagous to self-government), those arrangements were thoroughly ill-equipped to address the challenges faced in the localities as a result of industrialization and urbanization. The centre had little alternative but to act to reform the system. The nineteenth-century reformation resulted in local government emerging as a set of corporate institutions which appeared to owe their status to the State and which were organized to serve their publics. As a consequence of these reforms and the gradual growth of the

---

[298] Griffith, *Central Departments and Local Authorities* (above, n. 233), 506.
[299] Tocqueville, *Democracy in America* (above, n. 23), vol. 1, 60.
[300] Ibid.

administrative State, local authorities have emerged in the twentieth century as major institutions of governance. But this development has occurred largely because local authorities have become inextricably bound up in the affairs of central government.

After the nineteenth-century reforms, any appeal to a tradition of local self-government can no longer comfortably rest on ancient custom and history; the various shifts in the patterns of life and work and the comprehensive nature of the institutional reforms make such claims highly implausible. Nor, given the peculiarities of our constitutional arrangements, can such appeals be based on some authoritative set of constitutional norms. If tradition is to be invoked it must now be found to rest on modern practices and thus on a set of political understandings which have, over time, commanded widespread support. Furthermore, although attempts have been made to articulate justifications for local government in terms of the value of having intermediate institutions which interpose themselves between the individual and the State and of recognizing the role of local government in providing an exercise in political participation and political education, the primary justification for local government seems now to be rooted in its role as providing an efficient and effective institution for providing public services.[301]

Though the modern institution of local government has been regularly adjusted in the light of central imperatives, the value of the institution has throughout the twentieth century continued to be acknowledged. Local government was traditionally protected from becoming a subordinate creature of the central State as a result of the work undertaken by Parliament and the courts. Both institutions have ceded a great deal of ground to central government. Parliament, labouring under the pressures of a twentieth century workload, has relinquished the direct control over local administration which it once exercised through the private Bill procedure and, through the use of framework legislation, has enabled central and local government to negotiate arrangements for the provision of services. The courts, being unable to devise a 'jurist-law' capable of responding to the legal challenges of the administrative state, have acquiesced in the growth of an informal system of administrative law in which the central State performs a supervisory jurisdiction over the activities of local bodies. Nevertheless, the structure of central–local arrangements has been such as to acknowledge the claims of local authorities to represent the interests of their communities and to retain their capacity to initiate action to meet the needs of their locality.

That is, local government was far from having been fully absorbed into the central State system. The powers acquired by the centre did not serve to vest it with an overarching power of strategic direction. Such powers were, in reality,

---

[301] See L.J. Sharpe, 'Theories and Values of Local Government' (1970) XVIII *Political Studies* 153; W. Magnusson, 'Bourgeois Theories of Local Government' (1986) XXXIV *Political Studies* 1; K. Young, 'The Justification for Local Government' in M. Goldsmith (ed.), *Essays on the Future of Local Government* (Wakefield, 1986).

mainly available to ensure that the various conflicting interests were being fairly treated by local councils when exercising their extensive powers. Central involvement in local government was thus essentially the result of the nineteenth-century reforms placing 'the cash nexus' in a pivotal position in local affairs and local government being redesigned as a 'compulsory Association of Consumers'.[302] This reformation, particularly as reinforced by the twentieth century restructuring of functions, caused some contemporary commentators to define local government as an agency of collective consumption[303] and thus to identify a fundamental division in the allocation of state functions, with local government being concerned primarily with issues of consumption and the centre with matters of production.[304] Since this functional differentiation seemed to go hand-in-hand with particular types of politics – with those of the centre being characterized as a form of closed, corporatist politics based on economic policy and those of the localities constituting a more open type of politics rooted in social need – this form of analysis thus revealed the potential for a basic conflict between the institutions of central and local government over economic and social policy priorities.[305] From this perspective, local government could be seen to occupy an ambivalent position in relation to the central State; and, indeed, might well be viewed as the Achilles heel of the political system.[306]

This apparent potential for basic conflict had been insulated, primarily by the elaborate policy and professional networks which have emerged during the twentieth century to ensure co-ordination between central and local action. These networks were, however, themselves underpinned by the traditions of administrative politics and managerial professionalism which evolved in local government. From the mid-1970s onwards, the cement which held these communities together began to crumble in the face of economic strains. As a result of economic stagnation and fiscal retrenchment those tensions within the system of central–local government relations, which had been concealed by continous economic growth, the political consensus over the welfare state and an acceptance of the ability of the professional communities to overcome narrow conceptions of self interest and act in the public interest, became exposed. The increased political pressures generated by the changed economic conditions contributed to

[302] S. & B. Webb, *English Local Government, Vol. 4* (above, n. 46), 437–45.
[303] See, e.g., P. Saunders, *Social Theory and the Urban Question* (London, 1981), 180–218, 258–68.
[304] P. Saunders, 'Why Study Central–Local Relations?' (1982) vol. 8 no. 2 *Local Government Studies* 55; L.J. Sharpe, 'Functional Allocation in the Welfare State' (1984) vol. 10 no. 1 *Local Government Studies* 27.
[305] Saunders, 'Why Study Central–Local Relations?' (above, n. 304); id., 'Reflections on the dual politics thesis: the argument, its origins and its critics' in M. Goldsmith and S. Villadsen (eds.), *Urban Political Theory and the Management of Fiscal Stress* (Aldershot, 1986) ch. 1.
[306] P. Saunders, 'Local Government and the State', 55 *New Society* 550 (13 March 1981). It is because of the recognition of this cleavage that some political scientists expressed particular interest in the re-emergence of municipal socialism during the 1980s. See M. Boddy and C. Fudge (eds.), *Local Socialism?* (London, 1984). See further ch. 3 below.

the re-emergence of ideological politics[307] within both the major parties. And since the modern political party is 'a complex set of plural institutions'[308] this exacerbated the differences not only between but also within the parties, as radicals on each wing challenged the post-war consensus on the welfare state.

When in 1979 a Conservative Government was elected on a radical programme based on need to shift the boundaries between public and private, to promote market processes over planning techniques, and to assert the principle of consumer sovereignty, the consequences for the central–local government relations were evident. The collectivist character of local government services came to be seen as a basic impediment on the Government's objective of extending the sphere of market relations. Since professionals were viewed not as disinterested promoters of the public interest but as self-serving status groups who had erected barriers against innovation, the Government sought to challenge both the organizational structure of local government and also the influence of professional communities within the central–local network. Furthermore, although the resulting strains were felt throughout local government, in many of the conurbations the economic and political circumstances caused local Labour parties to redefine the relationship between local authorities and local communities and to rebuild a distinctive municipal socialist policy in which local government was viewed as an arena for opposing the capitalist State. These new forms of ideological politics on both right and left thus sought not only to challenge existing policies but also to alter the basic operating methods and decision-making processes in both central and local government. Consequently, it seemed highly unlikely that the central–local co-ordination network, which was based ultimately on a congruence of values, could withstand the political upheaval.

The Conservative Government's programme was driven essentially by the Benthamite principle of utility, albeit dressed in the modern garb of the value-for-money criteria of economy, efficiency and effectiveness. And the implementation of this programme also seemed to bear out many of the fears which have been expressed about the basic incompatibility between the principles of Benthamism and the retention of a system of local government. This sense of incompatibility stems primarily from the belief that, once the centre becomes wedded to the single-minded pursuit of efficiency, local institutions will come to be viewed purely in instrumental terms, and, especially when efficiency is equated with market values and the promotion of competition, this must inevitably lead to the denigration of local government. There is, however, also a process dimension to this argument since it is also the case that, if local government is viewed solely as an instrument for promoting economic welfare, the

[307] Ideological politics, which may be contrasted with administrative politics, results in the political parties providing specific and detailed programmes which they then work to translate into action: see M. Hill, *The Sociology of Public Administration* (above, n. 287), 210–16.
[308] R. Rose, *Politics in England* (London, 1980), 254.

system of local government is likely to be destabilized simply because the organizational requirements for efficiency are constantly changing.

While the economic, political and administrative upheavals are a critical part of the picture, the primary concern of this book is to examine the role which law has played in the light of the recent changes in the pattern of central–local government relations. As we have seen, the function of law within the twentieth century accommodation has been to establish a general framework for the conduct of central–local relations: the work of policy development and policy implementation was channelled through the policy and professional communities with very little active legal regulation, and the courts have played only a marginal role in policing local action, with the active supervisory work being undertaken primarily by central government agencies. The Conservative Government's strategy, however, had the effect of placing major strains on these policy networks, particularly as the Government was obliged to assert its hierarchical position in order to try to realize its objectives. This strategy had important implications for the role of law in the process. Once the conventions of the administrative network were challenged, affected parties turned to the law in search of answers to their grievances. Since the legislative framework had never been designed to establish an overarching regulatory structure, the statutes were all too often either thoroughly ambiguous or completely silent on the critical issue. This period is thus one in which the government has had to resort to the use of legislation for the purpose of speedily constructing a rule-based regime. Furthermore, once the conventional rules of the game had been undermined, affected parties, rather than seeking to resolve their differences through administrative processes, turned to the courts for a resolution of the dispute.

The contemporary period has thus been one in which both Parliament and the courts have been brought back into the central–local relationship. These have, however, been frustrating and controversial developments, with the parliamentary timetable once again becoming clogged up with local government business and the courts being dragged into a number of complex disputes which they seem ill-equipped to resolve. The root cause of the problem, it would appear, is that the centre has been seeking to use the central–local relationship as though it had been constructed in a hierarchical image of superior and subordinate. One objective of this chapter, however, has been to show that, notwithstanding the modern changes in our system of local government, this is not the case. One particularly important theme of this historical excursus has been to highlight the fact that the gaps and ambiguities in the legal framework of central–local relations are not the result of oversight but are a direct reflection of the attempt to express in law our historic traditions of local government.

This chapter thus provides a frame for addressing the significance of these contemporary developments. It has sought to identify the character of English local government and the continuing importance in the modern era of that tradition of local government. It has highlighted the extent to which our arrangements of government have rested not on formal institutional differentiation but on a shared value system and have been sustained by a particular political culture. In relation to law, it has emphasized the inextricable bond which exists within our traditions of governance between 'folk-law' and 'jurist-law'. What, finally, the chapter has sought to demonstrate is the extent to which the roots of the contemporary conflicts between central departments and local authorities lie deeply embedded in administrative, constitutional and legal history.

2

CONTEMPORARY TRENDS

On 1 April 1974 a new structure of local government came into existence, bringing to a resolution an intense period of inquiry and review which had taken place over much of the previous decade. This new system was designed to restore the status of local government which was in danger of being severely eroded owing to the fact that local government structures no longer 'fit[ted] the pattern of life and work in modern England'.[1] In promoting these reforms, the then Conservative government stated that it was 'determined to return power to those people who should exercise decisions locally, and to ensure that local government is given every opportunity to take that initiative effectively, speedily and with vigour'.[2] In the following twenty years, local government has been subject to a vast array of changes, many of which challenge the assumptions underpinning the reforms of the early 1970s. Cumulatively, these reforms have had a major impact on the institution of local government. The pace of change has been particularly pronounced since 1979 as successive Conservative governments have acted with great vigour to redefine the appropriate relationship between State and society and, as part of this endeavour, have sought to set in place a more limited role for local government. The model of local government emerging in the 1990s does not appear to be one which serves to strengthen local government's capacity for local initiative. Further, to the extent that the recent reforms have sought to return power to local people, their objective has been mainly to take power away from local councils. Local government, it would appear, has become part of the problem of finding democratic ways of living.

In this chapter, I will examine the thrust of the changes which have taken place over the last twenty years, with the objective of assessing the effect which these changes have had on the status of local government. For this purpose, those reforms which have had a significant impact on the political capacity of the institution of local government will be of particular importance. There are, I believe, four basic factors which have a major bearing on this issue: structure, functions, accountability and finance. The *structure* of local government obviously has a direct effect on institutional capacity, since it provides some indication of the appropriateness of the organization to undertake particular responsibilities. The range of local government *functions* is a manifestation of the relative importance of the institution within the general system of government.

---

[1] *Report of the Royal Commission on Local Government in England* (Chairman: Lord Redcliffe-Maud), Cmnd. 4040 (1969) vol. 1, para. 6(i).
[2] *Local Government in England: Government Proposals for Reorganization*, Cmnd. 4584 (1971).

The nature of the *accountability mechanisms* within the local government system provides an index of the extent of the institution's power of autonomous action. And the question of *finance*, and particularly the council's ability to draw upon its own sources of finance, has a powerful effect on its ability in practice to execute locally determined policies.

Before examining these recent changes, however, some benchmark must first be provided against which to assess the general impact of these reforms. I will therefore begin by sketching the distinctive pattern of local government which has emerged during the twentieth century.

The Modern Institution of Local Government

The institution of local government is a relatively modern phenomenon. Its emergence can be traced from the period after 1835 in which a reformed framework for local government was gradually put in place.[3] It was not until the early decades of the twentieth century, however, that the institution in its modern form could be said to have been established. At the end of the nineteenth century the basic structures had been set in place and local authorities were undertaking many important tasks. But the capacity of local government was still restricted by a heavy dependence on local rates for finance and it was not until the 1920s that any scheme for the equalization of the burden between rich and poor authorities was introduced or that central support for local services was provided on any significant scale.[4] Furthermore, at the turn of the century, the principles of plural voting and of one vote for every ratepayer still survived as the two principal forms of suffrage in English local government[5] and it was not until 1948 that the right to vote for local councillors was extended to every adult living in the area of the local authority.[6] If we are to find a distinctive pattern to local government, then, it must be found in the twentieth century.

During the twentieth century, however, local government has been subjected to almost continuous review and change. Major responsibilities have been removed from local government, new powers and duties have been given, a variety of new checks and control mechanisms have been devised, and reforms have been made to the structure of the institution. Given this process of more or less continuous change, it might plausibly be argued that there is no basic institutional identity to local government and that local authorities have simply been shaped in accordance with specific functional requirements of the central State. This argument carries a certain amount of weight. It should only be accepted, however, if the process of change affecting local government has been

---

[3] See 'The Reformation of Local Government' in ch. 1, 28–39.
[4] See Local Authorities (Financial Provisions) Act 1921; Local Government Act 1929.
[5] See B. Keith-Lucas, *The English Local Government Franchise* (Oxford, 1952), 221.
[6] Representation of the People Act 1948, Pt. II.

almost entirely random. In practice, this has not been the case. It is, I believe, possible to discern certain trends to the changes which have occurred and from analysing these trends the formative characteristics of local government may be distilled.

Many of the changes to local government result from the fact that during the twentieth century, as government has assumed a basic responsibility for the health of the economy and the welfare of the population, the scale of government has been transformed. With this transformation in the role of government has come major changes in the organizational arrangements of government. Central departments have a limited executant capacity; their primary function has been to establish a series of policy and resource frameworks within which a great number of semi-autonomous agencies provide services or regulate particular fields. Local government growth may be seen, in large part, as a reflection of these basic changes in government. The scope and scale of its activities has substantially increased as local government has, in conjunction with the centre, assumed responsibility for a broad range of services of critical importance to the welfare state. Local government, which now accounts for more than one-quarter of all public expenditure, has become incorporated into an extensive system of government in which a major task of the centre is that of 'securing coordinated policy actions through networks of separate, but interdependent, organisations where the collective capabilities of a number of participants are essential for effective problem-solving'.[7] That is, the modern institution of local government should essentially be seen as an agency which is both equipped with a considerable capacity for independent action but is also locked into an extensive network of government.

Formative characteristics of modern local government

Within this modern framework of government, certain basic characteristics of local government may be identified. These form a distinct pattern and, taken together, may be understood to be the formative characteristics of the modern institution of local government which has emerged in Britain during the twentieth century. There are four basic characteristics which have been of critical importance in shaping the institution of local government. These will be considered in turn.

1. *Multi-functionality*. As institutions of government, local councils have assumed responsibility for a broad range of functions. This characteristic may be seen in action in the manner in which institutional arrangements for the provision of local services were shaped during the transition from the nineteenth to the twentieth century. Consider, for example, the case of the education service.

---

[7] K. Hanf, 'Introduction' in K. Hanf & F.W. Scharpf (eds.), *Interorganisational Policymaking: Limits to Coordination and Central Control* (London, 1978), 2.

When Parliament decided in 1870 that an essential minimum of education should
be provided nationally, England and Wales was divided into school districts and
School Boards were established to meet this deficiency. In 1902, however, these
Boards were abolished and their functions were assumed by the counties or
county boroughs. A similar trend can be seen in relation to poor relief; the Board
of Guardians of the Poor was abolished in 1929 and its responsibilities allocated to county authorities. The underlying idea was that the local inhabitants
might look to a single institution for the basic services which government should
provide at the level of the locality. During the twentieth century, this principle of multi-functionality has also become associated with the idea of self-
sufficiency; that the authority will be able to organize and provide the service
for which it has responsibility. This idea of the multi-functional, self-sufficient
authority had a major impact on the reform debates of the 1960s and 1970s on
the relationship between the functions and size of local authorities.[8]

2. *Discretion*. On turning to the legal constitution of local government, we see
that local government law mainly utilizes the language of discretionary powers
rather than that of enforceable legal duties. Local housing authorities, though
under a duty 'to consider the housing conditions in and the needs of their district
with respect to the provision of further housing accommodation' have traditionally been simply empowered to provide housing.[9] Even when duties have been
imposed on local authorities, these have generally been cast in broad, subjective
terms. Thus the basic duty of the local education authority in the post-war period
has been 'to contribute towards the spiritual, moral, mental and physical development of the community by securing that efficient education shall be available to
meet the needs of the population of their area'.[10] In general, local councils have
been given broad enabling powers which has the effect, not only of marginalizing
the potentially restrictive impact of the *ultra vires* doctrine, but also equips them
with the capacity to innovate. Local councils have been given a broad discretion
which enables them to tailor activities or services to local needs. They have
generally been free to decide on the precise pattern of the services which they
deliver and even to re-define the nature of the service they provide. They are
equipped with the capacity of 'local choice'.[11] This discretion is essential because local authority services, being generally tied to a sense of place, need, as
a condition of effectiveness, to be responsive to local opinion. This is what
Laski called the 'genius of place'.[12]

---

[8] See, e.g., the Redcliffe-Maud Report, Cmnd. 4040, ch. VI.
[9] See, e.g., Housing Act 1957, ss. 91, 92.   [10] Education Act 1944, s. 7.
[11] J.D. Stewart, *Local Government: The Conditions of Local Choice* (London, 1983).
[12] H.J. Laski, *A Grammar of Politics* (London, 5th edn., 1967), 412: '[G]overnment is bound,
almost inevitably, to aim, not at variety, but at uniformity. It will seek to meet, not the special wants
of Liverpool, but those wants which are similar to wants just met in Hereford or Leicester. It cannot
grasp, in other words, the genius of place. Because . . . it is government from without, it fails to
evoke either interest or responsibility from the neighbourhood it controls.'

3. ***Taxation***. Local councils have possessed – in the form of a property tax levied as rates – an independent power of taxation which long predates the formation of the modern institution of local government.[13] This power of taxation has given local government a degree of financial independence from the centre which is unique amongst the subordinate institutions of government. The historical importance of the rates as a form of taxation is seen clearly reflected in the fact that it was only after the First World War that the yield from income tax exceeded that accounted for by rates.[14] Though central government grants in aid of local expenditure have, during the twentieth century, become the primary source of local government revenue, the retention of the rating power has given local government an important source of financial autonomy.

4. ***Representation***. Local councils, being the only governmental institutions outside of Parliament which are subject to direct periodic election,[15] are accorded a degree of political legitimacy which other agencies of government do not possess. Local councils are established both to express the wishes of, and to act on behalf of, their local communities. Local councils both represent, and are accountable to, their constituencies.

These four basic facets of local government – multi-functionality, discretion, taxation and representation – should be viewed as mutually reinforcing characteristics. As multi-functional bodies with broad discretionary powers, local authorities are equipped with the capacity to innovate and to determine local priorities. Further, without this basic competence it could be argued that there is no justification for the power of taxation. And, being elected bodies, local authorities are vested with the legitimacy to exercise broad discretionary powers – most crucially the power to tax – with which they are entrusted. They are, in short, complex organizations equipped with a capacity for effective governmental action and vested with a degree of political legitimacy which may authorize such action. These characteristics reveal the values on which the modern tradition of local government is founded.[16]

The modern institution

Local government has emerged this century as a multi-functional, representative institution which is vested with broad discretionary powers and a significant

---

[13] Rates go back at least to 1601, though it was not until 1925 that they were merged into a single general rate. See E. Cannan, *History of Local Rates in England* (London, 2nd edn., 1912); T. Travers, *The Politics of Local Government Finance* (London, 1986), ch. 1.

[14] Travers, *The Politics of Local Government Finance* (above, n. 13), 3.

[15] This position has been modified since 1979 as a result of the adoption of the principle of direct election to the European Parliament.

[16] For further examination of these values see: L.J. Sharpe, 'Theories and Values of Local Government' (1970) XVIII *Political Studies* 153; R. Greenwood & J.D. Stewart, 'The Institutional and Organisational Capabilities of Local Government' (1986) 64 *Public Admin.* 35; W. Magnusson, 'Bourgeois Theories of Local Government' (1986) XXXIV *Political Studies* 1.

capacity to undertake local initiatives. It is because of this tradition that the formal legal status of local government presents a potentially distortive picture. While constrained in principle by the *ultra vires* doctrine, local government has in fact been vested with considerable autonomy. Although formally subordinate, local government has, as a result of the changes in government during the century, acquired a relatively important position in an interdependent network of government. While the legal symbols of central power must be acknowledged, they should not be confused with the manner in which political power has traditionally been exercised between the centre and the localities.

This modern framework of local government has been fairly robust. Central departments of state certainly possess a very broad range of supervisory powers. In the event of disputes, however, the centre has rarely invoked its formal legal powers and has generally sought to proceed by way of bargaining and negotiation. When local authorities are accused of inefficiency or high-handedness, this has not generally resulted in immediate, direct action by central government; a degree of tolerance seems to have been accepted as part of the compact. Further, when new responsibilities requiring local delivery systems have emerged, the task has invariably been vested in local councils.

This pattern of governmental practice suggests that the modern institution of local government exists not simply because it is the agency which is able most efficiently to deliver particular services. While local government must, of course, strive to achieve efficiency, its status also serves to reflect certain basic political values. That is, local government should be seen not only as an agency for service delivery but also as an institution of community governance. Thus viewed, a degree of technical inefficiency may have been accepted as part of a constitutional settlement. Some degree of inefficiency is accepted as the price we may pay for maintaining robust local institutions which are able to mediate between the individual and the State, which are responsive to the interests of locality, and which provide some safeguard against an over-weening central executive.

Whenever the issue of local government reform has arisen during the twentieth century, such values have certainly been influential in shaping the reform agenda. The terms of reference of the Redcliffe-Maud Commission in the 1960s, for example, asked the Commission to review local government structure with regard to the need to ensure that functions be 'effectively exercised' and the need 'to sustain a viable system of local democracy'.[17] Furthermore, the Commission's Report included a succinct statement of the accepted position of the time:

> Local government is not to be seen merely as a provider of services. . . . The importance of local government lies in the fact that it is a means by which people can provide services for themselves; can take an active and constructive part in the business of government; and can decide for themselves, within the limits of what national

---

[17] Redcliffe-Maud Report, Cmnd. 4040 (1969) vol. 1, iii.

policies and local resources allow, what kind of services they want and what kind of environment they prefer. ... Local government is the only representative political institution in the country outside Parliament; and being, by its nature in closer touch than Parliament or Ministers can be with local conditions, local needs, local opinions, it is an essential part of the fabric of democratic govenment. Central government tends, by its nature, to be bureaucratic. It is only by the combination of local representative institutions with the central institutions of Parliament, Ministers and Departments, that a genuine national democracy can be sustained.[18]

The modern institution of local government was readily acknowledged to be the key agency for delivering governmental services at the level of the locality. Local councils were equipped with a significant capacity for initiative and the extent of their autonomy was a reflection of certain broadly accepted political values.

Strains on the Institution

The importance of this modern institution of local government is perhaps most readily acknowledged by the scale of its activities. Between 1890 and 1970, for example, the share of the national wealth which was consumed by local govern- ment increased almost fivefold.[19] This transformation in the scale of local goverment activities is basically the result of local government having become locked into a complex, interdependent, national network of government. It is thus on the character of this network that both the strengths and weaknesses of the institution have come to rest.

Although local government services have grown in importance during the twentieth century, this development has not progressed smoothly. The uneven pattern of growth is largely the result of a reallocation of local government functions which has taken place during this century, the general impact of which has been to cause local government to lose certain important trading services (such as gas, water and electricity). The loss of these responsibilities has never- theless been more than compensated for by the growing importance of local government's social welfare services. With the emergence of the welfare state, for example, the education, housing and social services responsibilities of local authorities have increased dramatically. But this shift in the balance of local authority services – away from production-related services and towards con- sumption-orientated services – has had a significant impact on the relationship between local government and the centre within this network.[20]

---

[18] Redcliffe-Maud Report, Cmnd. 4040 (1969) vol. iii. para. 28.

[19] C.D. Foster, R.A. Jackman & M. Perlman, *Local Government Finance in a Unitary State* (London, 1980), 102–6.

[20] For a broader discussion of the political and economic implications of this shift in the balance of local authority services see: P. Saunders, 'Why study central–local relations?' (1982) vol. 8 no. 2

There are two basic reasons why this pattern of local government growth has affected the central–local balance. First, it is a basic principle of public finance that there are limitations on a local authority's ability successfully to undertake independent policies of income redistribution.[21] This suggests that, as a result of functional reallocation, central government may legitimately claim to take an active interest in the policies of local authorities in order to ensure a degree of co-ordination and thus of effectiveness in service provision. The second reason is that the growth in local government expenditure throughout this century has been financed essentially by central government grants; the proportion of local expenditure which was met by central government grant, for example, increased from around 10 per cent in 1890 to nearly 50 per cent in 1970.[22] This degree of grant-dependency undoubtedly fosters a sense of hierarchy in the central–local relationship. These factors highlight two of the critical points of stress in this interdependent governmental network.

The twentieth century settlement has essentially been founded on the assumption that the centre and the localities shared a basic mutuality of objective and could be trusted not to interfere in one another's primary sphere of competence. The issues of what precisely were the objectives of the governmental system and how a demarcation might be drawn between local and central matters obviously remained uncertain. But, notwithstanding particular disputes and disagreements, the system seemed for much of the time to work adequately. Cushioning this system were two basic assumptions: first, that modern government would undergo a process of continuous growth; and, secondly, that the modern institution of local government would continue to be accepted as a vital component in the interdependent network of modern government. Throughout the post-war period these two basic assumptions were generally accepted. But the assumptions were underpinned by particular economic and political conditions: continuous economic growth and a political consensus concerning the welfare state. Once these conditions were eroded, the tension points in the network were exposed and the importance of the institution of local government came to be questioned. This is precisely what has occurred over the last twenty or so years.

Pressures during the 1970s

The problems which emerged in the 1970s arose primarily because of the economic strains in the aftermath of the OPEC oil crisis and the consequential

Local Government Studies 55; L.J. Sharpe, 'Functional Allocation in the Welfare State' (1984) vol. 10 no. 1 *Local Government Studies* 27; P. Saunders, 'Reflections on the dual politics thesis: the argument, its origins and its critics' in M. Goldsmith & S. Villadsen (eds.), *Urban Political Theory and the Management of Fiscal Stress* (Aldershot, 1986).

[21] W.E. Oates, *Fiscal Federalism* (New York, 1972), ch. 1.

[22] R.J. Bennett, *Central Grants to Local Governments: the Political and Economic Impact of the Rate Support Grant in England* (Cambridge, 1982), 44.

public expenditure crisis. But those economic difficulties also coalesced with a general sense of dissatisfaction over the performance of government. Such concerns have often been articulated by reference to the idea of governmental overload: the belief that, against a background of rising public expectations, the reach of government has become greater than its grasp, with the result that governmental action has all too often been associated with unacceptable levels of policy failure.[23] With these changing economic and political conditions, the entire structure of modern government came under close scrutiny and the major stress points within the central–local relationship were quickly revealed. The Government was thus obliged to respond to changed political–economic conditions from the very moment of birth of the reorganized system of local government. And in the process some of the basic assumptions of the system – that central and local government shared a basic mutuality of objective and that a powerful institution of local government was important – gradually came to be questioned.

There issues were largely evaded by the Labour Government of the 1970s. As the points of stress within the system became exposed, the centre, while seeking to bolster its hierarchical position, did so largely through a strategy of incorporation. That is, 'central government employed various institutions and processes to involve local government in central decision-making, hoping thereby to commit local government to central decisions'.[24] With the pressures for cutbacks in public expenditure during the 1970s, the Government used this strategy to try to persuade local government to comply with central government expenditure guidelines. As a consequence, the grant system came to be viewed not so much as a central contribution to local services with a semi-national character but rather as an instrument of central control over local government.

The Labour Government's fudge on the fundamental issues is exemplified by its response to the Layfield Report. The Government in 1974 established the Layfield Inquiry to 'review the whole system of local government finance'.[25] The Inquiry accurately identified the dilemma of control and accountability in a local system dependent on high and increasing levels of central grants. 'Effective control of expenditure', Layfield suggested, 'cannot be ensured in a system in which local accountability has been seriously weakened, unless central accountability provides that control.'[26] The Report recognized that an alternative – in the form of a revival of local accountability – existed but suggested that this would require a deliberate policy decision and a rejuvenation of the local tax

---

[23] See A. King, 'Overload: problems of governing in the 1970s' (1975) XXIII *Political Studies* 283; J. Douglas, 'The Overloaded Crown' (1976) 6 *Brit. J. of Political Science* 483; C. Offe, *Contradictions of the Welfare State* (London, 1984), ch. 2.

[24] R.A.W. Rhodes, 'Intergovernmental Relations in the United Kingdom' in Y. Meny & V. Wright (eds.), *Centre–Periphery Relations in Western Europe* (London, 1985), 33 at 59.

[25] *Report of the Committee of Inquiry into Local Government Finance* (Chmn: F. Layfield, QC), Cmnd. 6453 (1976), iii.

[26] Layfield Report, 72.

base. Without this, Layfield felt, there would be a continuation in the gradual shift of power to the centre.

In its response to Layfield, the Government outlined in general terms the basic responsibilities of central and local government but it declined to provide 'any formal definition'. This approach was rejected on the grounds that any attempt at a formal division of tasks 'would lack the advantages of flexibility and rapidity of response to new circumstances' and 'would be likely to break down under pressure'.[27] Further, the Government felt that there were evident disadvantages 'of both the centralist and localist approaches' and suggested that 'there is [no] clear case for the adoption of either'.[28] On the specific issue of finance, and the mounting concern of local dependency on central grants, the Government failed to propose any new tax for local government. By fudging the key issue, it thus created an environment in which the Layfield prediction proved essentially correct. 'As a poor response to a major problem', Tony Travers has commented, the Government's response to Layfield 'set the scene for the next government to change local authority finance with little real consultation.'[29]

The agenda for the 1980s

This is indeed precisely how the newly-elected Conservative administration acted. Rather than use exhortation within the existing network, the Government immediately proposed a new regime which, given its centralizing impetus, signalled the fact that the traditional structure was about to be fundamentally reformed. During the 1980s successive Conservative Governments have addressed the issue of central–local government relations, not only as an adjunct to their policies for reducing public expenditure, but also as part of a radical programme for restructuring the welfare state. As a result of this more explicitly ideological stance, many of the assumptions on which the modern institution of local government was founded have been directly challenged.

The key policies in the attempt by Conservative Governments to restructure the welfare state have been those which seek to reduce public sector employment, to shift expenditure away from social welfare services, and to reconstruct social policy on the principle of individualistic action rather than collectivistic organization. These general policies have had a profound impact on local government for a number of reasons: first, because, owing to the labour-intensive nature of their services and central government's lack of executant responsibility, local authorities employ more people than central government; secondly, because many local government services have been collectively organized; thirdly, because, as a result of functional reallocation, local government is heavily social-

---

[27] *Local Government Finance*, Cmnd. 6813 (1977), para. 2.8.   [28] Ibid.
[29] T. Travers, *The Politics of Local Government Finance* (London, 1986), 76.

welfare orientated; and finally because of local government's dependency on central government grants for their finances.

The challenge since 1979, then, concerns the attempt to discover a role for local government in a radically altered world. The events of the rather turbulent period since 1979 have complex origins, but what is clear is that the modern institution of local government was founded on a set of assumptions – concerning economic growth, the role of government in society, a basic consensus about the role of local government within the wider structure of government, and faith in a public service ethic – which in recent times have all come to be questioned. In order to examine the impact of these changes on the institution of local government, we will focus on those four factors – structure, functions, accountability and finance – which have already been highlighted as having a major impact on the issue of institutional capacity.

Financial Arrangements

From the outset, the Conservative Government was committed not only to a general reduction in public expenditure but in particular to cutting back expenditure on such services as education, housing and social services over which it had no direct control.[30] Recognizing the difficulties which this action posed, the Government thus advocated a basic reform of the system for distributing central grants to local government. The objective of this new system, which became known as the block grant mechanism, was to design a grant allocation system which would incorporate incentives to local authorities to reduce their expenditure. Though highly controversial, the reform had in fact been proposed as a 'combined grant' by the Department of the Environment in its evidence to the Layfield Inquiry[31] and, as a 'unitary grant', had been accepted in 1977 by the Labour Government.[32]

The enactment of the block grant mechanism in the Local Government, Planning and Land Act 1980 opened a new era in the central–local financial relationship. It was an era which, as Layfield had predicted, was marked by a creeping centralization of power. But it was also characterized both by 'hyperactivism'[33] and 'destabilizing incrementalism'[34] as central government lurched from one mechanism to the next in its quest to control local expenditure. Arising from the financial conflicts of the 1980s came the gradual realization that increasingly

[30] See, e.g., *The Government's Expenditure Plans*, Cmnd. 7841 (1980).
[31] Layfield Report, Appendix 7, 'Evidence by the Department of the Environment: Central Government Grants to Local Government: Some Possible Changes'.
[32] *Local Government Finance*, Cmnd. 6813, ch. 3.
[33] K. Minogue, 'On Hyperactivism in Modern British Politics' in M Cowling (ed.), *Conservative Essays* (London, 1978), 177.
[34] G. Bramley, 'Incrementalism run amok? Local government finance in Britain' (1985) 63 *Public Admin* 100.

there appeared to be no conspicuous mutuality of objective between central and local government and, ultimately, that the centre apparently no longer viewed the institution of local government as having an important role in the structure of governance. In order to consider this assessment, the changes introduced to the system of local government finance will be charted and their implications analysed.[35]

Block grant and expenditure targets

Local authorities raise the finance they need to run their services from four main sources: rates, fees and charges, grants, and by borrowing. Since local authorities are required to finance their affairs on an annual basis,[36] they are not generally empowered to borrow for revenue purposes. In respect of current expenditure, then, it is the first three sources, and the balance between them, which is of particular importance. Much of the growth in local government during the twentieth century has, for example, been financed by central government grants and, as a consequence, the burden on domestic ratepayers (expressed as a proportion of personal disposable income) has remained fairly constant throughout the postwar period.[37] And it is because of the growing importance of central grants that the method of allocating them has come to assume such a particular importance.

Since the 1950s, grant distribution has been governed by the principle that the bulk of grant aid should take the form of a general grant which is unhypothecated to specific services and after 1966 that general grant took the form of a Rate Support Grant (RSG). This type of general grant – where grant allocation is governed by general principles – protects local government against detailed central control by ensuring that grant is allocated in accordance with a common formula rather than being dependent on central approval of specific local authority services. The basic aims of the RSG have been to compensate authorities for differences in local taxable wealth (the resources element) and for disparities in spending needs (the needs element) and, since the establishment of this form of grant, the RSG distribution formula has been continually refined. However, as we have seen, from the mid 1970s onwards, this process of technical refinement has been coupled with a concern to provide incentives for local authorities to reduce expenditure.

The block grant mechanism enacted in 1980 was explicitly constructed around the concept of equalization so that up to a notional level of expenditure, called Grant-Related Expenditure (GRE), local authorities were to be fully compensated for differences in rateable values and spending needs. However, being a central assessment of a local authority's spending needs, GRE also served to

---

[35] The legal aspects of the changes which are sketched are examined in detail in ch. 5 below.

[36] See *Re Westminster City Council* [1986] 1 AC 668.

[37] C.D. Foster, R.A. Jackman & M. Perlman, *Local Government Finance in a Unitary State* (London, 1980), 316.

trigger an adjustment in grant. By incorporating a tapering provision so that marginal expenditure above GRE attracted a lower rate of grant (or, in the case of an authority with a high resource base, could even result in a negative marginal rate of grant), the block grant mechanism placed the burden of additional expenditure on local ratepayers. The block grant mechanism thus sought directly to address the apparent weakness that the post-war grant systems had actually encouraged local authorities to increase their expenditure, since, by doing so, they were able to attract more grant. By requiring the setting of individual assessments for each authority, however, an unprecedented degree of central involvement in local government finance was assumed.

Having introduced the block grant mechanism in the 1980 Act, the Government then found that for 1981/82, the first year in which the block grant mechanism was fully operational, local authorities had not reacted as anticipated to the grant tapering provisions. Many local authorities had opted to maintain service levels and to raise additional revenues from the rates. These projections caused the Secretary of State immediately to announce a new set of targets for local authorities which were based, not on some form of needs assessment as under the block grant mechanism, but on the historic expenditure levels of each local authority. This system of expenditure targets with its associated grant penalty arrangements was engrafted on to the block grant mechanism with retrospective effect in 1982.[38] The target system, which operated until 1986/87, had the effect not only of creating a much more powerful mechanism of expenditure control. It also served both to increase the complexity of the grant regime and to obscure the principles on which the block grant mechanism was based. Furthermore, it was a unilateral act by the centre which transformed the centre's capacity to control local government expenditure.

The Government's conduct in the early 1980s has been subject to widespread criticism. Such censure has not simply been because of the shift in the central–local balance, but also because of the rather inept manner in which the instruments of financial control were handled. The Government's action seemed to indicate uncertainty or confusion about its goals and, in part, these difficulties appeared to stem from a failure to appreciate the complexity of the system which it was seeking to influence. The most basic criticism was that the Government failed to recognize that intrinsic difficulties existed in using the block grant mechanism as a tool of expenditure restraint. Since the primary purpose of block grant was that of rate poundage equalization, the mechanism entailed a break in the link between the level of local expenditure and the size of the rate bill. The block grant mechanism thus comprised certain features which prevented it being used as a stringent mechanism for exerting general downward financial pressure on local government[39] and it is perhaps because of the Government's failure

[38] Local Government Finance Act 1982, Pt. II.
[39] C.D. Foster and R.A. Jackman, 'Accountability and control of local spending', *Public Money*, Sept. 1982.

fully to recognize this facet of the mechanism which caused much of its subsequent frustration.

In addition to that limitation, however, the reform of the grant system on the foundation of equalization also exposed certain structural weaknesses in the entire system of local government finance. The shift towards the equalization of rate poundages had the effect of establishing a close relationship between rate bills and rateable values; but, as a consequence, it highlighted basic inconsistencies in the valuation process and thus exposed weaknesses in the rating system.[40] Again, the Government did not appear to have been conscious of this effect of the block grant. Since the Conservatives had pledged in their 1979 election manifesto to reform the rating system, however, they obviously did not wish to put too great a strain on the rates. They were therefore placed in a rather difficult position. The most effective method of bringing about a reduction in local government expenditure would have been to reduce the proportion of local expenditure which central government was prepared to support. This was a method which had been shown to work, but only after a period in which rate demands had significantly increased.[41] And this seemed to be a consequence the Government was not prepared to countenance.[42]

It is precisely because of these complexities of the system and the tensions in Conservative policy that the Government tried to use the grant system to achieve too many conflicting objectives.[43] As a result, it entirely lost control over local government expenditure. By 1984 local government revenue expenditure was nine per cent higher in real terms than when the Conservatives took office and the consensus of official and academic opinion suggested that responsibility lay firmly at the Government's door.[44]

---

[40] R. Jackman, 'Local government finance' in M. Loughlin, D. Gelfand & K. Young (eds.), *Half A Century of Municipal Decline 1935–1985* (London, 1985), ch. 7, esp. at 158–61, 163.

[41] J. Barnett, *Inside The Treasury* (London, 1982), 75–6; L. Pliatsky, *Getting and Spending* (London, 1982), 112; J. Gibson, 'Local "overspending": why the Government have only themselves to blame', *Public Money*, Dec. 1983.

[42] Note also that the Government, in furtherance of its election pledge, in 1981 published a Green Paper on the issue, which implied that there were no viable alternatives to domestic rates: Department of the Environment, *Alternatives to Domestic Rates*, Cmnd. 8449 (1981).

[43] See Audit Commission, *The impact on local authorities' economy, efficiency and effectiveness of the block grant distribution system* (London, 1984). This study concluded that the system had provided few incentives for the improvement of efficiency and effectiveness and that managerial accountability had not been strengthened, local understanding of the system had not been furthered and central control had not been reduced.

[44] Audit Commission, ibid.; National Audit Office, *Report by the Comptroller and Auditor General. Department of the Environment: Operation of the Rate Support Grant System* (London, 1985); Seventh Report from the Committee of Public Accounts, Session 1985–86, *Operation of the Rate Support Grant System* (HC 47); J. Gibson, 'Local "overspending": why the Government have only themselves to blame', *Public Money*, Dec. 1983; J. Gibson, 'Why block grant failed' in S. Ranson, G.W. Jones & K. Walsh (eds.), *Between Centre and Locality* (London, 1985), 58; R. Jackman, 'The Rates Bill – a measure of desperation' (1985) 55 *Political Quarterly* 161; T. Travers, *The Politics of Local Government Finance* (London, 1986) ch. 8.

Rate-capping and beyond

Because of the difficulties it got itself into during the early 1980s, the Government felt obliged to take drastic action. This took the form of the Rates Act 1984, under which it acquired powers to control the amount of finance which local authorities could raise through the rates. This measure, a direct attack on 'the foundation stone upon which is built the whole structure of local taxation in England',[45] constituted an unprecedented centralization of political power. However, it is important to recognize that it was 'more out of exasperation than with a conscious sense of direction'[46] that the Rates Act was enacted. Furthermore, far from restoring control, rate-capping threatened 'to undermine what remain[ed] of financial accountability in local government'.[47]

The reason for this was essentially because the Government's directive strategy resulted in the shaking up, if not breaking up, of the policy network. What the Government failed fully to realize, however, was that the network had a crucial role to play in the effective implementation of its objectives. The Government's rejection of the strategy of incorporation – that is, of using the administrative network as a device of policy implementation – had a significant effect on the efficacy of the available control mechanisms. As directive rather than facilitative legislation, the 1984 Act marked a turning point in the drafting of local govenment finance legislation. It was drafted on the assumption that those to whom it was directed would act as utility-maximizers and would thus explore all available avoidance routes. The Act therefore sought to identify these in advance and tried to ensure that these routes could not successfully be taken. As directive legislation, the Rates Act itself was competently constructed. But the unprecedented powers acquired by the Government to control the amount which authorities could raise through the rates did not enable the Government to control the system. This was because, in the context of the overall system of local government finance, rate-capping was of marginal importance as a control mechanism.

The basic statutory framework laid down in the 1980 Act and on to which the 1984 Act was engrafted had been drafted in the traditional facilitative manner. Rate-capping, in conjunction with expenditure targets, simply caused local authorities to exploit the discretionary aspects of the basic framework either to avoid these control techniques or to ensure that they had a minimal impact. During the 1980s, a major 'creative accounting' industry emerged, in which local authority treasurers and lawyers working hand in hand with financial institutions sought, with some success, to exploit the flexibility within the basic framework.[48]

---

[45] J. Redlich and F.W. Hirst, *Local Government in England* (London, 1903), vol. I, 24.
[46] R. Jackman, 'The Rates Bill – a measure of desperation' (above, n. 44) , 170.
[47] Ibid.   [48] See ch. 6 below.

The problem here concerned the attempt to use law as a determinant of the balance between central and local power. The legal framework relating to local government finance had never been intended to establish the precise rules of the game; its function had been to provide a general framework through which (non-legal) regulatory norms could evolve. With a breakdown in the sense of partnership, both central and local government turned, in different ways, to the law to act as an umpire. It was a role for which the law was patently ill-equipped. The legislation had not generally been drafted with the possibility of adjudication in mind and therefore contained many obscurities. Also, since it did not establish a comprehensive regulatory framework, the Government was obliged – generally in response to gaps and deficiencies which local authorities had already identified and exploited – to rush to promote new legislation to resolve ambiguities and uncertainties. Eventually, frustrated by a number of legal challenges which had had the effect of threatening the entire system of local government finance established since 1980, the Government was obliged to obtain retrospective validation of all its expenditure decisions.[49]

Charging the community?

The Government responded to the difficult situation within which it found itself in the mid 1980s by proposing the most radical reform to the system of local government finance ever countenanced in modern times. Though touted as a set of reforms which were 'designed to ensure that local democracy and local accountability are substantially strengthened',[50] in actuality the reforms had the effect of greatly weakening the financial autonomy of local authorities and thus of undermining one of the basic pillars of the modern institution of local government.

These proposals were justified mainly by returning to the issue of the 'cash nexus' in modern local government,[51] though in this case the issue was dressd up in the contemporary language of public choice theory. The Government focused its attention on the relationship between three local groups which have a direct interest in local government: those who pay for (ratepayers), those who vote for (electors), and those who benefit from (consumers), local services. The financial reforms which were proposed flowed directly from the relationship between paying and voting and proceeded on the following analysis. In England, although there are 35 million electors, only 18 million are liable to pay rates, and of these only 12 million, or one-third of the electorate, pay full rates.[52] Further,

---

[49] Local Government Finance Act 1987, s. 4 which stated that any decisions of the Secretary of State under Part VI of the 1980 Act 'shall be deemed to have been done in compliance with those provisions' and those decisions 'shall have effect notwithstanding any decision of a court (whether before or after the passing of this Act) purporting to have a contrary effect'.

[50] Department of the Environment, *Paying for Local Government*, Cmnd. 9714 (1985), para. 1.51.

[51] See ch. 1 above, at 38.   [52] Ibid., para. 1.37.

on average, for every £1 raised locally from domestic ratepayers, £1.50 is paid by the non-domestic sector. So although 'the marginal cost of services to domestic taxpayers is reduced by a 60 per cent contribution from non-domestic ratepayers', there is 'no voting right attached to the payment of non-domestic rates'.[53] And, of course, around 50 per cent of local government revenue expenditure is met by central government grants.

In essence the Government's reforms, which were implemented in the Local Government Finance Act 1988, aimed to simplify the grant system, to reform the arrangements for the taxation of the non-domestic sector and to establish a closer nexus between voting and paying by making the marginal cost of local services payable by all voters equally. At the core of these reforms lay revolutionary reforms to the rating system, involving the nationalization of the non-domestic rate and the abolition of domestic rates and its replacement with a 'community charge' (effectively a poll tax). The reform of the non-domestic rate was designed to convert it from a variable, locally-determined tax into a uniform nationally-determined one, the revenues from which would be pooled and recycled to local authorities through the grant system as an equal amount per adult resident. The community charge in principle constituted a flat rate charge on each adult resident of the area.

The consequences of these reforms were profound. The nationalization of the non-domestic rate had the effect of increasing the proportion of central funding of local government to around 80–85 per cent. In addition to increasing central control, this resulted in the local tax having an extremely high gearing effect, which meant that small variations in a local authority's budget could produce great changes in the level of the charge. Furthermore, such variations might not come from changes in local expenditure at all but from technical adjustments to the grant allocation formula from one year to the next. The Green Paper itself pointed out that, 'if local accountability is to be effective, electors must be able to see how the price they pay relates to their local authority's expenditure decisions and the standard of services it provides'.[54] The combined effect of the high gearing effect and grant volatility indicated that this objective was unlikely to be achieved.

Though the impact of nationalization of the non-domestic rate was of fundamental importance, the community charge raised even more serious issues. It not only represented a distinct shift from a (household) tax on property to an (individual) tax on persons but also a shift away from the principle of ability to pay and towards the benefit principle of taxation; that is, that payment for the provision of public services should be proportional to the consumption of such services. Even on the benefit principle, however, it was difficult to justify the introduction of a flat rate charge. Local authorities provide a mixture of property and personal services, and there is in fact a significant correlation between

[53] Department of the Environment, *Paying for Local Government*, Cmnd. 9714 (1985), paras. 2.14–2.18.
[54] Ibid., para. 7.1.

property value and benefit obtained from local authority services.[55] The community charge was a highly regressive tax which was not justified even in terms of the benefit principle.

The community charge scheme could not adequately be explained by reference to public choice principles or on the basis of a shift from equity to benefit as the cardinal principle of local taxation. The scheme is best understood as forming an important part of a broader ideological vision of the institution of local government. Notwithstanding the widely adopted rhetorical use of the term 'poll tax', we should not lose sight of the precise intention of the Government in designating the new local tax a 'community charge'. What in effect the Government was saying was that local government was not in fact a tier of government which should be vested with the governmental power of taxation. It was essentially to be viewed as an administrative agency which provided certain services for which the principle of direct charging could not efficiently be applied; those who benefit from such services should thus pay a general charge to the agency responsible for securing the provision of these services.

Controls over capital expenditure

Central government has traditionally maintained control of local authority capital expenditure by imposing controls over borrowing. During the 1970s, the system was felt not to be effective: first, because an increasing proportion of capital expenditure was being financed by methods other than borrowing and was therefore not subject to control; and, secondly, because the system, in authorizing projects rather than a general level of expenditure over a defined period, was a rather unresponsive control mechanism. In Part VIII of the Local Government, Planning and Land Act 1980 new arrangements for central control of local authority capital expenditure were enacted. However, this system, which was designed to control the capital programme for a particular year, was constructed on the assumptions of the 1970s and, when Government began to use the grant system as an expenditure restraint mechanism, the ambiguities in the capital control system were exploited as part of the creative accounting movement which flourished in the 1980s.

Creative accounting tended to involve the rearrangement of the existing resources and commitments of the local authority across different time spans or between different accounting classifications, generally with the objective of maximizing the authority's revenue budget for the relevant year. This might, for example, involve the shifting of revenue items into capital expenditure, such as capitalizing maintenance and repairs costs in the housing revenue account in an improvement programme. It could involve the use of various techniques, such

---

[55] See G. Bramley, J. Le Grand and W. Low, 'How far is the poll tax a "community charge"? The implications of service usage evidence' (1989) 17 *Policy & Politics* 187.

as bartering or certain leasing arrangements, which boosted capital expenditure while circumventing the capital control system under the 1980 Act. Most controversially, however, it involved unlocking some of the equity in the local authority's capital assets in return for cash which was used to bolster revenue expenditure (e.g. through a sale-and-leaseback scheme) or to embark on capital projects whilst deferring the cost to future years, through deferred purchase schemes.[56]

While the schemes adopted in most local authorities could be viewed simply as an application of the techniques of active financial management to the local authority's capital assets with a view to maximizing value for money, the practices of some authorities in using the techniques to spend now while paying later caused much concern.[57] This led to central government action first in 1987 to outlaw deferred purchase deals[58] and then subsequently in 1988 to eliminate virtually all 'off balance sheet' transactions available to local government.[59] The sheer breadth of the restrictions imposed caught local authorities by surprise, particularly since the majority of the transactions affected made financial sense and did not jeopardize local authorities' financial stability. The restrictions signalled the fact that the Government had lost control of the system; by freezing the market, it was in effect able to acquire the breathing space it needed to devise and enact a new system of capital controls. This new system was enacted in Part IV of the Local Government and Housing Act 1989. This new regime repealed both the controls over borrowing in the 1972 Act and the system of capital expenditure controls in the 1980 Act and replaced them with a new system of credit controls which operated within a much more precise definition of capital expenditure.

We should finally consider the issue of capital receipts. Under the 1980 Act, local authorities were free to supplement their capital allocations with such proportions of their capital receipts from asset sales as the Government prescribed. With the Government's privatization initiative, and especially the vast sums generated from council house sales, re-investment of receipts could have resulted in aggregate local authority expenditure significantly exceeding the Government's cash limit without any local authority exceeding its allocation. The Government thus took steps to curb a local authority's ability to spend its capital receipts. Under the 1989 Act, for example, local authorities are obliged to set aside 75 per cent of capital receipts from council house sales and 50 per cent of any other capital receipt for the purposes of debt redemption. This restriction, together with other curbs on functions such as housing, have caused

---

[56] For a more detailed examination of these various schemes, see ch. 6 below.

[57] See, e.g., Audit Commission, *The management of London's authorities: preventing the breakdown of services* (Occasional Paper No. 2, 1987) which highlighted the case of eight London boroughs which, up to 1987, had cumulatively entered into deferred purchase arrangements amounting to over £550m.

[58] Local Government Act 1987, inserting new ss. 80A and 80B into LGPLA 1980.

[59] Local Government Finance Act 1988, ss. 130–132; inserting new s. 79A into LGPLA 1980.

concern to many authorities which are frustrated over their inability to use receipts from asset sales to meet the evident needs of their communities.

Local government finance in the 1990s

The key issues relating to local government finance in the 1990s may briefly be stated. Far from restoring local accountability, the community charge scheme must be understood as an extension of a process of centralization of power. The impact of the nationalization of the non-domestic rate, the volatility of central grant assessments and the high-gearing effect of the community charge seemed likely from the outset to combine to destroy the scheme's capacity to restore local accountability; and its highly regressive impact (together with the retention of capping powers) made it almost impossible for local authorities to diverge significantly from central government spending assessments. Its dismantling, within a year or two of the scheme's implementation, in fact had all the elements of grand tragedy: every informed person could see from the outset that the scheme was both unstable and unworkable. It offers a singular instance of 'a government putting a single piece of legislation at the forefront of its programme, forcefully implementing it, and then ignominiously abandoning it in the course of a single parliament'.[60] What in the end destroyed it was its widespread unpopularity amongst the public: the estimates that by the end of 1991 7.5 million liability orders had been issued, that non-collection of poll tax amounted to £1.5 billion and that 2,815 prison sentences had been imposed (the vast majority being suspended) for non-payment simply represent the tip of the iceberg in terms of the costs of the reforms.[61]

The Local Government Finance Act 1992 repealed the community charge and replaced it with the council tax which, as a banded property tax (albeit with personal discounts), marked a return to the basic principles of domestic rates. Criticism can certainly be levied both at the banding structure[62] and at the rather

---

[60] D. Butler, A. Adonis and T. Travers, *Failure in British Government. The Politics of the Poll Tax* (Oxford, 1994), 1.

[61] See P.A. Thomas, 'From McKenzie Friend to Leicester Assistant: the Impact of the Poll Tax' [1992] *Public Law* 208, 209. See also Butler, Adonis and Travers (above, n. 60), 180: 'The costs . . . were considerable. At least £1.5bn. was wasted on setting up, administering, amd replacing the community charge. In other words, £1.5bn–worth of taxpayers' money was spent on computers, staff, buildings, paper, postage, bailiffs, and all the other elements necessary to introducing and then abolishing the tax. In addition, the transfer costs to the national taxpayer had, by the end of 1993– 4, totalled well over £20bn. . . . [T]he capacity of local authorities to collect revenue, which had been exceptional (99 per cent) under domestic rates, was badly damaged. When the community charge was abolished in 1993, it was estimated that £2–2.5bn of tax was still unpaid. Collection will continue until the end of the century. Much of the money will never be recovered. It will take years for urban areas to move back to the high levels of tax collection achieved prior to 1990. Some councils may never do so.'

[62] Each dwelling is placed in a valauation band, from a list ranging from band A (properties valued at less than £40,000) to band H (properties valued at over £320,000). In less wealthy areas, in which a high proportion of properties are valued in band A, the system operates extremely crudely, with

rudimentary valuation methods which had to be adopted in order to enable the list to be drawn up expeditiously. However, the key issues of the 1990s will continue for some time to be the legacies of the 1988 Act reforms. The community charge scheme all but destroyed the integrity of the local tax system – indeed, it 'came close to undermining the whole structure of local government'[63] – and it has rendered extremely difficult any attempt to restore the taxing capacity of local government. Furthermore, given the high-gearing effect as a result of 80 per cent of local authorty expenditure being centrally provided, local authority budgets are increasingly being effectively determined by central government Standard Spending Assessments (SSAs).[64] Since the introduction of universal capping in 1992, even that limited freedom has disappeared and local councils' budgets seem now to be clustering around their SSAs.[65] The effect of these most recent changes has been to establish a system in which local authorities now assume a degree of formal responsibility out of all proportion to their ability actually to control services.

Functional Change

Neo-liberals might argue that the controversial reforms to the system of local government finance failed not fundamentally because of the unacceptability of the principle but rather as a result of mis-timing over the introduction of the reforms. On this analysis, the error of the community charge was that it was implemented before the major reforms to local government functions had been set in place. The scheme thus failed essentially because it attempted to introduce during the 1980s a local tax for a system of local government which was unlikely to materialize until the mid 1990s at the earliest.[66] In examining the recent reforms to local government functions, this argument might be borne in mind.

The primary objective of the Government's many reforms to local government functions since 1980 has been, so far as possible, to eliminate the redistributive dimension to local services and to restructure the collective organization

no significant distinction being made between properties which may be worth double those of others in the same valuation band.

[63] Butler, Adonis and Travers, *Failure in British Government* (above, n. 60), 2.

[64] See Audit Commission, *Passing the Bucks. The Impact of Standard Spending Assessments on Economy, Efficiency and Effectiveness* (London, 1993).

[65] See First Report of the House of Commons Environment Committee, Session 1993–94, *Standard Spending Assessments* (HC 90).

[66] It should be noted that in the original scheme, the poll tax was to be phased in over a ten year period. In 1986 the decision was made to cut the transitional phase to three years and then, at the Commons Report stage of the Scottish Bill (which was introduced one year earlier than that for England and Wales), an amendment was accepted to replace domestic rates with a poll tax immediately and without any transition: see Butler, Adonis and Travers, *Failure in British Government* (above, n. 60), 100–4.

of these services. The consequence has been to ensure that local services are provided in accordance with a market framework and that local government organizational arrangements are subjected to a range of market disciplines. A systematic attempt has thus been made to convert collectively organized redistributive services into trading services (or quasi-trading services) and then to subject these trading services, together with local public goods provided by local authorities, to market testing. It is envisaged (hence the slogan 'enabling not providing'[67]) that the local council might withdraw entirely from service provision and assume a role as a monitoring and regulatory agency with any redistributive issues being dealt with through nationally established schemes for income transfers. In order to consider this trend in detail, the changes introduced to a range of local government functions will be examined.

Public transport

The field of urban public transport provision provides a good illustration of the manner in which local authority responsibilities have been restructured in accordance with governmental objectives. During the 1960s, when local government structures were being reformed with the objective of strengthening the capacity of the system, a broad enabling framework was also established empowering county-level authorities in the main urban areas to assume responsibility for public transport.[68] These arrangements were strengthened after local government reorganization in the 1970s, when all county councils were placed under a duty to promote public transport services to meet the needs of their areas.[69] Since the 1970s, however, local authorities have been required to provide increasing amounts of subsidy to public transport undertakings in order to maintain a comprehensive network. In the 1980s, against a background of considerable disagreement between the centre and the localities over the means of promoting efficient urban transport systems, the system was fundamentally reformed.

Many of the large urban authorities had tried to maintain their networks by a strategy of freezing fares and increasing subsidies. They found, however, that their policies were undermined by the House of Lords which, in *Bromley LBC v. Greater London Council*,[70] struck down the GLC's supplementary precept to finance its fares policy on the ground that it was beyond the powers conferred in the Transport (London) Act 1969. This unexpected decision had the effect of destabilizing the system and the Government acted in an attempt to exploit these uncertainties by requiring authorities to justify the levels of revenue support to

[67] See, e.g., N. Ridley, *The Local Right: Enabling not Providing* (London, 1988).
[68] Transport Act 1968; Transport (London) Act 1969.
[69] Transport Act 1968, s. 9(3); Transport (London) Act 1969, s. 1; Transport Act 1978, s. 1.
[70] [1983] 1 AC 768. The issues surrounding this decision are examined in detail in ch. 4, 231–7 below.

public transport operators through a statutory cost-benefit process.[71] Its objective was, in the context of the uncertainties caused by the *Bromley* decision, to try to convert the general statutory duties of the authorities into justiciable constraints. When this exercise failed, more radical solutions followed.

The Transport Act 1985 brought in the most fundamental changes to local public transport policy since regulation had been introduced in 1930. First, in order to stimulate competition with municipal operators the system of bus licensing was deregulated.[72] Secondly, the public transport companies were reorganized and were obliged to operate at arm's length from the local authority and to run on commercial lines.[73] Thirdly, and consequentially, a new duty was imposed on local authorities not to inhibit competition in the provision of transport services.[74] Fourthly, the power of local authorities to provide service subsidies to transport providers was recast so as to enable them to provide subsidies only for routes and not networks, and then only in accordance with a strict tendering regime.[75] And finally the local authority's basic duty was altered from that of providing an *integrated* and efficient public transport system to meet the *needs* of the area to that of a residual, market support function of formulating policies to meet any appropriate public transport requirements that would not otherwise be satisfied.[76]

The overall effect of the 1985 Act has been to challenge the authority's traditional discretion in respect of the planning, financing and provision of public transport services. This has been achieved by a formal separation between service specification and service provision, by requiring service provision to be achieved through market competition, and by altering the governmental function to the residual one of planning only for the services that the market is not able to provide.

Housing

Although public transport provides a clear illustration of the general theme, developments affecting local government's housing responsibilities have probably had the most profound social impact. The emergence of the local authority role in housing during the twentieth century has been associated with a major social achievement. By the late 1970s local authorities had, since the 1930s, cleared nearly 2 million substandard houses; had, since 1949, provided grants to renovate more than 3 million houses; and had become responsible for managing around 30 per cent of the housing stock. Local government had also played a

---

[71] Transport Act 1983. For an analysis see: M. Loughlin, 'Lawyers, economists and the urban public transport policy process' in S. Glaister (ed.), *Transport Subsidy* (London, 1987).

[72] Transport Act 1985, Pts. I and II (deregulation was not extended to London).

[73] Transport Act 1985, Pts. IV and V.

[74] Transport Act 1985, s. 57(2) (providing a new s. 9A(6) of the Transport Act 1968).

[75] Transport Act 1985, ss. 88–92.   [76] Transport Act 1985, s. 57.

major role in the general improvement of housing conditions. As a result of the exercise of their management, regulatory and grant-providing powers, the number of households living in unfit or substandard housing had fallen from 7,500,000 in 1951 to 1,650,000 in 1976 and, over the same period, the number of over-crowded households fell from 650,000 to 150,000.[77] Since 1980, however, the Conservative government, starting from the assumptions that local author-ities have in general been poor managers of their housing stock, that owner-occupation is the desired tenure form, and that the market is the mechanism which is best able to provide good quality housing, has initiated a serious of major reforms which have radically transformed the role of local government in the field of housing.

The Housing Act 1980 set the tone of Government housing policy by intro-ducing three important reforms: the vesting of rights in council tenants to pur-chase the freehold of their homes on favourable terms; giving tenants formal legal rights, including security of tenure and certain rights in relation to housing management; and introducing a new housing subsidy system which provided incentives to authorities to raise rents to commercial levels and made it very diffi-cult for them to continue to provide for the general housing needs of their areas.

The most controversial of these reforms was the programme of council house sales: in 1982 sales peaked at over 200,000 but then started to decline as the pent-up demand began to dissipate. In an attempt to maintain the impetus the Government provided additional incentives in the Housing and Building Control Act 1984: procedures were streamlined; residential qualifications were reduced; the maximum discount was increased; rights were extended to cover leases; and rights to a 'shared ownership lease', in which tenants purchase a slice of the equity and pay a reduced rent on the remainder, were given.[78] By 1987, how-ever, local authorities still owned around 80 per cent of their original housing stock.[79] The Government then promoted potentially more fundamental measures in the Housing Act 1988. This Act provided for the compulsory disposal to the private sector of entire council estates through either the 'change of landlord' or 'Housing Action Trust'(HAT) schemes.[80] While the impact of these schemes might not have been as significant as the Government anticipated, they did mark a major shift in the official perception of local government's role in housing.

The trend towards reducing the local authority role in housing provision has been complemented by changes in the financial regime. The new housing subsidy system introduced in the 1980 Act gave the Government much greater

[77] See, Department of the Environment, *Housing Policy: A Consultative Document*, Cmnd. 6851 (1977).

[78] In the Housing Defects Act 1984, however, the Government felt obliged to give rights to assistance or to require the local authority to re-purchase the property to purchasers under the right to buy scheme of certain defective types of system-built housing.

[79] For an overview of the impact of the council house sales policy see: R. Forrest & A. Murie, *Selling the Welfare State* (London, 1988).

[80] Housing Act 1988, Pts. III and IV.

control over rental levels and, with falling subsidies, rents have increased dramatically during the 1980s. Since the consequence has been to increase the numbers of council tenants entitled to housing benefit, the overall effect has been a restructuring of subsidy: away from a socialized form organized by local authorities through the historic cost financing principle and towards a nationally-organized individualized income-related allowance. The new housing subsidy system is in effect a deficit subsidy system and, as a result of increased rental levels, by 1987/88 only 95 local authorities were in receipt of housing subsidy. However, local authorities still retained certain discretionary powers – particularly through rent-pooling arrangements or by making contributions from the rate fund – to shape council house rents. In the Local Government and Housing Act 1989 the Government acted to eliminate much of this remaining discretion of local authorities. This was achieved primarily by 'ring-fencing' of the Housing Revenue Account and by linking rents to the capital values of dwellings.[81]

Further initiatives have been taken by the Government in the 1990s in pursuance of this general housing strategy. The most important are to be found in the Leasehold Reform, Housing and Urban Development Act 1993 which introduced four major changes. First, it repealed the shared ownership scheme which had been introduced in the 1984 Act and replaced it with a 'rents-to-mortgages' scheme; this scheme is specifically designed to attract low-income tenants to buy since, in order to qualify, the tenant must have been in receipt of housing benefit for the previous year.[82] Secondly, arrangements are made for expanding tenant participation in local authority management agreements by introducing a 'right-to-manage' under which local authorities can be required to enter into management agreements with tenants' organizations.[83] Thirdly, arrangements are made for extending the system of compulsory competitive tendering (CCT) to housing management.[84] Finally, under the Housing Act 1985 local authorities are empowered, with ministerial consent, voluntarily to transfer their stock to the private sector and between 1988 and 1992 eighteen local authorities did so. The effect of such transfers, however, has been to increase the burden on the Exchequer through additional housing benefit payments.[85] The Government did not wish to discourage such transfers but did want to reduce the Exchequer burden. Consequently, in the 1993 Act provision is made for the Government to charge a levy on the receipts obtained by the transferring authority.[86]

---

[81] Local Government and Housing Act 1989, ss. 74–8.   [82] 1993 Act, ss. 108–20.

[83] 1993 Act, s. 132; inserting new s. 27AB into Housing Act 1985.

[84] 1993 Act, ss. 129–32. These are enabling measures which came into force on 1 April 1994 and under which the first contractors are expected to operate from 1 April 1996. On CCT see further below, 105–6.

[85] This is because, as a result of changes to Housing Revenue Accounts made by Part VI of the Local Government and Housing Act 1989, many local authorities are required to contribute to the cost of rent rebates.

[86] 1993 Act, s. 136.

The cumulative impact of the many changes introduced since 1980 to the role of local government in housing has been profound. Hitherto the primary agencies for bringing about improvements in housing standards, local authorities have come to be viewed as major obstacles to the achievement of further improvements. In the process, local authority discretion has been greatly reduced as a result of new rights vested in tenants and, more importantly, a range of new central government restrictions. Local authorities are now unable directly to act to meet the housing needs of their areas and are rapidly becoming landlords of poorer quality stock which is often available only for the least advantaged members of society.

Education

Though the timing of the major reforms varies, a similar pattern to that detected in relation to policies on public transport and housing may be seen to be emerging in respect of education; the largest and most important local government service. The key educational issue in the early 1980s was that of parental rights.[87] In the Education Act 1980 a system of parental choice was instituted which required local education authorities to comply with school preferences unless compliance would prejudice the provision of efficient education or the efficient use of resources.[88] These powers were subsequently entrenched by strengthening the parental role on school governing bodies and by augmenting the power of governing bodies.[89] While exit mechanisms were also set in motion on an individualized basis with the establishment of the assisted places scheme in 1980,[90] the main theme of education legislation during the early 1980s was that of strengthening the voice of the consumers of the service.

This emphasis changed during the latter half of the 1980s. The key event was the enactment of the Education Reform Act 1988 which, by enhancing voice mechanisms and extending exit arrangements, had a major impact on the local authority role in education. Voice mechanisms were enhanced primarily by the arrangements for open enrolment and local financial management. Open enrolment required each school to admit pupils up to the limit of its physical capacity[91] and this therefore meant that local authorities were no longer able to use an efficiency argument to justify their attempts to plan educational provision in their areas. Local financial management required every local authority to obtain the Secretary of State's approval for a scheme for financing its schools in accordance with a general formula.[92] In combination, open enrolment and local

---

[87] See M. Adler, A. Petch and J. Tweedie, *Parental Choice and Educational Policy* (Edinburgh, 1989).

[88] Education Act 1980, ss. 6–9.

[89] Education (No. 2) Act 1986; Education Reform Act 1988, Pt. I, ch. III.

[90] Education Act 1980, s. 17.   [91] Education Reform Act 1988, Pt. I, ch. II.

[92] 1988 Act, Pt. I, ch. III.

financial management subjected schools to market forces and considerably reduced the discretionary potential of local authorities to plan educational provision in their areas. The 1988 Act also greatly extended exit arrangements through
the establishment of 'grant maintained schools'.[93] The idea was for maintained
schools to opt out of local authority control and obtain their funding directly
from central government. This proposal to establish a new category of school
was explicitly designed to end the local authority's monopoly on the provision
of state education.[94]

In 1993 'the final stages in a transformation in education which will take
at least a decade to work through'[95] was set in place with the enactment of the
Education Act 1993. The most important innovation of the 1993 Act is the
establishment of a Funding Agency for Schools,[96] whose members will be appointed by the Secretary of State and which will be under his or her general
control. The Agency will not only take over responsibility for funding grant-
maintained schools but it is also envisaged that, once 10 per cent of pupils in
an area attend grant-maintained schools, the Agency will assume joint responsibility with the local authority for ensuring that there are sufficient schools in the
area;[97] and that, once the proportion reaches 75 per cent, the Agency could be
vested with sole responsibility.[98] Since the 1993 Act also makes various arrangements for extending opportunities for opting out,[99] it is clear that the Act envis-
ages a situation in which local authorities will lose their pre-eminent position as
providers of state education.[100]

According to the Government, 'five great themes run through the story of educational change in England and Wales since 1979: quality, diversity, increasing
parental choice, greater autonomy for schools and greater accountability'.[101]
Whatever anyone may think about these themes (and many would commend
each of them), the way in which the Government has both interpreted and
institutionalized these themes has been highly controversial. As construed by the
Government, these themes seem to require both the centralization of education
and the exposure of the system to market processes. These developments have
resulted in a systematic attempt to displace local authorities from the key role

[93] 1988 Act, Pt. I, ch. IV.
[94] It should be noted that the 1988 Act also took polytechnics and colleges of higher education
out of the control of local education authorities and placed them under the direction of a separate
funding council; the Polytechnics and Colleges Funding Councils (PCFC). This move was followed
by Part I of the Further and Higher Education Act 1992 which removed colleges of further education and sixth form colleges from LEA control and also placed them under the control of the
PCFC.
[95] *Choice and Diversity*, Cm. 2021 (1992), para. 15.1.
[96] Separate agencies are established for England and Wales: 1993 Act, ss. 3–6.
[97] A duty imposed on local authorities by the Education Act 1944, s. 8.
[98] 1993 Act, s. 12.   [99] 1993 Act, Pt. II.
[100] See N. Harris, *Law and Education: Regulation, Consumerism and the Education System*
(London, 1993).
[101] *Choice and Diversity*, Cm. 2021, para. 1.9.

which, thoughout the twentieth century, they have performed in the provision of education.

Direct provision of services

Since local government's statutory responsibilities are generally couched in the language of 'securing the provision' of various services, local authorities have always been empowered to contract with private bodies to secure that provision. In general, however, most local authorities, in accordance with the tradition of the 'self-sufficient authority', have taken the view that public services are most effectively provided by utilizing their own staff. Consequently, comparatively little work has been put out to tender. This basic pattern has, since 1980, been gradually called into question by central government and a growing range of local government functions have been subjected to the process of compulsory competitive tendering (CCT). This process, which complements the trends towards competition and privatization which we have already seen in relation to public transport, housing and education, presents a major organizational challenge to local government.

The principle of CCT was introduced in Part III of the Local Government, Planning and Land Act 1980 which not only required local authorities to establish their direct labour organizations (DLOs) as formal trading services and to account for them on a commercial basis, but also required a range of work to be put out to competitive tender. However, it was only in the mid 1980s, as the Government's general privatization programme came to be established, that its potential in the field of local government was fully recognized. The basic change came with the enactment of the Local Government Act 1988.[102]

The 1988 Act greatly extended the range of CCT in local government: seven specified activities – covering refuse collection, catering services, cleaning of buildings and streets, and the maintenance of vehicles and grounds – were phased in to the CCT regime on a rolling programme and the Secretary of State was empowered to extend the Act's scope to other local government activities.[103] The Act also considerably tightened the tendering regime, by imposing detailed procedures on local authorities and placing on them a general duty to do nothing 'having the effect or intended or likely to have the effect of restricting, distorting or preventing competition'.[104] Further, the Act prohibits local authorities from taking into account 'non-commercial considerations' in relation to the contracting for the supply of goods, materials and services.[105]

Although around 85 per cent of the total value of contracts in the first round

---

[102] See M. Radford, 'Competition Rules: the Local Government Act 1988' (1988) 51 MLR 747; K. Walsh, *Competitive Tendering for Local Authority Services: Initial Experiences* (London, 1991).
[103] In 1989 sports and leisure management was added to the programme: SI 1989 No. 2488.
[104] 1988 Act, ss. 4(5), 7(7).   [105] 1988 Act, s. 17.

was awarded by local authorities to their own direct service organisation (DSO),[106] this is not the critical factor in seeking an assessment of the impact of the Act on local government. The primary impact which the 1988 Act has exerted has been over local authority organizational structures: local authorities have been obliged, through an internal differentiation between client and contractor roles, to break down the corporate structure of the authority into semi-autonomous purchaser and provider units.[107] This presents a major challenge to the idea of an integrated self-sufficient authority. That this is part of an ongoing programme can be seen not only by the Government's proposals to extend CCT to housing management[108] but also by the requirement in the Environmental Protection Act 1990 that local authorities must separate regulatory and operational responsibilities in respect of waste disposal functions[109] and, more importantly, the provisions of Part I of the Local Government Act 1992 which extends the CCT regime to a range of professional services in local government.[110]

Institutional consequences of functional change

These many reforms to the way in which local authorities carry out their basic functions have had a major impact on the institution of local government. The general trend in the reforms to local government functions can be explained in a variety of ways: from redistributive services to trading services; from a collectivistic to an individualistic mode of organization of service delivery; from opaque practices to transparent mechanisms; from a provider role to a purchaser role. However they are to be characterized, it seems clear that the impact on both the discretionary powers of the authority and the principle of multi-functionality has been profound. While this trend is not universal, with, for example, a more complex picture emerging in relation to social services,[111] this has undoubtedly been the basic thrust of the recent reforms affecting local government functions.

---

[106] Audit Commission, *Realising the Benefits of Competition: The Client Role for Contracted Services* (London, 1993), para. 16.

[107] See P. Vincent-Jones, 'The limits of near-contractual governance: local authority internal trading under CCT' (1994) *J. of Law & Soc.* 214; id., 'The limits of contractual order in public sector transacting' (1994) 14 *Legal Studies* 364.

[108] Leasehold Reform, Housing and Urban Development Act 1993, ss. 129–33 (see above, 102).

[109] Environmental Protection Act 1990, Pt. II. The waste regulation functions were subsequently transferred to a newly established Environmental Agency: see Environment Act 1995, s. 2.

[110] In addition to housing management, these include legal, architectural, engineering, information technology, finance and personnel services: see *Competing for Quality*, Cm. 1730 (1991).

[111] See especially the new responsibilities vested in local authorities under the Children Act 1989 and the National Health Service and Community Care Act 1990, ss. 42–50, the general theme of which is to require the needs of those children and adults who are to be protected by the Acts to be individually and adequately considered and assessed. Nevertheless, the community care reforms do envisage the adoption of purchaser–provider distinction within local authorities and the more extensive use of private sector contracting: see Department of Health, *Caring for People: community care in the next decade and beyond*, Cm. 849 (1989).

These developments directly challenge the tradition of the self-sufficient local authority which has emerged during the twentieth century.

The general effect of these reforms has been to replace the traditional principle of institutional integration with that of institutional differentiation. This trend can clearly be seen occurring across the basic functions of local government. There are three main dimensions to this movement towards institutional differentiation. First, there is institutional differentiation *within* the local council, which may be illustrated by the changing relationship between maintained schools and the LEA or between the DSO and the purchasing local authority. Secondly, the principle of institutional differentiation may also be seen at work in promotion (generally through statutory requirements) of a growing number of contractual relationships between the local authority and a range of private bodies for the provision of public services, such as bus operators providing tendered services or private firms providing services under CCT arrangements. But there is also a third dimension to the principle which has hitherto only been addressed tangentially. In recent years the Government has also been promoting specific-purpose bodies to undertake tasks which previously had been the responsibility of local government. These agencies include: urban development corporations (UDCs);[112] training and enterprise councils (TECs);[113] London Regional Transport (LRT);[114] HATs;[115] grant maintained schools and the Funding Agency for Schools;[116] further education colleges;[117] and registered housing associations.[118]

[112] UDCs have been appointed by central government under Part XVI of the Local Government, Planning and Land Act 1980 for the purpose of regenerating designated areas (s. 135). These corporations are empowered, inter alia, to acquire land owned by public authorities in the area designated (s. 141) and the Secretary of State is empowered to make the corporation the local planning authority (s. 149) and the housing authority (s. 153) for the area and vest it with duties relating to building control (s. 151) and public health (s. 159). See also the Urban Regeneration Agency established under s. 158 of the Leasehold Reform, Housing and Urban Development Act 1993 to secure the regeneration of unused, underused or derelict land.

[113] The establishment of a network of locally-based TECs, with the responsibility for delivering Government-sponsored training schemes, has formed the basis of the Government's training strategy: see *Employment for the 1990s*, Cm. 540 (1988). TECs have between 9 and 15 board members, two-thirds of whom must be business leaders from the private sector, even though in some areas local authorities or health authorities are the largest employers. TECs have been devolved responsibility for training and enterprise programmes previously operated by the Training Agency (formerly the Manpower Services Commission).

[114] Under the London Regional Transport Act 1984 control of the London Transport Executive was transferred from the GLC to LRT, a body which is effectively under the control of central government.

[115] HATs are corporate bodies established when the Minister designates an area under the Housing Act 1988 (s. 62). The object of the HAT is to secure the effective management and improvement of housing accommodation in that area (s. 63). Its members are appointed by the Minister (s. 62) and the HAT must comply with any directions issued by the Minister (s. 72). The Minister may by order provide for the transfer to the HAT of local authority functions concerning planning, housing and public health (ss. 65–8).

[116] See above, 104.   [117] Further and Higher Education Act 1992, Pt. I.

[118] Housing associations must be registered to obtain grants from central government and loans from the Housing Corporation, whose primary function is to monitor the activities of the quasi-public housing sector: Housing Associations Act 1985.

These agencies are either specially established public bodies which are subject to central government control or bodies which, though technically private, exist essentially to perform public functions and are largely or wholly dependent on funding from central government for the performance of their functions. Because of their local character and essentially public functions, such bodies have become part of an institutionally differentiated structure of local governance.

This general process of institutional differentiation (many would say fragmentation) provides us with a much more complex picture of public sector action at the local level. In effect, the modern institution of local government seems to be in the process of being replaced by a complex local governance network in which the local council will simply be one – and not necessarily the most prominent – agency on the local scene.[119] It is within such a world – in which local councils are viewed as one agency amongst many and in which short-term central government policies can play such a powerful role in shaping the mosaic – that the poll tax may be characterized as a financing system which failed because it was introduced ahead of its time.

Accountability Mechanisms

The tradition of local government which has emerged this century is based on the idea of local councils as multi-functional authorities which are vested with broad discretionary powers to enable them to provide a range of services which meet the needs of their communities. Within this tradition, a distinctive pattern of accountability has emerged which tends to accentuate political mechanisms and to marginalize other forms of accountability. Many of the recent changes affecting local government, however, have been influenced by a desire to strengthen the mechanisms of accountability. The requirement that direct labour organisations operate as formal trading services may be viewed as a means of holding the authority to account for the service; vesting rights in consumers of services, such as tenants or parents of school children, evidently promotes accountability; and the Government even justified the poll tax as a reform which would enhance local democracy and local accountability.

However, as such examples illustrate, accountability is not simply a powerful concept; it is also a complex and multi-faceted one. In order to assess the impact which recent reforms have had on the status of local government, it is important to appreciate the way in which the various methods of holding local government to account have, in recent times, been adapted. This may be illustrated by considering the general discretion of local councils to provide services. At the outset, it should be recognized that the idea of a local government 'service' is

---

[119] See K. Walsh, *Public Services and Market Mechanisms. Competition, Contracting and the New Public Management* (London, 1995).

itself a political concept. Local government services display high levels of *heterogeneity*; they rarely involve the delivery of a single simple product and generally are intricate packages of different products falling under a common designation.[120] Consequently, local government services are often fairly *complex*, in the sense that a variety of different skills may be needed for their effective delivery. The heterogeneity and the complexity of local government services also results in there being a degree of *uncertainty* about the relationship between the resources supplied, the processes utilized and services provided.[121]

It is precisely because of these characteristics of local government services that decisions about them require the exercise of political judgment and thus are vested in elected representatives. Further, it is owing to the uncertainty about those processes that trust is vested in professionals to help ensure the delivery of high quality services. It is also because of these characteristics of local government services that the legal framework has traditionally been facilitative: our legal resources and legal culture are such that the legal system is unable to provide effective supervision of decision-making in conditions of complexity and uncertainty. The tradition of local government which has emerged has thus generated a distinctive pattern of accountability.

This pattern is based on the idea of the corporate authority. This idea suggests not only that decisions are taken by, or on behalf of, the entire council and that officers serve the council as a whole but also that local councils are free to regulate their own proceedings and that there are limits on the extent to which the corporate veil should be pierced. Much of the conduct of council business is thus regulated by convention rather than law and the standards of performance of officers is felt to be best enhanced by the promotion of professional standards. The principal control mechanisms are those which are applied as a result of central government supervision. And local accountability is primarily secured through the subjection of elected members to periodic elections.

The recent reforms to local government can be understood to reflect a sense of dissatisfaction over the performance of local government and the Government seem to have accepted that the traditional structure of accountability within local government should be viewed as forming part of the problem. The changing forms of accountability thus constitute an important dimension to the recent developments affecting the status of local government.

---

[120] Consider a simple example. Assume that the visit is considered as equally important an aspect of the local authority meals-on-wheels service as the regular delivery of a hot meal. If the authority were to determine that the service could be provided more economically by giving all recipients of the service a microwave oven and then providing them with a weekly supply of frozen meals, that decision, in pursuit of economy, would also have the effect of changing the nature of the service. What would need to be clarified was whether the change in the nature of the service was an intended outcome of the change in its mode of delivery.

[121] On these issues see further P. Day & R. Klein, *Accountabilities: Five Public Services* (London, 1987), 59–60.

The challenge

From the perspective of accountability, the essence of the challenge to the institution of local government posed by recent developments is to the ethic of discretion. This is manifested most clearly in the attempt to change the character of local services by altering the mechanisms of accountability for such services. This has taken place on a number of fronts.

The issue of the *heterogeneity* of services has been tackled by requiring local authorities to specify their service objectives with as great a degree of precision as possible. Where performance cannot easily be measured, authorities are encouraged to develop *performance indicators* which are designed to provide evidence of how well services are being provided. Key performance indicators are those which examine the relationship between the cost of a service and the resources created (economy), between the resources utilized and the service outputs (efficiency), and between service outputs and overall outcomes (effectiveness). This type of framework has been widely adopted in value-for-money (VFM) studies which have proliferated in local government in recent times.

The challenge to the issue of service *complexity* has taken the form of seeking to break down the large corporate authority into as many discrete units as possible with a view to rendering each of them more precisely accountable for the public resources which they consume. This is most clearly seen in the distinction drawn between client and contractor roles which has been a key feature of competitive tendering regimes. This organizational change designed to reduce service complexity is closely allied to the challenge to the *uncertainty* of aim of service programmes since the general response has been to require more precise, comparative and ultimately quantifiable performance targets to be developed. The basic thrust of this challenge is to subject discrete units of local services to a range of market disciplines, including the promotion of economic pricing policies for local authority services, the encouragement of direct competition with the private sector for the provision of services, and requiring the contracting out of local authority services to the private sector.

Such reforms possess a number of common features. The most obvious is that they all serve to confine, structure and check the traditional discretionary powers of the local authority and they therefore constitute a direct challenge to the idea of the corporate authority. Reforms along such lines challenge the traditional role of members and officer-professionals to shape the organization of the service and even to determine appropriate standards of performance. And it is precisely because they restrict discretion and require precise specification of service standards that they render local government decisions more susceptible to external accountability by consumers, local taxpayers, competitors, central departments, or review agencies. What is of particular importance, however, is that in this process of subjecting local government to these forms of accountability, the peculiarly *public* character of these services and the peculiarly *governmental* character of the institution becomes in danger of being undermined. In this light, the various reforms which have been promoted to reinforce these new forms of accountability should now be considered.

The structure of political accountability

Although during the early 1980s the Government contemplated a number of initiatives to alter the system of political accountability,[122] the most important reforms followed from the Widdicombe Inquiry into the conduct of local authority business which reported in 1986.[123] The Committee had been asked to pay particular attention to the roles of elected members and their relationships with officers and to make recommendations for strengthening the democratic process.[124] It identified as the key issue the fact that the formal framework did not recognize the existence of party politics in local government nor the needs of modern management and proposed a range of reforms based on the need to formalize the conventional practices and to bolster the professional position of officers.

Many of the Widdicombe recommendations were enacted in Part I of the Local Government and Housing Act 1989 which provided for the disqualification of members from being senior officers of a local authority[125], required all appointments to be made on merit[126], restricted the principle of co-option to council committees[127], and imposed a duty on the authority to allocate membership of council committees amongst the relevant political groups in proportion to their representation on the council.[128] In addition to the direct regulation of council members, the 1989 Act provided for indirect regulation through the differentiation of political and managerial tasks and through the imposition of new duties on officers.[129] Furthermore, since the new duties on designated officers

---

[122] The most radical was the proposal in the Local Government Finance Bill 1981 that a local authority would generally be permitted to levy a rate only within a ceiling specified by the Secretary of State and it would be permitted to levy a supplementary rate only if it were to gain the consent of its electors in a poll. The Government, however, failed to obtain the support of Conservative backbenchers who were concerned at the introduction of the principle of the referendum and the Bill was withdrawn. Note that in the Rates Act 1984 the Government acquired the power to impose the ceiling without the democratic safeguard proposed in the 1981 Bill.

[123] *Report of the Committee of Inquiry into the Conduct of Local Authority Business* (Chmn: David Widdicombe QC), Cmnd. 9797 (1986). See M. Loughlin, 'The Conduct of Local Authority Business' (1987) 50 MLR 64; P. McAuslan, 'The Widdicombe Report: Local Government Business or Politics?' (1987) *Public Law* 154.

[124] Ibid., para. 1.1.

[125] Local Government and Housing Act 1989, ss. 1–3. This provision is in response to the issue of 'twin-tracking' which was felt to compromise an officer's duties in serving the council impartially.

[126] 1989 Act, ss. 7, 8. Provision is made for the appointment of political advisers subject to specific restrictions: s. 9.

[127] 1989 Act, s. 13.   [128] 1989 Act, s. 15.

[129] These duties included the requirement that one officer be designated as the head of the paid service (s. 4), that an officer be designated with responsibility for financial administration (s. 6) and that a monitoring officer, charged with the responsibility for ensuring administrative propriety within

include the right of officers to determine the resources required to discharge their duties,[130] they marked a clear breach of the tradition of the corporate authority.

Some have suggested that these reforms to the structure of political account-ability, being skewed to the issue of politicization, failed to get to the heart of the leadership challenge facing local government.[131] Furthermore, it is important to note that the reforms marked a change in traditional assumptions underpin-ning the representative principle in local government as reflected through the idea of the corporate authority. In his classic work on central and local govern-ment, Norman Chester identified as two of three vital elements in our local government system the 'right of local electors to elect whom they please to their local Councils' and the 'necessity for a local Council to be able to rely com-pletely on the loyalty of its officials'.[132] The 1989 Act reforms impose significant restrictions on each of these principles.

Financial accountability

One of the primary methods of achieving accountability for the expenditure of public money by local government is through the procedures of external audit. External audit has since the nineteenth century been undertaken by the District Audit Service, an agency of central government. In 1983, however, audit ar-rangements were fundamentally reformed as a result of the establishment of the Audit Commission.[133] Under these new institutional arrangements the exercise of regularity audit remained basically unchanged, though the local authority's freedom under the 1972 Act[134] to choose between using the services of the district auditor or a private auditor was removed. Auditors are now appointed by the Audit Commission and the Government's intention was to ensure that a higher proportion of audit work was undertaken by private auditors.

The primary impact of this change on the status of local government, how-ever, comes not from the alteration of institutional arrangements for audit but because of amendments to auditors' powers. Under the 1982 Act auditors were placed under a duty to satisfy themselves that the local authority 'has made proper arrangements for securing economy, efficiency and effectiveness in its use of resources'.[135] Since the early 1980s the scale of VFM audit has substantially

the authority, be appointed (s. 5). On these developments see C.M.G. Himsworth, 'Officers, Mem-bers and Local Autonomy' in W. Finnie, C.M.G. Himsworth & N. Walker (eds.), *Edinburgh Essays in Public Law* (Edinburgh, 1991), 121.

[130] See, e.g., Local Government Finance Act 1988, s. 26(4) (community charges registration officer); 1988 Act, s. 114(7) (chief finance officer); Local Government and Housing Act 1989, s. 4(1)(b) (head of paid service); 1989 Act, s. 5(1)(b) (monitoring officer).

[131] For implicit Government recognition of this point see: *Local Government Review: The Internal Management of Local Authorities in England* (Department of the Environment, 1991). See also, J. Gyford, S. Leach and C. Game, *The Changing Politics of Local Government* (London, 1989) ch. 9.

[132] D.N. Chester, *Central and Local Government* (London, 1951), 351.

[133] Local Government Finance Act 1982, Pt. III.   [134] Local Government Act 1972, s. 154.

[135] Local Government Finance Act 1982, s. 15(1)(c).

increased. The Audit Commission has developed methodologies for wide-ranging organizational analysis covering most major areas of local government activity and has moved 'into the ambiguous and treacherous territory of advising local authorities on how to manage their policy-making and policy-implementation processes'.[136] The manner in which the Audit Commission has embarked on this task has been controversial, but there is little doubt that the Commission has been very influential.[137] Further, these developments entered a new stage with the enactment of Part I of the Local Government Act 1992. This Act, which was inspired by the Government's Citizen's Charter initiative,[138] empowers the Audit Commission to direct local authorities to publish comparative information on performance, thereby facilitating the publication of performance league tables.

Auditors have also acquired new powers, and the local authority's finance officer has been vested with new duties, to strengthen financial accountability. One concern which arose as a result of central–local conflicts during the mid 1980s over issues of finance was that the auditor possessed powers only to deal retrospectively with misconduct in local government. Under the Local Government Act 1988, then, the auditor was vested with two new powers. First, the auditor is empowered to issue a prohibition order against a local authority, the effect of which would be to require the authority to desist from making or implementing any decision or taking or continuing to take a particular course of action.[139] The second power permits the auditor to apply for judicial review of any decision, or any failure to act, which might have an effect on the authority's accounts.[140] The potential impact of these powers was reinforced by the duty imposed on the local authority's chief finance officer in section 114 of the Local Government Finance Act 1988 to make a report in any case of financial misconduct which arises within the authority. Once the report is issued, the authority is prohibited from pursuing the course of conduct referred to in the report until the report has been considered by the council. Since a copy of the report must be sent to the auditor, the exercise of this power will also alert the auditor to the possibility of financial misconduct.

The new institutional arrangements for audit, the new powers vested in auditors

---

[136] P. Day and R. Klein, *Inspecting the Inspectorates* (York, 1990), 16. See also M. Loughlin, *Administrative Accountability in Local Government* (York, 1992), ch. 3.

[137] For assessments, in addition to the studies by Day and Klein and Loughlin (above, n. 136), see: B. McSweeney, 'Accounting for the Audit Commission' (1988) 59 *Pol. Q* 28; M. Radford, 'Auditing for Change: Local Government and the Audit Commission' (1991) 54 MLR 912. For a self-assessment see: Audit Commission, *How Effective is the Audit Commission?* (London, 1991).

[138] *The Citizen's Charter*, Cm.1599 (1991). See further, Loughlin, *Administrative Accountability* (above, n. 136), ch. 6.

[139] Local Government Act 1988, s. 30, Sched.4 (inserting new ss. 25A–25C into the Local Government Finance Act 1982).

[140] Local Government Act 1988, s. 30, Sched.4 (inserting new s. 25D into Local Government Finance Act 1982). This power was successfully used by the auditor in *R* v. *Wirral MBC, ex parte Milstead* [1989] RVR 66.

and the new duties imposed on local government officers all serve both to structure the local authority's traditional discretionary power of action and to impose a powerful check on local government decision-making.

Administrative accountability

The main institutional mechanism for examining the propriety of local administration is the Commission for Local Administration, generally known as the Local Ombudsman, which was established under the Local Government Act 1974. The main function of the Local Ombudsman is to investigate complaints of maladministration in the conduct of local government business. Reforms have also been introduced in the 1980s to address concerns over the accessibility, jurisdiction and remedial powers of the Ombudsman. These issues will be considered in turn.

Under the 1974 Act the Ombudsman could not generally consider a complaint unless it had been referred by a councillor[141] and, for some time, this had been felt to impose a fetter which limited their effectiveness in addressing maladministration.[142] The principle of direct access to the Ombudsman received strong support from the Widdicombe Committee[143] and in 1988 was given statutory effect.[144] During the first year of direct access the number of complaints received by the Commission increased by 44 per cent,[145] a figure which, though not necessarily indicative of increased maladministration, does suggest growing public awareness of the Ombudsman's role and a greater willingness to use the procedure.

There are significant restrictions on the Ombudsman's jurisdiction. They may not question the merits of any decision. As Lord Donaldson put it: 'Administration and maladministration have nothing to do with the nature, quality or reasonableness of a decision.'[146] Nor may the Ombudsman challenge policy, a restriction reflected in the fact that they may not consider complaints concerning action which affects most or all of the inhabitants of an area.[147] And, since a complaint cannot be accepted if an alternative remedy exists,[148] the Ombudsman has no jurisdiction to consider complaints concerning unlawful action. Even within their designated sphere of general competence, there are a number of categories of exclusion including personnel matters, contractual or commercial matters, internal school proceedings, legal proceedings and the investigation of crime.[149]

---

[141] Local Government Act 1974, s. 26.
[142] See, e.g., Commission for Local Administration in England, *Annual Report 1984/85*, ch. 3
[143] Widdicombe Report, Cmnd. 9797 (1986) para. 9.64.
[144] Local Government Act 1988, Sched. 3, para. 5(2); amending Local Government Act 1974, s. 26(2).
[145] Commission for Local Administration in England, *Annual Report 1988/89*, 9.
[146] *R* v. *Local Commissioner, ex parte Eastleigh BC* [1988] 3 WLR 113, 119.
[147] 1974 Act, s. 26(7).   [148] 1974 Act, s. 26(6).   [149] 1974 Act, Sched. 5.

In recent years there has been some modification of these exclusions but they have been of marginal importance.[150]

More generally, the English Commissioners have been pressing to have the power to conduct investigations on their own initiative.[151] Despite support from Widdicombe,[152] the Government remained unpersuaded, mainly on the ground that it would entail a switch in the role of the Ombudsman from a grievance-handling mechanism into a general purpose watchdog and the effect might be to lose the goodwill of local authorities.[153] Nevertheless, the Government did recognize that there was scope for extending the Commissioners' role in improving the quality of administration by developing their capacity to prevent future maladministration. This was achieved by two legislative changes introduced in 1989: first by requiring local authorities to notify the Ombudsman of the steps they have taken to rectify any administrative shortcomings identified in an adverse report;[154] and secondly, by giving the Ombudsman specific powers to publish general guidance to local government on the principles underlying good administrative practice and on common administrative errors.[155] These changes signal an opportunity for the Commissioners to use their investigatory powers not simply to remedy injustice but also to try to assume the more general role of undertaking an administrative audit.

From the outset, a degree of concern has been expressed about the limited powers of the Ombudsman to enforce remedies. If the Ombudsman finds that there has been maladministration causing injustice, the local authority is obliged to consider the report and notify the Ombudsman of any action they propose to take. However, if the Ombudsman is dissatisfied with the proposed action the only action which can be taken is the issuance of a second report. In 95 per cent of cases in which injustice was found, satisfactory settlements have been reached;[156] but this still leaves 5 per cent of cases in which local authorities have refused to provide a satisfactory remedy. Widdicombe considered that this posed a challenge to the effectiveness of the system and recommended introducing the power of judicial enforcement of the Ombudsman's remedies.[157] The Government rejected this proposal but in the 1989 Act did try to strengthen the system by introducing new procedures to require councils to give full consideration to adverse reports and to provide a public explanation if they decide not to comply with the Ombudsman's recommendations.[158] Furthermore, the Government

---

[150] In 1988 the exclusion list was amended to enable investigations to be conducted into local authority action in connection with the investigation or prevention of crime (SI 1988 No. 242) and by s. 269 of the Education Act 1993 jurisdiction was extended to education appeal committees of grant-maintained schools.

[151] See, e.g., Commission for Local Administration in England, *Annual Report 1987/88*, 5.

[152] Widdicombe Report, para. 9.68.   [153] Cm. 433, para. 6.31.

[154] 1974 Act, s. 31(2B); inserted by Local Government and Housing Act 1989, s. 26.

[155] 1989 Act, s. 23.

[156] Commission for Local Administration in England, *Annual Report 1988/89*, 11–13.

[157] Widdicombe Report, para. 9.68.   [158] 1989 Act, ss. 26–9.

has stated that, if the new procedures failed to remedy the situation, legislation making the Ombudsman's recommendations legally enforceable would be introduced.[159]

In addition to the reforms bolstering the work of the Local Ombudsman, the Government also recently introduced reforms to strengthen complaints mechanisms within local government. In the 1989 Act the duty was imposed on local authorities to establish a monitoring officer whose function would be to report on any action or proposed action by the authority which would give rise to a contravention of law or code of practice or to maladministration.[160] The Government has also recently acquired powers to require local authorities to establish a complaints procedure relating to the discharge of their social services functions.[161] The general thrust of recent reforms has therefore been to open up, and render more effective, the various channels of pursuing grievances against local authorities.

The role of the courts

With the establishment of the modern institution of local government, central departments of State exercising administrative powers displaced the courts as the main agencies of control of local bodies. In part, as we have seen, this was because the discretionary character of many of the public services which local government provided was more appropriately regulated through the elaborate networks of central–local relations based on professional associations, policy communities and political affiliations than the sporadic, retrospective action of courts applying the *ultra vires* doctrine. One consequence of the many changes which have been introduced in reorganizing local authority functions and strengthening accountability mechanisms, however, is potentially to render local government more susceptible to judicial supervision.

The breaking open of the enclosed, corporate local authority through such reforms as the differentiation of political and managerial responsibilities, the formalization of the distinction between purchaser and provider functions, the requirement that service units operate on commercial lines and the imposition of new duties on local authorities to avoid anti-competitive practices all serve to subject local government to tighter forms of legal control than has generally been the practice this century. The vesting of new legal rights in the consumers of local authority services provides further opportunities to challenge the decisions of local councils. And the recent reforms to external accountability mechanisms – seen most clearly with audit reforms – tend to provide review agencies with new powers to subject local authorities to more active legal supervision.[162]

The result can be seen in the extent to which disputes concerning certain areas

---

[159] *The Citizen's Charter*, Cm. 1599 (1991), 43.   [160] 1989 Act, s. 5.
[161] National Health Service and Community Care Act 1990, s. 46.
[162] See I. Harden, *The Contracting State* (Buckingham, 1992), ch. 5; K. Walsh, *Public Services and Market Mechanisms* (above, n. 119), 213–20.

of local government decision-making, such as the allocation of pupils to schools, which have not hitherto generally ended up in the courts are now regularly the subject of judicial review.[163] One consequence of the general trend of recent reforms, then, is to enhance the legal consciousness of decision-makers in local government and potentially to strengthen judicial oversight. Certainly, applications for judicial review against local authorities have been increasing, with local government by the late 1980s overtaking central government as the primary target of judicial review.[164] Whether our legal system possesses the necessary intellectual or organizational resources to be able to handle effectively the control tasks which may be assigned to it remains open to question.[165]

Changing forms of accountability

Many of the reforms designed to strengthen the accountability of local government may be welcomed, both in terms of enhancing the idea of citizenship and of rendering the authority more responsive to the needs of those it exists to serve. But there is little doubt that in general the reforms challenge the idea of the corporate authority and, potentially at least, could significantly weaken the institution of local government. This argument is most likely to be articulated by those who regard public services as being *sui generis* since many of the reforms stem from the desire to simplify local services and thus render them fungible. The critical issue, then, is whether the customer service orientation which underpins many of the reforms can generate a language which is able adequately to encompass and express the interests which citizens hold in the processes of governance.[166]

Structural Reforms

The recent changes to local government functions have cumulatively had a major impact on the institution of local government. It is not surprising, then, that, sooner or later, the Government would turn its attention to the question of

[163] For an illustration, see the disputes which arose over the clash between parental choice rights and the local authority's policy of giving priority to applicants from its own area: *R* v. *London Borough of Greenwich Shadow Education Committee, ex p. Governors of John Ball Primary School* (1990) 88 LGR 589; *R* v. *Bromley LBC, ex p. C* [1992] 1 FLR 175; *R* v. *Royal Borough of Kingston-upon-Thames, ex p. Kingwell* [1992] 1 FLR 182; *R* v. *Royal Borough of Kingston-upon-Thames, ex p. Emsden* [1993] 1 FLR 179.

[164] See M. Sunkin, L. Bridges and G. Meszaros, *Judicial Review in Perspective: An Investigation of Trends in the Use and Operation of the Judicial Review Procedure in England and Wales* (London, 1993) which shows that in the late 1980s local authorities were respondents in 35 per cent of applications for judicial review as compared with 27 per cent against central government.

[165] This issue is discussed further in ch. 7 below, 399–416.

[166] See S. Ranson and J. Stewart, 'Citizenship and Government: The Challenge for Mangement in the Public Domain' (1989) XXXVII *Pol. Studies* 5; J. Stewart and K. Walsh, 'Change in the Management of Public Services' (1992) 70 *Public Admin.* 499, 510–16; K. Walsh, *Public Services and Market Mechanisms* (above, n. 119), 250–7.

local government structure. A structure established in the early 1970s and based on the assumptions about the self-sufficient, corporate local authority which had been articulated by the Redcliffe-Maud Commission seemed unlikely to be appropriate for the 1990s and beyond. The Government has not, however, addressed this question in the traditional manner by appointing a Royal Commission to investigate and report. Instead, the issue has been dealt with in an incremental fashion. During the 1980s structural reforms were introduced for London and the metropolitan areas, though at that stage they appeared primarily to be an adjunct to the Government's expenditure control policy, and it was only in the 1990s that structural reform throughout the rest of the country came to be officially considered.

Reorganization of metropolitan government

The Local Government Act 1985 provided for the abolition of the Greater London Council (GLC) and the metropolitan county councils (MCCs). This reform was touted on the basis that it 'will streamline local government', 'remove a source of conflict and tension', 'save money' and 'provide a system which is simpler for the public to understand'.[167] The Act, however, was introduced without any independent inquiry having been held and on the basis of a short White Paper which presented the case for change in ten paragraphs only and without any detailed evidence justifying these assertions. It was widely felt that the reform was a cynical response by the Government to the fact that all the authorities which were to be abolished were under Labour control and many were pursuing public transport, economic development and general expenditure policies which were in antagonism with the policies of central government.[168]

It was in fact rather difficult to defend the reforms on the ground of 'streamlining' since no simple transfer of functions from the county authorities to the districts and boroughs took place. Elaborate joint arrangements between the district-level authorities were required in relation to some of the transferred functions and new joint authorities in respect of police, fire and civil defence and passenger transport were required for the metropolitan areas.[169] This seemed to

---

[167] Department of the Environment, *Streamlining the Cities. Proposal for reorganising local government in London and the Metropolitan Counties*, Cmnd. 9063 (1983), para. 1.19.

[168] See, e.g., G.W. Jones, *Are the cities really being streamlined?* (Manchester Statistical Society, 1985), 3: 'The scheme was not brought forward after a review of how large urban areas should be governed, but more as compensation to ratepayers for the Government's failure to redeem an earlier pledge to abolish domestic rates. The dismantling of a tier of local government, and of one controlled by what the Government portrayed as profligate overspenders, could be presented as relief for hardpressed ratepayers.'

[169] Since the Home Secretary is the police authority for the metropolitan police district and LRT had in 1984 assumed responsibility for London's passenger transport functions, the London Fire and Civil Defence Authority was the only joint authority established for Greater London. The Inner London Education Authority was retained under Part III of the 1985 Act but, with effect from 1 April 1990, was abolished in the Education Reform Act 1988 (ss. 162–96) and its functions transferred to the London boroughs.

indicate that, although the Government was abolishing directly-elected metropolitan authorities, it still believed in the principle of metropolitan government. By replacing directly elected authorities with joint authorities consisting of district authority appointees, however, public accountability and effective political control was likely to be weakened and thus the power of the principle of representation eroded.

Major doubts remain about the effectiveness of the new arrangements.[170] From the outset, the Government's entire approach was essentially negative: 'The commitment to abolition seems to have come first, then its rationale, and only subsequently and belatedly the proposed alternative structure.'[171] Furthermore, in focusing on the symptoms rather than the critical issues it was felt that there was a danger that the reforms would be unstable.[172] While the transfer of responsibilities has in general been accomplished without as much disruption as had been feared, what has certainly become clear is that some of the arrangements are of bewildering complexity and this has inevitably led to a weakening and confusion of public accountability.[173] If the arrangements do prove unstable, however, the future is likely to be highly uncertain. Since the advocates of metropolitan government 'face formidable problems in defining an appropriate area, in allocating the right mix of powers, in achieving a modest redistribution, and in securing party political acceptance'[174] it is extremely difficult to envisage the circumstances in which what has been abolished could effectively be restored.

The local government review

The leading researchers into the consequences of abolition of the metropolitan county councils have argued that the 1985 Act reforms constituted a major structural change and created a general destabilizing momentum throughout the entire system of local government. On this analysis, abolition in the metropolitan areas provided a considerable boost to the campaigns of the large shire districts for a restoration of the county borough status which had been lost as a result of the 1972 Act reforms. Consequently, it was argued that 'few now expect the existing (1990) system to survive until the end of the century'.[175] The opportunity presented itself when the Government sought to pick up the pieces of local government finance after the abandonment of the poll tax. At this stage,

[170] See S. Leach, H. Davis, C. Game and C. Skelcher, *After Abolition. The Operation of the Post-1986 Metropolitan Government System in England* (Birmingham, 1991).

[171] B. Leach, 'The Government of the English Provincial Conurbations' (1985) vol. 11 no. 1 *Local Government Studies* 17, 29.

[172] G.W. Jones, *Are the cities really being streamlined?* (above, n. 168), 20.

[173] S. Leach and C. Game, 'English metropolitan government since abolition: an evaluation of the English metropolitan county councils' (1991) 69 *Public Admin.* 141; S. Leach et al, *After Abolition* (above, n. 170), 169: 'We are thus left with the conclusion that on any criteria of accountability, based on any conception of democracy, there has, since abolition, been a marked reduction in accountability.'

[174] K. Young, 'Metropolis, R.I.P.' (1986) 57 *Political Quarterly* 36, 45.

[175] S. Leach et al, *After Abolition* (above, n. 170), 1.

the Government undertook a wide-ranging departmental review of local government which went beyond the question of finance to consider the issues of internal management and structure.

On the issue of structure, this local government review suggested that 'there should be a move towards unitary authorities where these do not already exist'.[176] In relation to Wales the Government decided, after consultation, to replace the existing eight county councils and 37 district councils by 22 unitary authorities.[177] This proposal was enacted in the Local Government (Wales) Act 1994 and was designed to take effect from 1 April 1996. With respect to the non-metropolitan areas of England, a Local Government Commission was established in 1992 to conduct a review of areas and to recommend to the Secretary of State any structural, boundary or electoral changes as appear to it to be 'desirable having regard to the need – (a) to reflect the identities and interests of local communities; and (b) to secure effective and convenient local government'.[178] By the end of 1994, the Commission had completed its work. It recommended that no changes be made to the existing two-tier structure in 18 of the 39 county areas reviewed and that, in the other 21 counties, 50 new unitary authorities be created.[179]

The English process of using an independent commission to undertake structural review undoubtedly has particular strengths. It is a useful vehicle for seeking to depoliticize the exercise and for ensuring that the views of the localities are fully considered in the process. Nevertheless, the process was not without its difficulties and in fact the Commission's work has been subjected to a great deal of criticism, ranging from various methodological errors in the way it has acted[180] to the argument that the entire process is flawed on the ground that structure cannot adequately be reviewed without also addressing the general question of the role of local government in society.[181] Perhaps the main difficulty, however, has concerned the relationship between the Commission and the Government.

It was originally envisaged that the review work would be undertaken in five

---

[176] Department of the Environment, *Local Government Review. The Structure of Local Government in England: A Consultation Paper* (1991), 1.

[177] HC Debs. vol. 205 cols. 171–83 (3 March 1992).

[178] Local Government Act 1992, s. 13(5).

[179] For an overview of the Commission's work see: Local Government Commission for England, *Renewing Local Government in the English Shires* (London, 1995).

[180] See, e.g., S. Leach, *The Local Government Review. A Crisis of Credibility* (European Policy Forum, November 1993).

[181] See J. Stewart, 'The Flawed Process' in S. Leach (ed.), *The Local Government Review: Key Issues and Choices* (Birmingham, 1994), ch. 2. In *Renewing Local Government in the English Shires* (above, n. 179), the Commission itself apeared to have conceded this point: 'The Commission has been acutely conscious of the fact that its remit extended only to structure, and that it had no standing with respect to the powers of local authorities, their finance and their internal management. If in the future there is to be a thorough-going review of the structure of local government in England, it will be essential for the other aspects to be included. Unless they are, the process will be another exercise in structural determinism, in the mistaken belief that changes in structure alone will automatically ensure that the desired ends are achieved.' (para. 229).

tranches over a period of five years. The difficulty with adopting a rolling pro-gramme, however, was that Government decisions on initial phases would be likely to influence Commission thinking on subsequent stages, with the result that the philosophy of the exercise would be likely to shift during the process, causing different tranches of authorities to be treated differently. This problem was exacerbated after a change in Ministers led to an apparent loss of political will and uncertainty about the object of the exercise. In November 1993 it was decided that the process should be speedily concluded and that all review work be completed by the end of 1994. The Government then issued new policy guidance to the Commission. This guidance, which strengthened the presump-tion in favour of unitary authorities, placed great uncertainty over the status of the first tranche of reviews which were virtually complete and this led to two authorities successfully challenging the legality of the new guidance by way of judicial review.[182] In this case, the court held that the new guidance was tanta-mount to a direction and was outwith the Secretary of State's powers since, in effect, it sought 'to undermine the statutory criteria and add a further crite-rion'.[183] Though this legal challenge compounded the uncertainties, the Commis-sion was nevertheless able to complete its work by the end of 1994. But it was anything but a happy episode with the Chairman of the Commission effectively being sacked by the Government just before the Commission's final report was produced and the Government immediately establishing a new Commission to engage in a further review of the status of a group of former county boroughs which had not been recommended for unitary status.[184]

In 1994, Steve Leach delivered a rather harsh assessment on the local govern-ment review. He suggested that: 'What had become in 1992 and 1993 an exam-ple of *policy drift* – the survival of a policy initiative beyond the time when there is any real political commitment to it – is increasingly becoming a *policy fiasco*, with the potential for inflicting considerable harm both on local government as an institution and on the Government itself.'[185] Though harsh, it is difficult to refute. There can be no ideal solution to the question of local goverment struc-ture since tensions will always exist between centralism and localism, between unity and diversity, and between functional requirements and community iden-tities. It is, however, precisely because of the existence of these perennial tensions

---

[182] *R v. Secretary of State for the Environment, ex p. Lancashire CC* [1994] 4 All ER 165.
[183] Ibid., 177.
[184] HC Debs., vol. 255, col. 1183 et seq (2 March 1995); 'Review of the review', *Local Govern-ment Chronicle*, 10 March 1995.
[185] S. Leach (ed.), *The Local Government Review* (above, n. 180), 1. Cf. the comments of the Chairman of the Commission, Sir J. Banham, 'Whitehall farce or disaster diverted?', *Local Govern-ment Chronicle*, 5 May 1995: 'The structural review was seen as part of a wider reform process covering management and finance, if not the longer-term function of local government. This proved to be still-born with Michael Heseltine's departure from Marsham Street. . . . The Local Government Commission was established for political reasons, to deal with political problems. Longer-term considerations have simply not been on anyone's agendas over the past two-and-a-half years. . . . Ministers' unitary aspirations were not so much unfulfilled as unclear or even inconsistent.'

that the process through which reform of local government structures is considered is of such vital importance. By this benchmark, the recent reforms and review concerning the structure of local government have hardly served to strengthen the institution of local government.

The Status of Local Government

Throughout the twentieth century, the institution of local government has been a vital component of the British system of government. Although the functions of local government have been adjusted in the light of changing circumstances, the idea of the elected local council vested with discretion and resources and charged with responsibility for providing those public services which required a local mode of delivery has been generally accepted. However, the status of the institution not only reflects the fact that the local council is best placed to provide such services effectively. It also marks the recognition that, in our political tradition, the idea of democracy implies a sense of shared fallibility on the question of the public good. Local government promotes variety; it is only through the existence of local institutions equipped with a capacity for political choice that innovation occurs and learning is enhanced. Consequently, although central government has formally been granted very broad powers of supervision, respect for this tradition requires the centre not only to sanction diversity but also to tolerate apparent inefficiency. And the reason for this is that efficiency and effectiveness in the provision of public services is not simply a technical question but is one which is bound up with the idea of politics. It affects our sense of democracy.

In the modern world, public services cannot simply be defined as being matters of either central or local responsibility. An expectation has arisen that the State will ensure that the basic needs of all citizens will be met and, with the assumption by the State of responsibility for the management of the economy, central government must be in a position to control key economic variables. As a result, there is likely to be some shared responsibility between central and local government for virtually all services which local authorities provide. Consequently, the modern institution of local government should not be viewed as an essentially autonomous tier of government; it has become locked into a complex, interdependent network of government. This characteristic feature of the modern world does not necessarily indicate a decline in the importance of local government. But it does require those holding positions of power within the network to maintain a degree of tolerance and to harbour respect for difference.

Throughout the post-war period, cushioned by economic growth and a political consensus over the welfare state, the system operated adequately and with a basic level of respect for difference. Over the last twenty years, however, the stress points have become exposed and, as the Conservative administrations since 1979 has acted to recast the relationship between State and society, those conditions which have sustained the institution of local government within the interdependent network of modern government have subsided. Many of the specific reforms which have been introduced may, considered separately, be justified as part of a need for re-thinking government in a radically changing world. When viewed cumulatively, however, the reforms constitute a sustained attack on the modern institution of local government.

The recent reforms have altered the basic character of local government. The tradition of the self-sufficient, corporate authority which was vested with broad discretion to raise revenue and provide services has been directly challenged. Discretionary powers have been confined, structured and checked and the regime of local government finance is now such that it is virtually impossible for local authorities to diverge significantly from specific, centrally-determined spending assessments. Local government has, in effect, been transformed from being the basic institution with responsibility for providing those public services which require local delivery systems into a rather discredited agency which, though in fact retaining responsibility for many important services, no longer holds a necessarily pre-eminent status. Local councils have been stripped of governmental responsibility for certain services which continue to be public services but which are now provided by agencies which are funded directly from the centre. New governmental initiatives which are based on localities have invariably been promoted through special agencies which are subject to central control. And, in relation to those functions retained by local government, the centre has generally required councils to adopt a set of internal markets based on a purchaser–provider distinction, the establishment of local council provider units on a commercial basis and the use of competitive tendering for determining delivery of local services.

Some might argue that, far from marking the death of local government, the last twenty years is best understood as a period of transition which will give rise to rejuvenation. That is, the contemporary period should be viewed as a watershed marking the passage from an old-style bureaucratic model to a new, streamlined, responsive model of local government. On this analysis, the new model of the enabling authority provides a more effective system: one which replaces a system dominated by producer interests for one in which the consumer interest takes precedence; one which builds competition into the structure of local government and thus maintains incentives to enhance the efficiency of public services; one which, in differentiating service specification from service provision, requires the council to focus directly on its critical governmental responsibilities; and one which, consequently, maintains the flexibility to be well-placed to respond effectively to new challenges.

There are, however, a number of difficulties with this thesis of transition to the enabling model of local government. The problems are illuminated by focusing on two closely related issues: the idea of public services, and the ratchet effect of central control. The idea of public services has, as has already been indicated, a vital political dimension. Once public services are subjected to strict market disciplines, however, they are likely to lose their peculiarly political and hence public character; and if those basic attributes are relinquished, such services also lose their local character. Once local services are required to be provided in accordance with market criteria of economy and efficiency they lose the sense of variety which lies at the heart of the justification of local government. Further, if local services are to be provided according to market criteria then the tradition of tolerance in the central–local government relationship will rapidly disappear. The Redcliffe-Maud view that local councils 'can decide for themselves ... what kind of services they want'[186] will quickly be replaced by the belief that central government 'has a duty to intervene to ensure that local government provides services for the people who live in the area in the most efficient and economical way'.[187]

It is essentially because of these two trends that the positive attributes of the enabling model of local government do not significantly feature in the contemporary framework of local government. Recent reforms in pursuit of efficiency have sought to expunge the basic characteristics of public – and thus local – services and have thereby been associated with the centralization of power. If there exists an economic benchmark against which all services can be tested, then not only is variety replaced with uniformity but also the centre is no longer able to tolerate difference and is obliged to intervene in order to secure economy and efficiency. Once this position is reached, it rapidly leads to the centre using special agencies, which can more easily be controlled, to carry out local tasks. And if evidence is needed that the centre has not discovered the solution to these issues of governance, we need look no further than the record of its attempts to reorganize local government structures or reform systems of local government finance.

The recent reforms have thus served to diminish the status of local government within our system of government. Further, the reforms pose a serious challenge to the traditional view that it 'is only by the combination of local representative institutions with the central institutions of Parliament, Ministers and Departments, that a genuine national democracy can be sustained'.[188] Consequently, we might say that the reforms not only undermine the status of local government but also affect the distribution of political authority and the character of our democracy, in that the idea of democracy as 'an acknowledgement of shared fallibility and shared vulnerability' seems in danger of being supplanted with the idea that it is essentially 'a boast of political capacity'.[189] And it is in this sense that these recent developments affect not only the status of local government but also the character of our basic constitutional arrangements.

[186] Redcliffe-Maud Report, Cmnd. 4040, iii.
[187] M. Howard (Minister for Local Government), Official Report HC Standing Committee A, col. 48 (21 October 1987); quoted in M. Radford (1988) 51 MLR 747, 767 (above, n. 38).
[188] Redcliffe Maud Report, Cmnd. 4040, iii.
[189] J. Dunn, *Interpreting Political Responsibility* (Cambridge, 1990), 214.

3

THE CHALLENGE OF MUNICIPAL SOCIALISM

For a period during the 1980s there emerged a distinctive form of municipal socialism as the Labour councils controlling the major cities throughout the country sought to revitalize the cause of socialism within a rather inhospitable national climate.[1] In certain respects, the objective of these councils, in seeking to protect jobs and public services from the expenditure cutbacks and privatization initiatives, was essentially defensive. Nevertheless, many of the policies developed during this era should also be assessed in the light of basic social and economic changes which were taking place within their localities and which required those involved in Labour politics to re-examine the relationship between local councils and their communities. What is clear is that, however the phenomenon is best characterized, the municipal socialist movement of the 1980s seemed bound on a direct course of collision with central government.

The efforts of the Conservative administrations since 1979 to restructure the system of local government undoubtedly have created a great deal of turbulence in relations between central and local government. By actively pursuing this goal, the Government was obliged to subvert many of the conventional practices concerning the conduct of central–local relations and, as a consequence, the entire system became highly politicized. Local government thus came to be seen 'by all political parties as "political space" that could be used to pursue ideological objectives'.[2] The conflicts between central government and the municipal socialist authorities should, however, be viewed not only as a particularly acute aspect of this general tension in central–local government relations but also as one with distinctive dimensions. It is the objective of this chapter to illuminate one of these distinctive facets; viz., the manner in which law came to be utilized by the leading protagonists as an instrument to assist them in the realization of particular political objectives. Consequently, although I propose to examine various practices which have come to be associated with municipal socialism, my concern is not with the question of whether those policies are able effectively to address the economic and social problems of particular localities. I focus on the challenge of municipal socialism primarily because of the light

---

[1] For general accounts see: M. Boddy and C. Fudge (eds.), *Local Socialism? Labour Councils and New Left Alternatives* (London, 1984); J. Gyford, *The Politics of Local Socialism* (London, 1985); S. Lansley, S. Goss and C. Wolmar, *Councils in Conflict. The Rise and Fall of the Municipal Left* (London, 1989); G. Green, 'The new municipal socialism' in M. Loney et al (eds.), *The State or the Market: Politics and Welfare in Contemporary Britain* (London, 2nd edn., 1991), ch. 16.

[2] D. Burns, R. Hambleton and P. Hoggett, *The Politics of Decentralisation. Revitialising Local Democracy* (London, 1994), 18.

which the phenomenon may cast both on the role of law within the local government system and on the relationship between local authorities and central government.

We might begin, then, by reflecting on the fact that conventional arrangements have been of great importance not only to the conduct of relations between central departments and local authorities but also within the working practices of local government. In general, the law has operated to establish a highly flexible constitutive structure for local government. In law, decisions are taken by the council as a whole and the officers are obliged to serve the entire council. There was very little in the way of prescriptive legal rules concerning the internal organization of local councils and the formal framework did not reflect the existence of party politics in the system. To the extent that party politics was accommodated within the corporate structure of local government it had generally been the result of conventional understandings between party groups on how business should be conducted. Though our knowledge of conventional practices was patchy,[3] there seemed little doubt but that the sharpening of political intensity within local government had placed some of these informal arrangements under severe strain. At the extreme, there was the possibility of party groups seeking to assume total control of the council and exploit the legal limits of their ability to use the power of the authority for sectarian political purposes. The emergence of municipal socialism may thus enable us to develop our understanding of the rather tangled relationship between conventions and law in the workings of local government.[4]

In addition to highlighting the relationship between law and convention in the conduct of local government business, the practices of municipal socialism also reveal much of interest about the nature of the conflict in central–local relations during the 1980s. Since many of the practices of municipal socialist authorities were directly antagonistic to the policies being promoted by central government, an examination of the disputes which arose may provide some insight not only into the sphere of autonomous action possessed by local government and of the centre's willingness to tolerate difference and diversity within the system but also of the Government's capacity to dictate compliance with central prescription.

[3] See, e.g., the comments of W.J.M. Mackenzie, 'The Conventions of Local Government' (1951) 29 *Public Admin.* 345. Mackenzie suggests that one of the reasons is that local government 'is a subject repugnant to poets, and it is the poets . . . who do most to make a community conscious . . . of what in this technical sense we call its conventions' (345).

[4] At this point, it must be emphasized that the focus on municipal socialism is justified by the tensions which are raised in the central–local relationship. The problems which have arisen as a result of heightened political intensity within local government are manifest across the political spectrum. The most serious case to have arisen of a party group using council powers for sectarian purposes, for example, concerns the auditor's allegations that Conservative-controlled Westminster City Council had, during the late 1980s, used local authority powers for the purposes of gerrymandering. See *Westminster City Council. Audit of Accounts 1987/88 and Subsequent Years. Designated Sales. Note of the Appointed Auditor's Provisional Findings and Views* (Touche Ross, January 1994).

Furthermore, since the courts came to be drawn into many of the disputes that arose, this episode in the history of central–local government relations may cast some light on the ability of the judiciary to police the ambiguous and shifting boundaries between central and local government.

Economic and Social Change

Since the mid 1970s it has gradually been recognized that the Keynesian economic policies which governments had been pursuing since the Second World War, and which had been associated with a period of continuous economic growth, no longer appeared to be working.[5] In order to address the resulting economic crisis of low growth, falling profit rates and rising unemployment, governments were obliged to examine a range of alternative strategies. The Conservative Government's response was essentially to embrace monetarist economic policies so as to bring about a restructuring of the economy. Since the effects of these policies have included the shaking out of less efficient producers, the introduction of new methods of working in order to increase productivity and, against the background of rapidly rising levels of unemployment, to lower general wage costs,[6] the pursuit of these economic policies has resulted in a number of major social problems. These social problems have caused the Government to undertake a radical review of public policy. The consequences have been a reduction in the size of the public sector, a major reorganization of the public sector through the introduction of market-based techniques, and a systematic attempt to instil an ethos of individual responsibility amongst citizens.

These economic and social policies have had a particular impact on the major cities, whose economies have been based on the older manufacturing industries. Government policies have accelerated the processes of structural change in the economies of these cities, and it seemed highly unlikely that with any renewed economic growth there would be a corresponding increase in employment opportunities.[7] Commercial projects in the central urban areas may create new jobs for service-sector professionals – and there is always likely to be a secondary labour market consisting of insecure, unskilled and low-paid jobs – but the industrial sector was unlikely to generate significant new employment prospects.

[5] In the literature of the left, this theme is generally discussed in relation to the idea of 'Fordism'. For a discussion of the utility of the concept in the debate over changes in the local government system see: G. Stoker, 'Regulation theory, local government and the transition from Fordism' in D. King and J. Pierre (eds.), *Challenge to Local Government* (London, 1990), ch. 11; A. Cochrane, *Whatever Happened to Local Government?* (Buckingham, 1993), ch. 5.

[6] See C. Leys, 'Thatcherism and British Manufacturing' (1985) 151 *New Left Review* 5.

[7] See A.J. Scott, 'Locational patterns and dynamics of industrial activity in the modern metropolis' (1982) 19 *Urban Studies* 111; I. Begg and B. Moore, 'The changing economic role of Britain's cities' in V.A. Hausner (ed.), *Critical Issues in Urban Economic Development*, vol. 1 (Oxford, 1987) 44; S. Fothergill and G. Gudgin, *Unequal Growth: Urban and Regional Employment in the UK* (London, 1982).

It seemed apparent that we were entering a new stage of economic development in which, as a result of technological change, growth could occur without any conspicuous increase in employment opportunities.[8] Since economic growth may now take place without a significant proportion of the population being at all involved, the processes of economic development could thus become the cause of social marginalization rather than social integration. And this trend posed a major challenge for government, especially in relation to the industrial cities.

The Conservative Government's response, based on the promotion of market processes and individual responsibility (sometimes referred to as the return to 'Victorian values'), was felt by many within the cities to be wanting. Given the economic circumstances and the central government response, it was not surprising that many Labour-controlled local authorities sought to develop an alternative economic strategy. It was from this general review that one of the distinctive elements of municipal socialism emerged.

Labour's economic and social policies have traditionally been based on Keynesian ideas. Through the application of Keynesian techniques, it was felt that governments could effectively manage the economy and create the conditions for economic growth. Governments would then be in a position to siphon off some of the proceeds of economic growth for redistributive purposes. These economic and social policies were directly linked: demand management created growth, growth permitted redistribution, redistribution increased consumption, consumption promoted investment, and investment generated further growth. The pursuit of such policies also contributed to a process of functional differentiation within the administrative state, in which the centre retained responsibility for economic policy and local government came to be seen primarily as an agency of collective consumption.[9] When Labour began to re-examine its economic strategy, after the failures of Keynesianism first became evident in the policies of the Labour government during the 1970s, it was understandable that some would seek to alter the traditional role of local government within this scheme.

This challenge materialized primarily as a challenge to the politics of distribution. Labour, it was contended, had largely ignored the process of production and had come to define socialism solely in terms of distribution. What was needed was an economic strategy which was based on a recognition of the need to transform the processes of production.[10] The monetarist strategy of restructuring production through the market, it was argued, was entirely inadequate. Not only had it seriously weakened the British economy and simply used the market

---

[8] See: M. Piore and C. Sabel, *The Second Industrial Divide: Possibilities of Prosperity* (New York, 1984); L. Thurow, *The Zero Sum Solution* (New York, 1985).

[9] See P. Saunders, 'Why study central–local relations?' (1982) vol. 8 no. 2 *Local Government Studies* 55; L.J. Sharpe, 'Functional Allocation in the Welfare State' (1984) vol. 10 no. 1 *Local Government Studies* 27. See further ch. 1, 73–4.

[10] R. Murray, 'New Directions in Municipal Socialism' in B. Pimlott (ed.), *Fabian Essays in Socialist Thought* (London, 1984), ch. 15.

as a device for undermining the workforce, but it was also unable to develop policies for generating new jobs.[11] Labour should seek industrial restructuring through a planned intervention in production processes which would challenge inequalities within such processes, would transform the internal organization of public service agencies and could develop new technologies which were geared to labour skills and social needs.[12] Since Labour was out of power after 1979, it is perhaps only to be expected that these ideas came to exert an influence on the policies of Labour-controlled local councils. But it might also be noted that this shift in economic policy – based on a new regime of 'flexible specialization' – required a more local response.[13] The economic policies of municipal socialism thus sought to challenge the traditional pattern of functional allocation in which matters of economic policy (or production) were retained by the centre and local government was treated as an agency of social policy (or social consumption).

The Changing Nature of Labour Politics

The development of an economic dimension to local politics also reflected more general changes in the nature of Labour politics. The Labour party has, somewhat surprisingly perhaps, traditionally expressed scepticism about what might be called 'the municipal road to socialism'. There is, after all, a distinctive geography of inequality in Britain, in the sense that, as we travel away from London so too, in general, do we descend the hierarchy of power and wealth. As the party of the underprivileged, Labour might thus be seen also as the party of the localities.

At one level, Labour's traditional scepticism of local solutions may simply reflect the degree of centralization of power in the British system of government. There are, however, other factors at play. First, the adoption of Keynesian economic policies pushed it towards centralism, based on the argument that central direction was essential to the objective of effective management of the economy. This economic argument was reinforced by the requirements of egalitarianism since a fairly high degree of centralization seems a corollary to the promotion of equalization of service provision. Further, there are a number of considerations which concern the party's particular history. These include: parliamentarism, which leads to a vision of the party as essentially an electoral machine; the adoption at a critical stage of its history of the idea of the public corporation as the preferred model of public ownership; and the widespread acceptance of the assumption of 'permanent revolution', a belief that each time the party wins a general election it will retain power in perpetuity.[14]

---

[11] Ibid., at 214–16.   [12] Ibid., at 218–19.

[13] See J.R. Logan and T. Swanstrom (eds.), *Beyond the City Limits* (Philadelphia, Penn., 1990).

[14] For a discussion of these issues see: L.J. Sharpe, 'The Labour Party and the Geography of Inequality: a Puzzle' in D. Kavanagh (ed.), *The Politics of the Labour Party* (London, 1982), ch. 6.

Currents of decentralism have certainly existed within Labour party thought. The early Fabians, for example, envisaged that industry would largely be controlled by local authorities[15] and, during the early decades of the twentieth century, the idea of guild socialism was highly influential.[16] The formative period of municipal socialism in practice was during the 1920s when the Labour party first won control of many local authorities. During this period, although various attempts were made to use local authorities to challenge the established social order,[17] the cause of municipal socialism has tended to become associated with the idea of Poplarism.[18] Poplarism here refers to the policies of the Labour-controlled Poplar Borough Council and the Board of Guardians of paying higher rates of unemployment relief, higher wages to its lower grade workforce and generally attempting to act as a model socialist council. It was a policy which involved direct confrontation with central government and led to legal conflict.[19] It was also a policy which was not without its successes.[20] Nevertheless, even at that time, opposition to this form of confrontation existed within the Labour movement[21] and when a Labour Government was returned to power in 1929, it declined to implement its policy of providing local government with a power of general competence.[22] In retrospect, this proved to be a decisive turning point in the party's flirtation with the municipal road to socialism. Thereafter, the Labour party expressed more interest in nationalization than in municipalization and,

[15] See, e.g., S. & B. Webb, *A Constitution for the Socialist Commonwealth of Great Britain* [1920] (Cambridge, 1975), 236: 'There seems practically no limit to be assigned to the number and range of the industries and services that might advantageously be undertaken by Local Authorities.'

[16] See, e.g., A.J. Penty, *The Restoration of the Guild System* (London, 1906); G.D.H. Cole, *Guild Socialism Restated* (London, 1920).

[17] See S. MacIntyre, *Little Moscows: Communism and Working Class Militancy in Inter-War Britain* (London, 1980).

[18] B. Keith-Lucas, 'Poplarism', 1962 *Public Law* 52; N. Branson, *Poplarism, 1919–1925: George Lansbury and the Councillors' Revolt* (London, 1979).

[19] First, as a means of publicizing their grievances about the rate-burden on poorer authorities, the borough council in 1921 refused to levy precepts on behalf of other authorities. After the councillors had failed to comply with a court order requiring them to do so, they were imprisoned for contempt: see, *R* v. *Poplar BC (No. 2)* [1922] 1 KB 72. Secondly, as a result of their wages policies, the councillors were surcharged by the district auditor. The auditor's decision was subsequently upheld by the House of Lords: see, *Roberts* v. *Hopwood* [1925] AC 578, 594. See further ch. 4, 210–12; P. Fennell, '*Roberts* v. *Hopwood*: the Rule against Socialism' (1986) 13 *J of Law & Soc.* 401. For similar cases see: *Roberts* v. *Cunningham* (1925) 42 TLR 162; *Woolwich Corporation* v. *Roberts* (1927) 96 LJKB 757.

[20] The basic campaign for a scheme of rate equalization between the richer and poorer metropolitan boroughs was, for example, introduced by the Local Authorities (Financial Provisions) Act 1921. This scheme was initially negotiated with the Poplar councillors while they were in gaol for contempt and they were released, even though they had made no offer to purge their contempt by paying the precepts, only after the Minister of Health had sent a personal message to the Lord Chancellor urging him to ask the judges concerned to release the prisoners: see Keith-Lucas, 'Poplarism', 1962 *Public Law* 52, 60–2.

[21] See G.W. Jones, 'Herbert Morrison and Poplarism', 1973 *Public Law* 11.

[22] See W.A. Robson, *The Development of Local Government* (London, 1931), 206–10; Sharpe, 'Labour and the geography of inequality' in Kavanagh, *The Politics of the Labour Party* (above, n. 14), at 153–4.

to the extent that the party promoted local government, it tended to stress the efficiency arguments for, rather than the democratic dimensions to, the decentralization of power.

The recent rekindling of interest in the themes of municipal socialism has undoubtedly been fuelled by the fact that since 1979 Britain has been governed by Conservative administrations intent on pursuing centrally-imposed, market-orientated policies. There are, however, also a number of factors within socialist politics which has caused Labour to re-examine its policies on local government. In fact, over the last twenty years or so, socialist politics have been in a state of disarray. While socialism may have retained considerable strength both as a critical theory of contemporary society and as an ideal of the good society, it has not seemed able to present a convincing account of precisely how the transition from contemporary society to that ideal may successfully be accomplished. The parliamentary road to socialism, through the progressive extension of the public realm, was by the end of the 1970s beginning to lose much of its credibility[23] and the experiences of the revolutionary road scarcely provided an attractive alternative.[24] The re-emergence of municipal socialism may thus be viewed as part of a general process of seeking to reconstruct a socialist politics.

At the heart of this idea of municipal socialism lies a critique of centralism. This critique is based on the argument that, in establishing a centralist party structure in response to the existence of a centralized political system, the Labour party had adopted a rather uncritical view of the State as an agency of reform.[25] Certainly the fruits of post-war Labour economic and social policies seem to bear out some of these criticisms. Thus, centralist interventionism has not had a great deal of success either in terms of management of the economy or of providing an efficient and consumer-responsive model of public ownership.[26] Neither have the egalitarian arguments for centralism been clearly demonstrated; notwithstanding several decades of nationalized provision, the great disparities in standards of health care, for example, seem to have persisted.[27] In addition to these criticisms of centralist action, some of the assumptions which have pervaded Labour party thinking have recently been questioned. The idea of parliamentarism has been challenged on the ground that it is rooted in a very limited conception of democracy, and one which belies the party's own history.[28] And the assumption of 'permanent revolution' has been thoroughly undermined

---

[23] See R. Miliband, *Parliamentary Socialism* (London, 2nd edn., 1972); id., *Capitalist Democracy in Britain* (Oxford, 1984), ch. 2; E. Hobsbawm, *The Forward March of Labour Halted?* (London, 1981).

[24] See J. Dunn, *Rethinking Modern Political Theory* (Cambridge, 1985), ch. 5.

[25] See, e.g., London-Edinburgh Weekend Return Group, *In and Against the State* (London, 1980); M. Loney, *Community against Government* (London, 1983).

[26] See, e.g., T. Prosser, *Nationalised Industries and Public Control* (Oxford, 1986).

[27] See, e.g., Department of Health and Social Security, Report of a Research Working Group, *Inequalities in Health* (London, 1980).

[28] R. Williams, *Democracy and Parliament* (London, 1983); A.H. Halsey, *Change in British Society* (Oxford, 1978), 84–5.

by the apparent decline in working class politics,[29] the formation in 1981 of the Social Democratic Party, and the successive victories of the Conservatives in general elections since 1979.

This critique of centralism highlights many of the main themes which have shaped the new municipal socialism. In particular, the emergence of municipal socialism in the 1980s may be viewed as an attempt to reassert the values of collectivism in the context of a critical re-appraisal of the nature of the State, a recognition that traditional class loyalties would appear to be disintegrating, and an assertion of the importance of locally-based governmental action. Though the general circumstances are rather different from those associated with Poplarism during the 1920s, the power of the State has remained highly centralized. The policies of the new municipal socialism thus seemed likely to lead to a new era of conflict between central departments and local authorities.

Municipal Socialism and Central–Local Relations

In order to discern the impact which this emerging municipal socialism has had on central–local relations, the various dimensions to the strains experienced during the 1980s must be outlined. There are, first, certain basic institutional strains which often come to the foreground in a period of fiscal retrenchment. These strains arise in large part because local authorities provide many services of more than local significance and are heavily dependent on central finance for their ability to do so. Consequently, when central departments attempt to restrain expenditure on locally-provided services and use financial instruments to achieve this goal it is almost inevitable that this will create tensions throughout the system. There is invariably a political element to this strain, particularly since Labour-controlled authorities are likely to be highly committed to public services and therefore more resistant to expenditure cuts. Nevertheless, since restraint will affect all authorities to some extent, these tensions are essentially of an institutional character and reflect the structure of the central–local relationship which has emerged in the twentieth century.[30]

More overt political conflicts provide additional dimensions of strain and thus may exacerbate this basic institutional tension. Of these, we may first note those which stem from the controversial nature of the Government's programme. Here, the manner in which the reforms have been introduced has been particularly contentious and, to the extent that the Government has cut across the accepted ways of doing things, this has provided a further source of strain. Thus, although the market-orientated policies of the Conservative Government were likely to be strongly resisted by Labour-controlled authorities committed to the values of

[29] B. Hindess, *The Decline of Working Class Politics* (London, 1971); id., *Parliamentary Democracy and Socialist Politics* (London, 1983); P. Whiteley, *The Labour Party in Crisis* (London, 1983).
[30] See ch. 1, esp. 69–72.

collectivism, the manner in which the Government's strategy has been implemented has also caused controversy throughout the system. Finally, we might identify those central–local conflicts which arise, not so much from basic institutional strains nor from the Conservative Government's particular political programme or manner of its implementation, but rather from a set of new policies which were initiated during the 1980s by Labour-controlled local authorities. It is these policies which have become closely associated with the new municipal socialism and it is this particular dimension to central–local relations on which this chapter focuses.

The local authorities which have been most closely associated with the policies of municipal socialism tend to be located in the major urban areas which grew rapidly as a consequence of industrialization in the nineteenth century and in which there has been a long tradition of Labour party control of local councils. These are precisely the areas in which the impact of economic and social change has been most acute. De-industrialization has had a devastating effect on many of these local economies, often leaving the local authority as the major employer and investor in the area. De-urbanization has also placed strains on the local authority role, particularly in preserving the physical infrastructure of the area and maintaining social services in the face of a disproportionate loss of households which are less dependent on such services.[31] Furthermore, class de-alignment has complicated the conduct of party politics. Social role has tended to become more significant than class status in shaping self-identity, with the result that the loyalty of a class to a political party can no longer be taken for granted,[32] and this has had significant implications for the idea of the political party as a representative agency.

These various economic, social and political changes provide the context for the re-emergence of municipal socialism. First, the combined effects of cyclical and structural economic decline in their areas have required the local authority to re-examine its relationship with the local economy. Secondly, as the relative social needs of their areas have grown, authorities have tried to protect public services in the face of radical changes introduced by central government. Thirdly, against a background of contemporary countervailing trends away from collectivism,[33] these authorities have sought to re-assert the virtues of public provision of services. And fourthly, the greater diversity of allegiances to the Labour

---

[31] See K. Young and L. Mills, 'The decline of urban economies' in R. Rose and E. Page (eds.), *Fiscal Stress in Cities* (Cambridge, 1982), ch. 4; G. Bramley, 'Grant-related expenditure and the inner city' (1984) vol. 10 no. 3 *Local Government Studies* 15; *Rate Support Grant*, A submission to the Secretary of State for the Environment by the cities of Liverpool, Manchester, Newcastle-upon-Tyne and Sheffield (July, 1982).

[32] See P. Dunleavy, 'The political implications of sectoral cleavages and the growth of state employment' (1980) XXVIII *Political Studies* (pts. 3 & 4), 364, 527.

[33] See D.A. Dawson, 'Economic Change and the Changing Role of Local Government' in M. Loughlin, D. Gelfand and K. Young (eds.), *Half A Century of Municipal Decline 1935–1985* (London, 1985), ch. 2; J. Dunn, *The Politics of Socialism* (Cambridge, 1984), 47–8.

party, in combination with the more conditional nature of that support, has tended to affect both the character of local policies and the relationship between the local council and groups of potential supporters. It is in response to these various trends that the basic character of municipal socialism may be identified: a renewed interest in the economic activities of local government and, against a background of re-thinking the public service ethos and the relationship between the council and local communities, a desire to protect and promote public service provision.

Municipal socialism thus sought to reassess the record of achievement in local government. While there have undoubtedly been many achievements when evaluated in terms of the enhanced standards of public services in areas such as council housing, environmental health, personal social services and educational provision, reservations were expressed in particular about the manner in which these services traditionally have been provided. Formal bureaucracies have grown as the services have evolved and these have often displayed the classic problems concerning the responsiveness of bureaucracies to change. Some of these problems have been essentially cognitive failures which are common to many centralized planning systems.[34] Some, however, are political failures which stem from an inability to recognize that the main purpose of these organizations 'is not the production of a service but the solution of problems'.[35] The Conservative Government's response to these governmental failures has been to rely on market mechanisms. The new municipal socialists, by contrast, sought to reinvigorate the ideal of public service provision by devising mechanisms to make local councils more responsive to the communities they serve.

This has proved rather difficult in relation to basic services such as housing, public transport and education which have been the subject of major statutory reforms designed to ensure that local services are run in accordance with commercial principles and within a market framework. In these areas, central government has been vigilant to ensure the achievement of their objectives and would tolerate no opposition. In relation to council house sales, for example, the Conservative Government from the outset not only acquired extremely broad powers of intervention[36] but also displayed such an unprecedented degree of attentiveness in supervising progress with sales that effective resistance proved impossible.[37] Similarly, the attempt to maintain a low-rents policy was frustrated by central government's use of the new housing subsidy system in particular, the reformed rate support grant system in general, and eventually by ring-fencing housing

---

[34] See, e.g., A. Nove, *The Economics of Feasible Socialism* (London, 1982). For a classic study in local government see, N. Dennis, *People and Planning. The Sociology of Housing in Sunderland* (London, 1970).

[35] D. Donnison, *Urban Policy: A New Approach*, Fabian Tract 487 (London, 1983), 1.

[36] Housing Act 1980, s. 23; now Housing Act 1985, s. 164.

[37] See *R* v. *Secretary of State for the Environment, ex parte Norwich City Council* [1982] QB 808; K. Ascher, 'The Politics of Administrative Opposition: Council House Sales and the Right to Buy' (1983) vol. 9 no. 2 *Local Government Studies* 12; R. Forrest and A. Murie, *An Unreasonable Act? Central–Local Government Conflict and the Housing Act 1980* (Bristol, 1985).

revenue accounts to ensure that they operate on a break-even principle.[38] And any innovative manoeuvres by local authorities seeking to play the system, by for example devising schemes to take maximum advantage of government subsidy while maintaining low rents, met with swift Government reaction in the form of changes to the regulations.[39] In relation to the major programme of restructuring basic services there seemed to be little which local authorities could in practice do to resist the Government's intentions.

The fact that local authorities could not effectively oppose much of the new legislation introduced by the Government did not, however, mean that these councils had no flexibility to pursue their own policies. Although the legal powers of local government derive from the centre, flexibility and discretion had been built into the basic structures of local councils. This meant that, however single-minded the Government might be in the pursuit of its objectives, it was highly unlikely that it would be able to reorganize local authorities as entirely rule-bound organizations. Ultimately, it was this basic capacity for autonomous action which was explored by the municipal socialist authorities. And it is the manner in which the authorities exploited this capacity, the nature of Government's response to these local initiatives and the conflict which this engendered which forms the basis of this chapter.

For our purposes, what is particularly important about municipal socialism is the manner in which the movement undertook a systematic examination of the organizational arrangements, the statutory powers and the general institutional power of local government with a view to determining how the local authority might be adapted to the pursuit of socialist objectives. In effect, the exercise involved an examination of the legal framework of local government stripped of the embellishments of conventional norms in order that the legal boundaries of local authority action might more clearly be identified. A consideration of these initiatives thus provides a distinctive dimension to the basic themes of legality and locality which are explored in this book.

The chapter examines these various initiatives under four basic heads: organizational arrangements within local government; the use of the discretionary potential within the general statutory powers of local authorities; the utilization of the economic power bound up in the institution of local government; and finally the engagement in a strategy of direct confrontation with central government and use of the threat of non-compliance with legal duties as a means of highlighting local grievances. Before addressing each of these in turn, however, some attempt must be made to identify more precisely the particular group of local authorities with which we are concerned.

---

[38] See, e.g., Housing Act 1985, Pt. XIII; Local Government and Housing Act 1989, ss. 74–8, 162. See M. Loughlin, *Local Government in the Modern State* (London, 1986), 104–10; J. Driscoll, 'Public Sector Housing after the Local Government and Housing Act 1989' (1991) 54 MLR 244.
[39] See *R* v. *Secretary of State for Health and Social Security, ex p. Sheffield City Council* (1986) 18 HLR 6.

Identifying Municipal Socialist Councils

In a study published in 1988, Bennett and Krebs noted that most but not all local authorities whose rates after 1979 exceeded the modal distribution of tax rates by more than 30 per cent were Labour-controlled.[40] Further, all authorities which exceeded the mode by more than 50 per cent were Labour controlled and of this group 'a large number are readily identifiable as controlled by "new left" Labour councils'.[41] Bennett and Krebs concluded that it was the identification of a sub-group of Labour councils as being of the 'new left' 'which seems to offer most chance of defining the rather distinct behaviour of many high tax rate areas'.[42]

Commentators have, nevertheless, often acknowledged the difficulties involved in seeking to define precisely the constituents of this sub-group. This is not only because, throughout the 1980s, the group tended to vary over relatively short periods of time, as elections were won or lost or as different factions within the controlling group succeeded in establishing their authority, but also because, in Gyford's words, municipal socialism 'is best understood not in terms of a single coherent ideology but as a syndrome or a set of associated characteristics'.[43] These characteristics include the development of local economic and employ-ment strategies, the design of schemes for administrative decentralization to neighbourhood offices which might heighten the local community's involvement in public service delivery, and a concern for issues which traditionally had been absent from, or marginal to, local government such as police monitoring and the promotion of race and sex equality initiatives. Such characteristics have been most closely identified with the Greater London Council (GLC) and a large propor-tion of Labour-controlled inner London borough councils.[44] But there are com-plications. Sheffield City Council, though certainly part of the general movement, was mainly concerned with municipal enterprise and economic development initiatives[45] and Liverpool City Council was closely associated with the Militant tendency and displayed little interest in race and sex equality initiatives.[46]

Using a combination of expenditure figures, the existence of particular types of council committees and twinning arrangements with Eastern Europe or a South African front line state, Bennett and Krebs identified 24 local councils which in the late 1980s appeared to belong to the sub-group:

---

[40] R.J. Bennett and G. Krebs, *Local Business Taxes in Britain and Germany* (Baden-Baden, 1988), 87–8.

[41] Ibid., 293.   [42] Ibid.

[43] Gyford, *The Politics of Local Socialism* (above, n. 1), 18.

[44] Lansley, Goss and Wolmar, *Councils in Conflict* (above, n. 1), 16–22.

[45] D. Blunkett and G. Green, *Building from the Bottom: the Sheffield Experience*, Fabian Tract 491 (London, 1983).

[46] D. Hatton, 'The Fight Against Monetarist Policies in Liverpool' (1985) vol. 11 no. 6 *Local Government Studies* 20; P. Thompson and M. Allen, 'Labour and the local state in Liverpool' (1986) *Capital and Class* 7; G. Ben-Tovim, J. Gabriel, I. Law and K. Stredder, *The Local Politics of Race* (London, 1986), 101–3.

London: Camden, Greenwich, Hackney, Islington, Lambeth, Lewisham, South-wark, Brent and Haringey.
Metropolitan districts: Birmingham, Manchester, Liverpool, St. Helens, Shef-field, Walsall, Wolverhampton, Leeds and North Tyneside.
Non-metropolitan districts: Basildon (Essex), Leicester, Nottingham, Harlow (Essex), Scunthorpe (Humberside), and Langbaurgh (Cleveland).[47]

Bennett and Krebs acknowledged that the classification was not fully satis-factory and conceded that probably no entirely satisfactory categorization was possible. The list is, nevertheless, helpful. Certainly it is within this group – particularly if we add the GLC and the metropolitan county councils which were abolished in 1986 – that we find those local authorities which during the 1980s have been most regularly embroiled in legal disputes over the conduct of cen-tral–local relations.

Organizational Arrangements

The traditional pattern

Being an essentially nineteenth century construction, the legal framework of local government did not formally recognize the existence of party politics in local affairs. Local councils are executive bodies in which statutory functions are vested in the entire council. The process of adapting this corporate frame-work to the realities of party politics has been undertaken largely through the evolution of informal understandings by local party groups concerning the manner in which the decision-taking powers will be exercised. Such understandings have been particularly important since there were few statutory rules governing the internal organization of local councils. The power to delegate decision-making power to committees and sub-committees was extremely broad,[48] the nature of the committee structure was largely a matter for the authority itself to determine,[49] and there existed extensive powers to co-opt non-councillors onto committees.[50] In general, local councils were free to regulate their own internal procedures.

This system worked fairly smoothly, largely because of the evolution of an officer tradition of managerial professionalism and because of the prevalence of administrative politics in local government. Managerial professionalism drew

[47] Bennett and Krebs, *Local Business Taxes* (above, n. 40), 294–5. Cf. Lansley, Goss and Wolmar, *Councils in Conflict* (above, n. 1), 21–2.
[48] Local Government Act 1972, s. 101. There is, however, no power to delegate to a single member: *R* v. *Secretary of State for the Environment, ex parte Hillingdon LBC* [1986] 1 WLR 967.
[49] There are, however, a limited number of arrangements for which a local authority is obliged to appoint a particular committee: Local Government Act 1972, s. 101(9).
[50] Local Government Act 1972, s. 102.

its strengths from a combination of bureaucratic authority and professional ideals and its character was determined primarily through the operation of three principles: *functionalism*, which is the organization of the local authority along departmental lines in accordance with its major functional responsibilities; *uniformity*, which requires that 'the services of the authority are provided to a common standard and on a common pattern throughout the area of the authority'; and *hierarchy* or the top-down direction of the authority.[51] Administrative politics is a form of politics which is generally compatible with the dominant tradition of managerial professionalism since it exists when decision-making rests largely with officers who set the agendas and provide the primary source of policy innovation.[52] The officers, of course, still needed to be able to carry councillors with them and it is this factor, together with the passivity of most councillors, which may explain the compatibility of this tradition with the emergence of powerful council leaders.[53] It might also be added that the dominance of professional groups also assisted in the smooth-functioning of the central–local relationship, since the professionalization of policy systems provided a powerful method of securing the local adoption of centrally determined standards and practices.[54]

The challenge

These traditional working arrangements were directly challenged by the emergence of ideological politics in local government during the 1980s.[55] Ideological politics has had a far-reaching impact on the tradition of managerial professionalism. We have already seen that one of the factors which helped to shape the policies of the new municipal socialism was a perceived failure of bureaucratic solutions to policy problems. Indeed, one of the critical factors leading to the emergence of municipal socialist politics in particular localities has been the

[51] J.D. Stewart, 'The functioning and management of local authorities' in Loughlin, Gelfand and Young (eds.), *Half A Century of Municipal Decline 1935–1985* (above, n. 33), 98 at 99–102; J.D. Stewart, *The New Management of Local Government* (London, 1986); I. Cunningham and U. Fahey, 'Administrators and professionals in local government' (1976) vol. 2 no. 4 *Local Government Studies* 19.
[52] M.J. Hill, *The Sociology of Public Administration* (London, 1972), 210–14.
[53] See H. Elcock, 'Tradition and change in Labour party politics: the decline and fall of the city boss' (1981) XXIX *Political Studies* 439.
[54] See, e.g., P. Dunleavy, *The Politics of Mass Housing in Britain 1945–1975* (Oxford, 1981); id., 'Quasi-governmental sector professionalism: some implications for policy-making in Britain' in A. Barker (ed.), *Quangos in Britain* (London, 1982), ch. 11; M. Laffin, *Professionalism and Policy: The Role of the Professions in the Central–Local Government Relationship* (Aldershot, 1986).
[55] For the challenge on the political right by the trend towards what might be called 'municipal monetarism' see: Adam Smith Institute, *The Omega File: Local Government, Planning and Housing* (London, 1983); S. Platt, 'Skeleton Service', *New Statesman and Society*, 17 June 1988; N. Ridley, *The Local Right: Enabling Not Providing* (London, 1988).

existence of influential groups of Labour councillors who were younger than average, were weaned on a form of community politics which had emerged during the 1970s to challenge the policies of the 'local state'[56] and, often being public sector professionals themselves, seemed to be less likely to defer to the mystique of professional answers.[57]

This form of socialist politics undermined various aspects of the traditional arrangements. It appeared, first, to reject the existence of any clear distinction between politics and administration. Both the structure of the administration and the qualifications for particular posts in the administration, for example, were recognized as having significant political dimensions. Many of these authorities readily acknowledged the importance of political skills in the administration[58] and appointed people with readily identifiable political commitments to senior posts in the administration.[59] More contentious, perhaps, was the practice of what became known as 'twin-tracking'; that is, a councillor in one authority holding a senior administrative position in a neighbouring authority.[60] This blurring of the relationship between members and officers ultimately challenged the idea of the political neutrality of the tradition of managerial professionalism.

Though ideological politics 'puts great strains upon administrators',[61] the stress was exacerbated by the tendency of this new left politics also to be associated with the emergence of a bargaining style of politics. If the changing character of socialist politics had in part been occasioned by changes in class structures, with social role becoming more important than class to self-identity, then one might expect a greater diversity and fragmentation of interests and values. This in turn seemed likely to affect the character of politics, with the representative role of the political party being modified as the party accommodated the interests of various groups whose allegiance was conditional rather than ancestral. This style of politics is far removed from the tradition of the 'city boss'. It is a style which complicates the political process, since packages of policies must

---

[56] See C. Cockburn, *The Local State* (London, 1977); J. Benington, *Local Government Becomes Big Business* (London, 1976).

[57] See J. Gyford, 'Our Changing Local Councillors', *New Society*, 3 May 1984, 181; id., *The Politics of Local Socialism* (above, n. 1), 33–8; J. Gyford, S. Leach and C. Game, *The Changing Politics of Local Government* (London, 1989) chs. 2, 4, 5; Lansley, Goss and Wolmar, *Councils in Conflict* (above, n. 1), 9–22; Green, 'The new municipal socialism' (above, n. 1), 275–8.

[58] See, e.g., D. Blunkett (Leader of Sheffield City Council), 'Towards a Socialist Social Policy' (1981) vol. 8 no. 1 *Local Government Policy Making* 95, 102: 'the people who work for local authorities have got to be committed to a new type of politics'.

[59] 'The top echelons of the bureaucracy have got to be politically aware. It does mean that their jobs are insecure. That is the price people at the top have to pay.' P. Kodikara (Asst. Director of Social Services, Tower Hamlets LBC and Chair of the Social Services Committee, Hackney LBC, after his appointment as Director of Social Services, Camden LBC), *New Society*, 1 November 1984; quoted in Gyford, *The Politics of Local Socialism* (above, n. 1), 43.

[60] See Kodikara (above, n. 59). See further, D. Walker, 'Local interest and representation: the case of "class" interest among Labour representatives in Inner London' (1983) 1 *Government and Policy* 341.

[61] Hill, *The Sociology of Public Administration* (above, n. 52), 216.

be assembled through intra-party coalitions which exhibit signs of instability and this, in turn, further complicates the tasks of management in local government.[62]

How flexible was this legal framework of local government? Once the conventional understandings were removed and there was only the bare legal framework to impose limits, what was the extent of the power of the majority group to harness the organizational arrangements of the council to the realization of its political goals? In law, or so it appeared, the majority party could exercise an almost untrammelled executive power since the corporate nature of the council meant that there were few formal mechanisms of accountability to other elected members. Those in control could apparently dictate the committee structure of the authority, allocate committee places only to their supporters, co-opt on to local council committees people who were sympathetic to their objectives, appoint politically sympathetic officers to ensure that their policies were not frustrated in the process of implementation and generally assume command of the decision-making and management structures of the authority. During the 1980s, the courts for the first time were obliged, in a variety of contexts and with varying degrees of success, to reconcile the political character of local government decision-making with the general legal principles relating to administrative decision-making.[63]

The committee system

Given the scope and intensity of public business, the committee system has become 'the pivot of the system of local government'.[64] How far has it been transformed by the experiment with municipal socialism? It should be noted at the outset that little evidence has emerged of the extensive use of one-party committees. In 1985, one-party committees existed in around 20 per cent (and

[62] Also of great importance was the role of the District Labour Party in decision-making. See, e.g., Green, 'The new municipal socialism' (above, n. 1) at 276: 'The [Labour] party had created district parties in 1974 to separate local government issues from the industrial militancy and communist influence of Trades and Labour Councils. Within five years a new radical coalition . . . argued that these local parties should assert their constitutional right to make council policy and to select a panel of council candidates.' On the critical role of the district party in Liverpool politics see: M. Parkinson, *Liverpool On The Brink* (Hermitage, Berks, 1985), 26–7.

[63] See, e.g., *R* v. *Hammmersmith and Fulham LBC, ex p. Beddowes* [1987] QB 1050 (unsuccessful application to review sale of housing land which took place immediately before council elections altering political complexion of council); *R* v. *Waltham Forest LBC, ex p. Baxter* [1988] QB 419 (councillors entitled to take account of party loyalty and party policy as relevant considerations provided they did not operate to exclude all other relevant considerations); *R* v. *Bradford City Council, ex p. Corris* [1990] 2 QB 363 (no legal obligation upon a Lord Mayor, acting as chairman of the council, to exercise his casting vote in a non-partisan manner). And on the legal status of the political mandate in local government see below, note 94.

[64] H.J. Laski, 'The Committee System in Local Government' in Laski, Jennings and Robson (eds.), *A Century of Municipal Progress* (London, 1935), 82. For a more recent appraisal see J. Stewart, 'The Role of Councillors in the Management of the Authority' (1990) vol. 16 no. 4 *Local Government Studies* 25, at 29–30.

one-party sub-committees in about 30 per cent) of local authorities.[65] Most of these authorities, however, generally had only one such committee, the policy and resources committee. Since this has been standard practice in some authorities since the early 1960s,[66] and, given that it is a deliberative rather than executive committee, the generality of practice did not seem to cause major concern. It may have been the case that one-party sub-committees were becoming more common during the 1980s; perhaps most graphically illustrated by the exclusion of magistrates from some of the sub-committees of the Greater Manchester Police Authority.[67] But the power to restrict access of councillors and members of the public to such meetings became severely circumscribed by the provisions of the Local Government (Access to Information) Act 1985 and by recent cases which have determined that councillors have the common law right to inspect those documents and attend such meetings as are necessary to enable them properly to perform their duties.[68] Since such committees 'typically provided ... an arena for the majority party to discuss key items of business without the opposition, press or public being present'[69] their utility has been fairly limited since the 1985 Act.

Of perhaps greater importance to the cause of municipal socialism, however, was the exercise of their general powers to form new committees or sub-committees which would provide the organizational infrastructure to address a range of new issues. Such new issues have included policies on race, women, the police (especially in London where the Home Secretary acts as police authority for the Metropolitan Police[70]) and lesbian and gay initiatives. It is through an examination of the exercise of powers in these fields that we might obtain a better insight into the way in which municipal socialists were able to use local authority organizational arrangements to promote particular political objectives.

Race initiatives provide a good illustration of these developments. By virtue of section 71 of the Race Relations Act 1976, local authorities are under a duty to 'make appropriate arrangements with a view to securing that their various functions are carried out with due regard to the need (a) to eliminate unlawful racial discrimination; and (b) to promote equality of opportunity and good relations

[65] *Report of the Committee of Inquiry into the Conduct of Local Authority Business*, Cmnd. 9797 (London, 1986), 78–9 (hereafter the Widdicombe Report).

[66] H.V. Wiseman, 'The working of local government in Leeds' (1963) 41 *Public Administration* 51, 137. See also *Report of the Committee on the Management of Local Government* (Chmn: J. Maud) (London, 1967), paras. 24–33.

[67] *The Guardian*, 16 September 1986.

[68] *R* v. *Birmingham City Council, ex parte O* [1983] 1 AC 578 (access to files); *R* v. *Hackney LBC, ex parte Gamper* [1985] 1 WLR 1229 (attendance at meetings); *R* v. *Sheffield City Council, ex parte Chadwick* (1985) 84 LGR 563 (attendance at special sub-committee); *R* v. *Eden Valley DC, ex parte Moffatt, The Times*, 24 Nov. 1988 (holding that the general principles were equally applicable to informal working parties).

[69] Gyford, Leach and Game, *The Changing Politics of Local Government* (above, n. 57), 201.

[70] Metropolitan Police Act 1829, s. 1. On the GLC's role in this debate see: GLC, *A New Police Authority for London: A Consultation Paper on Democratic Control of the Police in London* (London, 1983).

between people of different racial groups'. During the 1970s few organizational reforms were introduced in furtherance of these special but rather vague duties; consultation with Community Relations Councils seemed to be the main form of consultation with ethnic minorities over local issues.[71] But during the 1980s things changed, to the extent that by 1985 there were in London alone fourteen authorities which had established race relations committees.[72]

There were a variety of factors which helped to bring about these changes. First, the Labour party seemed increasingly to be aware of the fact that, with the ethnic minorities constituting around one-third of the total population in some urban local authority areas, the black vote was important and their interests needed to be adequately represented. Additionally, a greater number of black councillors were being elected to local councils; for example, by 1987, three London boroughs had black leaders.[73] Perhaps the most important factor, however, was that of the urban riots of 1981 which had the effect of transforming race into a major political issue[74] and caused many local authorities to engage in a systematic re-examination of the impact of their practices on racial minorities.[75] These developments caused many local authorities (of which those of the 'new left' were heavily represented) to harness their corporate management techniques of policy review for the purpose of assessing the effects of the organization on different ethnic groups[76] and then to develop positive action programmes to promote racial equality.[77] The establishment of race relations committees supported by a race relations unit within the authority became the standard organizational reform for promoting many of these initiatives.

Similar organizational arrangements have been developed in relation to women's issues. By 1986, fifteen authorities had established women's committees, another eight had formed sub-committees and a further eleven had undertaken a formal initiative to develop positive action policies.[78] These institutional arrangements were designed to strengthen more general statements of equal opportunities

[71] Note that evidence of local consultation was a pre-condition to obtaining Urban Programme funding from the government under s. 11 of the Local Government Act 1966.

[72] J. Gyford, 'Diversity, Sectionalism and Local Democracy' in Widdicombe Report, Research vol. 4, *Aspects of Local Democracy*, 106 at 123.

[73] Lambeth (Linda Bellos), Haringey (Bernie Grant) and Brent (Merle Amory): see Lansley, Goss and Wolmar (above, n. 1), *Councils in Conflict*, 126.

[74] Lord Scarman, *The Brixton Disorders*, Cmnd. 8427 (London, 1981). See also, Fifth Report of the Committee on Home Affairs, Session 1980–81, *Racial Disadvantage*, HC 424.

[75] See, e.g., Department of the Environment, *Local Authorities and Racial Disadvantage: Report of a Joint Government/Local Authority Associations Working Group* (London, 1983).

[76] K. Young and N. Connolly, 'After the Act: Local Authority Policy Reviews under the Race Relations Act 1976' (1984) vol. 10 no. 1 *Local Government Studies* 13.

[77] For an overview see H. Ouseley, 'Local Authority Race Initiatives' in Boddy and Fudge, *Local Socialism?* (above, n. 1), 133.

[78] S. Halford, 'Women's Initiatives in Local Government' (1988) 16 *Policy and Politics* 251, at 252. Halford suggests (258) that Labour control of the authority is a necessary but not sufficient condition for such initiatives, and the decisive factor is the type of local Labour party. See also S. Goss, 'Women's Initiatives in Local Government' in Boddy and Fudge (eds.), *Local Socialism?* (above, n. 1), 109.

policies which many local authorities had adopted.[79] While no authority had the resources to compare with the GLC's women's committee,[80] the existence of such arrangements may be taken to indicate an intention to change the way councils work.[81] On a more limited scale, but perhaps with more controversial impact, was the commitment in a small number of authorities during the 1980s to develop gay and lesbian initiatives.[82]

These policy developments seemed to reflect the belief that 'a new politics could only be constructed by abandoning a simple reliance on the traditional working class, and constructing instead a "rainbow alliance" of oppressed groups, which would include women, blacks, young single people – and lesbians and gays – groups which, added together, would form a majority for socialism'.[83] The related organizational initiatives have challenged traditional practices on several fronts. First, the authority's power of co-option onto committees was extensively used so as to ensure adequate representation of the interests of these groups in the processes of policy formulation. This practice thus enabled the authority to tap community experience and to counter under-representation of these groups on the council. At the same time, it also posed a challenge to traditional notions of representative democracy. Secondly, these developments affected the tradition of managerial professionalism. The principle of functionalism, or departmental organization, was generally rejected since in practice small, centrally-based support units were established to promote a corporate approach. Furthermore, to the extent that these initiatives required positive action designed to promote social equality, the principle of uniformity of service provision was called into question. Finally, traditional ideas of career hierarchy were challenged by the tendency to employ officers at a senior level who were often not drawn from the general career structure of local government and who did not adopt traditional notions of officer neutrality.

In general, the implementation of these new initiatives posed major challenges to the traditional organizational structures of the local council. But these equality initiatives were essentially centrally-inspired and sought from the centre to implement a corporate strategy. Perhaps even more radical in the challenge to traditional structures have been the reforms which have been initiated to make

[79] See A. Coyle, 'The limits of change: local government and equal opportunities for women' (1989) 67 *Public Administration* 39.

[80] At the time of abolition the women's committee had an annual budget of £10m and the women's unit a staff of over 70: Lansley, Goss and Wolmar, *Councils in Conflict* (above, n. 1), 144–5.

[81] See S. Halford, 'Feminist change in a patriachal organisation. The experience of women's initiatives in local government and implications for feminist perspectives on state institutions' in M. Savage and A. Witz (eds.), *Gender and Bureaucracy* (Oxford, 1992), 155.

[82] See D. Cooper, *Sexing the City. Lesbian and Gay Politics Within the Activist State* (London, 1994) which examines experiences in Camden, Islington, Manchester and Nottingham (ch. 3) and Haringey (ch. 6).

[83] Lansley, Goss and Wolmar, *Councils in Conflict* (above, n. 1), 160–1.

the organization more responsive to the needs of communities by devising various schemes for the decentralization of service provision.

Decentralization

During the 1980s a variety of schemes for the decentralization of local authority services were devised, often, but certainly not always, by those authorities associated with the new municipal socialism. These schemes tended to build on the experiences of a number of area-based experiments which had been introduced since the late 1960s,[84] but in the 1980s they have generally emerged under a more radical banner. Decentralization has been championed as the solution to basic criticisms concerning the inflexibility, insensitivity and oppressiveness of local bureaucracies. Decentralization, it was argued, could promote participation, consumer-responsiveness and accountability and also would enable Labour to win back popular support for the public services.[85]

This drive to decentralization could potentially transform the traditional structures of local government. If understood as the devolution of local authority services to neighbourhood offices, it seemed directly to cut across the hierarchical principle reflected in the existence of functionally-organized departments. Further, once resources were devolved for allocation by area-based sub-committees, the principle of uniformity – of providing a common standard of service throughout the authority – was called into question. In addition to these administrative issues, major political challenges were posed, particularly since any real devolution of decision-making authority to neighbourhood units had the potential to erode the power of the majority party group. Though the issue of decentralization presented major managerial and political challenges, it seems clear that the local council possessed the legal powers necessary to establish radical schemes for the devolution of decision-making power. Local authorities possess very broad powers of delegation[86] and are empowered to extend extensive decision-making authority to area committees. If area committees were constituted as committees of the council, for example, they could co-opt up to one-third of their membership and, as sub-committees, there was no limit to the power of co-option.[87] Consequently, authorities were legally empowered, through co-option arrangements, directly to involve neighbourhood representatives in the decision-taking process.

It was perhaps because of the political and managerial difficulties that many authorities made symbolic commitments to such schemes but often did not achieve

[84] See R. Hambleton, *Policy Planning and Local Government* (London, 1978).

[85] See C. Fudge, 'Decentralisation: Socialism Goes Local?' in Boddy and Fudge (eds.), *Local Socialism?* (above, n. 1), 192 at 209–12; A. Wright (ed.), *Socialism and Decentralisation*, Fabian Tract 496 (London, 1984).

[86] Local Government Act 1972, s. 101.   [87] Local Government Act 1972, s. 102(3).

much progress.[88] In the case of Birmingham City Council, which in 1985 formulated an ambitious scheme involving the creation of 84 statutory parish councils throughout the city, the scheme foundered because they failed to obtain the approval of the Local Government Boundary Commission.[89] The most radical of the early schemes, however, was that which originated in Walsall where 23 neighbourhood offices were opened between 1980 and 1982, initially based on housing services but with the intention of devolving more services as experience was acquired.[90] The Walsall experiment was short-lived, mainly because Labour lost control of the council in 1982 and the more pioneering aspects of the scheme were abandoned. This service-led approach of incremental decentralization, nevertheless, proved a popular model for other authorities contemplating such schemes.

The most extensive schemes to have been implemented are those in the London Boroughs of Islington and (Liberal-controlled) Tower Hamlets.[91] Since 1986 Islington has developed a multi-service scheme based on 24 area offices providing for personal social services, housing management, community development, environmental health and welfare rights. This is essentially a scheme of administrative decentralization. At the same time, however, a network of neighbourhood fora were established to oversee the work of area offices and to assist in determining spending priorities.[92] Formally, these fora are advisory committees of the council which have consultation rights but no statutory decision-making powers. Notwithstanding these limitations, Burns, Hambleton and Hoggett have concluded that Islington has 'begun to create the pre-conditions from which effective forms of empowerment can develop', that the initiative 'is an experiment in neighbourhood democracy which has national significance' and that 'Islington has gone further than any other council in the UK in establishing reasonably stable arrangements for widening public involvement in local government decision-making.'[93]

---

[88] 'In Southwark and Camden . . . decentralisation was constantly on the agenda but little progress was made . . . in Hackney . . . the political and organisational momentum sunk within a miasma of uncertainty. In many boroughs, the plans collapsed under union opposition.' Lansley, Goss and Wolmar, *Councils in Conflict* (above, n. 1), 100. See also, Burns, Hambleton and Hoggett, *The Politics of Decentralisation* (above, n. 2), 109; K. Beuret and G. Stoker, 'The Labour Party and Neighbourhood Decentralisation: Flirtation or Commitment?' (1986) *Critical Social Policy* 4.

[89] See J. Collingridge, 'The Appeal of Decentralisation' (1986) vol. 12 no. 3 *Local Government Studies* 9.

[90] See C. Fudge, 'Decentralisation: Socialism Goes Local?' in Boddy and Fudge (eds.), *Local Socialism?* (above, n. 1), 192 at 195–8; J. Seabrook, *The Idea of Neighbourhood* (London, 1984).

[91] These schemes are examined in detail in Burns, Hambleton and Hoggett, *The Politics of Decentralisation* (above, n. 2). See also J. Morphet, 'Local Authority Decentralisation – Tower Hamlets Goes All The Way' (1987) 15 *Policy and Politics* 119; V. Lowndes and G. Stoker, 'An Evaluation of Neighbourhood Decentralisation' (1992) 20 *Policy and Politics* 47, 143.

[92] Burns, Hambleton and Hoggett (above, n. 91), 183. Cf. the Tower Hamlets scheme in which local councillors sit on the neighbourhood committees and exercise a wide range of powers: ibid., ch. 8.

[93] Ibid., 200.

The Widdicombe Inquiry

One basic characteristic of municipal socialism has been to identify the question of organizational form as a political issue. The various initiatives examined so far may all be understood to present challenges to the tradition of managerial professionalism in local government. As a result both of an intensification in local politics and of changes in its character, the conventional division between policy and administration has been called into question. Sectional interest groups now more commonly mediate the relationship between councillors and their constituents and councillors and officers. These groups may bring pressure to bear on, and through, councillors, causing an intensification of the political process. Such groups may also have a direct input into local government through consultation and co-option arrangements and thus lead to the tradition of representative democracy being challenged by forms of participatory democracy. At the same time, however, the re-emergence of ideological politics has often meant that the local party organization has sought more directly to influence local councillors, with the result that representative democracy is being challenged by ideas of delegate democracy.[94] These changes thus seemed essentially to reflect the changing nature of politics in local government.

It was as a result of these changes that in 1984 the Government announced its decision to establish a Committee of Inquiry to examine the conduct of local authority business. The recommendations of the Widdicombe Inquiry, whose report was published in June 1986,[95] was based on two key themes: the need to reinforce traditional understandings through a process of formalization of the working arrangements of local government, and the need to define more clearly the division between politics and administration.

The Committee took the view that, with the sharpening of political intensity in local government, conventional understandings concerning the conduct of politics were crumbling and that the solution was to endow certain traditional practices with formal legal status. The distinction between decision-taking and deliberative activities was fundamental to their recommendations. As regards

---

[94] For an examination of these configurations see J. Gyford, 'Diversification, Sectionalism and Local Democracy' in Widdicombe Report, vol. 4, 106 at 129–31. The issue of delegate democracy has been transformed into a legal issue most obviously in debates over manifestos and mandates, on which see: *Bromley LBC* v. *Greater London Council* [1983] 1 AC 768, 829 (Lord Diplock), 853 (Lord Brandon). See further J. Gyford, *The Politics of Local Socialism* (above, n. 1), 60: 'The Labour manifesto for the 1981 GLC elections was prepared over a two-year period by some two hundred people in six working parties, whose efforts culminated in a document 157 pages long. Having prepared such detailed proposals many activists were not prepared, once the elections were over, simply to hand the manifesto to elected Labour councillors and let them get on with the task of implementation. They saw themselves as not only the creators of the manifesto but also its guardians.'

[95] Widdicombe Report, Cmnd. 9797. For analysis see: M. Loughlin, 'The Conduct of Local Authority Business' (1987) 50 MLR 64; P. McAuslan, 'The Widdicombe Report: Local Government Business or Politics?' [1987] *Public Law* 154.

decision-taking activities, the Committee felt that the process should 'be open to public view, reflect the political control on the council, and should be confined to councillors'.[96] Consequently, they recommended that the political composition of such committees should reflect the composition of the council as a whole and that there should be no power of co-option on such committees.[97] In relation to deliberative activities their approach was more flexible. Political realities suggest that policies need to be developed in confidence and that if councillors are prevented from doing so within formal local authority structures they will simply be devised elsewhere. By suggesting that both co-option and the exclusion of councillors from deliberative committees was permissible, the Committee sought to ensure that policy formulation would take place in committees which would have access to officer advice.[98] The general objective of the Committee was thus to reinforce representative democracy and to seek an integration of the process of political formulation into the formal framework of local government.

The second key theme, that of drawing a clear division between politics and administration, was more complex. The Committee based their recommendations on a belief that politicization had resulted in councillors becoming involved in matters which ought not to concern them and that the remedy was to restore and entrench the tradition of managerial professionalism. Politicization had placed strains on the traditional roles of senior officers as professional managers of service departments, as advisors who ensure that the council are informed of all relevant considerations in making their decisions, and as arbitrators who stand outside of political conflicts between councillors and ensure that council business is conducted fairly and with propriety. It was felt that these roles had been undermined by certain changes in organizational arrangements and by the appointment of politically committed officers.[99] The Committee thus took the view that there was a need to strengthen the administrative tradition of establishing a permanent corps of politically neutral officers.

This was to be achieved mainly by clarifying, formalizing and enhancing the powers of the chief executive as head of the paid staff and by vesting in the chief executive overall responsibility for the propriety of council business.[100] The Committee recommended that certain officers, albeit strictly limited in number and seniority, could be attached to party groups; otherwise they must serve the whole council. Further, they held that twin-tracking infringed this principle and recommended that senior officers be statutorily disqualified from being councillors.[101]

The general thrust of the Widdicombe Report was that the recent sharpening of political intensity in local government potentially undermined traditional understandings of representative democracy and managerial professionalism and consequently that there was a need to bolster these conventions with the authority

---

[96] Widdicombe Report, para. 5.40.   [97] Ibid., paras. 5.40, 5.107.
[98] Ibid., paras. 5.55–5.60.   [99] Ibid., paras. 6.132–6.142.
[100] Ibid., paras. 6.152, 6.158, 6.166.   [101] Ibid., paras. 6.39, 6.217.

of the law. In their analysis, however, the Committee generally focused on the symptoms of political change without examining the causes which underpinned these changes in practice. By so doing, it could be argued that, in seeking to reconstruct the authority of the traditional regime, the Report's recommendations would serve only to exacerbate existing tensions.

Statutory reforms

The Government accepted most of the recommendations of the Widdicombe Committee on these matters,[102] which were given statutory effect by Part I of the Local Government and Housing Act 1989.[103] This Act provided that local authorities would be under a duty to ensure *pro rata* representation of the political parties on all local authority committees, sub-committees and appointments to other bodies;[104] the exception for deliberative bodies was thus not accepted. Enforcement of these requirements was left to the courts by way of judicial review.[105] The Government also largely followed Widdicombe on the issue of co-option and accepted the principle that only councillors should have voting rights on decision-taking committees. Members could still be co-opted, though they were not to have voting rights.[106]

The Government also shared the concern expressed by Widdicombe that, although the administrative tradition was that of an 'efficient, expert and politically impartial service',[107] local authorities had in law an almost complete discretion in the appointment of officers.[108] While they accepted the basic objective of the recommendations, however, they did not go so far as the Widdicombe proposals in establishing the chief executive as the buffer between politics and administration, mainly on the ground that it would place the chief executive in the contentious position of having to sit in judgment over elected members.[109] The 1989 Act thus simply required that an officer be designated as head of the authority's paid staff and that the duty of that officer would be to report to the authority on such issues as the organization and management of staff.[110] The Government did, however, introduce specific reforms which considerably bolstered the status of senior officers. First, a duty was imposed on the chief finance officer

---

[102] See, *The Conduct of Local Authority Business, The Government Response to the Report of the Widdicombe Committee of Inquiry*, Cm. 433 (London, 1988).

[103] See G. Ganz, 'The Depoliticisation of Local Government: The Local Government and Housing Act 1989, Part I' [1990] *Public Law* 224.

[104] Local Government and Housing Act 1989, ss. 15–17, Sched. 1; Local Government (Committees and Political Groups) Regulations 1990 (SI 1990 No. 1553).

[105] See, e.g., *R* v. *Greenwich LBC, ex parte Lovelace* [1991] 1 WLR 506; *R* v. *Plymouth City Council, ex parte Gregory* (1990) 89 LGR 478; *R* v. *Brent LBC, ex parte Gladbaum* (1989) 88 LGR 627.

[106] Local Government and Housing Act 1989, s. 13. For exceptions see: s. 13(4), (5); SI 1990 No. 1553, reg. 4.

[107] Cm. 433, 16.   [108] Local Government Act 1972, s. 112.

[109] Cm. 433, para. 5.7.   [110] Local Government and Housing Act 1989, s. 4.

to make a report in cases of financial misconduct.[111] Secondly, all authorities were required to appoint a monitoring officer whose functions were essentially those of a whistle blower. Thus, the monitoring officer was placed under a duty to keep under review the legality and propriety of the council's activities and to report to the council on any action which seemed likely to infringe legal obligations or certain codes of practice or to constitute maladministration.[112]

Further, the neutral status of the officers was reinforced by a number of measures. Twin-tracking was proscribed by disqualifying any person holding a 'politically restricted post' in local government from being a member of a local authority.[113] The 1989 Act also stated that the terms and conditions of service of any person holding a politically restricted post were to be deemed to incorporate such requirements restricting political activities as may be prescribed in regulations made by the Secretary of State.[114] All appointments to a local authority 'shall be made on merit',[115] with the Act vesting power in the Secretary of State to make regulations imposing a duty to adopt certain standing orders concerning the appointment and dismissal of staff.[116] This general prohibition in having regard to any person's political activities or political affiliations in making appointments, was modified by section 9 which made specific provision for the appointment of a strictly limited number of relatively junior staff to provide assistance to political groups on the council.

Organizational change

Politicization affected the entire structure of government during the early 1980s. While the policies of municipal socialism may be taken as the most visible manifestation of this phenomenon in local government, it certainly is arguable that the conduct of central government did more to undermine traditional working arrangements in government than anything which took place in the localities.[117] From this perspective, various controversial actions of the new left authorities provided the Government with the opportunity to deflect attention away from central government action, and the establishment of the Widdicombe

---

[111] Local Government Finance Act 1988, s. 114.

[112] Local Government and Housing Act 1989, s. 5.

[113] Local Government and Housing Act 1989, s. 1. Basically, the category includes all chief officers and their deputies and those officers designated in a list drawn up by the local authority in accordance with statutory guidelines (s. 2). Those so designated may, however, be exempted by regulations made by the Secretary of State or by the decision of an adjudicator appointed under s. 3 of the Act. See Local Government Officers (Political Restrictions) Regulations 1990 (SI 1990 No. 851).

[114] 1989 Act, s. 1(5).   [115] 1989 Act, s. 7.

[116] 1989 Act, s. 8. See further Cm. 433, paras. 5.37–5.48.

[117] See, e.g., ch. 7, 382–99. For further indications see, the Seventh Report from the Treasury and Civil Service Committee, Session 1985–86, *Civil Servants and Ministers: Duties and Responsibilities*, HC 92; Eighth Report of the Committee of Public Accounts, Session 1993–94, *The Proper Conduct of Government Business* HC 154; Seventeenth Report of the Committee of Public Accounts, Session 1993–94, *Pergau Hydro-Electric Project* HC 155.

Committee may be viewed as part of this exercise.[118] Though the Committee found little evidence of actual abuse of power, it seemed to take its cue from the actions of municipal socialist authorities in devising its recommendations for formalizing decision-making processes in local government. And in acting on many of these recommendations, the Government undermined the self-regulatory structure of local councils which provided a mainstay of the modern institution of local government.

Surveying central–local relations in 1951, D.N. Chester suggested that there were three 'vital elements' in local government which 'are so essential to its continuance as a real force that Departments should not be given power to interfere with them'.[119] These were:

(i)   The right of the local electors to elect whom they please to their local Councils.
(ii) The necessity for a local Council to be able to rely completely on the loyalty of its officials.
(iii) The freedom of a Local Authority, subject to the general doctrine of *ultra vires*, to spend the money it raises from local taxes in any way which pleases the local electorate to which it is responsible.[120]

The last, though it raises complex issues, is not of direct concern to us here, and though the first principle has been affected by the introduction of politically restricted posts, it is the second which is of most relevance. While it has never been the position that all local authority officers are merely the servants of the council,[121] the general principle reflects the idea that, as an institution of self-government, the local council should have autonomy in regulating its internal affairs. This principle was first breached by the Conservative government in imposing specific legal duties on local authority officers dealing with council house sales under the Housing Act 1980.[122] The Widdicombe-inspired reforms considerably extend this attempt to drive a wedge between the council and its officers through the attachment of statutory duties on the finance officer, the monitoring officer and the chief executive. To the extent that they are exercising separately conferred statutory duties, they are acting in their own right and not as agents of the council and it should be noted that, for the purpose of performing

[118] It should be noted that the Committee's establishment was announced to the Conservative party conference in 1984 by Patrick Jenkin, then Secretary of State for the Environment, in the following terms: 'There is a cancer in some local councils which runs much deeper than extravagant spending. In some of our cities local democracy is under attack . . . The conventional checks and balances are scorned. Councils squander millions on virulent political campaigns. Officers are selected for their political views; the rights of minorities are suppressed; standing orders are manipulated to stifle debates . . .' (*The Guardian*, 11 October 1984).
[119] D.N. Chester, *Central and Local Government* (London, 1951), 351.
[120] Ibid.
[121] The status of the chief constable (Police Act 1964, s. 5) and the chief finance officer (see *Attorney-General* v. *De Winton* [1906] 2 Ch. 106) are, for example, more complex.
[122] Housing Act 1980, s. 23(5); Housing Act 1985 s. 169(2).

these tasks, the local authority is under a duty 'to provide that officer with such staff, accommodation and other resources as are, *in his opinion*, sufficient to allow his duties ... to be performed'.[123]

Though the Government rejected some of the more controversial recommendations of Widdicombe, such as the proposal to establish the office of chief executive as a barrier between politics and administration in local government, it has undoubtedly promoted a clearer institutional differentiation. Analysing the impact of these reforms, Himsworth concluded that they amounted in effect to 'a partial severance of [local government's] political heart from its managerial head'[124] and suggested that, by placing distance between members and officers, the principle of officer loyalty had been undermined and 'another vital aspect of local government eroded'.[125]

Statutory Powers

The emergence of municipal socialism against a background of diametrically opposed Government policies caused many of these authorities to undertake a systematic examination of the scope and limits of their existing legal powers. Given the Conservative Government's legislative programme, many of the traditional collectivist policies associated with Labour-controlled authorities, such as subsidized council house rents and bus fares, could no longer be maintained. Local authorities wishing to retain redistributive objectives or to extend collectivist initiatives therefore had to search for new methods of doing so. Furthermore, the pressures placed on local authority budgets by general resource constraints, had forced many authorities, especially in the context of growing social needs, to seek to identify their policy priorities. Both the need to maintain or extend collectivist policies and the necessity of finding innovative methods of addressing basic needs required local authorities to engage in detailed scrutiny of the precise formulation of their statutory powers. The exercise resulted in various arcane statutory provisions for the first time coming to occupy a critical position in the processes of local government policy-making.

Redistributive policies

One result of increased politicization may be that authorities not only pay closer attention to the scope of their discretionary powers but also become more selective

---

[123] Local Government and Housing Act 1989, s. 4(1)(b) (head of paid service); s. 5(1)(b); Local Government Finance Act 1988 s. 114(7) (chief finance officer) [emphasis supplied]. These reforms complemented the arrangements providing for the statutory independence of the community charges registration officer in administering the poll tax reforms: Local Government Finance Act 1988, s. 26.

[124] C.M.G. Himsworth, 'Officers, Members and Local Autonomy' in W. Finnie, C.M.G. Himsworth and N. Walker (eds.), *Edinburgh Essays in Public Law* (Edinburgh, 1991), 121 at 139.

[125] Ibid.

over the provision of services within their areas. Such practices certainly challenge the traditional professional norm of uniformity of service provision. They might, however, also raise issues of legality. Thus, it might be argued that, although the channelling of resources to individuals or areas on the basis of need is perfectly legitimate, the primary motivation in actuality is that of discriminating in favour of those groups on whom the party depends for its continued majority. Arguments of this nature are very difficult to substantiate, particularly because it requires evidence of the motivation for, and not simply the impact of, local authority decision-making.[126] Such arguments were treated rather gingerly by the Widdicombe Committee which, though stating that 'it would in our view be wrong if a local authority were to give disproportionate priority to a particular section of the population across the range of its services',[127] did not consider 'practicable' any attempt 'to proscribe support for what might be described as "sectional" activities'.[128]

A good illustration of both this heightened sense of selectivity and of the creative use of discretionary powers is provided by the GLC's Stress Boroughs Scheme which was introduced in 1983/84. This scheme was instituted under the authority of section 136 of the Local Government Act 1972, a provision which empowers two or more authorities to enter into arrangements for the defraying of expenditure incurred by one of them in exercising functions exercisable by both. Under the Stress Boroughs Scheme, the GLC assumed responsibility for funding certain projects which, in the opinion of the borough councils in areas of high stress, were 'of strategic importance to Greater London and for which there was a special need which could not be met by available resources of the borough council'.[129] The redistributive advantage of this scheme is fully revealed only when the complex grant arrangements for financing local authorities are brought into the picture.

There were two principal financial consequences of the scheme. First, because of the impact of expenditure target penalties (and, later, the consequences of rate-capping), many of the inner London boroughs were bearing extremely high marginal costs on such discretionary expenditure.[130] The GLC, however, owing

---

[126] See, however, the case of (Conservative-controlled) Westminster City Council in relation to their policy of 'Building Stable Communities', which the auditor alleged was designed to maximize the Conservatives' electoral chances and thus was motivated by an improper and unlawful purpose: see the auditor's provisional report, above, n. 4. Note also that the episode highlights the limited penetrative capacity of judicial review and the manner in which these charges materialized only after an extensive investigation estimated to have cost over £1m: see *The Times*, 14 January 1994. Most recently, in July 1995 the Secretary of State for Scotland established a statutory inquiry into allegations that Labour-controlled Monklands DC had failed to appoint staff on merit as required by s. 7 of the Local Government and Housing Act 1989. Reporting at the end of December, this inquiry concluded that the allegations of bias against the council were unfounded: see 'Monklands cleared of jobs/religion bias', *Local Government Chronicle*, 5 Jan. 1996.

[127] Widdicombe Report, para. 8.81.   [128] Ibid.

[129] GLC, *Working for London. The Final Five Years* (London, 1986), 76.

[130] See ch. 5, 277–90.

to its very high resource base, did not by 1983/84 receive any block grant. Since all the GLC's income was raised from rates, the grant penalty regime did not apply and the council was able to spend all the revenue it raised without any fine on expenditure at the margin. The scheme thus mitigated the impact of targets on the boroughs. Secondly, since almost one-third of the GLC's precept came from the City of London Corporation and Westminster City Council, GLC expenditure had a significant resource redistributive effect. Most of the rate burden of the GLC was borne by industry and commerce and this led Ken Livingstone, the GLC leader, to suggest that the 'rating mechanism is the best method of redistributing wealth that the labour movement has ever had its hands on'.[131] The Stress Boroughs Scheme, the budget of which increased from £8m in 1983/84 to £77m in 1985/86,[132] in effect enabled funds to be diverted from wealthy areas to areas of deprivation and low rateable value.[133]

Schemes of this nature did not always work.[134] The existence of such proposals, however, are indicative of the extent to which the new left local authorities were prepared to examine their statutory powers in great detail for the purpose of identifying the limits of their power of autonomous action.

Economic development

The most obvious of the general discretionary powers which might be exploited by the socialist local authorities was that contained in section 137 of the Local Government Act 1972. This provision permitted local authorities to incur expenditure up to the product of a 2p rate on any purpose which in their opinion was in the interest of the area or some or all of its inhabitants. Section 137 is a provision which had been given a broad judicial interpretation.[135] Research undertaken for the Widdicombe Inquiry discovered that expenditure incurred under this provision had increased from £6m in 1975/76 to £136m in 1984/85,

---

[131] K. Livingstone, 'Interview' in Boddy and Fudge (eds.), *Local Socialism?* (above, n. 1), 260 at 265.

[132] GLC, *Working for London* (above, n. 129), 76.

[133] The Stress Boroughs Scheme may thus be viewed as an extension of the argument made by Poplar BC during the 1920s on the need for resource reallocation between richer and poorer authorities: see Branson, *Poplarism* (above, n. 18), chs. 3–7.

[134] In 1986, for example, Sheffield City Council tried to promote a scheme under which the districts of South Yorkshire would take over travel concession schemes, so that the precept-capped joint authority could minimize fares increases. This was designed to alleviate the combined impact of the Transport Act 1985 and the Local Government Act 1985 on South Yorkshire's cheap fares policy (for background see ch. 4, 237–47). The scheme, however, collapsed under the weight of various political and legal difficulties.

[135] See, e.g., *Lobenstein* v. *Hackney LBC* (1980)(unreported) in which the court upheld a grant under s.137 to the Olympic Association towards expenses in connection with the Moscow Olympics (there being two Hackney residents in the team). Note, however, that in *R* v. *District Auditor for Leicester, ex parte Leicester City Council* (1985) 25 RVR 191 the Court of Appeal held that local authority staffing and other overhead costs must be charged to the s. 137 account and would count against the expenditure limit.

almost half of which was being spent by the GLC and the metropolitan county councils.[136] That research also indicated that most of that expenditure (67 per cent) had been allocated to economic development and employment promotion measures. What these figures seemed to highlight was the manner in which the strategic metropolitan authorities had during the 1980s responded to the phenomenon of de-industrialization by harnessing their discretionary expenditure powers in an effort to develop an alternative to the Government's reliance on the market as the primary instrument of economic restructuring. The main opportunity to do so arose in 1981 when, after the elections of that year, local authority-controlled enterprise boards were established by the GLC, West Midlands CC, West Yorkshire CC and Lancashire CC.[137]

These boards symbolized a basic shift in the approach of local authorities to the issue of economic development. First, they signified a renewed interest of local government in the state of the local economy; in the West Midlands, for example, one-third of the jobs in manufacturing disappeared between 1978 and 1984, and the establishment of the board reflected the county council's determination to assist in the process of economic restructuring to create a more competitive local economy. Secondly, the local boards represented a new decentralized economic strategy, one which moved away from the Labour Government's centralized model of the National Enterprise Board of the 1970s.[138] Thirdly, the establishment of the boards marked a switch from the traditional local authority property-led economic development approach towards more active policies based on alternative economic strategies. This approach was most obvious in relation to the Greater London Enterprise Board which was committed to 'restructuring for labour' by involving workers in investment, production and marketing processes, by promoting equal opportunities policies in the firms the Board invested in, and by promoting the development of 'socially useful' products. Finally, in establishing the boards as arm's length companies, they moved away from the tradition of departmentalism towards a more flexible institutional structure which freed the boards from certain legal restrictions and attracted different types of officers.[139]

Significant differences existed between these boards, not only in terms of the resources they could command, but also the political-economic strategy they espoused and the commercial policies they followed. By the second half of

---

[136] Widdicombe Report, paras. 8.9–8.16. See also C. Crawford and V. Moore, *The Free Two Pence* (London, 1983).

[137] Labour assumed control of the GLC, the West Midlands CC and Lancashire CC in the 1981 elections. A fifth enterprise board was established on Merseyside in 1984.

[138] See Industry Act 1975.

[139] For analysis and review see: M. Boddy, 'Local Economic and Employment Strategies' in Boddy and Fudge (eds.), *Local Socialism?* (above, n. 1), ch. 7; J. Mawson and D. Miller, 'Interventionist Approaches in Local Employment and Economic Development: the Experience of Labour Local Authorities' in V. Hausner (ed.), *Critical Issues in Urban Economic Development*, vol. 1, (Oxford, 1986), 156; P. Totterdill, 'Local economic strategies as industrial policy: a critical review of British developments in the 1980s' (1989) *Economy and Society* 478; A. Cochrane and A. Clarke, 'Local Enterprise Boards: the Short History of a Radical Initiative' (1990) 68 *Public Admin.* 315.

the 1980s, however, a considerable degree of convergence had taken place. The primary reason for this was that, with the removal of their parent authorities as a result of the abolition of the GLC and the metropolitan county councils in the Local Government Act 1985, any possibility of additional grant-aid on a significant scale was removed and the boards were required to develop a strategy of partnership with the private sector in order to maintain their viability.

Nevertheless, the Government also felt that local government's 'ability to spend on economic development is governed not by properly focused powers ... but by a detailed interpretation of an assortment of powers' and this was 'not conducive to sensible decision-making on economic development issues'.[140] It therefore promoted legislation empowering local authorities to take 'such steps as they may from time to time consider appropriate for promoting the economic development of their area'.[141] This power is, however, strictly circumscribed by regulations and guidance.[142] The Government also introduced specific reforms concerning local authority controlled companies. Widdicombe had proposed that such companies should be 'pursued through machinery which operates *within* the organisation of a local authority'[143] and the Government, concerned not only with the scope of action of such companies but also with the fact that some authorities were using companies to engage in borrowing outside the rules governing local authority spending,[144] introduced a new regulatory framework. Under this framework, a controlled company may not carry out any activity which is *ultra vires* the local authority even if it is within the powers of the company. Further, the authority's general capital expenditure control regime will apply to the company so that any company borrowing or credit arrangements must be within the authority's overall credit ceiling.[145]

During the 1980s, a lively debate occurred on the left on whether these local enterprise board initiatives might form the basis for a socialist transformation.[146] Whether or not they were capable of doing so remains debatable. Action by central government – through the abolition of strategic metropolitan authorities in 1985 and the establishment of a restrictive regulatory regime in 1989 – meant that, whatever the radical potential of these initiatives might have been, by the end of the 1980s such boards were required to operate independently of local government and in accordance with commercial criteria.

[140] Cm. 433, para. 7.12.
[141] Local Government and Housing Act 1989, s. 33.
[142] Local Government (Promotion of Economic Development) Regulations 1990, SI 1990 No. 763; SI 1990 No. 789. See also Department of the Environment/Welsh Office Consultation Paper, *New Economic Development Power for Local Authorities in England and Wales* (August, 1989).
[143] Widdicombe Report, para. 8.114 (emphasis in original).
[144] Department of the Environment, *Local Authorities; Interests in Companies* (London, 1988), para. 3, Annex A.
[145] Local Government and Housing Act 1989, ss. 67–69.
[146] See, e.g., J. Benington, 'Local economic strategies: paradigms for a planned economy' (1986) 1 *Local Economy* 7; A. Eisenschitz and D. North, 'The London Industrial Strategy: Socialist Transformation or Modernising Capitalism?' (1986) 10 *Int. J. of Urban and Regional Research* 419.

Community groups

In considering the scope and use of the section 137 discretionary expenditure power, Widdicombe also discovered that, after economic development, much of the balance of expenditure was allocated to voluntary bodies.[147] While most of these projects were wholly non-contentious, Widdicombe acknowledged the existence of 'some concern in the evidence that local authorities are abusing their powers to grant-aid bodies which are party political in nature or which aim to promote peripheral, divisive or unnecessary causes'.[148] Examples specified by Widdicombe included the funding of national or international causes, women's peace organizations, and groups whose members 'represent small or controversial minorities'.[149] Widdicombe recognized that there were difficulties in seeking to legislate to tighten up the scope of discretion under section 137, but did recommend various changes.[150]

It was certainly the case that, especially in the metropolitan strategic authorities which possessed a much greater leverage capacity under section 137, the funding provided to community groups significantly increased during the early 1980s. The GLC, for example, established a Grants Sub-Committee which supported the voluntary sector 'because of the sector's ability to provide flexible, cost-effective services, to demonstrate innovation in response to changing needs, to encourage the involvement of members of local communities, and to provide particular opportunities for members of disadvantaged groups to articulate their views'.[151] Between 1981 and 1984 funding for voluntary organizations increased from £6m to over £50m, with the GLC providing grant aid to over 200 groups annually concerned with such matters as sport, the environment, women, the arts, police monitoring, ethnic minorities, the disabled, homosexual groups and resource, information and advice centres. This policy was part of an explicit strategy of moving towards a more open and participatory form of governance.

Opponents, however, singled out specific grants to such groups as 'the Karl Marx Library, *Spare Rib*, the Gay London Police Monitoring Group and assorted peace groups'[152] and the political controversy which this generated provoked the Government into action. Abolition of the GLC and the metropolitan county councils had both removed the most active authorities and had had the effect of halving the amount of section 137 money available in the metropolitan areas.[153] (It had, incidentally, also created major problems for the voluntary

[147] Widdicombe Report, para. 8.101.   [148] Ibid., para. 8.102.
[149] Ibid., para. 8.76.   [150] Ibid., paras. 8.90, 8.100, 8.109.
[151] GLC, *Working for London. The Final Five Years* (above, n. 129), 48.
[152] Lansley, Goss and Wolmar, *Councils in Conflict* (above, n. 1), 55.
[153] Note, however, that the Widdicombe Report recommended (para. 8.72) that the s. 137 limit for single-tier authorities should be double the level applying elsewhere and this was given statutory effect by amendments introduced in the Local Government and Housing Act 1989, s. 36(7) which inserted a new s. 137(4AA) into the Local Government Act 1972. With the removal of the domestic rates as a result of the poll tax reforms, the financial limit was reconstructed as a cash figure (£2.50 in two-tier and £5.00 in single tier areas) multiplied by the population of the area.

sector.)[154] Abolition was not, however, felt to be sufficient. This type of funding policy would appear to have motivated the Government in promoting section 28 of the Local Government Act 1988 which provides, inter alia, that a local authority must not 'intentionally promote homosexuality or publish material with the intention of promoting homosexuality'.[155] After Widdicombe, the Government also amended section 137. A new section 137A was enacted which imposed a duty on the authority to require any voluntary organization in receipt of financial assistance under section 137 to provide 'a statement in writing of the use to which that amount has been put'.[156] Section 137 was also significantly redrafted and the new provision required not only that the expenditure be in the interests of, but also 'will bring direct benefit to', the inhabitants and any such benefit must be 'commensurate with the expenditure to be incurred'.[157] The precise importance of these formulations remains unclear.

Information, publicity and campaigning activities

Local authorities have traditionally possessed broad powers to issue information and publicity.[158] Section 142 of the Local Government Act 1972, the most important of the provisions, empowered the authority both to make arrangements whereby the public on application may obtain information concerning services available within their area and also to arrange for the publication within their area of matters relating to local government. During the early 1980s a number of authorities, concerned particularly at the impact of Government expenditure cuts on local services, began to use these powers actively to publicize the implications of Government policies.

The early controversy arose in Scotland and concerned Labour-controlled Lothian Regional Council. In its own newspaper, the Council in 1982 criticized grant reductions as being 'based on utterly unrealistic figures' and as representing 'a threat to local democracy'. Conservative councillors challenged these

[154] The Local Government Act 1985 Act, s. 48 made provision for schemes for paying grants to voluntary organizations in Greater London and the metropolitan areas. The administration of the London scheme ran into certain legal difficulties: see, e.g., *R* v. *London Borough Grants Committee, ex parte Greenwich LBC* (1986) 84 LGR 781. And on the difficulties in practice see: National Council for Voluntary Organisations, *After Abolition. A Report on the Impact of Abolition of the Metropolitan County Councils and the Greater London Council on the Voluntary Sector – and the Outlook for the Future* (London, 1987).
[155] During the early 1980s, the GLC established a gay working party and spent around £1m in grants to support such lesbian and gay services as advice services, police monitoring and employment rights and produced *Changing the World: A London Charter for Gay and Lesbian Rights*. See GLC, *Working for London. The Final Five Years* (above, n. 129), 50–1; Lansley, Goss and Wolmar, *Councils in Conflict* (above, n. 1), ch. 9. On section 28 see: M. Colvin and J. Hawksley, *Section 28: A Practical Guide to the Law and its Implications* (London, 1989).
[156] Local Government and Housing Act 1989, s. 37.
[157] Local Government Act 1972, s. 137(1); as amended by Local Government and Housing Act 1989, s. 36(2).
[158] Local Government Act 1972, ss. 141, 142 and 144 (which should be read in conjunction with ss. 111 and 137).

passages on the ground that they exceeded the powers of the authority[159] and that they were calculated to promote the electoral advantage of the majority party. The court rejected the former claim, holding that 'to explain why the defenders have adopted a particular policy is to provide information on matters relating to local government' and that, since 'Parliament must have appreciated that party politics do prevail in local government', it can be assumed that they appreciated that an authority 'might well select for publication, information . . . which would show the majority group in a favourable light'.[160] The court did, however, uphold the claims of the petitioners on the latter claim and granted an interim interdict against distribution of the publication until after the forthcoming local elections. In a subsequent case in which the auditor challenged a local authority campaign which involved the supply of leaflets, badges and the like and which was based on the slogan 'Edinburgh District Council – Improving Services – Creating Jobs', the court, though endorsing the *Meek* guideline, held that, since the purpose was not to provide information but to campaign in opposition to the Government, that campaign was unlawful.[161]

In England, the main disputes arose in London, primarily over local authority campaigns against expenditure cuts, rate-capping and, later, the abolition of the GLC. But the GLC also made extensive use of advertising to highlight many of its policies, such as the 'Make London a Nuclear Free Zone' campaign.[162] The Government's concern was signalled by the fact that, when the Widdicombe Inquiry was established, the Secretary of State asked the Committee 'to submit an early interim report' on 'the use made by some local authorities of their discretionary powers to engage in overt political campaigning at public expense'.[163] Starting from an analysis of constitutional principles, however, Widdicombe adopted a rather sanguine approach. The Committee, finding that most local authorities spent less than 0.1 per cent of their gross budget and that only the GLC had spent as much as 1 per cent on information and advertising, took the view that there was 'much positive good to be gained from local authority publicity, that we do not take a narrow view of what it should properly cover, and that there is nothing objectionable about material dealing with matters of

---

[159] Local Government (Scotland) Act 1973, s. 88 which was drafted in similar terms to s. 142 of the 1972 Act.

[160] *Meek* v. *Lothian Regional Council* 1983 SLT 494, 495. We might also note the recognition of party control identified in the case. Lord Ross stated (496): 'It is clear from the minutes produced that publication of the *Lothian Clarion* is under the control of the policy and resources committee special sub-committee whose members are all members of the majority Labour group.'

[161] *Commission for Local Authority Accounts in Scotland* v. *City of Edinburgh District Council* 1988 SLT 767. The court also took the view (771) that: 'The situation might have been different if there had been any writing on the banners and other items indicating that further information could be obtained at specific addresses.'

[162] Lansley, Goss and Wolmar, *Councils in Conflict* (above, n. 1), 59, 68. By 1985 around 150 local authorities had declared themselves nuclear free zones: Gyford, *The Politics of Local Socialism* (above, n. 1), 16.

[163] Interim Report of the Committee of Inquiry into the Conduct of Local Authority Business, *Local Authority Publicity* (London, 1985), 1.

political controversy provided that it is properly handled'.[164] The Committee thus concluded that the existing legal framework should be retained, albeit with specific reforms designed to address particular problems.

Furthermore, by the time Widdicombe had reported on the primary issue of controversy, statutory reform seemed unnecessary since, at the behest of Westminster City Council, the courts had been asked to adjudicate on those issues. After the Inner London Education Authority (ILEA) was designated for rate-capping in 1984 the authority did not apply for redesignation under the Act.[165] Instead, being opposed to the Government's acquisition of these powers, ILEA organized a campaign to inform the public of the effects of the consequential service cuts. With a budget of £651,000 and using professional advisers the ILEA utilized mass advertising techniques, including posters and adverts bearing such graphic messages as 'What do you get if you subtract £75 million from London's education budget?' and 'Education cuts never heal. ILEA'. The decision to undertake this campaign was challenged by Westminster in an application for judicial review. Giving judgment, Glidewell J, accepting the guidelines which the Court of Session had adopted in *Meek*, held that, while local authorities were entitled to explain the effects of legislation and to describe the extent to which their actions would be curtailed by rate-capping, there was a difference between information and persuasion and that, where the primary purpose is persuasion, the authority's actions could not be a valid exercise of their powers under section 142. On this basis, the ILEA campaign was declared unlawful.[166]

By this stage, however, the GLC had responded to the Government's decision announcing its intention to abolish the authority by unveiling a major 'Awareness Campaign' to oppose abolition on the grounds that it was detrimental to the interests of Londoners. Costing around £12m[167] and culminating in the 'Say No To No Say' advertisements, the campaign won 23 major advertising awards in 1985 and, more importantly, saw the support of Londoners for the GLC case increase from 53 per cent in October 1983 to 74 per cent in September 1984.[168] This campaign was also challenged in the courts by Westminster City Council. Westminster first contested decisions by the GLC and ILEA to second staff to assist with the Democracy for London Campaign. In this case it was held that, while the ILEA's decision was made in the interests of good staff relations and was valid, the GLC's action, being motivated primarily for the purpose of

[164] Ibid, para. 162. The Committee also took note of the fact that between 1980/81 and 1983/84, the Government had spent £2.3m promoting the 'politically controversial issue' of the 'right to buy' under the Housing Act 1980: ibid., para. 117.
[165] Rates Act 1984, s. 3. See, below, 187–94.
[166] *R* v. *Inner London Education Authority, ex parte Westminster City Council* [1986] 1 WLR 28. The decision was not appealed, apparently because ILEA felt that the precise terms of the injunction agreed were fairly favourable.
[167] *The Times*, 26 July 1984. The Widdicombe Interim Report (para. 40) estimated that in 1984/85 the GLC's overall expenditure on information and publicity was £14m.
[168] GLC, *Working for London. The Final Five Years* (above, n. 129), 79.

conducting a political campaign was tainted with irrelevant considerations and was thus unlawful.[169]

Westminster had, on 11 January 1985, also obtained an *ex parte* injunction against the GLC's campaign against abolition pending trial on whether the campaign should be declared *ultra vires*. This injunction even prohibited the GLC from consulting legal advisers in relation to that campaign. On 17 January, the GLC sought to have the injunction lifted. Recognizing that timing was crucial, since money already committed by the GLC might be wasted if the campaign was halted and yet realizing that much could be spent *ultra vires* if the injunction was lifted, the court held that the injunction should remain in force. Nevertheless, the court accepted that the GLC should be able both to consult legal advisers and to exercise its legitimate powers under section 142.[170] This seemed to place the court in the position of having to vet each element of the campaign to determine whether or not particular leaflets or posters were lawful.

Meanwhile, notwithstanding the Widdicombe Interim Report and the court rulings, the Government had decided to proceed with legislation which restricted the publicity powers of local authorities. Part II of the Local Government Act 1986 thus confined local authority publicity powers to the provision of information on local government functions and services, strictly limited the use of section 137 for publicity powers, and provided that a local authority must not 'publish any material which, in whole or in part, appears to be designed to affect public support for a political party'.[171] Aside from the specific impact which this might have on publicity designed to combat racism, which might be construed as affecting support for the British National Party, the 1986 Act seemed in general to have 'a stultifying effect on local government participation in the democratic process'.[172] The Government had, however, been obliged to withdraw certain provisions from that Bill after defeats in the Lords[173] and it indicated that further legislation would be forthcoming. These new powers eventually materialized in sections 27 and 28 of the Local Government Act 1988. The latter provision, as we have seen, bans local authorities from promoting homosexuality, while section 27 amends section 2 of the 1986 Act primarily by identifying factors to which regard must be had in determining whether the material is

---

[169] *R* v. *Greater London Council and Another, ex parte Westminster City Council, The Times*, 31 December 1984.

[170] *R* v. *Greater London Council, ex parte Westminster City Council, The Times*, 22 January 1985.

[171] Local Government Act 1986, s. 2.

[172] H.F. Rawlings and C.J. Willmore, 'The Local Government Act 1986' (1987) 50 MLR 52, 63. See also H.F. Rawlings and C.J. Willmore, *Letting People Know. Local Government Publicity After the Local Government Act 1986* (London, 1986).

[173] The Government, for example, proposed to empower the Secretary of State to issue a binding code of conduct. This was defeated by the Lords by 119 to 108, Lord Denning arguing that: 'We shall find the freedom of debate and the freedom of speech undoubtedly circumscribed, not by the law, but by codes of practice' HL Debs, vol. 471 col. 873 (24 February 1986). The Government subsequently dropped this provision.

prohibited and by requiring authorities to have regard to any codes of practice issued by the Secretary of State concerning local authority publicity.

These statutory reforms have undoubtedly had a chilling effect on local government conduct. In 1986, for example, Glasgow District Council was advised by its solicitors to rewrite its annual budget explanation to ratepayers which commenced: 'Despite inflation, high interest rates and government cuts Glasgow district council has held its rate steady at 29.5p.' Everything before 'Glasgow' was considered to infringe the new legislative provisions and the statement was therefore amended.[174] These restrictions should also be placed alongside central government expenditure on publicity and especially the controversial advertising campaigns on privatization schemes.[175] They provide further evidence that, contrary to Widdicombe's proposition, local government, in the eyes of central government, has ceased to be 'more than the sum of the particular services provided'.[176]

Forward funding

When the Government decided to abolish the GLC and the metropolitan county councils, it had hoped to achieve that objective before May 1985 since the local elections then due might otherwise be turned into a referendum on that policy. When it was realized that for administrative reasons it would be impossible to abolish the authorities until April 1986, the Government then proposed that transitional bodies consisting of borough and district nominees should be established to run the authorities in their final year. This proposal was, however, defeated in the House of Lords.[177] Consequently, the Government decided that the term of office of the existing authorities should be extended until the date of abolition on 1 April 1986.[178] This arrangement, however, maximized the potential of the existing authorities, all of which were Labour-controlled, to continue with their policies. Though the Government acquired powers to require the authorities to obtain ministerial approval for certain decisions or schemes,[179]

[174] *The Guardian*, 21 March 1986.

[175] See, e.g., National Audit Office Report, Session 1989–90, *Publicity Services for Government Departments*, HC 46; 19th Report from the Committee on Public Accounts, Session 1989–90, *Publicity Services for Government Departments*, HC 81; C. Munro, 'Government Advertising and Publicity' 1990 *Public Law* 1; Report by Tony Blair MP, Shadow Energy Secretary, *Privatisation Advertising. The Selling of Water and Electricity* (London, 1989). See also Greenwich LBC's unsuccessful challenge to the launch of the Government's leaflet (at a cost of £970,000), 'The Community Charge: how it will work for you', which Greenwich argued that, although claiming to advise on the main points of the scheme, failed properly to explain the consequences of non-payment: *R v. Secretary of State for the Environment, ex p. Greenwich LBC, The Times*, 11 May 1989.

[176] Widdicombe Interim Report, para. 34.

[177] See HL Debs, vol. 453 cols. 1096–1139 (28 June 1984).

[178] Local Government (Interim Provisions) Act 1985, s. 2. See M. Loughlin, *Local Government in the Modern State* (London, 1986), 178–80.

[179] Local Government (Interim Provisions) Act 1984, ss. 5–9.

there was plenty of evidence which indicated that the authorities had, in anticipation, already acted.[180]

One particularly important question was whether the authorities would be
empowered to continue their policies after abolition by establishing units and
providing funds to finance activities beyond the date of abolition. The most
obvious source of authority for such action was section 111 of the Local Government Act 1972 which empowers local authorities to 'do anything (whether or
not involving the expenditure . . . of money . . .) which is calculated to facilitate,
or is conducive or incidental to, the discharge of any of their functions'. On its
face, section 111 simply incorporates in statutory form a common law principle
to the effect that the *ultra vires* doctrine ought not to be applied too rigidly to
the activities of local authorities. Nevertheless, previous authority existed, most
notably the decision of the House of Lords in *Manchester City Council* v.
Greater Manchester County Council,[181] to suggest that local authorities were
empowered to undertake the forward funding of projects.

The *Manchester* decision concerned a decision of the county council in 1978/
79 to pay £1.2m into a trust fund to meet the costs over the following seven
years of educating 400 children from their area at independent schools. This
payment, which was authorized mainly under section 137 of the 1972 Act, was
made against the background of the Education Act 1976 which had limited
the powers of local education authorities to award bursaries for their children
at non-maintained schools. The case thus seemed to raise two basic issues of a
quasi-constitutional nature. First, whether, when Parliament promotes a particular policy through statutory reforms to the powers of education authorities, it is
open to a local authority which is not an education authority to pursue a contrary
policy through the use of their general discretionary powers. Secondly, whether
an authority should have the power of forward funding, particularly since it
would appear to enable it to bind its successors. In this case, the House of Lords
took the view that no objection founded on the first issue could be sustained
since the county council's actions lay within the limits of the section 137 power.
On the second issue their Lordships held that, while local government finance
must be conducted on an annual basis, that principle is limited to the total
amount of expenditure incurred during the relevant year but does not apply to
expenditure on revenue account in that year. The county council's expenditure
was incurred when the money was transferred to the trust fund and the fact that
it was to be spent over a seven year period was immaterial. The *Manchester*
decision thus seemed to provide sound authority permitting the forward funding
of local authority schemes.

During 1985/86, then, 'the great cities', in Mary Goldring's words, 'rang to
the sound of clopping hooves and the slamming of stable doors behind fleeting
rumps'.[182] Much of this noise eventually reverberated around the Strand, generally

---

[180] See, e.g., *The Guardian*, 13 July 1984.   [181] (1980) 78 LGR 560.
[182] M. Goldring, 'Tombstone funding: life after death for the munificent seven', *The Listener*,
3 April 1986.

as a result of applications for judicial review brought by Conservative-controlled boroughs within the areas of the abolished counties. Solihull and Trafford MBCs, for example, each sought judicial review of their respective county authorities, challenging decisions to dispose of some of the revenue surplus in 1985/86 to voluntary bodies or on particular projects.[183] In each case, the contention that there was a legitimate expectation that the districts would be consulted before decisions were made was rejected. So too was the argument that the decisions infringed the principle of *Wednesbury* unreasonableness or were in breach of the authority's fiduciary duty to ratepayers;[184] the latter argument being rejected, notwithstanding the fact that, in *ex parte Trafford*, the applicability of grant penalties meant that one Greater Manchester CC project budgeted at £4m, would ultimately cost the ratepayer £13.2m. Furthermore, in the *Trafford* case, the court also held that the argument that forward funding of projects might be impugned was, on the authority of the earlier *Manchester* decision, of no validity.

On 3 March 1986 MacPherson J dispatched a great deal of this business. In addition to giving judgment in the *Solihull* and *Trafford* cases, he also determined an application by Westminster City Council and seven other London boroughs against certain decisions of the GLC.[185] The GLC had estimated that during 1985/86 it was likely to have a revenue surplus of around £281m, which would on abolition be distributed to the boroughs. The GLC, however, decided to use £76m to make certain forward funding arrangements which would meet expenditures in 1986/87: £40m to the new ILEA, £25m to voluntary organizations, and £11m to the Roundhouse arts centre. After Westminster had previously failed to prevent the GLC from spending up to £140m – money which had materialized in 1985/86 as a result of various creative accounting schemes – on the Stress Borough Scheme and on various arts projects,[186] this attack was specifically focused on the issue of forward funding. Again, MacPherson J held that the situation could not be distinguished from the *Manchester* decision in 1980 and that there was nothing to suggest that these forward funding arrangements, in form or substance, were unlawful.

[183] *R* v. *Finance Committee of West Midlands CC, ex parte Solihull MBC* (QBD) 3 March 1986 (unreported); *R* v. *Greater Manchester Council, ex parte Trafford MBC* (QBD) 3 March 1986 (unreported).

[184] See further ch. 4, esp. 250–6.

[185] *R* v. *GLC, ex parte Westminster City Council, The Times*, 4 March 1986. In *ex parte Trafford MBC* MacPherson J had considered 601 pages of affidavits and exhibits (transcript, 1), while in the *Westminster* case there was 'a body of affidavit evidence before me of about 500 pages of documents' (transcript, 1).

[186] *R* v. *GLC, ex parte Westminster City Council* (QBD) 7 August 1985 (unreported). It should be noted that many of these revenue surpluses materialized in the GLC and the metropolitan authorities because, as a result of the complexities of the grant regime and the consequent schemes for creative accounting, the true budgetary position of many authorities had been masked. Thus, in this case (transcript, 3) Mann J stated: 'The third consideration . . . concerns the treatment of 1984–85 balances or underspend for that year. The amount is £34m. It was open to the GLC to use a device by way of creative accounting whereby this sum was paid into a special fund and thus made available for 1985–86 without grant penalty.' On creative accounting schemes see ch. 6, 325–9.

Solihull and Westminster both appealed against these judgments. The Court of Appeal, though rejecting the Solihull challenge,[187] found in favour of Westminster on the issue of forward funding.[188] The GLC pursued the Westminster case in the Lords. In *Re Westminster City Council*,[189] the House of Lords affirmed the Court of Appeal's judgment and quashed the GLC's forward funding decisions. The decision on the proposed grant to the new ILEA appeared relatively straightforward: since the Local Government Act 1985 had made express and restrictive provisions for the funding of the new ILEA, it was held that the discretionary powers of the GLC could not therefore be construed as authorising payment of the grant. The question of grants to voluntary organizations and to the Roundhouse Theatre, however, proved more contentious.

In addressing this issue, the Lords held that the true principle of the *Manchester* case was that, provided expenditure falls to be defrayed in the year in question, it does not become *ultra vires* merely because it is expenditure of a capital nature or because it is an expenditure made in respect of costs which may not all be incurred in the year in question. The crucial issue, however, was whether the expenditure incurred was properly referable to the year in question. Their Lordships took the view that in the *Manchester* case it was so referable, because the expenditure related only to those children who were to begin their seven year curriculum in 1978; the expenditure was thus rendered necessary by, and consequential upon, the exercise by the county council in 1978 of its power to provide for the education of children in that year. In the *GLC* case, by contrast, it was held that there was nothing to link the running costs of these organizations in 1986/87 to an expenditure of, or to the exercise of a power or function of, the GLC in 1985/86. In fact, the payment seemed to be made simply to enable the GLC to do in 1985/86 that which it could not do in 1986/87.

This interpretation of the forward funding principle was, however, explicitly rejected by Lord Bridge. Lord Bridge could find nothing in the decision of the House in the *Manchester* case which supported the view that that decision depended on 'some special exception to a general rule against . . . "forward funding" by a local authority'.[190] The *Manchester* decision seemed to state quite clearly that, once the money was handed over, it constituted expenditure. Further, the argument of the majority in the GLC case, that there must be some element of continuity or nexus between the present year and future years, was felt by Lord Bridge to raise questions of degree which could not serve to define the limitations on an authority's *vires*. That argument, his Lordship contended, simply begged the question it sought to answer:

[187] *R* v. *West Midlands CC, ex parte Solihull MBC* (CA) 20 March 1986 (unreported).
[188] *R* v. *GLC, ex parte The Lord Mayor and Citizens of the City of Westminster, The Times,* 24 March 1986 (CA).
[189] [1986] AC 668.   [190] Ibid., 686.

In the *Manchester* case the purpose was to provide continuity of education for children in free or assisted places in such a way that it could not be interrupted by a change in the political control of the authority. In the instant case the purpose is to provide a purely temporary means of survival for voluntary organisations which have hitherto been supported from public funds by the GLC during a period of necessary uncertainty following abolition until it becomes clear whether or not their long-term survival will be made possible . . . Assuming the existence of the power, its exercise was not in either case under attack. I am unable to discern any criterion which I can understand and apply to make a valid distinction between the two cases by reference to the existence or non-existence of the power of forward funding.[191]

The decision of the House of Lords on the forward funding principle was, especially given Lord Bridge's cogent dissent, highly controversial. Although *Re Westminster* set the framework for subsequent actions involving the strategic authorities, it should be appreciated that it did not have the effect of prohibiting all further payments concerning the financing of future action.[192] It was clear, however, that, given the difficulties experienced by the Government in drawing up a legislative scheme which would enable the highly contentious policy of abolition to be implemented with the minimum degree of political disruption, the courts were likely to be drawn into the rather difficult, if not impossible, task of seeking impartially to hold the ring. The decision of the House in *Re Westminster* thus seemed only to confirm the beliefs of those who contend that the higher courts have a proclivity to protect what they perceive to be the interests of the central State.

Local control of policing

The police authority has traditionally performed an important role within the tripartite arrangements (between police authority, chief constable and Home Secretary) for the governance of police outside London.[193] Nevertheless, these arrangements have not generally been highly politicized. During the 1980s, however, a number of factors coalesced – including the phenomenon of urban riots of 1981 and 1985 and the policing of the miners' strike in 1984/85 – to reinvigorate the debate on democratic control over policing. This caused many police authorities, especially in the urban areas, to examine more closely, and to seek to

[191] Ibid., 689.

[192] See, e.g., *R* v. *GLC, ex parte London Residuary Body* (QBD) 5 December 1986 (unreported), a decision in which MacPherson J upheld payments of over £78m made on 27 March 1986 by the GLC to Satman Developments Ltd to undertake works on the former GLC housing stock which had previously been transferred to the boroughs. On the legal conflicts arising over the work of the London Residuary Body see M. Hebbert and A. Dickens Edge, *Dismantlers. The London Residuary Body* (London, 1994), esp. 55–6 (Satman), 81–93 (County Hall).

[193] See L. Lustgarten, *The Governance of Police* (London, 1986); I. Oliver, *Police, Government and Accountability* (London, 1986).

exercise, their statutory powers under the Police Act 1964. Such developments had the effect of bringing to light the many ambiguities in the role of police authorities within the tripartite arrangements.[194]

Under the 1964 Act, the police authority is under a duty 'to secure the maintenance of an adequate and efficient force' for their area.[195] It appoints the chief constable, determines the establishment of the force, provides equipment, fixes the budget and exercises financial control.[196] While the chief constable is responsible for the 'direction and control' of the force,[197] the authority may call for reports on any matter connected with the policing of the area[198] and, with the Home Secretary's approval, require the chief constable to retire in the interests of efficiency.[199] The structure is, however, riddled with ambiguity, most of it revolving around the influence of the police authority in shaping policing policies. The Royal Commission on the Police in 1962 had felt that there were certain aspects of policing policy, such as the means used to control public protests or the use of the police in industrial disputes, which were properly of concern to the police authority.[200] Since they did not make any specific recommendations on this question, however, the 1964 Act provisions were rather equivocal. These uncertainties remained largely untested during the 1960s and 1970s, but they came to be highlighted during the 1980s.

The issues were most graphically illustrated in relation to the miners' strike, which resulted in national co-ordination of police operations. This was achieved primarily through police activation of the National Reporting Centre which acted as a mechanism for establishing a system of 'mutual aid' between local forces.[201] The conduct of these operations, controlled by the Association of Chief Police Officers in close liaison with the Home Office, enabled the Government in effect to operate a national police force without the Home Secretary at any time invoking his powers of direction.[202] However, since police authorities were never at any stage consulted about these arrangements, it is hardly surprising that these actions resulted in friction between certain authorities and their chief constables. After all, not only might the deployment of constables to other parts of the country significantly affect the efficiency of the local force, but also it initially

---

[194] See B. Loveday, 'The Role of the Police Committee' (1983) vol. 9 no. 1 *Local Government Studies* 39; P.J. Waddington, 'The Role of the Police Committee: Constitutional Arrangements and Social Realities' (1984) vol. 10 no. 5 *Local Government Studies* 27; B. Loveday, 'The Role of the Police Committee – A Reply' (1984) vol. 10 no. 5 *Local Government Studies* 43.

[195] Police Act 1964, s. 4(1).

[196] Ibid., ss. 4(2), 4(3), 6(4), 8(4).   [197] Ibid., s. 5(1).

[198] Ibid., s. 12(2). Note, however, that the chief constable can refuse if he believes it would contain information, the disclosure of which would be contrary to the public interest, or that it is not required for the discharge of the police authority's duties. The authority must then appeal to the Home Secretary: s. 12(3).

[199] Ibid., s. 5(4).

[200] *Report of the Royal Commission on the Police*, Cmnd. 1728, paras. 88–91.

[201] Police Act 1964, s. 14(1). See Lustgarten, *The Governance of Police* (above, n. 193), ch. 8.

[202] Police Act 1964, ss. 14(2), 13(5).

appeared that the police authority was expected to meet the expenses of these operations.[203]

In South Yorkshire, antagonism between the chief constable and the police authority over matters of policing policy during the strike led the authority to exercise its statutory powers as a mechanism of control. The authority thus announced its intention of altering standing orders so as to restrict the chief constable's spending authority and to use its powers over the establishment to require the force to get rid of its dog and horse sections. These resolutions caused the Attorney-General in July 1984 to seek an interim injunction prohibiting the authority from taking further action. The Attorney-General's intervention turned out to be sufficient, since the police authority did not contest that action and backed down from its stance. Policing the miners' strike also caused conflict on Merseyside where the police authority encountered great difficulty in discovering the amount of aid the local force was providing to others. This, the authority claimed, jeopardized their ability to comply with their duty to maintain an adequate and efficient force: if significant numbers of officers were being redeployed, this must, it was argued, affect the efficiency of their force and, if it did not, it might indicate that the establishment of the force was excessive.[204]

The conflicts which arose over the miners' strike, however, highlighted more general tensions between the police authority and the chief constable which had been experienced in particular areas during the 1980s. Once the authorities sought to use their powers they encountered basic problems; not only were they entirely marginalized from the processes of policy-making, but they also confronted great difficulties in being adequately consulted about arrangements or even in obtaining basic information.[205] Further, the police authorities received little support from the courts when they were called on to adjudicate on these ambiguities.[206] There thus seemed little point in suggesting that police authorities

[203] The Home Secretary subsequently agreed to meet 75 per cent of the local costs of these operations above the product of a one penny rate: Home Office Circular, 59/84. See: B. Loveday, 'Central Co-ordination, Police Authorities and the Miners' Strike' (1986) 60 *Political Quarterly* 60; S. Spencer, 'The Eclipse of the Police Authority' in B. Fine and R. Millar (eds.), *Policing the Miners' Strike* (London, 1985), 34.

[204] See B. Loveday, *Report on the Role and Effectiveness of the Merseyside Police Committee* (Merseyside CC, May 1985), esp. 130–49.

[205] See, e.g., Merseyside Police Authority, *The Merseyside Disturbances: the Role and Responsibility of the Police Authority* (Merseyside CC, 1981); M. Simey, 'Police Authorities and Accountability: the Merseyside Experience' in D. Cowell, T. Jones and J. Young (eds.), *Policing the Riots* (London, 1982), Ch. 4.

[206] See *R* v. *Secretary of State for the Home Department, ex p. Northumbria Police Authority* [1989] QB 26. In this case, the police authority challenged the Home Secretary's decision to establish a central store of baton rounds and CS gas from which chief constables who required access to this equipment but who had been denied authorization by their local police authorities could obtain such equipment for use. The Divisional Court held that, although the Home Secretary had no statutory power to maintain the store, it could be established under prerogative powers. This decision seemed difficult to reconcile with the principle, established in *Attorney-General* v. *De Keyser's Royal Hotel Ltd* [1920] AC 508, that where a prerogative power had been superseded by statute it was in abeyance and could not be relied on. On appeal, it was held that the Home Secretary did in

should carefully examine the limits of their existing powers.[207] Once they tried to utilize these powers the authorities were faced with formidable barriers in the form of the chief constable's claim to constabulary independence,[208] reinforced by the tacit support of the Home Office and an acquiescent judiciary. The answer, it seemed, was to introduce legislation to make explicit the power of the police authority to determine the general policing policies of their areas.[209]

In the event, the tide has moved entirely in the other direction. Abolition of the metropolitan county councils removed directly elected bodies and replaced them with indirectly-elected joint authorities. Research conducted on the impact of abolition has suggested that the changes in policy orientation consequential on these reforms has been most significant in the area of policing policy. What has disappeared, the researchers concluded, was the tendency 'in Greater Manchester, Merseyside and (to a lesser extent) in South Yorkshire and the West Midlands' for the police authority 'to generate a lively and critical debate about certain aspects of policing and occasionally to pass motions which were embarrassing to the chief constable concerned'.[210] The reasons for this were mainly because in four of the six authorities Labour did not hold a majority (being dependent on magistrates for support) and also, lacking the organizational framework and policy networks of a singular authority it became harder for members 'to develop and sustain a well-informed critique of particular aspects of policing'.[211]

Radical changes to the governance of police were proposed by the Government in 1993.[212] Police authorities were to be reconstituted as independent corporate bodies consisting of 16 members, including eight local councillors, three local magistrates and five local persons appointed by the Home Secretary. A salaried chairman was to be appointed from the members by the Home Secretary. The chief constable was to be required to agree a policing plan with the police authority. Since the police authority were to be given no additional powers, it

---

fact have the statutory power to maintain a central store. Further, on the issue of prerogative power, the Court of Appeal also held that the Crown could not act under the prerogative if to do so would be incompatible with statute. Notwithstanding the police authority's claim that the action was in fact incompatible since it was inconsistent with the powers conferred on the authority by s. 4 of the 1964 Act, the court went on to hold that that statutory power did not expressly grant a monopoly to the police authority to secure the maintenance of an adequate and efficient force and they saw no reason to imply one.

[207] See, e.g., D. Regan, 'Enhancing the Role of Police Committees' (1983) 61 *Public Admin.* 97.

[208] *Fisher* v. *Oldham Corporation* [1930] 2 KB 364. See G. Marshall and B. Loveday, 'The Police: Independence and Accountability' in J. Jowell and D. Oliver (eds.), *The Changing Constitution* (Oxford, 3rd edn., 1994), 295 at 296–300.

[209] See, e.g., the Police Authorities (Powers) Bill (HC 1979–80, Bill 78) introduced by Jack Straw MP.

[210] S. Leach, H. Davis, C. Game and C. Skelcher, *After Abolition. The Operation of the Post-1986 Metropolitan Government System in England* (Birmingham, 1990), 111.

[211] Ibid. It should be noted that, although the Widdicombe Report recommended that, in principle, magistrates should not sit (or, at least, exercise voting rights) on police committees (para. 5.107), this proposal was not accepted by the Government: see Cm. 433, para. 2.13.

[212] *Police Reform: the Government's proposals for the police service in England and Wales* Cm. 2281 (1993).

appeared that this would be essentially a financial management plan. Police authorities would be required to supply performance information to the Home Secretary, who would acquire new powers to call for reports from, and issue directions to, the police authority.

These proposals in effect marked the destruction of the tripartite scheme, since it was clear that local government was no longer identified as having an institutional role in the governance of police. They were the subject of vigorous criticism[213] and, as a result of a number of Government defeats inflicted by the House of Lords, many of the most contentious aspects of these reforms were significantly amended.[214] Police authorities will now have 17 members, consisting of nine local councillors (a majority), three magistrates and five nominees.[215] The Home Secretary will not select the chairman and the nominees will emerge through a convoluted procedure rather than simply be appointed by the Home Secretary.[216] The impact of these reforms will, nevertheless, be considerably to strengthen central control and significantly to diminish local authority influence in the governance of the policing function.

Tightening the *ultra vires* regime

During the 1980s, many of the conventional understandings on how the statutory powers vested in local councils should be exercised lost much of their authority. This resulted in certain councils, of which those promoting a renewed municipal socialism were at the forefront, beginning to explore in earnest the precise legal limits of their rather general and ambiguous powers of autonomous action. Particular attention was paid to the general discretionary provisions under the Local Government Act 1972 which provided the legal foundation for much of the innovative action of local authorities in relation to joint action, economic development, grant-aid to community groups, campaigning activities and forward funding arrangements.

As we have seen, once these initiatives were developed central government took action to restrict many of the practices, including the formulation of a more precise and limited power in respect of economic development, a more circumscribed discretionary expenditure power under section 137, and statutory restrictions on publicity powers. However, given the prominent role of the strategic metropolitan authorities, especially the GLC, in developing many of these initiatives, it could also be argued that the manner in which their statutory

---

[213] See, e.g., the views of Lord Ackner, HL Debs, vol. 551, col. 510: '[T]he provisions in the Bill . . . propose a substantial move towards centralisation of policing and away from the tripartite relationship of police, Home Office and local police authorities. This tripartite relationship is clearly a constitutional safeguard of enormous importance which prevents policing falling under national political control.'

[214] See Earl Ferrers, HL Debs, vol. 552, col. 943 (1 March 1994).

[215] Police and Magistrates' Courts Act 1994, s. 3, Sched. 2; inserting new ss. 3A, 3B and Scheds. 1B and 1C into the Police Act 1964.

[216] Police Act 1964, Sched. 1B, para. 5; Sched. 1C.

powers were exercised played a significant part in the decision to remove them.[217] Consideration of the issue of policing tends to confirm this general trend; once utilized in ways which irritate the central State, the powers of local authorities will either be severely restricted or altogether removed from the province of local government. Finally, we might note that, whenever during the 1980s the judiciary were invited to adjudicate issues concerning the scope of the discretionary powers of local authorities, the general tendency, as cases such as *Re Westminster*[218] and *ex parte Northumbria Police Authority*[219] illustrate, has been to construe powers in a way which places limits on what often was traditionally understood to fall within the power of local government.[220]

Institutional Power

Local authorities have so far been examined as statutory bodies whose powers and duties are conferred by law. But the local authority may be viewed not only as a legally constituted agency of rule but also as an institution which exercises economic power.[221] As economic institutions, local authorities are, by any standard, important bodies. During the 1980s, for example, it was estimated that a medium-sized county council would be employing around 20,000 people and would hold a property portfolio worth over £500m on the open market.[222] Furthermore, as one judge remarked when discussing the complexities of the GLC's finances, '[t]he money involved is as much, I suspect, as the budgets of many small countries'.[223] When considering the capacity of municipal socialist authorities for autonomous action, this institutional economic power must also be taken into account.

During the 1980s, local authorities became increasingly aware of the power which they possessed as economic institutions. This was partly attributable to the growth in the use of corporate techniques which became a key feature of post-reorganization management practices. Reflection on the economic power of the local authority during the 1980s may also be related to the general tendency of institutions during periods of retrenchment to engage in a more comprehensive

---

[217] For an analysis of the competing explanations see: B. O'Leary, 'Why was the GLC abolished?' (1987) 11 *Int. J of Urban and Regional Research* 193.

[218] [1986] AC 668.   [219] [1989] QB 26 (above, n. 206).

[220] See also in relation to the construction of s. 111: *Hazell* v. *Hammersmith and Fulham LBC* [1992] 2 AC 1; *R* v. *Richmond upon Thames BC, ex parte McCarthy (Developments) Ltd* [1991] 4 All ER 897; *Allsop* v. *North Tyneside MBC* (1992) 90 LGR 462. See further on *Hazell*, ch. 6, esp. 344–54.

[221] See T. Daintith, 'The Techniques of Government' in J. Jowell and D. Oliver (eds.), *The Changing Constitution* (above, n. 208) ch. 8 (distinction between *imperium* to explain Government's use of law to achieve its objectives and *dominium* to describe the employment of the Government's use of wealth as an instrument of policy).

[222] J. Banham, 'Are we being served by local government? Some initial reflections' (1984) 55 *Political Quarterly* 273, 274.

[223] *R* v. *GLC, ex parte Westminster City Council, The Times*, 4 March 1985, per MacPherson J (transcript, 1).

examination of the nature and impact of their activities. The attempt by new left authorities to harness the economic potential of the authority to the realization of social and economic policy objectives may thus be viewed as a particular (and perhaps more radical) aspect of a general trend in local government during the 1980s.

The issues raised by the use of institutional power may be highlighted by considering the policy of promoting racial equality. During the 1980s, a considerable degree of pessimism came to be expressed about the capacity of legal processes to diminish racial inequality.[224] While legal instruments could achieve some advance in eliminating direct discrimination from public life, 'indirect' or institutional discrimination seemed to raise issues which the courts were ill-equipped to address.[225] Further, the issue of racial disadvantage in the fullest sense, meaning the inequalities which manifest themselves in under-achievement at school, higher rates of unemployment and concentration in poorer housing, seemed to be 'outside the effective reach of the law'.[226] The rights-based approach, in short, was viewed as being individualistic, based on the imposition of minimum standards and was, from the Government's point of view, inexpensive. It is also unlikely to have any significant effect on eradicating the patterns of racial disadvantage.

Local authorities are unusual amongst institutions in being vested with a special duty not only to avoid discrimination but also to seek the elimination of discrimination and to promote good race relations and equality of opportunity.[227] Research in 1980, however, showed that many local authorities had done very little in furtherance of these duties.[228] During the 1980s, many of the new left authorities attempted to remedy this position by developing a new set of race initiatives based on the objective of extending the scope of equality from the formal arena of legal relations to the entire field of social relations. Part of the response, as we have seen, was to establish committees and units to address race equality as a corporate objective.[229] The distinctive strategy which was adopted focused primarily on the economic power of the institution of local government.

This strategy implied a shift in emphasis away from equal treatment and towards more radical strategies of positive action. Thus, alongside the exercise of statutory powers, local authorities sought to utilize their potential as employers, landlords and contractors to address more directly the issue of disadvantage.[230] In relation to employment policies, for example, certain local authorities set

---

[224] See, e.g., L. Lustgarten, 'Racial Inequality and the Limits of Law' (1986) 49 MLR 68.
[225] Ibid., at 72; C. McCrudden, 'Institutional Discrimination' (1982) 2 *Oxford J. of Legal Studies* 303.
[226] Lustgarten (above, n. 224), 77.   [227] Race Relations Act 1976, s. 71.
[228] K. Young and N. Connolly, *Policy and Practice in the Multi-Racial City* (London, 1981).
[229] See above, 141–2.
[230] In 1984 Camden's Race Relations Unit, for example, took the view that, in addition to providing 'support and liaison with groups within the community' one of its primary functions was 'to look at institutional racism in the Council itself': quoted in J. Gyford, *The Politics of Local Socialism* (above, n. 1), 49.

equality targets and then devised special training schemes and altered recruitment practices in an attempt to realize them.[231] Many of these policies were pioneered by the London Borough of Lambeth, in which 30 per cent of the population is black. In 1978 Lambeth set equality targets and by the 1980s had achieved some conspicuous changes. Herman Ouseley noted that, whereas 'only 2 per cent of black households got the best quality accommodation in 1978, more than 30 per cent did so by 1981'; and this was accomplished not by 'positive discrimination' but simply by a race adviser ensuring 'that offers were made in accordance with needs and entitlements'.[232] Also, between 1978 and 1985 the proportion of the staff of the council from ethnic minorities increased from 8 per cent to 25 per cent.[233] Authorities adopting such policies also tended to adopt a firm policy of evicting tenants found guilty of racial harassment[234] and to require contractors to demonstrate compliance with the Race Relations Act.

What is particularly distinctive about such initiatives is the extent to which the local authority seeks, not so much to use its principal statutory powers, but rather to use its institutional power to achieve its policy objectives. Race is not the only initiative of this character. It may also be adopted in relation to policies on women or, perhaps most contentiously, in the pursuit of particular ideological objectives, such as those which cause us to reflect on the manner in which power relations have traditionally been bound up in municipal schemes. Examples of such policies include the renaming of streets, parks and municipal buildings or the use of town-twinning schemes as an expression of solidarity.[235] In order to examine the legal significance of the use of this power of *dominium*, the critical dimensions must first be identified. These appear to be those of ownership, employment, procurement and investment.

Ownership

The potential which local authorities possess to employ the economic power derived from their ownership and control of resources in furtherance of their

---

[231] For the statutory foundations of such policies see Race Relations Act 1976, ss. 5(a) (general occupational qualifications), 35 (special needs provisions), 37 (training and educational provision) and 38 (employment and training provision).

[232] H. Ouseley, 'Local Authority Race Initiatives' in Boddy and Fudge (ed.), *Local Socialism?* (above, n. 1), 133 at 150. See also, id., *The System* (London, 1981).

[233] Lansley, Goss and Wolmar, *Councils in Conflict* (above, n. 1), 124.

[234] Ibid., 125.

[235] See Lansley, Goss and Wolmar, *Councils in Conflict* (above, n. 1), 67–9. This ideological aspect was exaggerated, distorted and fabricated by sections of the media and used to promote an anti-Labour campaign. See, e.g., ibid., 126–7: 'Gradually . . . Labour's anti-racist policies became a major source of "loony left" attacks. Throughout 1986, the *Sun*, the *Daily Mail* and the *Mail on Sunday* ran a series of bizarre allegations about London boroughs, most of which centred on race. It was claimed, for example, that "Bernie Grant's Haringey" had banned the use of black dustbin liners as racist; that Hackney, Haringey and Islington Councils had banned the nursery rhyme "Baa Baa Black Sheep"; that Brent had paid for free trips for unemployed black youths to go to Cuba; that Camden had banned the word "sunshine" as racially offensive; that Haringey was committed to teaching West Indian dialect in schools. A study of ten of these stories by the Media Research Group of Goldsmiths College, London, found all to be either inventions or deliberate distortions.'

social and economic policies is immense. While this economic power is bounded by certain statutory duties or general legal principles applicable to administrative decision-making, the limits to such local authority action remained, in many areas, untested. To what extent, it might be asked, could local authorities use this power of *dominium* to promote specific ideological objectives? This issue has come to be fully reviewed in the courts only since the 1980s.

The leading authority on this question is *Wheeler* v. *Leicester City Council*,[236] a case concerning a dispute arising from the council's decision to prohibit Leicester Rugby Football Club from continuing to use a pitch owned by the authority. This ban resulted from the council's belief that the club had not aligned itself wholeheartedly with the council's stance of opposition to a tour of South Africa by the English Rugby Football Union. In seeking to understand the council's decision we might note that the British Government was a signatory to the Gleneagles Agreement of 1977. The Government, consequently, had undertaken to take every practical step to discourage sporting contact or competition between its nationals and those from South Africa. Furthermore, in 1982 Leicester City Council had adopted the principle of this Agreement. Since around 25 per cent of the population of Leicester was of Asian or Afro-Caribbean origin, this decision may be understood as one which reflected not only the beliefs of city councillors, but also the special interests of a substantial proportion of the local community. In these circumstances, it was perhaps not surprising that the council took the view that the rugby tour would constitute an affront to the city's ethnic minority population. Paying particular regard to their statutory duty to ensure that 'their various functions are carried out with due regard to the need . . . to promote . . . good relations between persons of different racial groups',[237] the council thus asked the rugby club to denounce the tour and to discourage three of its players from participating. The club's response, which denounced apartheid but stated that individual players, being amateurs, had freedom of choice to make their own decisions, was not felt by the council to be adequate.

The council's decision to suspend for 12 months the club's use of a recreation ground owned by the authority was challenged by way of judicial review. Both the Divisional Court and the Court of Appeal held that the ambit of section 71 of the Race Relations Act 1976 was not limited to the internal organization of the council's affairs and that they were entitled, when exercising their discretionary powers in relation to the recreation ground, to have regard to the purposes in section 71. They also held that the council's view, that a ban on a prominent club which had declined to condemn the South African tour could serve to promote race relations, was neither perverse nor unreasonable in accordance with *Wednesbury* principles.

On appeal to the House of Lords, however, this decision was reversed. Whilst accepting the interpretation of the lower courts on the ambit of section 71, their Lordships held that the council's actions were unreasonable in the *Wednesbury*

[236] [1985] 1 AC 1054. [237] Race Relations Act 1976, s. 71.

sense, amounted to a form of procedural impropriety and constituted a misuse of power. The rationale for this decision was, however, rather ambiguous, especially since the manner in which the council arrived at its decision had never been a central issue and the characterization of the council's decision as perverse appeared highly contentious. As one commentator put it, 'the House of Lords seems to have acted as a court of appeal from the Leicester City Council'.[238] The key issue seemed to be that of the misuse of power. The council, it was suggested, misused their powers by seeking to punish the club when it had 'done nothing wrong'.[239] Struggling to find an appropriate language, Lord Templeman reminded the House that 'the laws of this country are not like the laws of Nazi Germany'.[240] 'A private individual or a private organisation', his Lordship continued, 'cannot be obliged to display zeal in the pursuit of an object sought by a public authority and cannot be obliged to publish views dictated by a public authority.'[241] However, in refusing to follow the line of Browne-Wilkinson LJ's dissenting judgment in the Court of Appeal which addressed the dispute as a constitutional issue affecting fundamental rights,[242] the House exhibited some difficulty in fashioning a coherent and convincing judgment.

Browne-Wilkinson LJ, acknowledging implicitly that the polarization of political attitudes had had the effect of diminishing the effect of conventional practices, sought a remedy in a reinvigoration of the common law rights. He posed a basic question: can general powers conferred on an elected body for the administration of public property lawfully be used to punish those who lawfully decline to support the views held by that public body? This issue was, however, fudged by the House. Lord Templeman, for example, simply remarked that their decision 'does not mean that the council is bound to allow its property to be used by a racist organisation or any organisation which, by its actions or its words, infringes the letter *or the spirit* of the Race Relations Act 1976'.[243] The case seemed only to highlight the difficulties which the judiciary experience in reviewing the exercise of *dominium* powers. The courts seem to be required either to follow Browne-Wilkinson LJ in adopting a novel form of rights discourse or are rather inevitably drawn into the business of second-guessing the decision of the local authority. There are certain areas in which the issue might appear relatively clear.[244] But there are others which are ambiguous.[245]

The logic of this more active approach adopted by the courts can be seen at play in *R* v. *Somerset CC, ex parte Fewings*,[246] a case in which the court

---

[238] T.R.S. Allan, 'Racial Harmony, Public Policy and Freedom of Speech' (1986) 49 MLR 121, 123.
[239] [1985] AC 1054, 1079 (per Lord Templeman).   [240] Ibid., at 1080.
[241] Ibid.   [242] Ibid., 1061.   [243] Ibid., 1081 [emphasis supplied].
[244] See, e.g., *Webster* v. *Southwark LBC* [1983] QB 698 (local authority, contrary to s. 82 of the Representation of the People Act 1984, refused to grant the National Front the use of a hall in which to hold an election meeting).
[245] See, e.g., *R* v. *Barnet LBC, ex p. Johnson* (1990) 89 LGR 581 (consent to use council-owned park for community festival subject to conditions that land not to be used in connection with any political activity whatsoever struck down on grounds of uncertainty and discrimination).
[246] (1994) 92 LGR 674 (Div.Ct); [1995] 3 All ER 20 (CA).

addressed the question of whether the council was empowered to ban deer-hunting on council-owned land. Starting from the principle that a public body 'enjoys no such thing as an unfettered discretion',[247] Laws J in the Divisional Court identified the key issue as follows: 'was the subjective opinion of the majority of the councillors voting, that deer hunting is morally repulsive, a consideration which at law the council was entitled to regard as relevant?'[248] Laws J, taking the view that the question of whether or not hunting should be banned was an issue for the national legislature, concluded that the council's existing statutory powers, which enabled them to acquire land and take measures for 'the benefit, improvement or development of their area',[249] did not authorize decisions of this nature. At this stage, we might simply note that, although purporting to determine the limits of a statutory power, Laws J was also settling the effective boundaries of an institution of government. Although the decision of the Divisional Court was, by a majority, upheld on appeal, the Court of Appeal nevertheless adopted a less forthright stance, with their judgment hinging on a holding that the governing statutory provision had not properly been drawn to the attention of decision-makers.[250] Like *Wheeler*, *Fewings* seems to reflect judicial ambivalence towards the appropriate mode of construing the powers of local authorities: either a rigorous vocabulary of right/duty is utilized which has the effect of strictly limiting local authority discretionary power or the issue is, in effect, fudged.[251]

Employment

When vested with statutory responsibilities, local authorities have generally been required 'to secure the provision of' particular services to the locality. This formulation thus left the local authority free to decide whether to provide the service directly or to contract with the private sector. During the post-war period, however, local authorities have generally relied on directly-employed staff for the provision of core services and consequently have become major employers of labour. Furthermore, particularly as a result of the decline in manufacturing and the rise in unemployment from 1.5m to 3m between 1980 and 1983, local authorities often became the largest single employers in their areas and provided the main source of new employment opportunities. In this climate the objective of socialist authorities was primarily defensive: to retain employment opportunities and to ensure that the authority acted as model employers.

In this respect the policies were similar to those of Poplarism during the 1920s. The general environment had, however, substantially changed. Wage

---

[247] Ibid., 687.   [248] Ibid., 686.

[249] Local Government Act 1972, s. 120.

[250] This was the view of Sir Thomas Bingham MR who explicitly expressed no view on whether the same decision could have been reached on proper grounds. Simon Brown LJ held that the decision was within the local authority's powers, while Swinton-Thomas LJ held, to the contrary, that the ban could not fall within the power.

[251] See further ch. 7, 411–16.

negotiations in local government had become the subject of national agreements through the vehicle of a joint body, the Local Authorities Conditions of Service Advisory Body (LACSAB).[252] The main pressure to abandon these arrangements has tended to come from the Conservative Government, which felt that national agreements imposed a restraint on market forces and wished to see wage rates more closely linked to local economic conditions. Thus, although a related issue emerged when Camden LBC decided in 1979 to settle locally a national strike of local authority manual workers on terms which turned out to be favourable to their workforce,[253] the main employment policies of the new municipal social- ist authorities have generally been those which seek to protect the authority's employment base.

This protectionist objective was, however, subjected to a range of challenges from the Government. First, there were the general pressures to reduce the size of the local authority workforce which flowed both from financial constraints arising from reforms to the grant system and as a result of the extending influ- ence of value-for-money audit.[254] Many socialist authorities adopted policies of not making their employees compulsorily redundant and therefore, when re- quired to make savings because of financial restrictions, introduced voluntary redundancy schemes. Such schemes tended to include severance payments which were substantially higher than statutory requirements. In *Allsop* v. *North Tyneside MBC*,[255] however, the legality of such payments was successfully challenged by the auditor. In this case, the Court of Appeal held that the general discretionary powers of local authorities to appoint staff and and do anything incidental to the discharge of their functions did not empower local authorities to make enhanced redundancy payments to employees.

In addition to these general restrictions, a range of specific measures were introduced. The earliest were the reforms in 1980 which required local authority direct labour organizations to operate as a trading service; these organizations were also subject to statutory arrangements concerning financial accountability and the Secretary of State was empowered to close down any organization which failed to meet centrally devised financial objectives.[256] Public transport undertakings were also obliged to operate on a commercial basis at arm's length from local authorities in 1985.[257] Such reforms, especially when operated in

---

[252] See R.A.W. Rhodes, *The National World of Local Government* (London, 1985) ch. 5.

[253] In *Pickwell* v. *Camden LBC* [1983] QB 962 the Divisional Court refused to grant the auditor a declaration that the authority's decision was unlawful, stating that the issue for the court was not whether Camden had made a bad bargain but whether the evidence established that no reasonable local authority could have made a settlement on such terms. See further ch. 4, 248–50.

[254] See ch. 2, 89–91, 112–13.   [255] (1992) 90 LGR 462.

[256] Local Government, Planning and Land Act 1980, Pt. III. See M. Loughlin, *Local Government in the Modern State* 152–4; N. Flynn, 'Direct Labour Organization' in S. Ranson, G. Jones and K. Walsh (eds.), *Between Centre and Locality: the politics of public policy* (London, 1983), ch. 7. The Secretary of State, for example, closed down the London Borough of Haringey's DLO in 1986 after it had failed to meet designated financial targets.

[257] Transport Act 1985, Pts. IV and V.

conjunction with a growing interest by the centre in requiring local authorities to 'contract out' certain aspects of service provision to the private sector, posed a major threat to the authority's employment base.

These measures were strongly resisted by many local authorities for a number of reasons. First, given local unemployment rates, concern was expressed about the likely impact of labour force reductions not only on local households but also on the local economy. Further, local authority workforces had been established precisely because the private sector had refused to observe fair wage clauses, grant trades union recognition or, more recently, develop equal opportunities policies. Contracting out thus seemed likely to result, not only in a reduced workforce, but also in significant reductions in the wages and conditions of the relatively poorly paid workers who were retained.[258] Furthermore, this seems to have been the result, notwithstanding the legal protections accorded to workers under European law.[259] Though the socialist local authorities engaged in a general campaign during the mid 1980s,[260] their activities did little to prevent the extension of compulsory competitive tendering to a broad range of local authority services in the Local Government Act 1988.

Procurement

Although local authorities have traditionally relied on directly employed staff to provide core services, they have always engaged in a significant amount of

[258] See, e.g., K. Escott and D. Whitfield, *The Gender Impact of CCT in Local Government*, Equal Opportunities Commission Research Discussion Series No. 12 (Manchester, 1995). This research shows that, not only has employment in services subject to CCT under the 1988 Act been significantly reduced, but that, since most of these jobs were undertaken by women, competitive tendering has had the effect of significantly increasing economic inequalities between men and women.

[259] Thus, the Acquired Rights Directive 77/187, which was given effect in the UK by the Transfer of Undertakings (Protection of Employment) Regulations 1981 (TUPE), was designed to protect the rights of employees in the event of a relevant transfer of an undertaking to a new employer. There has been a great deal of confusion over the applicability of TUPE to CCT. See, e.g., *Dr Sophie Redmond Stichting* v. *Bartol* (1992) IRLR 366 (ECJ); *Christel Schmidt* v. *Spar und Leihkasse der Früheren Ämter Bordesholm Kiel und Conshagen* (1994) IRLR 302 (ECJ); *Dines* v. *Initial Health Services Ltd and Pall Mall Services Ltd* (1995) ICR 11 (CA). This confusion has been exacerbated by the fact that the European Commission also successfully brought an action against the UK Government for incorrectly implementing the Directive: *European Commission* v. *United Kingdom*, Case C/382/92 (8 June 1994). It should also be noted that, in anticipation of the success of the Commission's action, TUPE was significantly amended by the Trade Union Reform and Employment Rights Act 1993, s. 33 and the CCT regulations were amended: Local Government (Direct Service Organisations) (Competition) Regulations 1993, SI 1993 No. 848. Though these legal developments may ultimately place the future of the Government's CCT programme in jeopardy, their impact on those activities subject to this regime in the 1980s is likely to be limited.

[260] In November 1983, for example, Sheffield City Council organized a national conference on 'The Privatisation of Council Services'. The Council also commissioned a 'privatisation audit' which concluded that the privatization of 12 services (including cleaning, catering, refuse collection and parks and vehicle maintenance) would result in 1900 job losses and, through the multiplier effect, a further 548 jobs in the private sector. Though reducing the council's costs, it calculated that, over a five year period, the public cost of contracting out services in Sheffield would be £17m. See SCAT, *The Public Cost of Private Contractors* (London, 1985).

contracting for the provision of goods and services. Through this power of procurement local authorities are potentially able to exercise a significant amount of economic influence. In 1983, for example, it was estimated that Sheffield City Council was spending around £20m on contracts with 900 local firms.[261] During the 1980s, socialist local authorities began to examine how they might be able to use this purchasing power to assist them in the realization of their social and economic policy objectives.

What they discovered was that local authorities apparently possessed a great deal of discretion in determining how, and on what terms, services would be provided by contractors. The basic requirements were simply that they were required to make standing orders governing contracts for the supply of goods or materials or for the execution of works[262] and to maintain a list of persons willing to carry out construction and maintenance work.[263] Authorities thus began to amend standing orders and conditions of contract so as to ensure that private contractors complied with council policies and practices. In particular, contractors have been required to provide an acceptable health and safety policy statement, to comply with nationally negotiated pay and conditions agreements, to belong to an appropriate trade or employers' association (on the assumption that this helped to ensure compliance with pay and conditions provisions), to maintain adequate training programmes and to provide records to demonstrate compliance with anti-discrimination legislation.

Such controls were justified, especially in the context of competitive tendering between the local authority's direct labour organization and private contractors, on the ground of ensuring fair competition. In 1983, for example, direct labour organizations, though employing only 12 per cent of construction workers, provided 35 per cent of training places.[264] Some authorities even established special units to draft contract documentation, vet companies applying for acceptance on the approved list and monitor their performance.[265] Contract compliance was thus seen as a powerful device for protecting pay and conditions and for promoting equal opportunities in an environment in which the Government was encouraging the contracting out of service provision.[266]

Aspects of these procurement policies were subject to legal challenge in a number of cases. The first case, however, was not directly concerned with contract compliance arrangements but rather with the politics of solidarity. In 1986, the decision of Times Newspapers to move to Wapping had brought about a strike of their employees. When the newspaper group then considered the strikers

[261] D. Blunkett and G. Green, *Building from the Bottom* (above, n. 45), 11.
[262] Local Government Act 1972, s. 135(2).
[263] Local Government, Planning and Land Act 1980, s. 9(4)(a).
[264] W. Hall, 'Contract Compliance at the GLC' (1986) vol. 12 no. 4 *Local Government Studies* 17, 21.
[265] Ibid.
[266] See K. Minogue and J. O'Grady, 'Contracting Out Local Authority Services in Britain' (1985) vol. 11 no. 3 *Local Government Studies* 35.

to have repudiated their contracts of employment and proceeded to dismiss them, a long and acrimonious dispute ensued. As a gesture of support for the Times workforce, over 30 local authorities decided to ban the publications of Times Newspapers from their public libraries. This action resulted in Times Newspapers bringing an application for judicial review against the London boroughs of Camden, Ealing and Hammersmith and Fulham on the grounds that the decisions constituted an abuse of power and a breach of statutory duty. In *R* v. *Ealing LBC, ex parte Times Newspapers Ltd*,[267] the Divisional Court, follow- ing *Wheeler*, held that the ban had been imposed for an ulterior purpose; in the words of Watkins LJ, '[t]hat purpose was set by a political attitude to a so-called workers' struggle against a tyrannical employer with the object of punishing the employer'.[268] Since local authorities were under a statutory duty 'to provide a comprehensive and efficient library service for all persons desiring to make use thereof'[269] the court also held that the decision to remove these newspapers was one which no rational local authority could have thought was open to it to impose in discharge of its statutory duty.[270]

In *R* v. *Lewisham LBC, ex parte Shell UK Ltd*[271] the limits of contract com- pliance mechanisms were more directly examined. This dispute arose from the decision of the council to adopt a policy of boycotting all Shell products subject to alternative products being available on reasonable terms. The purpose of the boycott was to apply pressure on the Shell group to withdraw its interests in South Africa; such action being based on the council's anti-apartheid policy which it justified as part of its general duty to promote good race relations under section 71 of the Race Relations Act 1976. The council had sought to distinguish the case of *Wheeler* by focusing 'their judgment as to the effects on race rela- tions in their Borough of taking or not taking the action under consideration'[272] and thus attempted to restrict the issue to a *Wednesbury* challenge. The court accepted ('though on the present evidence the matter must be very near the line'[273]) that the council's decision not to continue to trade with Shell was not unreasonable in the *Wednesbury* sense. Nevertheless, the court held that the council had acted unlawfully. The reason was that the court took the view that *Wheeler* had established the proposition that 'a council cannot use its statutory powers in order to punish a body or person who has done nothing contrary to

---

[267] (1987) 85 LGR 316.   [268] Ibid., 326.

[269] Public Libraries and Museums Act 1964, s. 7(1).

[270] It might be noted that the 1964 Act imposed a duty on the Secretary of State 'to superin- tend . . . the public library service' (s. 1) and vested the Secretary of State with powers of investi- gation, default and direction enforceable by order of mandamus (s. 10). The respondents' argument (following *Pasmore* v. *Oswaldtwistle UDC* [1898] AC 387: see ch. 1, 49) that the courts should not intervene was, however, rejected on the ground that 'the statutory remedy involves a cumbersome procedure which is wholly unsuited to meet the requirements of a necessarily swift resolution of the issues arising out of the ban': 85 LGR 316, 331.

[271] [1988] 1 All ER 938.

[272] Opinion of Lord Gifford QC to Lewisham LBC: ibid., 945.

[273] Ibid., 952.

English law'[274] and thus held that 'the council was acting unfairly and in a manner which requires the court to intervene'.[275]

This conversion of *Wheeler* into a distinct head of review is bolstered by a case in 1988 in which the Secretary of State for Employment successfully sought judicial review of Liverpool City Council's decision to use its *dominium* powers through the award of grants to voluntary bodies in furtherance of its policy of opposing the Employment Training Scheme.[276] The council opposed that scheme on a number of grounds including the quality of the training, rates of pay, conditions of employment and the fact that it did not have trade union support. The Employment Secretary accepted that he could not compel the council to support the scheme but argued that its policy of amending its conditions of grant aid to ensure that no organization in receipt of grant took part in the scheme constituted an abuse of its discretionary powers. Here, the court had no difficulty in concluding that, although the council acted in good faith and believed that, 'as seen through its eyes', it had 'the best interests of Liverpool at heart',[277] the purpose of the action was 'the punishment or coercion of those voluntary organisations and others who would not "toe the line"'[278] and that, on the *Wheeler* principle, the policy was unlawful.

Though these judicial decisions were important in determing the limits of the local authority's use of its powers of procurement, the primary restrictions on this general contracting power were gradually imposed by statute. The Government initially moved rather slowly. In 1980 local authorities became bound by competition law so that any anti-competitive practice relating to the securing of services could be investigated and controlled by the Director-General of Fair Trading.[279] Also, after 1980 it became unlawful to require trade union recognition and trade union membership as a condition of a contract.[280] But the early controls on competitive tendering which were applied to certain types of works undertaken by direct labour organizations were relatively lax.[281] By the mid 1980s, however, it became clear that the Government wished to promote more extensive use of contracting for service provision in accordance with strictly commercial criteria.[282]

A good indication of the model of the tendering process which the Govenment had in mind was apparent in the Transport Act 1985. This Act deregulated local public transport provision, radically reorganized the corporate structure of

---

[274] Ibid., 951.   [275] Ibid., 952.

[276] *R v. Liverpool City Council, ex p. Secretary of State for Employment* (1990) 154 LG Rev 118.

[277] Ibid., 119.   [278] Ibid.

[279] Competition Act 1980, s. 2.   [280] Employment Act 1980, ss. 12–14.

[281] Local Government, Planning and Land Act 1980, s. 9. This regime did not restrict the authority's existing power to specify contract conditions or determine contracting procedures; it did not impose any duty to award the contract to the lowest tenderer (or to justify a decision not to do so); and vested in the Secretary of State the rather blunt supervisory power of closing down a direct labour organization which failed to meet specified financial objectives.

[282] See Department of the Environment, *Competition in the Provision of Local Authority Services* (London, 1985).

municipal bus undertakings and fundamentally altered the general responsibilities of local authorities in respect of public transport. The objectives were to stimulate private competition through deregulation, to ensure that competition worked by breaking up the market dominance of the public sector operators, and to recast the duties of local authorities away from the provision of network subsidies and towards subsidies for particular services. Tendering thus became critical since any service subsidies were to be allocated by tender. Consequently, in addition to placing local authorities under a general duty 'so to conduct themselves as not to inhibit competition',[283] the 1985 Act established a strict statutory framework governing the tendering process. This prohibited the local authority from including 'conditions with respect to the terms of employment of persons to be employed in providing any service' in any invitation to tender, required the authority to determine which tender to accept 'solely by reference to what in their view is the most effective and economic application of the funds at their disposal', and required reasons to be given for their decision.[284]

This type of restrictive framework was adopted when the Government considerably extended the range of compulsory competitive tendering for local authority service provision in the Local Government Act 1988.[285] Local authorities, when engaging in tendering, are under a general duty to refrain from doing anything 'having the effect or intended or likely to have the effect of restricting, distorting or preventing competition'.[286] They are obliged to give reasons for their decisions on the award of tenders,[287] and the Secretary of State is vested with very broad powers to intervene.[288]

Most importantly in relation to procurement powers, section 17 of the 1988 Act prohibits local authorities from taking into account 'non-commercial considerations' in relation to any contracts for the supply of goods, materials and services and for the execution of works. Matters prescribed by the Act to be 'non-commercial considerations' include terms and conditions of employment (including training and the use of self-employed labour), association with 'irrelevant fields of government policy', involvement in industrial disputes, international activities, political and industrial affiliations, and financial support for any institution.[289] In promoting this provision the Secretary of State argued that 'political discrimination in the award of contracts is an offensive and growing

---

[283] Transport Act 1985, ss. 57(2), 63(7), 92(1).

[284] Transport Act 1985, ss. 89(3), 89(7) and 90(3).

[285] The principle of CCT has since been extended beyond the original seven designated activities in the 1988 Act: see SI 1989 No. 2488; Leasehold Reform, Housing and Urban Development Act 1993, ss. 129–133; Local Government Act 1992, Pt. I. See ch. 2, 105–6.

[286] Local Government Act 1988, ss. 4(5), 7(7).   [287] Ibid., ss. 12, 20.

[288] Ibid., s. 13. See, e.g., *R* v. *Secretary of State for the Environment, ex p. Haringey LBC* (1994) 92 LGR 538 (unsuccessful application to challenge Secretary of State's order to remove the authority's power to collect refuse on the ground that the authority had engaged in an anti-competitive practice prohibited under s. 7(7)).

[289] Ibid., s. 17(4). The Secretary of State is empowered by s. 19(1) to specify additional non-commercial considerations.

practice' and that the Government thus intended to ban 'the unreasonable use of their contractual muscle by certain authorities'.[290] As subsequent litigation indicated,[291] these statutory restrictions effectively curtailed the attempts of socialist local authorities to use their powers of procurement to further their general social and economic policies.

Investment

As part of the general strategy of harnessing *dominium* power to the realization of the local authority's social and economic policy objectives, socialist local authorities also engaged in a re-evaluation of local government as an investor in the local economy. During the early 1980s, it was evident that local authorities were the biggest institutions then investing in Britain's provincial cities and attempts were thus made to ensure that this investment was adequately planned so that investment strategies were compatible with the general policies of the authority. This reappraisal took a variety of forms. Sheffield City Council, for example, felt that their Estates Department had adopted a rent-maximization view of its role which may have been detrimental to the general policies of the authority, and sought a solution in a reorganization of the Council's committee structure so that the department no longer reported to a separate committee but to the Planning and Environment Committee. Further, as we have seen, the establishment of local enterprise boards in the early 1980s was often justified on the need to invest funds in local industry in order to protect the local economy.

However, in recognition of the fact that even the local authorities' financial resources were small in relation to the scale of the economic challenges facing many major cities, efforts were made during the early 1980s, particularly by the enterprise boards, to secure the co-operation of local authority pension funds in their investment strategies.[292] Attempts to tap these potentially huge sums, however, proved difficult. Blunkett and Green, for example, while reporting that West Midlands County Council had 'gained for productive local investment a proportion of the new [pension fund] money flowing each year into its workers fund', also conceded that 'it has been a long and hard struggle, hedged around by narrow definitions of what is an acceptable return on an investment'.[293] These difficulties were reinforced as a result of the Vice-Chancellor's reaffirmation, in

---

[290] N. Ridley, HC Debs, vol. 119 cols. 83, 86 (6 July 1987); quoted in M. Radford, 'Competition Rules: the Local Government Act 1988' (1988) 51 MLR 746, 756.

[291] *R v. Islington LBC, ex parte Building Employers Confederation, The Independent*, 29 March 1989 (Divisional Court struck down several clauses in the council's Main Contracts Clauses document including those requiring contractors, in the performance of their contracts, to comply with the Sex Discrimination Act 1975, the Factories Act 1961 and certain health, safety and welfare regulations).

[292] For a discussion see R. Murray, 'Pension funds and local authority investments' (1983) 20 *Capital and Class* 89; R. Minns, 'Pension funds – an alternative view' (1983) 20 *Capital and Class* 104.

[293] Blunkett and Green, *Building from the Bottom* (above, n. 45), 12.

Cowan v *Scargill*,[294] of the principle that the duty of trustees was to act in the best interests of their beneficiaries and that their best interests 'are normally their best financial interests'.[295]

Such difficulties were compounded when certain local authorities began to explore the possibility of engaging in dis-investment strategies in relation to firms which, for example, retained links with the apartheid regime in South Africa. Here, the *Wheeler* principle, it seemed, would also apply directly to such action.[296]

Non-Compliance

It has generally been recognized, throughout the twentieth century, that, because central and local government are locked into a structure of mutual dependency, the relationship must be understood, if not in terms of partnership, then at least as operating within a framework of negotiation and bargaining. As we have seen,[297] as a result of the various tensions within this system and the determination to promote particular economic and social policies, the Conservative Governments of the 1980s have been forced to reconstruct the relationship in a more explicitly hierachical form. Though this caused conflict throughout the system, it has had a particular impact on those authorities promoting the policies of municipal socialism. The social and economic policies of municipal socialism, having run counter to those of the Government, became the particular target for many of the interventionist powers acquired by the Government under the recent tide of new legislation. Such action caused many socialist authorities to contemplate new versions of the Poplarist tactic of outright refusal to comply with Government directives.

Non-compliance has most commonly involved the exploitation of ambiguities within the statutory framework governing central–local government relations. With the collapse in authority of the conventional understandings and as a result of the consequential turn to law, numerous gaps and ambiguities were identified in a framework which had never been designed to prescribe detailed regulation of the central–local relationship. One of the most important examples of this practice was the manner in which local authorities devised new techniques of accounting in an effort to circumvent the increasingly restrictive regime of local

---

[294] [1985] 1 Ch. 270 (this case arose from the decision of the union representatives on the mineworkers' pension scheme to question certain investments, including those in oil and gas interests).

[295] Ibid., 287.

[296] Lewisham LBC, e.g., co-ordinated Joint Action Against Apartheid (JAAA) which represented 18 local councils. In one of JAAA's letters it was stated: 'In view of the success that Councils' boycotts have had on Barclays, I would urge your Council now to seriously consider severing its links with the Shell Company, including disinvesting any shareholdings that your Council may have ...'. See [1988] 1 All ER 938, 943.

[297] See ch. 2 above.

government finance devised by the Government during the 1980s.[298] This section, however, examines the adoption by socialist authorities of an explicit policy of direct refusal to comply with statutory requirements. These practices will be illustrated by reference to the issues of civil defence and rate-making.

Civil defence

Section 2(1) of the Civil Defence Act 1948 imposes a duty on local authorities to 'perform such functions as may be prescribed by the designated Minister' and the 1974 Regulations required local authorities, inter alia, to make plans for the continuation of essential services in wartime.[299] This responsibility generally fell to the Public Protection Committee of the county council and was not a particularly controversial or highly politicized business. During the early 1980s, however, the situation changed. The main reason for the change was the emergence of the peace movement. One major catalyst leading to the re-invigoration of that movement was a NATO review conducted in 1979 which had resulted in the decision to station American-controlled Cruise missiles in Britain. Against the background of these defence decisions, the Government also undertook a review of civil defence and issued the document, *Protect and Survive*. This document was viewed by the peace movement as an attempt on the part of the Government to use civil defence policy to enhance the credibility of NATO's strategy of deterrence. The peace movement, as an ingredient in a general campaign, thus tried to persuade local authorities not to co-operate in civil defence activities.

This campaign was quite successful. One symbolic indicator of its success was the fact that by 1985 around 170 local authorities in Britain had declared their areas to be 'nuclear free zones'.[300] A much more practical indication, however, is to be seen in the failure of the Government's civil defence exercise, 'Operation Hardrock'. This exercise, scheduled to take place in 1982, had to be cancelled owing to the refusal of 20 of the 54 county councils to participate.[301] In this situation there was little that the Government could do since the 1974 Regulations had not incorporated any duty on local authorities to keep civil defence plans under review and the Regulations did not vest any powers in the Home Secretary to compel authorities to make adequate provision.

The Home Office responded to this stance of non-compliance by issuing new civil defence regulations which imposed much more precise duties on local authorities.[302] These regulations required all local authorities to take part in training exercises, to keep plans up to date, to provide emergency control centres,

---

[298] See ch. 6 below.   [299] Civil Defence (Planning) Regulations 1974, SI 1974 No. 70.

[300] See I. Henderson, 'Local Government's Role in Emergency Planning' (1986) vol. 12 no. 4 *Local Government Studies* 10; L. Hilliard, 'Local Government, Civil Defence and Emergency Planning: Heading for Disaster?' (1986) 49 MLR 476.

[301] Ibid.

[302] Civil Defence (General Local Authority Functions) Regulations 1983, SI 1983 No. 1634.

to train staff and to recruit community volunteers. The regulations also required plans to be submitted to central government by the end of 1985. Throughout 1985 many local authorities indicated that they would refuse to comply, thus raising the prospect that the Home Secretary might be obliged to exercise default powers and appoint commissioners to undertake the exercise.[303] While this would not have been the first occasion on which commissioners had been appointed for this purpose,[304] the potential scale of defiance was much greater than on previous occasions.

In the event, though some authorities dragged their heels, were late in producing their submission and drafted plans of a rather rudimentary nature, the Home Office did not find it necessary to use its default powers. When faced with the ultimate sanction of the centre appointing commissioners to replace them, the local authorities saw little alternative to that of grudging compliance.

Rate-making in Liverpool, 1983/84

The most serious threat in recent times to the stability of the local government system materialized as a result of the stance adopted by certain Labour-controlled local authorities to the impact of financial controls imposed by expenditure targets and rate-capping. The key tactic, that of refusing to set a rate on the financial terms specified by central government, was one which exploited gaps and ambiguities in the legal framework of central–local relations.

This tactic owed much to the action of Liverpool City Council in relation to the fixing of its budget and rate for 1984/85. After almost a decade in which no party had an overall majority, Labour gained control of the City Council after the 1983 local elections. At the elections, Labour had given manifesto commitments not only to defend public services, create 1,000 new jobs, build council houses and reduce council house rents but also to refuse to increase rates to compensate for cuts in grants. From the outset it was clear that these commitments could not be achieved within the existing legal and financial framework. The situation was further exacerbated by the fact that the 1983/84 budget set by the previous Liberal administration had been achieved only by the adoption of certain creative accounting devices. This not only meant that actual expenditure was much higher than 'relevant expenditure' for grant purposes but it also placed additional pressures on the 1984/85 budget. Though the 1983/84 budget had been set at £218m, Labour in March 1984 proposed a budget of £262.4m. Further, though the impact of expenditure target grant penalties would mean a

---

[303] Civil Defence Act 1948, s. 2(1)(c).

[304] During the 1950s both Coventry and St Pancras refused to carry out their functions and commissioners were appointed to organize civil defence in these areas until the authorities capitulated. See: P.G. Richards, 'Questions about Local Authorities and Emergency Planning' (1979) vol. 5 no. 3 *Local Government Studies* 37.

grant of only £27.6m (as compared with £116m in 1983/84), they proposed a rate increase of only 9 per cent.[305]

Since local authorities are obliged to raise a rate sufficient to meet their estimated expenditure not met by other income,[306] this proposed budget was clearly unlawful. On 19 March the district auditor issued a report outlining the legal position and indicating that the proposed action was likely to amount to wilful misconduct which would expose the councillors to the risk of surcharge and disqualification.[307] At the budget meeting on 29 March, six Labour councillors refused to support the proposed budget and, there being no majority in favour of any proposal, the council entered 1984/85 without a budget or rate.

The City Council was able so to do for the simple reason that there was no statutory requirement that a rate be set by a particular date.[308] This thus provided the council with the opportunity of negotiating with the Government for a better deal. Nevertheless, it was also the case that the county council was entitled to take action to obtain its precept, whether by petitioning the Minister to appoint a receiver[309] or by way of judicial review.[310] Further, even though Labour-controlled Merseyside CC was not prepared to instigate these procedures, the Minister was also empowered to take such action. Since the Government not only decided against such legal action, but also continued to pay the City Council grant at a rate which assumed that it would meet its expenditure target, it was clear that the Government had determined on a conciliatory approach. Additional pressure was placed on the Government when, in the local elections in May, Labour was returned with an increased majority.[311] Negotiations continued throughout June and July and eventually, after certain concessions by the Government, on 11 July 1984, over three months into the year, Liverpool City Council fixed a budget and set a rate.

The council proclaimed the result a great victory,[312] a verdict endorsed by *The Times* whose leader column commenced with the statement that: 'Today in Liverpool municipal militancy is vindicated.' This leader went on to suggest that '[b]y exempting Liverpool from the consequences of spending above its target the government subverts its whole local government policy for the last five years'.[313] In fact, the position was fairly complex. The Secretary of State had

[305] See A. Midwinter, 'Setting the Rate – Liverpool Style' (1985) vol. 11 no. 3 *Local Government Studies* 25, 28.

[306] General Rates Act 1967, s. 2(1).

[307] L.C Stanford (District Auditor), *District Auditor's Report to the Liverpool City Council*, 19 March 1984 (pursuant to Local Government Finance Act 1982, s. 15).

[308] General Rate Act 1967, s. 2(1) (which stated that a rating authority must 'from time to time' make a rate); cf. s. 12(6) which requires precepting authorities to issue their precepts not less than twenty-one days before the beginning of the financial year.

[309] General Rate Act 1967, s. 15.   [310] *R. v. Poplar BC (No. 1)* [1922] 1 KB 72.

[311] This gave Labour a majority of 17, which meant that the 6 Labour councillors who voted against the March budget no longer held the balance of power.

[312] See, e.g., D. Hatton, *Inside Left* (London, 1988) ch. 6.

[313] 'Danegeld in Liverpool', *The Times*, 11 July 1984.

refused to exempt any item of expenditure for the purpose of assessing grant.[314] This was particularly important, since any attempt to do so would have had to apply to all local authorities,[315] and would affect the entire rate support grant settlement. The concessions made basically concerned aspects of capital expenditure and projects financed through specific grants. Thus, the Secretary of State agreed that a number of 'time-expired' Urban Programme projects which would otherwise have to be financed through the council's revenue budget could continue to be funded under the programme and that housing subsidy could continue to be paid on outstanding loan charges on council housing which had been demolished. These decisions involved a total cost to the Government of less than £10m. But, by taking projects out of the revenue budget and thus reducing the impact of grant penalties, they were worth around £20m to Liverpool City Council. In addition, although no firm assurances had been given, it was claimed that the Government had agreed to look favourably on Liverpool's capital spending programme for future years.[316]

As a result of these concessions, the City Council finally fixed a budget of £223m. In addition to the beneficial impact of Government concessions, this figure was achieved also by making certain downward revisions in the council's planned expenditure growth. Furthermore, notwithstanding the manifesto pledge to keep rates in line with inflation, it included a rate increase of 17 per cent.[317]

Rate-making and rate-capping

For many on the left, the stance adopted by Liverpool City Council had vindicated the use of a confrontational approach. Labour had assumed control of Liverpool in 1983 against a background not only of severe economic recession,[318] but also of the withdrawal of central government grants.[319] By refusing to set a rate on the financial terms set by the Government – and thus threatening

---

[314] Letter of P. Jenkin, Secretary of State for the Environment, to J. Hamilton, Leader of Liverpool City Council, 29 June 1984.

[315] Local Government Finance Act 1982, s. 8(4).

[316] 'I can give you an assurance that I will do my very best to ensure that allocations to Liverpool next year under the Housing Investment Programme and the Urban Programme, taken together, will enable the Council to make positive progress in dealing with the City's severe needs.' Letter from P. Jenkin to J. Hamilton, 29 June 1984.

[317] For a general assessment of the budget arrangements see A. Midwinter, 'Setting the Rate – Liverpool Style' 25 at 29–31.

[318] Unemployment in the city had risen from 39,000 in 1979 to 60,000 in 1983 and youth unemployment was recorded as almost 50 per cent in the 1981 census: see, Liverpool City Council, *Liverpool's Budget Crisis 1984: The Story of the Campaign* (Liverpool, 1984).

[319] Government rate support grants had decreased from £132.9m in 1975/76 to £115.8m in 1981/82 (in 1981/82 prices), which meant that RSG supported only 32.1 per cent of council expenditure in 1981/82 as contrasted with 38.9 per cent in 1975/76: Liverpool City Council, *Rates, Services and Jobs: the Campaign in Liverpool* (October 1983), Fig. 1 and Table 1. For a general analysis see P. Carmichael, *Central and Local Government Relations in the 1980s. Glasgow and Liverpool Compared.* (Aldershot, 1995), ch. 4.

to bring about a collapse of local government in Liverpool[320] – the City Council had placed the Government on the defensive. Rather than provoke a financial crisis by withholding grant or assert central control by seeking powers to appoint commissioners,[321] the Government adopted a conciliatory stance[322] and ultimately granted concessions to Liverpool. Liverpool's experience exerted a powerful influence on Labour-controlled local authorities which during 1984 were designated for rate-capping under the Rates Act 1984.

Throughout 1984, discussions took place within Labour local government circles about the possibility of engaging in a mass campaign of non-co-operation.[323] At this time, it was anticipated that the GLC and metropolitan county councils would be abolished in 1985 with transitional bodies consisting of borough and district nominees running the authorities in their final year.[324] The strategy thus emerged of developing a campaign, based on protecting jobs and services and promoting democracy, of both refusing to nominate representatives to interim bodies and of the rate-capped authorities refusing to set a rate. While it was declared that '[c]ollective action, achieving Government retreat, and not martyrdom, is the objective',[325] the difficulties of a strategy which threatened to bring about the collapse of local services could not be underestimated. When the Government abandoned its plans for transitional bodies, the non-co-operation strategy came to be fixed on rate-capping.

The Rates Act 1984 was the first clear example of the new style of tightly-drafted, directive local government legislation which severely limited the options available to a local authority.[326] If designated for rate-capping, an authority could apply to the Secretary of State for re-determination of its maximum expenditure level.[327] If it were to apply, however, not only was it required to

---

[320] On the legal issues surrounding the threat of local authority insolvency see: M. Grant, 'Rate-capping: the law and solvency', *Public Finance and Accountancy*, March 1984, at 19.

[321] See H. Clayton and D. Walker, 'Liverpool is told by Jenkin to borrow', *The Times*, 31 March 1984. The Government posessed no general power to replace elected local authorities with appointed commissioners. For a catalogue of the then existing default powers see: HC Debs, vol. 58 cols. 249–255w (11 April 1984).

[322] In a BBC radio interview after the results of the local elections Patrick Jenkin, the Secretary of State, said: 'There is no question of our even contemplating putting in commissioners until the situation has dramatically broken down in Liverpool, until the local council has shown beyond peradventure that they are not prepared to keep services going, they are not prepared to do what is necessary for the city to remain within the law.' *The Guardian*, 5 May 1984.

[323] The flavour of the debate may be gleaned from articles throughout 1984 in *New Socialist*. See, e.g., S. Weir, 'Raiders of the local state' (Jan./Feb., at 23); N. Fielding and P. Seyd, 'Cities in Revolt' (Sept., at 34); S. Hall, 'Face the Future' (Sept., at 37); F. Morrell and S. Bundred, 'No Short Cut' (Sept., at 40).

[324] See above, 161.

[325] D. Blunkett (Leader of Sheffield City Council and Chair of the Labour Party National Executive Committee Local Government Committee), 'Local Government Legislation. The Way Forward'. Paper to Labour Party Local Government Conference, *Forging the Links '84. A Strategy for Local Government*, Sheffield 6–7 July 1984.

[326] For an examination of the structure of the Act see M. Loughlin, *Local Government in the Modern State* (above, n. 38), 50–6. See further, ch. 5, 300–1.

[327] Rates Act 1984, s. 3(4).

provide such information as the Secretary of State may require, but, if the expenditure level were increased, the Secretary of State was empowered to impose 'such requirements relating to its expenditure or financial management as he thinks appropriate'.[328] Applying for re-determination thus amounted in effect to an invitation to the Secretary of State to undertake detailed scrutiny of the local authority's activities and to determine policies and priorities. In the light of these powers, the Labour authorities agreed that they would refuse to apply for re-determination and would only meet the Government collectively. Refusing to apply, however, also meant that it would prove almost impossible to subject the caps to legal challenge since the courts tend to require applicants to exhaust their statutory remedies before seeking judicial review.[329] The structure of the Act thus tended to push authorities opposed to capping into a stance of non-compliance.

Though the Labour authorities had agreed a strategy of non-compliance, there were in fact two distinct options. In addition to refusing to fix a rate, there existed the alternative of setting a limited rate but then embarking on a much higher spending programme, thus raising the prospect of local authority insolvency. That is, by assuming control over the rates, the Government not only brought about a fundamental change in the relationship between central and local government but also caused questions to be raised about the financial security systems of local authorities which had hitherto been underpinned primarily by the authority's unrestricted power to raise rates. The Rates Act 1984 for the first time raised the possibility of an unbridgeable gap developing between the expenditure of a local authority and the revenues available to it to meet its obligations. Furthermore, although this possibility had never entered into the design of financial security systems, audit procedures or judicial remedies, the 1984 Act contained no default powers.[330]

In July 1984, 18 authorities (17 of which were Labour-controlled) were designated.[331] In the following months, attention came to be focused on the 'no rate' rather than the 'deficit budget' option. Certain difficulties existed, however, in maintaining a collective stance on the former option. The most obvious concerned the fact that precepting authorities, having a statutory deadline, would be

---

[328] Ibid., s. 3(6).

[329] On the experience of the rate-capped local authorities seeking judicial review see ch. 5, 301–5.

[330] See further, M. Grant, *Rate-Capping and the Law* (London, 2nd edn, 1986), chs. 11–14.

[331] HC Debs, vol. 64, col. 828 (24 July 1984). The list included four precepting authorities (GLC, ILEA, Merseyside and South Yorkshire CCs); the London boroughs of Brent, Camden, Greenwich, Hackney, Haringey, Islington, Lambeth, Lewisham and Southwark; and the Labour-controlled districts of Basildon, Leicester, Sheffield and Thamesdown. It had been widely predicted that the criteria for designation would capture at least one non-Labour authority, not only to demonstrate the non-partiality of the procedure but also in the expectation that that authority would apply for re-determination and the procedures could be seen to operate fairly and benevolently. Conservative-controlled Portsmouth DC was duly designated. Expectations were confounded, however, when the council decided not to seek re-designation and agreed its limit.

in breach of statutory duty if they failed to set their precepts by 10 March[332] whereas the position of rating authorities, as the Liverpool episode illustrated, remained uncertain. On 19 February 1985, when leaders of rate-capped authorities met to discuss strategy, it became clear both that Merseyside CC and South Yorkshire CC would set a precept and that, before the financial year, the rating authorities would not be passing formal resolutions stating that they would refuse under any circumstances to set a rate. This left the GLC and ILEA exposed. ILEA at its meeting on 7 March approved a legal precept and with a majority of only four, the GLC Labour group faced difficulties in carrying any motion which would almost certainly result in surcharge and disqualification. After failing to resolve disagreements at its budget meeting on 8 March, the council reconvened on Sunday, 10 March, the last possible date for complying with the statutory deadline. As a result of various tensions within the Labour group, together with a degree of confusion, the GLC actually ended up, not only by setting a legal precept, but also in approving a precept which was below the maximum precept level.[333]

During March, most of the Labour-controlled rating authorities passed motions stating that it was impossible to set a rate 'at this time'. Indeed, though two of the rate-capped authorities had not proceeded with the strategy of non-compliance, the group was supported by Liverpool and Manchester who, though not rate-capped, contended that the impact of grant penalties made it impossible to set a rate which would enable them to protect jobs and services.[334] This time, however, it seemed clear that the Government would not be prepared to compromise. Furthermore, the courts were involved very speedily. On 5 March 1985, when granting leave to bring proceedings for judicial review against Hackney, the court granted interim relief in the form of orders prohibiting the council from making a rate demand contrary to its rate cap limit, from using any rates monies tendered by council tenants after 1 April until a lawful rate was set, and from using their temporary borrowing powers until a lawful rate was made.[335] This imposed immediate financial pressures on Hackney and served to place the other authorities on notice.

In granting interim relief, Mann J acknowledged that the case should be expedited but added that: 'It may be that this is the last occasion upon which the matter arises.'[336] Hackney, even though warned by the borough solicitor that the legal costs of defending the issue were prima facie surchargeable,[337] nevertheless continued to refuse to make a rate and on 16 April the application was heard. On this occasion, the court granted an order of mandamus requiring the

[332] General Rates Act 1967, s. 12(6).
[333] See 'Red-Faced Ken's Home Truths', *New Statesman*, 22 March 1985; J. Carvel, 'The panto-tragedy of the GLC rates vote', *The Guardian*, 14 March 1985.
[334] See, *The Guardian*, 5, 8 and 9 March 1985.
[335] *R* v. *Hackney LBC, ex p. Fleming* (Div.Ct.) 5 March 1985 (unreported).
[336] Ibid., transcript, 5.
[337] J. Carvel, 'The challenge of the out-of-pocket borough', *The Guardian*, 29 March 1989.

authority to make its rate but gave it until the end of May to comply. Giving judgment, Woolf J stated that, although there was no statutory date by which an authority was obliged to set its rate, the local authority was under a duty to exercise its discretion reasonably and with due regard to the interests of its ratepayers. And although the precise period depended on the facts of each case, he felt that 'in the absence of a reasonable explanation, not to make a rate by the beginning of a financial year or within a reasonable time thereafter – I have in mind weeks rather than months – would prima facie be unreasonable and, therefore, in breach of duty'.[338]

Before the *Fleming* judgment it had been clear that the local authorities were legally required to set their rate by 20 June, since delay beyond that date would result in irrecoverable losses being incurred.[339] As a result of that judgment, however, it became evident that, well before that date, local authorities were obliged to consider other particular legal duties. This situation was particularly serious because of the actions of central government. First, the Secretary of State 'had again and again and again made its position as clear as anyone possibly could that there would be no extra money available . . . and that the Government would not go back on, or re-open, the rate support grant report'.[340] This refusal to negotiate called into question the issue of whether the councillors had a 'reasonable explanation' for not making a rate. Secondly, the Department of Health and Social Security (in relation to the rate rebate element of housing benefit subsidy) and the Treasury Valuer (in relation to contributions in lieu of rates on Crown property) were refusing to make payments to local authorities until such time as a rate was made. Under these legal and financial pressures, the resistance of the authorities gradually crumbled and during April or May most authorities set their rates.[341] At the beginning of June only Camden, Greenwich, Liverpool and Lambeth were still holding out, and these eventually set their rates on 5, 8, 14 June and 23 July respectively.

In the view of the Audit Commission, however, the actions of Liverpool and Lambeth had come too late. Liverpool's situation requires particular attention. The 1984/85 budget settlement had been achieved mainly by creative accounting measures which meant that the basic financial difficulties had simply been postponed rather than resolved. These difficulties re-emerged in relation to the 1985/86 budget, particularly since, notwithstanding the negotiations with the Secretary of State in 1984, the grant settlement had not been favourable to Liverpool and the capital allocation was considered inadequate. The council was thus in the position of seeking a budget of £265.4m, though the expenditure target was

---

[338] *R* v. *Hackney LBC, ex p. Fleming* (1985) 85 LGR 626, 632.

[339] This was because of a provision in the General Rate Act 1967, s. 50, Sched. 10 which gave ratepayers the right to pay rates in 10 instalments payable at monthly intervals. Since 10 days' notice was required of the rate, the last date which permitted ratepayers to exercise this right was 20 June.

[340] [1987] 2 WLR 821, 849.

[341] See M. Grant, *Rate-Capping and the Law* (above, n. 330), 69 (Table 14).

only £222.1m. In these circumstances they joined with the rate-capped authorities and again deferred setting their rate. Faced with the stance of the Secretary of State, however, it became difficult to use the previous year's experience as a justification. Eventually, on 21 May, the district auditor wrote to every councillor advising them of the legal and financial risks and stated that unless the council 'makes a lawful rate at the earliest opportunity and in any event before the end of May I shall forthwith commence action' to undertake an extraordinary audit.[342] A budget meeting was eventually called, but not until 14 June. At this meeting, the leadership, conscious of the fact that 20 June was approaching, proposed a rate increase of 9 per cent. This left a shortfall of £29m on their budget plans and, though warned by officers of the consequences of deficit budgeting, this budget was carried.[343]

In June, however, the Audit Commission directed the district auditor to undertake an extraordinary audit of the accounts. On 11 June the auditor had written to councillors advising them that he was in the process of calculating the losses incurred as a result of their action and on 26 June a formal notice was issued to councillors that an extraordinary audit was to be held. The auditor, finding that it was impossible at that stage to calculate the loss of interest on rate income, focused on the loss of interest on those payments which the DHSS and the Treasury had refused to make until a rate was set. After considering councillors' representations, the auditor on 6 September certified that that loss, calculated at £106,103, was caused by the wilful misconduct of 49 Labour councillors and that they were jointly and severally liable for this sum. Since this loss involved a sum of over £2,000, the councillors were informed that they would also be disqualified.[344]

The audit procedures adopted in relation to Lambeth were virtually identical: similar notices of extraordinary audit were sent in June and almost identical certificates issued on 6 September. It thus seemed 'a natural inference that the auditors were acting in concert';[345] in actuality, the auditors were working under the supervision of the Audit Commission. When both Liverpool and Lambeth councillors appealed against the certificates under section 20(3) of the 1982 Act, the High Court, with the consent of the parties, heard the appeals simultaneously.[346] In dismissing these appeals, the High Court held that the auditors had acted fairly and that each council had acted unlawfully since their objective, that of threatening chaos if the Secretary of State did not make more funds available, was an improper reason for refusing to make a lawful rate by the beginning of

---

[342] See Local Government Finance Act 1982, s. 22.

[343] For a detailed analysis of these events see: (1986) 26 RVR 45, 58–68; M. Parkinson, 'Decision-Making by Liverpool City Council: Setting the Rate 1985–86' in *Aspects of Local Democracy. Research Volume IV. Committee of Inquiry into the Conduct of Local Authority Business* (London, 1986), ch. 2.

[344] See Local Government Finance Act 1982, s. 20(4).

[345] (1986) 26 RVR 45, 53 (*per* Glidewell LJ).

[346] *Smith* v. *Skinner; Gladden* v. *McMahon* (1986) 26 RVR 45.

the financial year. The councillors had not only caused the authorities to act in breach of their duty to 'make arrangements for the proper administration of their financial affairs',[347] but, since they had disregarded advice that what they were doing was wrong, were guilty of wilful misconduct.

The Liverpool (though not the Lambeth) councillors appealed and in the Court of Appeal pursued further the argument that the interests of fairness required that the auditor should have provided the councillors with an opportunity of an oral hearing before reaching a finding of wilful misconduct. It was contended that district audit practice had generally been to hold oral hearings[348] and evidence was provided that, of the 14 certificates of wilful misconduct which were issued between 1974 and 1980, in all but one of these an oral hearing had been offered.[349] In the light of this evidence, the Court found that, since the auditor's findings in effect challenged the councillors' credibility and honesty and given the seriousness of the consequences, the auditor acted unfairly in not providing them with an opportunity to make oral representations.[350] The Court held, however, that any such unfairness had been cured by the High Court hearing.[351] Since the Court was otherwise in general agreement with the lower court's findings, the appeal was dismissed.

The councillors appealed against this decision to the House of Lords. Their Lordships, however, not only unanimously rejected the appeal but also held that 'the district auditor did not act unfairly, and that the procedure which he followed did not involve any prejudice to the appellants'.[352]

The auditors' interventions thus resulted in 47 Liverpool[353] and 32 Lambeth councillors being surcharged and disqualified for holding public office for a period of five years. In his affidavit before the court John Hamilton, the Leader of Liverpool City Council, had explained their reasons for not making a rate until 14 June as follows:

Our financial problems were so severe that it appeared that we could not meet our budget costs without an unacceptable rise in the rates or an unacceptable cut in jobs and services. We believed that there was a reasonable prospect of obtaining increased financial resources that would alter the calculations and hence the level of rate we

[347] Local Government Act 1972, s. 151.

[348] See R. Jones, *Local Government Audit Law* (London, 1981), 277–8.

[349] *Lloyd* v. *McMahon* [1987] 2 WLR 821, 835.

[350] [1987] 2 WLR 821, 838–8 (Lawton LJ); 845 (Dillon LJ). Cf. Woolf LJ: 'While . . . it may have been preferable to offer an oral hearing, justice did not require such an offer [by the auditor]' (864).

[351] This finding was reached notwithstanding the fact that in the High Court all the evidence was given by affidavit and the councillors did not give evidence orally. Counsel for the appellants had, however, been provided an opportunity to seek a direction for an oral hearing but had considered that such a direction would not have been appropriate. See (1986) 26 RVR 45, 84; [1987] 2 WLR 821, 840, 848.

[352] [1987] 2 WLR 821, 873 (per Lord Keith).

[353] Of the original 49, two had died by the time of the appeal hearings: [1987] 2 WLR 821, 834.

would need to set. We believed this for a whole number of reasons which I will endeavour to set out below. Furthermore, we believed that there was no legal obligation to set a rate before the 20th June 1985. I state these as my personal beliefs absolutely and categorically.[354]

After acknowledging that 'political leaders from Robespierre, the sea-green incorruptible, to Gandhi the prophet of non-violence, have acted in the sincere belief that it was necessary to break the nation's laws in the interests of the nation's citizens', Lord Templeman provided a direct response to Hamilton: 'The sincerity of the appellants provides no defence to a charge that they deliberately delayed after they had been warned that it was wrong of them to do so.'[355] And it is by reflecting on the ambiguity of that word 'wrong' that we are brought closer to the issues of legal controversy which are thrown up by these developments.

Liverpool revisited: deficit budgeting

Liverpool's 1985/86 budget settlement had left an unresolved gap between expenditure plans and revenues available to finance them and thus raised fundamental questions about the credibility and legality of the budget. This situation was essentially inherited from 1984/85 in which related difficulties had emerged. On 16 January 1984, the city treasurer had produced a report which showed that the council was heading for a deficit on its revenue budget of £25.4m and, on the capital account, had commitments of £96.9m though having an allocation of only £64.6m. In the light of this report, the Secretary of State wrote to the council stating that he was minded to issue a direction prohibiting the council from entering any new commitments without obtaining his approval.[356] In February, however, the council entered into an agreement with Banque Paribas to sell their interests as mortgagees of council housing in return for a single capital receipt of £30m. This transaction, together with a number of creative accounting measures, meant that the council could keep within the limits of its capital allocation. After initially indicating that he 'was doubtful whether the council has the power to do what it is suggesting', the Secretary of State eventually informed the council that he would not be issuing a section 78 direction.[357]

The council might have secured a breathing space but the problems returned in relation to 1985/86. In addition to dealing with the auditor's action, the council also had a major task of running council services on a deficit budget. On

---

[354] (1986) 26 RVR 45, 67.   [355] [1987] 2 WLR 821, 888.

[356] See, Local Government, Planning and Land Act 1980, s. 78.

[357] See M. Parkinson, 'Decision-Making by Liverpool City Council' (above, n. 343), 50. The Secretary of State subsequently stated that he had approved the arrangement, despite doubts, because there were 'conflicting views about the legality of the procedure' and the Government intended to legislate 'to make the position absolutely clear': HC Debs, vol. 83, col. 1319 (25 July 1985). See Local Government Act 1986, s. 7. See further, ch. 7, 333–6.

19 July, the auditor wrote to councillors expressing concern about the deficit and suggested that 'the question of legality may need to be considered'.[358] The council officers proposed a number of creative accounting mechanisms, including a deferred purchase scheme, but the council resisted on the ground that these initiatives would result in future options being closed off. It was thus faced with the prospect, within a few months, of issuing dismissal notices to the majority of its employees and of placing an embargo on the ordering of goods and services. Consequently, as a tactic to retain its ability to spend while also placing pressure on the Government, the council on 6 September passed a resolution to issue redundancy notices to all its 31,000 workers, which notice would take effect on 31 December. This tactic split the trades unions, however, and on 2 October the National Union of Teachers obtained leave for judicial review of that decision.

At the expedited hearing on 14 November, the primary submission of the applicants was that the resolution to dismiss the teachers was unlawful and in breach of the authority's statutory duty under section 8 of the Education Act 1944 to provide schools for primary and secondary education. The court experienced little difficulty in determining that the authority's actions 'were not taken for educational reasons, but because the Council was not prepared to depart from the unlawful course it had embarked upon when it made its decision to make an unlawful rate'. Counsel for the council, while acknowledging that it was difficult to advance arguments in support of that decision, nevertheless submitted that the court should not grant relief on the ground that, since the fundamental problem concerned finance, the difficulties would continue unless and until the rate was set aside by the court. Counsel also pointed out that, not only had no ratepayer sought to have the rate set aside, but that the Attorney-General had also not applied to do so. Though recognizing the weight of that submission, the court, in granting a declaration, held that 'to refuse relief would be tantamount to giving tacit approval to illegal action deliberately pursued by the Council and would undermine the rule of law in this country'. Further, the court was not convinced that granting a declaration would have cataclysmic consequences: 'the situation could radically alter if the Council were prepared to indicate that they were no longer intent on pursuing their campaign to oppose Government policy by the adopted means and were, for example, to seek to set about putting their own house in order by arranging for the illegal rate to be quashed'.[359]

In the light of the court's decision, the NUT successfully sought to have their application amended to include a condemnation of the rate and on 22 November that application came before the court. On that date, however, the court agreed to defer the hearing for seven days to enable the council to prepare its defence.[360]

---

[358] Parkinson, ibid., 63.

[359] *R* v. *Liverpool City Council, ex p. Ferguson, The Times*, 20 Nov. 1985 (all quotations taken from transcript of judgment).

[360] A. Rawnsley, 'Liverpool rate case delayed', *The Guardian*, 23 Nov. 1985.

Meanwhile, in October, David Blunkett, as Labour party NEC spokesperson on local government, had proposed a deal under which other Labour authorities might be persuaded to assist Liverpool. The condition was that the council would allow representatives from the Association of Metropolitan Authorities (AMA) to examine the council's financial situation. The council agreed and a team chaired by Maurice Stonefrost, Director-General of the GLC, undertook an investigation. The Stonefrost Report, which was delivered on 29 October, accepted that the council was close to the point of insolvency but, largely following the council officers' initial proposals, proposed that a range of accounting devices might be used to help bring the revenue budget into balance. The report also suggested that the council might seek not to contest court action to quash the existing rate and thus issue a new rate which would involve a 15 per cent increase on the original.[361]

Throughout November, the Liverpool Labour party was placed under intense pressure to reach an accommodation and, towards the end of the month, an arrangement was eventually concluded. On 25 November, the city council's finance committee was in the position of being able to ratify the settlement which had been negotiated. The council was able to reconcile income and expenditure by adopting a number of measures. These included: taking advantage of £3m additional capital borrowing secured through the offices of the AMA;[362] the capitalization of repair and maintenance expenditure; entering into a deferred purchase agreement for £30m with a consortium of Swiss bankers; and by making expenditure reductions of £3m.[363] Through these actions, the budget crisis had been averted. The council's expenditure programme had been brought into alignment with available income and the action pending to quash the rate consequently was abandoned.[364]

Evaluation

The use, during the mid 1980s, of the Poplarist technique of non-compliance with legal requirements in order to highlight grievances and in an attempt to apply pressure on the Government to adjust its policies proved to be both highly controversial and relatively unsuccessful. The Government, in response to the action by Liverpool City Council in 1984, adopted a conciliatory approach and

[361] For a summary of the Stonefrost Report see, Carmichael, *Central–Local Government Relations in the 1980s* (above, n. 319), Appx. 3.

[362] This involved using the facility under the Local Government, Planning and Land Act 1980, s. 77, of entering into an agreement to enable local authorities to share the specified amount of prescribed expenditure between them.

[363] Parkinson, 'Decision-making by Liverpool City Council' (above, n. 343), 72–3. ('Gnomes of Zurich bail out Mersey's Trotskyists' ran the headline in *The Guardian* for 23 Nov. 1985.)

[364] This episode also caused the Labour party to undertake a major review. On 28 November, the Labour party National Executive Committee suspended the Liverpool District Labour party pending the outcome of an inquiry into its operation. This inquiry recommended major reorganization of the party and led ultimately to the expulsion of members of Militant from the party.

the council won significant, albeit marginal, concessions. This episode thus provided an incentive to the first round rate-capped authorities the following year to embark on a collective strategy of non-compliance in order to protest against the unprecedented character of central intervention in local government. But this political action of 1985 essentially failed.

Part of the reason for the failure was that the local councils were not nearly as united in their strategy as their public positions seemed to suggest. The public face of collective non-compliance masked major differences: while some councillors viewed their course as being one of direct confrontation with the Government, most seemed to have treated it simply as an opportunity to exploit an ambiguity in the legal framework and thus as a further round in the game of cat-and-mouse which characterized central–local relations of the period. And the fact was that most councils simply could not command a majority for outright confrontation through the maintenance of a blatantly unlawful position. This is perhaps unsurprising since previous history seemed to indicate that such action was likely to be sustained only in tightly-knit working class communities within which the councillors maintained particularly close ties of place and kinship.[365] These conditions of locality had been severely eroded not only by social and economic change but also as a result of local government reorganization. Furthermore, notwithstanding the façade of solidarity, the circumstances of particular councils were far from being identical: not only were precepting authorities statutorily obliged to set their precepts before the start of the financial year but also, because of the varying financial circumstances of rating authorities, they were likely to come under intense pressure (whether of a financial, political and legal character) at different times. The conditions for successful collective confrontational action were simply not present.

Another reason for failure was because of the stance adopted in 1985 by the Government. One reason for the conciliatory position taken in 1984 may have been that the Government already felt that they had their hands full as a result of the miners' strike which started on 6 March 1984. By 1985, however, the Government's attitude had hardened. One indication of this is provided by the Prime Minister's Carlton Lecture delivered on 26 November 1984. In this speech, Margaret Thatcher reflected on the threats to the social order just over a month after the IRA exploded a bomb at the Conservative party conference in Brighton.

---

[365] See, e.g., N. Branson, *Poplarism* (above, n. 18), Appx. B. See also the Clay Cross affair of the early 1970s. Clay Cross was a mining town of around 7,000 inhabitants which for over a decade had been represented entirely by Labour councillors. When the council refused to raise rents as required by the Housing Finance Act 1972 it had the strong support of the local community, a very high proportion of which were tenants of the council's 1,600 council houses. See *Asher* v. *Lacey* [1973] 1 WLR 1412; *Asher* v. *Secretary of State for the Environment* [1974] 1 Ch. 208; D. Skinner and J. Langdon, *The Story of Clay Cross* (Nottingham, 1974); A. Mitchell, 'Clay Cross' (1974) 45 *Political Quarterly* 165; R. Minns, 'The Significance of Clay Cross: Another Look at District Audit' (1973–74) 2 *Policy and Politics* 309; B. Jacobs, 'Labour Against the Centre: the Clay Cross Syndrome' (1984) vol. 10 no. 2 *Local Government Studies* 75.

'At one end of the spectrum', she stated, 'are the terrorist gangs within our borders, and the terrorist states which finance and arm them. At the other end are the hard left operating inside our system, conspiring to use union power and the apparatus of local government to break, defy and subvert the laws.'[366] By 1985, it appeared, the Government was determined to confront any challenge to its authority.

This seems particularly evident in the Government's response to the non-compliance tactic of rate-capped authorities. The losses identified by the auditors when acting against Liverpool and Lambeth, for example, were purely technical losses which were the direct consequence of a Government policy decision not to make specific payments concerned with rate rebate subsidy or contributions in lieu of rates on Crown properties until the rate had been set. There was no loss to the public purse in these calculations; what the councils had lost in interest had accrued to the benefit of central government. Further, in the complex world of financial transfers between central and local government, in which adjustments to grant payments in respect to a particular financial year are continuously made and often extend long beyond the close of the year, the precise calculation of loss of interest had a distinct air of artificiality to it. Certainly, the timing of grant payments is a matter of administrative practice rather than strict legal requirement, and it is extremely difficult to imagine any circumstances in which central government would be required to pay interest to local authorities on delayed grant payments.[367]

The process of extraordinary audit raises further important questions. Though the Secretary of State possessed the power under section 22(2) of the 1982 Act to require the Audit Commission to direct an extraordinary audit, this power was not exercised. Given the political consequences of extraordinary audit, it may be difficult to believe that the Commission's actions were undertaken without extensive consultation with the Government. Nevertheless, there seems to be no evidence of formal discussion having taken place. It appears that the Government simply expected the Commission to act as it saw fit in the circumstances. The actions of the Commission do, however, raise a number of questions. Why, in the light of the auditor's warnings in May about extraordinary audit, did the Audit Commission direct action only against Lambeth and Liverpool?[368] Why, if the loss of interest accrued from the time when the first payment would

[366] Quoted in H. Young, *One of Us* (London, 1989), 373.
[367] See *R* v. *Secretary of State for the Environment, ex p. Hackney LBC* [1983] 1 WLR 524 (holding, inter alia, that local authorities were only entitled to receive grant as and when the Secretary of State might decide and, since there was no statutory duty on the Secretary of State to pay grant at a particular time, a claim of interest founded on such a duty failed).
[368] On 9 May the District Auditors sent a statutory report (under s. 15 of the 1982 Act) to all authorities which had not then set a rate which stated, inter alia, that: 'I must now give the Council notice that unless it makes a lawful rate at the earliest opportunity and in any event before the end of May I shall forthwith commence action under section 20 to recover losses occasioned by the failure to make a rate from the members responsible for incurring them.'

normally be made, was action not undertaken against the other authorities?[369] Why, since the auditor deferred consideration of loss caused by delayed rate income, was this not subsequently investigated and further acted on?[370] The likely answers to these questions all seem to point to the fact that the primary concern was to make an example of the most confrontational of the councils by ensuring the surcharge and disqualification of the councillors. Once this had been successfully accomplished, there was no further incentive either to calculate the full extent of all losses or to proceed against other councils which had set their rates after the start of the year.[371]

The Government did eventually act to prevent any further use of the tactic of deferring the setting of the rate.[372] By that stage, however, the guidelines laid down by auditors and judges suggested that it was highly unlikely that any local authority would in the future contemplate adopting rate-deferral as a tactic to highlight its grievances with the Government.

Conclusions

The emergence of the municipal socialist movement during the 1980s was certainly in part the product of changes which were taking place in the character of Labour politics. Nevertheless, especially from a perspective of seeking to assess its impact on the role of law in central–local government relations, the movement's most distinctive feature has been its strategy of opposition to, or

[369] The auditors did, however, send notice to Camden, Hackney, Islington and Southwark to show cause why they should not be surcharged and, in the case of Hackney, restoration of the alleged loss was subsequently made to the council. See, Audit Commission, *Annual Report, 1987/88* (London, 1988), para. 27.

[370] It should be noted, however, that in Lambeth and Hackney appeals raised by objections relating to deferred rate-making were still continuing into the 1990s: see Audit Commission, *Annual Report, 1989/90* (London, 1990).

[371] It should also be noted that, in the case of most of these other councils, the auditor faced much greater difficulties in demonstrating that any loss incurred was attributable to wilful misconduct. Unlike Lambeth and Liverpool, these authorities had generally adopted the tactic of obtaining counsel's opinion on the reasons which might justify rate deferral and of identifying the actions they were taking which might justify deferral. See, for example, letter from Margaret Hodge, Leader of Islington LBC, to B.H. Skinner, District Auditor of Metropolitan Audit District, 26 April 1985 which stated, inter alia, that: 'We have been guided by an opinion from Leading Counsel'; that 'important [specified] matters justifying such a deferral arose'; that 'measures [have been] taken to minimize and cancel any possible losses which might accrue'; and which presented the argument that, contrary to the auditor's view, there was legal authority which justified off-setting savings against any losses which might arise. On this last point see *Pickwell* v. *Camden LBC* [1983] QB 962. The Audit Commission thus took the view that no action was taken against the other councils on the ground that 'while in some cases losses had resulted from late rate-making, wilful misconduct could not be established on the evidence presented and given the heavy burden of establishing this requirement. Without wilful misconduct there could be no action for recovery of the losses involved': Audit Commission, *Annual Report 1988/89* (London, 1989), para. 19.

[372] See Local Government Act 1986, s. 1 imposing a duty on rating authorities to make a rate on or before 1 April.

divergence from, the policies of the Conservative Government. This strategy is particularly significant for our purposes mainly because, in order to pursue collectivist policies in opposition to the wishes of central government, Labour-controlled local councils have been obliged to engage in a systematic examination of the legal and economic capacities of local government for autonomous action and to seek to harness these capacities in the service of distinctive social-ist policies. It is the general approach, and especially the specific identification and utilization of law as a power-conferring instrument, rather than the precise policy objectives which has been of particular interest to this study. Reflection on this general approach, for example, has certainly served to highlight the extent to which the conduct of local government affairs has traditionally rested on a set of conventional administrative practices. It has also thrown into relief both the flexibility and ambiguities of the traditional legal framework governing the conduct of local government affairs.

This movement has provided a primary stimulus for central government ac-tion. Many of the more interventionist and controversial powers acquired by central government in recent legislation have been acquired largely to ensure that the centre is equipped to respond speedily and effectively to evasive action or a more direct confrontational approach adopted by this group of Labour councils. In the process, both the courts and the legislature have been drawn into many of the disputes which have arisen.

The courts have in general been unable to provide a haven for local councils seeking the protections of the law for some of their more controversial policies. In being drawn into the process of clarifying the legal limits of local government power, the judiciary have generally adopted a narrow construction. Local govern-ment's campaigning power (even in support of an authority's own continued existence) has been defined in a fairly restrictive manner. So also, notwithstand-ing earlier authority upholding the power in flexible terms, has the power of local authorities to engage in forward funding of projects. And the use of *dominium* powers by local authorities has been subjected to a judicial gloss to the effect that they may not be exercised by local councils in such a manner as to cut across the expectations of individuals and groups unless those bodies have acted contrary to law. In resolving these disputes, the courts have accorded little, if any, weight to the argument that, since local authorities are institutions of gov-ernment, their powers ought be construed benevolently.[373]

The impact of municipal socialism has nevertheless been restricted and cur-tailed primarily by the actions of central government in promoting legislation to undermine collectivist organizational arrangements in local government and

---

[373] See, e.g., *R* v. *Somerset CC, ex p. Fewings* (1994) 92 LGR 674 (Div.Ct.) in which Laws J rejected the argument that powers conferred on an elected body ought to be interpreted more broadly: '[This argument] amounts to no more nor less than an invitation to adopt differential rules of statutory construction on the ground that democratic institutions ought to be encouraged. . . . I know of no principle of statutory construction upon which this argument could be supported.' (694).

generally to limit the discretionary powers of local authorities. Many of the most contentious disputes between central government and the municipal socialist authorities took place during the second term of the Thatcher administration. On the eve of the 1983 general election, Margaret Thatcher had intimated that the electoral prize to be fought for was 'the chance to banish from our land the dark, divisive clouds of Marxist socialism'.[374] Precisely what she had in mind was never made clear, but shortly after the election victory the Government promoted the Rates Act 1984, brought forward its proposals to abolish the (Labour controlled) GLC and metropolitan county councils and in 1984 established the Widdicombe Committee to examine the impact of politics on the conduct of local government business. The major battles raged throughout the period of the Conservative government's second term and, by the time the Government's main post-Widdicombe reforms materialized in 1988, the fight was effectively over.

The main reason for this was that, by the mid 1980s, many of the policies of the municipal socialist authorities, even those which were confrontational, were effectively part of a strategy to defend public services and to place the Government on the defensive until the next general election. The financial costs of this strategy were not insignificant. In January 1987, for example, the Audit Commission published a paper which suggested that 'large parts of London appear set on precisely a course which will lead to financial and management breakdown' and that there 'are very disturbing parallels between the situation in parts of London and that in parts of New York and Chicago'.[375] The paper singled out for special attention the creative accounting policies of eight London boroughs[376] which had negotiated deferred purchase arrangements amounting to over £550m. Since a large part of this money was being used to finance revenue expenditure – the Audit Commission estimated around £300m, representing 30 per cent of the revenue expenditure of these authorities – the Commission concluded that 'a cash gap of serious proportions is in prospect'.[377] Though the authorities in their response denied that these practices were irresponsible (arguing, for example, that it was not irresponsible to maintain home-helps, keep day-centres open or to keep homeless families off the streets), they did recognize that 'their long term use is neither sustainable nor prudent'.[378] When the Conservatives won

[374] Quoted in H. Young, *One of Us* (above, n. 366), 323.

[375] Audit Commission, Occasional Paper 2, *The management of London's authorities: preventing the breakdown of services* (London, 1987) 4, 2. On New York's difficulties during the 1970s see: E.M. Gramlich, 'The New York City Crisis: What Happened and What is to be Done?' (1976) 66 *American Economic Review* 415; R. Alcaly and D. Mermelstein, *The Fiscal Crisis of American Cities with special reference to New York* (New York, 1977); J. Shutt, 'Rescuing New York City, 1975–78', 3 *Papers in Urban and Regional Studies* 35.

[376] The London boroughs of Brent, Camden, Hackney, Haringey, Islington, Lambeth, Lewisham and Southwark, all of which figure prominently in the movement for municipal socialism.

[377] Audit Commission, *Management of London's authorities* (above, n. 375), 9.

[378] Association of London Authorities, *London's Financial Problems – Response to the Audit Commission* (London, 1987) para. 1.21. And so it turned out. In 1995 local authorities who under-

a third term in 1987 a reconfiguration of Labour politics was more or less inevitable. '[L]eft and right, hard and soft, are becoming irrelevant labels' reported Christian Wolmar. 'There are only two camps now, the dogmatists and the pragmatists, and the pragmatists . . . are in the ascendant.'[379] In effect, the challenge of municipal socialism was over.

The Conservative administration certainly had sensed that, in this respect, the 1987 general election was of critical importance. Thus, at 3.00 am on 12 June 1987, Mrs Thatcher, in a speech celebrating her party's success in the previous day's polls, announced that the challenge ahead was that of winning the inner cities. 'We have a great deal of work to do', she declared characteristically, 'so no-one must slack.'[380] The problem with some of the inner city areas, the Prime Minister ruminated, 'is that they are run by the militant Left'.[381] Following the election victory, the Conservative Government thus embarked on the most extensive and radical programme of local government reform ever introduced in a single parliamentary session,[382] the intended effect of which was to strip local councils of much of their power of discretionary action, to subject councils to a much greater degree of external scrutiny and to enable central government effectively to by-pass local councils in providing financial support for services to the locality.

took deferred purchase deals were seeking to renegotiate the loans. The consequences of failure to do so would have been disastrous: 'Islington says it would have had to abandon repair work on its housing until the year 2000, and impose rent rises if it had failed to renegotiate a £114 million loan. Lewisham's finance director Judith Armitt says the average rent of council tenants would have gone up by £10 a week or 10 per cent to pay for its loan of £17 million'; E. Dimbylow, 'The day of reckoning', *The Guardian Society*, 16 August 1995, 9.

[379] C. Wolmar, 'The fresh face of the capital's politics', *New Statesman*, 18 Sept. 1987, at 10.
[380] *The Guardian*, 13 June 1987.
[381] *The Times*, 13 June 1987.
[382] See Education Reform Act 1988 (opt out of schools); Housing Act 1988 (transfers of council estates), Local Government Act 1988 (CCT for a range of local government services); and Local Government Finance Act 1988 (fundamental reform of local government finance based on the poll tax).

4

FIDUCIARY DUTY IN PUBLIC LAW

The idea of trust is fundamental to an understanding of all political relationships. Without trust all attempts at establishing co-operative relations would founder and it is only through trust that the complex arrangements of government can operate effectively. It is, for example, only because of the existence of trust that, under conditions of risk and uncertainty, capital investment can be undertaken.[1] A socially extensive idea of trust is, however, rather difficult to establish. It is one thing to identify trust in friendship but quite another to situate it in the relationship between governors and governed. How, then, is a political relationship rooted in trust established? There would appear to be no simple answer to this question, though what does seems clear is that trust can be established only if 'relations are simplified, stylized, symbolized and given ritual expression; if, that is, they are coded in convention'.[2] This thus seems to suggest that the only society which is possible is one which is rooted in some sort of code; that is, a society in which 'the quality of persons is measured by the extent to which they observe this code'.[3] And this general line of inquiry seems to lead ultimately to the conclusion that the only viable type of society is an aristocracy.

Aristocracies, however, may take several different forms. The traditional form of aristocracy is founded on the notions of lordship, kingship and the majestic concept of sovereignty, all of which function in accordance with codes of honour. There are, however, modern variants of this aristocratic idea which may be seen to operate within the complex arrangements of modern government.[4] One famous version of this is the iron law of oligarchy propounded by Michels: 'Who says organization, says oligarchy.'[5] The general point underpinning these modern forms is that governing institutions, being locked into a system of functional interdependence, come to depend on the evolution of understandings and conventions to guide their action. These understandings, which are vital to the effective functioning of government, are most commonly reflected in the practices

[1] See N. Luhmann, 'Familiarity, confidence and trust: problems and alternatives' in D. Gambetta (ed.), *Trust. The Making and Breaking of Co-operative Relations* (Oxford, 1988), ch. 6.
[2] G. Hawthorn, 'Three Ironies in Trust' in D. Gambetta (ed.), *Trust* (above, n. 1), ch. 7 at 114.
[3] Ibid.
[4] See, e.g., G. Mosca, *The Ruling Class* (New York, 1939), who divides all governments into two types – the feudal and the bureaucratic; and N. Luhmann, *Trust and Power* (Chichester, 1979), Pt. I, who presents the view that there are two sorts of trust – a pre-modern sense founded on belief and a modern sense based on functional interdependence.
[5] R. Michels, *Political Parties* (Glencoe, 1958), 365.

of political elites, the codes of ethics of administrators and the values and standards of professions.

Within the British system of government these two basic senses of trust – one
rooted in sovereignty and the other in functional interdependence – seem to have
grown up alongside one another in an uneasy accommodation. During the eighteenth century, Adam Smith's identification of authority and utility as the two
main principles of government can be understood to reflect these two senses,[6]
as can Bagehot's famous distinction drawn in the nineteenth century between
the dignified and efficient aspects of the constitution.[7] But in what sense are
these ideas about trust reflected in the legal framework of government? The
orthodox view has been that the study of the constitution embraces an examination of the rules affecting the distribution and exercise of the sovereign power
of the state and that these rules comprise two sets: rules of law enforceable by
courts; and certain understandings, habits and practices which are not so enforced and which may be called constitutional conventions.[8] The effect of this
type of formulation has been to place consideration of the understandings within
which the character of the trust is located as beyond the properly legal. This
formulation also leads to the view that the courts are not generally concerned
with such understandings and exist essentially to perform the impartial role of
umpire.

Whilst it is true that, in the process of adjudication, the courts do not often
explicitly take into consideration these conventional understandings about the
modus operandi of the State, this orthodox view seems somewhat deficient.
Although the courts do not in any strict sense enforce constitutional conventions,
they do, without doubt, recognize and seek to give effect to conventional practices. Furthermore, once the blinkers imposed by a positivist conception of law
are removed and law is recognized to be an exercise in interpretation, the courts
can readily be understood to be an institution which serves to uphold the conditions of trust lying at the heart of political relationships. There are, of course,
limitations on the judiciary's ability to do so. The courts are, for example,
hampered by the ambiguous nature of the trust relationship, particularly as most
discussion of the idea of trust in relation to governance uses the term purely in
a metaphorical sense.[9] There are also certain institutional constraints on their

---

[6] A. Smith, *Lectures on Jurisprudence* (R.L. Meek, D.D. Raphael & P.G. Stein eds., Oxford,
1978).

[7] W. Bagehot, *The English Constitution* [1867] (R.H.S. Crossman ed., London, 1963).

[8] For the classic statement of this view see: A.V. Dicey, *Introduction to the Study of the Law of
the Constitution* (London, 8th edn., 1915), 19–31.

[9] See, e.g., F.W. Maitland, 'Trust and Corporation' in *Collected Papers* (Cambridge, H.A.L.
Fisher ed., 1911), vol. III, 321 at 403: 'Open an English newspaper, and you will be unlucky if you
do not see the word "trustee" applied to "the Crown" or to some high and mighty body. I have just
made the experiment, and my lesson for to-day is, that as the Transvaal has not yet received a
representative constitution, the Imperial parliament is "a trustee for the colony". There is metaphor
here. Those who speak thus would admit that the trust was not one which any court could enforce,
and might say that it was only a "moral" trust. But I fancy that to a student of *Staatswissenschaft*

ability to police the terms of the trust; a consideration which can, for example, be seen reflected in Lord Sumner's view that, although the courts 'are the ultimate judges of what is lawful and what is unlawful to borough councils, they often accept the decisions of the local authority simply because they are themselves ill-equipped to weigh the merits of one solution of a practical question as against another'.[10] Finally, concern is occasionally expressed over the question of whether the judiciary's grasp of the conditions of the trust relationship is sound. In particular, are the courts able to give adequate effect to the modern conventions rooted in functional interdependence or are they overly orientated, both culturally and institutionally, to the earlier understandings revolving around the idea of sovereignty?

These issues have generally not been brought sharply into focus, largely because the inter-governmental codes of practice which have evolved during the twentieth century have commanded general allegiance and, to the extent that disputes have arisen, they have not often come to the courts for resolution. During the last 15 years, however, this situation has changed. The impact of these changes has been particularly evident in the context of central–local government relations. Increasingly, the central–local relationship has come to be characterized in the language of conflict rather than partnership and, as a consequence, the courts have been prevailed upon to articulate the boundaries between the centre and the localities. In the process they have, in effect, been obliged to give specific effect to these codes.

In this chapter, I wish to focus on a specific facet of this general question of the importance of the idea of trust in understanding modern government. We know that, whenever the courts invoke the language of trust in seeking to characterize a governmental obligation, they invariably have in mind a non-justiciable idea of 'trust in a higher sense'.[11] But are there any circumstances in the public law context in which the courts are prepared to utilize the formal concept of the trust – in the sense of recognizing that a public body holds property in trust for others and thus that a technical separation of legal and beneficial interests has occurred – in order to construe a governmental relationship? The short answer to this question is apparently that there are not. Nevertheless, there is one particular relationship which the courts have identified as being similar to that between trustee and *cestui que trust*; *viz.*, that of the relationship between the local authority and its ratepayers. This relationship has been viewed by the courts as falling into the category of 'quasi-trust'; being 'in some respects' in the nature of a trust relationship. And gradually the term 'fiduciary' was adopted

legal metaphors should be of great interest, especially when they have become the commonplaces of political debate.'

[10] *Roberts* v. *Hopwood* [1925] AC 578, 606–7.

[11] *Tito* v. *Waddell (No. 2)* [1977] Ch. 106, at 216, 225 (per Megarry VC). See also *Town Investments Ltd* v. *Department of the Environment* [1978] AC 359 in which the House of Lords rejected the idea that a Minister was acting as a trustee for the Crown.

to characterize such a situation.[12] The idea has thus evolved that the relationship between the local authority and its ratepayers is one of a fiduciary nature.

This doctrine of a fiduciary duty which the local authority owes to its rate-payers, though only one thread in the net cast by the common law to afford protection against the exercise of public power, holds a particular interest for anyone seeking to understand the central–local relationship. Given the unique character of this doctrine, consideration of its nature and development may yield some valuable insights into the role of the judiciary in supervising local authority action. In particular, an examination of the use made of the doctrine may enable us to disclose something of the judiciary's role in policing political relationships amongst local interests and thereby, albeit indirectly, may explicate the sense of trust between the centre and the locality. An appreciation of the manner in which the doctrine has evolved may also enable us to reach certain conclusions about the ability of the courts adequately to articulate and enforce trust relations within modern government. If we are to view fiduciary duty simply as 'the formula through which the conscience of equity finds expression',[13] we might thus be in a position to measure the judicial notions of equity against modern conceptions of justice and fairness.

The Origins of the Fiduciary Concept

The source of the judicial doctrine which characterizes the relationship between local authorities and their ratepayers as being of a fiduciary nature is rather difficult to trace. The most obvious starting point for inquiry is that of the period in which the legal foundations of the modern system of local government were laid. For our purposes the critical events are, first, the enactment of the Municipal Corporations Act 1835 and, secondly, the emergence of the doctrine of *ultra vires* and its application to local authorities in the mid-nineteenth century.

The Act of 1835 brought about a legal revolution by re-establishing the original idea of the municipal corporation as the legal personification of the local community. It provided for a council elected by the local ratepayers which would hold its meetings in public and would have its accounts audited annually.[14] In removing the power of the 'freemen' of the borough to use the property of the corporation for whatever purposes they saw fit, the Act constituted 'a definite confiscation of private property rights and their dedication to public use under the control of a democratically governed authority'.[15] In the words of Ivor

---

[12] See, L.S. Sealy, 'Fiduciary Relationships' [1962] *Camb. L J* 69; E.J. Weinrib, 'The Fiduciary Obligation' (1974) 24 *Univ. of Toronto L J* 1.

[13] *Beatty* v. *Guggenheim Exploration Co.* (1919) 122 NE 378, 380 (New York Court of Appeals) per Cardozo J (on the idea of the constructive trust).

[14] See J. Redlich & F.W. Hirst, *Local Government in England* (London, 1903), vol. I, 111–33. See, also, above, ch. 1, 31–6.

[15] W.I. Jennings, 'The Municipal Revolution' in H.J. Laski, W.I. Jennings and W.A. Robson (eds.), *A Century of Municipal Progress. The Last Hundred Years* (London, 1935), ch. III, at 55.

Jennings, municipal corporations thus 'ceased to be forms of property and became instruments of government'.[16] During the remainder of the nineteenth century the principles of the 1835 Act were gradually extended to the other institutions of local government.

The Municipal Corporations Act assumes a particular significance for our purposes when it is considered alongside the developing doctrine of *ultra vires*. This doctrine emerged as such only in the nineteenth century. It was developed by the courts 'upon grounds of public policy and commercial necessity'[17] largely as a result of the need to determine the legal status of the new corporations, such as railway companies, which had been created by Parliament to carry out particular tasks. One effect of the application of the *ultra vires* doctrine to local authorities was to render unlawful the expenditure of money by a local authority unless that expenditure was for a purpose for which there was statutory authorization. But in formulating this doctrine the courts also had to attend to the question of how it might be enforced. One potential enforcement mechanism was through the equitable jurisdiction of the Chancery courts. And the peg on which to hang such an action was found in section 92 of the 1835 Act.

Section 92 required any surplus of borough funds, after all debts, salaries and specified expenses were paid off, to be applied 'for the public Benefit of the inhabitants and improvements of the Borough'. The section was of general significance in so far as it required the local authority to act for the public good. But, in the context of the emerging *ultra vires* doctrine, it also had a specific importance. In seeking to enforce the doctrine against local authorities, the courts were prepared to hold that section 92 had the effect of imposing on the municipal corporation a charitable trust in respect of its property.[18] As a consequence, the courts of equity were able to enforce the *ultra vires* doctrine by injunction on an information filed by the Attorney-General, who sued as protector of the rights of the public.[19] The early cases tended to concern the disposal of the property of the corporation. However, as local councils became charged with new statutory responsibilities, they could no longer depend on corporate property as the sole source of revenue and, increasingly, they resorted to the levying of rates. Nevertheless, the judiciary considered that the same principle applied; in asserting their control over *ultra vires* expenditure the courts held that their supervision extended not only to the disposal of corporate property but also to the use of the Borough Fund.[20]

---

[16] W.I. Jennings, 'Central Control' in Laski, Jennings & Robson (eds.), ibid., ch. XVIII at 420.

[17] S. Brice, *A Treatise on the Doctrine of Ultra Vires* (London, 3rd edn., 1893), xviii.

[18] *Attorney-General* v. *Aspinall* [1837] 2 My. & Cr. 613, 622–3 (per Lord Cottenham).

[19] See, e.g., *Attorney-General* v. *Aspinall* ibid.; *Attorney-General* v. *Poole Corporation* [1838] 4 My. & Cr. 17; *Attorney-General* v. *Wilson* [1840] Cr. & Ph. 1; *Attorney-General* v. *Lichfield* [1848] 11 Beav. 120.

[20] See, e.g., *Attorney-General* v. *Poole Corporation* [1838] 4 My. & Cr. 17, 21–2 (per Lord Cottenham LC): '[T]his statute [*sc.* the 1835 Act] creates a trust, in the corporation, of the Borough Fund . . . [T]he payment which this information seeks to prevent is a payment out of the Borough

The significance of these developments is found in the fact that, in order to enforce the *ultra vires* doctrine in equity, municipal property was characterized by the judiciary as being held on trust. According to Brice, the 1835 Act 'completely altered the nature of [municipal corporations], constituting them trustees of their corporate property for public purposes, and impressing a trust upon this property'.[21] And, of course, the concept of the trust is quintessentially in the nature of a fiduciary relationship. These developments might therefore cause us simply to assume that the genesis of the modern formulation of the concept of a fiduciary duty owed by a local authority to its ratepayers is to be found within these nineteenth century formulations devised by the judiciary to ensure the enforcement of the *ultra vires* doctrine in the courts of equity.

The matter is not, however, quite so straightforward. It is important to recognize, first, that, although the courts invoked the idea of the trust, they did so in a rather loose manner. The stress was placed firmly on the idea that the trust was for the benefit of the general public[22] and the judiciary specifically rebutted the notion that the council owed a special duty to its ratepayers.[23] The invocation of the idea of the trust thus seemed largely metaphorical; it was essentially a Chancery device enabling the courts to assert jurisdiction. It should also be recognized that the Chancery courts did not provide the sole means of enforcing the *ultra vires* doctrine. Alternative remedies were being developed at common law through the use of the prerogative writs and during the latter half of the nineteenth century these remedies were actively employed by the courts.[24] Furthermore, these common law remedies for many reasons, not the least of which was the fact that local government lawyers tended to be common

---

Fund, although created by means of the rate; and if this Court has jurisdiction to prevent or correct breaches of trust out of the Borough Fund generally, it must have equal jurisdiction over that portion of it which may have been raised by a rate; and this is totally beside the question whether this Court has any control over the rate itself.'

[21] Brice, *Ultra Vires* (above, n. 17), 192.

[22] *Attorney-General* v. *Compton* [1842] 1 Y & CCC 417, 427: 'The right to the fund is not vested in any single individual, or in any number of individuals. The beneficial right to the fund is in the public generally of that district, for whose benefit in a particular manner it is to be applied by the public officers of that district.'

[23] See, e.g., *Attorney-General* v. *Brecon* (1878) 10 Ch. Div. 204. This case concerned the question of whether the corporation could incur the costs involved in opposing a private Act which would have removed the council's power to approve the location of markets. In response to the argument that, since the majority of ratepayers were in favour of the Act, this was an improper expenditure, Jessel MR stated that: '[T]he corporation is governed by its town council, which is a representative body of all the ratepayers; and I am not aware of any means by which the town council can be controlled by the ratepayers except by the system of not re-electing them when the time comes round; which system is very likely to be enforced in the present instance if it should turn out that the town council have not acted in accordance with the views of the ratepayers'(228).

[24] See, e.g., *R* v. *Local Government Board* (1882) 10 QBD 309, 321 (per Brett LJ): '[M]y view of the power of prohibition at the present day is that the Courts should not be chary of exercising it, and that wherever the legislature entrusts to any body of persons other than to the superior Courts the power of imposing an obligation upon individuals, the Courts ought to exercise as widely as they can the power of controlling these bodies of persons if those persons admittedly attempt to exercise powers beyond the powers given to them by Act of Parliament.'

lawyers, became the standard form of challenge to the legality of local authority action.

At the turn of the century, then, the law did not seem to recognize any precise notion of a fiduciary duty owed by a local authority to its ratepayers. This strict sense of fiduciary duty was formulated only in the early decades of the twentieth century and, in particular, in the decade following the First World War. This was a period in which, with the emergence of the Labour party and as a result of the post-war extension of the franchise, local authorities across the country were coming, for the first time, under Labour control. Many of these Labour-controlled authorities began to use their powers in novel ways. In administering the Poor Law, for example, they were prepared to pay more generous sums in relief and they rejected the principle of 'less eligibility'.[25] This led to conflicts between the local authority and their ratepayers. During this period the ratepayers often sought the assistance of the Attorney-General.

An illustration may be provided by the case of *Attorney-General* v. *Fulham Corporation*.[26] Here, at the relation of a number of ratepayers, the Attorney-General sought an injunction to prohibit the defendants from using statutory powers which empowered them to provide facilities for the washing of clothes in order to run a business in the nature of a laundry. In granting the injunction Sargant J appeared especially to have been influenced by the fact that Fulham's scheme promoted the interests of 'classes that I do not think were intended to be benefited by the Acts in question', that the scheme was being run at 'a very substantial loss', and that it seemed 'an instance of the light-hearted way in which operations were conducted by persons who have not their own pockets to consider but who have behind them what they regard as the unlimited or nearly unlimited purse of the ratepayers'.[27] While the *Fulham* case may be viewed as a straightforward illustration of the operation of the *ultra vires* principle – that powers to provide basic facilities should not be interpreted as permitting the adoption of elaborate schemes of municipal enterprise – within the text of the judgment there may also be found some of the basic facets of the modern concept of fiduciary duty.

We have seen that during the nineteenth century local authorities were impressed with the characteristics of a trust essentially for the purpose of giving remedial effect to the *ultra vires* doctrine. Though the practical effect of enforcement of this doctrine in law and equity may have been the same, it is important to recognize that the principles involved are different. *Ultra vires* is based on the idea of *lack of power*, whereas the enforcement of trusts is rooted in the idea of *breach of duty*. This is a subtle, though important, distinction. It is entirely possible, for example, that although there may be no lack of power, action may give rise to a breach of duty. Given the fluidity of the emerging

---

[25] See Redlich & Hirst, *Local Government in England* (above, n. 14), vol. I, 98–111; M Rose, *The English Poor Law 1780–1930* (Newton Abbot, 1971), Pt. V.
[26] [1921] 1 Ch. 440.   [27] Ibid., 454.

principles of *ultra vires* in administrative law in the early decades of this century, the distinction is unlikely to be clear-cut. Nevertheless, this focus on the issue of duty rather than that of power does provide the court with a more interventionist handle for inquiring into such questions as the motive, purpose and impact of local authority action. In the *Fulham* case, for example, the essentially political issue of who benefits and who loses becomes more closely bound up with the legal question of whether or not the authority is empowered to run a laundry service. The focus on duty leads to a position in which the local authority is viewed as standing in an active *legal* relationship with their ratepayers such that they are under an obligation to maintain a balance between the services provided and the costs imposed on ratepayers. Finally, it may be the case that, once the analogy of the trust is invoked, the local authority's statutory powers may unconsciously come to be interpreted through the mental filter of the charitable trust, and thus be read as authorizing schemes for the relief of the poor but not for broader redistributive purposes.

While facets of the fiduciary concept can be seen in the *Fulham* case, it is not until the decision of the House of Lords in *Roberts* v. *Hopwood*[28] that the meaning of the concept is rendered explicit. This case concerned an appeal against the decision of the district auditor to surcharge members of Poplar Borough Council for maintaining a minimum wage for its employees which was not only in excess of wage rates in the area but also was paid to men and women alike. The council was empowered to pay their employees 'such salaries and wages as . . . [the council] may think fit'[29] and the precise issue of law was whether the maintenance of wage rates above those generally prevailing in the area was 'contrary to law'.[30] That the question of duty lay at the heart of the controversy was, however, clear from the fact that the auditor's justification for disallowance and surcharge was based on the argument that 'the Council cannot, as a fiduciary body, expend sums "so largely in excess of those which were needed to obtain the services required"'.[31] The councillors' appeal failed in the Divisional Court, succeeded by a majority in the Court of Appeal, but was rejected by the House of Lords. The importance of the idea of fiduciary duty to the resolution of this dispute can best be highlighted by contrasting the approaches taken in the Court of Appeal and the Lords.

What is most significant about the judicial method of the majority of the Court of Appeal was that the focus was almost solely on the issue of power. Scrutton LJ took the view that 'it is for the Poplar borough council to fix these wages, which are not to be interfered with unless they are so excessive as to pass the reasonable limits of discretion in a representative body'; that a 'wide margin should be allowed for error of judgment'; and that 'though the figures are near

---

[28] [1925] AC 578.   [29] Metropolis Management Act 1855, s. 62.
[30] Public Health Act 1875, s. 247(7).
[31] H.J. Laski, 'Judicial Review of Social Policy in England' (1926) 39 *Harv. L. Rev* 832, 834 (quoting from the brief submitted by the District Auditor to the House of Lords).

the line where interference should take place, I cannot find they have reached it'.[32] Atkin LJ adopted a more rigorous approach: 'The auditor's power . . . appears to me to be strictly limited to surcharging such payments as are beyond the powers of the council to make.'[33] He then examined the nature of the power and suggested that 'there is no reason for not giving the words of the section their plain and unrestricted meaning'.[34] As to the objection that this would enable the council to pay entirely extravagant wages ('such as . . . £30 a week to an office boy') Atkin LJ replied:

The answer . . . is to be found in the restriction that the council must act in good faith. They must determine the amount of wages as wages in an existing industrial system; they must not fix the amount as a dole or as a bribe, or with any object other than that of fairly remunerating the servant.[35]

Once it was established that local authorities had exercised their powers honestly and in good faith Atkin LJ felt that a heavy onus was placed on the auditor to make out a case and that '[w]here a case is admittedly near the line I can hardly conceive the circumstances in which the Court would allow the opinion of the auditor to over-rule the honest decision of the council'.[36] Atkin LJ adopted this approach because he felt that, if the test of legality were that of reasonableness, then the decisions of the elected local authority could easily be subverted by auditors and courts: 'Would it be open to the auditor to disallow the payment for four char-women out of forty-four if he thought forty sufficient, or ten dustmen out of 144 if his experience led him to the belief that the work could be done by 134?'[37] Furthermore, Atkin LJ specifically rejected the argument that the issue should be considered in terms of duty:

[W]e are dealing with powers given to public bodies consisting of representatives elected by the public on a wide franchise for comparatively short periods. I venture to doubt the legal value of the proposition of the Court below that 'the council are in a fiduciary position not merely towards a majority who have elected them but towards the whole of the ratepayers.' If it is sought to impose upon the councillors the liability of trustees to their cestuis que trust, the analogy fails. That trust and confidence are bestowed upon them is true; that they may not use the powers entrusted to them for their own advantage is also true. But for the proposition that there are any equitable rights in the ratepayers as such, which can be enforced by the interference of a court of equity with the honest administration of affairs, I know of no authority. The duty of the council is to the local community as a whole.[38]

Nevertheless, notwithstanding this powerful statement from a highly respected judge, the decision of the House of Lords to uphold the surcharge was justified

---

[32] *R v. Roberts, ex p. Scurr* [1924] 2 KB 695, at 721, 719, 721.   [33] Ibid., 722.
[34] Ibid., 725.   [35] Ibid.   [36] Ibid., 728.   [37] Ibid., 724.   [38] Ibid., 725–6.

essentially in the language of fiduciary duty. Lord Atkinson's speech set the tone in stating that the 'council would, in my view, fail in their *duty* if . . . they . . . allowed themselves to be guided . . . by some eccentric principles of socialist philanthropy, or by a feminist ambition to secure equality of the sexes in the matter of wages in the world of labour'.[39] Lord Atkinson then continued to articulate more precisely the character of that duty:

> A body charged with the administration for definite purposes of funds contributed in whole or in part by persons other than members of that body owes, in my view, a duty to those latter persons to conduct that administration in a fairly business-like manner with reasonable care, skill and caution, and with due and alert regard to the interests of those contributors who are not members of the body. Towards these latter persons the body stands somewhat in the position of trustees or managers of the property of others.[40]

Here we find the classic expression of the fiduciary duty which the local authority owes to its ratepayers. Though some of the other speeches sought to justify the decision on the ground that discretion is limited by the requirements of reasonableness, Lord Atkinson's speech provided the primary intellectual justification for the decision. Lord Sumner, for example, though focusing on the issue of powers was primarily concerned with the power of the auditor. On this issue he concluded that: 'I do not find any words limiting his functions merely to the case of bad faith, or obliging him to leave the ratepayers unprotected from the effects on their pockets of honest stupidity or unpractical idealism.'[41] And on turning to the local authority's powers Lord Sumner simply stated that: 'I can find nothing in the Acts . . . which authorizes them to be guided by their personal opinions on political, economic and social questions in administering the funds which they derive from the rates.'[42]

It is only with the decision of the House of Lords in *Roberts* v. *Hopwood* that the idea that a local authority owes a fiduciary duty to its ratepayers becomes firmly established as a legal principle. The duty, according to Lord Atkinson, is 'a legal duty as well as a moral one, and acts done in flagrant violation of it should . . . be properly held to have been done "contrary to law" '.[43] It is a concept which, though drawing loosely on nineteenth century Chancery cases, was precisely formulated only in the early decades of the twentieth century. Furthermore, this fiduciary concept seems to have been devised essentially to regulate the activities of (Labour-controlled) local authorities who came to recognize that, given the general discretionary powers of the local authorities and the fact that rates were payable as an incident of property ownership, the powers of local government could be used for general redistributive purposes.[44]

---

[39] [1925] AC 578, at 594 [emphasis supplied].   [40] Ibid., 595.
[41] Ibid., 604.   [42] Ibid.   [43] Ibid., 595.
[44] Consider, e.g., *Attorney-General* v. *Guardians of the Poor Law of Tynemouth* [1930] 1 Ch. 616. Here the Guardians had during the 1926 coal strike provided relief by way of loans to miners'

The Nature of the Fiduciary Obligation

Since the House of Lords in *Roberts* v. *Hopwood* lent its *imprimatur* to the idea of fiduciary duty, the concept has been invoked on numerous occasions. Nevertheless, whenever the courts have considered this fiduciary concept, they have generally alluded to it in a fairly imprecise manner and without either articulating the precise nature of the fiduciary obligation or explaining how the concept meshes with the general principles of administrative law which guide local authorities in the exercise of their powers. The idea of a fiduciary relationship between local councils and their ratepayers seems to suggest that, in some sense, the former act as agents for giving effect to the intentions of the latter. Any strict application of this principal–agency relationship would, however, entirely undermine the basic governmental character of local councils as representative institutions charged with the political responsibility of giving effect to the wishes of their electorates. Clearly, some more lax sense of fidelity must be implied. While the courts have been reluctant to specify the precise character of this notion of fidelity, it is nevertheless possible to identify two distinct, albeit related, dimensions to the fiduciary concept which have been elicited and which may throw some light on that issue. These two aspects may be termed the efficient management principle and the discrimination principle.

The efficient management aspect of the duty may best be explained in the words of Asquith LJ who in *Reading* v. *R*[45] suggested that 'a "fiduciary relationship" exists ... whenever the plaintiff entrusts to the defendant a job to be performed ... and relies on the defendant to procure for the plaintiff the best terms available'.[46] This sense of the fiduciary relationship between local councils and ratepayers may be explained in the following terms. Local councils are empowered by Parliament to undertake certain statutory responsibilities. In exercising their functions local councils are subject to active supervision by central government. However, in addition to this administrative relationship, a further dimension of accountability must be considered. Since much of the expenditure incurred by councils in carrying out these responsibilities is financed by local ratepayers, the courts have held that councils are under a legal duty to ratepayers to ensure that their money is expended wisely and with due regard to economy. It is this efficient management aspect of fiduciary duty which we see invoked in the controversy in *Roberts* v. *Hopwood*.

families. After the strike, loans repayments commenced and in 1929 the Guardians resolved to cancel the balance of the moneys owing. The ratepayers challenged this resolution and, notwithstanding the fact that the Guardians could in 1926 have lawfully provided relief as benefits rather than loans, the ratepayers succeeded in their action. Eve J justified his decision on the ground that: 'It never seems to have been appreciated that in respect of the property represented by the outstanding debts and the collection of the same the position of the Guardians in relation to ratepayers was of a fiduciary character and they could certainly not make present of it to the borrowers at the expense of the ratepayers.' (637).

[45] [1949] 2 KB 232.   [46] Ibid., at 236.

The discrimination aspect of fiduciary duty is, however, directed to a rather different concern. The discrimination principle seems to be activated not when the local authority is acting thriftlessly but rather when, acting under general discretionary powers, it seeks to benefit a small group disproportionately and at the expense of the general body. An early illustration of this type of concern was raised in *Board of Education* v. *Rice*[47] when Lord Loreburn LC stated:

> Suppose, for example, that the managers of a school were to say to the local authority 'we admit you are keeping our school efficiently, yet you are giving to other schools benefits you do not give to us', that would not be, in my opinion, a ground for complaint under the Act. I say nothing as to any remedy which ratepayers might have against the local authority upon the ground that it was misapplying public money in giving to the preferred school more than was justifiable.[48]

The implication here is that there exists some legal principle governing discriminatory expenditure under discretionary powers which is enforceable at the suit of the ratepayer. This supposed principle is not, however, easily articulated through the general principles of administrative law, except perhaps as part of a potentially unruly principle that discretionary powers must be exercised reasonably. In so far as it may be assumed to exist, it is best understood as an aspect of the concept of fiduciary duty. In this sense, the discrimination principle seems analogous to the responsibility of a trustee not unduly to favour one beneficiary at the expense of the general group of beneficiaries. That the principle can be interpreted in this light may be illustrated by the Court of Appeal's judgment in 1955 in *Prescott* v. *Birmingham Corporation*.[49]

The *Prescott* case concerned the exercise of Birmingham Corporation's general powers to operate a public transport system. Relying on its general discretionary power to charge such fares as it thought fit, the corporation introduced a scheme to allow certain categories of old people to travel without charge. This scheme, which cost the rate fund around £90,000 a year, was challenged by the plaintiff, a ratepayer, on the ground that it was *ultra vires* the local authority. The corporation mounted a strong defence, arguing that the legislation contained no equality clause and thus permitted discrimination and that, since the provisions concerning the charging of fares were permissive and not imperative, they therefore empowered the corporation, if so minded, to allow everyone to travel free. Birmingham cited authority for the proposition that a body authorized to levy a toll or rate could, in the absence of an equality clause, charge some more than others or even remit the charge for some.[50] The corporation recognized that discrimination could not be arbitrary or capricious but argued there was no *mala fides* in the operation of the scheme. Birmingham claimed, finally, that, if this

---

[47] [1911] AC 179.   [48] Ibid., at 183.   [49] [1955] 1 Ch. 210.

[50] See *Hungerford Market Co.* v. *City Steamboat Co.* (1860) 3 E & E 365; *Duke of Newcastle* v. *Worksop Urban Council* [1902] 2 Ch. 145; *Northampton Corporation* v. *Ellen* [1904] 1 KB 299.

scheme were unlawful, then so too would be schemes generally adopted to permit children to travel free or at half fares or to enable blind and disabled persons to travel free of charge.

At first instance, Vaisey J, while recognizing the force of the precedents, struck down the scheme on the ground that 'the corporation seem to me to be attempting . . . to usurp the functions of the legislature, and to redress what they appear to consider to be a nationwide grievance by local administrative methods'.[51] The learned Chancery judge felt that the scheme, in placing money 'drawn from the pockets of the total body of ratepayers at the disposal of a limited class of persons whose moral claim to free transport . . . may be less urgent than that of others outside the scheme, such as parents of large families or shop assistants . . . depart[ed] . . . from that principle of equality which is normally so important an ingredient of justice'.[52] 'Where,' Vaisey J wondered, 'is the process of discrimination and favouritism to stop?' In striking down the scheme he concluded that:

> If old people are to be financially helped partly by Parliament from the taxes and partly from municipalities from the rates, it seems to me that very unseemly competition would be set up between Parliament and the municipalities and between the municipalities themselves. The subsidising of particular classes of society is a matter for Parliament and for Parliament alone.[53]

Notwithstanding the articulation of a number of highly contentious statements, we can see in Vaisey J's judgment a relatively clear expression of the discrimination principle. On appeal to the Court of Appeal, the corporation fared no better. In dealing with the authorities holding that, in the absence of an equality clause, a body having a statutory power to charge tolls, rates or fares is empowered to discriminate in charging, the Court highlighted the distinction between consideration of the issue in terms of power and duty. The authorities cited stood for the proposition that 'the person discriminated against cannot object merely on the ground that he is charged more than the other man'.[54] However, it 'does not necessarily follow that nobody else can object'; if, for example, 'a trustee chose, from motives of philanthropy, to allow some person or class of persons, considered by him to be badly off, to travel free . . . , it may be that passengers charged the full fare could not object. . . . But . . . the cestui que trustent certainly could'.[55] Jenkins LJ, giving the judgment of the court, continued:

> Local authorities are not, of course, trustees for their ratepayers, but they do . . . owe an analogous fiduciary duty to their ratepayers in relation to the application of funds contributed by the latter. Thus local authorities running an omnibus undertaking at the

---

[51] [1955] 1 Ch. 210, 225.   [52] Ibid., 225–6.   [53] Ibid., 225.
[54] Ibid., 234–5.   [55] Ibid., 235.

risk of their ratepayers, in the sense that deficiencies must be met by an addition to the rates, are not . . . entitled, merely on the strength of a general power to charge different fares to different passengers or classes of passengers, to make a gift to a particular class of person of rights of free travel on their vehicles, simply because the authority concerned are of the opinion that the favoured class of persons ought, on benevolent or philanthropic grounds, to be accorded that benefit. . . . [I]t would amount simply to the making of a gift or present in money's worth to a particular section of the local community at the expense of the general body of ratepayers.[56]

In *Prescott* the discrimination aspect of the local authority's fiduciary duty to its ratepayers was firmly established. Though distinct, this discrimination principle can also be seen to mesh with the efficient management dimension to the concept. In *Prescott*, for example, Jenkins LJ, after articulating the discrimination principle, stated that 'it is clearly implicit in the legislation that . . . the undertaking was to be run as a business venture' and that this meant that 'fares fixed by the defendants at their discretion, in accordance with business principles, were to be charged'. This did not mean, Jenkins LJ continued, that the corporation should be guided by 'considerations of profit to the exclusion of all other considerations'. But it did mean that they should not 'go out of their way to make losses by giving away rights of free travel'.[57] While this statement presents itself as an exercise in statutory interpretation, it is not preceded by a detailed examination of the statutory scheme and is, I believe, better understood as an elaboration of a common law principle that, in the absence of statutory indications to the contrary, the courts will interpret general discretionary powers of this type to be exercised in accordance with 'ordinary business principles'. Thus interpreted, the principle can be understood simply as an elaboration of the efficient management aspect of fiduciary duty.

The final point to make on *Prescott* is that the general thrust of the judicial approach to the interpretation of this discretionary power seems to make sense only if local authorities are understood as being in some respect analogous to charitable trustees. Consider, for example, the way in which concessionary travel schemes for the blind and disabled were distinguished from Birmingham's scheme for pensioners. Vaisey J had attempted to differentiate these two types of schemes by reference to the former category's special need for transport and special difficulties in obtaining it.[58] The Court of Appeal, however, simply stated that:

> The practice of allowing free travel to blind and disabled persons may, or may not, be strictly justifiable, but may perhaps be classed as a minor act of elementary charity to which no reasonable ratepayer would be likely to object.[59]

This constitutes a fairly unsatisfactory conclusion to a rather muddled judgment. A local authority is not, in law, an eleemosynary institution; and the appeal

---

[56] [1955] 1 Ch. 235–6.   [57] Ibid., 236.   [58] Ibid., 225.   [59] Ibid., 236.

to 'ordinary business principles' provides little guidance on the legitimate limits to acts of 'philanthropy'.[60]

Notwithstanding these ambiguities and uncertainties, the general nature of the local authority's fiduciary obligation may now be identified. Two basic dimensions to the concept of fiduciary duty may be distinguished: an efficent management principle and a discrimination principle. While sharing certain characteristics in common, the two principles seem to be geared to different concerns. Although both aspects of the fiduciary concept focus on the use of a local authority's discretionary powers for redistributive purposes,[61] the efficient management principle is directed to the issue of redistribution across groups (from ratepayers to service beneficiaries) while the discrimination principle addresses the issue of redistribution within a general group, albeit also at the expense of the ratepayer. Each dimension to the duty enables the courts to engage in a more searching form of scrutiny than an inquiry focused simply on the question of power. And in both cases, the formulation of the principles seems to derive from the local authority being impressed with certain characteristics derived from the legal concept of the trust.

The Rationale for the Fiduciary Concept

We have seen that the imposition on the local authority of a fiduciary obligation in relation to its ratepayers is a twentieth century judicial development, that it operates in general to control the manner in which local authorities exercise their discretionary powers and, in particular, that it imposes on authorities legally enforceable duties both to manage their funds efficiently and not unfairly to discriminate within the general group of beneficiaries. While the fiduciary concept may indeed simply provide a 'formula through which the conscience of equity finds expression'[62] within public law, we should, nevertheless, examine the possible justifications for this exercise in judicial creativity. Our constitutional arrangements generally address matters of trust in governmental relationships through conventional understandings enforceable through political processes. This fiduciary concept is thus unique in casting the relationship between an institution of government and those from whom it draws a proportion of its finances in a specific legal form; there is, for example, no analogous fiduciary

[60] For a discussion see H.M. Fox, 'Judicial control of the spending powers of local authorities' (1956) 72 LQR 237, esp. 249–51, 259.

[61] It might be noted here that there are certain parallels with the manner in which fiduciary duty is interpreted in the private law of trusts. In particular, subject to the terms of the trust deed, the trustee is under a general wealth-maximizing obligation and cannot, for example, engage in investment which would lead to a redistribution of property between income beneficiaries and capital beneficiaries. See A.I. Ogus, 'The Trust as Governance Structure' (1986) 36 *Univ. of Toronto L J* 186.

[62] *Beatty* v. *Guggenheim Exploration Co.* (1919) 122 NE 378, 380.

relationship between central government and taxpayers.[63] Furthermore, since the concept provides only one thread in the web of arrangements for ensuring that local authorities do not abuse their powers, we should assess how it meshes with the general principles developed by the courts by way of judicial review through the prerogative orders. We might best begin to address this question by examining some political and economic arguments which might underpin and provide some justification for the fiduciary concept.

Parliament's power of the purse

One source of the fiduciary concept might be found in our constitutional traditions and, in particular, in Parliament's attentive control over taxation. While the fact that local government has been granted an independent source of finance might be indicative of the institution's governmental status, it could also be argued that this power, being analogous to a taxing power, was granted by Parliament subject to stringent safeguards. Specific controls exist to ensure that an adequate system of financial accountability has been set in place. The most important of these controls is that of external audit;[64] a mechanism which includes two extremely severe powers of personal liability for unlawful expenditure or loss caused by wilful misconduct,[65] and consequential disqualification for public office.[66] These penal powers, it might be argued, reflect the historic importance of Parliament's power over taxation; Parliament has jealously guarded its power of the purse and has signalled its intention to deal severely with any breach of the trust which it has placed in local councillors. When viewed in this light, the emergence of the fiduciary concept might thus be understood as a duty which has been fashioned by the judiciary to give effect to Parliament's will.[67]

While this argument, based on constitutional history, may go some way towards explaining the emergence of the fiduciary concept, it requires further consideration to be given to the nature of the judicial function. Why should the courts construct a novel and specific legal duty where Parliament is silent? Parliament has by statute imposed many restraints on the local authority's

---

[63] See, e.g., *R* v. *Inland Revenue Commissioners, ex parte National Federation of Self-Employed and Small Businesses Ltd* [1982] AC 617.

[64] See Local Government Finance Act 1982, Pt. III; R. Jones, *Local Government Audit Law* (London, 2nd edn., 1985); M. Loughlin, *Administrative Accountability in Local Government* (York, 1992), chs. 2 and 3.

[65] These provisions stem from legislation relating to the disbursement of poor relief by Commissioners. See Poor Law (Amendment) Act 1844, ss. 32, 35, 36.

[66] This additional penalty was enacted in the context of political conflict between local authorities and central government in the 1920s. See Audit (Local Authorities) Act 1927; B. Keith-Lucas, 'Poplarism', 1962 *Public Law* 52, at 74.

[67] See, e.g., *Attorney-General* v. *Wilson* (1840) Cr. & Ph. 1. Further evidence of this attitude may be found in the courts' tendency to adopt a restrictive approach to the interpretation of discretionary powers which are used by local authorities to raise money: see, e.g., *R* v. *Richmond-upon-Thames BC, ex parte McCarthy and Stone (Developments) Ltd* [1991] 4 All ER 897.

exercise of the rating power and remains free to legislate further limitations. Parliament might, for example, decide to devise specific procedural safeguards for ratepayers,[68] or remove the local authority's discretion in respect of categories of ratepayers who are not electors,[69] or it could resolve to limit the amount which local authorities can raise through the rates.[70] In such circumstances, an appeal to the general principle of parliamentary control over taxation does not, of itself, provide a justification for the fiduciary concept. To be convincing this form of argument requires supplementation by a specific theory of the judicial function. Furthermore, any such theory is likely to prove highly controversial. Here, reference need only be made to Atkin LJ's observation that the logic of the fiduciary obligation suggested that the courts could be required to determine as a matter of law whether the council needed only 40 rather than 44 staff to accomplish a particular function.[71]

Economic theories of local public finance

The nature of the fiduciary obligation fashioned by the judiciary can readily be understood in economic terms, with the efficient management and discrimination aspects of the duty equating with the ideas of productive and allocative efficiency respectively. Can economic theory also help to provide a rationale for the emergence of the concept? We might start perhaps by considering the views expressed by Vaisey J in *Prescott*. Vaisey J suggested that Birmingham's scheme had departed from a basic principle of equality and, if upheld, would lead to 'unseemly competition' between municipalities. He thus concluded that the 'subsidizing of particular classes' is a matter for Parliament alone.[72] Are these opinions supported by the weight of economic analysis?

On the face of things, much of neo-classical economic analysis of local public finance over the last 30 years has been based on rather different assumptions from those of Vaisey J. In this field, a great deal of work has been influenced by a model which was being sketched by Charles Tiebout just as the *Prescott* litigation surfaced. Tiebout's model envisaged a world in which different local communities offered different levels of public services. Tiebout hypothesized that, assuming perfect mobility, individuals will select the locality corresponding to

---

[68] See, e.g., Rates Act 1984, s. 13 which imposed a duty on local authorities to 'consult persons or bodies appearing to it to be representatives of industrial or commercial ratepayers in its area about its proposals for expenditure and the financing of expenditure in the next financial year'.

[69] See, e.g., Local Government Finance Act 1988, Pt. III establishing the principle of the 'uniform business rate'.

[70] See, e.g., Rates Act 1984 which conferred powers on the Secretary of State either selectively (Pt. I) or generally (Pt. II) to control the rates of local authorities.

[71] [1924] 2 KB 695, 724: see above, n. 37. It should also be noted that during the 1980s auditors were specifically placed under a *statutory* duty to satisfy themselves that the local authority 'has made proper arrangements for securing economy, efficiency and effectiveness in its use of resources': Local Government Finance Act 1982, s. 15(1)(c).

[72] [1955] 1 Ch. 210, 225–6.

their demands for services and that this would promote an efficient allocation of resources within the public sector. Far from being 'unseemly', competition between local authorities provides a parallel to the market solution for private goods and thereby promotes efficiency.[73] The Tiebout hypothesis seems ostensibly to point in an altogether different direction from Vaisey J's analysis. However, what must be borne in mind is the fact that this is a general theory which, arguably, builds in too many restrictive and unrealistic assumptions for the model to be able to provide a useful guide to policy-making.[74]

Perhaps the most surprising aspect of the Tiebout model is that it includes no examination of the system of local taxation. Consequently, although the model might ensure that the provision of local services matches the demands of households, it cannot ensure economic efficiency since that 'depends on the relative prices households have to pay ... which itself depends on the type of tax levied'.[75] Tiebout's model also implies that local councils will be in the business of only providing what economists call local 'public goods'. Public goods are those goods which, though needed, cannot efficiently be provided by the market. Public goods have two basic characteristics: non-excludability and non-rivalness. The criterion of non-excludability indicates that, once provided, it is difficult to exclude consumers from deriving benefits from the goods. If street lighting is introduced it will be almost impossible to charge consumers for the output they consume. The criterion of non-rivalness means that consumption by some does not reduce the amount available for others; in general, that more of the goods can be consumed without adding to the costs of the service. Once street lighting is introduced, additional consumers can benefit from the facility without imposing any additional costs. Since there are efficiency gains to be realized in producing the goods but it is inefficient for private producers to do so, they are provided by public bodies and the costs incurred are raised by taxation. Services which possess the characteristics of public goods include the provision of roads, parks, museums and police and fire services, and it is on the provision of these local public goods that the Tiebout model is based.

Once it is recognized that the Tiebout model is founded on the assumption that local government should not be in the business of providing services of a redistributive character, the model turns out in reality to be not so far removed from the assumptions made in *Prescott*. Indeed, when viewed in the light of the Tiebout hypothesis, Vaisey J's concerns begin to make certain sense. It seems, for example, to have become accepted as a basic principle of public finance

[73] C. Tiebout, 'A pure theory of local expenditures' (1956) 64 *J of Political Economy* 416.
[74] See W.E. Oates, *Studies in Fiscal Federalism* (Aldershot, 1991), ch. 16, 'On Local Finance and the Tiebout Model': 'The pure model ... involves a set of assumptions so patently unrealistic as to verge on the outrageous' (309); S. Rose-Ackerman, 'Tiebout Models and the Competitive Ideal: An Essay on the Political Economy of Local Government' in J.M. Quigley (ed.), *Perspectives on Local Public Finance and Public Policy* (Greenwich, Conn., 1983), vol. 1, 23.
[75] C.D. Foster, R.A. Jackman & M. Perlman, *Local Government Finance in a Unitary State* (London, 1980), 220.

economics that redistributive taxes should be centralized. The main reason for this is that, if local councils engage in redistribution on a significant scale, then incentives are created for the out-migration of high-income households and the in-migration of low-income households and these locational shifts (by reducing tax yield and increasing service demand) may ultimately frustrate the original objectives.[76]

Nevertheless, there remain a number of difficulties with the line adopted by Vaisey J. One problem is that the principle against local redistribution may come to be expressed in absolutist terms whereas it seems primarily to suggest only that sub-central government should take care in imposing what might be called non-beneficial taxes on highly mobile tax bases. We should note, however, that property rates provide a relatively immobile tax base. Furthermore, the degree of redistribution an authority is able to engage in is likely to vary according to the size of the authority; in this respect Birmingham Corporation might be better placed to redistribute effectively than a small rural council. But what renders Vaisey J's views highly suspect is his failure to acknowledge the role of central government grants in financing local services. During the twentieth century, as the range of redistributive services provided by local government has increased, so too has the proportion of local finance met by central government grants.[77] In effect, what has happened is that central government has, arguably, acted as local government's agent in collecting from more efficient and equitable tax sources the revenues which local government needs to undertake its redistributive functions effectively. In a system in which central grants provide such an important source of finance the economic relationship between the rate-payer and the council becomes more complex. The final difficulty concerns the idea of a 'redistributive service'. Here we mean simply a service which is collectively provided but which provides benefits only to a relatively small group. Local services which are often identified as falling into this category include education, housing and social services. The question of whether or not such services are to be classified as being public goods rather than private goods (and thus constitute redistributive services), however, is essentially a political question. If, for example, education is viewed as a process which serves only to increase the employment prospects of the individual then it is a private good. But if we believe that education improves the quality of life for all and contributes to the improved functioning of democracy then it should be classed as a public good: 'though non-excludability and non-rivalness do not apply to ... the actual provision of education, they do apply to the benefits we consider are being provided'.[78]

---

[76] W.E. Oates, *Fiscal Federalism* (New York, 1972), ch. 1; R. Musgrave, 'Who should tax, where, and what?' in C. McLure (ed.), *Tax Assignment in Federal Countries* (Canberra, 1983), ch. 1.

[77] For economic analysis of these changes see D.N. King, *Fiscal Tiers: The Economics of Multi-Level Government* (London, 1984), chs. 3–5.

[78] Foster, Jackman & Perlman (above, n. 75), 41.

Given the political character of this question, an explicit justification for judicial involvement is required.

Economic theory may indeed provide a basic perspective for beginning to appreciate the question of the fiduciary relationship between local authorities and ratepayers. Theories of local public finance based on formal models which have little bearing on the realities of government structures, however, are not of themselves able to provide a rationale for the fiduciary concept. In order to take this question further, we need to bring political and economic factors into closer alignment.

A political economy of local government

Much of the political–economic analysis of local government is drawn from public choice theory. Public choice theory tends to focus in particular on the relationship between three key local groups which have a direct interest in local government: those who pay for (ratepayers), those who vote for (electors), and those who benefit from (consumers) local government services. When considering the nature of fiduciary duty, the potential conflict between ratepayer and beneficiary was identified as the main point of tension. In *Roberts* v. *Hopwood* the beneficiaries were the local authority employees, in *Prescott* it was certain consumers of public transport services, and in both cases it was held that they unfairly benefited at the expense of ratepayers. If those who pay for and those who benefit from local services constitute distinct and separate groups then an issue of fairness might indeed arise. And in considering this question the role performed by the third group, the voters, is of particular importance, since the nature of their composition will indicate whether there is a tension between payers and voters and, consequentially, whether ratepayers can depend on the electoral process to act as an effective check on the expenditure decisions of the local council. It is through the relationships which have evolved between these three groups that we may discern a justification for the emergence of the fiduciary concept.

Before the 1835 Act reforms laid the foundations for the modern structure of local government, municipal corporations were closed, self-perpetuating bodies which were vested with the power to levy rates on a fairly broad group of ratepayers. A tension thus existed between the corporation and its ratepayers, since the latter group incurred the burden of taxation without being able to exercise a periodic check on expenditure policies through the election of its members. The reforms of the 1835 Act addressed this issue by extending the municipal franchise to ratepayers. On the assumption that most local government services of this period fell into the category of local public goods, it could be argued that the effect of the reforms was to bring the paying-voting-benefiting relationship into alignment. The ratepayers who pay for public services through local taxation also enjoy the benefits of them, and they exercise decision-making power through their accountable elected representatives.

Given the effect of these reforms, it may seem strange that the most influential nineteenth century cases which characterized the municipal corporation as holding its property on trust were decided shortly after the 1835 Act. When the cases are closely examined, however, any perplexity evaporates. This spate of cases generally materialized from the attempts by the unreconstructed corporations to evade the effects of the 1835 Act by disposing of the property of the corporation to their allies and traditional beneficiaries. Consider, by way of example, the situation regarding Leeds Corporation. Here, in the week following notice in the House of Commons of the Government's intention to introduce a Bill to reform municipal corporations, the members of Leeds Corporation met and resolved to transfer property of the corporation to certain private individuals. After the Act, the reformed corporation then acted as relators to an action seeking to make certain members concerned with these transactions personally liable to make good the funds. In *Attorney-General* v. *Wilson* they succeeded, Lord Cottenham LC holding that: 'This was not only a breach of trust and a violation of duty towards the corporation, whose agents and trustees they were, but an act of spoliation against all the inhabitants of Leeds liable to the borough rate.'[79] The mid-nineteenth century cases which in certain respects lay the foundations of the modern form of the fiduciary concept are essentially concerned with the special responsibilities of members of the unreconstructed corporations to their ratepayers.[80]

Though local authorities were impressed with the characteristics of a trust, the mid-nineteenth century case law should be understood as a specific response by the courts to a particular problem which arose as part of a process of modernizing local government. The trust concept was invoked to resolve the tension between ratepayer and corporation member which existed before the 1835 Act and which was rendered acute as a result of the reforms. Thereafter, the courts disavowed any specific trust relationship between ratepayers and the local authority. As Jessel MR indicated in 1878, 'I am not aware of any means by which the town council can be controlled by the ratepayers except by the system of not re-electing them when the time comes round.'[81] This is perhaps not surprising since, when they originally utilized the trust concept, the courts were seeking primarily to protect the public as the cestui que trust.

There is, however, a more basic reason why the courts did not establish a specific fiduciary relation between ratepayers and the local authority. The entire

---

[79] [1840] Cr. & Ph. 1, 26.

[80] We might note that these cases can thus be seen as attempts to address the issue of 'tombstone funding' similar to that which arose 150 years later as a result of the abolition of the Greater London Council and metropolitan country councils. For an examination of the modern issues see above, ch. 3, 161–5.

[81] *Attorney-General* v. *Brecon* (1878) 10 Ch. 204, 228.

thrust of local government franchise reforms in the nineteenth century had aimed at the establishment of a ratepayer democracy. Since local expenditure was raised almost entirely as rates, the burden therefore fell ultimately on the land-owners. It was felt to be 'a fundamental principle of free government'[82] that those who provided the funds should have the predominant voice in determining how they would be spent. This was achieved in the conduct of parochial busi-ness by the establishment of a system of plural voting; of giving voting power to ratepayers in proportion to their contribution to the poor rate.[83] Then in 1834, motivated by similar concerns, the administration of poor relief was transferred to Guardians.[84] With the reforms to the municipal corporations a ratepayer fran-chise was established and the vote was extended to the middle class, though not to the working class.[85] Given that a degree of harmony in the paying–voting–benefiting nexus could be anticipated in this system, any special legal relation-ship between ratepayer and member was rendered superfluous.

It is only at the turn of the century, as a result both of the changing nature of local government responsibilities and changes to the local government fran-chise, that the strains became apparent. During the second half of the century the municipalities, through their acquisition and use of powers, began to de-monstrate how local government could act as an agency for improving urban conditions. As a result, 'the people came to regard them in a new light – less as trustees of the rates, more as the providers of public services'.[86] Further, in 1888 elected county councils were established to govern rural areas and in 1894 plural voting was abolished.[87] Only as a result of these changes did it become possible for the working class to become involved in local government. And it is around this period that the Labour party began to organize with a view to gaining an influence in local government. By the end of the century, local government began to emerge as a powerful agency of governance which was subject to a form of democratic control. It is from these conditions that a precise concept of fiduciary duty came to be fashioned.

With these changes we see the emergence of a basic tension between rate-

---

[82] J.S. Mill, *Considerations on Representative Government* [1861] in id., *Three Essays* (Oxford, 1975) 142 at 279: '[T]hose who pay no taxes, disposing by their votes of other people's money, have every motive to be lavish, and none to economize. As far as money matters are concerned, any power of voting possessed by them is a violation of the fundamental principle of free government; a severance of the power of control from the interest in its beneficial exercise.'

[83] This was achieved by Sturges Bourne's Act of 1818. See B. Keith-Lucas, *The English Local Government Franchise. A Short History* (Oxford, 1952), ch. II.

[84] See the Poor Law Amendment Acts 1834 and 1844 which not only provided for plural voting for the election of Boards of Guardians but also extended the principle from occupiers to owners and thereby gave companies the power as owners to vote.

[85] See Keith-Lucas, *The English Local Government Franchise* (above, n. 83), ch. III in which he shows that the 1835 Act created a far narrower franchise than expected, a 'fact which modern writers have generally failed to understand' (58). See also S. & B. Webb, *The Development of English Local Government 1689–1835* (London, 1963), 174.

[86] Keith-Lucas (above, n. 83), 10.

[87] County Councils Act 1888; Local Government Act 1894.

payer and voter, particularly in relation to the use by the local authority of its powers for redistributive purposes. This tension is most clearly illuminated in relation to the administration of poor relief during the 1920s. By 1920 Labour had won control of a significant number of local authorities and, as the Fulham case illustrated,[88] had begun to use its powers in innovative ways. But Labour had also gained a majority in a number of poor law unions and, in the context of rising rates of unemployment, started to devise schemes which were less niggardly in the allocation of relief. This policy, which was most extensively adopted in the East End of London, became known as 'Poplarism' after the board which achieved greatest notoriety for its policies.[89] These policies of poor relief certainly imposed a major burden on ratepayers. But they also revealed more general structural deficiencies in the local government system, and one of the key objectives of Poplarism was to force central government to address these flaws.

In Poplar the burden on the poor law of the unemployed had in 1921 resulted in a rate for poor law purposes of 7s $2\frac{1}{2}$d (about 36p) in the pound, whereas in the city of Westminster it was only $4\frac{3}{4}$d (less than 2p). This was partly because in Westminster there were relatively few unemployed. But it was also the product of a great disparity in the taxable wealth of the two areas: in Poplar the average rateable value per head was £5 whereas in Westminster it was £42.[90] The response of Poplar to this apparent injustice was to try to persuade the Government to introduce a scheme for rate equalization. In order to force the Government's hand in March 1921 the Borough Council resolved to levy a rate sufficient only to meet the requirements of the Council and the Poor Law Guardians, and thus refused to collect the precepts of the London County Council and others, including the Metropolitan Police. The County Council successfully sought an order of mandamus requiring the precept to be issued[91] and the councillors, when they refused to comply, were imprisoned for contempt. The Government, however, being under pressure as a result of unrest around the country, urged the Lord Chancellor to ask the judges to release the prisoners so that they might attend a conference on the issue of rate equalization. Though the councillors gave no offer to pay the precepts, the Divisional Court discharged the prisoners and a scheme was negotiated and enacted in the Local Authorities (Financial Provisions) Act 1921.

Tensions of this nature – not only between ratepayer and councils, but also

---

[88] *Attorney-General* v. *Fulham Corporation* [1921] 1 Ch. 440. See above, 209–10.

[89] The jurisdiction of the Poor Law Union of Poplar coincided with that of the Poplar Borough Council which, as we have seen, in the 1920s developed wage policies which led the House of Lords in *Roberts* v. *Hopwood* (above, 210–12) to articulate the concept of fiduciary duty. On Poplarism see: B. Keith-Lucas, 'Poplarism', 1962 *Public Law* 52; N. Branson, *Poplarism, 1919–1925: George Lansbury and the Councillors' Revolt* (London, 1979).

[90] Keith-Lucas, 'Poplarism' (above, n. 89), 56.

[91] *R* v. *Poplar Borough Council* [1922] 1 KB 72; *R* v. *Poplar Borough Council, ex parte London County Council* [1922] 1 KB 95.

between poorer and more wealthy councils and between Labour-controlled authorities and central government – persisted throughout the 1920s. They provide
an illustration of the difficulties which exist when local authorities pursue independent policies of redistribution. Ratepayers in areas of high unemployment
were being required to pay more to provide assistance than in areas of greater
prosperity where unemployment rates were lower, and this burden threatened
the competitiveness of existing ratepayers and made the locality less attractive
for new investment. They were addressed by certain reforms and adjustments.
In the short term a system of sharing the cost of poor relief with the richer West
End authorities was instituted. The more general problem of the rates burden on
industry during the depression was dealt with in 1928 by a 75 per cent de-rating
of industry.[92] Finally, in the longer term, the responsibility for poor relief was
gradually wrested from local authorities and assumed by central government.[93]

   The idea of a fiduciary duty owed by a local authority to its ratepayers thus
seems to be a product of the peculiar conditions of a turbulent period. A transition was taking place from a nineteenth century local government system
based on the idea that the right to vote was conditional on making a direct
contribution to the funds which a local authority administered, to a twentieth
century system in which ratepayer democracy was being replaced by representative democracy. Poplarism had exposed the resulting antagonism: those who
vote for the policies were not closely aligned to those who pay their cost, and
– especially in the case of the single-purpose authority discharging a redistributive
function – those who benefit from the policy may be a distinctly different group
from those who provide the funds. '[T]o some people', Brian Keith-Lucas has
written, Poplarism 'must have seemed to be a justification of their worst fears
of the results of abolishing plural voting, the property qualification and *ex officio*
guardians.'[94] And perhaps to be included in that group are the members of the
House of Lords in *Roberts* v. *Hopwood*.

A modern rationale for the fiduciary concept?

The disjuncture in the paying–voting–benefiting relationship, evident in the pursuit
of redistributive policies by certain local authorities during the 1920s, seems to
provide the best justification for the emergence of the fiduciary concept. We
have yet to consider whether the courts were an appropriate institution to engage

---

[92] Local Government Act 1929.
[93] Poor relief was first given to county level authorities in 1929, an Unemployment Assistance
Board was established in 1934 to take over discretionary, means-tested unemployment relief, and
thereafter local authorities lost their responsibilities for poor relief in stages until the abolition of the
Poor Law in 1948.
[94] Keith-Lucas, *The English Local Government Franchise* (above, n. 83), 44. In addition to voting
restrictions, the Poor Law Amendment Act 1834 had imposed a property qualification on all Guardians and had given all Justices of the Peace an *ex officio* status as Guardians.

in this type of regulation. Leaving that question to one side, there remains a further basic issue to address: even assuming the judiciary were justified in articulating the concept of fiduciary duty in the circumstances of the 1920s, should the concept be confined to the peculiar circumstances of those times or does it still have a useful role to play within the modern framework of central–local government relations?

In many respects, the 1920s mark a transitional phase in central–local government relations. The principle of representative democracy had, by then, become well-established in local government and there have since been few major changes in the composition of the voting group. Since the 1920s, however, significant changes have occurred concerning the questions of who pays for and who benefits from local government services. Turning first to the question of benefit, it may be argued that the changes in the nature of local government services in modern times provide an important reason for retaining the fiduciary concept today. Not only did the share of the national wealth consumed by local government continue to increase throughout the century,[95] but a growing proportion of local expenditure was utilized for redistributive purposes. Although local government has relinquished responsibility for poor relief, many of its services have acquired an apparently redistributive dimension, through rate fund subsidies to council housing and public transport for example, and with the emergence of the welfare state the importance of such functions as education and social services has dramatically increased. By 1980 it was being suggested that 'the majority of local services are carried on in ways which are redistributive'.[96] Since '[a]ttacks on the equity of the rating system have almost always related not to the "beneficial" services but to what have been called the "onerous" services',[97] one might thus expect the fiduciary relationship between ratepayer and authority to have retained its significance.

This argument, however, ignores the major changes which have taken place since the 1920s in the sources of local government finance. The most important development has been the dramatic increase in the scale of central grants in aid of local government expenditure. In the 1920s less than one-quarter of local expenditure was financed through central government grants; by the late 1970s the relevant proportion was more than one-half.[98] The impact of this change can best be appreciated by considering the relationship between rates and grants as sources of local government finance. During the first two decades of the century the rates–grant yield ratio had remained steady at around 3:1. After 1920, however, the value of grants significantly increased, thereby considerably altering

---

[95] Local expenditure increased from about 5 per cent of GNP in 1900 to about 18 per cent in 1975: Foster, Jackman & Perlman, *Local Government Finance in a Unitary State* (above, n. 75), 78.

[96] Foster, Jackman & Perlman (above, n. 75), 206.

[97] E. Cannan, *The History of Local Rates in England* (London, 2nd edn., 1912), 168.

[98] These figures are derived from the statistical tables in Foster, Jackman & Perlman (above, n. 75), 145–8.

the ratio. By 1975 the rates–grant ratio was 1:2. The effect of these trends, it may be argued, has been to break the special relationship between the local authority and its ratepayers. The massive growth in central government grants since 1920 has certainly weakened, if not entirely destroyed, the clear link between local authority expenditure policies and ratepayer burden. The effect of grant systems has been such that, for example, it was not at all clear that an increase in expenditure by a local authority would impose a major, let alone disproportionate, burden on ratepayers.[99]

It is not, however, simply the scale of grants which weakens the link between the local authority and its ratepayers, but also the form of grant assistance. With the introduction of the principle of a block grant in 1929,[100] the financial regime began to shift away from a system of specific grants earmarked for particular services and towards the payment of a general or block grant paid in accordance with the needs of the locality and the resources available to the authority to address those needs. Under a general grant system, it will invariably be difficult to identify the incidence of benefit and burden of many of the local authority's policies. Consequently, as a result of both the scale and the form of central government grant since the 1920s the idea of a special status for ratepayers in the paying–benefiting relationship would appear to have been all but destroyed.

We have seen that local authorities first came to be impressed with the characteristics of a trust in the aftermath of the 1835 Act which laid the foundations for the emergence of a modern system of local government. We have also seen that the courts devised a specific concept of fiduciary duty only in the 1920s; that is, only once the principle of representative democracy in local government had become established and local councillors had sought to use general discretionary powers for redistributive purposes. In each of these circumstances, the judiciary seem to be grappling with particular problems within a local government system in transition. Since the 1920s, however, the system has fundamentally changed: local councils have now clearly emerged as representative bodies rather than as trustees of the ratepayers; they provide public services for the benefit of all inhabitants of the locality, not simply those who pay rates; with the growth in the importance of central grants, local councils have come to be funded by every taxpayer not only the ratepayer; and thus we come full circle because the 'fact that every citizen today pays taxes in one form or another . . . justifies a claim for universal suffrage in local government'.[101]

What these developments seem to signal is the fact that in the modern era the voting–paying–benefiting relationship in local government has become highly

---

[99] It is worthy of note that, notwithstanding the dramatic increase in local expenditure since the Second World War, the burden on domestic ratepayers, expressed as a proportion of personal disposable income, has remained fairly constant: see Foster, Jackman and Perlman (above, n. 75), 316.

[100] Local Government Act 1929.

[101] B. Keith-Lucas, *The English Local Government Franchise* (above, n. 83), 11.

complex. The question of benefit is itself (as has already been indicated) a highly political issue. This has been recognized at least since the deliberations of the Kempe Committee in 1914 which suggested that many local authority services were 'semi-national goods' since they yielded benefits not only to the locality but also to the nation and argued that, since the nation was buying services from the local authorities, it should contribute to their costs.[102] What in effect has occurred since the 1920s is that, in acknowledgement of these complexities, we have developed a modern structure of trust relations organized through an elaborate administrative network founded on a bedrock of functional interdependence. Local authorities vested with a broad range of discretionary powers and central departments with extensive supervisory duties are now locked into a highly complex administrative system which assumes responsibility for the delivery of an extensive range of public services. Furthermore, the conventions which have emerged to guide and regulate the system have not generally been expressed in legal form. In part this has been because our legal system and legal culture has been unable to adjust to these new circumstances; the judiciary, being rooted in an ancient idea of aristocracy founded on traditional codes, seem to be both institutionally and culturally ill-suited to regulate the system. Within the modern structure of central–local government relations, a judiciary which was equipped with an ancient baggage of simple concepts seemed no longer to be in a position to perform an effective supervisory role.

Reactivation of the Fiduciary Concept

The concept of fiduciary duty came to be seen as almost irrelevant to the postwar system of local government. Although the concept was critical to the judgments in the *Prescott* case, it was the discrimination principle rather than the more extensive efficient management principle which was formative in that case. Furthermore, *Prescott* actually provides an excellent illustration of the nature of the changes which have taken place since the 1920s, since it was widely recognized that the decision 'created a very awkward position in municipal finance',[103] that it cut across the grain of the modern framework of the central–local relations, and that its impact on public transport systems immediately had to be remedied by statute.[104] While the fiduciary concept occasionally surfaced in

---

[102] *Report of the Departmental Committee on Local Taxation*, Cd. 7315 (London, 1914).

[103] *Litherland UDC* v. *Liverpool Corporation* [1958] 1 WLR 913, 915 (per Harman J).

[104] Public Service Vehicles (Travel Concessions) Act 1955. See Harman J in *Litherland* v. *Liverpool* (above, n. 103) at 915: 'Having regard to the widespread use of schemes of this sort, this decision created a very awkward position in municipal finance, and, in order to clear the matter up, Parliament thought right to enact the [1955 Act]. The statute gives a kind of indemnity for past illegal acts [and] provides . . . that any local authority operating a public service vehicle undertaking may "make arrangements" for the granting of concessionary fares.'

challenges to the legality of local authority action, especially in respect of council house rents schemes,[105] such challenges were invariably unsuccessful.[106]

The rationale for the fiduciary concept has in effect been destroyed as a result of the post-war settlement in which central departments and local authorities have forged an executive partnership to ensure the provision of a range of cradle-to-grave welfare services. In the process, central government has become the primary funder of local services through a grant system which, since the 1929 Act, has come to be fashioned on three fundamental principles: that grant aid should be provided as a general grant which leaves to the local authority the decision about how much actually to spend on particular services; that grant should be based on an assessment of the locality's needs; and that the system should seek to compensate authorities for disparities in taxable wealth.[107] Since grants are paid in recognition of the fact that non-locals may benefit from locally provided services, that certain local groups may benefit disproportionately from local services, and that certain less wealthy authorities may not be able to afford to provide a general level of services which society regards as an incident of citizenship,[108] the special relationship between local ratepayers and the council has effectively been broken.

Nevertheless, the combination of further technical refinements to the grant system together with recent changes in central policies have served during the 1980s to bring a version of the efficient management aspect of fiduciary duty back into consideration. In 1980 the system of grant allocation was refined and came to be explicitly constructed on the concept of equalization.[109] This meant that, in theory, all local authorities would be able to provide a nationally uniform standard of service at an equal rate poundage cost to its ratepayers. However, this final stage in the process of technical refinement of the grant system, coincided with a period in which central government's policies have been to impose restraints on the growth in local government expenditure. The Government has therefore attempted to use the grant system as an instrument for encouraging local authorities to reduce expenditure. Initially this was achieved through a tapering provision in the block grant mechanism which meant that expenditure above a designated level attracted grant at a lower rate. The Government felt,

---

[105] See *Belcher* v. *Reading Corporation* [1950] 1 Ch. 380; *Summerfield* v. *Hampstead BC* [1957] 1 All ER 221; *Evans* v. *Collins* [1964] 1 All ER 808; *Luby* v. *Newcastle under Lyme Corporation* [1965] 1 QB 214.

[106] The only other case in the post-war period up to 1980 in which the concept has formed a major aspect of a successful challenge appears to be *Taylor* v. *Munrow* [1960] 1 WLR 151, a case in which the Divisional Court upheld the auditor's decision to surcharge councillors of St Pancras UDC who had refused to raise rents in accordance with the provisions of the Rent Act 1957 on the ground that, as a matter of policy, they opposed the principle of means-testing.

[107] See R. Jackman, 'Local Government Finance' in M. Loughlin, M.D. Gelfand & K. Young (eds.), *Half A Century of Municipal Decline 1935–1985* (London, 1985), 144 at 162.

[108] See D.N. King, *Fiscal Tiers* (above, n. 77), ch. 4.

[109] This is the block grant system established under Local Government, Planning and Land Act 1980, Pt. VI.

however, that this taper was not sufficiently powerful and in 1981 instituted a system of expenditure targets which imposed grant penalties on local authorities which failed to cut back on historic expenditure levels.[110] The impact of these tapers and targets has been to transfer onto local ratepayers a greater burden of the marginal costs of local authority decisions which incur expenditure above the relevant centrally-determined levels. In such circumstances the fiduciary concept, with its in-built sense of balance between service benefits and ratepayer costs, could potentially assume a new lease of life.

It was not long before this issue was tested. The occasion was the switch in control of the Greater London Council (GLC) from Conservative to Labour in the May 1981 elections. The Labour party had included in its election manifesto a proposal to seek to reverse the high-cost, low patronage spiral of decline on London's public transport system by reduction of fares through the injection of greater amounts of public subsidy. In furtherance of this policy the new GLC administration reduced fares on London Transport Executive's (LTE) transport system by 25 per cent and issued a supplementary precept to meet the costs of any consequential revenue deficit.

The fares cut was estimated to require an extra £30 million in revenue support. However, owing to the impact of the new block grant mechanism, the cost to the GLC was much greater. First, as a result of the equalization mechanism within the block grant, the GLC, because of its very high resource base, was one of a small number of authorities which was on a negative marginal grant slope throughout the entire range of its conceivable budgetary options. The effect of the taper within the block grant mechanism was therefore to steepen the slope of grant loss. The decision to increase expenditure in order to finance the reduction in fares thus had the effect of incurring further loss of rate support grant. In addition to this direct consequence of the block grant mechanism, the Secretary of State in 1981 announced expenditure targets for individual local authorities in accordance with a formula based on historical patterns of expenditure. Any authority exceeding the expenditure target in 1981/82 would in effect incur a fine in the form of grant penalties. The combined impact of the block grant mechanism and expenditure targets meant that the supplementary precept issued by the GLC in 1981 was roughly twice the amount actually required for fares reductions on London Transport.

This supplementary precept was challenged by the London Borough of Bromley by way of judicial review. Bromley, a Conservative-controlled outer London borough which was not served by any underground stations, was concerned that the burden on its ratepayers was not proportionate to any benefits they were likely to derive and founded its challenge primarily on the fiduciary concept.[111]

---

[110] These developments are examined in more detail in ch. 5, below, esp. 269–71.

[111] See 'Bromley Council v Greater London Council: Counsel's Opinion' [1991] *Public Law* 499 which reproduces the opinion received by Bromley. The opinion does not examine the statutory framework in any detail and casts the case almost entirely on the precedent of *Prescott*.

Its application was dismissed by the Divisional Court which held that: 'Matters of this kind are for the appropriate authority and eventually the electors, and not for the Court to determine.'[112] On appeal, however, the Court of Appeal over-turned that decision and quashed the supplementary precept. This decision was unanimously affirmed by the House of Lords.[113] This is not the place to examine in detail the intricate complexity of this decision; a complexity which flows from the fact that five opinions were given, each of which, against a background of common law principles, provides varying interpretations of the statutory scheme.[114] What is of vital importance, however, is the fact that the fiduciary concept played a powerful role in the shaping of each of the opinions.

In four of the opinions the fiduciary concept was treated essentially as a principle of statutory interpretation. Lords Wilberforce and Scarman focused primarily on the GLC's duty, under section 1 of the Transport (London) Act 1969, 'to develop policies ... which will promote the provision of integrated, efficient and *economic* transport facilities'[115] and concluded that, when interpreted in the light of the fiduciary duty which a local authority owes to its ratepayers, the Act did not empower the GLC to adopt a fares policy which unduly benefits transport users at the expense of ratepayers.[116] Lords Keith and Brandon focused primarily on the duties of the LTE and, reading the 1969 Act in the light of the common law principle that unless a contrary intention is clearly expressed transport authorities should run their services on ordinary business principles, could not discern anything in the Act to negate that principle.[117] Though differing in emphasis, it is worthy of note that the authoritative source of each of these approaches is that of *Prescott*.[118] When considered in this light it is clear that, however formulated, the fiduciary concept provided the key to the decision. The result seemed to be that the 1969 Act, though permitting grant financing of public transport 'which it may not be practicable or possible to avoid' did not empower the GLC to provide grants 'as an object of social or transport policy'.[119]

In the final opinion to consider, Lord Diplock, disagreeing with the others on the question of statutory construction, held that there was nothing in the statutory framework 'which impose[d] any limitation on the power of the GLC to make grants'.[120] His opinion, however, is of particular importance since he was able to concur in the result only by elevating the fiduciary concept to the status of a quasi-constitutional principle. Examining the GLC's constitutional status and statutory duties in conjunction, Lord Diplock identified three groups to

[112] *R* v. *Greater London Council, ex parte Bromley LBC* (unreported) 3 November 1981 (Div.Ct). Lexis transcript of judgment.
[113] *Bromley LBC* v. *Greater London Council* [1983] 1 AC 768.
[114] See M. Loughlin, *Local Government in the Modern State* (London, 1986), 70–5.
[115] Emphasis supplied.
[116] [1983] 1 AC 768 at 814 (Lord Wilberforce), 841–2 (Lord Scarman).
[117] Ibid., 834–5 (Lord Keith); 847–50 (Lord Brandon).
[118] Ibid., 815 (Wilberforce); 838 (Scarman); 831 (Keith) and 851 (Brandon).
[119] Ibid., 846 (per Lord Scarman).   [120] Ibid., 827.

whom the GLC owed duties in relation to public transport: potential passengers; residents of Greater London who benefit from the general mobility of the transport system whether or not they use public transport; and the ratepayers, to the extent that they contribute to the cost of the system. He considered that there was a certain symmetry between passengers and residents but that there was no such coincidence between these two groups and the third; the ratepayers 'constitute only 40 per cent of the residents and that 40 per cent bears only 38 per cent of the total burden borne by all ratepayers'.[121] Having thus identified a tension between service beneficiaries and ratepayers Diplock was then able to bring the fiduciary concept into play. He suggested that, if the issue under consideration was merely one of lowering fares by 25 per cent and transferring its cost to ratepayers, it would be difficult to suggest that the GLC was in breach of its fiduciary duty. But here the loss of rate support grant meant that the GLC's decision did not simply concern the allocation of a total financial burden but was also 'a decision to increase the burden so as nearly to double it and to place the whole of the increase on the ratepayers'.[122] For Diplock that was clearly 'a thriftless use of moneys obtained by the GLC from the ratepayers and a deliberate failure to employ to the best advantage the full financial resources available to it by avoiding any action that would involve forfeiting grants from central government funds. It was thus a breach of the fiduciary duty owed by the GLC to the ratepayers'.[123]

The decision of the House of Lords in *Bromley* undoubtedly constitutes a landmark in the development of the fiduciary concept. For the majority, the concept furnished a powerful common law principle through which to make sense of the statutory scheme in the 1969 Act. And in Lord Diplock's account the concept assumed a status as part of the constitutional foundations of local government. But what sort of landmark does the decision provide?

Some consider that the case illustrates the fact that, in the guise of the fiduciary concept, the principle of proportionality forms part of our law.[124] In this version *Bromley* is seen as marking a stage in a gradual process of developing modern principles of administrative law. Others have sought to appropriate the case in support of a view that the normative material of law is inherently ambiguous and can be used to justify any decision.[125] In this interpretation *Bromley*, although

---

[121] Ibid., 829.   [122] Ibid., 830.   [123] Ibid.

[124] See, e.g., J. Jowell, 'Courts and the Administration in Britain: Standards, Principles and Rights' [1988] 22 *Israel Law Rev.* 409, 418: 'Local authority expenditure that is so excessive and is thus said to offend the fiduciary duty of the authority to its ratepayers in effect offends the principle of proportionality – because of the failure of the authority rationally to have balanced the benefits achieved by the expenditure against the burdens suffered by ratepayers.' See also J. Jowell & A. Lester, 'Beyond *Wednesbury*: substantive principles of administrative law', 1987 *Public Law* 368 at 381–2; J. Jowell & A. Lester, 'Proportionality: neither novel nor dangerous' in J. Jowell & D. Oliver (eds.), *New Directions in Judicial Review* (London, 1988), 51 at 62.

[125] See, e.g., A.C. Hutchinson, 'The rise and ruse of administrative law and scholarship' (1985) 48 *MLR* 292, 304–14; P. Goodrich, *Legal Discourse. Studies in Linguistics, Rhetoric and Legal Analysis* (Basingstoke, 1987), 192–204.

having important policy implications, exemplifies the general process of legal analysis. Each of these types of analysis seems deficient: *Bromley* provides neither an index of legal rationalization nor a general illustration of law's irrationality. It is certainly true that those speeches which sought to interpret the Transport (London) Act through the spectacles of fiduciary duty were not only extremely convoluted but also bordered on the incoherent. But, by ignoring such obvious signposts to interpretation as the legislative history and by utilizing an anachronistic concept as their guide, the Law Lords effectively succeeded in turning sense into nonsense.[126] If the Lords had referred to the White Papers and ministerial statements on the objectives of the 1969 Act, there could have been little doubt but that the Act marked a major change in policy and provided a legal framework for providing subsidies to public transport as an object of transport policy.[127] In introducing the Bill, for example, the Transport Minister stated that:

> The main powers that the [Greater London] Council will have . . . will be to pay grant to the Executive for any purpose it thinks fit and to issue directions to the Executive. This gives the Council the right to prescribe policy lines to be followed and to take financial responsibility for its decisions. . . . The Council might wish, for example, the Executive to run a series of services at a loss for social or planning reasons. It might wish to keep fares down at a time when costs are rising and there is no scope for economies. It is free to do so. But it has to meet the cost.[128]

During this period the Government had suggested that: 'To attempt to solve these [public transport] problems in exclusively commercial terms is to bring the Victorian mentality to the solution of modern needs.'[129] Over a decade later, this is precisely what the Law Lords sought to do. That error was compounded by the fact that the interpretation which the majority gave to the 1969 Act simply did not make sense. In suggesting that LTE must operate in such a manner as to try to keep its subsidy requirement to a practical minimum Professor Sir Christopher Foster, a leading transport economist, has convincingly argued that the Lords fell into a logical error:

> [T]here is a profound economic problem with this approach since there is no such minimum independent of the quantity of service, and the amount of subsidy needed is

---

[126] Cf. *Magor & St. Mellons RDC* v. *Newport Corporation* [1950] 2 All ER 1226, 1236 (per Lord Denning): 'We do not sit here to pull the language of Parliament and Ministers to pieces and make nonsense of it. That is an easy thing to do, and it is a thing to which lawyers are often prone.'

[127] See Ministry of Transport, *Transport in London*, Cmnd. 3686 (1968). The reform of arrangements in London was part of a more general review of transport policy in the 1960s. See, Ministry of Transport, *Transport Policy*, Cmnd. 3057 (1966).

[128] Mr Richard Marsh, Minister of Transport, HC Debs, vol. 775 cols. 1247–8 (17 December 1968). Even Mrs Margaret Thatcher acknowledged in the debate that: 'The purpose of the Bill is to achieve a new concept in transport planning . . .' (col. 1255).

[129] *Transport in London*, Cmnd. 3686, para. 9.

a consequence of the scale and type of services provided. No one doubts that there is some level, or levels, of services the LTE could provide which would eliminate the need for revenue subsidy. One example is this – it could close down most of its bus services and run most of its train services profitably. Thus one cannot talk about the minimum level of subsidy without specifying service levels. In 1981 the GLC changed its mind on the level of services it wanted provided and that new level of services implied a reduction in fares if the services were to be used as fully as the GLC wanted. Thus it is arguable that the new higher level of subsidy represented a new practical minimum in relation to the new service level. There is a logical error here which cannot be escaped.[130]

These difficulties in the majority's approach to the question of statutory construction were implicitly recognized by Lord Diplock. Diplock realized that seeking to make sense of the Act through the lens of fiduciary duty rendered the Act nonsensical; indeed, his opinion can be read as providing a cogent critique of the majority's approach. But, after providing an interpretation of the Act which was consistent with the goals of the policy-makers of the time, Diplock then invoked the fiduciary concept as a basic constitutional principle. Though making sense of the 1969 Act, Diplock's use of the fiduciary concept had the potentially more profound effect of rendering incoherent the new block grant mechanism. In order to substantiate this view, Lord Diplock's treatment of fiduciary duty must be examined in some detail. His analysis is divisible into two parts: the identification of a conflict of interest between service beneficiaries and ratepayers, and the content given to the concept in the context of the operation of the rate support grant system.

On the issue of conflict of interest between service beneficiaries and ratepayers, Lord Diplock's analysis is both formalistic and incomplete. Although he did not discern any basic tension between passengers and residents he did suggest that only 40 per cent of residents were ratepayers. By this, he presumably meant that only 40 per cent of residents were heads of households and thus under a legal liability to pay rates. When viewed in anything other than formal legal terms, however, rates cannot be seen simply as a formal burden on the head of household; it must be understood as a general tax on the household. Certainly this is the standard way in which economists examine the question of the burden of rates.[131] When viewed from the perspective of household burden, however, it is difficult to see how the category of domestic ratepayers is distinguishable from that of residents. And if domestic ratepayers can be equated with residents there is unlikely to be a basic tension between domestic ratepayers and passengers. However, as Lord Diplock points out, 62 per cent of rates are paid by commercial and industrial ratepayers. Unfortunately the significance of this

[130] C.D. Foster, 'Urban Transport Policy after the House of Lords' Decision' (1982) vol. 8 no. 3 *Local Government Studies* 105, at 107.
[131] See, e.g., Foster, Jackman & Perlman, *Local Government Finance in a Unitary State* (above, n. 75), ch. 6 ('The Incidence of Rates').

statistic is not explained, though it seems implicit in Diplock's analysis that the relationship between non-domestic ratepayers and service beneficiaries is one of conflict. This, however, is not necessarily the case. Non-domestic ratepayers could benefit significantly from an increase in the general mobility of the transport system: either in greater accessibility (of customers or clients to them or of their products to various outlets), or in the alleviation of increased-cost inspired wage demands of employees. Given Lord Diplock's failure to examine this question, it is not at all clear why his analysis demonstrates an imbalance between service beneficiaries and ratepayers in using rates to finance a reduction in fares on the transport system. Yet, without this fundamental imbalance, the invocation of the fiduciary concept does not seem justifiable.

Lord Diplock did not need to follow through his analysis in detail because ultimately he held that the GLC breached its fiduciary obligation, not simply as a consequence of imbalance, but essentially because, as a result of its rate support grant implications, the decision to reduce fares constituted a thriftless use of the ratepayer's money. This conclusion was reached, however, without any examination of the nature of the block grant system. If the system had been properly considered Lord Diplock would have realized that, as a result of the techniques used to achieve greater equalization, the GLC (because of its extremely high resource base) received negative marginal rates of grant throughout the entire range of budgetary choice.[132] If the strict logic of his analysis were adhered to, the only safe budgetary position of the GLC would have been at an expenditure position requiring its budget to be more than halved and at which it would not raise any precept whatsoever because its expenditure would be financed entirely from central government grant. This seems patently absurd.[133]

But that is not all. Lord Diplock not only failed to examine the nature of the grant system which gave rise to this situation, but also ignored the mechanism by which actual grant loss was assessed. He noted that the £69 million cost of fares reduction resulted in the loss of £50 million of rate support grant. What was not mentioned was the fact that almost one-third of that grant loss was attributable to penalties for exceeding the expenditure target announced by the Secretary of State that year. At that time, however, the system of expenditure targets lacked any statutory foundation and penalties could not actually be levied until the system was retroactively authorized in 1982.[134] If that proportion of loss

---

[132] For an examination of why some authorities gain, and others lose, grant at the margin see: R. Jackman & C.D. Foster, 'The Accountability of Local Authorities', *Public Money* (September, 1982), 11.

[133] Cf. C.D. Foster, 'Urban Transport Policy after the House of Lords' Decision' (above, n. 130), at 115: 'Whether an authority loses grant [at the margin] does not depend at all on its transport needs or policies, but on something totally alien, esoteric and very complicated: which itself derives from a principle of local finance – the equalisation of rate poundage in relation to needs and the imposition of a grant taper on marginal expenditure by central government.'

[134] Local Government Finance Act 1982, s. 8(10).

attributable to the system of targets were discounted, would the reduced rate of penalty still cause Diplock to conclude that the GLC had breached its fiduciary duty? Unfortunately we have no way of knowing because, although elaborating on this grant-rate balancing aspect of fiduciary duty, Lord Diplock provided no formula to enable us to appreciate when the scales may have been tipped too much in favour of the service beneficiaries.

The *Bromley* decision reactivated the fiduciary concept in highly controversial circumstances. Viewed through the lens of fiduciary duty, the generally accepted meaning of the 1969 Act was grossly distorted, resulted in an interpretation which, in an economic sense, was nonsensical and undermined a key policy of the newly elected administration at the GLC. It even caused the GLC's Comptroller of Finance to comment that 'it is difficult to avoid the reaction that a judge is substituting his or her "balance" between collective "good" and individual "good" for that of the elected body'.[135] But the manner in which Lord Diplock employed the concept had potentially more important consequences since it seemed to result in the creation of a novel and very powerful legal doctrine for restraining local government expenditure. In a study of the emergence of fiduciary duty in private law Ernest Weinrib has concluded that the concept served to promote two basic values: 'the primary notion of the control of discretion and the penumbral desirability of protecting commercial structures and the market-place within which they operate'.[136] In the context of *Bromley* it is tempting to conclude that the fiduciary concept serves precisely the same function in public law.

Fiduciary Duty and Urban Public Transport Policy

The *Bromley* decision had a major and direct impact on public transport policy throughout the country. The effect of the five opinions, each of which adopted a slightly different approach and emphasis, was to generate a great deal of uncertainty. The one general consensus which did emerge was that the decision

---

[135] M.F. Stonefrost, 'An Administrator's Viewpoint on *R* v. *GLC, ex p. Bromley LBC*' (unpublished paper presented to Oxford University Faculty of Law, 2 March 1983) at 9. Cf. H.S.E. Gravelle, 'Judicial Review and Public Firms' (1983) 3 *Int. Rev. of Law and Economics* 187, at 200–1: 'The *Bromley* decision attracted much unfavourable comment. It was suggested that the judges were in effect making policy by imposing their particular and narrow view of the proper objectives of a public transport system . . . To a considerable extent these criticisms are misconceived, being based on a misunderstanding of the *ratio decidendi* and on a naive positive theory of public firm behaviour. . . . Given the previous case law on the subject, it is difficult to argue that the majority of the Law Lords adopted an interpretation which is obviously at variance with the intention of the Act's drafters.' Gravelle's account, however, is based on a naive grasp of legal interpretation (especially on the generally accepted relationship between common law and statute law), an apparent ignorance of the policy framework which shaped the 1969 Act, and on a fundamental misunderstanding of what economic analysis has to offer by way of helping us to understand the case.

[136] E.J. Weinrib, 'The Fiduciary Obligation' (1974) 24 *Univ. of Toronto L J* 1, 22.

had destroyed any stable foundation for public transport policy.[137] The impact of
the decision on the policies of the shire counties was less serious, primarily as
a result of differences in the drafting of their enabling statute and also because
of the more modest scale of their revenue support operations.[138] In London and
the metropolitan areas, however, the crisis was acute.

Public transport policy in the metropolitan areas

Although the legal framework governing public transport provision in the metropolitan areas was contained in the Transport Act 1968 rather than the Transport (London) Act 1969 which governed the *Bromley* dispute, the two Acts were
very similar in design and reflected a common philosophy.[139] Furthermore, after
May 1981 all six metropolitan authorities were under Labour control and all
were providing revenue subsidies to public transport undertakings. Following
the *Bromley* decision in December 1981, the metropolitan authorities immediately sought legal advice on the significance of that decision for their policies.
These opinions were almost unanimously restrictive and caused intense political
controversy. In Greater Manchester, for example, following counsel's opinion
indicating that they were exposed to legal challenge as a result of their general
levels of subsidy, the county council resolved to raise fares by 15 per cent.[140]
And on Merseyside, the leadership, after receiving counsel's opinion, decided at
the preliminary budget meeting to maintain fares levels rather than implement
the second stage of its planned fares cuts.[141]

It was South Yorkshire CC, however, which was placed under the most severe
pressure. In South Yorkshire the Passenger Transport Executive (PTE) had
frozen fares on its undertakings since 1975 and had been able to make good the
shortfall as a result of revenue grants from the county council. In January 1982
the PTE obtained counsel's opinion which stated that 'there is nothing in the
1968 Act to alter the basic rule that the undertaking must be run on ordinary
business principles or to give any power of making a grant for policy or social

---

[137] See, e.g., Report of Honorary Secretary, Society of County Secretaries, *R* v. *GLC & Another,
ex parte Bromley LBC* (Winchester, 12 April 1982), 4: '[I]t is not easy to see how any confusion
about the law resulting from the GLC case is to be dispelled. . . . While local authorities . . . will
be well-advised to take legal advice and to give it proper attention, no Counsel however
senior can be expected to spot in advance with certainty at what point on the "gradient" [of grant
penalty] an authority will slip into illegality.' See also, Stonefrost, 'An Administrator's Viewpoint'
(above, n. 135), 8: 'An "if you do this, then the Courts might . . ." climate, however strong, is not
a stable legal or administrative basis for major decision [making] on important public services.'

[138] See Society of County Secretaries Report (above, n. 137). The Transport Act 1978, s. 1
imposed on the counties a similar duty to that on the GLC but in requiring them to promote 'a co-
ordinated and efficient system of public passenger transport' the 1978 Act significantly omitted the
word 'economic'.

[139] See, Ministry of Transport, *Transport Policy*, Cmnd. 3057 (1966); Ministry of Transport,
Public Transport and Traffic, Cmnd. 3481 (1967).

[140] 'Fares subsidy in disarray', *Local Government Chronicle*, 22 January 1982, 65.

[141] 'Judge aids fares confusion', *Local Government Chronicle*, 29 January 1982, 95.

reasons' and that the 'Authority has been acting unlawfully and in breach of its fiduciary duty to the ratepayers by making grants beyond that which is authorised by the Act and the Executive has been acting unlawfully in that . . . it has not been seeking to "break-even"'.[142] The Authority's own advice emphatically reinforced that received by the PTE. In an extensive, 39-page opinion, leading counsel not only suggested that there was a 'strong likelihood' that the Authority would lose any legal challenge to its policies but also that 'a continuance of the existing transport policy would be regarded as unreasonable and that surcharge would be very likely to result'.[143] Given the weight of this legal advice, in early February the PTE recommended that from April 1982 fares should rise on average by 75 per cent.[144] The county council, however, were very reluctant to abandon the central plank of their transport policy without exploring all possible options. After hearing that the powers of metropolitan authorities to make grants under the 1968 Act was being challenged in an action against Merseyside CC they succeeded in obtaining counsel's opinion which, though unable to give any 'guarantee that Councillors will not be the subject of an order' for surcharge, suggested that the Merseyside action 'could be used as a reason for shelving the issue temporarily'.[145] This provided South Yorkshire CC with the breathing space they required.

There were in fact two actions which challenged the powers of metropolitan authorities to provide revenue grants under the 1968 Act. These actions involved the county councils of the West Midlands and Merseyside. In each of these authorities, as with the GLC, Labour had won control at the 1981 elections and, in furtherance of their election pledges, each had issued a supplementary precept to finance a reduction in fares on their public transport undertakings. In both cases the commencement of proceedings for judicial review to quash the precepts had been delayed until the *Bromley* dispute had been resolved. Since this delay seemed sensible, leave out of time was granted.

In the light of the eventual outcome of the West Midlands challenge, we should consider the decision-making process of the newly-elected county council. Labour's manifesto, after a considerable amount of research and discussion, had contained a proposal to reduce public transport fares by 25 per cent and, after Labour had won the election by a substantial majority, the view was taken that a clear mandate for the proposal had been obtained. On 10 June 1981 the Authority considered a report from the Director General of the PTE which included, inter alia, a proposal that, in achieving an average reduction of 24 per

[142] Report of Chief Executive to South Yorkshire CC, *Transport Policy. Summary of advice given to the PTE by Mr Malcolm Spence QC* (16 February 1982), para. 3.
[143] Opinion of Sir Frank Layfield QC and William Hicks, *South Yorkshire County Council. Transport Policy* (29 January 1982), paras. 35, 36.
[144] Joint Report of the Chief Executive, County Treasurer and PTE, *Passenger Transport Budget 1982/83* (S Yorks CC, nd), para. 17.
[145] Opinion of Harry Sales, *South Yorkshire CC. Transport Policy* (10 February 1982), paras. 26, 19.

cent, individual fares reductions should vary between 14 and 33 per cent. This report was accepted by the Authority, was considered at further meetings and on 25 June a special joint meeting of the Policy and Resources, Highways and Passenger Transport Committees formulated proposals for a reduction in fares on bus and rail services averaging 23 per cent from September 1981 and thereafter for a freezing of fares. The Policy and Resources Committee then received reports detailing the financial implications (which included grant loss) of the new Council's policy decisions[146] and met with representatives of the West Midlands CBI and Ratepayers' Association before the County Council agreed on 13 July to implement the new policies and to issue a supplementary precept to finance them.[147]

After the *Bromley* decision the West Midlands CC supplementary precept was challenged by Solihull BC and Guest, Keen & Nettlefolds Ltd. West Midlands CC obtained counsel's opinion which, contrary to the opinions received in South Yorkshire, considered that 'the difference in the material provisions of the Acts of 1968 and 1969 are such that the ... *Bromley* case does not conclude the problems in the instant case' and took the view that 'the West Midlands County Council has the power (subject to the proper exercise of its discretion) ... to make a general reduction in fares'.[148] The opinion, however, went on to address that exercise of discretion and concluded that:

(a) The County Council ... paid scant regard to the effect their new transport policies would have or the increased burden that would fall on the ratepayers by reason of the imposition of a government grant penalty for overspending. ... [W]e are of the view that in failing to have any or any sufficient regard to that factor the County Council failed to take into account a proper consideration and therefore acted illegally. ...

(b) In our opinion, the evidence also shows that a substantial majority of the Councillors regarded themselves as bound by the terms of their manifesto in circumstances which ought to have resulted in a re-think of their policies. ...

(c) Further, there is no evidence that proper regard was given to the precise level of the fares reductions. ...

(e) In their deliberations, it is our view that the Council also had regard to an irrelevant consideration, namely the attainment of philanthropic purposes, that is to say, help to the unemployed and disadvantaged. ... [T]he Transport Act 1968 puts on local authorities a duty to provide an integrated and efficient transport system. That is the purpose of the Act and the Act cannot be used as a tool of general social policy unconnected with the attainment of that purpose.[149]

---

[146] In addition to public transport policies (costing £17.8m), there were proposals to restore cuts in highways' maintenance budget (£2.3m) and establish the West Midlands Enterprise Board (£8m).

[147] These facts are taken from Joint Opinion of William Glover QC and Robert Griffiths, *In the Matter of a Supplementary Precept of the West Midlands County Council* (26 January 1982).

[148] Ibid., paras. 37, 43.   [149] Ibid., para. 55.

This opinion is reproduced in some detail because it clearly highlights the intrusive character of review of local authority decision-making which seems to take place whenever the fiduciary concept is invoked. The opinion is also important because, so far as West Midlands CC were concerned, they had received judgment on the challenge to their supplementary precept. In the light of that advice, on 25 January 1982 the County Council passed a resolution declaring the supplementary precept for 14 pence in the pound null and void and issuing a new precept for 5.75 pence. The effect was to remove the costs of financing the public transport policy with the result that fares would increase by around 70 per cent.

At the judicial review hearing scheduled for the following day, Woolf J accepted the County Council's concession and, for the avoidance of doubt, granted an order of certiorari to quash the original supplementary precept.[150] In giving judgment, however, Woolf J stressed the fact that the order should in no way be taken to reflect on the merits of the arguments on the construction of the 1968 Act.[151] This was important since, on the day following judgment, an application challenging Merseyside CC's supplementary precept was made and this case also was heard before Woolf J. Consequently, three weeks later, on 17 February, Woolf J gave judgment in the *Merseyside* case on precisely those issues.[152]

The general situation and the council's decision-making procedures in the *Merseyside* case were almost identical to the scenario at the West Midlands CC. On Merseyside, the previous administration had resolved to increase fares by 15 per cent from July 1981 but when Labour assumed control in May of that year, in furtherance of their manifesto proposals, they reversed that decision and proposed a 10 per cent cut in its place, making in effect a 25 per cent reduction in budgetary terms. The council held a similar schedule of meetings to those in the West Midlands and in August confirmed the policy and the supplementary precept. After these decision-making procedures were explained in affidavit evidence, counsel for the applicants[153] sought leave to cross-examine the Chairman of the Passenger Transport Committee 'to fill in the gaps in the affidavit evidence'.[154] Woolf J, however, refused leave on the ground that he 'did not

---

[150] *R* v. *West Midlands CC, ex p. Solihull MBC and Guest, Keen & Nettlefolds Ltd*, 26 January 1982 (unreported). Whether Woolf J would have accepted counsel's views had the issue been vigorously argued remains a matter of speculation. See *R* v. *Amber Valley DC, ex p. Jackson* [1984] 3 All ER 501 (Woolf J held that, although the evidence indicated that the local planning authority were 'politically predisposed' to grant permission, it was 'almost inevitable now that party politics played so large a part in Local Government, that the majority group on a Council would decide on the Party line' and that it was wrong, on this basis, to infer that the council committee would not take account of all relevant considerations.) See also *R* v. *Waltham Forest LBC, ex p. Baxter* [1987] 3 All ER 671.

[151] *R* v. *West Midlands CC* (above, n. 150), transcript, 8.

[152] *R* v. *Merseyside CC, ex parte Great Universal Stores Ltd* [1982] 80 LGR 639.

[153] It is worthy of note here that the leading counsel who advised West Midlands CC also acted for the firm who were the applicants in the Merseyside litigation.

[154] (1982) 80 LGR 639, 645.

consider that an exploratory cross-examination of this sort was appropriate on an application for judicial review'.[155] Furthermore, in rejecting that aspect of the challenge founded on the exercise of discretion, Woolf J not only rejected the general claim that 'the County Council after the election did no more than arbitrarily give effect to the provisions of the manifesto'[156] but also specifically refuted: (i) the argument that, given that the Council failed to consider any figure other than the 10 per cent reduction set out in the manifesto, it should be inferred that they improperly regarded themselves as committed to it;[157] (ii) the suggestion that a 'sinister interpretation is to be inferred from the speed with which matters were dealt with';[158] and (iii) the claim that, since it was conceded that account was taken of 'the high cost of public transport and the hardship that that would continue to bring to the sizeable proportion of the County population whose sole source of income is state benefits', irrelevant considerations had been taken into account.[159] In rejecting these procedural claims Woolf J, to my mind, also effectively disposed of counsel's views concerning the legality of the process followed by West Midlands CC.

On the important matter of the construction of the 1968 Act, Woolf J held that the regime established by that Act was slightly but, nevertheless, significantly different from that of the 1969 Act and that 'it is not possible to apply the reasoning of the *GLC* case to the interpretation of the 1968 Act'.[160] Woolf J also held that the Authority had the power under the 1968 Act to subsidize the PTE in furtherance of its objectives of providing an integrated and efficient system of public transport and that, since the decision 'did not incur the automatic penalty' which had been of such importance in *Bromley*, it could not be said that the Authority 'had acted inconsistently with its fiduciary duty to its ratepayers'.[161]

The *Merseyside* decision was of great significance. It was, for example, only because of that ruling that South Yorkshire CC was able to maintain its cheap fares policy which had come under pressure from the weight of legal advice. The court in *Merseyside* seemed, in effect, to be indicating its disinclination to follow the approach which the majority in *Bromley* had adopted of using the fiduciary concept as a lens through which to discern the meaning of the relevant Act. Why, then, was it not the subject of an appeal? The answer, it seems, lies in the fact that Woolf J expressed his concern that, not only had the applicants held their hand until the *Bromley* case had been finally resolved, but also had failed to warn the council that they were proposing to bring this action. Consequently, Woolf J took the view that, even if he had found that the council had misinterpreted the provisions of the 1968 Act, he would, as a matter of discretion, have denied the applicants the relief which they sought.[162] Given this view, the applicants had few material incentives for pursuing the issue in the Court of Appeal.

---

[155] (1982) 80 LGR 639, 645. [156] Ibid., 655. [157] Ibid., 657. [158] Ibid.
[159] Ibid., 658. [160] Ibid., 655. [161] Ibid., 658. [162] Ibid., 659.

Public transport policy in London

Meanwhile, back at the GLC matters were in a state of chaos. The Comptroller of Finance, when asked if there was a 'fit' between the legal judgment and administrative requirements, commented:

> A considerable amount of time was spent in the courts in exchanging various dictionary . . . interpretations of words such as 'economic' and 'business principles'. I therefore looked up the word 'fit' in the Oxford Pocket Dictionary. Its first meaning is 'a sudden seizure of hysteria, apoplexy, fainting, paralysis or epilepsy'. . . . [T]his meaning is an accurate description of the degree of fit between the legal results and administrative requirements since the case.[163]

It was not just the restrictive interpretation given which created the difficulties but also the fact that, from a public policy perspective, it was thoroughly unhelpful to be seeking to provide practical guidance on the basis of five opinions with different nuances.[164] Furthermore, the Comptroller of Finance recognized that, in practical terms, a public transport system could be operated on a break-even principle.[165] However, '[w]hat almost immediately followed was that none of the many interested parties wished to interpret the judgements in that way'.[166] As recorded by the Comptroller of Finance:

> Although the Solicitor General's interpretation was wholly consistent with the interpretation given to the Council, the Attorney General almost immediately issued a statement that the GLC's interpretation was 'too harsh' – presenting an unresolvable administrative problem as to who decided and on what basis the extent to which a financial duty which the GLC and London Transport were enjoined to achieve and which could be achieved, need not be pursued. The Attorney General also granted welcome but temporarily based relief by stating that the London Transport Budget for 1982 could be approved without breach of the fiduciary duty of the Council – an intriguing but curiously based advance absolution on behalf of the Council against a possible action by ratepayers in respect of a budget which the Council had not considered.[167]

---

[163] Stonefrost, 'An Administrator's Viewpoint' (above, n. 135), 6.

[164] It resulted, for example, in counsel advising the GLC and LTE being unable to agree on the implications of the decision for public transport fares. After 'long conferences' a joint opinion was produced which began: 'It is already known that there is a divergence of view between us as to the proper interpretation of the House of Lords Judgments . . . The effect of this divergence is that Counsel for London Transport consider that the GLC is entitled to provide a higher level of subsidy for the current year than is considered to be permissible by Counsel for the GLC . . .', R. Alexander QC, P. Weitzman QC and J. Goudie (Counsel for GLC), J. Drinkwater QC and C. Lockhart-Mummery (Counsel for LTE), *Joint Opinion. London Transport Fares* (25 January 1982).

[165] Stonefrost, 'An Administrator's Viewpoint' (above, n. 135), 7. See also, London Transport Executive, *Facts about Public Transport* (March 1982): 'London Transport could so arrange its services . . . so as to break even. . . . This would have to be achieved by further massive increases in fares combined with substantial further reductions in services.'

[166] Stonefrost, ibid.   [167] Ibid.

The Government would not, however, agree to the introduction of legislation to validate the GLC's scheme.[168] As a result, the GLC was required to submit a revised budget for 1981/82 in which public transport fares were raised to roughly twice the level of those under their original scheme. The key issue at the time was whether that would be sufficient or whether further staged increases would be needed.[169] After seeking additional legal opinion on the subject, however, during 1982 there gradually emerged a different view. This was that, provided the GLC approached its decision in a careful procedural manner, it could for 1983/84 reduce its existing fares by 25 per cent. As the Finance Comptroller expressed it, 'although initially expressed as an alternative interpretation of [*Bromley*, it] was, to me, more of an "if and then the court might" statement and not an interpretation of the four [Law] Lord judgements'.[170] It was, in short, an attempt to exploit a climate of criticism of the Lords' judgment. The GLC then prepared a scheme, called the 'Balanced Plan', involving fares reductions equivalent to 25 per cent. At this stage, however, and in a reversal of roles from the immediate aftermath of *Bromley*, the LTE were advised that they could not receive this proposed subsidy without being in breach of their duties under the 1969 Act. Since, once again, they were unable to agree on the precise nature of their powers and duties under the Act the GLC applied for judicial review, seeking a declaration that its proposed action was a lawful exercise of its powers.

It is unclear whether this was by design, but the effect of bringing an action concerning the prospective decision had the effect of separating the question of fiduciary duty as a constitutional principle from that of the role of fiduciary duty in providing an aid to statutory interpretation. Since the overall budget had not been compiled and the grant decisions of central government had not been determined, the consequences of the public transport policy decision on the GLC's expenditure and grant profile could not be assessed by the courts. In *R* v. *London Transport Executive, ex parte Greater London Council*, the Divisional Court took the view that the *Bromley* decision had been 'widely misunderstood and indeed misrepresented'.[171] In construing the 1969 Act, the Court

---

[168] Cf. the aftermath to the *Prescott* case (above, 229). The Government did, however, promote the Travel Concessions (London) Act 1982 in order to avoid doubts concerning the legality of London Transport's concessionary fares scheme for pensioners. Note that 'the block grant penalties on the ratepayers were as proportionately harsh for "free" travel for the elderly as they were for reduced fare levels for the rest of travellers' (Stonefrost, 'An Administrator's Viewpoint' (above, n. 135), 8). Is this the charitable trust conception of local government reflected in a statutory form?

[169] Counsel for the GLC took the view that 'the proposal for a 100 per cent fare increase in March 1982, without any further fare increase of a similar magnitude later in the year, cannot be reconciled with the Judgements', *Joint Opinion. London Transport Fares*, para. 2. However, if fares rose steeply, Camden LBC had threatened to challenge the legality of the GLC's actions on the ground that it would be failing in its duty under s. 1 of the 1969 Act to provide 'integrated, efficient and economic transport facilities and services': see *R* v. *LTE, ex p. GLC* [1983] 1 QB 484, at 493.

[170] Stonefrost, 'An Administrator's Viewpoint' (above, n. 135), 7.

[171] [1983] QB 484, at 490.

held that, provided the GLC had regard to its statutory duty to promote 'an integrated, efficient and economic' public transport system, the balance to be struck between farepayers and ratepayers was a matter of discretion for the GLC, subject only to the requirement that 'if the balance was arbitrary or clearly unfair, then it would be invalid under the *Wednesbury* principle'.[172] In granting the GLC its declaration, the Divisional Court, though paying lip service to the *Bromley* precedent,[173] seemed in actuality, and in parallel with the decision of that court in the *Merseyside* case, to be seeking to distance themselves from the attempt by the Law Lords in *Bromley* to use the fiduciary concept as a lens through which to interpret the Act.

Central government action

By January 1983, then, after a period of confusion of just over 12 months, the Divisional Court, through critical judgments on both the 1968 and 1969 Acts, had managed to marginalize the significance of the fiduciary concept as a guide to statutory interpretation and had restored some semblance of order and balance to the statutory framework governing urban public transport. By this time, however, central government had already resolved to take action. In July 1982 the Government announced that a Bill would be introduced which would establish a 'clear and consistent legal framework' for the payment of urban public transport revenue subsidy and would provide the basis for 'a reasonable, stable and lawful subsidy regime'.[174] The primary objective of the Transport Act 1983, however, was not simply to clarify the power to provide revenue subsidies for public transport. While, in framing the Act, the Government seemed implicitly to recognize that the Lords got it wrong in *Bromley*,[175] they also sought to use the opportunity to impose a greater degree of central control over the exercise of the revenue grant power, to depoliticize that process, and to convert the statutory limitations on the power to provide subsidies into justiciable constraints.[176]

Under the 1983 Act transport executives were required to carry out a cost-benefit exercise to demonstrate the transport benefits that result from the levels of subsidy provided. The objective here was to objectivize the statutory duty on authorities to provide 'efficient' or 'economic' public transport systems; if subsidy costs exceeded transport benefits then authorities could perhaps be found to be in breach of their statutory duties. Furthermore, in determining the level of revenue subsidy to be provided to executives, local authorities were required

---

[172] Ibid., 491.   [173] See especially the judgment of Glidewell J, ibid., 510–13.

[174] Department of Transport, *Public Transport Subsidy in Cities*, Cmnd. 8735 (1982), paras. 3, 12.

[175] In the 1983 Act, s. 7(3) of the 1969 Act, which had been interpreted in *Bromley* as imposing limitations on the power of LTE to accept subsidies, was repealed and was replaced by a provision which made it clear that the financial duty of the executives was a technical accounting duty: Transport Act 1983, s. 2.

[176] For a more detailed examination see: M. Loughlin, 'Lawyers, economists and the urban public transport policy process' in S. Glaister (ed.), *Transport Subsidy* (London, 1987), 101.

to have regard to 'the need to achieve a proper balance between the interests of ratepayers in their area and the interests of transport users'.[177] Although on its face this provision seemed simply to place the procedural dimension of the fiduciary concept on a statutory footing, it was also indicative of a key theme of the 1983 Act. This theme is seen most clearly in relation to the power of the Secretary of State to issue guidance to each authority as to the maximum level of subsidy it would be appropriate to provide. What was unusual about this power to issue guidance is that it took the form of a 'protected expenditure level' (PEL). That is, if the authority's revenue subsidy did not exceed the amount in the guidance then it 'shall be regarded for all purposes as a proper exercise of that power'.[178] The function of this unusual provision was made explicit by the Government in its explanation of the purpose of the PEL:

> Councillors will then be able to take decisions on the overall amount of current expenditure, and in doing so will need to take account both of the targets set by the Secretary of State for the Environment and of the guidance by the Secretary of State for Transport. If, nevertheless, the Authority should decide for a higher level of subsidy, councillors will know that they run the risk of surcharge should their action be challenged by the Auditor and found by the Courts to be unlawful. Ratepayers will continue to have the right to challenge expenditure above the indicated level where they think it is unreasonable.[179]

What this seems to indicate is that, far from attempting to remove the uncertainties which resulted from the *Bromley* decision, the Government was in fact seeking to exploit those uncertainties and harness them to its particular policy objectives. And it sought to do so primarily by structuring the 1983 Act scheme in such a way as to exploit the uncertainty inherent in the notion of fiduciary duty as a constitutional principle.

The Government nevertheless failed in this objective. One difficulty was that, even on the Department of Transport's own model, all authorities were obtaining net benefits on the levels of subsidy provided.[180] However, perhaps more significantly, PELs did not function as anticipated. In the critical first year of operation, the GLC and five of the six metropolitan authorities all provided revenue support at a level higher than their PELs. While these authorities were, in all probability, also incurring grant penalties as a result of their expenditure policies, none was challenged by way of judicial review. An assessment of why this form of fiduciary challenge failed to materialize requires us to examine the impact of the reactivated fiduciary concept on the general expenditure policies of local authorities. However, following the failure of the 1983 Act, the Govern-

[177] Transport Act 1983, s. 4(3).   [178] Transport Act 1983, s. 5(2).
[179] Cmnd. 8735, para. 13.
[180] See S. Glaister, 'The Allocation of Urban Public Transport Subsidy' in S. Glaister (ed.), *Transport Subsidy* (above, n. 176), 27.

ment sought much more radical solutions to the question of urban public transport policy.[181]

Fiduciary Duty and Local Expenditure Policies

The *Bromley* decision, quite clearly, had a major impact on public transport policies in the early 1980s and played a pivotal role in a process through which the Government was able to transform the regulatory and financial frameworks in that field. But, by reactivating the fiduciary concept in a more general sense – especially in the formulation articulated by Lord Diplock – the decision potentially had a more far-reaching effect. Furthermore, since no detailed guidance was provided in that case to indicate precisely how the balance between ratepayers and service beneficiaries should be struck, this aspect of the fiduciary concept seemed inherently ambiguous. This feature of the fiduciary concept could, in itself, operate to destabilize existing local authority programmes.

Counting costs in Camden

Some initial indications of the impact of the fiduciary concept on general expenditure policies may be gleaned from an examination of challenges at the beginning of the 1980s to the policies of the London Borough of Camden. During the 1970s Camden had acquired a reputation as a high-spending – some would say profligate – authority.[182] Even before the *Bromley* action, the general level of expenditure by Camden had caused ratepayers to bring legal action alleging a breach of fiduciary duty.

In *Barrs* v. *Bethell*[183] three ratepayers claimed that Camden's policies of not increasing council rents, of refusing to make cuts in services and in making no reduction in the size of its direct labour organization had resulted in a loss of rate support grant and imposed an unfair burden on ratepayers. Evidence was provided which showed, for example, that for every £1 of rent collected to meet

---

[181] In the London Regional Transport Act 1984 responsibility for public transport in London was taken away from the GLC and placed under central control. The Local Government Act 1985 went even further, by providing for the abolition of the GLC and the metropolitan county councils, and placing public transport in the metropolitan areas under the control of joint authorities. Finally, the Transport Act 1985 de-regulated the system of public transport, subjected it to market competition and left local authorities with the residual role of securing through tender the provision of services which, though desired, would not be provided by the market.

[182] See, e.g., A. Henney, *The Costs of Camden* (London, 1981); id., *Inside Local Government. A Case for Radical Reform* (London, 1984), 200–4, 267–9, 365–7. For a specific illustration see *Sovmots Investments Ltd* v. *Secretary of State for the Environment* [1979] AC 144, a case in which Camden sought to acquire the maisonettes in the Centre Point office block as part of their housing stock even though the costs were such that, on the council's own projections, the authority would incur a loss of around £3,000 per unit per annum: see [1977] QB 411, at 423.

[183] [1981] 3 WLR 874.

council housing costs, over £2 was contributed by the ratepayers. Citing primarily the authorities of *Roberts* v. *Hopwood* and *Prescott*, the ratepayers argued
that Camden's policies had infringed their fiduciary obligations. Having brought
this action for a declaration in the Chancery Division, however, Camden argued
that the ratepayers lacked standing. After carefully considering the relevant
authorities, Warner J held that, other than by way of judicial review, a ratepayer
had no standing to sue a local authority without the leave of the Attorney-
General. Since local authorities 'are particularly vulnerable to actions by busy-
bodies and cranks' the law provided 'a filter in the form of a requirement that
either the consent of the Attorney-General to a relator action or the leave of the
court for an application for judicial review should be obtained'.[184] But was it not
the case that the Court of Appeal held that the plaintiff ratepayer in the *Prescott*
case was entitled to pursue a declaration in the Chancery Division on the ground
that the local authority was in breach of its fiduciary duty? Warner J, after
recognizing that fact, stated:

> But the report of counsel's argument . . . show[s] that no point was taken as to the
> plaintiff's locus standi. None of the authorities on that topic were referred to. The
> inference seems to me to be irresistible . . . that the Court of Appeal assumed that
> the plaintiff had locus standi to bring the action without addressing its mind to the
> question.[185]

The leading post-war authority on fiduciary duty had thus proceeded simply,
and erroneously, on the assumption that a ratepayer possessed the standing to
bring an action for a declaration.

In addition to judicial review and obtaining the Attorney-General's leave, there
exists the statutory procedure of audit through which a ratepayer can challenge
local authority expenditure. This was the route taken in the case of *Pickwell* v.
Camden LBC.[186] This case arose from the decision of Camden to settle locally
a national strike of manual workers employed by local authorities. In January
1979 the workers had taken strike action in furtherance of their claim for a basic
wage of £60 per week and a reduction in the working week to 35 hours. On 13
February the Labour group voted 14–13 in favour of a local settlement, a decision which was ratified by the council by 31 votes to 24. The local settlement
meant that, in comparison with the national settlement reached on 8 March,
workers in Camden were, depending on grade, being paid between 5.5 and 26.7
per cent above national rates. The auditor considered that, on the authority of
Roberts v. *Hopwood*, this 'Camden supplement' was 'contrary to law' and sought
a declaration to that effect. The auditor calculated that, over the three years to
1980/81, the unlawful expenditure totalled £950,000 and asked the court for
consequential orders making the councillors personally liable for this sum.

[184] [1981] 3 WLR 892.   [185] Ibid., 886.   [186] [1983] 1 QB 962.

The Divisional Court, however, refused the declaration. What is particularly interesting is that, in doing so, the court seemed to cast doubt on the view that the fiduciary concept had any independent status in public law. Forbes J intimated that:

> Of course it is plain that a local authority owes a fiduciary duty to its ratepayers: it also owes a duty, laid on it specifically by Parliament, to provide a wide range of services for its inhabitants, be they ratepayers, electors or neither. It is entitled as an employer to have regard to the interests and welfare of its workforce, as any good employer should. It must therefore often be involved in balancing fairly these interests which may frequently conflict.[187]

Forbes J then suggested that, for it to be demonstrated that 'a local authority has deliberately topped the balance in favour of one interest over others', it must be shown, whether the issue is addressed in terms of taking into account irrelevant considerations or of acting unreasonably in *Wednesbury* terms, that it was acting 'beyond the power which was entrusted to it'.[188] In this case, it was clear that the council 'was faced with a position where vital services had been so disrupted that real hardship was being caused, not only to the elderly and the handicapped, but to the commercial concerns who pay rates but have no elective voice' and thus 'we are worlds away from Poplar in the 1920s where a calm and deiberate decision to indulge in what then passed for philanthropy was being taken'.[189] Forbes J concluded that: 'I remain wholly unsatisfied that the district auditor has made out a case for declaring the decision ... unlawful.'[190]

These findings were reinforced by Ormrod LJ who, in addition, specifically considered *Bromley* and held that 'it would not be right to regard this case as authority for the general proposition that this fiduciary duty opens up a route by which the courts can investigate and, if thought appropriate, interfere with any exercise of their discretionary powers by local authorities'.[191] Such an approach, Ormrod LJ felt, would cut across the view that it 'is not for the court to substitute its own view of what is a desirable policy'[192] and 'would completely undermine the principles of the *Wednesbury* case'.[193] '[T]he question for this court,' Ormrod LJ continued, 'is not whether Camden made a bad bargain for the ratepayers, or were precipitate in making the offer to the strikers, or could have achieved a cheaper settlement by waiting, or made a better bargain by different tactics. These are matters for the electorate at the next election. The question for the court is whether the evidence establishes that no reasonable local authority could have made a settlement on such terms.'[194]

---

[187] Ibid., 987.   [188] Ibid., 988.   [189] Ibid., 995–6.

[190] Ibid., 996.   [191] Ibid., 1004.

[192] *Luby* v. *Newcastle under Lyme Corporation* [1964] 2 QB 64, 72 (per Diplock LJ): cited by Ormrod LJ at [1983] 1 QB 1003.

[193] [1983] 1 QB 962, 1004.   [194] Ibid., 1004.

The two Camden cases are of interest for the light they cast on the leading authorities which have expounded the concept of fiduciary duty. In *Barrs* v. *Bethell* the court in effect held that the ratepayer in *Prescott* did not have the standing to bring that action. The *Pickwell* case went much further since fiduciary duty was clearly subsumed under the general principles of administrative law. Furthermore, Ormrod LJ, when explaining the changes in the auditor's powers during this century, in effect provided an explanation of the decision in *Roberts* v. *Hopwood*:

> [The auditor] has ceased to be the adjudicator with power to disallow and surcharge, and has become the applicant; the court is no longer an appellate court, reviewing the decision of the district auditor; it is now a tribunal of first instance, adjudicating directly upon the actions of the local authority, and making the initial decision itself. The district auditor is now in the invidious position of a quasi-prosecutor with responsibility for deciding to launch, and for conducting the proceedings in this court. The court must now find the primary facts for itself and make the effective decision . . .[195]

There is one direct consequence of these changes: whereas the Poplar councillors were seeking to challenge an order of the auditor, in the audit regime after 1972 the burden of proof is placed firmly on the auditor. In these circumstances, it would appear that the auditor will require something quite exceptional in terms of proof in order to establish breach of fiduciary duty.

Dealing with the Diplock dictum

The *Pickwell* case did not, however, explicitly consider the concept of fiduciary duty which had been elaborated by Lord Diplock in *Bromley*. In the context of the block grant mechanism established in 1980 and the system of expenditure targets engrafted on to it in 1981, the Diplock dictum potentially constituted an extremely powerful doctrine of expenditure restraint. It also seemed to take all the key actors in the local government system by surprise. The Government, being concerned about the potential arbitrariness of its impact, in March 1982 made available to the local authority associations a legal opinion on its meaning. This opinion took the view that '[e]xpenditure by a local authority above its GRE or target is certainly not made unlawful by that fact alone' and that 'the fact that an authority is on "negative marginal rate" of grant does not of itself demonstrate that the authority is in breach of its fiduciary duty'. But it continued:

> It is however very probable that if an authority is challenged in Court on the level of its expenditure or on a specific item of expenditure, the Court would expect to see that the authority had considered very carefully the full possibilities and implications of alternative lower levels of different items of expenditure in relation to the different

[195] [1983] 1 QB 998.

costs to the ratepayers and that the further an authority spends above its GRE or target, the heavier will be the onus of justification.[196]

It seemed virtually inevitable that, against the background of rate increases to meet the shortfall left by grant reductions, the Diplock dictum, even after the gloss placed on it by the Government, would be used to found challenges both to general levels of local authority expenditure and also to specific items of expenditure. One of the first, *British Leyland Cars* v. *Birmingham DC and Coventry City Council*,[197] took the form of an appeal to the Crown Court under section 7 of the General Rate Act 1967. In this case, the appellants contended that the rates levied by the respondents for 1982/83 were unlawful on the grounds that the councils had failed to pay sufficient regard to Government guidelines on local authority expenditure and to the impact of a rate increase on industrial ratepayers. In dismissing this appeal, Sir John Willis found that the councils had had regard to all relevant factors and that, in relation to the argument that the authority were in breach of their fiduciary obligations, stated that counsel was 'in effect inviting me . . . to substitute the opinion of the court for that of the authority. There is nothing in the General Rate Act empowering the court to undertake such an exercise.'[198] After another Crown Court ruled that it had no jurisdiction to consider this type of challenge under the 1967 Act[199] the Government acted by making it clear that this form of challenge may proceed only by way of judicial review.[200]

The first challenge by way of judicial review concerned an application by the Borough of Kensington & Chelsea to quash the entire GLC precept for 1982/83.[201] This application was based on two items in the GLC's budget which, it was contended, revealed a breach of the authority's duty to its ratepayers. The first item concerned the 'transferred property deficit'. The GLC had decided to increase rents on their housing stock by £1 per week for 1982/83. Since the Government had assumed a rent increase of £2.50 for the purpose of calculating housing subsidy, this decision meant that a rate fund contribution would be required to make up the difference. In the interests of rent harmonization, the GLC also proposed to apply the limited rent increase to its former housing stock which, since the 1970s, had gradually been transferred to the boroughs. Under the transfer arrangements the GLC retained responsibility for any deficits incurred in respect of the transferred properties. Consequently, it was decided that

---

[196] This document was made available to the local authority associations and a copy placed in the House of Commons library: see HC Debs, vol. 19 col. 118w (2 March 1982).

[197] [1982] RVR 92.

[198] Ibid., 97. For a similar type of challenge against the rate levied by Newcastle upon Tyne City Council, which also failed, see: 'Ratepayer loses test case', *The Guardian*, 15 December 1981.

[199] See *Municipal Journal*, 12 February 1982, 179.

[200] Local Government Finance Act 1982, s. 4.

[201] *R* v. *Greater London Council, ex p. Royal Borough of Kensington & Chelsea*, *The Times*, 7 April 1982.

if any boroughs were prepared to limit the rent increase on the transferred stock to £1 per week the GLC would meet the deficit.

Kensington challenged this decision to extend the rent limit to transferred properties as being in breach of the GLC's fiduciary duty. In presenting its arguments the two basic aspects of the duty were differentiated. Thus, it was argued that the GLC must keep a proper balance between ratepayers and council tenants (the efficient management principle) and also that it must keep a proper balance between ratepayers *inter se* and therefore that it must not discriminate between ratepayers in different boroughs (the discrimination principle). The Divisional Court dismissed the argument based on the efficient management principle fairly summarily on the ground that it had no substance. In respect of the discrimination principle McNeill J had this to say:

> It seems to me that . . . the scope within which illegality based on discrimination within the fiduciary duty of a local authority or within the *Wednesbury* principles exists is very limited in the absence of statute. Bearing in mind that the present case is concerned with local authority housing, a social need subsidised by common acceptance both by the tax payers and the rate payers, I should find it very difficult to find illegality based on discrimination, except perhaps in some very strong case, which this certainly is not.[202]

The second budgetary item challenged in this case was a special contingency balance of £30m which the GLC had included in its budget in addition to the standard contingency reserves on capital and revenue accounts. Kensington argued that the standard reserves adequately covered all contingencies and that this balance was an attempt to evade anticipated constraining legislation in the form of the proposed abolition of the power to levy supplementary rates and precepts[203] and as such was not a proper exercise of the GLC's discretion having regard to its duty to ratepayers. McNeill J held that, given the degree of financial uncertainty during this period, the GLC was not only justified in creating this fund but also suggested that a local authority would be 'failing in its duty to its ratepayers if it did not endeavour, in budgeting for its annual requirements by way of precept and rate, to assess the consequences of future legislation affecting its functions'.[204]

In dismissing Kensington's application, McNeill J had some harsh words for those who might seek to use the courts as part of an essentially political campaign:

> It is a matter of real concern that the Divisional Court, exercising the power of judicial review, is increasingly . . . sought to be used for political purposes superficially dressed up as points of law. The proper remedy in such matters is the ballot box and not the

---

[202] Transcript, 15. For authorities which support this view in the context of housing rents see: *Belcher* v. *Reading Corporation* [1950] 1 All ER 221; *Evans* v. *Collins* [1964] 1 All ER 808; *Luby* v. *Newcastle under Lyme Corporation* [1965] 1 QB 214.
[203] See Local Government Finance Act 1982, s. 2.   [204] Transcript, 30.

court. . . . The impropriety of coming to this court when, as I suspect to be the position in this case, political capital is sought to be made – even though unsuccessfully – out of judicial review cannot be overstressed.[205]

This decision, especially when read in conjunction with *Pickwell* and in the context of the general tone adopted by the court in *R* v. *LTE, ex parte GLC*, seemed to be indicating quite clearly that the courts were not prepared to give credence to any active notion of the fiduciary concept founded on the Diplock dictum. Nevertheless, these judgments did not prevent further challenges based on the logic of Lord Diplock's speech. Indeed when, in 1983, a business rate-payer sought judicial review to quash Greenwich LBC's general rate for 1983/ 84 the nature of the challenge, for the first time, was directed to the core of the Diplock dictum.[206] The applicant's argument was not concerned with the legality of any particular item of expenditure but was based on the general contention that, in spending above its expenditure targets and incurring grant penalties, Greenwich's budget failed to maintain a balance between ratepayers and service beneficiaries. Greenwich's expenditure target was £52m and at that level it would have received grant amounting to £32.4m. Since Greenwich had budgeted to spend £62m, however, it received only £26.7m in grant and its decision to spend £10m more than its target therefore entailed a loss of £5.7m of grant which had to be made up by an increase in the rates. The Divisional Court once again refused the application. The court held that the council, having taken into account all relevant considerations, could interfere only if the council's decision was 'so outrageous that no right thinking person could support it' and it was felt that 'the material before the court comes nowhere near establishing such a state of affairs'.[207] Any more active claim for fiduciary duty was described as a 'dangerous and seductive argument' since it could all too easily lure the court into substituting its own view of the way in which the rating authority should have exercised its discretion.

Challenges of a similar nature arose once again in the mid-1980s, especially in the context of the worsening picture of financial stability in certain London authorities.[208] Nevertheless, in line with the earlier authorities, the Divisional Court rejected any applications seeking to use the fiduciary concept in such a way as to engage in a more intrusive form of review than that indicated by the basic principles of administrative law.[209] The only novel version of the concept

[205] Ibid., 28. [206] *R* v. *Greenwich LBC, ex p. Cedar Transport Group Ltd* [1983] RA 173.
[207] Ibid. [208] For the general background see, below, ch. 6, at 330.
[209] Most noteworthy were the challenges to general rate increases of over 60 per cent in Ealing and Waltham Forest for 1987/88. In each case, Labour had gained control of the council in the previous year and was seeking to implement its manifesto proposals. The Divisional Court in each case construed fiduciary duty simply as a relevant consideration to which the authority should have regard. See *R* v. *London Borough of Ealing, ex p. Dunstan*, 15 June 1987 (QBD, unreported); *R* v. *Waltham Forest LBC, ex p. Waltham Borough Ratepayers Action Group*, 29 July 1987 (QBD, unreported); [1987] 3 All ER 671 (the appeal addressed only the issue of fettering of discretion).

which emerged during this period was the attempt to introduce a temporal dimension; that is, to use the concept not to only require the maintenance of a balance between ratepayers *inter se* but also between present and future ratepayers. The argument here was that attempts by local authorities to obtain additional income in the current financial year, the cost of which would be borne in future years, could be construed, if the burden on future ratepayers was great, as being in breach of fiduciary duty. The best example is to be found in an auditor's statutory report on the accounts of the London Borough of Haringey in April 1987. This report, which concerned the use of a variety of mechanisms to defer the cost of revenue projects in 1987/88, stated:

> ... the Council has a fiduciary duty to its ratepayers to be financially prudent while striking a fair balance between the interests of present and future ratepayers and the recipients of services. It is not enough for the Council to consider the proposed effect of any expenditure in a single financial year. It is also necessary to look beyond that year to the full year effects in the succeeding year and subsequent years. None of the budget reports which I have seen contains the information necessary to enable members to carry forward this exercise.[210]

This dimension to the fiduciary concept, which may be viewed as an elaboration of the discrimination principle, has not been fully considered by the courts.[211]

These cases have been considered in some detail so that the tenor of the judiciary's response to fiduciary challenges may be appreciated. The general message is that the courts have worked actively and consistently to nullify any elaborate conception of fiduciary duty as a quasi-constitutional principle affording an independent head of review. The Divisional Court quickly recognized that the use of the fiduciary concept as a balancing mechanism in relation to general expenditures would inevitably lead the court into the exercise of second-guessing the decisions of elected local councils. This would undoubtedly raise an issue of legitimacy, since any active use of the concept would result, to an unusual degree, in the legalization of the political process. It would also impose major institutional strains, as the court in the *Greenwich* case implicitly recognized when it took cognizance of the fact that, in 1983/84, 173 of the 457 local authorities in England and Wales were budgeting to spend at a level that exceeded their expenditure target.[212] The courts thus worked quickly to subsume the fiduciary concept under general principles of administrative law, which rendered the fiduciary concept entirely subservient to the *Wednesbury* principles. Fiduciary duty was construed as imposing an obligation of a purely procedural

---

[210] Statutory Report of the District Auditor on 1985/86 Accounts of Haringey LBC, 14 April 1987, para. 22.

[211] It was initially raised in the *Waltham Forest* case (above, n. 209) but was later dropped: 'A further claim for a declaration relating to the financing of revenue and capital expenditure by a scheme of deferred purchase and parallel loan is not now pursued by the applicants' (Transcript, 1).

[212] [1983] RA 173.

nature. It was interpreted simply as serving to identify one of the relevant considerations to which the local authority must have regard. Having considered the
issue, however, the local authority's decision could be impugned only if it was
found to be grossly unreasonable.

It is precisely because of the character of these post-*Bromley* judgments that
the Government's attempt to utilize the fiduciary concept as a mechanism of
restraint under the Transport Act 1983 failed.[213] Nevertheless, when viewing
matters in retrospect, we should not underestimate the degree of legal uncertainty which existed in the period immediately following the *Bromley* decision.
All authorities incurring grant penalties were potentially exposed to legal challenge. But the GLC and the ILEA, as authorities with newly-elected Labour
administrations which were seeking to develop services but were placed on a
negative marginal grant curve, were particularly vulnerable. They survived only
because the courts were not prepared to carry through the strict logic of the
Diplock analysis. In the immediate aftermath of *Bromley* local authorities were
sent rushing to counsel for advice concerning the legality of both new and existing policies. During this period, business at the local government bar flourished.

This aspect of the post-*Bromley* picture provides a further cause for concern.
During this period, there was a perception that we might be entering a new era
of legalization of political decision-making. As it has turned out, this did not
happen. But in the process what emerged was a related phenomenon of the
politicization of law. With the realization that the law might come to intrude
more pervasively in the conduct of local politics, councils became more politically adept in their use of law and lawyers. A good example is provided by the
housing rents policy of the GLC, the fruits of which were subject to challenge
in the *Kensington* case. What happened was that, in the context of budget preparations for 1982/83, the GLC sought counsel's advice on the legality of freezing rents for that year. Since the Government was assuming that for subsidy
purposes rents would rise by £2.50, the effect of a rents freeze would be to
transfer the burden of this shortfall to the rate fund and this would have the
consequent effect of increasing expenditure, which would entail the loss of rate
support grant. Counsel's opinion was therefore sought on whether a rent freeze
would be in breach of the GLC's fiduciary duty. Counsel was presented with six
options on rent increase/rate burden choice ranging from rent freeze in option 1
to rent increase of £2.50 in option 6. Counsel's opinion was that options 1 and
2 were unlawful on the ground that they would impose a disproportionate burden on ratepayers but that options 3–6 were lawful. Option 3 involved an increase in rents of £1 and the GLC duly recommended a rent increase for 1982/
83 of £1.00 per week.[214] We should not be naive about the type of exercise on

---

[213] See, above, 246–7.

[214] For a synopsis of this and other opinions on this issue see: 'Law and Local Authorities:
counsel's opinions on budgets and rents', *Public Money*, June 1982, 49 at 54–6.

which the GLC were embarking. On the face of things, it is difficult to imagine a more clear cut example of the legalization of political issues. But it is also not difficult to construct a scenario in which counsel can be viewed playing a role in the GLC's general political strategy. During the 1980s, then, there emerged a new political art in local government circles; the art of using counsel's opinion to protect policy decision-making. Whether this aspect of the post-*Bromley* world – shopping around or first taking informal soundings before formally briefing counsel – has resulted in an improvement in the processes of local authority decision-making remains open to doubt.

Whither the Fiduciary Concept?

We have seen, then, that *Bromley* did not mark the opening of a new era in judicial supervision of local government decision-making and, with the benefit of hindsight, the decision may be viewed essentially as an aberration. *Bromley* provides a singular example of the court misconstruing a statute, being unable to offer clear guidance as to its meaning and failing to appreciate the significance of some of its opinions. It was perhaps for these reasons that the Divisional Court felt it necessary to work so hard to restore the *status quo ante*. It may also not be entirely fanciful to suggest that it is partly because of errors such as *Bromley* which led the House of Lords ten years later to relax the rule prohibiting reference to parliamentary material as an aid to statutory interpretation.[215] However, in addition to these judicial manoeuvres which have had the effect of marginalizing the impact of the fidicuary concept, there are certain more general reforms of an institutional nature which have been recently introduced and whose impact might in effect be to ensure that the concept of fiduciary duty may no longer carry any credence within the field of public law. These reforms concern judicial review procedure and the reforms to the system of local government finance.

Procedural reforms in judicial review

Bromley was decided during a period in which the courts were working to establish the principle that judicial review should be the exclusive procedure for addressing issues of public law. This principle is now firmly established and one consequence of the reform is that the Divisional Court has come in effect to constitute a distinct administrative division of the High Court.[216] The consequence of this reform is that all challenges to public bodies which seek to invoke the fiduciary concept will come to the Divisional Court by way of judicial

---

[215] *Pepper* v. *Hart* [1992] 3 WLR 1032.

[216] See, e.g., L. Blom-Cooper, 'The new face of judicial review: administrative changes in Order 53', 1982 *Public Law* 250.

review. And this procedural reform is, I believe, likely to have a significant effect on the status of fiduciary duty in public law.

The primary reason for this view is that the fiduciary concept is essentially a creation of the courts of equity and arguably is one which has never been fully absorbed by the Queen's Bench Division. We have seen that the origins of the concept lie in the characterization by the courts of equity of municipal property as being held on trust for the purpose of enforcing the *ultra vires* doctrine. Furthermore, with the singular exception of *Roberts* v. *Hopwood*, the Divisional Court arguably has never during the twentieth century accorded the fiduciary concept an independent status. Whenever that concept has been raised in the Divisional Court it has been viewed primarily as a procedural requirement; it may be a relevant consideration to which local authorities should have regard but, provided they have considered their duty to ratepayers, the authority's decision will not be impugned by the courts unless it is categorized as being *Wednesbury* unreasonable. Thus, the leading post-war decision of *Prescott* arose from an application for declaratory relief in the Chancery Division; and, as we have seen, significant doubts have been expressed as to whether the court properly addressed the question of standing.[217] Furthermore, while *Bromley* proceeded by way of judicial review, the Divisional Court in that case dismissed the application on the ground that it was for the GLC rather than the courts to hold the balance between farepayers and ratepayers and it was not until the issue reached the appellate courts that the fiduciary concept was taken seriously. And we have seen that the post-*Bromley* Divisional Court cases have all served to interpret the fiduciary concept simply as a subset of the *Wednesbury* principles.

Given both the general importance and the anomalous position of *Roberts* v. *Hopwood*, we might reflect briefly on the circumstances of that case. This case concerned the exercise of audit powers and it should be recalled that it was in fact the auditor who first invoked the fiduciary concept in that dispute.[218] This is significant because, at that time, the auditor possessed the statutory power of surcharge, which meant that the councillors, should they wish to contest the auditor's findings, were obliged to appeal against that decision to the Divisional Court. The Court's role, then, was that of reviewing the decision of the auditor rather than directly addressing the question of the legality of the councillors' actions. The reasonableness of the auditor's judgment rather than the reasonableness of the councillors' actions provided the focus of the challenge in the courts; and this may go some way towards explaining the Divisional Court's decision in that case. We might note, however, that since that period the powers of auditors have been amended. Instead of determining the issue, the auditor is in the position of presenting a *prima facie* case to the Divisional Court, which

---

[217] *Barrs* v. *Bethell* [1982] 1 All ER 106.
[218] See Laski, 'Judicial Review of Social Policy in England' [1926] 39 *Harv. L Rev.* 832, 834.

body has become the tribunal of first instance. And since that reform, that court's attitude to the fiduciary concept has significanctly changed.[219]

The general point of importance is that, with the establishment of the special procedures for addressing public law challenges to local authority action, the influence of the fiduciary concept has waned. The Crown Office list judges who have been appointed to determine these cases have expressed no interest in the idea of a specific, judicially enforceable fiduciary duty which the local authority owes to ratepayers and as those judges are promoted to more senior positions in the ranks of the judiciary their influence is likely to extend more widely.

Reform of local government finance

The other issue to consider in assessing the continuing power of the fiduciary concept is that of the Conservative Government's programme of local government reform, and in particular reforms to the system of finance introduced in the late 1980s. The general tenor of these reforms, it may be argued, renders the judicial enforcement of a concept of fiduciary duty to ratepayers redundant since the basic objective has been to reorganize the entire system of local government in the image cast by the fiduciary concept.[220] This development may be seen most clearly in relation to the reforms to local government finance.

The basis for the fiduciary concept, as we have seen, lies in the relationship between those who pay for, those who vote for, and those who benefit from local services. At the heart of the concept lies a tension between those who benefit from services and those who finance their cost, though the nature of the electorate may come to perform a pivotal role since it may indicate whether that potential tension is capable of being remedied through the ballot box. When, during the late 1980s, the Government embarked on the most radical reform of local government finance this century, the type of thinking which was most influential was precisely that which underpinned the fiduciary concept.[221] Under the community charge or poll tax scheme,[222] the Government attempted in effect to bring about fundamental readjustments in the voting-paying-benefiting relationship so as to render the concept of fiduciary duty redundant.

In seeking to justify the poll tax scheme the Government argued that its basic objective was in fact to bring the voting-paying-benefiting relationship into alignment. The two basic reforms of the 1988 Act – the nationalization of non-domestic rates and the abolition of domestic rates and their replacement with a 'community charge' – each served to undermine the fiduciary concept. Nationalization of the non-domestic rate converted it from a variable, locally-determined tax into a uniform, nationally-determined one and thus removed the

---

[219] See *Pickwell* v. *Camden LBC* [1983] 1 QB 962.   [220] See, above, ch. 2.

[221] See Department of the Environment, *Paying for Local Government*, Cmnd. 9714 (1985).

[222] Local Government Finance Act 1988. See also Abolition of Domestic Rates etc. (Scotland) Act 1987.

critical link between business ratepayers and the local council. Furthermore, the community charge which replaced domestic rates was payable as a flat rate charge on every adult resident of the area, which meant that the marginal cost of local services would be payable by all the electorate equally. Consequently, since all local taxpayers would contribute an equal share to the cost of the services provided by a council elected on a franchise consisting of all the local taxpayers, any conceivable rationale for the fiduciary concept had disappeared.[223]

While the community charge scheme has since been abolished and replaced by the council tax, a banded property tax,[224] it is arguable that the general effect of these recent reforms has been to render illegitimate any attempt to invoke the fiduciary concept. Since the 1988 Act was constructed on a model which made judicial enforcement of the duty redundant, Parliament has signalled quite clearly that the fairness of the balance between local taxpayers and service beneficiaries is a matter for Parliament rather than the courts. The subsequent modification of the community charge scheme to provide a fairer balance in the relative contributions of local taxpayers is indicative of the fact that Parliament is attentive to these issues and thus there is no longer any residual role for the courts in such matters.

Conclusions

The character of the British constitution is such that we are greatly dependent for the effective functioning of our governing arrangements on the emergence of a sense of trust. This sense of trust requires us to place faith in those on whom we confer authority to act responsibly and fairly in carrying out their responsibilities. This idea seems to be rooted in a belief that it is not possible to specify boundary rules in advance: trust thus emerges as a way of coping with the task of governing under complex and changing circumstances. There is, however, one area in which the judiciary have in fact been prepared to define the boundaries of governmental authority by reference to this sense of trust. In articulating the concept of a fiduciary relationship between local councils and their ratepayers, the courts, by imposing a legally enforceable duty on local authorities, have to that extent substituted the trust placed in elected representatives with a sense of trust in the ability of the judiciary to determine the limits of fair political action. In this chapter the emergence of the idea of this fiduciary concept in the field of public law has been traced. We have seen that there have been three critical periods over the last 150 years in which the concept has been forged and

[223] This basic point was not recognized by a number of commentators who simply assumed that the idea of fiduciary duty would automatically extend to community charge payers. See, e.g., C. Himsworth and N. Walker, 'After Rates' [1987] PL 586, at 610; J. Goudie, 'Local authorities and fiduciary duty' in M. Supperstone & J. Goudie (eds.), *Judicial Review* (London, 1992), 265, at 267.
[224] Local Government Finance Act 1992.

that each period may be understood as marking a transitional phase in the development of the modern system of local government. By focusing on these periods we might thus acquire some insight into the position of the judiciary in our structures of governance.

The initial period was in the immediate aftermath of the Municipal Corporations Act 1835 when municipal corporations were impressed with the character of a public trust. The aim of the judiciary in utilizing this device was to give effect to the legislative policy which had established the municipal corporations as institutions of government. The Chancery courts used the flexibility of their equitable jurisdiction to ensure that borough funds were applied to public purposes and thereby assisted in the establishment of a modern system of local government. The *ancien régime*, a self-perpetuating oligarchy of freemen of the borough, had their rights to corporate property confiscated and transferred to elected councils. At this stage, however, there existed no precise notion of a fiduciary duty to ratepayers; the duty of the council seemed to be one which was owed to the community as a whole and the concept of the trust was invoked essentially to ensure that the corporations, being governmental institutions, used their resources for furtherance of the collective good.

The idea that the council owed an enforceable fiduciary duty to its ratepayers did not emerge in any precise form until the 1920s. The system of local government operating during the nineteenth century, which is perhaps best characterized as that of a ratepayer democracy, was one in which the council could be trusted to act in harmony with the interests of those who financed their activities precisely because it was directly accountable to that group through regular elections. With the extension of the franchise, however, especially after 1894, strains between the interests of electors and ratepayers became more evident and these strains were exacerbated as a result of the growing success of the newly formed Labour party in local elections. The tension between voters, ratepayers and beneficiaries of council services was reflected in a particularly stark form in the movement generally known as Poplarism and it was therefore hardly surprising that it was in the context of a decision of Poplar BC in this period that the House of Lords enunciated a more specific version of the fiduciary concept.

In common with the first period, the 1920s may be also viewed as a period of transformation. If the post-1835 situation concerned the conversion of municipal corporations into institutions of local government, the 1920s was the period in which the full fruits of that reform process were revealed in the emergence of democratic party politics based on a wide franchise. At this stage, however, and unlike the post-1835 period, the judiciary did not act to further the modernization process. Rather, a more precise version of the fiduciary concept was fashioned for the purpose of bolstering the nineteenth-century system; the special legal status accorded the ratepayer and the language relating to the 'philanthropy', 'honest stupidity' and 'unpractical idealism' of elected representatives all reveal a Victorian mentality amongst the judiciary. But the 1920s is to be understood as a transitional phase in the development of local government not simply because of the growth in party politics but also because of the changing nature of the relationship between central and local government. After 1920 a major extension took place in the use of central grants in aid of local expenditure and, accompanying this, a recognition of need to use grants to bring about some form of equalization in respect of differential resources and needs. These changes are symptomatic of the emergence of an interdependent central–local network in which much more complex patterns of trust were being delineated.

The consequence of these changes was that the fiduciary concept had virtually no resonance within the modern system which emerged after the 1920s. Ideas of 'trust' and 'duty' certainly were of relevance but they were to be understood not as legal concepts but largely in terms of professional norms located within the complex structure of the central–local relationship. The ideas were embedded within a modern rather than a traditional aristocratic code of conduct. These changes were not really accommodated by the judiciary until after the Second World War; as may be illustrated by Lord Greene MR's judgment in *Wednesbury*, which served both to marginalize *Roberts* v. *Hopwood* and to re-orientate the focus of review to the misuse of power rather than breach of duty.[225] By this time, it had become abundantly clear that the issue of 'duty' was primarily regulated through the administrative network of central–local government relations and the role of the courts in this system was relatively marginal. Although the fiduciary concept was occasionally invoked in the post-war period, it appeared, most notably in *Prescott*, in the form of the discrimination principle rather than the more extensive efficient management principle. Furthermore, its utilization in that case seemed only to undermine settled understandings and it resulted in action being quickly taken by Government to nullify its effect.[226] The post-war experience seemed only to confirm that the concept imposed a forced simplicity on a complex system and was an anachronism which the courts should shelve.

How, then, are we explain its reactivation in the 1980s? What is particularly interesting here is that, once again, the 1980s may be understood as a period of transition for local government. On this occasion it seemed that the entire post-war settlement, based on networks operating with a fair degree of mutual trust within a very general legal framework, was crumbling. The centre's response was to assert its status within a hierarchical structure and to bring about a fundamental restructuring in the central–local relationship. This context may explain precisely why, even though the legal analysis of the House of Lords in *Bromley* was patently inadequate, the Government not only refused to act to nullify its

---

[225] *Associated Provincial Picture Houses Ltd* v. *Wednesbury Corporation* [1948] 1 KB 223, at 232: *Roberts* v. *Hopwood* 'is no authority whatsoever to support the proposition that the court has power, a sort of overriding power, to decide what is reasonable and what is unreasonable. The court has nothing of the kind.'

[226] Public Service Vehicles (Travel Concessions) Act 1955: see, above, 229.

impact but actually sought to exploit the uncertainties of the judgment for its own purposes. As we have seen, the courts did not take any further initiative to transform the concept into an overriding instrument of review. In so acting the judiciary clearly took cognizance of their limited institutional competence to engage in managerial supervision of the general expenditure policies of local authorities. Nevertheless, the initial destabilizing impact which *Bromley* had caused, greatly assisted the Government in the pursuit of its general objectives. The Government's actions in the early 1980s had undermined the sense of trust in the framework and the *Bromley* decision had served to deflect responsibility for that action. Thereafter the Government moved to reorganize the system, to break many of the codes and conventions and to restructure the central–local relationship in precise legal form.

The developments which have occurred since *Bromley* seem to indicate that in future the idea of a fiduciary duty which local councils owe to their local taxpayers is unlikely to resurface as an enforceable legal duty. Certainly, the judiciary have since 1981 worked actively to subsume the fiduciary concept within the general principles of administrative law. However, perhaps of even greater importance have been developments in the field of legislation. Since 1980 the Government has extensively reorganized the system of local government. In the new system which has emerged in the 1990s there is little room for any sense of trust. Acting presumably on the basis that the idea of trust provides too insecure a foundation for the system, the Government has forged a hierarchical central–local relationship based on precise powers and duties. Discretion has been replaced by rules and the primary form of law has shifted from a facilitative to directive style of law. In this new local government system based on limited powers, specific duties and broad central powers of supervision intended to be actively exercised there is simply no longer any need for a general concept of a fiduciary obligation owed to local taxpayers. The judicially-developed concept of fiduciary duty is dead precisely because the entire structure of local government has been reorganized in its image. And the difficulties which the judiciary have experienced of accommodating representative local government within the structures of governance have now come to be shared by the central executive.

5

OF TAPERS, TARGETS AND CAPS: CENTRAL CONTROLS OVER LOCAL EXPENDITURE

Writing in 1912, Edwin Cannan explained how, in producing a new edition of his classic study on *The History of Local Rates*, he had undertaken the 'extra-ordinarily difficult task' of including an additional chapter on the relationship between expenses borne by local rates and those contributed by central government grants.[1] 'There are', he reflected, 'probably not a dozen persons in England who could pass an examination on the principles which determine the distribution between the various localities of the proceeds of the national taxes allocated to them by the Local Government Act 1888, and the Acts which have followed it.'[2] The arrangements, Cannan was to conclude, amounted to 'eclecticism *in excelsis*'.[3] Cannan was scarcely alone in holding this conviction. His views were, for example, echoed by none other than Sidney Webb, a man blessed with a remarkable ability to dig out the most obscure of details and subject them to rational analysis. Writing at the same time as Cannan, Webb arrived at the conclusion that the system of central grants in aid of local expenditure is 'a chaos which practically no one understands'.[4]

In the early decades of the twentieth century there existed a great multiplicity of grants allocated according to a range of differential criteria.[5] Indeed, the Royal Commission on Taxation in 1901 had concluded that one of the basic reasons for the lack of public demand for reform was the vast complexity of the system.[6] Another reason perhaps was that, during this period, central grants contributed only around one-fifth of local expenditure.[7] As the burden of local expenditure increased during the 1920s, however, a greater proportion of that expenditure came to be met by central grants and, as a result, pressure emerged for the reorganization of the grant system. This was achieved in the Local Government Act 1929 which replaced many of the specific grants with a general grant. With the enactment of this general grant, the principle of grant allocation

---

[1] E. Cannan, *The History of Local Rates in England* (London, 2nd edn., 1912), v–vi.

[2] Ibid., vi.   [3] Ibid., 152.

[4] S. Webb, *Grants in Aid* [1911] (London, 2nd edn., 1920), 7.

[5] It has been estimated, for example, that in 1918 local education was supported by 57 grants which were calculated by reference to different rules: D.N. Chester, *Central and Local Government* (London, 1957), 170.

[6] Report of the Royal Commission on Local Taxation, Cd. 638 (1901), 1.

[7] C.D. Foster, R.A. Jackman and M. Perlman, *Local Government Finance in a Unitary State* (London, 1980), 133 (Fig. 1.5.1).

for the first time reflected the fact that local authorities had different rateable resources and different spending needs. New demands during the 1930s led to new forms of specific grant, however, and it was not until the introduction in 1948 of a more extensive 'equalization grant' that the principle of the modern grant system was properly established.[8] Furthermore, it was only after reforms in 1958 that the principle of the general grant in practice governed the allocation of the great bulk of central government grant aid.[9] In 1966, by which time central grants provided more than half of local expenditure, the basic grant was renamed the Rate Support Grant[10] and, though subject to subsequent adjustments, it has remained the basic form of grant ever since.[11]

These changes in grant regimes can be understood as a reflection of some basic changes which have taken place in the central–local government relationship. During the twentieth century the scale of government has been transformed as government has assumed a basic responsibility for the health of the economy and the welfare of the population. With this transformation in the role of government have come major changes in the organizational arrangements of government. Central departments have a limited executant capacity; their primary function has been to establish a series of policy and resource frameworks within which a vast number of semi-autonomous agencies provide services or regulate particular fields. Local government growth, in large part, reflects these basic governmental changes. The scope and scale of its activities has substantially increased as local government has, in partnership with the centre, assumed responsibility for a broad range of services of critical importance to the welfare state. Local government, which now accounts for more than one-quarter of all public expenditure, has become incorporated into an extensive system of government in which a major task of the centre is that of 'securing coordinated policy actions through networks of separate, but interdependent, organisations where the collective capabilities of a number of participants are essential for effective problem-solving'.[12]

As part of this compact, local government growth has been financed largely by central government grants. One indication of this is the fact that, when expressed as a proportion of personal disposable income, the domestic rate burden has remained remarkably constant throughout this century.[13] The compact has been regarded by many as a wholly beneficial arrangement for ensuring the effective provision of governmental services. This view was succinctly expressed by Webb when he stated that:

[8] Local Government Act 1948, Pt. I.

[9] Local Government Act 1958, Pt. I (rate deficiency grant).

[10] Local Government Act 1966, Pt. I.

[11] In 1988, as a result of the abolition of domestic rates, it was renamed the Revenue Support Grant: see Local Government Finance Act 1988, Pt. V.

[12] K. Hanf, 'Introduction' in K. Hanf & F.W. Scharpf (eds.), *Interorganisational Policymaking: Limits to Coordination and Central Control* (London, 1978), 2.

[13] Foster, Jackman and Perlman (above, n. 7), 316.

It has become an axiom of political science that, with our English administrative machinery, Grants in Aid of Local Government are indispensable – (i) for any equitable mitigation of the inequalities of burden; (ii) to secure effective authority for the necessary supervision and control of the National Government; (iii) to encourage the kind of expenditure most desirable in the interests of the community as a whole; and (iv) to make it possible to attain to anything like a universal enforcement of the 'National Minimum' that Parliament has prescribed.[14]

This development has, however, also been a perennial cause of concern. Cannan succinctly articulated this concern when he expressed the view that 'the demand for a transfer of expense from the localities to the State' would undermine the liberties of the 'English people' and would lead to 'a country governed by experts who will create efficiency in every branch of national life – regardless of expense'.[15] He concluded that:

The New Chadwickianity which is being preached is not founded on a crude system of centralisation involving the disappearance of the organs of local self-government, nor on coercion enforced by reluctant law courts. It leaves all the old forms intact and proposes to lay no rude hands on the persons of recalcitrant councillors. It is founded on the ingenious expedient of inducing the nation to allow itself to be taxed to supply funds which are to be redistributed between the various localities according to general regulations laid down by parliament, one of which is that the locality must satisfy the inspectors of some Government department that the service in respect of which the grant is made is 'efficient'. By this expedient the citizen delivers himself bound hand and foot into the custody of the official expert . . .[16]

In place of Webb's utilitarian interest in the greatest good of the greatest number, Cannan seeks to shift the focus of concern to the issue of process. Financial dependency on the centre, he suggests, will not merely stifle local initiative but will also replace political decision-making with official control. Cannan also implies that, through the use of carrots rather than sticks and framework legislation rather than specific duties, the effect will be that law will effectively be displaced as a medium for maintaining a balance between central and local interests. Webb was not oblivious to the constitutional significance of grants-in-aid. He accepted that 'the Grant in Aid . . . has become a governmental instrument of extraordinary potency for good or ill, of greater actual importance in the lives of the people than parts of the Constitution to which more attention is directed'.[17] Further, he recognized that whether local government 'hardens into a stagnant bureaucracy, smothered in red tape and rendering the very minimum of utility to the community; or blossoms and develops into an

[14] Webb, *Grants in Aid* (above, n. 4), 26.
[15] Cannan, *History of Local Rates* (above, n. 1), viii.
[16] Ibid., viii–ix. For the significance of Cannan's reference to Chadwick see, above, ch. 1, 29–36.
[17] Webb, *Grants in Aid* (above, n. 4), 2.

ever-improving, ubiquitously-serving agency ... depends very largely on the particular conditions upon which its Grant in Aid is made'.[18] The gulf which separates Cannan and Webb is measured not only by their differences on the relationship between representatives and officials, law and administration, traditional forms and scientific structures, but also, ultimately, on their sense of the desirable balance between public and private.

Though these basic tensions can, of course, never fully be dissolved, the establishment of the principle of the general grant may be viewed as an attempt to alleviate some of the concerns which arise from local government's growing dependency on grant aid. General grants seek to achieve equalization without making the payment of grant dependent on official approval of specific packages of services; they enable central government to devise a general policy and resources framework without becoming embroiled in matters of detail; and they provide strong encouragement for the provision of a nation-wide arrangement of basic services without the centre engaging in an intrusive investigation into the efficiency of particular services in particular localities.

This attempt at reconciliation is not, however, achieved without certain costs. From its very inception, the idea of the general grant has been 'criticized for its complexity, especially in the formula, for being inhibitive of the active interest of the local ratepayer, for making development of services too stereotyped and uniform, and for not giving enough encouragement to careful administration'.[19] These criticisms concerning issues of complexity, accountability and service responsiveness were defused only to the extent that, alongside the grant allocation mechanism, there developed an administrative culture through which the potentially antagonistic interests of the centre and the localities could be mediated. This required a degree of give and take, a willingness to have regard to the interests and concerns of the various parties, and an acceptance of the idea that disputes and disagreements should be resolved through negotiation and bargaining rather than by insisting on formal powers and duties. As a result of this compact, the entire question of grant allocation has, despite its admitted constitutional significance, been largely removed from the legal sphere. Framework legislation has been used essentially to validate the general scheme, but disputes over matters of grant allocation never ended up in the courts and lawyers have tended to regard the issues as being beyond their realm.[20]

All this changed in the 1980s. As attempts were made to use the grant system

---

[18] Webb, *Grants in Aid*, 2–3.

[19] Sir J. Stamp, 'The Finance of Municipal Government' in H.J. Laski, W.I. Jennings and W.A. Robson (eds.), *A Century of Municipal Progress* (London, 1935), chap. XVI at 386.

[20] The standard legal texts gave the subject the most cursory treatment. See, e.g., C. Cross, *Principles of Local Government Law* (London, 6th edn., 1981) which devoted only 9 pages in a book of 700 pages to the subject; K. Davies, *Local Government Law* (London, 1983) which deals with grants in 6 pages. See also P. Liell, *Council Houses and the Housing Act 1980* (London, 1981) which examines in detail the tenants' charter and the right to buy but nowhere considers the importance of the changes to the housing subsidy system introduced by the 1980 Act.

to promote accountability and responsiveness, and generally to restrain expenditure, conflict between the centre and the localities ensued. This had the effect of subverting the compact, and thus of undermining conventional administrative understandings concerning grant arrangements. And, with the removal of this insulation, the issue of complexity assumed a new intensity. The primary reason for this was that the grant 'losers' turned – possibly for the first time – to the law for guidance concerning their rights and liabilities. And once lawyers had arrived on the scene, the residue of trust between the parties within the system rapidly dissolved. At this stage the issue of the complexity of the grant system, which Cannan had identified as a major problem earlier this century, assumed a new form. Allocation of grant may have been based on principles but, from the lawyer's perspective, those principles appeared to have been buried beneath the jargon of economically literate officials. Michael Elliott expressed this view tersely when he suggested that: 'GREs, HIPs, Schedules of GRPs, Capital Receipt Underenhancement, 100 per cent virement, 10 per cent tolerance, principles for multipliers, transitional clawback – these are the stuff not of a governmental system that serves its community as best it can, but of one which has largely lost its "service" objectives and elevated a concern for its own processes into a pathological narcissism.'[21]

This chapter examines this recent experience in which lawyers and the courts have become involved in the business of trying to use the law to establish a normative framework governing grant allocation. As we shall see, it has been a rather unhappy episode in the history of central–local government relations. This is not, however, to suggest that lawyers have been at fault. 'There is no point', as Elliott rightly points out, 'in blaming lawyers for revelling in the unclear and the unclarified, the dispute-inducing and the oversubtleties of meaning – this is what they are paid to do.'[22] Rather, the experience provides a penetrating insight into the difficulties which arise when a relatively simple, external review agency is dragged into the business of trying to regulate the continuing, complex relations of two key institutions locked into an interdependent network of government.

The Block Grant Mechanism

The origins of the block grant mechanism

The twentieth century settlement in the system of central–local relations was based on the fundamental assumption that central departments and local authorities shared a basic mutuality of objective and could be trusted not to interfere in one another's primary sphere of competence. The issues of what precisely

---

[21] M. Elliott, 'Local Government in Schleswig-Holstein – the Intrusion of Law' (1982) vol. 8 no. 1 *Local Government Studies* 16, at 17.

[22] Ibid., 17.

were the objectives of the system and how a demarcation could be drawn between local and central matters obviously remained contested. But, notwithstanding particular disputes and disagreements, the system seemed for much of
the time to work adequately. What cushioned the system were the assumptions
that government in the twentieth century would experience continuous growth
and that local government would continue to enjoy the status of a vital component of that system of government. During the 1970s, however, the foundations
on which this settlement was based began to crumble. Many of the resulting
antagonisms came to be reflected through the financial relationship.

The clearest indicator of difficulties arose from the challenge to the assumption of growth. With the pressures for cutbacks in public expenditure during the
1970s, the grant system came to be seen not so much as a central contribution
to local services with a semi-national character but rather as an instrument of
central control over local government. These strains can be seen reflected in the
Government's decision in 1974 to establish the Layfield Committee to 'review
the whole system of local government finance'.[23] Layfield accurately identified
the dilemma of control and accountability in a local system dependent on high
and increasing central grants. 'Effective control of expenditure', the Report
indicated, 'cannot be ensured in a system in which local accountability has been
seriously weakened, unless central accountability provides that control.'[24] It
recognized that an alternative – in the form of a revival of local accountability
– existed but felt that this would require a deliberate policy decision and a
rejuvenation of the local tax base. Without this, Layfield suggested, there would
be a continuation in the gradual shift of power to the centre. The Labour Government responded to Layfield by outlining the responsibilities of central and
local government but rejected 'any formal definition' since that 'would lack the
advantages of flexibility and rapidity of response to new circumstances' and
'would be likely to break down under pressure'.[25] The Government felt that
there were evident disadvantages 'of both the centralist and localist approaches'
and suggested 'there is [no] clear case for the adoption of either'.[26]

The Government response failed to propose any new tax for local government
and, by fudging the key issue, created an environment in which the Layfield
prediction proved essentially correct. 'As a poor response to a major problem',
Tony Travers has commented, the Government's response to Layfield 'set the
scene for the next government to change local authority finance with little real
consultation.'[27] The Conservative Government which assumed power in 1979
was from the outset committed to reducing expenditure on services, such as
education, housing and social services, for which it had no direct control.[28] It

---

[23] *Report of the Committee of Inquiry into Local Government Finance* (Layfield Report), Cmnd.
6453 (London, 1976), iii.
[24] Ibid., 72.   [25] *Local Government Finance*, Cmnd. 6813 (London, 1977), para. 2.8.
[26] Ibid.   [27] T. Travers, *The Politics of Local Government Finance* (London, 1986), 76.
[28] See, e.g., *The Government's Expenditure Plans*, Cmnd. 7841 (London, 1980).

thus immediately proposed reform of the grant system to provide incentives for local authorities to reduce their expenditure. This new system, which was enacted in Part VI of the Local Government, Planning and Land Act 1980, was known as the block grant mechanism.

The enactment of the block grant mechanism opened a new era in the central–local financial relationship. It was an era which, as Layfield had correctly predicted, was to be one of growing centralization of power. But it was also characterized both by hyperactivism and 'destabilizing incrementalism'[29] as central government lurched from one mechanism to the next in its quest to control local expenditure. Arising from this confusion over finance came the growing realization, not only that the Government was seeking to assert its pre-eminence in the relationship, but also that increasingly there was no conspicuous mutuality of objective between central and local government and ultimately that the centre no longer viewed the institution of local government as having an important role in the structure of governance.

The characteristics of the block grant mechanism

Since the 1950s, as we have seen, grant distribution has been governed by the principle that the bulk of grant aid should take the form of a general grant unhypothecated to specific services and after 1966 that general grant took the form of a Rate Support Grant (RSG). The basic aims of the RSG have been to compensate authorities for differences in local taxable wealth (the resources element) and for disparities in spending needs (the needs element) and since its establishment the RSG distribution formula has been continually refined. From the mid 1970s, however, this process of technical refinement has been coupled with a concern to incorporate incentives for local authorities to reduce expenditure.

In its evidence to Layfield the Department of the Environment had proposed combining the needs and resources elements, thus enabling this 'combined grant' to achieve full equalization with a much lower grant total. This combined grant, however, involved central government making an assessment of each local authority's spending need and this therefore implied an unprecedented degree of central supervision of each local authority's expenditure plans. It was suggested, in support of the proposal, that its effect would be to clarify the relationship between central and local government, since local government would assume responsibility for spending above the assessed needs figure. The Department nevertheless conceded that the combined grant 'would have the appearance of a major change in the whole philosophy of the grant system'.[30] Layfield took the view that such a grant could fit either a centralist or localist approach but

---

[29] G. Bramley, 'Incrementalism run amok? Local government finance in Britain' (1985) 63 *Public Administration* 100.

[30] Layfield Report, Appendix 7, 'Evidence by the Department of the Environment: Central Government Grants to Local Government: Some Possible Changes', para. 3.7.1.

expressed the concern that grant allocation should not be used as a short-term regulator of local expenditure.[31] In its response, the Labour Government advocated the introduction of a 'unitary grant' which was, to all intents and purposes, the combined grant proposal.[32] When the Conservatives took office in 1979 they took over the essence of this proposal, renaming it the 'block grant'.

The block grant was explicitly constructed around the concept of equalization so that up to a notional level of expenditure, called Grant-Related Expenditure (GRE), local authorities were to be fully compensated for differences in rateable values and spending needs. GRE, however, being a central assessment of a local authority's spending needs, also served to trigger an adjustment in grant. By incorporating a tapering provision above GRE so that marginal expenditure above GRE attracted a lower rate of grant (or, in the case of an authority with a high resource base, could result in negative marginal rate of grant) the block grant mechanism placed the burden of additional expenditure on local ratepayers. The block grant mechanism thus sought to deal with an apparent weakness in post-war general grant systems of providing incentives to local authorities to increase expenditure in order to attract more grant.

Having introduced the block grant mechanism in the 1980 Act, the Government then found that for 1981/82, the first year in which the block grant mechanism was fully operational, local authorities had not reacted as anticipated to the grant tapering provisions. Many local authorities had opted to maintain service levels and raise the necessary additional revenue from the rates. These projections caused the Secretary of State immediately to announce a new set of targets for local authorities which were based, not on some form of needs assessment as under the block grant mechanism, but on the historic pattern of expenditure of each local authority. This system of expenditure targets with its associated grant penalty arrangements was engrafted on to the block grant mechanism with retrospective effect in 1982.[33] This target system, which operated until 1986/87, had the effect not only of creating a much more powerful mechanism of expenditure control. It also served both to increase the complexity of the grant regime and to obscure the principles on which the block grant mechanism was based. Furthermore, it was a unilateral act by the centre which transformed the centre's capacity to control local authority expenditure.

The Government's conduct in the early 1980s has been subject to widespread criticism. Such censure has not simply been because of the shift in the central–local balance, but also because of the rather inept manner in which the instruments of financial control were handled. The Government's action seemed to indicate uncertainty or confusion about its goals and, in part, these difficulties appeared to stem from a failure to appreciate the complexity of the system which it was seeking to influence.

---

[31] Layfield Report, 215–6, 225–6.
[32] *Local Government Finance*, Cmnd. 6813, ch. 3.
[33] Local Government Finance Act 1982, Pt. II.

The most basic criticism was that the Government failed to recognize that intrinsic difficulties existed in using the block grant mechanism as a tool of expenditure restraint. Since the primary purpose of block grant was that of rate poundage equalization, the mechanism entailed a break in the link between the level of local expenditure and the size of the rate bill. The block grant mechanism thus incorporated certain features which prevented it being used as a stringent mechanism for exerting general downward financial pressure on local government[34] and it is perhaps because of the Government's failure fully to recognize this facet of the mechanism which caused much of its subsequent frustration. Beyond that, however, the reform of the grant system on the foundation of equalization also exposed certain structural weaknesses in the entire system of local government finance. The shift towards the equalization of rate poundages had the effect of establishing a close relationship between rate bills and rateable values; but, as a consequence, it also highlighted certain basic inconsistencies in the valuation process and thus exposed weaknesses in the rating system.[35] Again, the Government did not appear to have been conscious of this effect of block grant. Since the Conservatives had pledged in their 1979 election manifesto to reform the rating system, however, they obviously did not wish to put too great a strain on the rating system.[36] This therefore placed them in a difficult position. The most effective method of bringing about a reduction in local government expenditure was to reduce the proportion of local expenditure which central government would support. This was a method which had been shown to work, but only after a period in which rate demands had significantly increased.[37] This, however, was probably a consequence the Government was not prepared to countenance.

It is precisely because of these complexities of the system and the tensions in Conservative policy that the Government tried to use the grant system to achieve too many conflicting objectives.[38] As a result, it entirely lost control over local government expenditure. By 1984 local government revenue expenditure was 9 per cent higher in real terms than when the Conservatives took office and the consensus of official and academic opinion suggests that responsibility for this

[34] C.D. Foster & R.A. Jackman, 'Accountability and control of local spending', *Public Money*, September 1982.

[35] R. Jackman, 'Local government finance' in M. Loughlin, M.D. Gelfand & K. Young (eds.), *Half A Century of Municipal Decline 1935–1985* (London, 1985), ch. 7, esp. at 158–61, 163.

[36] Note also that the Government, in furtherance of its election pledge, in 1981 published a Green Paper on the issue which implied that there were no viable alternatives to domestic rates: Department of the Environment, *Alternatives to Domestic Rates*, Cmnd. 8449 (London, 1981).

[37] J. Barnett, *Inside The Treasury* (London, 1982), 75–6; L. Pliatsky, *Getting and Spending* (London, 1982), 112; J. Gibson, ' "Local Overspending": why the Government have only themselves to blame', *Public Money*, December 1983.

[38] See Audit Commission, *The impact on local authorities' economy, efficiency and effectiveness of the block grant distribution system* (London, 1984), which concluded that the system had provided few incentives for the improvement of efficiency and effectiveness and that managerial accountability had not been strengthened, local understanding of the system had not been furthered and central control had not been reduced.

state of affairs lay firmly at the Government's door.[39] The Government became caught in a vortex leading to an irresistibly increasing centralization of control: from block grant to expenditure targets; then to the acquisition in the Rates Act 1984 of powers to control the amount of rates which local authorities could raise; and then ultimately to the fundamental and rather disastrous reforms to the entire system of local government finance in the Local Government Finance Act 1988. This was not so much the result of conscious policy choice as being caught up in a system, the complexity of which it failed fully to appreciate.

Discretion and constraint in grant distribution

One critical dimension of the disputes over grant distribution arrangements during the 1980s has been the manner in which the law was invoked to adjudicate over the fairness of either the process or the actual allocation of grant. In order to begin to appreciate the significance of this development, the basic legal framework for the distribution of the rate support grant must first be outlined.

The most evident feature of the legal framework governing grant allocation in Part VI of the Local Government, Planning and Land Act 1980 was the extent of discretionary power exercised by the Secretary of State. The Secretary of State was obviously able to determine both the aggregate amount available for rate support grants and the portion of that amount which would be available for specific and supplementary grants and the domestic rate relief grant.[40] Those powers were hardly contentious, however, since they are basic to the processes of government. Further, the general discretion available to devise a formula for allocating the remainder as a block grant was also, in general terms, uncontroversial. But, in addition to those broad powers to shape the contours of the system, the Secretary of State was also vested with powers which potentially could be used to adjust the component parts in such a way as to affect individual authorities' entitlement to block grant. Thus, there existed powers: to adjust a local authority's calculation of 'relevant expenditure' and 'total expenditure';[41] to set the principles on which the grant-related poundage (GRP) is calculated and GRE determined;[42] to apply a multiplier, for a variety of purposes, to increase or decrease the amount of grant an authority might otherwise obtain;[43] and to disregard certain categories of expenditure for grant penalty purposes.[44]

---

[39] Audit Commission, *The impact on local authorities' economy, efficiency and effectiveness of the block grant distribution system* (London, 1984); National Audit Office, *Report by the Comptroller and Auditor General. Department of the Environment: Operation of the Rate Support Grant System* (London, 1985); House of Commons, 7th Report from the Committee of Public Accounts, Session 1985–86, *Operation of the Rate Support Grant System* (HC 47); J. Gibson, 'Local "overspending": why the Government have only themselves to blame', *Public Money*, December 1983; J. Gibson, 'Why block grant failed' in S. Ranson, G.W. Jones & K. Walsh (eds.), *Between Centre and Locality* (London, 1985), 58; R. Jackman, 'The Rates Bill – a measure of desperation' (1985) 55 *Political Quarterly* 161; T. Travers, *The Politics of Local Government Finance* (above, n. 27), ch. 8.
[40] Local Government, Planning and Land Act (LGPLA) 1980, ss. 54, 55.
[41] LGPLA 1980, ss. 56(8), 54(5).   [42] LGPLA 1980, ss. 57, 58.
[43] LGPLA 1980, s. 59.   [44] Local Government Finance Act 1982, s. 8(4).

In exercising many of these powers the Secretary of State was required to apply the same set of principles to all authorities or to all local authorities in the appropriate class. This seemed to provide an important safeguard, but the efficacy of this protection crucially depended on the scope for unilateral determination of the potentially relevant criteria: it could, for example, still be possible to target particular authorities and then to devise either the principles or the classes to ensure that they would be differentially considered.

In general, the breadth of the discretionary power of the Secretary of State suggested that resort to the courts for an adjudicative resolution of disputes would be unlikely to be particularly helpful. Nevertheless, during the 1980s, as the traditional assumptions in the conduct of central–local relations came under strain, this is precisely what occurred. The main reason why this was a thoroughly unsettling experience was essentially because of the manner in which Part VI of the 1980 Act, which established the basic statutory foundation for the payment of rate support grant, had been drafted. Being framework legislation it had not been drafted with the idea of adjudication in mind; its function was simply to confer power and competence rather than to establish the rules of the game. Furthermore, since the objective was to validate a complex mechanism with a technical economic logic, the drafting exercise was scarcely straightforward. It was presumably felt that the legal framework should not be too precise, since this might unduly inhibit the Government's ability to adjust the allocation formula to take account of new circumstances. But it should also not appear too discretionary, since that would undermine the protection accorded to local government within a largely centrally-financed system of the general, unhypothecated grant. The result of these competing pressures was establishment of an elaborate legal framework whose most basic characteristic was extreme opacity.

The Transition to Block Grant

Although the block grant mechanism became fully operational in 1981/82, the Conservative Government's determination to exert downward financial pressure through the grant system was such that the 1980 Act also contained transitional arrangements for 1980/81.[45] The objective of these arrangements was, so far as possible, to place the grant distribution arrangements for that year on a similar basis to the fully operational block grant mechanism. It did so essentially by giving the Secretary of State the power to withdraw grant from local authorities levying high rate poundages. Since the old system did not incorporate any centrally-determined assessments of spending need, however, there was bound to be a degree of rough justice within these arrangements.[46]

---

[45] LGPLA 1980, ss. 48–50.
[46] For details of the mechanics of the transitional arrangements see M. Loughlin, *Local Government in the Modern State* (London, 1986), 35–6.

In *R* v. *Secretary of State for the Environment, ex parte Brent LBC*[47] six London boroughs which had been adversely affected by the use of these transitional powers applied for judicial review and sought to quash the Secretary of State's decisions on the grounds of illegality, irrationality and procedural impropriety. The irrationality challenge was fairly summarily dismissed by the court, which was perhaps not surprising since the Secretary of State's decisions had been incorporated in subordinate legislation which had been subjected to affirmative resolution.[48] The court also rejected the challenge, under the head of illegality, founded on the question of whether the Secretary of State, as required by the Act,[49] had laid down in the Order the principles on which grant withdrawal would be effected. On this point, the court held that the multipliers which had been applied to grant entitlement were laid out in such detail that 'the instructed reader can discern the underlying principles'.[50] But the London boroughs did succeed on the issue of procedural impropriety. The Divisional Court held that, since the Secretary of State's decision affected the local authorities' rights to substantial sums of grant aid, the applicants had a right to be heard and that, because the Secretary of State had refused to listen to new representations *after* he had obtained the statutory power under the 1980 Act, his decision, being in breach of his duty of fairness, should be quashed.

Ex parte Brent, though directly concerned only with the transitional arrangements, is of primary importance in the recent history of central–local government financial relations. Its main significance was to signal unequivocally the changes wrought in the character of the central–local relationship. The effect of these changes can most readily be appreciated by having regard to the impact which the decision seemed to have had on the three institutions involved: local authorities, central departments and the courts.

Most obviously, the case provides a clear indication that local authorities were prepared to respond to the directive strategy of the Government by way of legal challenge in the courts. That this was to become the norm was underlined by the events which immediately followed the Divisional Court's ruling. After the judgment, the Secretary of State, having listened to local authority representations, decided to maintain grant abatement. This decision also was challenged in the courts, albeit, on this occasion, unsuccessfully.[51] This might suggest that the local authorities had obtained little reward for their efforts. This, however, was not strictly correct. Although the Secretary of State maintained grant abatement, because of the delays occasioned by the court hearings, the abatement provisions were determined on the basis of outturn rather than budgeted expenditure. And one consequence of that adjustment was to enable Hackney LBC to avoid

---

[47] [1982] 2 WLR 693.
[48] Rate Support Grant (Principles for Multipliers) Order 1980 (SI 1980 No. 2047).
[49] LGPLA 1980, s. 49(4).   [50] [1982] 2 WLR 693, 724.
[51] *R* v. *Secretary of State for the Environment, ex p. Hackney LBC* [1983] 3 All ER 358 (Div. Ct.); [1984] 1 All ER 956 (CA).

abatement altogether, thereby resulting in its saving almost £1 million in grant.[52] The *Brent* challenge thus provides an early illustration of the tactical use of the courts. Given the amounts of money which were generally at stake, the complexity of the arrangements for disbursing it, the opacity of the legislative framework, the fluidity of the general principles of administrative law which were potentially applicable, and the general uncertainty of the political and economic environment, local authorities soon recognized that, regardless of the strength of the legal arguments, there existed many incentives for initiating legal action over adverse grant expenditure determinations.

The *Brent* litigation appears also to have influenced central government behaviour. In general terms, the action alerted the Government to the fact that they were entering a new era of central–local relations; an era in which the Government would be required to pay particular attention to legal formalities in conducting business with local government. One specific event which may well have been influenced by the impact of the *Brent* action concerns the manner in which the system of expenditure targets was introduced. When expenditure targets were first announced in 1981 they appeared to lack any statutory foundation. The most obvious administrative method, that of applying multipliers to the grant entitlements of all authorities which did not comply with their expenditure target, seemed to fall foul of protections which prohibited the use of multipliers for the purpose of decreasing the amount of grant payable to an authority.[53] Nevertheless, what the Secretary of State initially proposed was to increase the grant-related poundage[54] schedules across the board; this would have the effect of reducing the amount of grant payable to each authority. Multipliers could then be used to *increase* the amount of grant payable to individual authorities which *complied* with their target.[55] The fact that this proposal could be touted itself reveals a great deal about the structure of Part VI of the 1980 Act. In the event, however, the Secretary of State decided not to proceed in this manner. Instead, he announced that retroactive powers would be sought to legitimate the use of expenditure targets from 1981/82. These were acquired in the 1982 Act.[56] This adoption of the legislative rather than administrative method of implementing expenditure targets seems to have been influenced by the probability that the administrative method would have been challenged and thus the risk that the target system may have been struck down by the courts.

The *Brent* case is also important in providing some indication of the likely attitude of the courts to action of this nature. Although arguments directed to each of the three principal heads of review were presented, the court seemed

---

[52] See [1983] 1 WLR 524 at 533: 'Hackney ... was able to show on outturn figures they qualified for the ... waiver and consequently on 9 August 1982 they were paid £929,416, being the amount by which their rate support grant for 1980/81 had been reduced'.

[53] LGPLA 1980, s. 59(2), (3).   [54] LGPLA 1980, ss. 57, 58.

[55] See, *Statement by the Secretary of State for the Environment to the Consultative Council on Local Government Finance*, 2 June 1981.

[56] Local Government Finance Act 1982, s. 8(10).

much more comfortable with the procedural aspects of the issue. This reflects a general feature of judicial review which was highlighted by Lord Brightman when he suggested that judicial review 'is concerned, not with the decision, but with the decision-making process'.[57] The court seemed particularly reticent when considering the question of irrationality. There were in fact two forms of irrationality argument in *Brent*. The explicit one, that the Secretary of State reached a decision that no reasonable minister could have reached, was, on the evidence, difficult to sustain. But the illegality or *ultra vires* issue in fact contained a disguised rationality argument. What the London boroughs were actually seeking to argue was that the requirement that the principles on which the multipliers were determined be specified in the Order meant that the Secretary of State must disclose the philosophy or rationale for the use of multipliers. In effect, that the use of multipliers must be rationally related to the objects of the Act. This was firmly rejected by the court. The court held that a distinction must be made between primary and secondary principles. The primary principle, laid down in section 48, is simply that the Secretary of State may reduce the rate support grant of any authority whose rate exceeds the 'notional uniform rate'. Since this 'primary principle' is essentially a broad discretionary power it is unlikely to incorporate any rigorous rationality requirement. The principles referred to by the applicants were merely secondary principles which served to indicate how the reduction determined by the Secretary of State was to be effected.[58] By adopting this formal distinction, the court ensured that it would not be drawn in to the role of acting as a general arbiter of the fairness and rationality of the Government's use of its powers to allocate grant aid.

One reason for adopting such an approach may have concerned the question of institutional competence. The affidavits and exhibits presented in the *Brent* case amounted to nearly 1,000 pages. The complexity of the issues raised was such that the court not only held a pre-hearing review but was also provided with a 'glossary of terms, a reading guide, a chronological statement of events and an outline of the submissions to be made'.[59] This enabled the court to examine the subject in advance of argument and considerably assisted its ability to produce a detailed explanation of the rate support grant system, as well as the facts and issues of the dispute in its judgment. This departure from traditional practice seemed to be an essential pre-condition to the judiciary being able to deal with the issues seriously. But the scale of the exercise and complexity of the issues might also have indicated that the extension of active judicial supervision to the field of central–local government relations should not lightly be instigated.

The legal challenge to the transitional arrangements in the *Brent* case thus signalled certain basic changes in the conduct of central–local government

---

[57] *R* v. *Chief Constable of North Wales Police, ex parte Evans* [1982] 1 WLR 1155, 1173.
[58] [1982] 2 WLR 693, at 724.   [59] Ibid., 735.

relations. Local authorities which were subject to the new forms of control would, it seems, examine carefully the nature of the central power and the manner in which it was being exercised with a view to subjecting such decisions to review in the courts. Central departments would thus be obliged to ensure that they properly exercised their legal powers. Furthermore, since local authorities had certain incentives to pursue cases which might only have a remote chance of ultimate success, this heightened degree of legal consciousness had a general impact on the central–local relationship which was relatively independent of the likely success of challenge in the courts. Finally, in *Brent* the court seemed to indicate that, while arguments rooted in procedural propriety would be entertained, those founded on rationality and fairness would not. And the reason for this was that it would require the court to assume a role which it was institutionally ill-equipped to perform.

Expenditure Targets in the Courts

The system of expenditure guidance, or targets, was accorded a statutory foundation in the Local Government Finance Act 1982. The 1982 Act repealed the protections in section 59 of the 1980 Act against the use of multipliers for the purpose of reducing grant and inserted a new power enabling multipliers to be used in order to make adjustments in the amount of block grant payable to an authority 'by reference to guidance issued by the Secretary of State and designed to achieve any reduction in the level of local authority expenditure . . . which he thinks necessary having regard to general economic conditions'.[60] This was scarcely a narrowly drawn power. The primary restraint on its exercise was the requirement that any such guidance 'shall be framed by reference to principles applicable to all local authorities'.[61]

The introduction of expenditure targets resulted not only in displacing the block grant tapering provisions as a restraining mechanism, but also in entirely obscuring the principles on which the block grant system was based.[62] Furthermore, since the introduction of expenditure targets coincided with the resurrection of the concept of fiduciary duty by the House of Lords in *Bromley LBC* v. *GLC*,[63] during the early 1980s there was the distinct possibility that these targets could be judicially transformed into ceilings on expenditure. This concern was heightened as a result of the Government's use of the power. In the first two years of its operation there was a maximum penalty to be paid and the system was thus used to fine local authorities which exceeded their targets. From 1983/ 84 onwards, however, a continuous and progressive penalty mechanism, through

---

[60] Local Government Finance Act 1982, s. 8(1); inserting a new s. 59(6)(cc) into the 1980 Act.
[61] LGPLA 1980, s. 59(11A).
[62] See Loughlin, *Local Government in the Modern State* (above, n. 46), 38–45.
[63] [1983] 1 AC 768. See, above, ch. 4, 231–7.

the use of a rising scale of multipliers, was applied for expenditure above target. By increasing the severity of the penalty scheme each year the Government was able, even without a threat of legal challenge founded on the fiduciary concept, to make the cost of non-compliance with the target politically or economically infeasible for the great majority of local authorities.

Targets and breach of statutory duty

The first major challenge to the legality of expenditure targets came from the London Borough of Hackney. Hackney, an inner London borough, was experiencing high levels of social stress. Since it had performed worst on the index of deprivation derived from the 1981 Census,[64] Hackney was, at that time, generally viewed as being England's poorest borough.[65] In the context of public expenditure reductions, the Labour-controlled authority was experiencing great difficulties in its attempts to cater for the needs of the borough. During the early 1980s, although Hackney's expenditure had steadily increased, it had been able largely to avoid grant penalties through the adoption of certain short-term measures. This strategy culminated in a decision to use the whole of its available balances of £10m to hold down the rate increase for 1983/84. This decision had the effect of reducing its total expenditure calculation for grant purposes, thereby resulting in saving £6.4m of RSG.

The consequences of this strategy, however, were exposed when the borough made preparations for its 1984/85 budget. Although its expenditure target had been set at £79m, Hackney required an expenditure of around £100m for an essentially standstill budget. At that level of expenditure, however, because of the tightening of the penalty rate, Hackney would incur a grant penalty in the region of £15–19m. Consequently, if the authority wished to maintain service levels, it would be obliged to increase its rates by 40–60 per cent.[66] Hackney thus petitioned the Secretary of State arguing that the announced expenditure target was unattainable in practice and that the Secretary of State should exercise his power under section 8(4) of the 1982 Act to disregard certain items of Hackney's expenditure for grant purposes.[67] The Secretary of State refused to do so and confirmed Hackney's target at £79m.

Hackney thereupon applied for judicial review, challenging the legality of the

---

[64] See, London Borough of Hackney, *The Case for Hackney* (1983) which reveals that Hackney had the highest proportion of single parent households (10.6%), second highest rate of overcrowding (9%), fifth highest number of households lacking basic amenities (11.9%) and seventh largest population loss since 1971 (18.1%). In addition, Hackney had the second highest unemployment rate in Greater London (15.3%).

[65] For a study of Hackney see, P. Harrison, *Inside the Inner City* (Harmondsworth, 1983).

[66] See, Joint Report of Chief Executive, Director of Finance and Director of Personnel to Policy & Resources Committee, *The Budget and the Rate 1984/85: Prospects and Options* (London Borough of Hackney, 9 November 1983).

[67] See [1986] 84 LGR 32, at 41–3.

expenditure guidance issued by the Secretary of State.[68] The principal argument pursued by Hackney was that the Secretary of State's expenditure guidance should be capable of being attained without the local authority having to act in breach of its statutory duties and failing to comply with accepted local authority functions and responsibilities. This argument was rejected in the Divisional Court on the ground that there was nothing in the Act to indicate this limitation on the use of expenditure guidance powers. Targets served only to establish a level beyond which the local authority could not look to central government for funding; they were not ceilings since expenditure above the target could still be financed by rates. In reaching this conclusion Forbes J was particularly concerned with the competence of the courts to deal with the sort of arguments presented. Forbes J considered that, given the manner in which a local authority's statutory responsibilities are formulated, the question of whether or not they can be performed at a given level of expenditure could not be viewed as a matter of 'pure fact'. The exercise was essentially evaluative and therefore a matter of policy with which the courts could not interfere; the court was 'simply not equipped to evaluate the mass of evidence . . . which it would be necessary to assemble' in order to test the validity of such policy judgments.[69]

In the Divisional Court the role of principles in structuring the discretion of the Secretary of State, an issue first addressed in *ex parte Brent*, was also raised. Section 59 of the 1980 Act required that guidance 'shall be framed by reference to principles applicable to all local authorities'[70] and stated that these principles 'shall be specified in the Rate Support Grant Report'.[71] In this case, Hackney argued that, since the Rate Support Grant Report had merely produced the formulae by which the guidance had been calculated, it had failed to comply with the statutory requirements. Again, the key issue was whether the term 'principles' in the statute required the Secretary of State to disclose the philosophy or the rationale for his guidance. On this question Forbes J felt that, since *Brent* had not been entirely clear on this point, it was necessary to make explicit the fact that the reference to 'principles' in the 1980 Act meant simply 'a self-sufficient proposition intended to be applied to a set of relevant circumstances'.[72] Consequently, 'the Secretary of State could well specify simply the mathematical principles (i.e., the formula or formulae) by the application of which the guidance figure for any local authority could be found'.[73]

On appeal, the point relating to the principles safeguard was not pursued and the challenge came to focus primarily on the question of attainability. On this issue, the Court of Appeal upheld the Divisional Court's judgment. The Appeal Court felt that the claim in effect amounted to a requirement that the Secretary of State must 'consider individually the position of each local authority and . . .

---

[68] *R* v. *Secretary of State for the Environment, ex parte Hackney LBC* (1984) 148 LGR 691 (Div. Ct.); (1986) 84 LGR 32 (CA).

[69] (1984) 148 LGR 691, at 712.   [70] LGPLA 1980, s. 59(11A).

[71] LGPLA 1980, s. 59(8).   [72] (1984) 148 LGR 691, 750.   [73] Ibid.

adjust the guidance that he gives according to the level of those commitments, provident or extravagant, wise or unwise, into which that authority may have chosen to enter according to the way in which it has seen fit to carry out their statutory duties and responsibilities'.[74] This interpretation, the court held, was not intended by Parliament. This was clear from the fact that, in framing guidance, the Secretary of State was under no obligation to consult with each local authority and, far from being obliged to consider the individual position of each local authority, was required to frame the guidance by reference to principles applicable to all authorities.

One general issue which arose from the Hackney challenge concerned the local authority's motive in pursuing its action in the courts. It must have been clear at the outset that the authority would face a difficult task. Could it be the case that the judicial review action was viewed as part of the Council's general political campaign against growing central controls over local expenditure? If it is to be so viewed, then two questions arise for consideration. The first is simply whether it is justified in cost-benefit terms. While the action certainly generated a significant amount of publicity and brought to the attention of the national media Hackney's grievances concerning the system of expenditure control, it was also undoubtedly an expensive exercise.[75] The second question raises the more difficult issue of whether, by virtue of adopting such a litigation-based strategy, there existed a danger of obfuscating the basic political issues. This point may be highlighted by considering the advice received by Hackney while preparing for their legal challenge. Counsel's advice stated that:

> A case can be wholly undermined and litigation can fail if it can be shown that an authority has undertaken unjustifiable or unreasonable expenditure or failed to eradicate obvious inefficiency and extravagance. . . . Statements which are alleged to have emanated very recently from Liverpool, even if Liverpool has a very strong case that it is being maltreated by the present Block Grants system, would inevitably undermine any case it might wish to bring and therefore it is necessary to be vigilant at all times in the coming months and years that nothing is said or decided which would unnecessarily undermine Hackney's case.[76]

The message here is that, if a local authority is seeking to maximize its chances of pursuing legal action tactically, then it may have to modify other aspects of its general political strategy.

---

[74] (1986) 84 LGR 32, 47.

[75] In a letter soliciting contributions from local authorities towards the cost of mounting an appeal against the first instance judgment it was estimated that the Divisional Court case alone had cost Hackney £35,000: Letter from Secretary of Association of Metropolitan Authorities to Chief Executives of Member Authorities, *London Borough of Hackney* v. *Secretary of State for the Environment*, 10 April 1984.

[76] Roger Henderson QC, *Advice to London Borough of Hackney* (28 October 1983) at 8. On the Liverpool situation see, above, ch. 3, 185–7.

Targets, principles and fairness

In strict legal terms, probably the most important point arising from *ex parte Hackney* was the clarification given by Forbes J that any reference to the term 'principles' in the statute would be treated by the courts as a purely formal criterion. If correct, this then raised the general question of whether there were any significant statutory restrictions imposed on the Secretary of State to prevent him discriminating between individual authorities in the process of allocating grant. Under the 1980 Act the Secretary of State was required to set a local authority's GRE and GRP 'in accordance with principles to be applied to all local authorities'.[77] It is also stated that in constructing principles for determining GRP 'the principles . . . shall apply to all authorities belonging to the appropriate class'.[78] Further, the power to use a multiplier to adjust the distribution of block grant may only be exercised 'in accordance with principles to be applied to all local authorities' or 'in accordance with principles to be applied to all local authorities belonging to the appropriate class'.[79] Finally, as we saw in *Hackney*, when the power was given to use multipliers for implementing the target system, the guidance issued by the Secretary of State for achieving such expenditure reduction 'shall be framed by reference to principles applicable to all local authorities'.[80] If principles were to be construed as being purely formal, perhaps these statutory protections would in practice be of little significance.

Nevertheless, these provisions seem to have been designed to control against certain types of discriminatory action. While the Secretary of State may legitimately shift the allocation of grant between, for example, urban and rural authorities, the intention was to safeguard against entirely individualized decisions. But did these provisions in fact accord that degree of protection? Consider, for example, the process for devising targets for 1983/84. Two generalized sets of targets were formulated, but the Government, apparently wishing specifically to penalize the GLC, also devised a third. This third target was announced provisionally to the Consultative Council on Local Government Finance as being one which would apply to all local authorities spending more than 20 per cent above their 1981/82 budget. When the Government subsequently discovered that this target would not only apply to the GLC but would also catch Corby and Milton Keynes, it quickly revised the target to apply only to those local authorities spending 25 per cent above 1981/82 budget. As finally constructed this third target caught only one local authority, the GLC. Since the target was 'designed to achieve [a] reduction in the level of local authority expenditure . . . which [the Secretary of State] thinks necessary having regard to general economic conditions'[81] and was formally constructed in universal terms, it seemed that there

---

[77] LGPLA 1980, s. 57(1). [78] LGPLA 1980, s. 58(1).
[79] LGPLA 1980, s. 59(5). [80] LGPLA 1980, s. 59(11A).
[81] LGPLA 1980, s. 59(6)(cc).

was little the GLC could do, even though the target had in practice been devised solely to apply to that authority.

The most important legal challenge to the system of expenditure targets did, nevertheless, raise a similar question. This action concerned the fairness of the construction of targets for 1985/86. In 1984/85 the base point for determining the expenditure target of all local authorities was either their previous year's target or their GRE, whichever was higher. In 1985/86 the establishment of the base point was more complicated. For authorities whose budgeted total expenditure was less than or equal to 1984/85 GRE, the 1985/86 target was 1984/85 GRE plus 3.75 per cent. For authorities spending above GRE, the 1985/86 target would be the 1984/85 target plus 3.75 per cent. This construction appeared, at first glance, to follow a similar pattern to the previous year's arrangements. The changes, however, operated to the particular disadvantage of a small group of authorities; those whose 1984/85 expenditure was greater than GRE and whose GRE was greater than target. The ten local authorities which fell into this group were thus denied the protection of determining their base position by reference to the higher of the two indicators; a form of protection which had been afforded to all local authorities in the previous year and to the vast majority in 1985/86. This group of traditionally low spending authorities (identified as such by virtue of the fact that their targets were below GRE) considered that the penalty imposed on them for spending above GRE in 1984/85 was wholly disproportionate to the extent to which they had done so.[82]

Three of the authorities from this group applied to the Divisional Court to quash the Secretary of State's guidance on the grounds of *Wednesbury* unreasonableness. This application was unsuccessful and two of the authorities, Nottinghamshire CC and Bradford MDC, pursued the issue to appeal. In the Court of Appeal the authorities' specific contention – which may be read both as a rationality and a proportionality argument – failed to win the support of the court. On this issue the court held that, whenever a line is drawn, hard cases are almost certain to occur and that, when that occurs, it does not necessarily follow that the principle on which the line was drawn is irrational.[83]

In the course of argument, however, the Court of Appeal latched on to a more basic point of statutory interpretation; and one which potentially had a profound effect. In addition to the irrationality challenge, the applicants had argued that the 1985/86 expenditure guidance was unlawful because it had not been framed 'by reference to principles applicable to all local authorities' as required by section 59(11A) of the 1980 Act. The guidance had in fact divided local author-

---

[82] Consider, for example, the case of Nottinghamshire CC. Its 1984/85 budget was less than 0.002 per cent higher than its GRE. As a consequence of the 1985/86 guidance, however, its relevant target, at which grant penalties would apply, was a figure which was £6,750,000 below its GRE (see [1986] 2 WLR 1, 23). Note that the relevant figure was the 1984/85 *budget* rather than outturn expenditure. Had the council appreciated the significance of its budget in relation to future grant entitlement it could surely have made the relevant adjustments.

[83] *Nottinghamshire CC* v. *Secretary of State for the Environment* (unreported) CA, 3 October 1985.

ities into two classes – those spending at or below GRE and those that were not – and applied different principles to the two classes. Furthermore, since local authorities had made out their 1984/85 budgets many months before the Secretary of State issued his guidance in December 1984, it followed that neither of the two sets of principles could be applicable to all authorities. In three separate but unanimous judgments, the Court of Appeal endorsed this argument and quashed the Secretary of State's decisions. The Court held that, in framing the guidance, the Secretary of State may not discriminate on the basis of the past spending performance of local authorities since to do so would breach the protections accorded by section 59(11A). That did not mean that the Government was not able to take account of the extent to which guidance had been followed but that 'the scheme of the legislation is that the discrimination against overspending is to take place at the second stage when the multiplier is fixed and not in the fixing of the guidance'.[84]

This decision had major consequences for the system of local government finance. It did not simply render unlawful the targets set for Nottinghamshire and Bradford but seemed to indicate that the entire 1985/86 target system was unlawful. Furthermore, although the targets for 1981/82 and 1982/83, being based on a uniform criterion of past expenditure, were not affected by the decision, in order to use the system to maintain an impetus for expenditure reduction, the Government had since 1983/84 found it necessary to adopt some form of two tier test. The Court of Appeal's judgment thus cast doubt on the legality of the target system utilized since 1983/84. Furthermore, since rate-capping had also been introduced from 1985/86[85] and rate-capped authorities had been designated on the basis of compliance with expenditure targets, the validity of that process was also called into question.

In these circumstances, the Secretary of State's decision to appeal to the House of Lords was scarcely surprising; after all, at issue now was the sum of over £1,000m which the Government had withheld in grant penalties under the target system since 1983. The Government, however, faced an uphill struggle; in the words of one commentator, 'the likelihood of [reversal] cannot appear strong in the light of the clear and unanimous reasoning of the Court'.[86] Nevertheless, in *Nottinghamshire CC* v. *Secretary of State for the Environment*[87] the House of Lords unanimously reversed the Court of Appeal's judgment. In a convenient division of labour Lord Bridge examined the issue of statutory interpretation and Lord Scarman the question of *Wednesbury* unreasonableness.

In seeking to construe the true meaning of section 59(11A), Lord Bridge addressed three facets of statutory interpretation: the purpose of the statutory scheme laid down in Part VI of the 1980 Act; the relevance of the precise

---

[84] Transcript of judgment, 8 (*per* Dillon LJ).   [85] Rates Act 1984; see, below, 299–301.

[86] M. Grant, 'Targets, goalposts and judges' (1985: unpublished paper) at 5 (copy on file with author).

[87] [1986] 2 WLR 1.

statutory language adopted; and the circumstances in which section 59(11A) had been enacted. On the issue of purpose, Lord Bridge considered that, on the Court of Appeal's interpretation, the target system could be used only to require an overall reduction or to restrict the overall increase of local government expenditure across the board by a given percentage. This interpretation seemed to be 'very startling in the context of this legislation and in the light of its evident purpose', given that the basic aim of the 1980 Act reform was to replace a system under which control could be achieved only by reducing aggregate rate support grant with a new mechanism in which more discriminate grant constraints could be applied.[88] Bridge recognized that 'if the statutory language leads inescapably to these consequences, they must be accepted' but that 'it would be wrong to construe ... section 59(11A) without regard ... to the apparent scheme of the legislation'.[89]

Within this general context, Lord Bridge then reflected on the statutory language adopted. The most puzzling feature of the 'principles' safeguards in Part VI of the Act was the fact that whereas section 59(11A) referred to 'principles applicable to all local authorities', all but one of the other provisions[90] used the phrase 'principles to be applied to all local authorities'. In wrestling with the possible differences between these phrases Lord Bridge, after considering various explanations, admitted that he 'could not help feeling ... that we were back among the medieval schoolmen debating nice theological differences about angels dancing on the head of a pin'.[91] In the end, his Lordship could 'see no way to avoid the conclusion that the draftsman is using the phrases ... as completely interchangeable'.[92] He thus concluded that 'the subsection is capable of bearing either of the meanings which the parties urge your Lordships to put upon it'.[93] In these circumstances Lord Bridge felt that a purposive approach dictated an interpretation in favour of the Secretary of State.[94]

Lord Bridge finally considered the circumstances in which section 59(11A) had been enacted. He recognized that the 1982 Act retrospectively validated the guidance issued for 1981/82 and 1982/83 and that the latter year's guidance was issued in a Rate Support Grant Report which had been considered by the House of Commons some months before the 1982 Act was enacted. Bridge suggested that the guidance issued in that Report had made precisely the same sort of differentiation between authorities which the respondents were arguing was unlawful. He felt that this was significant because 'to the extent that the meaning

[88] [1986] 2 WLR 1, 16.   [89] Ibid., 17.
[90] The exception is s. 61(5) which required that, when the Secretary of State specifies fresh determinations in any supplementary reports, those determinations 'shall be exerciseable only in accordance with principles applicable to all local authorities'.
[91] [1986] 2 WLR 1, 17.   [92] Ibid., 18.   [93] Ibid., 19.
[94] 'I should be extremely reluctant to accept that the draftsman of the legislation by so small a difference of language intended to achieve so fundamental a difference in legislative effect with consequences which, as I have already pointed out, seem to me out of accord with the scheme and underlying purpose of the [1980 and 1982] Acts': ibid., 17.

of provisions given retrospective force is open to doubt, the nature of the guidance by reference to which those provisions will operate, having been set out in a report submitted to and approved by the House of Commons before the enactment of the statute, is available as a contemporanea expositio of the draftsman's purpose'.[95] That is, Parliament could hardly have intended an interpretation such as would render unlawful the guidance which it had so recently approved, and for which the Act had provided retrospective validity. For these reasons, Lord Bridge concluded that, on the issue of the construction of section 59(11A), the Government was entitled to succeed.

When applying for judicial review, the primary submission of Nottinghamshire CC had been that, even if the guidance had complied with the requirements of the statute, it offended a basic principle of public law. That is, it imposed such a disproportionate burden on certain local authorities relative to others that it must be viewed as being a perversely unreasonable exercise of discretionary power by the Secretary of State. This issue was considered by Lord Scarman. Scarman, however, refused to examine the detail of the guidance. This unusual failure even to present the essence of the applicants' case was explained on the ground that such an examination would be justified only if a prima facie case had been made that the Secretary of State 'had acted in bad faith, or for an improper motive, or that the consequences of his guidance were so absurd that he must have taken leave of his senses'.[96] In this case Lord Scarman felt that the evidence came nowhere near to establishing any of these propositions.

The justification for the adoption of this approach was that the issue involved the 'exercise by the Secretary of State of an administrative discretion which inevitably requires a political judgment on his part and which cannot lead to an action by him against a local authority unless that action is first approved by the House of Commons'.[97] In essence, Lord Scarman seemed to be saying that these matters, concerning the limits of public expenditure by local authorities and the incidence of the financial burden between taxpayers and ratepayers, were fundamentally matters of politics. Such decisions were therefore matters for the Secretary of State and the House of Commons and not for the courts. 'Judicial review', Scarman concluded, 'is a great weapon in the hands of the judges: but the judges must observe the constitutional limits set by our parliamentary system upon the exercise of this beneficent power.'[98]

The speeches of Lords Bridge and Scarman were unanimously approved by all the Law Lords. In the process of doing so, however, Lord Templeman provided a gloss on the nature of judicial review, feeling it necessary to remind agencies that judicial review 'is not just a move in an interminable chess tournament'.[99] He added:

---

[95] Ibid., 20. [96] Ibid., 5. [97] Ibid., 4.
[98] Ibid., 8. [99] Ibid., 23.

I hope that in future local authorities will bite on the bullet and not seek to persuade the courts to absolve them from compliance with the Secretary of State's guidance. . . . [P]ersuasion should be offered not to the judges, who are not qualified to listen, but to the department, the minister, all members of parliament and ultimately to the electorate.[100]

It has been suggested that the *Nottinghamshire* decision 'shows three Law Lords displaying a fine understanding of the legislative, political and constitutional contexts in which judicial review operates'.[101] This assessment seems rather wide of the mark, particularly since little evidence of 'understanding' of the relevant contexts may be discerned from the speeches. This lack of understanding is revealed most clearly in Lord Bridge's confused and muddled speech on the nature of the statutory framework. The analysis of the context of the statutory reforms is, for example, pretty unconvincing. Lord Bridge criticized the Court of Appeal's interpretation, that guidance could require only an overall across the board reduction in expenditure, on the ground that the basic purpose of the 1980 Act was to provide more discriminatory arrangements for grant allocation. The 1980 Act, through GRE and the grant tapering provisions, certainly did seek this objective. But it should also be recalled that those complex and delicate arrangements were felt by the Secretary of State, during the first year of system's operation, to be rather too subtle; a more powerful mechanism for encouraging expenditure restraint was required. This mechanism – the system of expenditure targets – was used in 1981/82 to require an across-the-board expenditure reduction from a specific historic base. This target system was thus applied in a manner which entirely obscured the principles on which the 1980 Act system had been constructed. Given this context, it seems difficult therefore to make the argument that, because the 1980 Act adopted a more discriminatory mechanism, expenditure targets should also be read in this light. Furthermore, the nature of the 1982 Act reforms also seem to support the view that the target system was basically conceived as an across-the-board mechanism of control. The Act stated, for example, that the guidance is 'designed to achieve any reduction in the level of local authority expenditure' which the Secretary of State 'thinks necessary having regard to general economic conditions'.[102] The tenor here suggests a concern with macro-economic conditions and aggregate local authority expenditure rather than a system which is finely tuned to the particular circumstances of individual authorities. In this context, the Court of Appeal's interpretation scarcely seems 'startling'.[103]

Given this context, it would appear that Lord Bridge was not justified in concluding that, since the statutory language is ambiguous, a purposive approach

[100] [1986] 2 WLR 1, 23.
[101] S. Lee, 'Understanding judicial review as a game of chess' 102 *LQR* 493, 496.
[102] LGPLA 1980, s. 59(6)(cc); inserted by Local Government Finance Act 1982, s. 8(1).
[103] [1986] 2 WLR 1, 16 (*per* Lord Bridge).

favoured the Secretary of State's interpretation. But was the statutory language ambiguous? A detailed reading of the case might suggest that perhaps the only actor who appreciated the significance of the precise statutory language was the draftsman. Lord Bridge concluded that the Act was ambiguous and thus could bear the interpretation favoured by each of the parties on the ground that no discernible difference could be identified between the use of the phrase 'principles to be applied to all local authorities' and that of 'principles applicable to all local authorities'. He thus held that the draftsman intended to use the phrases interchangeably. This may not in fact be the case. There is in actuality a subtle but potentially significant distinction between the phrases, particularly as employed within the framework of the 1980 Act. While both phrases are, in a linguistic sense, notoriously ambiguous with respect to time, there is a discernible distinction between them. As utilized within Part VI of the 1980 Act, while the former seems capable of bearing a future meaning the latter does not. And whereas the latter is capable of carrying a past connotation, the former is not. Thus, when the legislation was concerned with the construction of GRE and GRP the phrase 'principles to be applied' (present–future) is used. However, when the statute provides for fresh determinations to be made in supplementary reports the phrase 'principles applicable' (present–past) is adopted because the reports will refer to conditions which are already extant. The precise significance of the use of 'principles applicable' in section 59(11A) was that it referred to conditions which were already in existence.

This linguistic analysis is important in so far as it may indicate that the statutory formulations were not as ambiguous or arbitrary as their Lordships apparently believed. But this analysis also has a particular significance since it provides support for the formulation adopted by the Court of Appeal. The expenditure guidance had been set in accordance with past conditions and, in order to be in accordance with 'principles applicable to all local authorities', that guidance was required to adopt criteria which were generally applicable to all authorities. The Court of Appeal's interpretation thus seems preferable, not least because the House of Lords' analysis seems to strip section 59(11A) of any importance as a structural constraint on the discretionary power of the Secretary of State. This approach is reinforced by examining the form of the Rates Act 1984. Lord Bridge dismissed any consideration of the 1984 Act as providing an aid to the construction of the Acts of 1980 and 1982 on the ground that it was in all probability impermissible but, in any case, was unhelpful and irrelevant.[104] Nevertheless, the drafting logic may be seen by considering a specific difference between the Bill and the Act in what became section 2(5):

> The power to designate an authority shall be exercised in accordance with principles determined by the Secretary of State and, in the case of an authority falling within any

---

[104] [1986] 2 WLR 1, 9.

of the classes specified in subsection (6) below, these principles shall be the same for all authorities falling within that class [or for all of them which respectively have or have not been designated under this section in the previous year].

The phrase in parenthesis was not included in the Bill as originally drafted. It was added later, presumably to enable the Secretary of State to discriminate within a group of authorities (e.g., metropolitan district councils) between those which had and had not been rate-capped in the previous year. Its significance for our purposes is that it provides an indication that, in the mind of the draftsman at least, without explicit power the Secretary of State would not be entitled to discriminate between authorities on the basis of past conduct. It thus provides further support for the view that there was a certain integrity in the drafting of these statutes and that the Court of Appeal's interpretation of them was the one which made most sense.

We should finally consider Lord Bridge's observation that, if the Court of Appeal's interpretation was correct, it would suggest that the 1982/83 guidance which Parliament had in 1982 sought retrospectively to validate was also unlawful; and this seemed, on the face of things, implausible. There are two points to consider on this issue. First, it is not at all clear that the 1982/83 guidance did in fact exceed the limits of the power as construed by the Court of Appeal. The limitations on grant penalties identified by Lord Bridge in the 1982/83 guidance[105] appeared to be in the nature of general safety nets which were justifiable under section 59(6) of the 1980 Act. Secondly, even if Lord Bridge's analysis is correct, what are we to make of it? Lord Bridge conceded that this argument came into play only if (as I have argued to the contrary) the statute is ambiguous. Nevertheless, while there may be reasons why the judiciary may feel obliged to construe ambiguous legislation in a light favourable to the Government, this should not blind us to the reality of the process. The *Nottinghamshire* dispute is best understood as an indication of the difficulties we experience when, because of a breakdown of trust, law comes to be used as a primary instrument in the regulation of central–local financial relations. The system was simply too complex, the economic context changing too rapidly and the political issues too intense for the conduct of relations to be capable of being adequately governed by general legislation.

The analysis of the statutory framework undertaken by the House of Lords in the *Nottinghamshire* case leaves much to be desired. Lord Bridge presented an inadequate account of statutory context concerning the introduction of expenditure targets, failed to understand the significance of the precise statutory language utilized and, as a result, was unable to follow the Court of Appeal in giving that language its 'ordinary and natural meaning'.[106] We can but hope that the view expressed by one commentator, that Lord Bridge's opinion 'will be-

---

[105] [1986] 2 WLR 1, 19–20.
[106] *Nottinghamshire CC* v. *Secretary of State for the Environment* (CA: unreported). Transcript, at 28 (*per* Slade LJ).

come the standard judicial introduction to a fearsomely complex area of statute law',[107] will not come to pass.

Lord Scarman's analysis of the general public law challenge was also not without its limitations. Contrary to the views of some commentators, I do not believe his speech should be interpreted as establishing the 'proposition' that 'it was not open to the courts to hold the action of a Minister to be unreasonable once that action had been approved by Parliament'.[108] Lord Scarman was concerned not so much to delineate the proper relationship between Parliament, the executive and the courts as to highlight the limits to the institutional competence of courts. His speech reinforced the concerns expressed by Forbes J in the *Hackney* case on the ability of the courts to act as a forum for examining the rationality and fairness of the Government's actions in operating the expenditure target system. Nevertheless, it is unfortunate that Scarman did not see fit even to explain the grievances of the applicant local authorities. By failing so to do, we are presented with the unusual position of the applicants' primary complaint not actually being examined in the court's judgment. This may not, in itself, be especially serious. It does become so, however, when the tone of one of the speeches suggested that that issue had not been properly understood,[109] since it then appears that the court might not in fact have fully appreciated the nature of the applicants' grievance.[110] Lord Scarman's speech should simply be read as an indication that the judiciary felt extremely uncomfortable with these central–local disputes being addressed in the courts and as providing a signal that local authorities should pursue their grievances through alternative channels.

[107] S. Lee, (1986) 102 *LQR* 493, 494 (see above, n. 101).

[108] R. Ward, 'Biting on the bullet: the constitutional limits of judicial review' (1986) 49 *MLR* 645, 647; C.T. Reid, 'Parliament, the executive and the courts', 1986 *Camb. L J* 169, 170.

[109] Lord Templeman ([1986] 2 WLR 1, 26) expressed the issue thus:

> Nottingham's budget for 1985/86 exceeded their guidance for 1984/85 by £7,200,000. And Nottingham had overspent their guidance in the two preceding years. Out of 413 local authorities there were only 10, including Nottingham and Bradford, whose 1984/85 budgeted expenditure exceeded GRE where GRE itself was above target.

Lord Templeman here adopts a formulation which confers the impression that Conservative-controlled Nottinghamshire was in the top ten of a league table of 'highspenders', a characterization that has also influenced the commentators (see Ward, 49 MLR 645, 646). This is quite erroneous. It arises because Templeman's formulation suggests that there is a cumulative target system of which guidance is the first stage and GRE the second. This is incorrect. Nottinghamshire was probably exceeding its guidance because the target system had initially been pegged at 1978/79 expenditure which may have been a year of particularly low spending. Consequently, although exceeding guidance the authority was still spending within the range of its GRE; that is, within the notional expenditure for equalizing the distribution of rate support grants.

[110] It also had the consequence that subsequent cases misunderstood the nature of the dispute. In the leading case on charge-capping, for example, Leggatt LJ, giving the Divisional Court judgment, mischaracterized the position in *Nottinghamshire* when stating that: 'The guidance given differentiated between high-spending and low-spending authorities, that for high-spending authorities being based on the previous year's guidance rather than on the authorities' grant-related expenditure.' (*Hammersmith LBC* v. *Secretary of State for the Environment* [1990] 3 All ER 589, 603). By reference to GRE, which involved an assessment of providing a common standard of service, Nottinghamshire CC was in fact a low-spending authority.

Principles, rationality and the courts

The basic theme which flows through the cases challenging the Government's use of expenditure targets concerns the question, first raised in the *Brent* case on the transitional arrangements, of the meaning of the requirement that guidance must be based on general principles. What does this requirement mean? Does the requirement prevent the Government from targeting particular authorities? Does the requirement entail a modicum of rationality in the relationship between targets imposed and objectives to be achieved? And will the courts give legal force to such constraints?

Forbes J was undoubtedly correct in stating that the term 'principle' meant simply 'a self-sufficient proposition intended to be applied to a set of relevant circumstances'.[111] However, what is of particular importance about this formulation is not its formality but rather the fact that it suggests that principles are devices which constrain the influence of irrelevant factors. The idea that like cases should be decided alike is a well-established principle of formal justice. What the principle leaves open, of course, is the question of which likenesses are the relevant ones. The courts experience no great difficulty in reasoning on the basis of this principle in respect of the vast majority of cases which arise for consideration; the principle, after all, lies at the foundation of the doctrine of precedent. The problems encountered by the courts in giving significant effect to the principles requirement in the context of local government finance are a consequence of the fact that they feel ill-equipped to define and apply the criteria of relevancy and irrelevancy.

The principles requirement in local government finance legislation would seem to prohibit the Government from targeting local authorities purely on the basis of party political considerations. It would also seem to indicate that targets should have some relationship to the achievement of their economic objectives. What the courts have tried to signal, however, is the fact that they possess neither the cognitive nor material resources to address either these relevancy or rationality issues. The reason for this is that such questions are rooted in a politico-economic discourse which cannot easily be translated into law. The courts should not be criticized for this jurisdictional limitation. In the *Nottinghamshire* case, however, the House of Lords committed a basic error in allowing its anxiety about the limits of its jurisdictional competence to shield central government through a distorted reading of the meaning of the statutory requirements.

After Targets

In July 1985 the Secretary of State announced that from 1986/87 the system of expenditure targets would be abandoned.[112] The Government thereafter proposed

---

[111] (1984) 148 LGR 691, 750.   [112] HC Debs., vol. 83, col. 1316 (25 July 1985).

to control local authority expenditure through the block grant distribution arrangements in conjunction with the power of rate control. This change did not, however, mark the emergence of a new, more consensual system of grant distribution. Nor did the abolition of targets cause local authorities to heed Lord Templeman's advice to 'bite on the bullet' and refrain from rushing to the courts in contentious matters of public financial administration.[113] Rather, it simply caused local authorities to switch attention away from the particular statutory provisions relating to targets and towards the general statutory framework governing grant distribution in Part VI of the 1980 Act.

Capping windfall gains

With the abolition of targets, the Government was particularly concerned to ensure that local authorities did not make windfall gains on grants. The Government sought to ensure that this did not happen in 1986/87 by capping the grant allocation of such authorities through the use of multipliers. This was permissible provided the multipliers were being used for the purpose of 'limiting the change in the amount of block grant payable to an authority for the year from the amount payable in the previous year'.[114] The Secretary of State's determination to give effect to this objective was, however, challenged in the courts by Birmingham City Council, one of the capped authorities. Birmingham's primary argument was that the Secretary of State had exceeded his powers under section 59 because he had used a notional base position for determining the previous year's grant rather than Birmingham's actual grant entitlement for 1985/86. This argument was accepted by the Divisional Court which granted a declaration that the Secretary of State's determination was *ultra vires*.[115]

Before the Court's judgment was delivered, however, the Minister, having no doubt been advised that the Government was likely to lose the case, made a statement in the House of Commons to the effect that Birmingham's interpretation of the provision rendered the system unworkable and defeated the objective of the 1986/87 capping and safety-netting provisions. That interpretation, furthermore, would cast doubts not only on the legality of the current year's settlement but also on all grant determinations since 1981/82. The Minister therefore stated that the Government would be introducing a Bill 'to remove any doubts about the Secretary of State's powers in relation to multipliers for past years and for the future'.[116]

That Bill was introduced on 13 June 1986 and was enacted on 21 October as the Rate Support Grants Act 1986. The 1986 Act provided for the retrospective validation of all determinations under section 59 of the 1980 Act which had been specified in Rate Support Grant Reports approved by the House of Commons

[113] [1986] 2 WLR 1, 23.   [114] LGPLA 1980, s. 59(6)(a).
[115] *R* v. *Secretary of State for the Environment, ex parte Birmingham City Council* (unreported) (15 April 1986).
[116] HC Debs., vol. 95, col. 359 (10 April 1986) (William Waldegrave, Minister for the Environment).

on or before 21 January 1986.[117] The 1986 Act also amended section 59 of the 1980 Act in order to give greater discretion to the Secretary of State in the use of the power to apply multipliers to grant entitlements[118] and, more generally, the Government utilized the opportunity to introduce certain amendments to Part VI of the 1980 Act which would minimize the possibility of subsequent legal challenges. By way of illustration, one example may be provided. Previously, the 1980 Act had required Rate Support Grant Reports to 'specify the considerations leading the Secretary of State to make any such determination'.[119] The Government conceded that it 'would be totally impossible for reports to meet this requirement' since 'a detailed description of the considerations underlying each of the grant-related expenditure determinations would alone require a document several times the size of the present RSG Report'.[120] The Act therefore replaced this duty with the requirement that the Report specify 'such explanation as the Secretary of State thinks desirable of the main features of the determination'.[121]

By taking drastic action to legitimate all previous determinations involving the use of multipliers and by tightening up the drafting of the legislation and transforming certain objective duties into subjectively formulated requirements, the Government presumably hoped that, taking its cue from the opinions expressed by the Law Lords in the *Nottinghamshire* case, matters of public financial administration could in future be kept out of the courts. Nevertheless, if this had been the expectation, it was soon to be frustrated.

Challenging expenditure determinations

Less than two months after the Rate Support Grants Act 1986 had received the Royal Assent the Government was obliged to make a further statement in the House of Commons concerning rate support grants.[122] The Secretary of State informed the House that a discrepancy had been discovered within the conventions which had been followed by some local authorities in calculating their expenditure figures. In turn, this had cast doubts on the manner in which two key concepts which underpinned the 1980 Act scheme – those of 'relevant expenditure'[123] and 'total expenditure'[124] – had in practice been constructed.

Basically, the problem was as follows. 'Relevant expenditure' was the net expenditure of the local authority after income from fees and charges had been subtracted. 'Total expenditure' was relevant expenditure less specific and supplementary grants. It was therefore the total which was eligible for block grant; and it was also indicative of expenditure which falls to be defrayed from the rate fund. The difficulty arose because there had been no detailed statutory prescrip-

---

[117] 1986 Act, s. 1.   [118] 1986 Act, s. 2.
[119] LGPLA 1980, ss. 60(6)(b), 61(6).
[120] HC Debs., vol. 100, col. 80 (23 June 1986), per William Waldegrave.
[121] 1986 Act, Sched. 1, para. 8.
[122] HC Debs., vol. 107, cols. 1051–1060 (16 December 1986) (Nicholas Ridley, Secretary of State for the Environment).
[123] LGPLA 1980, s. 54(5).   [124] LGPLA 1980, s. 56(8).

tion of what a local authority was obliged to include in its accounts of revenue transactions. In addition to the rate fund, local authorities also maintained other accounts, such as the housing revenue account, the accounts of trading undertakings and special funds. What remained unclear was the relationship between the rate fund and these other accounts. Should these other accounts be viewed as forming part of the rate fund (in which case the net surplus or deficit on those accounts should be included in total expenditure)? Or, more narrowly, was it only the transfers from the rate fund into these other accounts which should be treated as expenditure for block grant purposes? This question seemed simply to concern technical matters of accounting. On this rather arcane question, however, rested the legal foundations of the entire block grant system and thus the legality of the distributions of tens of billions of pounds in grant since 1981.

This ambiguity had been identified immediately after the enactment of the 1980 Act. At that stage, during a period in which conventional practices still appeared to carry authority, the Government had dealt with the matter simply by issuing Circular advice to the effect that the narrower interpretation should be adopted.[125] After the *Birmingham* challenge, however, the Government lawyers undertook an exercise of carefully examining the provisions of the 1980 Act[126] and, during this process, a discrepancy in the practices of local authority expenditure returns came to light. The Government sought the advice of the Attorney-General on the matter and, on receiving an opinion to the effect that the Government's recommended accounting practices were legally incorrect, determined that clarificatory legislation was required.

However, the issue did not simply emerge as a result of governmental review. The London Borough of Greenwich had also initiated action in the courts and, on the day following the Secretary of State's parliamentary statement, Greenwich by consent obtained a declaration that the Rates Limitation Order 1986 was *ultra vires* in so far as it related to Greenwich on the ground that the calculation of its expenditure base for the purpose of designation for rate-capping was unlawful.[127] The general effect of these developments was not only to place in doubt the legality of all rate support grant settlements since the introduction of block grant; it also meant that, until the matter was rectified, the Secretary of State was unable to determine the rate support grant settlement for 1987/88 or to designate authorities for rate-capping. The Government's proposed solution was, as a matter of urgency, to introduce legislation 'to validate . . . all past decisions involving the use of relevant or total expenditure and allow decisions to be properly taken for the remainder of the present rate support grant system'.[128]

The Local Government Finance Act 1987, which had been introduced in Parliament on 18 December 1986, was enacted on 12 March 1987. It dealt with three main issues. The 1987 Act first placed a duty on local authorities to

---

[125] DoE Circular letter, 13 February 1981.   [126] *The Guardian,* 17 December 1986.
[127] *R* v. *Secretary of State for the Environment, ex p. London Borough of Greenwich* (unreported) 17 December 1986 (Webster J).
[128] HC Debs., vol. 128, col. 1051 (16 December 1986).

maintain a rate fund revenue account and gave very broad powers to the Secretary of State both to specify the kinds of expenditure or income which were to be regarded as being of a revenue nature and also to determine the manner in which those items were to be debited or credited to that account.[129] Secondly, since these errors had created special problems in relation to authorities which were to be rate-capped, the Act made certain adjustments to the mechanics of rate limitation for 1987/88.[130] The 1987 Act in effect suspended the normal rate-capping procedures for 1987/88 and instead incorporated formulaically determined maximum rates and precepts, the understanding of which required a considerable grasp of algebra.[131] Finally, and perhaps most importantly, the Act validated all past rate support grant determinations.[132] Here the provisions of the Act went beyond a simple retrospective validation of past practices. The practices of certain local authorities in making transfers to special funds for the purpose of maximizing block grant entitlement during the period since 1983/84 were, for example, retrospectively invalidated even though it was not at all clear that, at that time, those practices were unlawful.[133] Furthermore, the breadth of the power secured to sanction retrospective validation caused a great deal of concern. The relevant parts of section 4 stated:

4.   (1) Anything done by the Secretary of State before the passing of this Act for the purposes of the relevant provisions [i.e., Part VI of the 1980 Act] . . . shall be deemed to have been done in compliance with those provisions.

. . .

(6) Subsection (1) above shall have effect notwithstanding any decision of a court (whether before or after the passing of this Act) purporting to have a contrary effect.[134]

These provisions were extraordinarily wide. During the Parliamentary proceedings, attempts were made, albeit without success, to limit retrospection to the calculations made by the Secretary of State concerning relevant or total expenditure. It seems that, by this stage, the Government wished to ensure, once and for all, that local authorities would in fact have no choice but to bite on the bullet in matters of grant allocation decision-making.

The rate support grant process for 1987/88

The impact which all this complexity and confusion exerted on the processes of public financial administration may be gleaned by examining the process leading

---

[129] Local Government Finance Act (LGFA) 1987, ss. 1–3.
[130] LGFA 1987, ss. 6–8.   [131] LGFA 1987, Sched. 2.
[132] LGFA 1987, ss. 4–5 (England and Wales); ss. 13–14 (Scotland).
[133] LGFA 1987, s. 5.   [134] See also LGFA 1987, s. 6(2), (6).

to the approval of the rate support grant (RSG) for 1987/88. The process generally commences with the Government's announcement of its provisional determinations on the RSG during the summer. After a period of consultation, the Rate Support Grant Report, which includes the details of grant support to local authorities, is laid before and approved by the House of Commons in December. Then, on the basis of these grant allocations, local authorities prepare their budgets in order to be able to issue precepts by 10 March[135] and make a rate by 1 April.[136] The procedures relating to the 1987/88 settlement, however, were fundamentally to deviate from this pattern.

The procedures began as normal with the Secretary of State's announcement in July 1986 of his decisions on rate support grants and rate limitation.[137] Dissatisfaction had been expressed about the proposed settlement, particularly from the Conservative-controlled shire counties, and this caused the Government to issue a second consultation document at the end of October. Nevertheless, an early Report was still expected since the Government asked for responses to the second round of consultation within three weeks. On 19 November the Secretary of State revealed that he had received representations on the settlement not only from the local authority associations but also from over 200 local authorities.[138] Nevertheless, he still expected to announce decisions on the settlement in December. Events, however, did not proceed as anticipated.

On 3 December the Secretary of State issued an unprecedented third Consultation Paper.[139] At the time it was generally believed that this was required as a result of certain policy changes which were to be introduced in order to limit the maximum grant losses of local authorities. Since these changes would generally operate to the advantage of Conservative-controlled shire counties, Opposition members felt that the changes were influenced by the belief that a general election was to be held shortly after the start of the new financial year. This additional period of consultation meant that the Report could not be laid before January. On 16 December, however, the Secretary of State made his announcement concerning the errors in calculating relevant and total expenditure. At this stage he also revealed that he had first become aware of these errors in October,[140] and this raised the question of whether the initial delays had been occasioned primarily by the need to find time to devise and draft new legislation.

---

[135] General Rate Act 1967, s. 12(6).

[136] Local Government Act 1986, s. 1. This specification of this duty resulted from the protest action of certain local authorities designated for rate limitation in 1985/86 of deferring making a rate until after the start of the financial year: see, above, ch. 3, 187–94.

[137] HC Debs., vol. 102, col. 181 (22 July 1986).

[138] HC Debs., vol. 105, col. 234w (19 November 1986).

[139] HC Debs., vol. 106, col. 925 (3 December 1986).

[140] HC Debs., vol. 107, col. 1054 (16 December 1986). This caused Dr John Cunningham, the Opposition front bench spokesperson, to ask: 'For how long has the Secretary of State known of this situation? . . . Does it, for example, explain his refusal to make a rate support grant statement, as he promised he would, as long ago as mid-November?' (col. 1052).

Certainly the consequence of the December announcement was that the RSG Report could not be laid until new legislation had been enacted.

In order to ensure that administrative chaos did not ensue, the Secretary of State announced that the cut-off date for consultation on the settlement would remain 19 December and that a *de facto* RSG settlement would be made in January.[141] In mid-January 1987 the Secretary of State announced his 'firm intentions' for the 1987/88 RSG settlement.[142] Indeed, the consultation requirements provided one clue as to why such broadly drafted retrospective validatory clauses were required in the 1987 Act. If the provisions were less than all-embracing, then, on the authority of the *Brent* case,[143] further consultations would have been required after the power had been obtained and since the 1987 Act was enacted only on 12 March, this would be too late to enable precepts to be set by the statutory date and certainly too late to complete the administrative requirements of the budgetary process by 1 April.

Nevertheless, even these 'firm intentions' did not prove to be quite so fixed. On 23 February the Department of the Environment wrote to inform local authorities of various revisions to the settlement. These alterations were required because the Department had discovered an error in the compilation of one element in the GRE calculation. This was particularly serious for the rate-capped authorities because their maximum rates, which were set out in the Local Government Finance Bill,[144] had been determined by reference to block grant entitlement. However, there was more to come, particularly since local authorities had been considering the possibility of legal action. The initial legal challenge came from Birmingham City Council which applied for a declaration that the Secretary of State had no power to anticipate legislation in this manner and thus that the RSG Report should be issued promptly. This application was unsuccessful.[145] It was followed by an application for judicial review by the London Borough of Greenwich. After Greenwich had succeeded in its application to quash its Rate Limitation Order,[146] its action proceeded in an amended form. This amended application sought to challenge the Secretary of State's decision to redetermine the multipliers for assessing block grant for the London boroughs which were contained in the Rate Support Grant Report 1986/87. In a judgment issued on 26 February 1987, Taylor J granted a declaration that the Secretary of State's decision was *ultra vires*.[147]

---

[141] HC Debs., vol. 107, col. 1059. This power to determine a cut-off date for considering representations was only made explicit in the 1986 Act which gave the Secretary of State the power to disregard any information received after a specified date: see LGPLA 1980, s. 65(3) (inserted by Rate Support Grants Act 1986, Sched. 1, para. 13).

[142] HC Debs., vol. 108, col. 147 (13 January 1987).

[143] [1982] 2 WLR 693: see, above, 274–7.   [144] LGFA 1987, Sched. 2.

[145] *R v. Secretary of State for the Environment, ex p. Birmingham City Council*, *The Independent*, 25 February 1987; *The Times*, 30 March 1987 (Div.Ct.).

[146] *R v. Secretary of State for the Environment, ex p. London Borough of Greenwich* (unreported) 17 December 1986 (Div.Ct.).

[147] *London Borough of Greenwich v. Secretary of State for the Environment* (unreported) 26 February 1987 (Div.Ct.).

This decision, the substance of which is considered below, further complicated the RSG process. Although the judgment concerned the 1986/87 settlement, it had a reverberative effect on the 1987/88 process. Consequently, on 5 March 1987, after some local authorities had already announced their budgets and made their rates and five days before precepts were required by law to be fixed, the Secretary of State announced that, as a result of the *Greenwich* judgment, further amendments would have to be made to the RSG figures announced in January.[148] After allowing a short period for consultation those modifications were then made.

The 1987/88 RSG Report was eventually laid before the House and approved on 25 March 1987, only six days before the start of the new financial year. The relief felt by the Secretary of State was palpable. Opening the parliamentary debate he stated that:

> Despite all the difficulties that have arisen this year, I am glad that we have been able to lay the report ... before the new financial year starts, so that grant can be paid. I am extremely grateful to Opposition Members for their help and support in achieving this great success.[149]

Given the obstacles it was indeed an achievement. But it is scarcely an experience which instils confidence that the Government had developed sound principles of public financial administration.

Hoist with their own petard?

The period between 1985 and 1987 in many respects represents the nadir of the Government's strategy relating to rate support grant distribution. It is a period characterized by miscalculation, legal action, retrospective legislation and the looming threat of administrative chaos. If one also brings into the equation the Opposition claims that the Government were guilty of 'political fiddling of the system' designed 'to buy off the much-leaked Tory revolt' over their local government expenditure policies,[150] then it is evident that the Government had become enmeshed in a highly complex web from which it was proving extremely difficult to extricate itself. The power and resilience of the legal threads of this web are well illustrated in the Divisional Court's judgment in *London Borough of Greenwich* v. *Secretary of State for the Environment*.[151]

This action was rooted in the Government's attempt to ensure that the expenditure consequences of abolition of the GLC and the metropolitan counties would be neutral at the ratepayer level. The consequential grant adjustments were incorporated in the RSG Report for 1986/87. After that Report had been

---

[148] HC Debs., vol. 111, col. 1042 (5 March 1987).
[149] HC Debs., vol. 113, col. 440 (25 March 1987) (Nicholas Ridley).
[150] HC Debs., vol. 113, col. 449 (25 March 1987) *per* Dr John Cunningham.
[151] Unreported, 26 February 1987 (Div.Ct.).

laid before the House of Commons, however, the London Borough of Bromley drew attention to the fact that, although it had inherited some 60 miles of metropolitan roads from the GLC, its budget for road maintenance had dropped from over £3m to a negligible amount. The Department then discovered that a mistake had been made in the method by which the effects of transferring highway maintenance were to be assessed. After consultations, the Minister stated that the error would be rectified by redetermining the multipliers and issuing a supplementary report. Greenwich, which anticipated that it would lose between £2.2m and £3.8m in grant as a result of the redetermination, applied for a judicial review of the Minister's decision.

It was common ground that the Secretary of State was empowered to vary a multiplier provided that 'he is satisfied that the variation is required in consequence of the principles specified by him in relation to the original determination not having been correctly applied to it on the basis of the information available to him when it was made'.[152] The case for Greenwich rested on two main arguments. First, it was argued that the error did not result from an incorrect application of a principle specified by the Secretary of State. Secondly, it was argued that, even if they were wrong on that point, the Rate Support Grants Act 1986 operated to prohibit redetermination. These arguments will be addressed in turn.

Greenwich's argument on the first point was that the so-called 'Bromley error' arose not from an incorrect application of the principles but flowed from the fact that the wrong principle had been chosen, and it was contended that the Act did not permit a variation of a multiplier on this ground. Greenwich maintained that the Government had allocated GLC expenditure on highway maintenance to successor authorities by utilizing a method of taking the difference between pre-abolition and post-abolition GREs. It was this method which had generated the figures said to produce the Bromley error. Further, the method had in fact been correctly applied on the basis of information available to the Secretary of State at the relevant time. The real problem was that, having subsequently discovered its consequences, the Government wished to change the method. Greenwich contended that this method constituted a 'principle' and that the Act did not empower the Secretary of State to alter principles. The Government disputed this view. The primary principle was that multipliers should be determined to prevent ratepayers either gaining or losing as a result of the abolition of the GLC and the exercise of taking the difference between pre-abolition and post-abolition GREs was merely a method or formula for putting the principle into effect. The adjustment to the formula was thus required to ensure the correct application of the principle.

As a matter of logic, it would appear that the Government's case was stronger. The difficulty with the argument was that it was the precise antithesis of the line

---

[152] LGPLA 1980, s. 61(4A); inserted by Rate Support Grants Act 1986, Sched. 1, para. 10.

which it had pursued in the *Brent* and *Hackney* cases. In *Greenwich*, Taylor J examined the relevant dicta in those judgments and, following their tenor, upheld Greenwich's argument. Taylor J concluded that the method, the mathematical mode of determining and allocating transferred expenditure on highway maintenance, constituted a principle. Although it was not the main principle, in the sense of being the underlying aim, purpose or rationale, following Ackner LJ in *Brent*, it was to be classified as a secondary principle. The Government's earlier formalistic approach had served to confound it and to operate tactically in favour of the applicant authority. But, as Taylor J observed, 'it cannot be open to the Secretary of State at will to label some of his criteria "principles" and others mere methods or formulae'.[153]

Greenwich's second argument also had an ironical dimension. The borough council argued that, even if the principles specified by the Secretary of State had been incorrectly applied, the Secretary of State could not rely on the power in section 61(4A) of the 1980 Act to make adjustments. This was because of the effect of the Rate Support Grants Act 1986, section 1 of which stated that all determinations under section 59 of the 1980 Act which had been specified in Reports approved by the House of Commons on or before 21 January 1986 were to be deemed to have been properly enacted. Since the RSG Report making the initial grant allocation to successor authorities had been approved by the House of Commons on 20 January 1986, the Secretary of State was unable to argue that the principles had not been correctly applied. This argument was also upheld by the court, Taylor J suggesting that, in effect, 'the Secretary of State is hoist with his own petard'.[154]

The topsy-turvy world which had thus been created as a result of these developments may perhaps best be summed up by the words of the Secretary of State in the course of trying to explain away the difficulties experienced by the Government during this period:

> Large numbers of authorities are taking cases to the courts ... The result of that process ... is delay, uncertainty and confusion. That is not the Government's fault. It is the fault of those who insist on litigation on every possible occasion.[155]

Rate Limitation: From Targets to Caps

Many of the legal problems which the Government encountered in allocating grants to local authorities during the 1980s appeared to stem from the fact that the legislative framework had not been constructed with the idea of adjudication in mind. That is, Part VI of the 1980 Act adopted the traditional form of establishing a facilitative framework through which the details of grant distribution

---

[153] Transcript, at 19.   [154] Transcript, at 10.
[155] HC Debs., vol. 111, col. 1046 (5 March 1987).

could be administratively determined. Difficulties arose precisely because, as a result of economic and political change, bargaining was replaced with direction, conventional understandings ceased to carry much authority, and local authorities reacted defensively to central direction by turning to the legal framework in search of constraints on the central executive's discretionary power. The complexity of the system in conjunction with the opacity of the legislation resulted in ambiguity, confusion and, occasionally, chaos as a range of problems unfolded more rapidly than the centre's ability to redraft the framework to bring it into alignment with a central directive strategy.

When in 1983 the Government proposed to cap the rates of high-spending authorities, however, the likelihood that any exercise of such directive powers would be subject to legal challenge was already apparent. The Government thus made a conscious decision to design the legislation in such a manner as to minimize the possibility of executive decisions being subject to judicial review. The Rates Act 1984 contained few obvious pegs which could be used by recalcitrant local authorities to mount a legal challenge in the hope of frustrating the Government's ability to realize its objectives. This point was presumably what Dillon LJ had in mind when he commented that: 'In contrast to earlier legislation on local government finance, the 1984 Act is remarkably simple and straightforward in its terms.'[156]

The scheme of the Rates Act 1984

Under the selective rate-capping scheme[157] the Secretary of State was empowered to designate an authority for rate limitation if it appeared to him that its expenditure was likely to exceed GRE and 'to be excessive having regard to general economic conditions'.[158] The procedure required the Secretary of State first to determine a maximum expenditure level for the designated authorities.[159] That expenditure level did not, however, constitute a legally binding ceiling, but simply provided the basis for determining the maximum rate, once the RSG settlement had been announced. The primary constraint on the exercise of these discretionary powers was that both designation and determination of a maximum expenditure level had to be undertaken in accordance with 'principles determined by the Secretary of State' and which would be the same for all authorities falling within specified classes.[160] As we have seen, such a formulation provides a limited degree of protection against manipulation since, as it became evident,[161] the formulae could easily be skewed to capture variable groups of authorities.

---

[156] *London Borough of Greenwich* v. *Secretary of State for the Environment, The Times,* 27 February 1987 (CA). Transcript, 1.

[157] Rates Act 1984, Pt. I. Part II of the Act, which empowered the Secretary of State to control the rates of all local authorities, was never brought into operation.

[158] 1984 Act, s. 2(2).   [159] 1984 Act, s. 3(1).   [160] 1984 Act, ss. 2(4), 3(2).

[161] See HC Debs., Standing Committee G, col. 203 (7 February 1984).

Once a maximum expenditure level had been fixed a designated authority was able to apply for redetermination of that expenditure level. Here, however, it was apparent that particular attention had been paid to the form of drafting: applications had to be accompanied by such information as the Secretary of State required; the Secretary of State was empowered, on considering an application, to fix an authority's expenditure level at a lower figure; and, if he decided to increase the expenditure level, he was able to impose on the authority 'such requirements relating to its expenditure or financial management as he thinks appropriate'.[162] Any authority seeking redetermination seemed, in effect, to be inviting the Government to undertake detailed scrutiny and control of its affairs.

Finally, it should be noted that the authority was invited to accept the maximum rate. If this limit were accepted, the maximum would be fixed by administrative direction; if not, it was prescribed by an order laid before and approved by a resolution of the House of Commons. Any authority intending to contest its maximum rate was thus caught in a double bind: if the rate cap was accepted, acquiescence would make subsequent challenge difficult; if it was not, the incorporation of the maximum in subordinate legislation would suggest that the figure could be challenged in the courts only on limited grounds. The scheme of the Rates Act thus suggested that the opportunities for successful judicial review would be rather circumscribed.

Judicial review as a surrogate redetermination process

In the first round of rate-capping, the eighteen designated authorities declined to apply for re-determination of their maximum expenditure levels. The Secretary of State, presumably wishing to demonstrate that the statutory procedures were workable, gave assurances that he had no intention of using his powers in an interventionist manner and extended the date for re-determination applications.[163] Nevertheless, the authorities remained unprepared to apply and, instead, sought to make informal representations. Their aim was to utilize general principles of administrative law in order to establish in effect a shadow set of negotiation procedures to that outlined in the 1984 Act. When the Secretary of State, no doubt conscious of procedural proprieties, listened politely but refused to concede the possibility of establishing alternative procedures, the authorities turned to the courts for assistance.

The most important of the first round capping challenges was *R* v. *Secretary of State for the Environment, ex parte Greater London Council and Inner London Education Authority*.[164] In this case the GLC and ILEA applied for judicial review to quash the maximum precept set for the authorities. The applicants sought primarily to test the rationality of the capping process. They argued first

---

[162] 1984 Act, ss. 3(4)–(6).
[163] HC Debs., vol. 65, col. 681 (22 October 1984).
[164] Unreported, 3 April 1985 (Div.Ct.).

that the Secretary of State's refusal to disclose the reasoning process which led
him to fix the maximum precept amounted to a form of procedural impropriety
since it prevented them from being able sensibly to determine whether to accept
the proposed maximum precept or to apply for re-determination. The authorities
also sought to challenge not the reasonableness of the decision itself but the
soundness of the chain of reasoning which formed the basis of the decision.
Before dealing these substantive issues, however, the Divisional Court first
considered the role of the court in relation to judicial review of the Rate Limitation Order.

On this procedural issue, the Secretary of State had argued that, while the
court may have the power to quash the Order on the ground that it is *ultra vires*
in the strict sense that it goes beyond the powers conferred by the statute or that
a statutory pre-condition to the laying of the Order had not been performed, it
had no jurisdiction to consider either the merits of his decisions on rate-capping
or the processes by which he arrived at them. That is, since the Order had been
the subject of an affirmative resolution of the House of Commons, judicial
review was permissible on the ground of illegality but not for procedural impropriety or irrationality. In rejecting this argument the Court held that, since fairness was not an abstract concept, it had to be evaluated in the light of all the
circumstances of a particular case and, further, that there was nothing in the
1984 Act which suggested that Parliament intended to take away the court's
jurisdiction to review on the ground of procedural impropriety. On the irrationality point the court held that the 'debate in the House on affirmative resolution
and the investigation by the court of a *Wednesbury* complaint are of a quite
different character and are directed towards different ends; the two are
complementary'.[165]

Nevertheless, although the court rejected the Government's challenge as a
matter of principle, it also accepted that in practice the grant of review on such
grounds was likely to be rare. Furthermore, the court expressed significant reservations about its role in respect of challenges of this nature. Giving the judgment of the court, Mustill LJ suggested that, while the court's function is to
supervise administrative decision-making, it must also ensure that it is not drawn
into the sphere of electoral politics. In this type of dispute, in which the Secretary of State is required to make judgments which are economic and political in
character, that exercise is particularly difficult. Furthermore, Mustill LJ recognized that there were also practical constraints on the court's role. In addition
to the burden placed on the court by the fact that 'there were numerous affidavits
and affirmations, with copious exhibits', the steps taken by the Secretary of State
involved 'the delicate balancing of considerations which are not susceptible of
the formal reasoning appropriate to a court of law' and 'there is a danger that
if this kind of inquiry is to become widespread, there will be a real impediment

[165] Transcript, 31.

to the proper conduct of government, using the word in its widest sense, with at the same time the danger that the important and salutary role of judicial review may thereby become discredited'.[166]

After addressing these concerns, the court turned to consider the substantive issues. It experienced little difficulty in rejecting the argument that fairness required the Secretary of State to disclose the assumptions on which his decisions were based, holding that this claim could be sustained only if the denial of information had frustrated the procedures contemplated by the Act, and that there was no basis for the claim: 'there is no reason why the negotiations could not have been initiated even in the face of the Department's reticence'.[167] In the course of the action, however, additional information came to light about the assumptions and calculations made by the Secretary of State and, on the basis of this information, the GLC challenged the soundness of the chain of reasoning leading to the setting of the GLC's maximum precept. This issue concerned the manner in which the GLC's reserves had been calculated. In addressing this question, the court highlighted both the institutional and constitutional limitations to its ability properly to examine this question. Even if it were viewed as a technical dispute, the court acknowledged that the issues 'cannot be thoroughly explored within the confines of an application of this kind'.[168] However, the court also recognized that underlying the technical dispute lay 'a solid core of broad political and economic judgment on which the parties are fundamentally opposed'[169] and concluded that:

> There is no 'right' answer to this question, nor is there a 'right' method by which to arrive at an answer. We accept that the court has formal jurisdiction to examine the reasoning of a decision maker for the purposes of judicial review. We can envisage cases of crass and obvious errors in the choice of application of a process of reasoning which ought to have been governed by logic where the court might be prepared to intervene. But the disputes relating to reserves are not of this kind. They are for Parliament, the council chamber and, ultimately, the polling station; not for the court.[170]

While refusing to place formal limits on its jurisdiction, the court nevertheless 'felt . . . considerable reserve about the legitimacy of at least part of the exercise embarked on by the two authorities'[171] and gave few indications in its 96-page judgment that local authorities might find support for their position through the pursuance of judicial review.

The *GLC* case was not, however, the only application from authorities which had been rate-capped for 1985/86. A major concern of a number of the rate-capped authorities was the fact that, since the expenditure levels of designated authorities were made on the basis of the previous year's budget, that figure significantly understated the actual spending of authorities because of their use

---

[166] Transcript, 22–3.   [167] Transcript, 44.   [168] Transcript, 57.
[169] Transcript, 58.   [170] Transcript, 59.   [171] Transcript, 24.

of a variety of creative accounting techniques.[172] This meant that the expenditure cuts required by the Secretary of State were often much greater than the official figures seemed to indicate. The Secretary of State appeared to recognize that this was the case, and urged authorities to apply for re-determination.[173] The response of Greenwich, however, was not an application for re-determination but, ultimately, an application for judicial review of the Secretary of State's failure to adjust the maximum rate set for the borough in the light of information which had informally been provided concerning their use of special funds to bolster expenditure. In *London Borough of Greenwich* v. *Secretary of State for the Environment*[174] the Court of Appeal upheld the Divisional Court's refusal to quash the maximum rate set for Greenwich. The court held that, in light of the fact that Greenwich's budgetary returns to the Department of the Environment failed to provide any information about their use of special funds and given their refusal to apply for re-determination, it was not open to the authority subsequently to complain about the refusal of the Secretary of State to adjust the maximum rate on the basis of information informally provided. The Court of Appeal also reiterated the point made in the *GLC* case concerning the claim that the requirements of fairness placed the Secretary of State under a duty to provide information about his calculations. Pointing to the minister's responsibility to Parliament, the court rejected the idea that 'the common law has ever imposed such a general duty of disclosure on ministers of the Crown or their departments in the absence of a statutory requirement of disclosure.'[175]

Despite the Court of Appeal's rejection of Greenwich's case, a similar application was made by the London Borough of Islington in relation to the 1986/87 rate-capping process.[176] Islington had again refused to seek re-determination, though a number of authorities in the second round had applied. Islington did, however, provide detailed information to the Department on their use of special funds so as to indicate that their previous year's actual expenditure level had been significantly understated and council leaders had met with the Minister to explain their position. Islington's objective was essentially to provide the Government with the information needed to demonstrate that it was in a similar financial position to those authorities which had applied for re-determination. When the Secretary of State upwardly re-assessed the expenditure limits of the authorities which had applied but refused to adjust Islington's maximum rate, Islington applied for judicial review. The authority's basic case was that, by prescribing a maximum rate on the basis of the original expenditure level, the Secretary of State had failed to take into account a relevant consideration; viz., whether, having regard to the information provided, that expenditure level was still appropriate. This argument was fairly summarily rejected by the court on the

[172] On the various practices which led to this gap see, below, ch. 6.
[173] See M. Grant, *Rate Capping and the Law* (London, 2nd edn., 1986), 42.
[174] *The Times*, 19 December 1985.   [175] Lexis transcript of judgment.
[176] *R* v. *Secretary of State for the Environment, ex p. London Borough of Islington* (unreported) 26 March 1986 (Div.Ct.).

ground that, although the Secretary of State was obliged to take into account Islington's representations on the proposed maximum rate, as a matter of statutory construction he could not take into account representations as to the validity of the expenditure level; that could be done only through a formal application to re-determine the level.

The *Islington* decision marked a clear rejection of the attempt by local authorities to utilize the procedures of judicial review for the purpose of establishing alternative procedures for re-negotiating the rate cap. Webster J's judgment went further, however, since he also held that, in a strict sense, he lacked jurisdiction to consider Islington's challenge. Webster J accepted the formal line of argument, which the court had rejected in the *GLC* case, primarily because of the opinion of the House of Lords in the *Nottinghamshire* case,[177] which had been handed down only a few days before the *Islington* hearing. Following Lord Scarman's opinion in *Nottinghamshire*, Webster J held that, in the absence of some exceptional circumstance, it was inappropriate for the courts to intervene on the ground of 'unreasonableness' in such matters of public financial administration and that Lord Scarman's reference to *Wednesbury* unreasonableness should be interpreted liberally as also excluding challenge on the ground of 'relevant considerations'.[178]

GRE, caps and rationality

As we have seen, the system of expenditure targets was abandoned from 1986/87 and from that year onwards expenditure control was to be achieved through the block grant mechanism and rate-capping arrangements. Since GRE was an assessment of the local authority's expenditure needs, it might be expected that there would be some relationship between GRE and the maximum expenditure level designated by the Secretary of State for a rate-capped authority. If, for example, the expenditure level was fixed at a point significantly below GRE could the authority mount a variant of the *Hackney* challenge, contending that the ceiling was unattainable and thus irrational? And, after *Nottinghamshire*, would the courts have jurisdiction to consider such an application?

This issue did not in fact materialize in this form. Instead, the courts were asked to adjudicate on an interesting variant of this argument. With the abolition of the metropolitan county councils in 1986, a number of their functions were allocated to single-purpose joint authorities.[179] These joint authorities were deemed to have been designated under the Rates Act[180] and thus had their maximum

---

[177] [1986] 2 WLR 1. See, above, 282–9.

[178] Webster J thus rejected the argument that the collecting of material upon which a decision is based should be considered to belong to a stage of the decision-making process which precedes the decision itself and therefore that an error at that stage constitutes procedural impropriety rather than irrationality. He did so because, in practical terms, it seemed impossible to divide up decision-making in such a manner. It is worthy of note that in the *GLC* case, the court considered that errors in the decision-making process fell under the head of procedural impropriety: see transcript, 18–19.

[179] Local Government Act 1985, Pt. IV.   [180] LGA 1985, s. 68(6).

expenditure levels fixed by the Government. In the case of such single-purpose authorities, the relationship between the expenditure level and the GRE assessment for that service could easily be ascertained. West Yorkshire Police Authority was one such joint authority. For 1986/87 its expenditure level had been set at £60.6 million but, after submitting an application for re-determination, the Home Secretary increased the figure to £63.2 million. This figure was not below the police authority's GRE; on the contrary, with a GRE of £50.7 million, the authority's maximum expenditure level had been fixed at a point 25 per cent above its GRE. However, in these circumstances the authority came to the conclusion that its GRE, which influenced its entitlement to grant, must have been wrongly assessed. The authority thus applied for judicial review to quash the Secretary of State's determination of the authority's 1986/87 GRE.[181]

The police authority's basic argument was that, since GRE was intended to represent an assessment of the cost of providing a common standard of service with average efficiency, it should bear some relationship to its expenditure level. The argument ran as follows. The Home Secretary has a general duty to use his powers to promote the efficiency of the police[182] and is empowered to pay grants to police forces only if satisfied that the police service is being efficiently and properly maintained.[183] The Home Secretary had never suggested that West Yorkshire's police force was being inefficiently run and, on the basis of the authority's submission, had increased its expenditure level. Furthermore, an affidavit from the Chief Constable had indicated that if police spending were to be restricted to its GRE assessment the force would no longer be able to provide an adequate or efficient standard of police service. In the light of these facts, the authority argued that its expenditure level was a relevant consideration to which the Environment Secretary should have had regard in setting its GRE. And as he had not, the GRE assessment for the authority contained in the RSG Report should be quashed.

In considering the application, McCowan J accepted the Secretary of State's argument that the fixing of GRE did not have the function of setting a target expenditure but simply affected the distribution of liability for any given level of expenditure as between taxpayer and ratepayer. GRE was a formulaic assessment which was determined by the Government first deciding on the service control total – that is, the aggregate figure for current expenditure on police services – in the light of its public expenditure plans and then dividing that total amongst police authorities in accordance with a set of principles applicable to all authorities. Consequently, the Environment Secretary's function in setting GRE levels was quite different from that of the Home Secretary's in setting expenditure levels; the latter had responsibility for the performance of police

[181] *R* v. *Secretary of State for the Environment, ex p. West Yorkshire Police Authority* (unreported) 1 July 1986 (Div.Ct.).
[182] Police Act 1964, s. 28.
[183] Police Act 1964, s. 31; Police (Grant) Order 1966, art. 2.

functions whereas the former did not. Once this distinction was appreciated it became clear that, though expressed in the language of irrelevant considerations, the police authority's claim was in reality a disguised rationality argument. In essence, the argument was that the system had produced irrational results. When viewed in this light, the Divisional Court's decision to reject the application can be readily understood. McCowan J, following Webster J's interpretation in *Islington* of Lord Scarman's *Nottinghamshire* guidelines, held that the police authority's claim went to the reasonableness of the decision and therefore, since the RSG Report had taken effect after obtaining the consent of the House of Commons, the court was not competent to investigate the nature of the complaint.

Rate-capping and the courts

From the perspective of those local authorities seeking to challenge the Government's use of rate-capping powers, the experience of calling on the courts for aid and assistance has been altogether unsatisfactory. The Rates Act had been tightly drafted as directive legislation and there were few complexities or ambiguities which could be exploited. The judiciary had little difficulty in identifying the challenges as essentially political claims dressed up as points of law and had no reservations in suggesting that the appropriate arenas for addressing those issues were to be found in Westminster and Whitehall rather than the Strand. Although the signal sent by the House of Lords in the *Nottinghamshire* case had struck an uncertain note in relation to litigation concerning the 1980 Act, the message was clearly received by the courts when dealing with rate-capping challenges. That message was reinforced in relation to the third round of rate-capping in 1987/88 because, as a result of the calamities leading to the enactment of the Local Government Finance Act 1987, the normal statutory procedures of the 1984 Act had been abandoned and were replaced with formulaically determined caps laid down by statute.[184] In one sense, this represented the highest expression of the insulation from judicial scrutiny of governmental controls over the expenditure of individual local authorities. However, it should also be pointed out that, by this stage, local authorities had effectively abandoned the strategy of trying to use the courts as a shield against the impact of rate-capping.

Charge-Capping

The introduction of the poll tax

In January 1986 the Government published *Paying for Local Government* which outlined its proposals for a radical change in the system of local government

---

[184] Local Government Finance Act 1987, Sched. 2.

finance.[185] The Green Paper advocated the nationalization of the non-domestic rate with recycling to local authorities on a per capita basis, the phased replacement of domestic rates with a flat-rate community charge (generally referred to as a poll tax) and the simplification of the grant system. These changes were implemented in the Local Government Finance Act 1988. The only significant modification was that the community charge was not to be phased in, but would replace domestic rates with effect from 1990/91. These changes, the most revolutionary to the system of local government finance in modern times, were highly controversial.

It is not part of my objective here to evaluate the general impact of these reforms.[186] But it is necessary to outline the basic reforms to the grant system. The starting point for the new grant allocation exercise is the assessment by the Government of the total sum which it would be appropriate for local government to incur on revenue expenditure (known as Total Standard Spending or TSS) and the amount of central government money which will be available to support that spending (known as Aggregate External Finance or AEF). In order to allocate that money to local authorities through the Revenue Support Grant (RSG), the Secretary of State makes an assessment of what it is necessary for each local authority to spend in order to provide a common level of services. These are known as Standard Spending Assessments (SSAs). SSAs replace GRE assessments and seek to simplify the system of grant distribution by replacing the 63 components of GREs with a simpler structure based on only thirteen separate components of expenditure need.[187] The sum of each of the relevant SSA elements produces a single SSA for each local authority. This SSA can then be used as the basis for distributing RSG in the following manner:

RSG = SSA *less* income from business rate *less* assumed poll tax income

Local authorities were permitted to spend above their SSA but this would have to be financed entirely from local resources by levying a higher than standard poll tax. Consequently, it can readily be seen how these reforms were justified as seeking to restore local accountability to the system. The Government promoted the reforms on this basis since they would: provide 'a more direct and fairer link between voting and paying, with more local voters contributing towards the cost of providing local authority services'; ensure that 'the payments [made] towards local services do not conceal from local voters the true costs of increased spending'; establish 'clearer grant arrangements, so that the clear

---

[185] Cmnd. 9714.

[186] See, J. Gibson, *The Politics and Economics of the Poll Tax: Mrs Thatcher's Downfall* (Warley, 1990); D. Butler, A. Adonis and T. Travers, *Failure in British Government. The Politics of the Poll Tax* (Oxford, 1994).

[187] See Department of the Environment, *Standard Spending Assessments – Background and Underlying Methodology* (London, 1990).

consequences of increases or reductions in spending are felt directly and straight-forwardly by local domestic ratepayers'.[188]

Given these objectives of the reforms, however, what is surprising is the fact that in Part VII of the 1988 Act the Secretary of State acquired the power to cap the level of a local authority's community charge. This was justified on the ground that 'in the first years of the new system when due to the transitional arrangements . . . the accountability pressures would not be fully in place there might be a greater need for it to exercise its powers to secure reduction in excessive budgets and the resulting charges'.[189] Under the 1988 Act, the Secretary of State's power was, strictly speaking, not to cap the charge but rather to cap the authority's budgeted expenditure. The Secretary of State could designate an authority if, in his opinion, its budgeted expenditure was 'excessive' or if there was an 'excessive increase' in expenditure in relation to the previous year.[190] Designation was to be made 'in accordance with principles determined by the Secretary of State' and 'those principles shall be the same . . . for all authorities falling within that class'.[191] The Secretary of State was obliged to inform the authority of the proposed maximum expenditure, which figure the authority might either accept or challenge.[192] If challenged, the Secretary of State, 'after considering any information he thinks is relevant' was required to make an order, to be approved by resolution of the House of Commons, stating the maximum expenditure.[193] The system of charge-capping thus closely fol-lowed the rate-capping arrangements.

Challenging charge-capping

On 3 April 1990, the Secretary of State, following the introduction of the new system with effect from 1 April, exercised his powers under the 1988 Act to designate 21 councils for charge capping.[194] Common principles were applied to all authorities which, though complex, were geared to local authorities which were budgeting to spend in excess of 12.5 per cent above their SSA.[195] Not-withstanding the demoralizing experience of the local authorities which had challenged the exercise of rate-capping powers, and despite the fact that the Government had had the benefit of that experience when drafting Part VII of the 1988 Act, nineteen of the capped authorities applied for judicial review of

[188] *Paying for Local Government*, Cmnd. 9714, para. 1.54.
[189] Affidavit of Mr Paul Rowsell, Assistant Secretary, Department of the Environment: see [1990] 3 All ER 589, 598.
[190] 1988 Act, s. 100(1).   [191] 1988 Act, s. 100(4).
[192] 1988 Act, s. 102(1), (5).   [193] 1988 Act, s. 104.
[194] Only 20 authorities were actually designated on 3 April. Since the London Borough of Lam-beth had been unable to agree a budget until after the start of the financial year, that authority was not designated until 10 April.
[195] See [1990] 3 All ER 589, 600–1.

the Secretary of State's decision.[196] Given the 'acute political controversy'[197] surrounding the Act in general, together with the fact that all the capped councils were under Labour control, it was perhaps imperative on political grounds that charge-capping be challenged. But was there any significant possibility of success?

The applicants certainly did not conserve on legal resources. They employed a 'galaxy of counsel'[198] who collectively presented arguments which ran through the entire spectrum of possible administrative law challenges to ministerial decision-making and the issue was pursued to the House of Lords. That it was always going to be an uphill struggle may be signified by the fact that the applicants failed to convince one of the eleven judges involved to decide in their favour on even one of the multifarious issues raised during the proceedings. While commending the lawyers 'for the very considerable, and largely success-ful, efforts which they made to avoid duplication of arguments whilst ensuring that every conceivable point was made in the interests of their respective cli-ents'[199] the judiciary not only dispatched the case with remarkable speed,[200] but also clearly signalled that, in future, there should be no further challenges of a speculative nature.

The applicants raised many specific arguments, some of which were variants of those raised in rate-capping challenges, but the main issues can conveniently be considered under the heads of illegality, irrationality and procedural impro-priety. The critical issue, however, was likely to be the attitude which the courts would adopt to Lord Scarman's view in *Nottinghamshire* that, in matters of public financial administration where the minister's judgment needs the ap-proval of the House of Commons, the courts may not legitimately review the decision on the ground of irrationality. Would this apply in *Hammersmith* given that the challenge was to designation, a process which both preceded and was distinct from capping, and only capping was subject to parliamentary approval? Should Lord Scarman's opinion be treated as a formal restriction on the juris-diction of the courts or simply a warning that the courts should be wary in this

[196] *Hammersmith & Fulham LBC* v. *Secretary of State for the Environment* [1990] 3 All ER 589. For an examination of the case see: C.M.G. Himsworth, 'Poll Tax Capping and Judicial Review' [1991] *Public Law* 76.

[197] [1990] 3 All ER 589, 628 (per Lord Bridge).

[198] [1990] 3 All ER 589, 628 (per Lord Bridge). Ten QCs were employed to represent the applicants in the Divisional Court hearing.

[199] [1990] 3 All ER 589, 627 (per Lord Donaldson MR) (CA).

[200] The Divisional Court heard the case between 5–11 June 1990 and delivered judgment on Friday, 15 June. The Court of Appeal 'began the pre-reading of relevant papers on the same day and continued the process on Monday, 18 June and the morning of 19 June, oral argument beginning at 2 pm on that day and ending at noon on Wednesday, 27 June' ([1990] 3 All ER 589, 613). The Court of Appeal delivered judgment on 3 July and seven days later (on 10 July) hearings com-menced in the Lords. On 17 July, at the conclusion of the hearing, their Lordships dismissed the appeals and gave their reasons for doing so in an opinion delivered on 4 October. The process from the date of first hearing in the Divisional Court to oral decision of the Lords had taken exactly six weeks.

field of substituting their view of the reasonableness of the action for that of the minister? And, given the overlap in practice between the three heads, just how extensively might Lord Scarman's restriction be viewed?

The courts made short shrift of the first question: although designation was not directly subject to parliamentary approval it was part of a general process which was and hence was not to be distinguished on this ground.[201] But there were significant differences expressed on the important question of jurisdiction. The Divisional Court held that '[p]ublic financial administration is a matter peculiarly within the province of Parliament to the exclusion of the courts' and that 'the applicants are therefore confined . . . to attacks on the legality and on the procedural propriety of what has been done'.[202] The Court of Appeal, however, believed that the Divisional Court had misunderstood *Nottinghamshire* since in that case Lord Scarman was asserting jurisdiction but 'at the same time warn[ing] against the risk of the courts exceeding that jurisdiction by considering not whether the decision was irrational in the sense of being perverse . . . but the wholly different question of whether the decision was reasonable, in the sense of being sensible or politic'.[203] Giving the judgment of the House, Lord Bridge, who of course sat in the *Nottinghamshire* case, adopted a formalistic tone more in tune with the Divisional Court's interpretation and held that 'since the statute has conferred a power on the Secretary of State which involves the formulation and the implementation of national economic policy and which can only take effect with the approval of the House of Commons, it is not open to challenge on the grounds of irrationality short of the extremes of bad faith, improper motive or mainfest absurdity'.[204] In adopting this approach, the court was able summarily to reject a number of the applicants' challenges. One complaint, for example, was that, by using SSAs as the criterion for determining whether the budget was excessive, the Secretary of State had used an inappropriate base. While the Court of Appeal rejected this argument on its merits,[205] the House of Lords did so simply on the ground that, being a reasonableness challenge, the complaint was inadmissible.[206]

Although the court did not apply the formal restraints on the irrationality challenge to the sphere of procedural propriety, it is evident that their general approach to the rationality question also influenced their attitude towards complaints of a procedural nature. Lord Bridge considered that, while procedural fairness is to be viewed as an important principle when 'citizens may be affected in their person, their property and their reputation' or when public authorities are accused of having acted 'unlawfully or discreditably', the procedural challenges in this dispute seemed to be rooted in differences of political judgment and '[i]n this statutory context I am very doubtful whether it would be appropriate for the court to imply terms in the statute derived from the doctrine of audi alteram

---

[201] [1990] 3 All ER 589, 603–4. [202] Ibid., 604. [203] Ibid., 615–16.
[204] Ibid., 637. [205] Ibid., 618–19. [206] Ibid., 637.

partem'.[207] The court was therefore not prepared to imply any requirements to supplement the procedures laid down in the 1988 Act: there was no duty to consult local authorities before determining the principles for designation; there was no requirement on the Secretary of State subsequently to give reasons for setting a particular maximum expenditure to enable authorities adequately to be able to challenge that amount; and the Secretary of State was under no obligation to disclose to the authority information received from various sources and which he may have taken into account in determining whether to, or how he would, exercise his capping powers.[208]

This left only the illegality challenge, which, since the Secretary of State had carefully followed the statutory procedures, was an extremely difficult argument to sustain. The main point under this head was that, since the Secretary of State's capping powers are triggered only if he believes that the authority's proposed expenditure is 'excessive', then, by analogy with the *Tameside* case,[209] the Secretary of State was obliged to apply *Wednesbury* standards: is this a budget which is greater than any reasonable local authority could properly regard as being sensible? The court regarded the analogy as being false[210] and concluded that excessive meant only that the Secretary of State 'thinks it is more than it should be'[211] and that the 'setting of a norm of local government expenditure is essentially a matter of political opinion'.[212]

Having so comprehensively rebuffed the local authorities' challenge to charge-capping, Lord Bridge, after recognizing the predictability of such a challenge materializing in the first year of the use of these controversial powers under a politically contentious system, concluded in effect by reiterating the concerns expressed by Lord Templeman in *Nottinghamshire*. He stated:

> I hope your Lordships' decision will serve to make it clear for future years that no similar challenge has any prospect of success unless an authority is in a position to show that the Secretary of State has acted in bad faith or for an improper motive or can point to some failure to comply with the procedural requirements which the Act clearly spells out.[213]

The *Hammersmith* decision should not be taken to mean that there was no longer any flexibility within the legal framework of local government finance to

---

[207] Ibid., 637–8. [208] Ibid., 637–40.

[209] *Secretary of State for Education and Science* v. *Tameside MBC* [1977] AC 1014.

[210] '[*Tameside*] was a decision on different statutory language in a wholly different statutory context and it has no relevance whatever to the construction of s. 100 of the 1988 Act. If one asks in the circumstances of an individual case whether a local education authority has acted unreasonably in the discharge of its statutory functions, this is clearly a question which admits of an objective answer. If one asks, however, . . . whether a local authority's budgeted expenditure for a year is excessive, it is plain that there can be no objective criterion by which to determine the answer.' [1990] 3 All ER 589, 634, *per* Lord Bridge.

[211] Ibid., 605. [212] Ibid., 634. [213] Ibid., 640.

enable local authorities to win tactical victories.[214] What it did was to indicate very clearly that the function of the courts was essentially that of ensuring that the statutory requirements were adhered to: in this field, in which discretionary action was rooted in the exercise of political judgment, there was no room for utilizing a more robust tradition of judicial review in which 'justice of the common law' would operate to 'supply the omission of the legislature'.[215]

Towards Universal Capping

From the moment of its introduction, it was quite clear to those with any understanding of the complexities of local government finance that the community charge scheme was unstable and could not last.[216] The community charge was abolished in the Local Government Finance Act 1992 and, with effect from 1 April 1993, was replaced with the council tax.[217] For our purposes, however, it is important to appreciate the fact that the basic system of central controls remained intact and that the council tax simply replaced the community charge as the basic method of raising the 20 per cent of local authority finance which is now derived from local sources. We are not so much concerned here with the relative merits of community charge and council tax as methods of raising local finance but rather with the functioning of the basic system of local government finance.

As a result of the practical difficulties caused by in-year capping (that is, applying caps after budgets had been set) in the first year of charge-capping, from 1991/92 the Government adopted the practice of announcing its capping intentions in advance of local authorities fixing their budgets. Furthermore, in 1992/93 the Government removed the threshold which had previously excluded many of the smaller district councils from capping, thus potentially exposing all

[214] See, e.g., *R* v. *Lambeth LBC, ex p. Secretary of State for the Environment, The Times*, 9 October 1990 (CA). Lambeth had set its community charge at £547.98 on the assumption of a collection rate of 90 per cent. When it was designated and a lower budget expenditure was fixed by the Secretary of State, Lambeth revised its community charge based on that lower expenditure level but on the assumption that only 85 per cent of those liable would pay. This was unsuccessfully challenged by the Secretary of State: provided the revised forecast could reasonably be made on the basis of the existing data, the authority was entitled to revise its estimate. Note, however, that this decision caused the Government to promote the Community Charges (Substitute Setting) Act 1991 to reverse its effect.

[215] *Cooper* v. *Wandsworth Board of Works* (1863) 14 CB (NS) 180, 194.

[216] See, e.g., the Conservative Government's 1981 Green Paper, *Alternatives to Domestic Rates* (Cmnd. 8449) which had concluded that a poll tax would be feasible only as a supplement to another major revenue-raising tax, since only in this form could its 'enforcement difficulties' and its 'effect . . . on those on lower incomes' be minimized (para. 7.14). The following White Paper suggested that a poll tax would be 'hard to enforce' and 'expensive to run' and proposed that this option 'should be rejected' (*Rates*, Cmnd. 9008 (1983), para. 2.9).

[217] The council tax is a tax on property which is set at a scale rate across eight bands (A–H) determined by a process of valuation. See Local Government Information Unit, *Council Tax Guide* (London, 1994).

local authorities to central government caps. The consequence of these two developments has been a significant shift towards universal capping of local authority expenditure. Although formally the number of local authorities actually capped each year remains very low, the provision of advance criteria means that each authority is presented annually with a target expenditure which must not be exceeded. Thus, in 1993/94 327 of the 449 English and Welsh local authorities, which collectively accounted for 92 per cent of total local government spending, set their budgets at, or within 1 per cent of, their capping limit.[218] Central government now effectively determines the budgets of the vast majority of local authorities.

The critical element in this process is the Standard Spending Assessment. Since 1990 the primary measure of 'excessive' expenditure[219] has been that of a budget set at more than 12.5 per cent of the authority's SSA and, where a calculation of an 'excessive increase'[220] in budget over the previous year is made, the criterion has been a percentage increase (2.5 per cent in 1993/94), though this cap is applied only if the authority's budget exceeds its SSA. Given the centrality of SSAs not only to the exercise of ensuring a fair distribution of grant but also to the exercise of determining the limits of a local authority's expenditure, a great deal of concern has been expressed about the manner in which SSAs have been constructed.

An early legal challenge to the rationality of SSAs occurred in *R* v. *Secretary of State for the Environment, ex parte Avon CC*,[221] which action concerned the allocation of RSG in respect of the police service. Following local government reorganization under the Local Government Act 1972, Avon CC and Somerset CC had established a combined police force. The amalgamation scheme meant that Avon, with approximately 67 per cent of the combined population, was served by 76 per cent of the combined force. As a result of this division, the cost per head of population for police was significantly greater in Avon than in Somerset. This cost-sharing formula, which had been approved by the Home Secretary, was generally accepted as being fair. However, under the new system of local government finance, the amount of RSG allocated to Avon and Somerset through the police service block of the SSA had been apportioned purely by reference to their respective populations; and the effect of this mismatch was that, if each authority were to spend at the level of their SSAs, the community charge, instead of being standardised at £278, would be £281 in Avon and £271 in Somerset. Since this system had been touted as seeking to restore local accountability, and seemed both to penalize Avon chargepayers and expose Avon

---

[218] Memorandum by Local Authority Associations, 'Review of Standard Spending Assessments' in First Report of the House of Commons Environment Committee, Session 1993–94, *Standard Spending Assessments* (HC 90), 60 at 64.

[219] Local Government Finance Act 1988, s. 100(1)(a).

[220] Local Government Finance Act 1988, s. 100(1)(b).

[221] Unreported, 31 July 1990 (Div.Ct.).

councils to unwarranted criticism, Avon CC argued that the RSG distribution was irrational and perverse. In refusing the application the Divisional Court relied primarily on the authority of the *Nottinghamshire* case.[222] Nolan J stated:

> The significance of House of Commons approval . . . is that it places an obstacle so great as to be almost insuperable in the way of the argument that the decision was perverse. Indeed, as I read Lord Scarman's speech as a whole, he regarded it as virtually inconceivable, in the absence of bad faith and deception on the part of the Minister concerned (itself almost inconceivable), that the House of Commons ever would approve a decision which was perverse.[223]

Given the tenor of this judgment, it was evident that the courts felt entirely unable to review the process of grant distribution. If SSAs were to be subject to scrutiny, it would have to be through administrative and parliamentary methods. During 1993/94 both the Audit Commission[224] and the House of Commons Environment Committee[225] undertook investigations into SSAs.

The general message of these reports was that, although the SSA mechanism is suitable for the purpose of equalizing councils' ability to meet local needs, great pressure has been placed on the mechanism as a result of SSAs being used for tasks for which they were not originally designed. The reports accepted that there could be no truly objective system since the process of assessing needs must inevitably involve an exercise of political judgment. As the Audit Commission report recognized:

> The use of formulae offers some safeguard against capricious ministerial behaviour but does not extinguish its possibility. Indeed, formulae, because they are little understood, can draw a disguising veil across the values which lie behind them. No formulation is value-free, but formulae can disguise what those values are.[226]

Consequently, while transparency should certainly be encouraged, these decisions ultimately rest on value stances. Furthermore, in developing such needs assessment systems, it may be important to keep the mechanism as simple as possible on the ground that simplicity enhances understanding and hence promotes accountability. At the same time, however, it should be recognized that there must always be a trade-off between simplicity and fairness in the construction

---

[222] At this stage, the House of Lords had decided the *Hammersmith* case in favour of the Government but had not yet given reasons; the court nevertheless remained bound by the Court of Appeal's judgment on the matter.

[223] (1990) 89 LGR 498, 511.

[224] *Passing the Bucks. The Impact of Standard Spending Assessments on Economy, Efficiency and Effectiveness* (HMSO, 1993).

[225] First Report from the House of Commons Environment Committee, Session 1993–94, *Standard Spending Assessments* (HC 90).

[226] *Passing the Bucks* (above, n. 224), vol. 1, 19.

of the system.[227] The shape of SSAs – with trade-offs being made between discretion against formulaic decision and simplicity of indicators against fairness of needs assessments – will ultimately be matters of judgment.

The problems raised in relation to SSAs, however, are not so much the product of their particular design but rather that of the various functions which SSAs are now expected to perform within the system of local government finance. These tensions have been exacerbated as a consequence of the acute pressures which have been imposed on that system in recent times. Since SSAs were developed in 1989, the proportion of local government income raised by local taxes has, as a result of the introduction of the 1988 Act reforms, fallen from over 50 per cent to about 20 per cent and this change in the central–local balance has had a major impact on the attempt to use the system to restore local accountability. One reason is because of the high gearing effect at the margin. This results in a 1 per cent increase in expenditure costing 5 per cent on the local tax; and the greater the needs of the authority, and hence the higher the SSA, the greater the gearing ratio for spending above SSA.[228] This gearing effect in itself causes problems for the objective of promoting local accountability. But it must also be recognized that, without year on year stability in a local authority's SSA, the accountability objective becomes virtually unrealizable. Even though the Government has tried hard to minimize changes in SSAs as a result of changes of methodology or data, significant year on year changes have been experienced largely because of changes in the control totals between the service blocks which are a product of changes in the Government's public expenditure policies.[229] This can result in changes of up to 30 per cent in a local authority's SSA from one year to the next;[230] and, with that degree of grant volatility, rational planning by local authorities becomes extremely difficult and the attempt to use changes in council tax levels as an index of either profligacy or efficiency will be highly dubious.

Given the current climate of severe expenditure restraint, the high level of central support for local services has also provided an additional source of pressure on local government. The Government recognizes that SSAs are not spending targets and that RSG is a block grant which is not hypothecated to specific services.[231] However, the total SSA is constructed from the control totals

---

[227] The Audit Commission Report raises such issues by utilizing an example and asking whether it is fair that Cambridge has a higher SSA per head for district services than Hartlepool. For an explanation as to how this came to be the case see *Passing the Bucks*, vol. 1, 24–5.

[228] See *Passing the Bucks*, vol. 1, 28 (Exhibit 13) which shows that, as a result of variations in needs assessment, the decision to budget at 10 per cent above SSA would require a council tax increase of 28 per cent in Mole Valley (low SSA), 56 per cent in Doncaster (medium SSA) and 96 per cent in Tower Hamlets (high SSA).

[229] See, Memorandum of the Department of the Environment, 'Revenue Support Grant Settlement' in House of Commons Environment Committee Report (above, n. 225), Minutes of Evidence, 1 at 3: 'SSAs . . . should be relatively stable over time. In practice it has been quite difficult to achieve this.'

[230] *Passing the Bucks* (above, n. 224), vol. 1, 21 (Exhibit 10).

[231] See House of Commons Environment Committee Report (above, n. 225), Minutes of Evidence, 54.

within the seven main service blocks and the SSA formula operates to allocate a particular share of the various service control totals each authority should have. While these are then aggregated to provide the authority's block figure, which is in principle available to the authority to spend as it chooses, there has been pressure from some central departments to seek to ensure that control totals are actually spent on that particular service. The Secretary of State for Health, for example, saw 'little point in having a system whereby central government distributes money according to one set of criteria (SSAs) and local government spends it according to another (local discretion)'.[232] Though it is widely accepted that this use of SSAs is unjustified, the emergence of what the Audit Commission calls a 'performance culture' has resulted in some government departments becoming less tolerant of these differences. The problem has been concisely explained by the Audit Commission in the following terms:

> [T]he tendency to judge local services in terms of the relevant service component of the local SSA is gaining momentum. The government has stated its intention of fixing the funding of grant maintained schools with reference to the education component of the SSA for the area. This gives local authorities which wish to retain control of their school systems a strong incentive to ensure that local authority funding of schools is not less than SSA, thereby reducing the incentive for schools to 'opt out'. As education is the largest service, the hypothecation of its SSA is likely to incline all other service budgets towards their SSA.[233]

This threat of incremental hypothecation places an unjustifiable degree of refinement and specificity on the SSA system. More importantly, it has the potential to strike at the heart of the discretionary power of local government.

However, perhaps the greatest threat of all has been the use of SSAs as a basis for the capping of local government expenditure. With universal capping since 1992, even the limited freedom of action permissible under a high gearing regime disappears. As we have seen, local authority budgets are increasingly being determined by caps based on SSAs. In these circumstances, in which '[a]ll authorities are effectively capped, many to their SSA with no margin above it', the Audit Commission felt that 'saying [SSAs] should be "no less fair" than GREs is not enough'[234] and the local authority associations have suggested that, while '[f]lawed SSAs can be tolerated to a degree when restricted to their orginal purpose of facilitating grant distribution ... it is a very different matter when they are used in ways which conflict with local accountability'.[235] The trajectory

[232] Letter from Mrs Virginia Bottomley, Secretary of State for Health, to President of the Society of County Treasurers, 8 January 1993. Quoted in House of Commons Environment Committee Report (above, n. 225), ix.
[233] *Passing the Bucks* (above, n. 224), vol. 1, 12. See also Department for Education Consultation Paper, *A Common Funding Formula for Schools 1994–95* (December 1993).
[234] *Passing the Bucks* (above, n. 224), vol. 1, 25.
[235] Memorandum by Local Authority Associations, in House of Commons Environment Committee Report (above, n. 225), Minutes of Evidence, 60 at 64.

of current Government policy, with local councils' budgets increasingly clustering around their SSAs and pressures being applied to persuade councils to determine service priorities in accordance with SSA service analysis, seems to be
leading to 'a system in which councils assume a degree of accountability out of
proportion to their ability to control services'.[236] These recent developments
pose a major threat to the viability of a strong institution of local government.

Conclusions

During the course of the twentieth century, we have turned almost full circle in
our understanding of the financial relationship between central and local government. In the first decade, central support for local government met only one-fifth
of its cost; during the last decade, only one-fifth of local government expenditure is *not* being met by central government grants. When the century opened,
concern was being expressed about the multiplicity of central grants; as it comes
to a close, the primary concern is the multiplicity of purposes for which a single
block grant is being used. In the early years, central grants-in-aid were generally
associated with an enhanced quality of public services and the 'universal enforcement of the national minimum'; today, the grant regime is commonly viewed
as one which stifles innovation and seeks what might be termed the 'universal
imposition of a national maximum of local expenditure'.

Concern has always been expressed about the dangers involved in using central grants to fuel the growth in local government service functions. We have,
for example, already seen Cannan, in the role of Cassandra, arguing in 1912 that
central grants would undermine local government through the substitution of
local initiative by a centralized instrumental rationality, and suggesting that this
would result in both the replacement of politics with administration and the
displacement of law as a medium regulating the balance between central and
local government. Given the strength of the tides of change, Cannan may perhaps more appropriately be viewed in the role of Canute. But even those, like
Webb, who took a thoroughly positive view of the changes were not unware of
the potential problems. Our legal culture, being imbued with the traditional
values of the common law, was viewed as being unable to adapt to the regulatory issues of the modern world of government and faith was thus placed in the
establishment of a compact between central and local government. It was this
compact, which would be underpinned by the development of a public service
ethic amongst officials, that would provide the best hope for reconciling traditions of local government with the emergence of the positive State. During the
last twenty years or so, as gradually there has occurred a loss of faith in the idea
that governmental action is to be equated with progress and with the incorporation

---

[236] *Passing the Bucks* (above, n. 224), vol. 1, 29.

of market techniques for promoting economy and efficiency into governmental programmes, the cracks in the network were revealed. As central government increasingly used the grant system as a tool of both general and specific expenditure control, the compact was undermined. With the disintegration in authority of conventions, local authorities turned to the law to provide a regulatory framework governing the central–local financial relationship.

This chapter has focused specifically on that experience. It has been a rather disheartening episode though, since the twentieth century system has been constructed on the displacement of law as a primary medium of regulating the central–local relationship, this was perhaps only to be expected. Lord Donaldson was therefore only partially correct when, in the *Hammersmith* case, he suggested that, since central departments and local authorities are vested with powers and duties, the 'role of the judiciary is essentially that of a referee' and that the 'referee is only involved when it appears that some player has acted in breach of the rules'.[237] The Master of the Rolls was only partially correct in his assessment because what was not explicitly acknowledged was the fact that the traditional 'game' of central–local government relations was a complex one in which one of the basic 'rules' was that the parties did not go to the courts to resolve their disputes. The structure of the legal regime governing central–local relations established a broad, facilitative framework, the objective of which was to legitimate an administrative structure within which disputes would be resolved through adminstrative processes. The foundational legislation thus used statutory language of a general, discretionary and opaque character.

When, as a result of the disintegration of the traditional rule-book, local authorities, largely from a sense of frustration, turned to the courts for a resolution of their grievances, the traditional statutory language often served only to confound the judiciary. The complexity of the system in combination with the ambiguities and lacunae within the statutory framework presented the courts with considerable difficulties. This has been compounded by the hyperactivism of the Government. As it gradually realized the consequences of its policies, the Government quickly embarked on the task of redefining the system as a set of judicially enforceable rules. The problem was that, for a period during the 1980s, the complexities of the system outstripped the Government's capacity to reorder the rule structure of the game. The only solution then was to resort to the drastic remedy of retrospective legislation; of changing the rules of the game after the event in order to bring them into line with the Government's desired version of the nature of the game.[238]

However, once the courts are drawn into the exercise and are expected to perform the role of referee, the question then arises of where they are to find the rules. Lord Donaldson's answer, that 'the rules are made by Parliament

---

[237] [1990] 3 All ER 589, 614.
[238] Lord Donaldson, ibid., alluded to this dynamic situation in suggesting that the courts 'are continually being faced with the need to study, interpret and apply new versions of the rules'.

supplemented by and against the background of the rules of the common law',[239] served to identify the critical issue. The statutory rules, having been devised by the Government and being constantly amended to suit the requirements of the moment, are unlikely to assist local government. Furthermore, even in circumstances where the statute might afford a degree of protection to local authorities, the courts have tended, in cases such as *Nottinghamshire*, to resolve ambiguities in the statutory formulation to the benefit of the Government. The critical issue is that of the character of the game: is it a game which is constituted by the statutory rule book or should it be viewed as a more complex game in which the statutory rules are supplemented by common law values? This is the point which Lord Donaldson fudged since the function of the referee is not simply that of giving effect to the rules; through the activity of enforcing the rules, the referee is also, of necessity, elaborating on the character of the game.

The response of the courts since 1980 has been rather mixed. Some judges have in effect been trying to act on the assumptions of the traditional rule-game in which the courts were not expected to act as referee; a view most clearly expressed by Lord Templeman in *Nottinghamshire* when he suggested that local authorities should 'bite on the bullet' and not come rushing to the courts with their grievances. Given the universal pretensions of law, however, the courts are generally reluctant to concede that they lack the jurisdiction to provide an authoritative ruling on the meaning of legislation. They have, nevertheless, on occasion been torn between providing a commonsensical reading (with potentially devastating consequences) and that of adopting a convoluted approach in order to give effect to the Government's objectives. But what of the role of judicially-developed principles of administrative law? During the early 1980s, as can be seen in the *Brent* case, the courts seemed to recognize the importance of the concept of procedural fairness in regulating the conduct of central–local government relations. As the judiciary gradually realized the scale of the task involved in using law as a primary technique of regulation in this field, they marked the retreat: judicial review would be undertaken on the ground of illegality but not on grounds of irrationality or procedural propriety. The former restriction was most clearly signalled by Lord Scarman in *Nottinghamshire*, while the latter was demonstrated in *Hammersmith* through Lord Bridge's intimation that audi alteram partem had no significance in this field. In general, the courts seem to have been indicating that they simply lacked both the institutional capacity and constitutional legitimacy to perform the exercise being demanded of them. Consequently, because of their limited competence as umpires of a more complex rule-game, the judiciary have gradually worked their way to the position of holding that central–local government financial relations is a relatively simple game constituted solely by the statutory rules.

This leaves us in a rather difficult position. The old compact seems to have

---

[239] [1990] 3 All ER 589.

disintegrated, the courts are unable to develop an adequate regulatory frame-work, the current accountability structures are blurred and confused and, what-ever the rhetoric of the Government, the thrust of recent developments seems to be leading us inexorably down the road of centralization. What is unclear is whether this has been a conscious strategy or the largely unintended by-product of the Government's frustration at being unable to manage the complex system of central–local government relations to further its own policy objectives. What is clear, however, is that, if we are indeed heading irreversibly down the road of centralization, our existing governmental arrangements are entirely inadequate for the task of ensuring that ministers will be properly held to account for the system for which they will have assumed primary responsibility.

6

INNOVATIVE FINANCING IN LOCAL GOVERNMENT

The status of local government within our system of government is not easily determined from a purely legal point of view. Local authorities, being corporate bodies established by statute, are viewed by many lawyers as being relatively simple institutions. The general statutes (the Local Government Acts) provide a constitutional structure, in the form of a common management, financial and decision-making framework, and various functional statutes (such as Housing, Education, Planning, and Social Services Acts) equip that corporate body with a set of more or less precise responsibilities. Since both types of statute provide a range of controls – both internal and external – over the exercise of these powers, we are tempted to evaluate the relative autonomy of local government by examining this checklist of powers and constraints. This type of approach is, however, likely to be highly distortive. And the reason for this is primarily because the functions performed by law within the system are dependent on a more basic set of practices concerning the structure of governance. Consequently, although law in a sense establishes the framework of the local government system, it does not define that system.

If we are to understand the modern institution of local government we must first recognize the fact that local government has become locked within an extensive network of government. The status of local government is thus largely a product of its function within this interdependent network. This network is often not explicitly recognized in law and is accommodated by the widespread use of framework legislation; law, that is, which is facilitative rather than restrictive and which often confers powers without specifying controls. In effect, law cedes some of its control functions to a variety of administrative networks. These informal networks, being generally built on divergent interests, have both an ambiguous status and nature. The boundaries of these networks, and the power relations within them, are constantly shifting. Nevertheless, because of high structural interdependencies and because of the overall complexities of the fields which they regulate, these networks are of great importance to the achievement of system stability and performance. Although the image projected from a traditional legal perspective is that of a central authority imposing its will on dependent bodies, when we take account of the actual workings of government a more complex picture emerges; while the centre possesses a great array of special powers, it too is also locked into a highly complex network which it cannot easily control.

I wish to highlight both the centre's position within that network and the fact that law performs limited control functions within our system of government precisely because, since 1980, the Government has sought radically to alter the status of local government. The resulting changes to the structure, functions and financial arrangements of local government have been implemented very speedily and in a highly charged political atmosphere and have required the assertion of a strong central will. As a consequence, the attempt at consensus-building has regularly been jettisoned, the authority of conventional understandings has waned and very significant strains have been imposed on the administrative network. A further important consequence of this strategy is that the Government has sought to use law in an instrumental sense to perform a primary control function; the new arrangements have been constructed on more formalized and restrictive premises and, with the replacement of mediation with adjudication, the courts have been brought more directly into the system.

These developments raise some basic questions about our system of government. What are the limits to the Government's ability to achieve its objectives by means of central direction? To what extent is the Government able to undermine the authority of the traditional administrative network without paying a significant price in terms of diminished system performance or outright policy failure? And, in particular, does law possess the capacity effectively to discharge its new regulatory functions within this restructured system? In this chapter, aspects of these questions will be addressed by way of an examination of the responses of local authorities to the Government's attempts to restrict their expenditure programmes. What we shall see is that, with the disintegration of conventional restraints, many local authorities began to exploit the ambiguities within the legal framework of local government and attempted to protect their budgets through the adoption of a variety of 'creative accounting' devices and through the use of new types of financial instruments; that many of these innovative devices operated to frustrate the Government's ability to achieve its objectives; and that the Government was drawn into the exercise of having to draft increasingly restrictive forms of legislation to curb these practices.

Trends in Local Government Finance

Local authorities have traditionally raised the finances they need to undertake their functions from four main sources: rates, fees and charges, grants from central government, and by borrowing. Local authorities are required to finance their affairs on an annual basis[1] and are not generally empowered to borrow for revenue purposes. In respect of current expenditure, then, it is the first three sources (and the balance between them) which has been of particular importance.

---

[1] See *Re Westminster City Council* [1986] 1 AC 668, esp. 704, 707, 710, 713.

Much of the post-war growth in local government expenditure has been financed by central government grants. By the mid 1970s, however, this trend was causing the Government some concern and during the 1980s the Government took action to reduce the burden on the central Exchequer of local government programmes. In an attempt to reduce these burdens, the Government introduced a great number of changes to the system of local government finance: the real value of central government grants steadily reduced throughout the decade; grant distribution arrangements were amended to target grant to authorities which complied with specific Government expenditure guidelines; a variety of reforms were introduced to persuade, or even direct, authorities to increase their yield through fees and charges for services provided; powers were acquired to cap the amount which local authorities could raise from the rates; control over non-domestic rate levels was centralized; and the system of domestic rates was abolished and replaced first with the poll tax and later the council tax.[2]

The Government anticipated that the existence of these new pressure points would provide the appropriate signals to local authorities that they must reorganize their priorities, reduce expenditure and not seek to protect their programmes by financing them through increases in local taxes. This expectation proved, initially at least, to be ill-founded. One important reason for this was that the effect of imposing these unprecedented centralizing measures in a unilateral manner was to subvert the administrative network. Since the Government had altered the 'rules of the game', it could not expect local government to respond to exhortation in the conventional manner. In the words of an Audit Commission report on this subject, 'local authorities have responded rapidly, predictably and (from their point of view) sensibly to the pressures induced by the uncertainties'.[3] During the period up to the late 1980s, then, the Government became caught in a vortex of progressive centralization, largely in an attempt to apply the brakes to a system which was threatening to get out of control. This trend culminated in fundamental reforms to the entire system of local government finance.[4]

During the 1980s, the rules of the central–local financial relationship thus became those specified in legislation. Having been drafted in accordance with the conventions of the traditional network, however, many of these rules were both ambiguous and less than comprehensive. Consider, for example, the accounting requirements for local government expenditure. Local authority accountancy practices were certainly underpinned by statute but that legal framework was rather general,[5] and much of the detail was left to administrative guidance

---

[2] For details see, above, ch. 5.

[3] Audit Commission, *The impact on local authorities' economy, efficiency and effectiveness of the block grant distribution system* (London, 1984), 23.

[4] Local Government Finance Act 1988 (poll tax and nationalization of non-domestic rates); Local Government and Housing Act 1989, Pt. IV (new system of capital expenditure controls).

[5] Local Government Act 1972, Pt. VIII; The Accounts and Audit Regulations 1974.

or professional standards.[6] As a former Director of Finance of the London Borough of Hammersmith and Fulham suggested, it was 'a direct reflection of the successful self-regulatory activities and the absence of any major structural shortcomings in local authority accounts that the regulations contain so little detail compared to, say, the Companies Acts'.[7]

Under the framework which emerged in the post-war period, detailed central prescription was felt to be unnecessary because professional self-regulation together with the acceptance of the authority of conventional practices ensured the integrity of the accounts. When central government during the 1980s unilaterally sought to impose its will, however, many actors within the system turned from conventional practices to the legal requirements. On so doing, the extent of discretion and flexibility within the system, which had hitherto been latent, became all too apparent. And when central government utilized centrally-determined expenditure assessments as specific targets and attached grant penalties, local authorities began to exploit the ambiguities and gaps in order to minimize the impact of these central controls. We have already seen how these expenditure controls were challenged by local authorities in the courts.[8] In this chapter, we shall examine not so much how local authorities challenged expenditure controls but rather how they sought to avoid them by shifting expenditures between various funds in order to adjust their expenditure figures to maximum advantage.

Techniques of Creative Accounting

This exercise of playing the game strictly in accordance with the rules prescribed by law resulted in the emergence of the practices of 'creative accounting'. Creative accounting is a rather ambiguous concept. The practice generally creates no new local resources for a local authority. The effect is simply to rearrange the existing resources and commitments of the authority across different time spans or between different accounting classifications. But because of the regime of centrally determined targets and caps operating during the 1980s, the effect of applying the techniques of 'active management' to local authority accounts could potentially have a significant impact on an authority's entitlement to grant or on the revenue resources available to it in a particular year. The need to make expenditure cuts, for example, might be avoided simply by shifting money between accounts (that is, between funds which exist only on paper). If, for example, a local authority is budgeting to spend above target and is thereby incurring penalties, it could increase its grant entitlement by perhaps £2 or £3 for each £1 by which its budgeted expenditure figure is reduced. There has

---

[6] Local Government Audit Code of Practice (DoE, 1973). More detailed guidance is provided by the Chartered Institute of Public Finance and Accountancy (CIPFA), the main professional body.

[7] C. Holtham, 'Local Government: Internal Control and External Reporting' in D. Henley et al. (eds.), *Public Sector Accounting and Financial Control* (London, 1983), 84.

[8] See, above, ch. 5.

been no shortage of schemes for achieving this effect. During the 1980s a major industry, with local authority treasurers and lawyers working hand in hand with financial institutions, has evolved. Its potential importance has been great. One study has suggested that, over the period 1981/82 to 1985/86, increases in grant entitlement of up to 50 per cent could have been engineered by creative adjustment of a local authority's 'relevant expenditure' figure.[9]

The main creative accounting device in the sphere of revenue expenditure has been simply to shift expenditures between different local authority accounts. This has been achieved mainly by the establishment of *special funds*. Because money moved into a special fund counts as expenditure for that year, this exercise could be used to maximize grant entitlement. If, for example, an authority is spending below target it could optimize its grant position by shifting a sum representing the difference between actual expenditure and target into a special fund. 'Relevant expenditure' would then equal its target (its maximum grant point). The authority could then use that money in the following year when it would not count as expenditure. If actual expenditure in the following year was at target, this meant that the money from the special fund could be used to boost actual expenditure above target without incurring any penalty. The evidence suggests that the amount of money in local authority special funds increased significantly during the 1980s.[10]

Another important method of shifting expenditure across accounts has been to shift between revenue and capital expenditure. Traditionally, the definition of what counted as revenue or capital expenditure had been largely a matter of convention and, despite the introduction in 1981 of a new system of capital expenditure controls,[11] the legal framework was not particularly specific in its definitions of revenue and capital matters. Consequently, an authority which was proposing to spend above target but was within its capital expenditure allocation, could try to reduce its relevant expenditure figure by shifting some expenditure formerly treated as being of a revenue nature into a capital account. This process, the *capitalization of revenue expenditure*, has been an important source of grant maximization. It has been most commonly used in respect of housing expenditure where maintenance and repairs costs (part of revenue-borne expenditure) could be capitalized into an improvement programme. This, for example, was one of the range of measures which Liverpool City Council adopted to alleviate its 1984–85 budgetary difficulties.[12]

[9] P. Smith, 'The potential gains from creative accounting in English local government' (1988) 6 *Government and Policy* 173. 'Relevant expenditure' is the 'expenditure for that year falling to be defrayed out of the rate fund of a local authority': Local Government, Planning and Land Act (LGPLA) 1980, s. 54(5). This is the authority's expenditure base for assessment of grant.

[10] Audit Commission, *The impact on local authorities' economy, efficiency and effectiveness of the block grant distribution system* (London, 1984), 26 (Exhibit 8).

[11] LGPLA 1980, Pt. VIII.

[12] See A. Midwinter, 'Setting the rate – Liverpool style' (1985) vol. 11 no. 3 *Local Government Studies* 25. See further ch. 3, 185–7, 194–5.

This form of capitalization of revenue expenditure, however, was useful to the authority only in circumstances where it was not already committed to the limit of its 'prescribed expenditure' on capital projects. Prescribed expenditure consisted basically of the sum of three elements: 110 per cent of the amount specified by the Minister as the local authority's capital allocation for the year; an amount equal to a prescribed proportion of the authority's net capital receipts; and an amount equal to the authority's trading profits for the year.[13] When the authority was running up against its prescribed expenditure limit, however, it might be required to consider various ways in which it could boost its capital expenditure. The obvious ones – generating additional capital receipts from asset sales or increasing its trading profits – were, however, unlikely to appeal to many authorities which otherwise would wish to protect their programmes. More innovative arrangements were therefore devised.

These arrangements took a variety of forms. Initially, an important option was to try to bolster the capital expenditure programme above capital allocation by finding novel ways of generating *additional capital receipts*. This required authorities to identify assets which could be sold without perceptibly affecting their policies and programmes. One of the most controversial forms of asset sale for this purpose was the sale by local authorities of their interest as mortgagee of their housing stock. In one well-publicized case, Liverpool City Council, as part of the package to alleviate its 1984–85 budgetary crisis, sold its mortgagee interest to Banque Paribas for £30 million.[14]

Another method was to exploit the looseness of the definition of prescribed expenditure in the 1980 Act by acquiring capital assets which were outside the capital control system. The main methods of doing this were by *medium term leasing* and by the *bartering of assets*. Under the 1980 Act system, if a local authority entered into a leasing arrangement the transaction counted as prescribed expenditure and the capitalized value of the leased asset became a call upon the capital expenditure allocation, even if the payments were made monthly or yearly. However, the leasing of land and buildings did not count as capital expenditure if the lease was for less than 20 years.[15] Leasing for less than 20 years therefore became very attractive to authorities which were at the limit of their prescribed expenditure. Bartering was another method of avoiding capital controls. This generally involved the authority transferring property to developers in return for other parcels of land or perhaps the vesting in the authority of new buildings, or the carrying out of improvements on behalf of the authority. Since no money changed hands, such deals fell outside the capital control system.

In addition to methods of bolstering prescribed expenditure limits or avoiding

[13] LGPLA 1980, s. 72; Sched. 12. Local Government (Prescribed Expenditure) (Consolidation and Amendment) Regulations 1987, SI 1987 No. 2186.

[14] See, e.g., HC Debs., vol. 255, col. 1319 (25 July 1985). See further ch. 3, 194.

[15] LGPLA 1980, Pt. VIII, esp. s. 80. Local Government (Prescribed Expenditure) Regulations 1983, SI 1983 No. 296.

their impact, some local authorities also engaged in various forms of *debt re-scheduling*. These arrangements caused particular concern because many were devised not simply in furtherance of efficient debt management but rather with the objective of converting some of the equity locked in assets into income. One method of doing this was by the technique of *lease and leaseback* or *sale and leaseback* of the authority's operational assets. Under this method the authority assigned to a financial institution a leasehold or freehold interest in some of its property portfolio (e.g., the town hall, office buildings, libraries or some of its commercial estate) in return for cash. Since the property was leased back, the authority continued to use the asset and therefore, throughout the period of the arrangement, paid rent to the institution. In effect the authority was receiving an up-front premium in return for rental payments. In some cases these rental payments were commuted into a lump sum which was payable by the authority at the end of the arrangement. The advantage to the authority of this arrangement was that, although money was being borrowed in fact, it did not count as borrowing in law and expenditure controls were therefore circumvented. This method had the additional benefit to the authority that the money which was borrowed by the disposal of capital assets could be used to finance deficits on revenue account. Thus, in 1987 the London Borough of Brent entered into a sale and leaseback deal with Guinness Mahon in respect of its town hall; an arrangement which enabled the authority, which had been rate-capped, to reduce the scale of its required expenditure cuts from an estimated 38 per cent to 20 per cent.[16]

Another method of achieving similar objectives was through *advanced purchase* and *deferred purchase* schemes. The effect of such schemes was, through the use of a financial institution or other intermediary, to transfer expenditure artificially to an earlier or later year than that in which the work was actually undertaken and would normally be paid for. Advanced purchase schemes enabled the authority to maximize the use it made of prescribed expenditure limits in a manner analogous to the use made of special funds in relation to revenue expenditure. Deferred purchase schemes allowed an authority to acquire the use of assets under arrangements in which interest was rolled up for a certain period (typically three years). In effect, the cost of borrowing was being deferred, with the cost being met at some point in the future. Many of the deferred purchase deals struck by local authorities in the mid 1980s concerned very large sums; Hammersmith, Camden, Sheffield and Manchester, for example, were all reported to have negotiated agreements under which they had each borrowed in the region of £100m.[17]

---

[16] HC Debs., vol. 129 cols. 331–2 (9 March 1988).

[17] HC Debs., vol. 111 col. 763 (3 March 1987) (Minister for Local Government). The nature of such schemes may be illustrated by considering the example of Sheffield City Council which had borrowed £100m under a deal in which it was expected to pay back £175m over 7 years. This deal, which was concluded between the City Council, a housing association and the Nationwide Building

While there were others, such as certain schemes which utilized the powers of joint funding of activities to circumvent particular restrictions[18] or to set up arm's length companies to carry through particular projects,[19] those which have been outlined provided the main techniques of the creative accounting game which flourished in local government during the 1980s. It was a game born of the fact that self-regulation seemed no longer to command authority. When one turned to the legal rules, however, it became clear that they had not been devised as instruments of control but had been drafted primarily to provide legal support for the conventional arrangements which had evolved. It was therefore hardly surprising to find that the legal framework provided many opportunities for avoiding the impact of the new control powers acquired by central government.

The Problems of Creative Accounting

The problems posed by the growth in creative accounting practices have been most clearly identified by auditors. In 1987 the Audit Commission noted that there was nothing wrong with creative accounting if it meant simply that local authorities 'take advantage of the opportunities to reduce borrowing costs offered by new types of financial instrument'. Problems arise, however, when these techniques are used essentially as devices 'to evade controls and as an alternative to bringing the budget into balance'.[20] This latter sense of the term, which auditors believed to be increasingly prevalent during the 1980s, was roundly condemned both by the Government[21] and by the audit authorities. Creative accounting in this sense was felt to stand for the 'manipulation of standards' and 'implies inconsistency in the treatment of accounting transactions in order to gain some benefit'.[22] Such practice 'offends one of the basic tenets of accountability, that users should have confidence that financial statements

Society, involved the construction of 2,000 houses, of which 1,200 were to be available for the local authority, 200 for the housing association, and 600 for sale. See A. Stewart, *Planning, Housing and Jobs. The Sheffield Report* (University of Warwick, 1988), 38.

[18] On joint funding with health authorities see: M. Grant, *Rate Capping and the Law* (London, 2nd edn. 1986), 89. In addition, the GLC's Stress Borough Scheme, introduced in 1983/84, made use of the powers in s. 136 of the LGA 1972 and the redistributive potential of its precept to alleviate the impact of targets on certain inner London authorities (see ch. 3, above, 152–3).

[19] These companies were then able to borrow money on the financial markets and such borrowings, although generally underwritten by the local authorities, did not count as local authority borrowing and therefore did not count against their prescribed expenditure total.

[20] Audit Commission, *Annual Report and Accounts, Year ended March 31, 1987* (London, 1987), 13.

[21] *Paying for Local Government*, Cmnd. 9714 (1986), paras. 7.15–25.

[22] Commission for Local Authority Accounts in Scotland (Accounts Commission), *Report and Accounts, 1987* (Edinburgh, 1987), 6.

fairly represent the financial position and performance of the authority in question'.[23] In general, it was considered that there is 'nothing creative in misleading people into believing that painful decisions can be postponed at no cost'.[24]

The extent of use of these practices has varied considerably within local government. In 1986 the Accounts Commission asked the Controller of Audit to report on the use of such practices in Scotland. This investigation led the Commission to conclude that 'it appears that the situation in Scotland does not at present give grounds for as much concern as we had feared'.[25] In England and Wales, the situation seemed, in certain areas at least, much more serious. An Audit Commission report on local government in London, for example, highlighted the case of eight London boroughs which, up to 1987, cumulatively had entered into deferred purchase arrangements amounting to over £550 million.[26] The Commission expressed particular concern over these arrangements because a large part of that sum was acknowledged by the boroughs to be financing revenue expenditure and therefore 'without further creative accounting measures a cash gap of serious proportions is in prospect'.[27] Indeed, from 1987–88 this gap was estimated by the Commission to represent about 30 per cent of the 1985–86 revenue expenditure of this group of London boroughs. With deals of this scale and nature being negotiated it was clear that certain authorities were storing up trouble for the future.

Many of the deals negotiated by London boroughs and metropolitan authorities prior to 1987 were apparently intended to enable them to maintain their expenditure programmes until after the general election of that year. When that election failed to produce a change in government, the gamble seemed to have failed and the costs of creative accounting began to catch up with them. This problem was perhaps most graphically illustrated by the fact that the London Borough of Haringey was required to set a rate for 1989–90 which was 56 per cent higher than the previous year, even after budgeting for rent rises of 60 per cent. The main reason for this massive increase was as a result of £21 million of debt repayments which it was required to make on a number of deferred purchase agreements which had been negotiated during a period in the mid 1980s when it had been rate-capped.[28] Arrangements on the scale entered into by certain authorities had clearly affected the financial viability of those councils.

---

[23] Commission for Local Authority Accounts in Scotland (Accounts Commission), *Report and Accounts, 1987* (Edinburgh, 1987), 3.

[24] Audit Commission, *Review of the First Term and Annual Report and Accounts, Year ended March 31, 1986* (London, 1986), 4.

[25] Accounts Commission, *Report and Accounts 1987*, 6.

[26] Audit Commission Occasional Paper no. 2, *The management of London's authorities: preventing the breakdown of services* (London, 1987).

[27] Ibid., para. 34.

[28] See, 'Curtain up in the town hall', *The Economist*, 8 April 1989, 40. A further reason for Haringey's budgetary crisis was the court ruling that it could not spend capital receipts for revenue purposes: see *Stockdale* v. *Haringey LBC* [1989] RA 107 (see below, 331).

The Legality of Creative Accounting Techniques

Although these various techniques involve pushing the law to its limits, they aim essentially to exploit the ambiguities and uncertainties in the legal rules and do not, in general, cross the borderline into illegality.[29] In fact the courts have generally been careful not to categorize such arrangements in pejorative terms. In *R* v. *Secretary of State for Health and Social Services, ex parte Sheffield City Council*, a case which concerned an attempt by the authority to alter the terms of its tenancy conditions in order to enable tenants to maximize their entitlement to housing benefit, Forbes J stated:

> The background to this case . . . is that we have a cental government of one political persuasion determined to seek to curb local authority spending, and we have local authorities of an opposite political persuasion equally determined to resist that endeavour by central government. In that atmosphere it seems to me unwise to label proposals either of central government or of local authorities with slightly pejorative designations like 'devices' and that sort of thing . . . What to a politician of one political persuasion looks like a device to a politician of the opposite persuasion might be regarded as a perfectly legitimate and indeed wholly laudable manoeuvre. I therefore want as far as possible to avoid being dragged into any suggestion concerned with the labelling of proposals as either devious or laudable. It is no part of the court's business to get dragged into the political arena.[30]

Nevertheless, certain of the more arcane schemes have been declared unlawful. In *Stockdale* v. *Haringey LBC*,[31] for example, the Court of Appeal struck down an attempt by the authority to use moneys paid into its Loans Fund to maintain its expenditure programmes. In 1985/86 Haringey, being rate-capped and already borrowing up to its prescribed expenditure limit, found itself with a shortfall on its programme for repair and maintenance of buildings and highways. It therefore decided to take £7.7m from its Loans Fund to finance this programme. This sum represented the amount paid into the Loans Fund from the accounts of various service committees of the council by way of their annual provision for the repayment of the principal sums of loans previously made. But because these payments were not in fact required for the repayment of loans in that year the council decided to use that amount to bolster that year's expenditure programme. It was this decision which was challenged by the auditor and the Court of Appeal, upholding the Divisional Court, held that the 1972 Act permitted the authority to spend from that account only the amount which had been, or could be raised by borrowing within the permitted limits. The Court of

---

[29] Audit Commission, *The management of London's authorities*, para. 23: 'The moves discussed above [running down financial reserves, capitalization of revenue expenditure and deferred purchase arrangements] did not involve any illegality; but that does not necessarily make them desirable.'
[30] (1986) 18 HLR 6, 12.   [31] [1989] RA 107.

Appeal also held that money paid into a fund under a statutory provision for a particular purpose, in the absence of statutory authority to the contrary, could only be used for that purpose. Since Haringey had no power to spend beyond its prescribed expenditure limit and no power to direct money from the fund to other purposes its decision was unlawful.

Of more general significance is the case of *R* v. *Wirral MBC, ex parte Milstead*.[32] This case involved an attempt by the borough council to factor receipts on council house sales for the years 1989/90 to 1992/93 to a company called Legendbroad. Factoring essentially involves the sale of property in which the right to receive a sum of money at a later date is sold for an amount equivalent to that amount, less a discount representing the value of the use of the money between payment of the purchase price and the receipt of the debt assigned. In this case the council calculated the amount it would receive from council house sales over the relevant period at £10m. Under the factoring arrangement Legendbroad would make an upfront payment to the council of £7.285m. It is difficult to see the benefit of such an arrangement to the council without appreciating some of the technicalities of capital expenditure controls. Local authorities under the regulations were permitted to spend only a certain proportion (20 per cent in the case of council house sales) of capital receipts. But, because of the process of 'cascade', there was an advantage to authorities in having the capital receipt paid earlier rather than later. If an authority obtains capital receipts amounting to £1m in year one, £200,000 is prescribed expenditure for that year. But in the following year 20 per cent of the balance of £800,000 can be taken as prescribed expenditure, and so on. Consequently, as a result of the process of cascade, factoring arrangements of this nature could bring significant benefits to local authorities.

On the auditor's application, however, the Divisional Court struck down this factoring agreement as being *ultra vires*. Wirral argued that the agreement was incidental to the selling of council houses and was therefore authorized by section 111 of the 1972 Act. The Court, however, disagreed: 'If power to sell the proceeds of sale of Council houses to Legendbroad is incidental to the power of sale of the houses, I do not see where the line can be drawn. Why is not investment in a speculative gold mine or on a hoped for Derby winner equally incidental, save only for the sanction of *Wednesbury* unreasonableness?'[33] The Court also held that the payment from Legendbroad was not a 'capital receipt' for the purpose of calculating prescribed expenditure since it was not a sum received by the council in respect of a disposal of land.

This judgment was of general importance because a number of local authorities had considered using factoring arrangements as a means of bolstering their capital expenditure programmes. Thamesdown Borough Council, for example, sought judicial review of its auditor's action in relation to a factoring agreement

---

[32] [1989] RVR 66.　　　[33] Ibid.

which it too had entered into with Legendbroad, but eventually the authority submitted to judgment.[34] Nevertheless, notwithstanding these actions, it seemed quite clear that the great majority of the schemes which were being devised, even those which might appear financially imprudent, did not cross the bounds of legality.

Central Government Action

If these various accounting schemes were to be widely adopted throughout local government, their impact would be such as significantly to undermine the Government's system of expenditure controls. Given the fact that the great majority of the schemes were not unlawful, the Government was obliged to take direct action. The initial response, however, was simply one of exhortation. In February 1987, for example, the Secretary of State informed Parliament that:

> A local authority's debt and its creditworthiness have always been its own responsibility. The Government do not stand behind local authority debt. The great majority of local authorities understand the importance of maintaining their creditworthiness and behave in accordance with the rules of financial good practice.[35]

While this signal was undoubtedly directed primarily to the financial institutions, the audit authorities were also, at this stage, seeking to exhort local authorities into compliance with sound financial practices.[36] It seemed clear, however, that, within the prevailing climate of central–local government relations, exhortation would be unlikely to achieve much. Resort was therefore made to restrictive legislation.

One of the earliest forms of restriction was introduced in the Rate Support Grants Act 1986. As a result of a number of highly technical changes to the block grant distribution system in the 1986 Act,[37] the Government prevented local authorities seeking to maximize their grant entitlement in any year by a method which enabled authorities, at the end of the year, to transfer the difference representing the shortfall between outturn expenditure and target into a *special fund*. Later that year the Government also effectively closed off the possibility of a local authority generating *additional capital receipts* by the device of selling its interest as mortgagee. This was achieved by section 7 of the Local Government Act 1986, which required any local authority proposing to dispose of its mortgagee interest to obtain the prior written consent of the mortgagor.

---

[34] See *R* v. *Arthur Young, ex parte Thamesdown BC*, QBD, 15 February 1989 (unreported).
[35] HC Debs., vol. 110 col. 743w (19 February 1987).
[36] See, e.g., Accounts Commission, *Report and Accounts 1988*, 25.
[37] Rate Support Grants Act 1986, Sched. 1.

The most important changes, however, came in 1987 and 1988. In July 1986 the Secretary of State for the Environment announced that legislation would be introduced to outlaw *advanced and deferred purchase schemes*.[38] This objective was achieved in the Local Government Act 1987 which inserted new sections 80A and 80B into the 1980 Act, the effect of which was to treat capital expenditure as being incurred by an authority in the year in which the works are carried out, regardless of when payments are actually made. This enactment was followed by a second measure, announced by the Secretary of State on 9 March 1988, which imposed new restrictions on three forms of creative accounting: *medium term leases, barter,* and *lease and leaseback* or *sale and leaseback.* When the 1986 announcement was made, it had been preceded by a period of consultation, with the result that an estimated £2 billion worth of deals had been rushed through before the proposal was able to take effect.[39] In order to avoid a similar occurrence in relation to leasing and bartering schemes, those restrictions took effect, without consultation, from the day of announcement. The restrictions were thus implemented by way of amendments to the prescribed expenditure regulations[40] and were intended to be made permanent after subsequent consultations. The 1988 restrictions were later made permanent by the Local Government Finance Act 1988.[41]

The Government's aim in taking this action was to prevent local authorities using what were considered to be 'artifical' devices to incur expenditure above the levels permitted to them under the capital control system. The problem was that the Government's strategy, both in using its existing powers[42] and acquiring new powers,[43] was taking it in both a highly centralist and ultimately unworkable direction. As the Audit Commission commented: 'The general picture . . . is of loopholes being identified and exploited until blocked by fresh controls;

---

[38] HC Debs., vol. 102 col. 183 (22 July 1986).

[39] HC Debs., vol. 129 col. 326 (9 March 1988).

[40] SI 1988 no. 434, amending the Local Government (Prescribed Expenditure) (Consolidation and Amendment) Regulations 1987 (SI 1987 no. 2186).

[41] LGFA 1988, ss. 130–2, which amended the 1980 Act mainly by inserting a new s. 79A. The effects of these restrictions were essentially that (1) assets acquired by barter would score as prescribed expenditure on the basis that assets were being acquired freehold and for cash and (2) the period of leasing which escaped capital expenditure rules was reduced from 20 years to 3 years. The effect of the latter provision was not only to eliminate many of the leasing advantages (since local authorities will be required to enter into shorter and more expensive leases) but it also made lease and leaseback arrangements much less attractive.

[42] The Secretary of State was empowered to issue a direction to an authority which he believed to be exceeding its prescribed expenditure limit, the effect of which was to prevent the authority from taking on any new contractual commitments without Ministerial approval: LGPLA 1980, s. 78. Such a direction was issued to three London borough councils in January 1989: see *The Economist,* 8 April 1989, 40.

[43] In addition to the restrictions outlined above, new powers were given to auditors to enable them to issue a 'prohibition order' and to apply for judicial review of any decision which might have an effect on the authority's accounts: see LGA 1988, s. 30; Sched. 4 (inserting new sections 25A-D into Local Government Finance Act 1982). The prohibition order does not appear yet to have been used; the *Wirral* case (above, n. 32) was the first case initiated by the auditor under the s. 25D power.

after which the emphasis moves on to identifying fresh loopholes.'[44] It was thus generally recognized that the solution did not lie in further rules to block the loopholes through which creative accounting operated since this was likely to lead only to ever more complex and convoluted schemes. What ultimately was needed was the restoration of order in the system.

By 1988 the Government appeared to recognize that an entirely new system of capital expenditure controls was required. This goes some way towards providing an explanation for the Ministerial statement of 9 March 1988. That announcement, without warning and despite being ostensibly aimed at a small group of 'irresponsible' authorities, had the effect of eliminating virtually all the 'off balance sheet' transactions available to local government. The sheer breadth of the restrictions imposed by that announcement caught local authorities by surprise, particularly because the great majority of the transactions affected made financial sense for local authorities and did not in any way jeopardize their financial stability. By adopting such an all-encompassing restriction, however, the Government was thus able to freeze the market. This then provided the Government with the breathing space it needed to be able to devise and introduce a new system of capital controls.

On 7 July 1988 the Secretary of State was able to announce that the existing system was to be abandoned[45] and, after issuing a Consultation Paper,[46] a new system was enacted in Part IV of the Local Government and Housing Act 1989. This new regime, which took effect on 1 April 1990, repealed both the controls over borrowing in the 1972 Act and the system of capital expenditure control in the 1980 Act and replaced them with a new system of credit controls which operated within a much more precise definition of capital expenditure. At the same time, the Government also took action to establish a much more restrictive regime relating to local authority interests in companies[47] and established, in particular, that the activities of companies that are either controlled or influenced by local authorities are to be treated as those of the authority for the purpose of the capital control system introduced in the 1989 Act.[48]

The establishment of this new system marked the end of the creative accounting industry of the 1980s. However, since complex control systems must inevitably depend to some extent on self-regulatory structures, the 1990 Act system provided a necessary but not sufficient condition for the restoration of stability. This was implictly recognized by CIPFA which, in the late 1980s, established a steering group (including the Audit Commission, the local authority associations and the Department of the Environment) with the aim of developing a modern system of capital accounting to be introduced in the 1990s. As the Audit Commission commented: 'A key feature [of the proposed new system] is the

[44] Audit Commission, *Report and Accounts, Year ended 31 March 1988*, para. 29.
[45] HC Debs., vol. 136 col. 1199 (7 July 1988).
[46] Department of the Environment, *Capital Expenditure and Finance* (London, 1988).
[47] Local Government and Housing Act 1989, Pt. V.   [48] Ibid., ss. 39(5), 70.

move away from dependence on law and statute to determine the accounting treatment of transactions and towards an approach based more on common sense and economic substance. Only in this way will the proliferation of creative accounting devices be halted.'[49]

Local Government and the Banks

If the Government had felt that, by 1988, it had got the problem under control it was to be sorely mistaken. At precisely the moment at which the Government was introducing a new capital control system designed to eradicate the problems caused by the use of creative accounting techniques, new dimensions to the trend of innovative financing in local government were being revealed. These practices generally concerned the relationship between local authorities and the banks. Traditionally, the local government sector has obtained much of the capital finance for its projects through the Public Works Loan Board (PWLB), which offers loans at favourable rates. There is, however, no obligation on local authorities to use the PWLB for their borrowing requirements and during the 1980s the majority of local government loans were raised in the City. In the context of the financial revolution of the 1980s, there were undoubtedly competitive deals to be struck. But these deals carried particular risks; and towards the end of the decade some of these risks appeared to be materializing.

One highly dramatic event which had a major impact on certain local authorities concerned the decision of the Bank of England in July 1991 to wind up the Bank of Credit and Commerce International (BCCI) because of widespread fraud within the bank. At the time of the closure, BCCI had assets of $1.6 billion but worldwide liabilities of $10.64 billion, including £3.25 billion owing to British depositors. This group of British depositors included 30 British local authorities which had deposited a total of £82 million with the bank. Of these, however, one authority, the Western Isles Island Council, had lost £24 million.[50] Furthermore, of this sum, £17 million had been borrowed by the Council from City institutions in advance of need, without statutory authority and for the purpose of being re-deposited with BCCI at a higher rate of interest. The loss, which was entirely unexpected[51] and which accounted for almost half of the Council's budget, was primarily attributable to the entrepreneurial activities of the Council's treasurers.[52] This loss has had a profound impact on the Council,

---

[49] Audit Commission, *Report and Accounts. Year ended 31 March 1988*, para. 22.

[50] See Second Report of the Treasury and Civil Service Committee (TCSC), Session 1991–92, *Banking Supervision and BCCI: The Role of Local Authorities and Money Brokers*, HC 26.

[51] The council actually deposited an additional £1.5m with BCCI only 15 minutes before the bank was closed: see Memorandum of Western Isles Island Council, TCSC Report, Appx. 7, 126.

[52] The question of how this occurred was the subject of a private report to the council by Professor Alan Alexander and a report from the Controller of Audit to the Accounts Commission under s. 102(3) of the Local Government (Scotland) Act 1973: see TCSC Report (above, n. 50), vii.

which was obliged to obtain a 30 year loan sanction for £24m, adding an estimated £3m a year to its costs[53] and requiring an almost fivefold increase in the poll tax between 1991/92 and 1992/93 (from £26 to £122) and major cuts in services.[54]

Of more general significance was that of the arrangements made by local authorities in establishing companies for the purpose of avoiding capital control limits. These companies were generally established to undertake particular projects. They obtained the finance needed for such schemes from the banks, with the local authority acting as guarantors of these loans. When some of the projects failed, however, the legal problems began to surface. The leading case is that of *Credit Suisse* v. *Allerdale BC*.[55] In this case the council set up a company to undertake a leisure development scheme in Keswick. The company borrowed money from the bank, and these debts were guaranteed by the authority. The scheme proved to be unsuccessful and eventually the company went into liquidation. When the company called in the credit guarantee, however, the council argued that, since the project was *ultra vires* the council, the guarantee was void and unenforceable. When the bank took legal action to enforce the guarantee and recover £6 million in loans made to the company, the High Court dismissed the claim and upheld the council's argument that, since the guarantee had been made for an improper purpose, it was unlawful. This decision created a great deal of uncertainty in the financial markets. As other schemes failed, further litigation followed, not all of which seemed entirely consistent with the *Allerdale* judgment.[56]

These legal uncertainties compounded the problems of those local authorities which had entered into deferred purchase arrangements during the mid 1980s. During 1995 many of these deals were coming to term and many local authorities were seeking to refinance their loans. Because of the uncertainties generated by the *Allerdale* judgment, and in particular the speculation that all off-balance sheet transactions designed to circumvent the capital control system might be unlawful, the authorities experienced great difficulties in doing so.[57] The best

---

[53] TCSC Report (above, n. 50), xxvii.

[54] See S.J. Bailey and S. Galloway, 'Financial Crisis in the Western Isles' (1993) vol. 19 no. 2 *Local Government Studies* 149.

[55] (1995) 1 Lloyd's Rep. 315.

[56] See, e.g., *Credit Suisse* v. *Waltham Forest LBC*, *The Times*, 2 November 1994 (bank successfully sued under a local authority guarantee after a joint venture company established by the council and a private body to provide housing accommodation for the homeless went into liquidation). Cf. *Morgan Grenfell & Co.* v. *Sutton LBC*, *The Times*, 23 March 1995 (local authority loan guarantee on behalf of an unregistered housing assocation was *ultra vires* because the Housing Associations Act 1985 empowered local authorities only to loan to registered associations).

[57] See, 'Allerdale to disarm the loan arrangers', *Local Government Chronicle*, 5 May 1995: 'The legal uncertainty means councils are unable to refinance an estimated £1 billion of deferred purchase loans – most of which are due before the end of 1996. At least one council has already bitten the bullet and repaid a loan, forcing it to shelve a large proportion of its capital allocation.' See further, E. Dimbylow, 'No closer on Allerdale', *Local Government Chronicle*, 16 June 1995.

hope for both local authorities and the banks lay in an Appeal Court judgment which would provide a clear and authoritative framework. However, although *Allerdale* had been scheduled for appeal hearing in the autumn of 1995, it was by no means certain that the appeal would proceed.[58] In the interim, there was considerable uncertainty in the financial markets.

Perhaps the most dramatic events of all, however, concerned local authority involvement in the swaps market. Before examining the problems which have arisen in this sector, the nature of this market must briefly be explained. In many respects the swaps market stood as a symbol of the financial revolution of the 1980s. This market, which did not exist at the start of the decade and which was born as an offshoot of the Eurobond market, was by the end of the decade the fastest growing sector of the international capital markets which far outstripped the scale of the Eurobond market. The child thus came to dwarf the parent.

Most of the market (around 80–85 per cent) comprises interest rate swaps.[59] The principle of the interest rate swap (IRS) is straightforward. Two borrowers enter into an agreement to exchange interest rate payments on their debts. Party A has debt at a floating rate of interest. He believes that interest rates are about to rise and therefore would like it fixed at the current market rate. Party B (known as the counterparty) is someone with fixed-rate debt who thinks that interest rates are about to fall. She would therefore prefer to have a floating rate debt. The swaps market facilitates the exchange of risk on these debts. Party A, with floating rate debt, pays fixed rate payments to his counterparty; in exchange Party B pays him at the floating rate.[60]

The primary advantage of the IRS is that it enables a commercial undertaking to reduce its exposure to risk. But the swaps market has grown so rapidly not only because it provides a useful facility for actively managing debt but also because of its inherent flexibility. Thus, for example, more complicated swap structures can be devised which enable the swaps market to be used not only for debt management but also for tax planning or even for speculation. In addition to being used for a range of purposes, the swap principle can be applied to a variety of objects. Alongside the IRS a market has developed for currency swaps and even commodity swaps. The currency swap operates on similar principles to the IRS, albeit with currency rather than interest rates. It enables companies with multi-currency cash stocks which they may need at various times in the future to utilize a swaps market to maximize their yield. Commodity swaps are

---

[58] The main problem concerned the legal costs of the action. See, 'doubts on Allerdale fuels City loan fear', *Local Government Chronicle*, 9 June 1995: 'Credit Suisse would not reveal how much the case had cost so far, but Allerdale has already spent over £650,000. The complex nature of the High Court ruling means that it could take up to 20 days to be heard and the cost for the bank could be as high as £500,000. There is a good chance the case would have to go to the House of Lords, adding to the cost.' The case was eventually listed for hearing in February 1996.

[59] *Euromoney*, October 1988, 36.

[60] In practice, the parties, rather than paying the sums they have agreed to, will make a settlement on a net payment basis on fixed dates.

less common; they are mainly used by oil producers and consumers which are exposed to future commodity prices.[61]

The swaps market has also devised a number of instruments for reducing or increasing the extent of the risk to which the parties may be exposed in the swap transaction. One form is that of caps, floors and collars which hedge the swap so that payments between the parties are not exchanged until interest rates rise (caps) or fall (floors) or either rise or fall (collars) above or below specified rates. But the most important development in the swaps market has been the incorporation of options into swap structures; these are called swap options or (in the business) 'swaptions'. The swap option is an option to enter into a swap on agreed terms either at a future date or over a specified period. With the swap option the counterparty will pay an option fee upfront in exchange for a right to enter a future swap on what it expects will be favourable terms. Swap options, however, are more controversial. As one financial analyst commented: 'I would not mention swaptions in the same breath as swaps, caps and floors. The latter are hedging instruments; swaptions are primarily arbitraging tools.'[62]

The flexibility provided by the swaps market has certainly been an important factor in the rapid growth of the market and has undoubtedly attracted speculators. That is, the market is being used not only for the purpose of hedging debt portfolios but also enhancing profit opportunities. This is because a swap is itself a self-contained transaction which neither assumes a pre-existing contract nor affects any obligations under any existing contract; it is essentially the purchase of an income.

Local Authorities and the Swaps Market

Local authorities have for many years been actively using money market tools to manage the interest risks on their debt portfolios. When the swaps market emerged during the 1980s, local authorities recognized the opportunities it presented and became one of the largest and most active types of players in the UK swaps market; it has been estimated, for example, that in the 1980s they accounted for around one third of all sterling-based swaps business.[63] Probably the most common transaction in which they were involved was to use swaps to turn a portion of fixed-rate loans from the Public Works Loan Board into floating rate debt. Initial assessments indicated that just under 100 British local authorities had used swaps,[64] although subsequently it was estimated that 130 authorities

---

[61] See, *Euromoney. Supplement on Risk Mangement*, April 1989, 31.

[62] L. Lynn, Vice-President, Citicorp, New York, quoted in *Euromoney Supplement on Risk Management*, 43.

[63] *The Economist*, 18 March 1989, 128.

[64] An Audit Commission survey in 1989 indicated that 78 local authorities in England and Wales had been involved in the swaps market: see [1990] 2 WLR 1038, 1067. In addition, a number of Scottish authorities were known to have negotiated swaps deals, although the precise number was unknown.

had been dealing in the swaps market.[65] Swaps were viewed as a device which enabled local authorities to retain flexibility in the management of their borrowings[66] and potentially to save money by reducing the cost of borrowing. However, because of the flexibility of the market, swaps could be viewed, not only as a means of protection against movements in interest rates, but also as an innovative route round the complex rules that limit local government's borrowing power and hence as an aspect of creative accounting. The swaps market might even be seen as an opportunity for local authorities to generate extra income by speculating on interest rate movements.

Some insight into the nature of local authority involvement in the swaps market may be gleaned from examining the profile of swaps entered into by Westminster City Council in the period 1983–89. As Figure 1 shows, Westminster entered into nine transactions in two spurts of activity (1983/84 and 1988/89) involving principal sums of between £5m and £30m. On the face of things, these transactions seemed to be part of the general strategy of the authority to manage its debt efficiently.

During the late 1980s, however, evidence began to emerge which suggested that certain local authorities, under the pressure of grant penalties and rate-capping, were seeking to use the swaps market as a means of generating additional income. Once again, London authorities were at the forefront of this group. In 1987, for example, the London Borough of Haringey's financial dealings were the subject of a statutory report in the public interest[67]. This report, in addition to dealing with lease and leaseback deals and deferred purchase schemes, also covered the use of interest rate swaps. The auditor highlighted two swap transactions which Haringey had entered into in 1987 for periods of nine and five years, in each of which fixed rates were being swapped for floating. These two swaps involved an aggregate principal of £180m, nearly 40 per cent of the council's total loan debt. What was unusual about these transactions was that the authority not only took on an obligation to pay the floating rate but also exchanged its entitlement to receive fixed rates from its counterparty at 9.14 per cent for a package of an entitlement of 5.57 per cent (i.e., almost half the fixed rate) together with a front-end premium of £30m. That is, it converted an income stream of £44m into an up-front payment of £30m. This payment was then

---

[65] See *Financial Times*, 8 May 1991. These figures were obtained as a result of a British survey conducted by the Chartered Institute for Public Finance and Accountancy (CIPFA). See also: Memorandum of Bank of England, 'Local Authority Swaps' in Second Report of the Treasury and Civil Service Committee, Session 1990–91, *The 1991 Budget*, HC 289. Minutes of Evidence, 15 at 16.

[66] In 1978, after the Treasury expressed concern about the shortening maturity of local authority debt, local authorities drafted a voluntary code of practice setting out guidelines for maintaining long term borrowing: see N.P. Hepworth, *The Finance of Local Government* (London, rev. 6th edn., 1988), 150–2, 327; W.B. Taylor, 'Borrowing by local authorities in the UK', *Nat.West Bank Q. Rev* August, 1983, at 60. Swaps enable local authorities formally to keep to these guidelines, since they do not count as borrowing.

[67] *Haringey LBC, Audit of Accounts 1985–6, Statutory Report* (14 April 1987). This report was prepared by the auditor under s. 15(3) of the Local Government Finance Act 1982.

Fig. 1 Westminster City Council's Swaps Transactions 1983–89.

Date	Agreement with	Amount (million)	Period (years)	Terms	Comments
Feb 15, 1983	Lloyds & Scottish	£5	2	WCC pays L&S Libor L&S pays WCC 11.4375%	Net gain to WCC of £76,941
Aug 25, 1983	UDT	£5	5	WCC pays UDT Libor UDT pays WCC 11.8125%	Net gain to WCC of £244,715
Oct 17, 1983	Nordic Bank	£5	5	WCC pays N Libor N pays WCC 10.75%	Net gain to WCC of £47,231
Dec 1, 1983	Hambros Bank	£5	5	WCC pays H Libor H pays WCC 11%	Net gain to WCC of £36,605
Apr 3, 1984	Kleinwort Benson	£10	5	WCC pays KB 10.75% KB pays WCC Libor	Net loss to WCC of £11,721
Jul 8, 1988	American Insurance Group	£30	15	WCC pays AIG Libor AIG pays WCC 10.01%	–
Jul 8, 1988	American Insurance Group	£30	5	WCC pays AIG 9.11% AIG pays WCC Libor	Two AIG swaps linked
Sep 23, 1988	Barclays Bank	£10	5	WCC pays B Libor B pays WCC 10.85%	Linked to swap with Manufacturers Hanover
Mar 23, 1989	Manufacturers Hanover	£10	4.5	WCC pays MH 10.8% MH pays WCC Libor	Linked to swap with Barclays

WCC = Westminster City Council

Source: *Euromoney Corporate Finance April 1989*, 15

to be credited to the loans pool interest account with the result that the loans pool interest rate (the rate charged on outstanding loans to services) was substantially reduced and a balance of £18m could be used to meet revenue expenditure. The auditor was concerned about the legality of these arrangements and urged the council to review their decisions on these transactions. However, after obtaining counsel's opinion, Haringey reconsidered its decision but arrived at the same conclusion and the auditor refrained from taking further action pending clarification of the question of the legality of a local authority's use of swaps.

As the Westminster profile illustrates, many of the early forays of local authorities in the swaps market were advantageous. As interest rates began to rise in the late 1980s, however, the pressures on local authorities increased and, since many were swapping fixed for floating rates, profits on the transactions started to turn into losses. At this stage, the Audit Commission began to take a more active interest and, although the Commission's solicitor issued an opinion in July 1987 to the effect that swaps which were part of the normal process of debt management were lawful, the Commission also expressed doubts about the legality of certain transactions. The Commission's initial target was those authorities which had acted as intermediaries for others in swap transactions. On 13 August 1987 the Commission issued a statement suggesting that, while interest rate swaps were a legitimate tool of debt management, local authorities which acted as intermediaries in swap transactions were acting beyond their powers.[68] The Commission's objection was that, since intermediary authorities were not managing their own debt, they could not be said to be facilitating the discharge of their functions.[69]

Since a number of local authorities questioned this interpretation, the Audit Commission sought counsel's opinion. In a comprehensive joint opinion in June 1988 Roger Henderson QC and John Howell came to the conclusion that local authorities had no power to enter into swaps transactions. This opinion, however, revealed one issue on which counsel were unable to agree; that of interest rate swaps which constitute 'parallel contracts'. Such swaps are so-called when they are arranged: in parallel to an existing borrowing debt; where the notional principal of the swap is no more than the total of outstanding debt; and where the expected profit from the swap is to be used to reduce interest rate variation risks imposed on that authority by its previous borrowing. On this issue, Mr Henderson considered that, provided the purpose of the transaction is the prudent management of the authority's loan portfolio, the contract could be justified as being 'conducive or incidental to the discharge of . . . their [borrowing] functions'.[70] Mr Howell, however, felt that, since parallel contracts did not form a

[68] The reason why an authority acts as an intermediary is generally to enable a relatively creditworthy local authority to be positioned between the ultimate swapping party and the counterparty, in return for which the intermediary takes a small payment.
[69] Audit Commission, *News Release*, 13 August 1987.
[70] I.e., in accordance with Local Government Act 1972, s. 111.

special category of swaps, they also were unlawful. Further, he argued that, since borrowing is not a function of the authority but simply an ancillary power to enable the authority to exercise its functions, a swap could not be viewed as being incidental to the exercise of a local authority's functions.[71] Other than for this disagreement, however, counsel's opinion suggested that local authorities had no powers to engage in swaps transactions. In July 1988 the Audit Commission issued a general statement to that effect, stating explicitly that swap options had no statutory backing and concluding that where the swaps transaction 'is designed to generate income or profit and has no relation to the structure of the authority's own debt, auditors may challenge income received or expenditure incurred as items of account contrary to law'.[72]

On 27 July 1988, after receiving counsel's opinions from the Audit Commission, Anthony Hazell of Deloitte Haskins & Sells, the auditor for the London Borough of Hammersmith and Fulham, informed the council that, owing to the scale and nature of its operations, some or all of its swaps transactions may have been entered into unlawfully. Hammersmith first became involved in swaps in 1983, while it was under Conservative control, but its trading operations had substantially increased after 1987 (when under Labour control) and, in addition to IRS, it had bought and written swap options, gilt options and interest rate caps, floors and collars and had acted as intermediary in swap transactions with other councils. Though at this stage matters were unclear, it was later revealed that Hammersmith had entered into a total of 592 transactions, mainly between 1987/88 and 1988/89, with a total notional value of over £6 billion.[73] That is, the council had been dealing in the swaps market in notional sums which cumulatively amounted to a figure which was nearly 20 times its total debt and was more than 100 times its annual turnover.[74] In July 1988, at the height of its trading activity, Hammersmith had 0.5 per cent of the *world's* swaps market.[75]

On 1 August 1988 the council's Director of Finance informed the auditors that he was suspending all swaps transactions but that he would continue to manage existing swaps as part of an interim strategy designed to reduce the council's exposure to loss. During the period in which Hammersmith pursued this strategy the council sought leading counsel's opinion on the legality of their transactions. The advice of Anthony Scrivener QC was to the effect that swaps were lawful provided they were part of a strategy of interest risk management

---

[71] The argument which formed the basis of this disagreement was elaborated upon by counsel in two separate opinions (by John Howell on 21 June 1988 and Roger Henderson QC on 8 July 1988) which followed the delivery of the joint opinion.

[72] Audit Commission, *News Release*, 14 July 1988.   [73] [1990] 2 WLR 17, 53 (Appendix B).

[74] It should nevertheless be recognized that the notional principal sum can be a misleading figure since at any one time the figure is likely to be less than that aggregate because certain transactions will have lapsed or been settled. Also, if an authority enters into a swap option and subsequently enters into another transaction to hedge its exposure on that option, while the risk to the authority may have been reduced, the notional principal sum of its swap transactions will have increased.

[75] *The Independent*, 2 November 1989.

but that, if the objective was to trade for profit, the transactions were *ultra vires*.[76] This opinion did not, however, provide advice to the council about the legality of its interim strategy. On 23 February 1989 the auditor produced a statutory report in the public interest on Hammersmith's transactions and informed the council that it should desist from any further activity unless supported by legal opinion. At this stage Hammersmith approached the Secretary of State for the Environment and sought his sanction to make £2.3m in payments (and £650,000 in receipts) that the council should have made and received on swaps.[77] On 28 February the Secretary of State refused to grant his sanction and Hammersmith accordingly suspended all its swaps market activities. At this stage the council still had in existence 297 deals, involving a notional principal sum of nearly £3 billion.[78]

After February 1989, all local authorities gradually followed Hammersmith's example and suspended their swaps market activities. Since this would be likely to place the authorities in default on their transactions, they tended to set aside in special accounts the cash equivalent plus interest of any outstanding swap settlement payments, so that the sums could eventually be passed to counterparties once the legal position had been clarified. In March 1989 representatives of 70 banks and other financial institutions, the main counterparties of local authorities, met and established a Steering Group to co-ordinate action.[79] The banks then decided to initiate legal proceedings against any local authorities which defaulted on interest-rate swap payments and writs were subsequently issued against a number of local authorities, including Ogwr DC, Harlow DC and Blackburn DC.[80]

On 30 May, however, the auditor applied to the Divisional Court under section 19 of the Local Government Finance Act 1982 seeking a declaration that items of account in Hammersmith's Capital Market Fund were contrary to law. As a result of this application, the banks decided not to proceed with their writs against local authorities pending the outcome of the auditor's action against Hammersmith.

The Hammersmith Litigation

Over the years up to 1989 Hammersmith had received £37m in premiums from swaps and options products. These profits had accrued mainly in the early period,

---

[76] See [1990] 2 WLR 17 at 27.

[77] *The Economist*, 18 March 1989. Under the Local Government Finance Act 1982, s. 19 the Secretary of State is given powers to sanction payments which would otherwise be unlawful.

[78] [1990] 2 WLR 17, 53 (Appendix B).

[79] *Euromoney Corporate Finance*, May 1989 at 20. The banks were also invited to sign a memorandum of agreement under which all out of pocket expenses, including legal fees, were to be borne equally by all the participating institutions.

[80] See *Financial Times*, 25 April 1989, 28 June 1989, 16 July 1989.

however, and with the rise in interest rates in the late 1980s Hammersmith's portfolio exposed the authority to significant losses. By February 1989, when it ceased operations, only £12.5m remained in the council's Capital Markets Fund, as £24.5m had been spent on settling payments for deals in which the authority owed money.[81] At the close of operations Phillips & Drew, the council's financial advisers, calculated that if Hammersmith's portfolio were allowed to run as it stood it would result in a loss of £13m, thereby eliminating any previous profit in its Capital Markets Fund. But that assumed that interest rates matched the forecasts in February; if the forecasts were 1 per cent out either way the council would either reap profits of £90m or incur losses of £118m.[82] In fact, interest rates rose sharply after February 1989 and in November 1989 it had been estimated that Hammersmith's portfolio had a negative value of around £200m.[83]

Once the council had realized the financial position with respect to its Capital Markets Fund, it was obviously in Hammersmith's own best interests to accept the auditor's argument that all of its transactions between 1987 and 1989 were unlawful. A judicial declaration could not simply be entered, however, without potentially jeopardizing the interests of two groups. First, there were the interests of other local authorities, the vast majority of whom had each entered into only a few swap transactions for debt management purposes,[84] and whose interests might significantly diverge from those of Hammersmith. Take, for example, the case of Glasgow DC which in November 1989 had 11 active swaps transactions involving a notional principal of £140m, a sum which represented less than 10 per cent of the council's outstanding debt. Those transactions had, to that date, saved the authority £3.8m in interest costs and, because they generally (and perhaps unusually) involved the swapping of floating for fixed rates, while the high interest rates continued the savings to the authority were estimated to be increasing at an annual rate of £3.4m.[85] Clearly, the interests of all authorities on the legality of swaps transactions were far from identical. Secondly, we should consider the interests of the counterparties, who were particularly concerned that, if items of account were declared contrary to law and an order made for rectification of the accounts, their private rights to enforce outstanding contracts might be prejudiced. In order to protect their commercial interests, then, five of the banks were joined as respondents to the action.[86]

---

[81] *Euromoney Corporate Finance*, May 1989, at 20.

[82] *Euromoney Corporate Finance*, April 1989 at 14.

[83] *The Independent*, 2 November 1989.

[84] The Audit Commission estimate in 1989 suggested that of the 77 other authorities in England and Wales then known to have engaged in swaps, 59 had entered into fewer than five deals and only 10 authorities had entered into more than 10 deals: [1990] 2 WLR 1038, 1067.

[85] Report by Director of Finance, City of Glasgow DC, *Loan Swaps in the aftermath of the Hammersmith & Fulham decision*, 8 November 1989.

[86] Cf. *Re Hurle-Hobbs* [1944] 2 All ER 261 in which the Court of Appeal had held that a contractor was not entitled to be represented on an appeal against disallowance of local authority expenditure on sums paid to him on the ground that his legal rights were not affected by the disallowance.

The legal issues

In *Hazell* v. *Hammersmith and Fulham LBC*,[87] the courts were asked to address three main legal issues. The first issue was whether the transactions entered into by Hammersmith were capable of being within the powers conferred on local authorities by Parliament; this we may call the issue of *power*. Secondly, whether, even if the powers existed, Hammersmith's activities constituted a proper exercise of those powers; the issue of *purpose*. And, thirdly, there arose a question of *restitution*: if Hammersmith's actions were declared unlawful, should the courts order that all payments be restored to the payers? In order to simplify the proceedings, the Divisional Court ordered that this third issue be deferred.[88] The action thus focused on the legality of swaps transactions.

On this question of legality it is possible to identify three basic positions: (1) that local authorities lack the *power* to enter into any form of swap transaction (the Howell view)[89]; (2) that, while local authorities possess the basic power, swap transactions may be entered into only for certain *purposes*: either (a) transactions which constitute 'parallel contracts' (the Henderson view)[90] or (b) for the purpose of interest rate risk management (the Scrivener view);[91] and (3) that local authorities may enter into swap transactions even when their purpose is to trade for a profit. Since the consensus of legal opinion was that position (3) was untenable,[92] the issue came to be polarized between (1) and (2); and since Mr Howell represented the auditor in this action and Mr Scrivener appeared for Hammersmith, the issue specifically focused on their competing views.[93]

Local authorities possess no express powers to enter into swaps transactions, which is hardly surprising since the basic statutory provisions on finance are contained in the Local Government Act 1972, a measure enacted at a time when the swaps market did not even exist. Furthermore, swaps transactions do not seem to involve borrowing by the authority.[94] If, then, these transactions are lawful they must fall within a local authority's discretionary powers. The key

---

[87] [1990] 2 WLR 17 (Div.Ct.); [1990] 2 WLR 1038 (CA); [1991] 2 WLR 372 (HL).

[88] [1990] 2 WLR 17 at 29.   [89] Above, pp. 342–3.

[90] Above, p. 342.   [91] Above, pp. 343–4.

[92] See, e.g., *London County Council* v. *Attorney-General* [1902] AC 165; *Attorney-General* v. *Fulham Corporation* [1921] 1 Ch. 440; *Attorney-General* v. *Smethwick Corporation* [1932] 1 Ch. 562.

[93] There was also an intellectual reason for absorbing the parallel contracts position into the more general risk management position. There is, for example, considerable uncertainty about the meaning of the parallel contracts position. Does it refer to a single loan or can it be applied to a group or pool of loans? If the former, it would seem simply to be a technical requirement. If the latter, it seems to collapse into the interest rate risk management position.

[94] Swaps do not fall within any of the specific categories of instrument by which an authority has authority to borrow (LGA 1972, Sched. 11) and if a proposed borrowing does not fall within one of the fund-raising methods permitted under the Act, Treasury approval must be obtained. Consents, however, had never been sought in respect of swaps. This is not surprising since, although the payment which a local authority received under a swap is calculated by reference to a notional sum, that principal is never borrowed or received by the authority.

provision is section 111 of the 1972 Act, which seeks to modify a strict application of the *ultra vires* doctrine to local authorities by empowering an authority 'to do anything . . . which is calculated to facilitate, or is conducive or incidental to, the discharge of any of their functions'. Since section 111(3) specifically states that 'a local authority shall not by virtue of this section raise money . . .' it seems clear that swaps transactions for the purpose of income generation do not fall within the authority conferred by section 111. But could swap transactions for the purpose of debt management fall within the confines of section 111?

The Howell view was that, for two main reasons, they could not. The first reason was that, being an independent transaction, the swap must intrinsically be viewed as a means to purchase an income; consequently, all such transactions were concerned with income generation. Secondly, it was argued that, since borrowing is not itself a function of a local authority,[95] swaps designed to manage its debt portfolio cannot be regarded as being incidental to a local authority function. The Scrivener view, by contrast, was based on the fact that local authorities have powers of borrowing and investment and an attendant duty to take reasonable care to manage their investments and borrowings prudently. Accordingly, it would be proper for a local authority to take the best advantage from the volatility of interest rates by repaying an existing loan and substituting it for a replacement loan on different terms. Since swaps are instruments which enable the same result to be achieved, but can achieve that objective more cheaply, simply and speedily, the use of swaps for the purpose of interest rate risk management should fairly be regarded as being incidental to or consequential upon a local authority's powers of borrowing and investment. These contrasting opinions set the basic parameters within which the courts considered the issue.

The Divisional Court

The auditor's application was heard by the Divisional Court over eleven days in October 1989 and on 1 November the Court issued its judgment.[96] The Court, following the Howell view, held that a local authority had no statutory authority to enter into swaps transactions and thus held that all 592 transactions entered into by Hammersmith between 1987 and 1989 were *ultra vires* the council. Although borrowing and investing were recognized to be functions of a local authority, the court held that swaps transactions lacked the necessary degree of nexus to be categorized as being incidental to those functions. Swaps transactions were capable only of being 'incidental to the incidental': since it is an incident of borrowing that one pays interest, swapping interest payments was viewed as being incidental to the incidental.[97] But could not 'debt management' or 'interest rate risk management' be viewed as a function of a local authority?

[95] Cf. *Re Westminster LBC* [1986] AC 668, 714 (per Lord Oliver): 'expenditure of money is not in itself a function of the authority'.
[96] [1990] 2 WLR 17.   [97] Ibid., 36–7.

On this issue the Court held that, viewing the structure of the 1972 Act as a whole, it would be to subvert the financial integrity of the Act to construe these activities as local authority functions because, although Schedule 13 expressly authorized debt restructuring, that power was narrowly confined. Consequently, although the Court felt that 'properly controlled activities of this nature could provide a useful tool . . . to the council' it was held that it was 'not for the court to confer powers on the Council which the language of section 111 does not confer'.[98]

Having disposed of the issue on the question of power, it was unnecessary to deal with the second question; the issue of purpose. Nevertheless, the Court did also give its opinion on the question of whether, if local authorities possessed such powers, Hammersmith had properly exercised them. On this issue the Court concluded: that there had been no proper delegation of the authority's powers to its officers;[99] that the authority's Capital Markets Fund had never been validly established;[100] and that the dealings from April 1987 to August 1988 were unreasonable on *Wednesbury* principles, but that its activities from August 1988 to February 1989 (when Hammersmith pursued its interim strategy) were not.[101]

The Court of Appeal

On appeal from the decision of the Divisional Court, the Court of Appeal, giving judgment on 22 February 1990,[102] overturned that decision and, following the Scrivener view, unanimously held that local authorities were empowered to negotiate swaps contracts provided they were entered into for a lawful purpose. The Court also held, again contrary to the views of the Divisional Court, that swaps transactions entered into for debt management purposes 'are a novel method of achieving an unexceptional end' and that debt management 'is fairly to be regarded as incidental to or consequential upon a local authority's powers of borrowing and investment'.[103] Further, the Court, taking 'a sensibly liberal interpretation',[104] held that the detailed statutory code regarding borrowing and investing in Schedule 13 of the 1972 Act was not inconsistent with local authorities being able to enter into swaps transactions as part of interest rate risk management. In so finding the Court specifically rejected Mr Howell's argument that swaps were in the nature of income generating instruments on the ground that when a swap is negotiated as part of the process of managing risk, 'the commercial substance of the transaction is no more a means of "raising money" than would be taking out an insurance policy, or varying the rate of interest payable on a loan by agreement with the lender'.[105]

The Court of Appeal's approach thus raised the question of how the line was

[98] [1990] 2 WLR 38.   [99] Ibid., 39–41.   [100] Ibid., 41–2.   [101] Ibid., 42–5.
[102] [1990] 2 WLR 1038.   [103] Ibid., 1064.   [104] Ibid., 1066.   [105] Ibid., 1070.

to be drawn between the permissible objective of interest rate risk management and the impermissible activity of trading. While accepting that parallel contracts clearly fell within risk management, the Court was unwilling to provide detailed guidance: first, because it did not arise for decision in the proceedings, and secondly because insufficient evidence on this point had been provided to enable them to address this question properly. The Court, nevertheless, found no difficulty in concluding that all of Hammersmith's transactions up to July 1988 were tainted with the improper purpose of trading and were therefore unlawful.[106] But what of the interim strategy? Could it be lawful to seek to undo damage caused in the course of effecting an unlawful purpose or was the council required 'to stand and watch the flood-waters rise, impotent to raise a sandbag'?[107]

Although the Court was unable to find much authority bearing closely on this problem, it took the view that the law has 'eschewed a rigid, doctrinaire principle that all transactions tainted by lack of *vires* or illegality are necessarily and for all purposes void'[108] and concluded that:

> The correct principle . . . is that, if a local authority has unwittingly and in good faith exceeded its powers, but is with good reason uncertain whether or not it has done so, it has implied power for such period as it reasonably takes to resolve that uncertainty to take such steps as it reasonably and prudently can to limit and reduce the loss which its earlier conduct may cause to its ratepayers or community charge payers.[109]

Applying this principle, the Court felt that the purposes of the council after July 1988 were radically different from those in the earlier period since the council was not seeking to make a profit but was taking defensive steps to protect its financial interests. Consequently the Court held that the transactions entered into during the period of the interim strategy were not unlawful.

The House of Lords

Both the auditor and the council sought and obtained leave to appeal to the House of Lords[110] which eventually[111] issued their judgment on 24 January 1991.

---

[106] Ibid., 1072–4.   [107] Ibid., 1076.   [108] Ibid.   [109] Ibid., 1076–7.

[110] The auditor did so only after taking counsel's opinion on the factors which he might legitimately take into account in considering whether to seek leave to appeal and whether he was permitted (in considering the general issues raised by the action) to consult with the Audit Commission. After being advised that he was entitled to take more general considerations into account and that he was able to consult with the Commission on the nature of those issues, he sought leave. The juridical foundation for the Court of Appeal's decision to grant leave to Hammersmith, however, remains unclear. The Court accepted most of Mr Scrivener's arguments and the idea of granting leave to a defendant on the basis that only a majority, rather than all, of its transactions is unlawful seems peculiar. What Hammersmith's appeal signalled was that it was proposing to alter its line of argument and align itself with the Howell position and, as a result, Hammersmith's case was presented in the Lords by new leading counsel.

[111] The House encountered certain difficulties with the form of their own proceedings. If they were to determine that all swaps transactions were *ultra vires* they would be relieved of having to

The issues were well balanced with the Divisional Court having adopted the Howell interpretation and the Court of Appeal having found in favour of the Scrivener construction. But since both the auditor and Hammersmith advocated a strict approach to the issue of *vires*, this left the banks in the position of arguing that swaps transactions for debt management purposes were within the powers of a local authority.

The House of Lords, speaking through Lord Templeman, found in favour of the approach adopted by the Divisional Court.[112] Accepting that borrowing is a 'function' of local authorities, the critical issue was whether swaps transactions were incidental to the borrowing function. Lord Templeman utilized dicta from certain nineteenth-century cases involving a building society, a statutory river company and a railway company to highlight the point that the issue was not whether the contracts were incidental to borrowing 'but whether swaps transactions are incidental to a local authority's borrowing function having regard to the provisions and limitations of the Act of 1972 regulating that function'.[113] That is, the power was not incidental simply because it was convenient or desirable or profitable but depended on the nature of the statutory scheme. After examining in some detail the statutory provisions governing local authority borrowing contained in Schedule 13 to the 1972 Act, Lord Templeman concluded that Schedule 13 established 'a comprehensive code' and that this code was 'inconsistent with any incidental power to enter into swaps transactions'.[114] The issue of whether local authorities should have this power was thus a matter for Parliament to decide.

A critique

In preferring the strict constructionist approach of the Divisional Court in *Hammersmith*, the Lords seemed to have been swayed both by their perceptions of the nature of the swaps market and the reasons for local authority involvement in it. In both respects, however, their grasp of the issues appears to be singularly limited. Lord Templeman, giving the leading opinion, displayed only the most limited understanding of the operation of financial markets in general,[115] and swaps markets in particular. Consider, for example, his illustration of the workings of the swaps market:

> If a local authority borrowed £10m in 1986 for five years at 10 per cent per annum and LIBOR in 1987 was 12 per cent, the local authority would be unlikely to contemplate

consider a number of further arguments and therefore could ration the time spent on the case. But could their Lordships' findings on the *vires* question be signalled in advance of the conclusion of hearing? It was eventually decided that they could and at the beginning of November, in a gap in the dates set aside for hearing, a 'provisional' ruling was sent to the parties that the House was minded to find all swaps transactions *ultra vires*: *Financial Times*, 2 November 1990.

[112] [1991] 2 WLR 372.   [113] Ibid., 384–5.   [114] Ibid., 387.

[115] Lord Templeman, for example, seemed to be under the impression that Eurodollar interest rates have some connection with Sterling LIBOR: [1991] 2 WLR 372 at 379.

a swap. But if in 1987 LIBOR was 10 per cent and the local authority believed that LIBOR would fall to eight per cent, the local authority might be minded to enter into a swap. In that event the local authority would agree to pay a bank LIBOR every year and the bank would agree to pay interest at 10 per cent on a notional sum of £10m until 1991.[116]

Why does Lord Templeman assume in the final sentence that the bank will pay interest at 10 per cent on this transaction? There seem to be two possible explanations. It may have been believed that the bank takes on the *actual* fixed rate negotiated by the local authority in 1986; if so, this is simply incorrect. Alternatively, it could have been assumed (wrongly) that because LIBOR is 10 per cent in 1987 the fixed rate for a swap will also be 10 per cent. In reality, the fixed rate for a five year swap is likely to be significantly different from the LIBOR rate.[117] The reason for this is that the fixed rate depends on the relationship of medium-term to short-term sterling rates and this relationship tends to be rather volatile. Whichever assumption one makes, however, what is clear is that their Lordships have failed to grasp the most elementary aspects of this (admittedly rather sophisticated) market.

Once the issue of the relationship between fixed swap rates and floating LIBOR rates is understood, it is evident that, contrary to Lord Templeman's assumption, a local authority might well contemplate entering into a swap in the situation hypothesized in that first sentence. Suppose, for example, that in the circumstances outlined by Lord Templeman the five year fixed rate in 1987 was 14 per cent, 2 per cent above LIBOR. The local authority has gained 4 per cent by borrowing in 1986. The authority can lock into that gain in 1987 by entering into a swap to pay the floating rate. The net effect of these arrangements would be to ensure that the local authority is able to borrow at LIBOR minus 4 per cent a year (commencing in 1987 at a rate of 8 per cent). Alternatively, the fixed swap rates in 1987 might be 10 per cent, 2 per cent below LIBOR. The authority might then wish to swap fixed for floating in the belief that LIBOR will fall and will average under 10 per cent over the next four years. The point here is that there are many circumstances in which, in the situation postulated by Lord Templeman, it would be rational for a local authority to enter into a swap arrangement.

This failure by Lord Templeman to get to grips with the nature of the market is highlighted in his consideration of the evidence submitted by the treasurer of Westminster City Council. Lord Templeman clearly thought the treasurer was talking nonsense when providing an example of a council swapping an 11 per cent a year fixed rate of interest for a variable rate of 10 per cent: 'The treasurer does not explain why a bank would be willing to accept a variable rate of 10 per

---

[116] [1991] 2 WLR 372, at 379.

[117] In June 1986 the fixed 5 year swap rate did actually coincide with LIBOR. In May 1988, however, the fixed rate was 1.5 per cent higher; and in October 1989 it was almost 3 per cent lower.

cent while agreeing to pay a fixed rate of 11 per cent.'[118] But when there is a positive yield curve (that is, when fixed swap rates are above LIBOR) this happens as a matter of course. When the treasurer then suggested that if LIBOR rose above 11 per cent he would enter a reverse swap to pay a fixed rate of 11 per cent, again Lord Templeman is mystified: why should a bank enter into such a transaction? But although the treasurer cannot guarantee relocking at 11 per cent, the process is quite straightforward. With LIBOR at 10 per cent and five year rates at 11 per cent the treasurer swaps into floating. If after a year LIBOR rises too high for his liking he can create an average rate of 11 per cent for the five year period provided four year rates are no more than about 11.35 per cent a year. This is certainly conceivable since, because of the volatility of short-term rates, it is possible for LIBOR to be above 12 per cent and fixed swap rates to be under 10 per cent. At the date of the House of Lords' judgment, for example, LIBOR was at 12.37 and four year swap rates at 10.83; precisely the circumstances necessary for the treasurer to be able to enter into that hypothetical reverse swap.[119]

Having failed to get to grips with the basic nature of the swaps market, Lord Templeman added spice by his consideration of the scale of Hammersmith's activities. The overall impression seems to be that this market is an opaque mystery and, since neither the Law Lords nor Hammersmith understand it (why otherwise would it expose itself to such massive losses?), local authorities should not be permitted to transact in it. Hence the highly coloured views of Lord Templeman:

> A swap transaction undertaken by a local authority involves speculation in future interest trends with the object of making a profit in order to increase the available resources of the local authorities.[120]

> Debt management is not a function. Debt management is a phrase which has been coined in this case to describe the activities of a person who enters the swap market for the purpose of making profits which can be employed in the payment of interest on borrowings.[121]

> A swap contract . . . is more akin to gambling than insurance.[122]

These views, equating the market with speculation and gambling, are resonant of the old cases in which the courts experienced difficulty in distinguishing investment from gambling.[123] Here terms such as 'gambling' assume a symbolic

---

[118] [1991] 2 WLR 372, at 380.

[119] For actual illustrations of this process in action see the two sets of linked swap transactions entered into by Westminster City Council in 1988 and 1989 in Fig. 1, above.

[120] [1991] 2 WLR 372 at 385.　　　[121] Ibid., at 388.　　　[122] Ibid.

[123] See *Universal Stock Exchange* v. *Strachan* [1896] AC 166; A.C. Page and R.B. Ferguson, *Investor Protection* (London, 1992), 5–7.

quality and become a substitute for rational analysis of whether or not the use of swaps involves the assumption of inappropriate or unacceptable risk. It is difficult, for example, to see how the purchase of swap caps can, under any circumstances, be viewed as gambling. Furthermore, Lord Templeman's remarks fly in the face of the evidence that swaps are regarded as everyday tools of financial management by large organizations and are viewed essentially as instruments for the mitigation of risk.

The pejorative characterization of the market by the House of Lords thus seemed mainly to be based on a misunderstanding of its operation. However, it was also skewed by the circumstances of one exceptional authority's relationship to that market. Thus Lord Templeman stated that: 'The greater the volatility of interest rates, the greater the risk of loss to a local authority as a result of swaps transactions.'[124] But this assumed that local authorities entered the market solely for the purpose of taking on floating rate swaps. While this perception was undoubtedly affected by Hammersmith's transactions it is not strictly accurate. One bank heavily involved in swaps had estimated that in about one-third of the local authority swaps on that bank's books the authority was paying the fixed rate.[125] More generally the court seemed to be influenced by the fact that, since Hammersmith's motives in entering the market seem speculative, the market itself must be viewed as such.

Once this picture of the activities under scrutiny has been painted, the approach to statutory construction falls into place. Schedule 13 to the Local Government Act 1972 was held to establish a comprehensive code which is inconsistent with any incidental power to enter into swap transactions. But this interpretation depends on a particular characterization of the way in which the Act functions. Central to this view is the role of the PWLB. Lord Templeman indicated that the Board offers loans to local authorities at fixed or variable rates[126] on advantageous terms, that it permits authorities to replace one borrowing with another and to change from variable to fixed rate interest, and therefore that the Board, which accounts for 80 per cent of local authority borrowings,[127] had all the flexibility needed to enable an authority properly to manage its borrowings.

But is this characterization of the role of the PWLB accurate? Although by the end of the 1980s 80 per cent of local authority borrowing was through the PWLB, in the early 1980s (at the beginning of the period in which the swaps market grew) the Board provided for only 35 per cent of local authority borrowing. Moreover, there are a number of mechanisms within the Board's arrangements which restrict its flexibility. First, until September 1989 (i.e., after the

---

[124] [1991] 2 WLR 372 at 388.

[125] Private information. See also the example of Glasgow DC above, n. 85.

[126] Lord Ackner seems to imply (wrongly) that the PWLB provides only fixed rate loans: [1991] 2 WLR 372 at 399.

[127] Ibid., at 386 (per Lord Templeman), at 399 (per Lord Ackner).

freezing of local authority involvement in swaps markets) there was an anti-prepayment bias in the Board system. An authority which had a fixed rate PWLB loan below the current term rates had a valuable commodity. But if it was felt that interest rates were going to fall, it could be foreseen that it would become less valuable. Before September 1989, however, the Board would not pay the authority anything for extinguishing that loan.[128] The only way to reverse the position and retain an advantage was by a swap. Secondly, a borrower can switch from floating to fixed rates under Board loans only on interest payment dates. If therefore an authority has a PWLB floating rate loan with a six month interest period and becomes convinced one month into that period that the rates are likely to rise over the next few months, nothing can be done immediately without a swap facility. Thirdly, the mechanism required by the Board in moving from fixed to variable is to prepay the fixed loan and take out a new variable loan. PWLB rules, however, prescribe limits (quotas determined by formulae) on the amount of preferential funding a local authority can take out in any one year. The new loan will count against this quota and may therefore act as an impediment to flexible management of its debt. Finally, the PWLB mechanisms contain no equivalent of the purchase of interest rate caps and collars. In general, the PWLB system of the 1980s was neither the panacea nor the predominant source of borrowing suggested by the House of Lords judgment.[129]

The general point of this analysis may now be articulated. Given that the Lords were presented with two credible and competing interpretations of the powers of local authorities, their choice must have been determined by such factors as their understanding of the nature of local government, their views on the character of the activity local authorities were engaged in, and their perception of the consequences of finding one way or the other. What I have tried to show is that, in their jaundiced view of the swaps market and their idealized characterization of PWLB mechanisms, the House of Lords failed to provide a satisfactory account of the local authority debt management mechanisms. Their judgment may have been affected by the particular circumstances of Hammersmith. But its impact was felt across the entire system of local government.[130]

---

[128] PWLB Circular No. 87 para. 24. This position was corrected by Circular No. 88 (25 September 1989).

[129] A number of the above points are outlined in a paper submitted to the Department of the Environment jointly by the British Banks Association (BBA) and CIPFA, *Swaps and Local Authorities*, 7–8 (22 August 1990).

[130] We might also note that, in order to maintain a degree of consistency in their restrictive interpretation of the scope of s. 111, the Lords were obliged to overturn the decisions of both the Divisional Court and Court of Appeal in *R* v. *Richmond upon Thames BC, ex p. McCarthy & Stone (Developments) Ltd* [1991] 4 All ER 897; a case in which they held that local authorities were not empowered under s. 111 to charge fees for pre-planning application consultations with developers.

The Case for Retrospective Legislation

The *Hammersmith* judgment had the effect of rendering all the swaps transactions of local authorities *ultra vires* and void. Any obligations apparently created by the transactions were unenforceable. No further payments could be made by local authorities, nor any received. That is, no private law rights were conferred by these swaps transactions. But what consequences did the ruling have for contracts which throughout the 1980s had been entered into by local authorities and on which payments, in either or both directions, had been made? This is the third question which had been raised by the litigation; the issue of restitution. Since this issue had been deferred by the Divisional Court, however, the *Hammersmith* case provided little guidance, Lord Templeman simply stating that the 'consequences of any ultra vires transaction may depend on the facts of each case'.[131] This raised the prospect of a litigation nightmare with attempts being made to unravel several thousand transactions, involving around 130 local authorities and 80 banks.

The general uncertainties of this entire legal process had been almost of as much concern to the banks as the issue of default. The banks had, for example, generally matched their fixed-rate outflows to councils with fixed rate inflows which they had taken on (e.g., by purchasing a gilt-edged government bond); thus, when a swap was liquidated, the bank would also sell the gilts. One problem which had faced the banks since 1989 was that, since they did not know which swaps would eventually be declared unlawful and which would not, they were unable to take effective pre-emptive action (by selling gilts attached to a swap). For these reasons, it became very difficult to assess the cost to the banks if local authorities failed to meet their side of the contracts; estimates seem to have varied from £150m to £1bn.[132] What was not uncertain, however, was that the banks were prepared to take vigorous action to protect their interests.

Before the Hammersmith litigation had commenced, the banks, concerned at the impact which uncertainty and default might have on the reputation of the City of London as a well-run financial centre,[133] lobbied the Government for legislation to ensure that all local authority contracts entered into in good faith should be deemed to be enforceable. The Government, however, wished to see the legal process run its normal course.[134] After the House of Lords judgment, various parties returned to this issue. It is perhaps important to note that most local authorities wished to fulfil their contracts. None had speculated on the scale of Hammersmith. In most local authorities the losses were relatively small and

---

[131] [1991] 2 WLR 372 at 390.

[132] *The Economist*, 18 March 1989, at 128 (£150m); *Financial Times*, 2 November 1989 (£400m); *The Independent*, 2 November 1989 (£500m); *The Times*, 2 November 1989 (£1bn).

[133] *The Economist*, 6 May 1989, at 109; also 18 March 1989, at 128.

[134] HL Debs., vol. 511 cols. 397–407 (11 October 1989).

these authorities had generally made provision within their budgets to continue to make payments. They would not therefore be taken by surprise if required to do so. Furthermore, some authorities remained net gainers in their transactions. More generally, there was a feeling within many local authorities that they were honour-bound to maintain these deals. Finally, there was a fear within local government that, if they were not allowed to make these payments, credit would become more expensive for the entire sector.

Consequently, after *Hammersmith* not only the banks but also certain sections of the local government world advocated the enactment of legislation validating existing swaps transactions. While this would be retrospective in nature, it was argued that it would simply legalize the position which virtually everyone believed to be the case. CIPFA, for example, proposed that new legislation be introduced which would both establish 'debt management' as a function of local authorities, thereby conferring limited powers to use swaps as tools of debt management, and also retrospectively validate those swaps transactions which had been entered into and which were a proper function of debt management.[135] The banks also once again argued for retrospective legislation on the ground that this would be the only way of restoring the damage caused to the international reputation of the London financial markets. The banks suggested that, if all transactions were validated, they 'would be willing to work out, with H.M. Government, ways of mitigating the impact of the proposal on the community charge payers in the very small number of local authorities where the payment in full or immediately would be unduly burdensome'.[136] And they also pointed out that the issue of retrospection had not previously caused the Government any difficulties.[137]

Despite the fact that the banks' case was strongly supported by the Bank of England,[138] the Government announced in May 1991 that although it had 'received a number of representations for a variety of different schemes of legislation to enable local authorities to make payment under past arrangements which have been found to be unlawful', it would not 'seek to alter existing legal obligations'.[139] The Government's decision undoubtedly caused Hammersmith

[135] CIPFA, *Swaps*, A submission to DoE, 20 February 1991.
[136] BBA, *Interest Rate Swaps used by Local Authorities: the banks' proposal for rectifying the damage done by the Hammersmith and Fulham case*, Parliamentary Brief (n.d.), 1.
[137] The BBA pointed to the retrospective legislation introduced in relation to the Woolwich Equitable Building Society case (see Finance Act 1986, s. 47) and also noted that, following *Hammersmith*, the Government of Hong Kong had acted retrospectively to validate the past, present and future swaps contracts entered into by two statutory railway corporations (BBA, above, n. 135, 1). The banks might also have referred to several recent examples in the area of local government finance: see, Local Government Finance Act 1982, s. 8(10); London Regional Transport (Amendment) Act 1985; Rate Support Grants Act 1986; Local Government Act 1987; Local Government Finance Act 1987, s. 4.
[138] See R. Leigh-Pemberton in Second Report of the Treasury and Civil Service Committee, Session 1990–91, *The 1991 Budget*, HC 289. Minutes of Evidence, paras. 130–2.
[139] HC Debs., vol. 190 cols. 402–3w (7 May 1991).

to breath a sigh of relief since retrospective validation of all its deals would have exposed the authority to losses of around £200m; a sum which represented a bill of around £4,000 per community charge payer in the borough.

Unravelling Swaps Transactions

Given the failure of various parties to convince the Government of the necessity of retrospective legislation, attention came to focus on mechanisms for unravelling the swaps transactions. It quickly became clear that this would be a complex, uncertain, expensive, time-consuming and essentially arbitrary process. The rapidly developing law of restitution was unable to offer any clear and authoritative guidance on the restoration of payments in this situation; however it was presented, the judiciary would inevitably be placed in the position of making it up as they went along. Litigation would thus be complex, uncertain, expensive and time-consuming. Furthermore, as the Bank of England recognized, 'restitution is arbitrary in its effect, involving the unwinding of transactions already settled to the satisfaction of both parties and totally undoing the contribution to risk management which was originally intended'.[140] In the dynamic world of capital markets there was simply no way of restoring the *status quo ante*. Restitution of payments would serve to penalize those prudent local authorities which had successfully used the swaps market to hedge against interest rate movements.

Notwithstanding these uncertainties and complexities, legal advice was soon circulating throughout the local government system. The Audit Commission was quickly off the mark, issuing a Technical Release for the guidance of auditors, the general tenor of which suggested that full restitution of payments should be made.[141] This message was reinforced by counsel's advice obtained by CIPFA, albeit with one important reservation. Recognizing the uncertainties involved, counsel suggested that perhaps a valid distinction could be made between closed and open deals, on the basis of the principle that payments in settlement of honest claims are irrecoverable.[142] This was potentially a very important distinction. Although it had been estimated that the banks could obtain around £125m on full restitution of payments,[143] they would not fare so well if time-expired deals were excluded, because in general local authorities tended to be net gainers in the earlier transactions and net losers in the more recent deals. However,

---

[140] Memorandum of the Bank of England, 'Local Authority Swaps' in Second Report of the Treasury and Civil Service Committee, Session 1990–91, *The 1991 Budget*, Minutes of Evidence, 15 at 17.

[141] Audit Commission, *Capital Markets Activity. Interest Rate Swaps etc*, Technical Release 16/91 (May 1991).

[142] Mr Roger Henderson QC, *Advice to CIPFA*, 6 February 1991, 9–10.

[143] *Financial Times*, 8 May 1991.

much of this advice seemed to be imposing a forced simplicity on a highly complex legal and factual situation and there seemed no alternative to obtaining authoritative higher court rulings in relation to a range of transactions.

As has been mentioned,[144] shortly after the suspension of local authority swaps activities in February 1989, the banks issued a number of writs against various authorities for the enforcement of swaps contracts. When the auditor commenced action against Hammersmith in May 1989, however, the banks decided not to proceed, pending the outcome of the Hammersmith action. After the House of Lords' judgment the writs were then converted into restitutionary actions. By May 1991, when the Government announced that retrospective legislation would not be introduced, it was estimated that 12 banks had issued 69 writs against 32 local authorities[145] and that many more were threatened. Furthermore, the anticipated test case on restitution – an action by Citicorp Investment Bank against Ogwr DC which had been listed for trial commencing 4 March 1991 – failed to materialize when, at the eleventh hour, the parties reached an out-of-court settlement under which the authority fully repaid the net principal payments on both open and closed deals and made a partial payment of interest.[146]

Since there were no other cases listed for early trial and local authorities were not rushing to volunteer their transactions as suitable for a test case, a free-for-all seemed inevitable. At this stage, however, the commercial court determined to offer its assistance. Early in July Evans J, the presiding judge of the commercial court, being concerned at the proliferation of writs seeking restitution against local authorities in respect of swaps transactions, sought an investigation. This search revealed the existence of around 150 outstanding writs on this issue. In an unprecedented action, Evans J then wrote to all the parties offering the court's assistance in avoiding unnecessary duplication of hearings and invited the parties to attend a hearing on 31 July to explore the possibility of mounting a single or representative hearing regarding the key legal issues.

At this hearing, Steyn J made a general order that the lead actions should comprise six cases (three chosen by the banks and three by the local authorities) and that all other swap actions should be stayed. The judge also made a cost-sharing order in favour of the local authority defendants in the lead actions. These six lead actions were scheduled to commence in March 1992. On the eve of the trial, however, five of the six actions were settled, thereby defeating the purpose of the original selection. A second general hearing of all the parties was held on 8 June 1992 and a new set of lead cases selected.

In the second round of lead cases the High Court established that the banks were entitled to restitution of the money paid under the void contracts.[147] While

---

[144] Above, 344.   [145] *Financial Times*, 8 May 1991.
[146] *Financial Times*, 4 March 1991.
[147] *Westdeutsche Landesbank Girozentrale* v. *Islington LBC*; *Kleinwort Benson Ltd* v. *Sandwell BC* (1993) 91 LGR 323.

the court's analysis in reaching that conclusion was criticized,[148] the *Islington* decision has been confirmed by the Court of Appeal which required repayment of the principal with compound interest not simply from April 1990 (when the Divisional Court ruled that Hammersmith's transactions were *ultra vires*) but from June 1987 (when money was first paid to Islington by the bank).[149]

While the basic principle seems now to have been established that the local authorities were placed in a fiduciary position in respect of the moneys paid by the banks under *ultra vires* swaps transactions, many technical issues remain to be resolved. The legal disputes are likely to continue for some considerable time.[150]

Law in the Conduct of Local Government Business

One important issue remains to be considered. Given the professional status of officers and the formal constraints on local authority decision-making, how was it possible for Hammersmith to cultivate swaps operations on such a scale and thus to leave itself in an extremely exposed position? This question was examined by an independent inquiry, consisting of leading counsel and two former local authority chief executives, appointed by Hammersmith to investigate the history and circumstances of the council's capital market activity.[151] The Veeder Inquiry, which was appointed in February 1990, finally reported in July 1991.

The Inquiry found that, although Hammersmith had been engaging in swaps transactions from 1983, until 1987 the scale of swaps was quite limited, the principal purpose was debt management and that, viewed in the light of contemporaneous practice, 'there was nothing untoward but much to commend in the way the council's debt was managed by the finance officers.'[152] The significant change in practice came about in May 1987 when the council entered into its first swap option and thus crossed 'the watershed between debt management and income generation'.[153] Thereafter the scale and nature of Hammersmith's capital markets activities substantially increased. The most dramatic period was from November 1987 to July 1988; during this period Hammersmith entered into 390 new transactions, representing 70 per cent of its entire capital market activities.[154] At the commencement of this period the nett running total of notional

---

[148] A. Burrows, 'Restitution of payments made under swap transactions', *New Law Journal*, 2 April 1993, 480.

[149] [1994] 1 WLR 938.

[150] See, e.g., *Kleinwort Benson Ltd* v. *South Tyneside MBC* [1994] 4 All ER 972; *South Tyneside MBC* v. *Svenska International plc* [1995] 1 All ER 545.

[151] V.V. Veeder QC, John Barratt and Michael Reddington, *The Final Report of the Independent Inquiry into the Capital Market Activities of the London Borough of Hammersmith and Fulham* (Hammersmith & Fulham LBC, 1991).

[152] Inquiry Report, ch. 10, 55. (Each of the chapters of the Inquiry's Report are independently paginated.)

[153] Inquiry Report, ch. 12, 15.   [154] Inquiry Report, ch. 13, 1.

principal had just exceeded the total of Hammersmith's debt; eight months later the nett running total exceeded Hammersmith's debt by a factor of 12.[155]

All of this took place as a result of the decisions of officers within the Finance Department and without any formal reporting to council or its finance committee or without the leading members even being informally briefed.[156] The use of swaps and other derivative instruments was viewed throughout as being a technical matter of ensuring the minimization of borrowing costs rather than an issue of principle to be put to members. Briefly what appears to have happened is that an enterprising and innovative culture had been built up within Hammersmith's Loans Division, but between November 1986 and November 1987 the key officers left the authority and those who assumed responsibility responded to this culture without the experience to handle the tasks wisely. These officers thus failed to recognize either the financial or legal risks involved in these activities and committed grave errors of professional judgment. The Inquiry also found that 'there was a most serious managerial failure . . . to ensure adequate supervision and control' of Hammersmith's swaps activities.[157] Furthermore, when in May 1988 the Director of Finance left Hammersmith, the two officers primarily identified as bearing operational responsibility for their capital markets activity were promoted to become Director and Deputy Director of Finance. Whatever merit these appointments may have had, these internal promotions had the effect of ensuring that there was no occasion for the sort of general review of operations which often follows a new senior appointment.

It might be noted, finally, that when, in January 1988, the chair of the finance committee was briefed in entirely positive terms on Hammersmith's swaps activities, being informed that they were generating around £1m a year, the finance chair was of the view that the practice should not be reported to the committee except in the most general of terms. The reason for this was that, given Hammersmith's general financial constraints, if this source of additional finance were reported to the committee, there would be great pressure to spend it on revenue projects. As the Inquiry reported: 'With the benefit of hindsight, it is of course a tragedy . . . that the [finance committee] was not fully informed, formally or informally, of [Hammersmith's] Capital Market activities.'[158] Consequently, it was the action of external audit agencies that led to a brake being applied.

In July 1988, having heard rumours in the City, the Controller of Audit at the Audit Commission telephoned Hammersmith's chief executive to express concern about the scale of their swaps activities. The chief executive, taking his advice from the new Director of Finance, reassured the Commission that there

---

[155] Inquiry Report, ch. 12, 31; ch. 13, 1.

[156] The chair of the finance committee was first informed of the use of swaps on 29 January 1988 but only in general terms and in that presentation 'would have learnt nothing to alert him . . . to the questionable legality or financial prudence' of these activities (ch. 14, 31) and the leader of the Council 'did not have any knowledge of [Hammersmith's] involvement in Capital Market activities until . . . July 1988' (ch. 16, 5).

[157] Inquiry Report, ch. 23.   [158] Inquiry Report, ch. 14, 41.

was no need for concern.[159] At the end of July, however, following the Audit Commission's receipt of counsel's opinion,[160] the auditor intervened. Between July 1988 and February 1989 there followed the period of the Interim Strategy, which was designed to wind down Hammersmith's operations and reduce its exposure to risk. The implementation of this strategy was found by the Inquiry to be 'materially defective'.[161] In part, this seemed to be as a result of a degree of confusion between the legality and prudence of Hammermith's activities. With the auditor's intervention, attention was focused on legality and, until February 1989, no one at Hammersmith seemed to accept that their activities had exposed the authority to the risk of serious financial loss.[162]

Hammersmith's financial situation was not exposed to proper scrutiny within the council in the period between July 1988 and February 1989 essentially because it was felt that confidentiality had to be maintained throughout the operation of the Interim Strategy in order to protect Hammersmith's market position. Consequently, the first report to councillors on the authority's capital market activities was received on 28 February. Nevertheless, even in this report the chief executive sought to emphasize the fact that the council had a surplus in its Capital Markets Fund and stated that 'it is believed that our 4/5 year strategy would indeed produce profits'.[163]

If there is a general moral to be drawn from the events unravelled by the Veeder report it may be that neither formal systems operating within a local authority[164] nor new statutory responsibilities imposed on officers[165] can provide an adequate substitute for the development and maintenance of the highest standards of professional competence and ethics. There has recently been much criticism made of the traditional public sector ethos which is characterized as being orientated to failure-avoidance rather than the pursuit of enterprise and success. The new philosophy tends to emphasize the need to devolve responsibility downwards, to counteract risk aversion with a 'bias for action' and, consequently, to provide mechanisms for supporting potential failure. The Hammersmith experience provides some salutary lessons in the dangers of adopting an enterprise

[159] The Director of Finance, writing to the Chief Executive in July 1988 stated: 'It is . . . clear that the Audit Commission do not really understand the whole question of interest rate swaps and how they can beneficially be used by Local Authorities . . .', Inquiry Report ch. 17, 4.

[160] See above, 342–3.   [161] Inquiry Report, ch. 15, 38.

[162] Inquiry Report ch. 15, 38; ch. 17, 68.

[163] Inquiry Report, ch. 20, 13. The chief executive (Tony Eddison) also published an article in the *Health Services Journal* on 6 April 1989 in which he stated: 'Now that the realisation has dawned that Hammersmith and Fulham had not suffered any financial losses and that its financial strategy, if it is allowed to continue, could produce a healthy surplus in the early 1990s, the press have disappeared. The enterprise culture is fine, it seems, as long as public servants do not make a success of it.'

[164] See, e.g., C. Holtham, 'Developing a system for measuring departmental performance', *Public Money and Management*, Winter 1988, at 29.

[165] See, e.g., LGFA 1988, s. 114 (duty on chief finance officer report in any cases of financial misconduct); Local Government and Housing Act 1989, s. 5 (duty on local authority to appoint a monitoring officer charged with ensuring administrative propriety within the authority).

orientation without proper safeguards or adequate scrutiny of its implications for the entire activities of the organization.

While focusing on the specific task of explaining precisely what happened and how it occurred, the Veeder Inquiry did not ignore the complex factors that shaped the environment within which these events unfolded. These, the Inquiry recognized, included: 'the "cat-and-mouse" financial game played betweeen central and local government with increasing intensity from 1983 onwards'; 'the pressures on Councils and their officers to find loop-holes in, and means of outwitting, the systems of central government control on expenditure'; 'the resulting distortion of normal prudential values in local government finance, moving away from practical common-sense exercisable by Council members as laypersons to legalisms and technicalities which could be followed only by experts'; 'the pressures on senior local government officers arising from the far-reaching successive changes in the financing and management of local authorities imposed by central government'; and 'the uncertainties regarding local authorities' borrowing and ancillary powers under the 1972 Act [and] the use by local authorities of the Swaps market since 1982, without material challenge from external auditors and the Audit Commission until July 1988'.[166] The basic theme which links these various factors is that of the instrumentalization of law within the local government system. What the Hammersmith experience highlights is the difficulty of utilizing law as a mechanism of regulation and control in circumstances in which there is an extremely limited degree of legal consciousness amongst the main actors within the system.

Conclusions

Conventional understandings have played a vital role not only in the conduct of relations between central and local government but also within the decision-making arrangements of local government. The Local Government Acts accord local authorities a great deal of discretion concerning the management of their activities. That discretion has been mediated through a local government tradition of 'managerial professionalism'. John Stewart has identified this tradition as one which aimed to 'ensure service delivery in accordance with rules laid down and good professional practice' and which 'appear[ed] to solve the problem of control in what is often a large-scale organization'.[167] And, in his magisterial study of central–local government relations in the 1960s, John Griffith highlighted the professionalism of officers as 'the greatest single force which enables local authorities to carry out, with much efficiency, the considerable tasks

---

[166] Inquiry Report, ch. 23, 2–3.

[167] J.D. Stewart, 'The functioning and management of local authorities' in M. Loughlin, D. Gelfand & K. Young (eds.), *Half A Century of Municipal Decline 1935–1985* (London, 1985) 98, at 102.

entrusted to them'.[168] This tradition served not only to regulate relations between members and officers but also to instil the belief that officers need not be subject to precise formal regulation. In practice, the self-regulatory activities of the professions would ensure the promotion of the highest standards of conduct.

With the strains of the last decade or so, however, the local government system has become highly politicized. One dimension may be seen in the central–local government relationship, where the sense of partnership has been replaced by increasingly antagonistic relations. Another, however, may be seen in relation to the decision-making processes within local government. Once local authorities began to examine the *legal* limitations on their powers free from the mediating influence of central guidance or professional practice, then both the power relations and control structures implicit in the tradition of managerial professionalism came to be challenged. In effect, the Widdicombe Inquiry which was established in the mid 1980s was charged with examining this question.[169] However, in recommending a range of reforms which were designed to bolster the status of officers and to formalize the relationship between members and officers,[170] Widdicombe dealt only with one facet of the recent strains. The Widdicombe Committee, by focusing on power relations and thus on officer checks on members, rather neglected the issue of control structures: *quis custodiet ipsos custodes?* While politicians no doubt applied various pressures to discover and exploit innovative methods of financing in local government, the relationship forged between the Western Isles Island Council and BCCI or between Hammersmith and the swaps market alongside other examples of the creative accounting movement which flourished in the 1980s, were essentially officer-inspired and officer-implemented.

[168] J.A.G. Griffith, *Central Departments and Local Authorities* (London, 1966), 534.
[169] *Report of the Committee of Inquiry into the Conduct of Local Authority Business*, Cmnd. 9797 (1986).
[170] For a discussion see ch. 3, 146–8.

7

THE JURIDIFICATION OF CENTRAL–LOCAL GOVERNMENT RELATIONS

There has never existed within the English constitutional tradition a juridical relationship of hierarchy between the central State and local institutions. This feature of our system of government lies at the core of our tradition of local government and has been a key factor in determining the character of the central–local relationship. Parliament, as the institution which represented the interests of localities in the central State apparatus, has traditionally formed the primary link which connects these two tiers of government. The main business between local institutions and the central State has habitually been transacted through Parliament. Further, it is because of this critical link that no distinct system of administrative law has developed in this country. The Act of Parliament in effect became the form through which both the general law was altered and administrative orders were issued. Parliament's role in mediating central–local relations may thus be viewed as an expression of each of two principles which Dicey identified as 'pervad[ing] the whole of the English constitution'; viz., Parliamentary sovereignty and the rule of law.[1] The executive was obliged to act through Parliament and, in using the form of an Act of Parliament, we ensured that we were ruled by one indivisible body of ordinary law applicable in the ordinary courts. Our traditions of *locality* were thus interwoven with our traditions of *legality*.

In the nineteenth century, as a consequence of the processes of industrialization and urbanization, there occurred what many have viewed a 'revolution' in government.[2] For our purposes, what is especially important about this revolution is that it was fuelled primarily by a major expansion in the capacity of local government. In the process, local government was reconstituted by being placed on a statutory foundation and becoming charged with a growing number of regulatory and executive responsibilities. At this stage, law was utilized primarily for the purpose of conferring enabling powers on local authorities, though later certain duties were also imposed. The reforming statutes also tended to vest a range of supervisory powers in central departments. These nineteenth-century changes thus brought about a shift in the character of the central–local relation-

---

[1] A.V. Dicey, *Introduction to the Study of the Law of the Constitution* (London, 8th edn., 1915), 402.

[2] See, e.g., O.O.G.M. MacDonagh, 'The Nineteenth-Century Revolution in Government: A Reappraisal' (1958) 1 *Historical Journal* 52; H. Parris, 'The Nineteenth-Century Revolution in Government: A Reappraisal Reappraised' (1960) 3 *Historical Journal* 17.

ship. The private Act procedure came to be replaced by executive action (through provisional orders and the like) and increasingly the central–local government relationship was governed by a set of conventional administrative practices which evolved within a general and facilitative statutory framework.

Though the nineteenth-century reformation may be understood as a process of 'statutorification'[3] of local government, this was not accompanied by a juridification of the central–local government relationship. That is, even though the central–local relationship was placed on a legal foundation, the structure of positive law did not serve to define the character of the relationship. Statutorification did not, for example, result in the courts coming to play an active role in circumscribing the boundaries to local government's authority and in determining the character of the central–local relationship. The main reason for this was because of the facilitative character of the statutory framework. In seeking both to confer broad discretionary powers on local authorities and extensive supervisory powers on the central authorities, the primary function of the statutes was to formalize an administrative relationship between the centre and the localities and to marginalize the role of the judiciary. These statutes should not be read as instituting a set of legal norms governing conduct; rather they should be viewed as establishing an interlocking administrative framework through which such understandings could evolve in the course of practice.

In order to appreciate the significance of this point in relation to the theme of juridification, we need to consider further the nature of the powers acquired by central government. Though many of these powers were highly interventionist in form, it should first be noted that, if we were to focus on the inventory of central powers, we would obtain a highly skewed picture of the system. The reason for this is that these powers were never intended to be regularly used. Their primary function was to provide the centre with an ultimate threat and they were therefore designed mainly to facilitate the forging of a central–local partnership. It is also important to note that, before the twentieth century, these central powers were not used to provide a general public policy steer; central government simply did not possess the capacity to use these powers to formulate and implement a central policy on policing, housing, education and the like. Basically, the supervisory powers acquired by the centre were used primarily to provide a longstop – a final check on local action.

What this means is that the statutory framework of the reformed system was in effect designed to establish an informal – a non-juridified – system of administrative law. The basic function of central government was to use this extensive, though rather haphazard, network of appeal, audit, inquiry and approval powers to provide a check on the fairness and propriety of local authority action. Furthermore, notwithstanding the occasional *cause célèbre*, this central jurisdiction was one which was generally acknowledged by the courts. The judiciary in

---

[3] G. Calabresi, *A Common Law for the Age of Statutes* (Cambridge, Mass, 1982), ch. 1.

effect recognized that the central authority was better situated to supervise the manner in which the discretionary powers vested in local authorities were being exercised.[4] Anyone seeking to understand the central–local relationship therefore needed to consider the administrative norms which were evolving through practice. Since such norms were a product of the general political culture, the function of the statutory framework could only be properly understood by first appreciating the political culture within which it was embedded. To reiterate Maitland's point, 'jurist-law' had to be construed against a background of 'folk-law';[5] and, in this context, judicial acknowledgement of the political culture which sustained the system resulted essentially in the displacement of jurist-law as an active medium for regulating the system. Further, it is precisely because of the recognition of this relationship between 'folk-law' and 'jurist-law' that the judiciary did not feel impelled to venture too far into the realm of 'legal metaphysics' and develop regulatory principles of public law. For such reasons, statutorification did not lead to juridification.

It is, I believe, only by appreciating the importance of political culture that we may make sense of the twentieth-century accommodation. By political culture I have in mind a rather broad notion, one which is able to embrace cross-party consensus on the role of government in society and the traditions of administrative politics and managerial professionalism in local government. These cultural traditions enable us to understand both the function of the statutory framework and the importance within the central–local relationship of the various policy networks.[6] This elaborate network performs a vital role in serving to co-ordinate and harmonize the activities of government. The network not only creates the channels through which the centre and the localities are able to mediate their differences; it also provides a vital forum for enabling political shibboleths to be transformed into detailed and workable policies.

In addition to these critical exchange functions, the network also seems to perform certain functions of a more explicitly constitutional nature. By this, I mean that it is only through the workings of the network that a resolution is effected between a number of tensions which exist within our prescriptive constitution. Arguably, the primary constitutional function of this network has been to enable a reconciliation to be effected between our traditions of local government and the centre's claims to sovereign authority. That is, although we have prided ourselves on our tradition of local government, such a claim tends to rest rather uncomfortably alongside the basic legal principle of the constitution: that Parliament has the power to pass whatever laws it desires. The reconciliation of

---

[4] See, e.g., *Board of Education* v. *Rice* [1911] AC 179 and *Local Government Board* v. *Arlidge* [1915] AC 120. See further, W.J.L. Ambrose, 'The new judiciary' (1910) 26 LQR 120; A.V. Dicey, 'The development of administrative law in England' (1915) 31 LQR 148.

[5] F.W. Maitland, *Township and Borough* (Cambridge, 1898), 14. See, above, ch. 1, 20–3.

[6] See, above, ch. 1, 60–72. For an illustration of this point see the work of a leading public lawyer on the system: J.A.G. Griffith, *Central Departments and Local Authorities* (London, 1966).

the centre's sovereign legal right with the traditions of local self-government is, in effect, what has been accomplished through the practices of this network. The informal understandings which have evolved concerning spheres of competence, consultation arrangements and the like may be understood to reflect a form of constitutional settlement. Though the practices have been neither fixed nor entrenched, the pattern has not been without identity.

The elaborate network of linkages which has evolved between the centre and the localities in the twentieth century may thus be taken to reflect both the requirements of modern governance and the niceties of constitutionally acceptable conduct. While the practices of the network continued to fulfil conditions of both efficiency and legitimacy, the rather amorphous constitutional aspects to these practices could happily remain indeterminate. The difficulties have arisen largely because, in pursuit of the goal of efficiency in government, the centre has in recent years felt itself obliged to act contrary to many of the assumptions and practices of this network. Given the character of these arrangements, the attempt to disentangle the twin precepts of efficiency and legitimacy and to repackage the assemblage of practices as formal constitutional norms seems highly implausible. But the existence of such problems similarly should not cause us entirely to ignore this dimension to recent developments. If reforms introduced by the State encounter resistance, this may certainly affect their effectiveness. Further, to the extent that such resistance is rooted in the concern that those reforms cut across the generally accepted ways of doing things, we might say that the State is itself subverting the conditions of legitimacy.[7]

These basic facets of the twentieth-century accommodation in the central–local relationship have a particular relevance when seeking to undertake an assessment of the significance of recent developments. The contemporary strains in central–local government relations are rooted ultimately in a crisis of politics. As the post-war political consensus on the welfare state gradually began to fall apart, as ideological politics became polarized between Thatcherite policies from the centre and municipal socialist policies of the urban local authorities, and as self-regulatory structures and professionalized networks came to be challenged in the names of transparency, efficiency or consumer rights, the stress points in the system of central–local government relations were rapidly revealed. The legal significance of these important political changes could scarcely have been more profound. As the authority of the conventional practices of the administrative network were undermined, law has been dragged from the background into the foreground of the central–local relationship. And it is this transformation of law from that of providing a facilitative framework into that of establishing a regulatory regime which constitutes the juridification of central–local government relations.

---

[7] See R. Barker, *Political Legitimacy and the State* (Oxford, 1990), ch. 9.

This process of juridification has thrown up a wide range of highly complex issues which have been hidden from legal consciousness largely because of the work undertaken by the conventional practices of the administrative network. To the extent that the idea of local self-government has retained its significance in the modern era it has been rooted in the practices of the network rather than embodied in the requirements of the law. Furthermore, it has mainly been because of the efficacy of this administrative network in providing a medium for resolving disputes that lawyers have been shielded from the need to address some basic questions concerning the character of law in the modern administrative State. What is particularly important about developments since 1979, then, is that these difficult questions which have remained buried in an uneasy accommodation have now been uncovered. The meaning and significance of the themes of locality and legality within our structures of governance have thus been exposed for examination.

In this concluding chapter, I propose to examine a number of issues which arise as a result of this transformation in the role of law in central–local government relations. I shall focus in particular on the impact of this basic change on two key institutions of government. First, the exercise of converting the legal framework from that of a facilitative arrangement into a regulatory regime has required the Government to embark on a major legislative programme. This has, of course, had the effect, once again, of bringing Parliament more directly into the central–local relationship. We should therefore examine the general impact of this change. Secondly, the disputes which have been generated as a result of the restructuring of the system have led to the courts being invited to adjudicate on a broad range of issues which hitherto have not been considered appropriate for judicial resolution. Given the general circumstances in which this task has been thrust upon them, it has become difficult to interpret jurist-law against a backcloth of folk-law and, consequently, there has been an impetus to delve into legal metaphysics and to articulate an autonomous conception of legality. Again, this is a trend of some significance, particularly since it seems to require the development of distinctive principles of public law. What is also evident, however, is that the institutional changes associated with the juridification of central–local government relations raise a basic constitutional issue which has implications beyond this particular sphere of government. This constitutional question concerns the nature of the relationship between law and governance in the British system and the impact of recent developments on that relationship. Given the importance of this issue, this study of change in the character of the central–local relationship may also be viewed as a study in microcosm of trends affecting British government in general. Before examining the utilization of legislation as an instrument of regulation and of adjudication as a primary mechanism of dispute resolution, I therefore propose to consider some general questions concerning politics, law and governance.

Reflections on Politics, Law and Governance

There is little doubt that the concept of juridification is alien to the English style of thought. The concept seems to derive primarily from German theorists such as Max Weber who sought to analyse the implications of the general processes of secularization and rationalization on the character of modern life.[8] As part of these processes, it was argued, the legal order tended to develop the characteristics of a formal rationality which served as a normative foundation for society. It is this tendency to formalize all social relations in juridical terms which we may understand as the process of juridification. This tendency towards greater legalization – what Habermas has called the 'colonization of the life-world'[9] – has been the subject of extensive debate in recent times. To the extent that these debates have revolved around the concept of juridification, they have been instigated mainly by German scholars.[10] The important point, for our purposes, however, is that these debates did not seem to engage perceptively with British concerns in the sphere of public law. Why might this be so?

In order to address this question, our starting point should be to reflect both on the peculiar character of our constitutional tradition and on the general impact of the growing rationalization of social and political life on our arrangements of government. By way of introduction to this theme, we might consider the argument developed by Michael Oakeshott in his celebrated essay on 'Rationalism in Politics'.[11] This essay is an elaboration of what Oakeshott calls 'the character and pedigree of the most remarkable intellectual fashion of post-Renaissance Europe'.[12] The 'fashion' he is alluding to is that of 'Rationalism', by which he means essentially a belief in the sovereign authority of reason. Authority and tradition, the customary ways of doing things, are the prime targets of the Rationalist's challenge. The claims of these practices, the Rationalist contends, must be subjected to the tribunal of the intellect and be rendered formal, orderly and precise. Oakeshott's main objective is to show that this style of Rationalism has had a pervasive impact on the conduct of modern politics. Rationalism, he argues, is not simply one style of politics; it 'has become the stylistic criterion of all respectable politics'.[13] Modern politics has become

---

[8] See M. Weber, *Economy and Society* (New York, G. Roth and C. Wittich (eds.), 1968), esp., vol. 2, ch. 8.

[9] J. Habermas, *The Theory of Communicative Action. Vol. 1 Reason and the Rationalization of Society* (Cambridge, 1981); id., 'Law as Medium and Law as Institution' in G. Teubner (ed.), *Dilemmas of Law in the Welfare State* (Berlin, 1986), 203.

[10] See, esp., G. Teubner, 'Juridification. Concepts, Aspects, Limits, Solutions' in Teubner (ed.), *Juridification of Social Spheres* (Berlin, 1987), 3. Note, however, that the Americans, who have been labouring under the acute burden of over-legalization, have also participated. See, e.g., D.M. Trubek (ed.), *Reflexive Law and the Regulatory Crisis* (Madison, Wisconsin, 1983); C. Joerges and D.M. Trubek (eds.), *Critical Legal Thought: An American–German Debate* (Baden-Baden, 1989), Pt. 5.

[11] See M. Oakeshott, *Rationalism in Politics and other Essays* (London, 1962), 1.

[12] Ibid., 1.   [13] Ibid., 21.

the politics of programme, of technique, and of ideology. Though focused on the issue of politics, Oakeshott's essay may not only help us to identify something of the character of the British constitution and of the role of law within government but also to highlight a number of contemporary issues posed by rationalization. By focusing on the manner in which modern politics 'have become fixed in the vice of Rationalism' and by indicating that 'much of their failure . . . springs . . . from the defects of the Rationalist character when it is in control of affairs',[14] he presents an interesting perspective through which we may make sense of a range of constitutional questions.

One critical aspect of Oakeshott's essay is the argument that the source from which the deficiencies of Rationalism spring is that of a doctrine of human knowledge. Oakeshott identifies two sorts of knowledge; technical knowledge and practical knowlege. Technical knowledge is that type of knowledge which is susceptible of precise formulation; it is the type of knowledge which can be formulated into rules and may be taught and learned. Practical knowledge, by contrast, cannot be the subject of rule-formulation. It 'exists only in use'[15]; it is a form of traditional knowledge which cannot be taught and learned, but may only be imparted and acquired. Oakeshott suggests that, though these two sorts of knowledge do not exist separately, and both are involved in any form of human activity, they are nevertheless distinguishable. He illustrates the distinction by considering such activities as cookery, painting and religion. In a practical art like cookery 'nobody supposes that the knowledge that belongs to the good cook is confined to what may be written down in the cookery book; technique and what I have called practical knowledge combine to make skill in cookery wherever it exists'.[16] Similarly in a fine art such as painting in which 'a high degree of technical knowledge . . . is one thing; the ability to create a work of art . . . is another'.[17] And on religion, Oakeshott submits that, though it would 'be excessively liberal to call a man a Christian who was wholly ignorant of the technical side of Christianity, who knew nothing of creed or formulary, . . . it would be even more absurd to maintain that even the readiest knowledge of creed and catechism ever constituted the whole of the knowledge that belongs to a Christian'.[18]

Thus viewed, the error of Rationalism is essentially that of discounting practical knowledge. Since practical knowledge cannot be precisely formulated and generally expresses itself simply as the customary way of doing things, it often gives an appearance of imprecision which the Rationalist finds anathema. The error of the Rationalist, then, is to assume that the only kind of useful knowledge – that which satisfies the Rationalist's particular standard of certainty – is technical knowledge. It is thus an error of a fairly simple sort; the error of mistaking a part for the whole.

This excursus on human knowledge enables us more clearly to link Oakeshott's

---

[14] See M. Oakeshott, *Rationalism in Politics and Other Essays* (London, 1962), 28.
[15] Ibid., 8.   [16] Ibid.   [17] Ibid.   [18] Ibid., 8–9.

concerns directly to constitutional issues. For what Oakeshott claims in respect of cookery, painting and religion may also be extended to the activities of politics, law and governance.

The conduct of modern politics

In modern politics, Oakeshott argues that traditions of behaviour have given way to political programmes. Attitudes have been replaced by doctrines and customary practices have become transformed into ideologies. One consequence is that the conduct of contemporary politics has become riddled with ideological discourse. Across the political spectrum, various formulae have been devised to provide political guidance and, with this institutionalization of 'comparatively rigid systems of abstract ideas',[19] technique may be said to have triumphed. The idea of politics as 'the activity of attending to the general arrangements of a set of people whom chance or choice have brought together', as a 'conversation', or simply as the 'pursuit of intimations'[20] – that is, as a practice rooted in traditions of political behaviour and which is not reducible to logic or technique – has been all but jettisoned.

Oakeshott is often viewed as a unique voice in modern politics; a conservative – even a reactionary – thinker harking back to a traditional social order in which everyone had a given place. There are, no doubt, aspects of Oakeshott's work which may readily be construed in that light. Nevertheless, if we focus on Oakeshott as a thinker engaged in a genuinely philosophical analysis of human activity, his work may help us to acquire an insight into many of the central issues of contemporary politics. Consider, for example, the analysis presented by Charles Taylor in his 1991 Massey Lectures.[21] In these lectures Taylor identified individualism, instrumental reason and the question of political freedom as constituting the three key features of the contemporary politics. What is particularly noteworthy is that the characteristics of Oakeshott's idea of 'Rationalism' seem to lie at the core of each of them. In order to illustrate this point, I shall briefly consider each in turn.

The modern social world is one which, in an important sense, is founded on the self; it is a regime in which, more than at any other stage of our history, people have a right to choose for themselves their own pattern of life. For many, this form of individualism may be viewed as being the finest achievement of modern civilization. But, as Taylor emphasizes, it is a freedom which has been won 'by our breaking loose from older moral horizons' and only by discrediting the sense that we belonged to some larger order, some 'great chain of Being'.[22] Although this traditional order may have imposed restrictions on us, it also helped to confer meaning on the activities of social life. Consequently, the

[19] Ibid., 21.
[20] 'Political Education' in *Rationalism in Politics* (above, n. 11), 111 at 112, 125, 133–4.
[21] C. Taylor, *The Malaise of Modernity* (Concord, Ont., 1991).   [22] Ibid., 3.

emergence of modern individualism has generally been associated with a narrow-ing or flattening of our experience as we begin to shut out those issues (relig-ious, political, historical) which transcend the concerns of the self. On the downside, then, modern individualism seems to lead to a sense of disenchantment; a loss of a higher sense of purpose and, ultimately, to a culture of narcissism.[23]

The second feature of modernity which Taylor highlights is that of instru-mental reason, by which is meant 'the kind of rationality we draw on when we calculate the most economical application of means to a given end'.[24] This instrumental rationality is, of course, directly analogous to Oakeshott's idea of Rationalism. Taylor emphasizes that instrumental reason should not be viewed solely in negative terms. This scientific or technological imperative has not only provided the engine for enormous wealth generation but, through exaltation of productive labour and the utilization of an instrumental stance towards nature, it has enabled us to realize our status as autonomous, rational agents. Neverthe-less, there are many who are now coming to view technological civilization not so much as a symbol of progress but as a manifestation of decline. We may perhaps see this view reflected most obviously in the emergence of an environ-mental movement founded on a belief that, as a result of this striving for dom-ination, we have lost a vital contact with the natural rhythms of life. Related concerns have been expressed in a sense of dissatisfaction with the culture of the consumer society; an anxiety which may reflect the Platonic idea that a life of endless accumulation not only distracts us from higher things but may itself constitute a form of slavery.[25] Instrumental reason, which may in one sense be viewed as liberating, has threatened to take over our lives as the metric of efficiency or wealth maximization becomes our sole criterion of the good. This form of instrumental rationality has also had a major influence on our social and political arrangements. Being no longer grounded in the order of things, our governing institutions have become the subject of redesign; they have become bureaucratized and, in the fashionable jargon, subject to a continuous process of re-invention. This process, in turn, accentuates the sense of distance between institutions and communities and it induces us to see the relationship in an essentially instrumental perspective.

The final aspect of modernity which Taylor highlights is one which assesses the likely implications of individualism and instrumental reason for the conduct of political life. At this point, we may draw in particular on Tocqueville's studies of the political implications of modernity. Tocqueville suggested that the

---

[23] For a selection of the literature on this theme see: D. Bell, 'The cultural contradictions of capitalism' in D. Bell & I. Kristol (eds.), *Capitalism Today* (New York, 1970); A. Bloom, *The Closing of the American Mind* (London, 1987); C. Lasch, *The Culture of Narcissism. American Life in an Age of Diminishing Expectations* (New York, 1979); P.E. Slater, *The Pursuit of Loneliness. American Culture at the Breaking Point* (London, 1971).

[24] *Malaise of Modernity* (above, n. 21), 5.

[25] See the discussion of this theme in Taylor's essay 'Legitimation Crisis?' in his *Philosophical Papers, vol. 2. Philosophy and the Human Sciences* (Cambridge, 1985), ch. 10.

trends towards individualism and instrumentalism have a tendency to fashion the kind of society in which the individual becomes confined 'entirely within the solitude of his own heart' and does not seek actively to participate in the affairs of government.[26] This, he argued, creates the danger of a new variety of despotism rooted in an 'all-powerful form of government ... elected by the people' and which would 'combine the principle of centralization and that of popular sovereignty'.[27] This new variety would be a 'soft' form of despotism. Though more extensive, it would also be more mild and consequently 'it would degrade men without tormenting them'.[28] What Tocqueville thus envisaged was the emergence of 'an immense and tutelary power'; a power which 'is absolute, minute, regular, provident and mild' and which 'covers the surface of society with a network of small complicated rules, minute and uniform, through which the most original minds and the most energetic characters cannot penetrate'.[29] The only defence against this threat, Tocqueville felt, was a vibrant political culture in which the people actively participate in the several levels of government. The difficulty is that individualism and instrumentalism militates against this and a vicious cycle of civic decline is set in motion. In general terms, Tocqueville was seeking to highlight the dangers of a system of parliamentary democracy. Though that achievement may universally be acclaimed in positive terms, Tocqueville warned that '[t]o create a representation of the people in every centralized country is ... to diminish the evil that extreme centralization may produce, but not to get rid of it'.[30]

Is something like this happening in our highly centralized and bureaucratic political world? We can certainly feel the resonances of Tocqueville's thought running across the spectrum of modern political commentary, from Hailsham's concerns about 'elective dictatorship'[31] to Foucault's views about 'governmentality' and 'disciplinary power'.[32] Taylor, however, conceives Tocqueville's fears in a slightly different manner: 'The danger is not actual despotic control but fragmentation – that is, a people increasingly less capable of forming a common purpose and carrying it out.'[33] As people feel less and less tied to their fellow citizens, the difficulties of forming political groupings to express common purposes through democratic action become exacerbated. Yet, '[t]o lose the capacity to build politically effective majorities', Taylor argues, 'is to lose your paddle in mid-river. You are carried ineluctably downstream, which here means further and further into a culture enframed by atomism and instrumentalism.'[34] In some

---

[26] A. de Tocqueville, *Democracy in America* [1835] (New York, P. Bradley ed., 1990) vol. 2, 99.

[27] Ibid., vol., 2, 319.   [28] Ibid., vol., 2, 317.

[29] Ibid., vol., 2, 318–19.   [30] Ibid., vol., 2, 320.

[31] Lord Hailsham, *The Dilemma of Democracy. Diagnosis and Prescription* (London, 1978), ch. xx.

[32] M. Foucault, 'Governmentality' in G. Burchell, C. Gordon and P. Miller (eds.), *The Foucault Effect. Studies in Governmentality* (London, 1991), ch. 4; M. Foucault, *Discipline and Punish. The Birth of the Prison* (Harmondsworth, 1977).

[33] *Malaise of Modernity* (above, n. 21), 112.   [34] Ibid., 118.

senses, then, this threat is more serious than that posed by the instrumentalization of social life; instrumental reason may reduce the scope for freedom of action, but the 'loss of political liberty would mean that even the choices left would no longer be made by ourselves as citizens, but by an irresponsible tutelary power'.[35] At the very least, Taylor suggests that the difficulties in maintaining an active culture of self-government have brought about an important change in the character of modern politics. The politics of democratic will-formation seems now to be in danger of being supplanted by the politics of the rights-bearing subject.

These three features – individualism denoting the loss of meaning, instrumental reason signifying an eclipse of ends, and the issue of self-government touching on the loss of political freedom – each address issues of vital importance to the conduct of modern politics. Further, though there is certainly no consensus on how these issues might best be addressed or resolved, we might note that at the core of each of these concerns is the concern, examined by Oakeshott, of politics being reduced to a matter of technique.

The culture of the common law

But of what relevance is Oakeshott's essay to the question of law? In order to address this question, we must return to the distinction between technical and practical knowledge and the claim that the only sort of knowledge which the Rationalist recognizes is technical knowledge. Though Oakeshott's concern is with the emergence of Rationalist politics – ideological politics or the 'politics of the book' – it should be evident that the thrust of his argument is equally applicable to developments in the law.

Our legal traditions are rooted in the idea of the common law as a body of ancient custom which exists 'time out of the mind of man'. By its nature, custom is a set of usages which evolve through time. Though these usages are acknowledged, interpreted and recorded by judges, the common law is best understood as a body of unwritten law. We acquire knowledge of the common law, then, not simply by the analysis of texts, but primarily by acquiring an education in a tradition of behaviour. Once the common law is understood in this manner, we can extend much of Oakeshott's thought directly to law. 'We acquire habits of conduct', Oakeshott suggests, 'not by constructing a way of living upon rules or precepts learned by heart and subsequently practised, but by living with people who habitually behave in a certain manner.'[36] We might say that education in the law involves the acquisition of 'habits of conduct in the same way as we acquire our native language'; that is, imitatively, unreflectively, by living with the native people and by appreciating that '[w]hat we learn here is what may be learned without the formulation of its rules'.[37]

---

[35] *Malaise of Modernity* (above, n. 21), 10.
[36] 'The Tower of Babel' in *Rationalism in Politics* (above, n. 11), 59 at 62.   [37] Ibid.

The common law habit of thinking is, at root, a form of practical knowledge. The rules are not the well-spring of knowledge, but are to be understood essentially as cribs which may be used effectively only by someone educated in the traditions of the common law. At the core of the common law mode of thinking lies the idea of precedent. In the hands of the common lawyers, precedent is anything but a formalistic, backward-looking doctrine. *Stare decisis* certainly ensures that the present is linked to the past, but the function of the judge is creative and the idea of precedent may be viewed as 'a useful fiction by which judicial decision conceals its transformation into judicial legislation'.[38] Precedent is thus the device which enables us to reconcile continuity with innovation, order with progress, and to proclaim that the common law is always immemorial and always up-to-date. Oakeshott encapsulates this habit of thinking when he elaborates on the idea of a tradition of behaviour. He acknowledges the fact that such a tradition 'may . . . appear to be essentially unintelligible' and continues:

> It is neither fixed nor finished; it has no changeless centre to which understanding can anchor itself; there is no sovereign purpose to be perceived or invariable direction to be detected; there is no model to be copied, idea to be realized, or rule to be followed. Some parts of it may change more slowly than others, but none is immune from change. Everything is temporary. Nevertheless, though a tradition of behaviour is flimsy and elusive, it is not without identity, and what makes it a possible object of knowledge is the fact that all its parts do not change at the same time and that the changes it undergoes are potential within it. Its principle is a principle of *continuity*: authority is diffused between past, present and future; between the old, the new and what is to come. It is steady because, though it moves, it is never wholly at rest.[39]

The challenge to the common law tradition in modern times has come from the growing use of legislation. Legislation has always been recognized as constituting an important source of law. It may, in particular, be needed in order to extricate the law from the dead ends to which gradual evolution occasionally leads or to provide a framework for addressing new issues which arise. Notwithstanding these beneficial effects, in the mind of the common lawyer, legislation is also viewed as a dangerous device. In Hayek's words: 'It gave into the hands of men an instrument of great power which they needed to achieve some good, but which they have not yet learned so to control that it may not produce great evil.'[40] This has been the refrain of many lawyers, especially with the emergence since the nineteenth century of the modern administrative state. The thrust of

[38] A.V. Dicey, *Law of the Constitution* (above, n. 1), 18.
[39] 'Political Education' in *Rationalism in Politics* (above, n. 11), 111, 128. In a note to this passage Oakeshott adds: 'The critic who found "some mystical qualities" in this passage leaves me puzzled: it seems to me an exceedingly matter-of-fact description of the characteristics of any tradition – the Common Law of England, for example . . .'.
[40] F.A. Hayek, *Law, Legislation and Liberty. Vol. 1 Rules and Order* (London, 1973), 72.

their concern has been that the volume of legislation rides roughshod over 'acquired habits of conduct', that it has the effect of distorting 'our native language', and that it destroys the sense of law as an engagement which 'may be learned without the formulation of its rules'.

Further, since the great mass of modern legislation seems to have been produced in response to the demands of Rationalist politics, it may thus be seen to have injected ideological considerations into the fabric of the law. Throughout the twentieth century the implications of this trend have been vigorously debated and views on this issue have remained highly polarized.[41] In one camp we have the common lawyers arguing that social legislation destroys the moral fibre of the nation,[42] while in the other the thrust of the argument has been that a judiciary steeped in the culture of the common law has operated systematically to distort and marginalize the progressive effects of social legislation.[43] What, ultimately, this debate concerns is the most appropriate conception of legality rooted within our system of governance. As legislation has come in modern times to supplant the common law as the primary source of law, rather than being viewed as a reflection of the custom of a people which evolves through traditional practices, law comes to be equated with the command of a sovereign. To put the issue at its simplest, law ceases to be an exercise in practical knowledge and comes to be viewed as a form of scientific knowledge; and the lawyer, no longer the purveyor of practical wisdom, is obliged to adopt the techniques of the engineer.[44]

---

[41] For an argument that public law discourse in the twentieth century has been polarized between 'normativist' and 'functionalist' styles of thought, see M. Loughlin, *Public Law and Political Theory* (Oxford, 1992).

[42] See, e.g., A.V. Dicey, *Lectures on the Relation between Law and Public Opinion in England during the Nineteenth Century* (London, 1905), 256: 'The beneficial effects of State intervention, especially in the form of legislation, are direct, immediate and, so to speak, visible, whilst its evil effects are gradual and indirect. . . . State help kills self-help'; G.W. Keeton, *The Passing of Parliament* (London, 1952), 11–14: 'When Holdsworth, Lord Hewart and Dr Allen attacked the extension of administrative powers of legislation and adjudication, it was with the knowledge that each successive delegation . . . represented a fresh victory for policy over private right . . . The days of individualism have ended, for the time being at any rate. Everywhere, to a greater or a lesser degree, the collectivist state is triumphant. . . . So far, it is clear, we have not arrived in Moscow. We do not yet have the one-party state. Today, the executive is not quite all-powerful, although it is beyond question that it has increased very considerably in power over the past quarter of a century.'

[43] See, e.g., H.J. Laski, 'Judicial review of social policy in England' (1926) 39 *Harvard L Rev.* 839; W.A. Robson, *Justice and Administrative Law* (London, 1928); W.I. Jennings, 'The courts and administrative law – the experience of English housing legislation' (1936) 49 *Harvard L Rev.* 426; J.A.G. Griffith, 'Judges in Politics: England' (1968) 3 *Government & Opposition* 485; P. McAuslan, 'Administrative Law, Collective Consumption and Judicial Policy' (1983) 46 MLR 681.

[44] Oakeshott, *Rationalism in Politics* (above, n. 11), 34: '. . . professional education is coming more and more to be regarded as the acquisition of a technique, something that can be done through the post, with the result that we may look forward to a time when the professions will be stocked with clever men, but men whose skill is limited and who never had a proper opportunity of learning the *nuances* which compose the tradition and standard of behaviour which belong to a great profession'. For a recent examination of this issue, see: A.T. Kronman, *The Lost Lawyer. Failing Ideals of the Legal Profession* (Cambridge, Mass., 1993).

The character of the British constitution

This discussion on law may readily be extended into a deliberation over the character of the constitution. The spirit of the British constitution may be viewed essentially as an extension of the methods of the common law; *jus non scriptum* becomes transposed into the idea of the unwritten constitution. If we seek to identify the British constitution in the modern sense of the rules establishing and regulating the exercise of governmental power, we find that it is made up of a miscellaneous collection of statutes and practices, none of which constitute higher law and most of which make little sense unless interpreted in the light of innumerable political understandings. The point which Oakeshott highlights is the fact that the British constitution may be made to work only by way of a political education in a particular tradition of behaviour.

The key to the constitution, then, is the political experience of our rulers. 'The well-established hereditary ruler, educated in a tradition and heir to a long family experience', Oakeshott suggests, 'seemed to be well-enough equipped for the position he occupied; his politics might be improved by a correspondence course in technique, but in general he knew how to behave.'[45] Oakeshott extends this point by claiming that, even in the most favourable circumstances, 'knowledge of the political traditions of [a] society ... takes two or three generations to acquire'.[46] The contentious political issues which flow from these assertions may be placed to one side. Simply as a matter of analysis, what Oakeshott's observation highlights is the extent to which the constitution works, not because of an institutional separation of powers and the like, but because of a shared value system of the governing class. The governing class was educated in these practices from birth, and such values were given institutional expression through the traditions of public schools, Oxford and Cambridge colleges and the system of 'club government'.[47]

This perspective casts an interesting slant on a range of constitutional challenges presented in the twentieth century and certainly illuminates the intense nineteenth-century debates about the likely impact of democracy on the workings of the constitution.[48] For Oakeshott, Rationalism in politics is born of political inexperience. As new and politically inexperienced social classes obtain access to political power, they acquire a political doctrine in place of a tradition of political behaviour. They then come to treat with contempt that which they do not understand. Some Rationalists – Oakeshott singles out Bentham – explicitly seek to 'cover up all trace of the political habit and tradition of their society with a purely speculative idea'.[49] Gradually, the rule-book politics of

---

[45] *Rationalism in Politics* (above, n. 11), 24.   [46] Ibid., 30.

[47] W. Bagehot, *The English Constitution* [1867] (London, R.H.S. Crossman ed., 1963), 156. On this theme see, above, ch. 1, 26–8.

[48] See J. Roper, *Democracy and its Critics. Anglo-American Democractic Thought in the Nineteenth Century* (London, 1989), Pt. III.

[49] *Rationalism in Politics* (above, n. 11), 25.

Rationalism assumes its grip. Even in 1947 Oakeshott could write that 'the political tradition, which, not long ago, was the common possession of even extreme opponents in English politics, has been replaced by merely a common rationalist disposition of mind'.[50]

From this perspective, the critical problem of the twentieth century has been the impact which this emerging ideological politics has wrought on our anti-Rationalist constitutional arrangements. In the eyes of many, it has resulted in what may be called 'the waning of constitutional understanding'.[51] And it is this development which has caused those such as Lord Hailsham to characterize our system as one of party government or 'elective dictatorship'.[52] The efficient secret of this system has become the fact that government generally may take whatever action the governing party MPs are prepared to tolerate. For growing numbers of citizens, however, this appears to provide a thoroughly inadequate safeguard. One difficulty, however, is that the apparent remedy for our ailments – the adoption of a written constitution incorporating entrenched rights – seems from the traditional perspective not simply to be a corrective to Rationalist politics but also a further stage in the growing rationalization of society. Oakeshott, for example, viewed the impact of the American and French Revolutions and the Rationalist constitutions which they inspired as the extreme case of an entire society being reconstructed on rationalistic lines.[53] The paradox for conservatives has thus become whether, in order to protect the political values they hold dear, they should embrace the system of thought which they have traditionally rejected.[54]

Rationalization and governance

This analysis would seem to indicate that the critical issue in twentieth-century British government has been that of seeking to accommodate the emergence of

[50] *Rationalism in Politics*, 32.
[51] N. Johnson, *In Search of the Constitution* (London, 1977), ch. 3.
[52] *The Dilemma of Democracy* (above, n. 31), ch. xx.
[53] *Rationalism in Politics* (above, n. 11), 27: 'The Declaration of Independence is a characteristic product of the *saeculum rationalisticum*. It represents the politics of felt need interpreted with the aid of an ideology. And it is not surprising that it should have become one of the sacred documents of the politics of Rationalism, and, together with the similar documents of the French Revolution, the inspiration and pattern of many later adventures in the rationalist reconstruction of society.' Cf., M. Oakeshott, 'Contemporary British Politics' (1947–8) 1 *Cambridge Journal* 474, 489–90: 'The common law rights and duties of Englishmen were transplanted throughout the civilised world. . . . In this process some of their flexibility was lost; the rights and duties were exported; the genius that made them remained at home. Peoples, desirous of freedom, but dissatisfied with anything less than the imagination of an eternal and immutable law, gave to these rights the false title of Nature. Because they were not the fruit of their own experience, it was forgotten that they were the fruit of the experience of the British people. . . . What went abroad as the concrete rights of an Englishman have returned home as the abstract Rights of Man, and they have returned to confound our politics and corrupt our minds.'
[54] See N. Johnson, 'Constitutional Reform: Some Dilemmas for a Conservative Philosophy' in Z. Layton-Henry (ed.), *Conservative Party Politics* (London, 1980), 126.

ideological (Rationalist) politics with our anti-Rationalist legal and constitutional traditions. Though the gradual extension of democratic politics has evolved hand in glove with the growth of the administrative state, this has not resulted in fundamental constitutional reform. Rather than seeking to deal with the growth of government functions by reorganizing the State along orderly juridical lines, our objective has been to bring these extensive governmental responsibilities within the fold of the traditional arrangements. This has been achieved mainly by developing structures which were able to build on experience and to sustain and cultivate the new forms of practical knowledge which these governmental responsibilities required.

This type of accommodation has had important consequences for the role of law in government. Rather than adopting a Rationalist approach of seeking to define and formulate in law the precise powers, duties and procedures of public authorities, flexible frameworks have been established through which the working relationships of public bodies could emerge in the light of experience. These working practices, which have become central to the effective functioning of modern government, are reflected primarily in the conventional understandings of political élites, the codes of ethics and working habits of administrators and the values and standards of those professions – such as engineers, accountants, social workers, education administrators and lawyers – which have come to play an important role in the functioning of this extensive administrative system. The hallmark of this style is to be found in the pervasiveness of 'self-regulation' in the British administrative system.[55] The result has been that, in the course of forging an administrative state within the boundaries of the traditional framework, we have, in effect, developed a largely non-juridified structure of administrative law. At some level or other, the judiciary have taken cognizance of these arrangements, though in practice this has generally meant that the courts have withdrawn from the active supervision of many areas of modern governance. We have retained a common law conception of law, but the consequence has been that we have failed to think juridically when developing guidance, control and evaluation mechanisms in modern government.

For a period, this accommodation worked well enough. However, as the inexorable process of rationalization of society continued to pose new challenges for government, the strains became evident.[56] Since the 1970s, a great deal of concern has been expressed throughout the western world about the growing burden of government programmes and the apparent inability of government to maintain the requisite degree of responsiveness to new social and economic developments. A vigorous debate has ensued over governmental performance, which has been expressed in such terms as the problem of 'overload in

[55] See, e.g., D. Vogel, *National Styles of Regulation: Environmental Policy in Great Britain and the United States* (London, 1986); R. Baggott, 'Regulatory reform in Britain: the changing face of self-regulation' (1989) 67 *Public Admin.* 435.

[56] See D. Marquand, *The Unprincipled Society. New Demands and Old Politics* (London, 1988).

government',[57] of 'pluralistic stagnation'[58] or of an 'institutional sclerosis'[59] within the apparatus of government. Further, it is largely as a consequence of these political debates over government performance, that lawyers began to discuss the problems of regulatory overload, of over-legalization and of juridification. What is significant, however, is that, although Britain was certainly identified as being affected by the phenomenon of overload, the issue of over-legalization did not engage with the British experience of the administrative state. And the reason for this was precisely because, for the reasons identified, the administrative state in Britain had not evolved in a highly juridified form.

From the late 1970s, then, the apparatus of government has been identified as being part of the problem of devising effective government policies and of maintaining innovation and responsiveness in government. The policies pursued since then have generally been founded on a set of individualistic values and, being based on the single-minded pursuit of efficiency, rooted in a means-end rationality. In short, the programme developed by the Government has been the epitome of Rationalist politics. Whether the programme constitutes an effective response to the issue of government performance remains open to debate. For the purpose of this study, however, the critical point is that the implementation of this ideological programme has imposed severe strains on the traditional government arrangements based on the primacy of practical rather than scientific knowledge. As these self-regulatory frameworks have been undermined in the name of efficiency or consumer rights, the legal structures of government have increasingly been employed as normative frameworks. In Britain, rather than being identified as part of the problem of government effectiveness, the phenomenon of juridification has become a feature of the proposed solution.

This programme has had an acute impact both on the institution of local government and on the pattern of central–local government relations. We must not be starry-eyed about local government. Local government undoubtedly exhibited many of the less desirable features which have afflicted modern government generally. Having been absorbed into the framework of modern governance, local government has become highly bureaucratic and, in many respects, remote from the local communities it exists to represent and serve.[60] However, notwithstanding these deficiencies, the institution of local government has in recent years provided a rallying point for those who express scepticism that a Rationalist, neo-liberal programme based on the entrenchment of hierarchy and the construction of markets represents undiluted progress. The defence of the

[57] See, e.g., A. King, 'Overload: Problems of Governing in the 1970s' (1975) 23 *Political Studies* 283; J. Douglas, 'The Overloaded Crown' (1976) 6 *Brit. J of Political Science* 483; C. Offe, *Contradictions of the Welfare State* (London, 1984), ch. 2.

[58] S.H. Beer, *Britain Against Itself: The Political Contradictions of Collectivism* (London, 1982), Pt. I.

[59] M. Olson, *The Rise and Decline of Nations: Economic Growth, Stagflation and Social Rigidities* (New Haven, 1982), 78.

[60] See the discusssion, above, in ch. 1, 72–7 [The Triumph of Benthamism?].

institution of local government may thus assume importance for those who are already concerned at the degree of centralization in the British system of government, who lament the apparent decline in active participation in the affairs of government, or who oppose the idea that politics can be reduced to a matter of economics. The sceptics may not all be pulling in the same direction;[61] nor need they idealize the existing practices of local government. What, in essence, they are articulating is the importance of trying to keep an institutional space open for expressing and negotiating difference; in effect, for retaining some sense of locality in the conduct of politics.

The Government's programme thus raises a number of complex political questions, many of which seem to revolve around Taylor's concerns about the issues of individualism, instrumentalism and self-government. Our concern, however, has been primarily with the role assumed by law in the implementation of the programme. This turn to law has been in many respects a disconcerting affair. As we have seen, legislation in this field was not designed to establish over-arching norms regulating the central–local relationship. Consequently, the search for answers to contemporary disputes within the body of these statutes has generally proved to be a rather frustrating exercise. However, given the complexities of the relationship, so too has been the attempt to use law as a medium for carrying through a fundamental reform of the system. In order to analyse this experience, the impact of these changes on both Parliament and the courts must be examined. Before doing so, however, we might briefly reflect on the manner in which this attempt to use law as a primary mechanism for regulating central–local relations is related to the theme of rationalization.

Consider first the role of legislation. It is often said that local government legislation generally takes the form of framework legislation; that is, legislation which provides a skeletal structure, leaving the details to be provided by secondary legislation or administrative guidance. This focus on the concept of framework legislation does not, however, capture the basic change in legislative style which has been effected since the late 1970s. In general, we have continued to see the enactment of framework legislation. What is most significant is that the style of this framework legislation has changed from *facilitative* legislation to that of *instrumental* legislation; that is, from legislation which provides a flexible structure enabling norms to emerge through working practices to that of legislation which is designed to establish the norms and regulate the relationship. And the critical difference between these two styles of framework legislation is

---

[61] Many of the most ardent critics of modern individualism, for example, have been the neo-conservatives, while the critique of instrumental reason has been most closely associated with the Frankfurt school of critical theory: see, e.g., J. Habermas, *Towards a Rational Society* (London, 1971); id., *Knowledge and Human Interests* (London, 1971); id., *Theory and Practice* (Boston, 1973). Furthermore, while neo-conservatives are more likely to defend the traditional patterns of local government, the theme of the need for renewal of politics in localities has featured prominently in modern communitarian thought: see S. Mulhall and A. Swift, *Liberals and Communitarians* (Oxford, 1992); D. Bell, *Communitarianism and its Critics* (Oxford, 1993).

that, while the former is anti-Rationalist in character, the latter is the embodiment of Rationalism.

Furthermore, the Government's use of instrumental legislation has also been the source of major difficulties. Perhaps the most important has been the tendency, especially in relation to local government finance, to fall foul of the 'synoptic delusion'. This error, which Hayek regards as being a basic characteristic of what he calls 'constructivist rationalism', refers to 'the fiction that all relevant facts are known to some one mind, and that it is possible to construct from this knowledge of the particulars a desirable social order'.[62] This is a problem which is common to all complex systems in which attempts are made to improve the effectiveness of the system through the imposition of some central will. Such action often fails simply because of the systemic limits imposed, whether through a limited knowledge of particular facts or a limited understanding of how the system works, on the centre's ability to reconstruct such systems afresh. A related problem has been that of hyperactivism.[63] That is, as particular failures are gradually registered by the centre, or as the centre feels the need to establish either more precise objectives or a different set of objectives, new legislation is promoted to rectify faults or make necessary adjustments. Because of the formalities and time delays of the legislative process, however, this type of legislative hyperactivism often generates its own spiral of failure.

These legislative problems have been exacerbated when law is invoked as the primary method of dispute-resolution. Since so much of the traditional legislation in this field had never been drafted with the idea of adjudication in mind, the tendency since the early 1980s of trying to use the judiciary as an umpire in central–local government disputes has often been an unsettling and frustrating process. Just as Rationalism in politics creates pressures for rationalistic structures of government, this in turn contributes to the growing rationalization of law. One consequence has been the fact that since 1979 the public law workload of the courts has substantially increased. This trend, however, has often served only to expose the fact that, in clinging on to the cultural traditions of the common law, we have not been able to develop a modern jurisprudence of public law.

Parliament and Central–Local Government Relations

Throughout the twentieth century, the central–local relationship has been essentially an administrative relationship which has been facilitated through frame-

---

[62] Hayek, *Law, Legislation and Liberty, vol. 1* (above, n. 40), 14.

[63] K. Minogue, 'On Hyperactivism in Modern British Politics' in M. Cowling (ed.), *Conservative Essays* (London, 1978) 117, 120–1: '[H]yperactivism . . . is a morbid condition partly . . . because it tends to induce activity before experience has generated enough understanding of our situation to allow us to act wisely.'

work legislation. One consequence of this modern settlement has thus been that Parliament has ceased to be the primary link which mediates relations between local and central government, its main function becoming that of legitimating change through the approval of the Government's proposals for new legislation. The nature of this facilitative legislation has been such that major policy changes could often be negotiated and implemented without the need to return to Parliament for a new grant of authority. A good example of this is to be found in the field of education where, notwithstanding major changes in education policy throughout the post-war period, the Education Act 1944 continued into the 1980s to provide the basic statutory foundation for the system.[64] The basic function of such framework legislation was thus to provide a visible means of legal support for a regulatory system which emerged as a result of deliberations through administrative networks.

As we have seen, since 1979 the Government has sought to marginalize, undermine or by-pass these administrative networks and to govern by way of central direction. The existing legal framework, however, not having been drafted for such purposes, simply contained too many gaps and ambiguities to be susceptible to conversion into an instrument of command-and-control regulation. Consequently, the Government's strategy required the establishment of a more explicit hierarchical structure governing the central–local relationship and, in turn, this necessitated the promotion of a major programme of local government legislation. The scale of this programme is highlighted by the fact that in 1989, during the parliamentary debates on the Local Government and Housing Bill, it was acknowledged that this was the fiftieth Bill affecting local government which had been introduced by the Government in the ten years of Conservative rule.[65] This in fact seems to have been a fairly modest estimate since a subsequent study concluded that, in the period between 1979 and 1992, 143 Acts having a direct application to local government in England and Wales were enacted, of which 58 contained major changes.[66]

The scale and complexity of the Government's legislative programme since 1979 has certainly been unprecedented. What is particularly interesting is that its effect has been, once again, to bring Parliament into the process of mediating the central–local relationship. This experience has not, however, been an especially happy one for any of the parties involved. The scale of the programme has

[64] See, e.g., D.E. Regan, *Local Government and Education* (London, 1977), 11–12: 'It is clear . . . that MPs on all sides fully appreciated the importance of the measure. They were conscious of legislating for a generation. Indeed the Butler Act has served for even longer . . . Of course the structure of an educational system does not entirely determine the content of the education provided. Since 1944 there have been profound changes in teaching methods, educational philosophy, school design, the role of head teachers, and much else. A child at school in 1945 would find much strange if he were to return in 1976. Nevertheless these changes have occurred within an enduring framework.'
[65] HC Debs., vol. 147 col. 165 (N. Ridley), col. 177 (Dr J. Cunningham) (14 February 1989).
[66] Report of the Hansard Society Commission on the Legislative Process, *Making the Law* (London, 1992), 19, 291.

imposed a major strain on parliamentary procedures and the speed with which the Government has often felt required to act has resulted in many aspects of the legislative process being highly truncated or, in some cases, effectively abandoned. In its desire to bring about the transformation of local government, the Government has often felt obliged to ride roughshod over Parliamentary concerns.

Consultation

Within the twentieth century accommodation in central–local government relations, it has become standard practice that the Government will consult affected local authorities before initiating new legislation.[67] Further, in relation to subordinate legislation, this practice is often incorporated in a statutory requirement.[68] And when the Government announces proposals for fundamental change in the system of local government, it has generally been assumed that the action should not be taken until the issues have been examined by independent inquiry. Webster J, in a case in which the court held that the Government had been in breach of its statutory requirement to consult the local authority associations over the drafting of new social security regulations, defined consultation in the following terms:

> [T]he essence of consultation is the communication of a genuine invitation to give advice and a genuine consideration of that advice. . . . [T]o achieve consultation sufficient information must be supplied by the consulting party to the consulted party to enable it to tender helpful advice. Sufficient time must be given by the consulting to the consulted party to do that, and sufficient time must be allowed for such advice to be considered by the consulting party.[69]

By the standards imposed by this test, the Government's recent consultative practices concerning proposals affecting local government have fallen far short of the norm.

The traditional practice of establishing an independent inquiry before initiating fundamental change has certainly been forsaken. Royal Commissions were established during the 1960s, for example, to consider patterns of local government before embarking on a major reorganization of the system[70] and during the 1970s an official inquiry was established to consider the issue of local

---

[67] See, e.g., R.A.W. Rhodes, *The National World of Local Government* (London, 1986), 391–3.

[68] See, e.g., Local Government, Planning and Land Act 1980, ss. 54(4), 56(10); Social Security and Housing Benefits Act 1982, s. 36(1).

[69] *R* v. *Secretary of State for Social Services, ex p. Association of Metropolitan Authorities* [1986] 1 WLR 1, 4.

[70] *Report of the Royal Commission on Local Government in Greater London*, Cmnd. 1164 (1960) (Herbert Report); *Report of the Royal Commission on Local Government in England*, Cmnd. 4040 (1969) (Redcliffe-Maud Report).

government finance.[71] By contrast, during the 1980s basic reforms to structure and finance have been promoted without any such independent inquiry[72] and in the 1990s a comprehensive review of structure, finance and management arrangements of local government was undertaken purely by internal departmental review.[73] When, on the basis of this review, it was determined that further local government reorganization should follow, a statutory Local Government Commission was indeed established to make detailed recommendations for England.[74] The work of this Commission, however, has been racked with controversy.[75]

Given both the political conviction and the governmental agenda of Conservative administrations since 1979, it is perhaps not surprising that the use of Royal Commissions to advise on policy reform has been all but jettisoned.[76] Nevertheless, the complexity of contemporary government is such that, simply as a precondition to the effective implementation of policy, a certain degree of consultation with affected parties is often essential. The traditional manner of undertaking such public consultation has been through the issue of Green Papers outlining various options and inviting comments and then subsequently publishing a White Paper to explain the Government's proposals. Since 1979, however, the tendency has been to divert from these standard practices.

The practice of issuing formal Green Papers has, it would appear, been abandoned, since no such papers have been issued since 1988.[77] In effect, Green Papers have been replaced by informal consultative documents, or else White Papers are now expected to perform this role. But fewer White Papers have been published; there was, for example, no White Paper issued to explain the major changes to the system of school government introduced by the Education Reform Act 1988. Furthermore, even when such Papers are issued, they often are published too late in the process to enable affected parties to have a significant impact on policy formulation. Thus, although the Government had announced in

---

[71] *Report of the Committee of Inquiry into Local Government Finance*, Cmnd. 6453 (1976) (Layfield Report).

[72] See Local Government Act 1985 (abolition of GLC and metropolitan county councils) and Local Government Finance Act 1988 (abolition of domestic rates, establishment of uniform business rate and introduction of community charge).

[73] Department of the Environment, *Local Government Review. The Structure of Local Government in England: A Consultation Paper* (April 1991); *A New Tax for Local Government* (April 1991); *The Internal Management of Local Authorities in England* (July 1991).

[74] Local Government Act 1992, Pt. II. Not, however, in relation to Wales where a unitary model of reorganization was imposed: Local Government (Wales) Act 1994.

[75] See, above, ch. 2, 119–22.

[76] Note, however, how perceptions change. In the nineteenth century Toulmin Smith railed against the use of such Commissions on the ground that nomination was under the control of the Government and that 'all the real bearings of the case, all the actual facts and conditions and requisites are distorted or effectually smothered, and a vast blue book is produced, which it may be safely relied on that no one will read, but with the pretended results proclaimed in the first few pages of which the indolent many find it most convenient to content themselves': J.T. Smith, *Government by Commissions Illegal and Pernicious* (London, 1849), 18.

[77] See *Making the Law* (above, n. 66), Appx. 8.

the Queen's speech in June 1987 that there was to be 'major reform of housing legislation', no White Paper was published until the end of September, after the legislation had been drafted and only six or seven weeks before the Bill itself was published.[78] Perhaps the best example, however, concerns the consultation process in relation to the extension of compulsory competitive tendering to professional services in local government. The consultation document was published contemporaneously with the Bill in November 1991. That document invited responses by 31 January 1992. By this date, the Bill had not only passed through all its stages in the Lords but had also reached the committee stage in the Commons. Since the Minister regularly responded to Parliamentary questions on the Bill's proposals by stating that the matter remained the subject of consultation, this consultation timetable thus served to frustrate detailed Parliamentary debate on the Bill.[79]

Furthermore, of the consultative documents which are produced, there has been a distinct change in style. These documents seem increasingly to take the form of promotional literature rather than papers which explore options or explain the reasoning which has caused the Government to take action. The White Paper, *Streamlining the Cities*, for example, by its very title suggested a marginal change to metropolitan government rather than what was in reality a fundamental reorganization of the local government system. In that Paper, the Government's case for abolishing the Greater London Council and the metropolitan county councils was outlined in only ten paragraphs and then it was simply asserted that abolition 'will streamline local government . . . will remove a source of conflict and tension . . . will save money [and] will also provide a system which is simpler for the public to understand'.[80] These are highly contentious statements for which the Government provided little evidence. On the basis of the subsequent research findings, they appear not to have been justified.[81]

The promotional character of such papers is symbolically reflected by the change in format introduced in the late 1980s. With the switch to glossy booklets produced in a larger format, the style of presentation seems to have been accentuated to the detriment of detailed analysis of the proposals. The White

---

[78] Cm. 214 was published on 29 September and the Bill was given its first reading on 19 November.

[79] See, *Making the Law* (above, n. 66), 295–6.

[80] Department of the Environment, *Streamlining the Cities. Proposals for reorganising local government in London and the Metropolitan Counties*, Cmnd. 9063 (London, 1983), para. 1.19.

[81] The major project undertaken by the Institute of Local Government Studies, University of Birmingham, on the consequences of the abolition of the metropolitan county councils concluded that: 'Nobody seriously argues anymore that the 1986 reorganisation involved merely the removal of unnecessary powers from local government or the direct transfer of power from the MCCs and GLC to the districts and boroughs. . . . It can be demonstrated that abolition led to increases in expenditure and posts rather than decreases. As we show, joint action for anything other than a very limited range of services should be seen as an additional (indirectly elected) tier of local government which actually undermines, in a fundamental sense, the "unitary authority" principle. It also raises major issues about processes of resource allocation, public comprehensibility and, in particular, public accountability.' See S. Leach, H. Davis, C. Gane and C. Skelcher, *After Abolition. The Operation of the Post-1986 Metropolitan Government System in England* (Birmingham, 1991), 2, 5.

Paper explaining the proposal to remove further education colleges from local authority control, for example, justified the reform in a single sentence:

> Colleges lack the freedom which we gave to the polytechnic and higher education colleges in 1989 to respond to the demands of students and of the labour market.[82]

No further reasons were given, nor were any statistics provided. Yet, on this basis, 'a reorganisation of the public sector accounting for £2 billion per annum of public expenditure was proposed to Parliament'.[83]

The general experience, then, has been one of fewer consultative documents being issued, containing less information and analysis, and often being produced on a timetable which seems to defeat the ostensible objective of the exercise. In this sense, consultation with local government over new legislation seems to have followed a similar trend to the conduct of business through the Consultative Council on Local Government Finance (CCLGF). The CCLGF, having been established in the 1970s as a forum for negotiations between central and local government over grant distribution arrangements, has during the 1980s been increasingly used not for negotiation or even consultation but simply for the announcement by the Government of decisions unilaterally determined.[84] In general, the processes of consultation have been transformed mainly into machinery for informing affected parties of firm proposals.

Parliamentary procedures

The scale and complexity of the Government's programme in seeking to establish a more precise legal framework governing the central–local relationship has imposed major strains on parliamentary procedures. The exigencies of time, in conjunction with the complexity of the task of drafting directive rather than facilitative legislation, has caused the Government regularly to use parliamentary procedures primarily for the purpose of tidying up the rough drafts of legislation which have been introduced as Government Bills. Furthermore, given the specific time pressures within Parliament, this in turn has required the Government to take action strictly to ration the period which may be set aside for parliamentary discussion on these Bills.

These problems are certainly in part a consequence of deficiencies in the consultative process. Since consultation documents have often been prepared at the same time as instructions were being sent to parliamentary counsel, any

---

[82] *Education and Training for the 21st Century*, Cm. 1536 (1991), para. 9.2.

[83] *Making the Law* (above, n. 66), 296 (Evidence of the Local Authority Associations).

[84] This trend reached its nadir in 1988 when the Secretary of State took the unprecedented step of announcing the main features of the 1989/90 settlement *in advance* of the CCLGF meeting established to discuss the working parties' reports. See Association of County Councils, *Rate Support Grant (England) 1989/90* (London, 1989), 54.

changes to be made in the light of consultation have generally taken the form of amendments to Bills already placed before Parliament.[85] Thus, in its study of the legislative process in 1992, the Hansard Society Commission noted that 'all our evidence suggests that in many cases Government amendments are necessary to remedy defects in the bill which are already known to those who prepared and drafted it'[86] and that too many Bills were introduced 'half-baked', that is, 'with detail remaining to be worked out and consequently large numbers of Government amendments having to be tabled in Parliament'.[87]

This tendency to legislate 'on the hoof' has been a particularly noticeable feature of recent local government legislation.[88] Its impact may most graphically be seen in the number of Government amendments made to local government Bills in the House of Lords (that is, generally at the tail-end of the legislative process). In 1987/88, for example, the Government promoted a total of 1,259 amendments of this type to three Bills affecting local government.[89] In the following session, there were 606 amendments of this type made to the Local Government and Housing Bill alone.[90] Many of these amendments have been introduced in great bulk and at short notice – during the Lords' consideration of the Housing Act 1988, for example, 100 amendments were tabled in one day – and this makes it almost imposssible to digest and debate their implications. It is this failure on the part of Government to finalize its proposals before introducing a Bill which the Hansard Society Commission felt constituted 'the basic defect in the legislative process' and amounted to 'a grave indictment of those Governments' approach to law-making'.[91]

The general impact of these practices in curtailing debate has been compounded by the increasing tendency of the Government strictly to ration the amount of time which may be spent in parliamentary discussion on the Bill. Most of the major Bills affecting local government which have been introduced since 1979 have been the subject of an allocation of time motion. The effect of applying this guillotine has been significantly to restrict detailed examination of many of the Bill's provisions.[92]

---

[85] See, e.g., *Making the Law* (above, n. 66), 339–41 (memorandum of G. Roscoe, former lawyer in the Department of the Environment).

[86] Ibid., para. 116.   [87] Ibid., para. 173.

[88] An illustration of the nature of the change is provided by way of contrast with the Education Act 1944. It had originally been intended to publish that Bill in July 1943 simultaneously with the White Paper. However, because of various drafting problems, publication of the Bill was actually deferred until December 1943. By the time the Bill was published, it was reported to have gone through at least fifteen versions. See, R. Aldrich and P. Leighton, *Education: Time for a New Act?*, Bedford Way Paper No. 23 (London, 1985), 13.

[89] Education Reform Act 1988 (569 amendments); Housing Act 1988 (273 amendments); and Local Government Finance Act 1988 (417 amendments).

[90] *Making the Law* (above, n. 66), 301.   [91] Ibid., para. 182.

[92] The following Bills affecting local government have since 1979 been subject to an allocation of time motion: Education (No. 2) Bill 1979–80 (twice); Housing Bill 1979–80 (twice); Transport Bill 1982–83; Housing and Building Control Bill 1982–83; Rates Bill 1983–84; Rating and Valuation (Amendment) (Scotland) Bill 1983–84; Local Government Bill 1984–85 (twice); Transport

This mode of legislating has had the effect of generating its own cycle of legislative hyperactivity. Legislation on the hoof does not result simply in a greater number of Government amendments being introduced at a late stage of the parliamentary process; it also tends to lead to new legislation being introduced which is designed to correct and amend errors of the earlier legislation. The clearest example of this trend may be found in relation to statutes concerning local government finance. During the 1980s, the introduction of legislation seeking to redraft, amend and repeal earlier legislation covering this subject became virtually an annual event. In 1980 a major Act establishing a new system of grant distribution and capital expenditure control mechanism was enacted.[93] Not only was this subject to amendment in 1982[94] but between 1984 and 1989 a total of 11 further Bills were promoted for the purpose of amending and reforming the financial regime under which local government operated.[95] Nor was this the end of the process. In 1991 no fewer than four Bills were introduced to amend or clarify the community charge system,[96] culminating in the following year with major legislation designed to repeal that system and replace it with a council tax.[97]

This practice of legislating on the hoof is confined neither to highly technical fields nor to politically contentious legislation. The Bill which became the Children Act 1989, for example, had all-party support. It entered Parliament as a measure of 121 pages, containing 79 clauses and 11 schedules. As a result primarily of Government amendments, including Parts which were not contained in the original Bill,[98] it was eventually enacted as a measure containing 108 sections and 15

Bill 1984–85 (twice); Local Government Finance Bill 1986–87 (twice); Abolition of Domestic Rates etc. (Scotland) Bill 1986–87 (twice); Education Reform Bill 1987–88 (twice); Local Government Finance Bill 1987–88 (twice); School Boards (Scotland) Bill 1987–88; Housing Bill 1987–88; Self-Governing Schools etc. (Scotland) Bill 1988–89 (twice); Local Government and Housing Bill 1988–89; National Health Service and Community Care Bill 1989–90 (twice); Community Charges (General Reduction) Bill 1990–91; Local Government Finance Bill 1991–92 (twice); Education (Schools) Bill 1991–92 (twice); Local Government Bill 1991–92; Education Bill 1992–93 (twice).

[93] Local Government, Planning and Land Act 1980, Pt. VI.

[94] Local Government Finance Act 1982.

[95] Rates Act 1984 (rate-capping); Education (Grants and Awards) Act 1984 (education support grants); Rate Support Grants Act 1986 (amending block grant distribution arrangements); Housing and Planning Act 1986 (urban development grants); Local Government Act 1986 (date for rate-setting); Local Government Finance Act 1987 (validating rate support grant decisions); Rate Support Grants Act 1987 (abandoning recycling of grant to local authorities); Local Government Act 1987 (adjustments to education block grants and capital expenditure arrangements); Local Government Finance Act 1988 (introducing community charge etc.); Rate Support Grants Act 1988 (providing for transition from rate support grant to revenue support grant regime); Local Government and Housing Act 1989 (amending community charge system and introducing a new capital control system).

[96] Community Charges (General Reduction) Act 1991, Community Charges (Substitute Setting) Act 1991, Caravans (Standard Community Charge and Rating) Act 1991, and the Local Government Finance and Valuation Act 1991.

[97] Local Government Finance Act 1992.

[98] The First Division Association has explained this practice thus: 'Frequently, the drafting timetable slips ... The target date for introducing the bill, however, comes to be seen as an absolute,

schedules totalling 218 pages. This was not the end of the story. Various errors were then subsequently identified, with the result that the Government found it necessary to insert 42 paragraphs amending the 1989 Act into a Bill proceeding through Parliament in the following session.[99]

The style of local government legislation

Much of the new legislation affecting local government has been more directive in nature. Extensive powers have been vested in Ministers to oversee conduct in local government. Precise duties have been imposed on local authorities to undertake particular tasks. A broad range of powers to hold local authorities to account for their activities has been conferred on a wide range of agencies or interest groups. These trends do not, however, signal the abandonment of framework legislation. If for no other reason, the pace of change has required the Government to rely, so far as practicable, on delegated powers. Nor have these changes generally produced a more direct and accessible legislative style; the complexity of the system and the lack of clarity about the Government's objectives have invariably combined to frustrate simplicity in the drafting of statutes. Ambiguity, complexity and the vesting of broad powers in Ministers have always been facets of local government legislation. The most important features of this new style of local government legislation, then, are that these new powers are intended to be extensively used and the new legislation is designed to define the precise boundaries of the central–local relationship.

In order to appreciate the significance of the change in style of local government legislation, it is thus essential to consider not only the actual style of drafting but also to acknowledge the fact that the function of these statutes in the regulatory framework has fundamentally altered. It is this basic functional change which ultimately determines the distinctiveness of this legislation. The powers acquired by Ministers were intended to be used as drafted, the duties imposed on local authorities were designed to be fully enforced, and the legal framework established was devised to govern.

An early indication of the significance of these changes is provided by Part I, chapter I of the Housing Act 1980 which introduced the statutory right of council tenants to purchase their freehold on favourable terms. Knowing that it would be politically controversial, the Secretary of State acquired very broad powers under section 23 to intervene and 'do all such things as appear to him necessary or expedient' where it appears that tenants 'have or may have difficulty in exercising the right to buy effectively and expeditiously'.[100] Though

---

either because of pressure from the Parliamentary business managers or because the Minister fears that delay will be perceived as indecision. Bills are therefore commonly introduced with significant parts missing ... These parts then have to be introduced by Government amendment, at a later Parliamentary stage ...': *Making the Law* (above, n. 66), 166.

[99] Courts and Legal Services Act 1990, Sched. 16.   [100] See now, Housing Act 1985, s. 164.

described by the Minister as a default power,[101] the provision was actually more intrusive, since it was exercisable even if a local authority was not actually in default in carrying out their duties. What was particularly unusual, however, was the vigilance of the centre in ensuring that these rights were able to be exercised expeditiously. The first formal notice under section 23 seeking information was issued only five weeks after the commencement date of the Act and by the time Norwich City Council was approached on 30 April 1981, just less than eight months after commencement, 33 local authorities had already received similar notices.[102]

By this stage, although Norwich had accepted the tenant's right in 803 cases, they had not completed one sale. Throughout the rest of 1981, discussions took place between the local authority and the Department. The rate of progress, however, was not sufficient to satisfy the Secretary of State who, on 3 December, served a notice of intervention. In *R* v. *Secretary of State for the Environment, ex parte Norwich City Council*[103] this notice was the subject of an application for judicial review. This application was dismissed by both the Divisional Court and Court of Appeal. Though contrary opinions were expressed in the Court of Appeal about the reasonableness of the local council's actions,[104] it was held that this question was irrelevant to the issue before the court. Though expressing the opinion that '[l]ocal self-government is such an important part of our Constitution that . . . the courts should be vigilant to see that this power of the central government is not exceeded or misused',[105] the court was unanimous in holding that the Secretary of State had not exceeded his powers. Perhaps the most significant aspect of the case is the language used by the court in explaining the Secretary of State's power. Section 23 was found to be 'a most coercive power',[106] was considered 'Draconian in its terms'[107] and was felt to be 'without precedent in legislation of this nature'.[108] The courts found in favour of the Secretary of State because, 'short of seeking to exclude altogether any power of review by the courts, the wording of s. 23 has clearly been framed by Parliament in such a way as to maximise the power of the Secretary of State and to minimise any power of review by the court'.[109]

---

[101] During the Committee stage of the Bill John Stanley stated: 'There is nothing new in providing in legislation powers for Ministers to take over the statutory duties of local authorities where those local authorities are failing to discharge their duties.' HC Debs., Standing Committee F, Session 1980–81, col. 491.

[102] See R. Forest and A. Murie, *An Unreasonable Act? Central–local government conflict and the Housing Act 1980* (Bristol, 1985), 31–3.

[103] [1982] QB 808.

[104] Lord Denning MR considered that: 'The Council here showed too little concern for the rights of the tenants. They should have given them a higher priority. They were unreasonable not to do so.' (ibid., 827). Kerr LJ, however, stated that: 'In my view the council could not possibly be regarded as having acted unreasonably in approaching their obligations under the Act on this basis.' (ibid., 830).

[105] Ibid., 824, *per* Lord Denning MR.   [106] Ibid.   [107] Ibid., 828.

[108] Ibid., 829.   [109] Ibid., 828.

This example highlights both the breadth of the powers acquired by the centre during the 1980s and its vigilance in supervising local action. It may be taken as a model of central oversight of local authorities when required to implement contentious initiatives.[110] Nevertheless, notwithstanding the fact that there is now a greater awareness that such measures are likely to be subject to judicial scrutiny, the Government has not always managed clearly to signal its intentions. Mustill LJ was undoubtedly expressing the frustrations of many judges who in recent years have had to immerse themselves in the mysteries of local government finance when stating that: 'I find it impossible to discern with any accuracy the spirit of section 35(5) [of the Local Government Finance Act 1988] simply because I believe that in all the flurry of legislation, evasive action and counter-legislation, the point under review has not been fully thought out.'[111] As a result of such difficulties, there has been a tendency during the 1980s for draftsmen to cut back on the statutory protections accorded local authorities in the grant distribution process. Many of the protections in Part VI of the 1980 Act, such as the requirement of equitable treatment within classes of authority, have, for example, gradually been removed. By 1988 there was simply a requirement on the Secretary of State to place a report before the Commons specifying the basis for grant allocation.[112] Furthermore, whenever the Government has felt frustrated by judicial interpretation of such obscure or ambiguous provisions, it has felt few qualms about using retrospective legislation to reaffirm its position.[113]

In considering the character of this new style of local government legislation, regard must also be had to the issue of framework legislation. Notwithstanding the unprecedented scale of primary legislation concerning local government, much of this legislation provides only a skeletal framework. Such legislation thus cannot easily be examined and amended by Parliament since not only the details but often also the substance and the principles of the legislation remain unspecified. Given the lack of parliamentary time for scrutiny of delegated legislation, the inadequate nature of that scrutiny (in particular, the inability to amend), and the difficulties of viewing the various pieces as part of an overall

---

[110] Cf., e.g., the powers of the Secretary of State in relation to compulsory competitive tendering: Local Government Act 1988, ss. 11–13. See, e.g., *R* v. *Secretary of State for the Environment, ex p. Knowsley MBC, The Independent*, 25 September 1991, where the Court of Appeal held that, since the Minister had not acted unreasonably, the courts could not review the decision that certain local authorities had acted anti-competitively in accepting a bid for a service contract from their own Direct Service Organization which was higher than that of a private contractor.

[111] *R* v. *Lambeth LBC, ex parte Secretary of State for the Environment* [1991] COD 132 (CA). Note that, after the Minister's application to have the level of the charge quashed was refused, a Bill was promoted to ensure that the Secretary of State's view on the capping level fully feeds through into a new reduced level of community charge: see Community Charges (Substitute Setting) Act 1991.

[112] Local Government Finance Act 1988, s. 78A.

[113] See, e.g., London Regional Transport (Amendment) Act 1985; Rate Support Grants Act 1986; Local Government Finance Act 1987, s. 4; Local Government and Housing Act 1989, s. 52.

picture, there are particular reasons for believing that these practices undermine the effectiveness of parliamentary scrutiny. Many of these difficulties are well-illustrated by the Local Government and Housing Act 1989. Though the 1989 Act contained a number of important reforms, such as imposing political restrictions on local authority members, specifying the economic development powers of local authorities and introducing a new capital control system, it is almost impossible to grasp the nature or significance of these reforms without also examining the many regulations passed under the authority of the parent Act.[114]

Finally, particular attention should be paid to the use of 'Henry VIII clauses'. Henry VIII clauses, so-named from the Statute of Proclamations which conferred on Henry the power to make proclamations with full legislative force, are provisions enabling primary legislation to be amended by secondary legislation. Though such clauses have been a perennial source of controversy in discussions on administrative law in Britain,[115] it should be noted that they were were rarely used before 1945 and then almost exclusively in the field of local government legislation.[116] Further, though they have become a more standard feature of framework legislation since the war, they have not generally been used in contentious circumstances.[117] During the 1980s, however, they have often been used in contentious local government legislation. A typical provision is to be found in section 101 of the Local Government Act 1985 which provides that:

(1)   The Secretary of State may at any time by order make such incidental, consequential, transitional or supplementary provision as appears to him to be necessary or expedient –

   (a)   for the general purposes or any particular purposes of this Act or in consequence of any of its provisions or for giving for effect to it . . .

(2)   An order under this section may in particular make provision –

   . . .

   (c)   for amending, repealing or revoking (with or without savings) any provision of an Act passed . . . before the abolition date.[118]

---

[114] On this issue see the evidence of the Society of County Secretaries in *Making the Law* (above, n. 66), 350–1.

[115] See, e.g., Report of the Committee on Ministers' Powers, Cmd. 4060 (1932), 56–62 (Donoughmore Committee).

[116] The Henry VIII clause had first appeared in the Local Government Act 1888 and up until 1930 had been incorporated in only eight Acts, six of which concerned local government matters (ibid., 36, Annex II). See further, J. Willis, *The Parliamentary Powers of English Governmental Departments* (Cambridge, Mass, 1933), 152. The Donoughmore Committee had recommended that it 'should be abandoned in all but the most exceptional cases' and it was not used from that date until after 1945: see Lord Rippon of Hexham, 'Henry VIII Clauses' (1989) 10 *Statute Law Rev.* 205.

[117] Such provisions generally have been used either to provide a mechanism for up-rating penalties in line with inflation or for the making of transitional or consequential provisions.

[118] For similar examples see, Local Government Finance Act 1988, s. 147, Education Reform Act 1988, s. 52(7) and the Children Act 1989, s. 15. Note, however, that the original formulation of the

The general point to be emphasized is that the most significant change in the drafting of recent local government legislation is not so much its unprecedented style, but rather the fact that these new central powers are intended to be actively used and establish a precise regulative framework.

Parliament and the poll tax

The impact of these various practices may be illuminated by considering, as a specific example, the manner in which the Government introduced the community charge (or poll tax) system. The Local Government Finance Act 1988 enacted what is generally recognized to be the most radical reform to the system of local government finance this century. From a parliamentary perspective, it provides a remarkable illustration of the Government's ability to promote major legislation and then to abandon the reform and repeal and replace the measure all within the course of a single Parliament. Notwithstanding its short life, however, it has had a profound impact on government: it brought the entire system of local government finance to the brink of collapse, was a major factor in the downfall of the Prime Minister in November 1990, and, despite the fact that it was touted as restoring local accountability, was the critical event in the period between 1988 and 1993 which saw the expenditure of all local authorities being in effect determined by the centre. On a conservative estimate, the measure cost the country £1.5bn[119] and left local councils with vast numbers of unpaid bills which they will still be trying to collect well into the next millenium. How could this have been allowed to happen?

The Government had expressed some concern about the system of local government finance on assuming office in 1979. A departmental review was undertaken which culminated in a Green Paper whose general conclusion was essentially that there are no alternatives to domestic rates.[120] Consequently, when introducing its rate-capping proposals, the Government stated that 'rates should remain

clause in the Children Bill (to 'modify or repeal' the primary legislation) was subjected to a powerful attack in the Lords by Lord Simon of Glaisdale as 'a constitutional outrage' (HL Debs., vol. 502 col. 1295, 20 December 1988). This caused the Lord Chancellor to agree to alter the wording by replacing that phrase with the word 'amend'. There are also a significant number of more specific forms of Henry VIII clauses such as the power under s. 5(4) of the Local Government Finance Act 1992 to amend council tax bands or under s. 8 of the Local Government Act 1992 to extend the range of activities subject to CCT.

[119] D. Butler, A. Adonis and T. Travers, *Failure in British Government. The Politics of the Poll Tax* (Oxford, 1994), 2. This study also suggests that that figure increases 'to over £20bn if transfers from national taxation are included' (ibid.).

[120] Department of the Environment, *Alternatives to Domestic Rates*, Cmnd. 8449 (1981). Reflecting on this paper, Butler, Adonis and Travers commented that: 'In retrospect, it is extraordinary that such an effective poll tax demolition job should have been overridden within three years by those – including many of the same people – who produced the poll tax.' *Failure in British Government* (above, n. 119), 35.

for the foreseeable future the main source of local revenue for local government'.[121] Foreseeability in government must certainly be less than three years,[122] however, since in January 1986 the Government announced its proposed poll tax reforms.[123] It is interesting to note that *Paying for Local Government* is the first consultative document to have abandoned the traditional format in favour of a larger, glossy design replete with charts and tables. In their authoritative study, Butler, Adonis and Travers confirm the impression that the change in presentation went hand-in-hand with a substantive change. They note in particular that the critical Figure 11, which was designed to show that the community charge would be more progressive than rates, 'was an early example of the government's efforts at presentational delusion' and was 'in reality, not comparing like with like'.[124]

During 1986 the decision was made to cut the transitional period for replacing domestic rates with the poll tax from ten years to three. Since the Secretary of State for Scotland was determined, against the background of the highly unpopular rates revaluation in 1985, to have the reform enacted before the 1987 general election, the Scottish legislation was the first to be introduced. Production of the Scottish Bill then revealed some of the difficulties:

> Drafting the Bill . . . turned out to be 'something of a nightmare', in the words of [one] of those [officials] involved. The more they got into complexities, the more concerned became the Scottish Office – ministers as much as officials – at the problems of implementation.[125]

Nevertheless, at the Commons report stage of the Scottish Bill, and against the advice of officials, Ministers accepted an amendment to introduce the poll tax in 1989 without any transitional phase. This then provided the model for the English legislation which was introduced in the following session.

After being granted a second reading in December 1987, the Local Government Finance Bill went to Committee stage. In order to placate Conservative doubters, the Secretary of State agreed to ensure that their voice would be heard in committee. In order to ensure a Government majority, however, that Committee, with 44 members, was almost double the size of the standard standing committee. This committee nevertheless conducted its business at breakneck speed, convening only one week after the second reading debate and meeting three times a week instead of the usual two. As to the Committee's impact, we might note the assessment of Butler, Adonis and Travers:

---

[121] Department of the Environment, *Rates*, Cmnd. 9008 (1983), para. 2.15.

[122] In actuality it was less than two years since the Prime Minister identified the Chequers meeting of Sunday, 31 March 1985 (18 months after the *Rates* White Paper) as the date on which 'the community charge was born': M. Thatcher, *The Downing Street Years* (London, 1993), 648.

[123] Department of the Environment, *Paying for Local Government*, Cmnd. 9714 (1986).

[124] *Failure in British Government* (above, n. 119), 91.   [125] Ibid., 102.

As with most controversial government Bills, the standing committee was a futile marathon. Between mid-January and mid-March 1988, the committee held 35 sessions sitting for a total of 120 hours. . . . A colossal amount of committee time was spent on the first few clauses . . . after which the government resorted to a guillotine so that most of the later clauses went through with virtually no debate. . . . The axe fell after 70 hours and 17 of the Bill's 129 clauses, the guillotine motion allocating a mere 18 sittings to the outstanding clauses and sections – including all the arrangements for the community charge register, rebates and administration. The government did not lose any of the 173 votes held during the committee stage . . . In the bill's entire passage through the Commons, only five or so minor opposition amendments were accepted, two of them changing the word 'March' to 'January'.

The committee stage was mostly a matter of posturing . . . The government introduced a mass of amendments of its own to improve the mechanics of the Bill. For the rest, it was scrutiny by slogan and soundbite.[126]

Thus the Bill which, when introduced in the Commons, contained 131 clauses and twelve schedules and was 100 pages in length, left it as a measure of 150 clauses and sixteen schedules. The Bill, now extending to 151 pages, had increased in size by over 50 per cent, not because of extensive parliamentary scrutiny, but essentially because of the tabling by the Government of over 200 amendments.

The influence of the Lords was not much greater. Though their Lordships managed to carry two relatively minor amendments against the Government,[127] the Bill which returned to the Commons was longer again; this time because of a further 417 Government amendments introduced in the Lords. Consideration of these amendments by the Commons was subject to a guillotine.[128] When enacted on 29 July, the Local Government Finance Act 1988 was a measure extending to 179 pages and consisting of 152 sections and thirteen schedules.

Though the system was designed to take effect on 1 April 1990, gaps, anomalies and uncertainties were rapidly appearing. The Government tried to address these by a growing body of delegated legislation, much of it produced at a very late stage and many of these regulations being themselves the subject of rapid amendment. Further, the Government was also required to make significant amendments to the 1988 Act system during the following session. This was achieved by adding a large number of provisions, mainly in the Lords, to the Local Government and Housing Bill.[129] By this stage it was becoming apparent that, when viewed in terms of household burden, the vast majority of people would be worse off under the new system. As the protests grew, the Government

---

[126] *Failure in British Government* (above, n. 119), 116–17.

[127] One extended the rebate system to student nurses and the other extended the rebates available to disabled people.

[128] HC Debs., vol. 137 col. 1100 (20 July 1988).

[129] See Local Government and Housing Act 1989, Sched.5, which included basic changes to the safety net arrangements and introduced a new system of transitional relief, at a cost to the Exchequer of nearly £500m, covering the period 1991–94.

gradually realized that the poll tax was a major political catastrophe. This caused a new swathe of amendments to be introduced which, though doing little to mitigate the unpopularity of the reform, did significantly complicate its implementation. In the words of Butler, Adonis and Travers, the poll tax 'was advancing from the mere baroque to vulgar rococo, as the flailing efforts of ministers to dampen down political hostility produced an ever-moving target at which local authorities had to aim'.[130] By December 1990 the Prime Minister had been replaced and Michael Heseltine, who had throughout been a stern critic of the poll tax,[131] was once again installed as Secretary of State for the Environment.

Heseltine immediately announced a departmental review of local government structure, finance and management arrangements. In March, two weeks before the start of the new financial year and after virtually all poll tax bills had been sent out, the Chancellor of the Exchequer announced a £140 reduction in all poll tax bills, thus causing local authorities to have to start afresh with their collection arrangements. In April it was then announced that the poll tax would be replaced with the council tax.[132] In order to get the new tax up and running by 1993 property revaluations had to be carried out and therefore the Local Government Finance and Valuation Act 1991 was rushed through Parliament. In the following session the Local Government Finance Act 1992, which introduced the new scheme, was enacted.

The Hansard Society Commission was not inaccurate when suggesting that 'the collapse of the community charge legislation resulted from the Government's failure to ensure, by discussions with those most directly involved, that it would be workable in practice and that the charges could be collected'.[133] Whether that comment captures the full flavour of this episode which 'almost everyone involved in the design and implementation of the poll tax now recognises ... as a public policy failure of the first magnitude'[134] is another matter.

Norms of rule-making

There is a significant amount of research which indicates that, in circumstances in which the parties are obliged to maintain continuous relations with one another, the optimum regulatory strategy is one based on a co-operative approach.[135]

[130] *Failure in British Government* (above, n. 119), 145.

[131] See in particular his speech in the second reading debate in which he reminded MPs that in the review he undertook in 1981 the poll tax had been rejected out of hand, that the tax would not improve accountability, that its crude regressive nature would provoke profound discontent and that: 'Responsibility for the poll tax will be targeted precisely and unavoidably at the Government who introduced that tax. That tax will be known as the Tory tax.' HC Debs., vol. 124 col. 1141 (16 December 1987).

[132] Department of the Environment, *A New Tax for Local Government* (April, 1991). This consultation document was informal, short and decidedly not glossy.

[133] *Making the Law* (above, n. 66), para. 114.

[134] Butler, Adonis and Travers, *Failure in British Government* (above, n. 119), 302.

[135] See, e.g., I. Ayres and J. Braithwaite, *Responsive Regulation: Transcending the Deregulation Debate* (New York, 1992).

Nevertheless, in moving away from the traditional manner of conducting central–local relations – a bargaining approach in which the norms of the system emerged through the practices of the network – the Government may have felt that it had little alternative if it wished to realize its radical objectives. Even if the necessity of adopting a central directive strategy is accepted, however, there is plenty of evidence to suggest that many of the policy failures of this period were the product of the Government's failure fully to realize the consequences of its own basic strategy. In particular, the Government did not seem to recognize that the impact of its actions would have the effect of transforming the function of local government legislation from that of providing a facilitative framework through which the rules of the game could emerge to that of embodying the rules of the game itself. Thereafter, it seemed to be caught up in a hyperactive cycle of seeking to fill in the gaps, resolve the ambiguities or simply to alter the rules, all largely in response to various forms of evasive action taken by local authorities. In short, the Government did not seem to appreciate the complexity of the system it was seeking to regulate and direct.

In *The Morality of Law*, Lon Fuller identified eight precepts which constituted what he called an 'internal morality of law'. Fuller argued that the sovereign authority could fail to make law if: (i) there was a failure to devise any rules so that every issue was decided in an ad hoc manner; (ii) there was a failure to make known to affected parties the rules to be observed; (iii) rules were announced with retrospective effect; (iv) there was a failure to make the rules understandable; (v) contradictory rules were enacted; (vi) rules were proclaimed which required conduct beyond the powers of the affected parties; (vii) rules were changed so frequently that affected parties could not orientate their action by them; and (viii) there was a basic lack of congruence between the rules announced and their actual administration.[136] Though Fuller insisted that these norms must be viewed as moral criteria, some have argued that they are best understood as precepts of efficacy.[137] Without wishing to become embroiled in this jurisprudential debate, I wish here simply to take Fuller's precepts as providing some basic standards against which the functional effectiveness of a legal or administrative system might be gauged.

Putting the precepts into a positive formulation, it could be argued that central government failed in its directive strategy of the 1980s essentially by failing to promulgate a rule-system which was of sufficient generality, accessibility, prospectivity, intelligibility, coherency, attainability, stability, and congruency to be able to provide an effective guide to local authority action. The clearest

---

[136] L.L. Fuller, *The Morality of Law* (New Haven, rev. edn., 1969), ch. II.

[137] Certain critics have thus taken the view that Fuller's precepts betray a confusion between morality and efficacy. For a discussion see: Fuller, *The Morality of Law*, ch. V, 'A Reply to Critics'. Cf. N. Luhmann, *A Sociological Theory of Law* (London, 1985), 164–5 (adopting the view that Fuller's precepts are best viewed as 'legal norms of legal norm-making' and thus as criteria of reflexivity in modern law).

illustration of this point may be found in relation to the way in which the Government altered the system of financing local government during the 1980s. During the critical period of the early 1980s, for example, the Government changed the system with such rapidity that it became exceedingly difficult for local authorities to engage in any form of sensible financial planning. One index of the volatility of the system is provided by the fact that, between 1979/80 and 1983/84, local government had to operate under no fewer than seven different grant systems.[138] Furthermore, the complexity of the system was such that, in the words of the Audit Commission, 'few people understand fully the basis on which grant is distributed'.[139] The Commission also had major doubts about the coherence of the system, suggesting that 'the present system is being used to try to secure at least four different objectives which are not mutually compatible'.[140] The clearest indication of the failure of this directive strategy, however, is found in the Secretary of State's decision in 1987 not only to use legislation retrospectively to validate all past grant determinations, but also to enact a provision which stated that the Secretary of State's grant determinations 'shall have effect notwithstanding any decision of a court . . . purporting to have a contrary effect'.[141]

Though the experience with respect to local government finance certainly provides the clearest illustration of this theme of legislative hyperactivism, it is arguably simply the most extreme example of a general trend, which has also been replicated in such local government service areas as housing, education and public transport. Parliament has thus been brought back into the business of mediating the central–local government relationship. Rather than enabling that institution once again to act as the voice of the localities at the centre, however, the episode serves only to highlight the degree to which the institution of Parliament has itself become an instrument of Government.

The Judiciary and Central–Local Government Relations

The process of transforming the legal framework into a regime which defines the character of the relationship between central and local government has not only imposed major pressures on Parliament. This new regime is also one in which the courts are apparently expected to perform the role of umpire in central–local disputes. Since the traditional facilitative framework was devised on the implicit understanding that the conduct of central–local relations was essentially an internal rule-game, this modification has presented a significant challenge for the

[138] G.W. Jones and J.D. Stewart, 'The Layfield Analysis Applied to Central–Local Relations under the Conservative Government', vol. 8 no. 3 *Local Government Studies* 47, 55–6.

[139] Audit Commission, *The impact on local authorities' economy, efficiency and effectiveness of the block grant distribution system* (London, 1984), 1.

[140] Ibid.

[141] Local Government Finance Act 1987, s. 4(6). For a more detailed examination of these issues see, above, ch. 5.

judiciary. The nature of the changes were clearly signalled by Lord Woolf in 1986 when he stated that:

> I find it difficult to believe that there has been any other period of our legal history where a sphere of law has developed in such a rapid and exciting manner as administrative law over the period since I started practice. . . . While it was rare before I was appointed [to the High Court in 1979] to have one public body challenging before the courts a decision of another, it is now commonplace to have central government attacking local government decisions, local government attacking central government decisions and one local authority challenging the decisions of another.[142]

What adjustments have been required by courts as a result of the assumption of this new responsibility? How well have the judiciary responded to the challenge? In considering these issues we must at the outset acknowledge the point made by Lord Woolf that this process of bringing the courts into the business of regulating the central–local relationship has proceeded in tandem with the emergence of a distinctive public law jurisdiction of the High Court. The evolution of the judicial role in regulating central–local conflicts has thus been bound up in the general processes of the development of the court's public law jurisdiction. Before focusing on the jurisprudential issues raised by these changes, we should first consider the manner in which these recent developments relate to general trends in the development of English public law.

The public law jurisdiction

In the early 1980s, at precisely the time at which the courts were being prevailed upon to resolve central–local disputes, the judiciary were in the process of completing a major project, which had commenced in the immediate post-war period, of modernizing court procedures 'for preventing the abuse of power'.[143] The basic principles of administrative law had been overhauled,[144] a streamlined 'application for judicial review' had been established,[145] and the principle that

---

[142] Sir H. Woolf, 'Public Law–Private Law: Why the Divide?', 1986 *Public Law* 220.

[143] A. Denning, *Freedom Under The Law* (London, 1949), 126.

[144] The major milestones were: *R* v. *Northumberland Compensation Appeal Tribunal, ex parte Shaw* [1951] 1 KB 711 (resurrection of the power to review for error of law on the face of the record); *Ridge* v. *Baldwin* [1964] AC 40 (reinvigoration of principles of natural justice and leading to emergence of principles of procedural fairness); *Conway* v. *Rimmer* [1968] AC 910 (Minister's claim of Crown privilege could be subjected to judicial review); *Padfield* v. *Minister of Agriculture* [1968] AC 997 (subjectively formulated discretionary powers vested in ministers could not confer an unfettered discretion); *Anisminic* v. *Foreign Compensation Commission* [1969] 2 AC 147 (all errors of law effectively went to jurisdiction); and *Council of Civil Service Unions* v. *Minister for the Civil Service* [1985] AC 374 (prerogative powers are in principle reviewable in accordance with the same principles which apply to powers rooted in statute). It was precisely because of these developments that, in the last case (at 410), Lord Diplock felt able to reformulate the principles of judicial review under the heads of illegality, irrationality and procedural impropriety.

[145] RSC Ord. 53, SI 1977 No. 1955; Supreme Court Act 1981, s. 31. These reforms thus replaced the prerogative orders, which Lord Denning had in 1949 identified as 'not [being] suitable for the winning of freedom in the new age': *Freedom under the Law* (above, n. 143), 126.

judicial review provided the exclusive procedure for addressing public law claims had just been enunciated.[146] In effect, a distinct public law jurisdiction of the High Court had been fashioned. Since most of the central–local disputes have proceeded by way of judicial review, this recent experience throws some light not only on the ability of the judiciary to rise to the challenge of resolving such disputes, but also on the general strengths and limitations of judicial review. This experience thus provides a singular illustration of the nature of this newly formulated public law jurisdiction.

Probably the most impressive aspect of judicial review has been the speed with which the courts have been able to resolve many of these highly complex central–local disputes. One objective of the reforms has been to uphold 'the public interest in good administration' and this requires that 'public authorities and third parties should not be kept in suspense as to the validity of a decision the authority has reached ... for any longer period than is absolutely necessary'.[147] In furtherance of this objective, the judiciary have ensured that many of the disputes which raise major issues concerning the powers of central departments or local authorities have been able to progress through the court system with extraordinary speed. In *Bromley*, for example, Lord Scarman commented that the 'speed with which these proceedings were taken through the Divisional Court and the Court of Appeal was a remarkable achievement by the two courts and an indication of the value of the procedure of judicial review'.[148] The timetable was even more striking in the *Westminster* forward funding case: the Divisional Court gave judgment on 3 March 1986, the Court of Appeal by 20 March and the issue was argued before the House of Lords between 24 and 26 March, judgment finally being delivered on 17 April.[149] Given the scale and complexity of the action, the speed with which the courts were able to dispose of the community charge capping case was perhaps the most impressive of all: although consuming a total of 25 court days, the procedure took only six weeks from the date of first hearing in the Divisional Court to oral decision of the Lords.[150]

Such speed in the dispatch of cases of a highly complex nature, however, cannot be achieved without incurring certain costs or without requiring a number of adjustments to be made in the traditional methods of disposing of judicial business. One obvious time-saving device would be to switch from the standard practice of full oral advocacy of the entire case in open court towards a requirement of advance submission of written briefs, thereby enabling a saving to be

---

[146] See *O'Reilly* v. *Mackman* [1983] 2 AC 237. See further, H. Woolf, *Protection of the Public – A New Challenge* (London, 1990).

[147] *O'Reilly* v. *Mackman* [1983] 2 AC 237, 280–1 (*per* Lord Diplock).

[148] *Bromley LBC* v *Greater London Council* [1983] 1 AC 768, 836.

[149] *Re Westminster City Council* [1986] AC 668.

[150] *Hammersmith & Fulham LBC* v. *Secretary of State for the Environment* [1990] 3 All ER 589. See, above, ch. 5, 310 (n. 200). For a reminder that the use of the expedited procedure can have consequential effects on the development of other areas of law see: A. Rodger, 'Reflections on *Junior Books*' in P.B.H. Birks (ed.), *Frontiers of Liability, vol. 2* (Oxford, 1994), 64.

made on the time required in court for oral hearing. Though the English tradition is founded on oral advocacy, there has been some movement in the direction of written submissions in addressing central–local disputes since the early 1980s. The earliest signal that some adjustment would be required was provided in the *Brent* case. At the end of a judgment which contained a skilful analysis of the grant system and a detailed explanation of events leading to the decision challenged, Ackner LJ commented:

> Having learned a few weeks before the hearing that the affidavit and exhibits numbered close on 1,000 pages we had a pre-hearing review. At our request we were most helpfully provided with a useful glossary of terms, a reading guide, a chronological statement of events and an outline of the submissions to be made. This enabled us to save much hearing time by some useful advance reading.[151]

Since *Brent*, these techniques have been adopted virtually as standard practice in relation to complex central–local disputes.[152] Necessity is the mother of innovation. Certainly, it is difficult to see how, without this heavy reliance on the pre-hearing reading of papers and skeleton arguments, such judicial business could be effectively dispatched.

These procedural adjustments, however, raise more general questions concerning the purpose of public law proceedings. The basic objective, it would appear, is to ensure and to promote elementary standards of fairness, reasonableness and legality in the conduct of public administration.[153] But the public law jurisdiction is highly discretionary. Applicants for judicial review must obtain leave before proceeding and, given the need for speed and the limited judicial resources available, 'this necessarily involves limiting the number of cases in which leave to apply should be given'.[154] Further, the legal principles which are applied are highly flexible and, notwithstanding judicial protestations that they are in no way concerned to challenge policy decisions,[155] the degree of malleability of these principles suggests that the law–policy division is less clear-cut than is often supposed. Remedies are also discretionary, with the courts showing 'a proper awareness of the needs of public administration'[156] in fashioning any

---

[151] *R* v. *Secretary of State for the Environment, ex p. Brent LBC* [1982] 2 WLR 693, 735.

[152] In the community charge capping case, for example, we were informed that the Court of Appeal 'began the pre-reading of relevant papers on the same day [as the Divisional Court gave judgment] and continued the process on Monday, 18 June and the morning of 19 June, oral argument beginning at 2 pm on that day': [1990] 3 All ER 589, 613.

[153] See Lord Woolf, 'Droit Public – English Style', 1995 *Public Law* 57, 64.

[154] *R* v. *Panel on Takeovers and Mergers, ex p. Guinness plc* [1990] 1 QB 146, 177–8 (*per* Lord Donaldson MR).

[155] See, e.g., H. Woolf, 'Public Law–Private Law' (above, n. 142), 225: 'Under public law, . . . it is not for the courts to specify what is reasonable and its views on policy questions are normally of no relevance. The explanation for the more limited role of the courts in relation to public duties is that the statute or other authority which creates the duty places the responsibility for the decision on the public body responsible for making the decision.'

[156] *R* v. *Monopolies and Mergers Commission, ex p. Argyll Group plc* [1986] 1 WLR 763, 774 (*per* Lord Donaldson MR).

relief. What in effect is happening is that, with the formalization of a system of public law, the judiciary have been obliged to grapple with a range of issues which essentially concern the nature of their role in the conduct of public law litigation.

The issues raised by these developments may most concisely be identified by drawing a highly-stylized distinction between the private law and public law models of adjudication.[157] In the private law model, adjudication is seen as a bi-polar, self-contained episode where the controversy is over a set of completed events and right and remedy are interdependent. The public law model, by contrast, is one in which: the scope of the action is not exogenously given but is shaped by the parties; the party structure is not rigidly bi-polar but amorphous; fact inquiry is predictive and legislative rather than historical and adjudicative; relief is forward-looking, flexible and with important consequences for absentees; the remedy is not imposed but negotiated; its administration requires the continuing participation of the court; the judge plays an active role throughout; and the action concerns a grievance about the operation of public policy. Within these characteristic tendencies of public law litigation many of the tension-points in the emerging public law jurisdiction may be discerned.

Many of these tendencies have been evident in the major cases we have examined in this study. In the *Nottinghamshire* case, though the action was initiated by a small number of local authorities seeking to pursue a relatively discrete claim of unfair treatment, that question had been effectively lost from view by the time the case reached the Lords, and the issue at the forefront of deliberations before the House in reality concerned the nature of the entire legislative scheme for distributing central government grants and the role of courts in policing that system.[158] Furthermore, although in that case the court was apparently seeking to maintain a differentiation between governmental and judicial processes, it was obliged to do so essentially by shaping the action into a form in which it could make a 'legislative' pronouncement. On one level, the *Bromley* decision[159] also seems to illustrate the extent to which the courts are distanced from perceiving themselves as managers of public policy programmes; how else can we explain the apparent absurdity of our highest court, though concurring in the result, giving five different opinions on how best to interpret the nature of the 1969 Act scheme? Nevertheless, when we consider the aftermath of that decision, not only in relation to public transport policy but also in the light of the legality of local authority expenditure policies in general, a strong case can be made for the argument that we make sense of the subsequent case law not in terms of a faithful following of the *Bromley* precedent but rather by reference to the judiciary's perception of the need to modify that decision in

[157] See A. Chayes, 'The Role of the Judge in Public Law Litigation' (1976) 89 *Harvard L Rev.* 1281.
[158] *Nottinghamshire CC v. Secretary of State for the Environment* [1986] 2 WLR 1. See, above, ch. 5, 282–9.
[159] *Bromley LBC v. Greater London Council* [1983] 1 AC 768.

order to alleviate some of the discordant public policy consequences which seemed to flow from that judgment.[160]

The case of *Hazell* v. *Hammersmith LBC*, however, seems to provide the best single illustration of the issues thrown up by the emerging public law model of litigation. Though that case presented itself as an action between the auditor and one (rather atypical) authority, the manner in which it was shaped resulted in an action which sought to determine the general question of whether local authorities could lawfully engage in swaps transactions on capital markets. That this was in the nature of a 'legislative' determination is evident from the fact that these sophisticated financial instruments did not even exist when the statutory framework was set in place in 1972 and the court was thus obliged to reach a resolution by reference to the basic structure of the statutory framework and general principles of administrative law. One difficulty, however, was that the bi-polar dispute not only excluded affected parties but also was highly skewed, since the defendant authority actually had a material interest in the success of the auditor's restrictive argument. This led, in consequence, to the joinder of several banks to the action. But this still meant that the views of many of the 130 and more local authorities which had used swaps as an instrument of debt management were never fully presented. The case also threw up a number of unusual features of the adjudicative process: judgments being delivered either before or after the closing of City financial markets to minimize any disruptions which they might occasion;[161] the auditor feeling obliged to seek counsel's opinion on whether he was permitted to consult other parties (and thus to obtain a broader governmental view) before seeking leave to appeal against the Court of Appeal's decision; and, in order to ration the time spent on the case, the House of Lords taking the unprecedented step of issuing a 'provisional' ruling on the question of *vires*.[162] Further, the issues were scarcely resolved as a result of the Lords' ruling. In that case the court addressed only the general issue of *vires* and, for the purpose of simplifying the proceedings, had ordered the deferral of the question of whether, if the transactions were unlawful, all payments made should be restored.[163] After *Hazell*, the issue of restitution thus came to the forefront. Since no obvious test-case existed, the Commercial Court, being concerned at the proliferation of actions (there being around 150 outstanding writs on this issue) took unprecedented action when offering the court's assistance in managing the action by hosting meetings between the parties in the hope of arranging for a set of representative actions.[164]

These examples draw out a number of facets of the difficulties faced by courts when becoming involved in this type of public law litigation. The judiciary are required to play a much more active role in shaping the nature of the issue which

---

[160] See, above, ch. 4, 237–56.
[161] See, *The Times*, 2 November 1989; *The Independent*, 23 February 1990.
[162] *Financial Times*, 2 November 1990.   [163] [1990] 2 WLR 17, 29.
[164] See, above, ch. 6, 357–9.

is presented for resolution and in the form of relief granted. This degree of discretion potentially creates problems since the courts could be drawn into the business of having effectively to manage the implementation of public policy programmes.[165] Also, because of the need for a bi-polar dispute over a multi-party issue in circumstances in which the courts are often required to articulate principles which have an impact on activities not before the court, considerable uncertainties can be generated. A good example of this problem is provided by the *Allerdale* litigation, in which the High Court judgment created uncertainties about the legality of various forays of local authorities in the financial markets but where, because of the cost, complexity and limited interests of the plaintiff in that action, it seemed unlikely that their appeal would be pursued.[166] In general, one basic danger of juridification in this field is that the courts would rapidly come to play a central role in the management of public business.

This phenomenon of judicial managerialism has become a feature of the contemporary American court system, where it has generated a great deal of heated debate.[167] In the emerging public law jurisdiction in England, the issue must be addressed against the background of a rapidly expanding judicial review caseload.[168] Some have argued that the resulting delays simply require redress through the appointment of more judges.[169] This cannot provide a solution to current difficulties, however, without some fundamental questions first being asked about the nature and purpose of the system. Lord Lane has referred to judicial review as being analogous to a motorway; once provided, the public have an incentive to use it. Picking up on that figure of speech, Lord Woolf suggested that in the 1990s there is 'a danger of it becoming as overcrowded as the M25'.[170] This is a useful analogy. The reason why solutions such as the M25

[165] One example of this occurred in 1985, in the run-up to the abolition of the GLC, when the court was placed in the position of almost having to vet each item of the GLC's information and publicity campaign. See, above, ch. 3, 160.

[166] *Credit Suisse* v. *Allerdale BC* (1995) 1 Lloyd's Reports 315. See, above, ch. 6, 337–8.

[167] See, e.g., J. Vining, 'Justice, Bureaucracy and Legal Method' (1981) 80 *Michigan L Rev.* 248; J. Resnik, 'Managerial Judges' (1982) 96 *Harvard L Rev.* 376; id., 'Failing Faith: Adjudicatory Procedure in Decline' (1986) 53 *Univ. of Chicago L Rev.* 494; O. Fiss, 'The Bureaucratization of the Judiciary' (1983) 92 *Yale L J* 1442.

[168] During the 1980s, the judicial review caseload increased more than threefold and in the 1990s has continued to grow at a rate of increase at well over 20 per cent compound a year. See, M. Sunkin, 'What is happening to judicial review?' (1987) 50 *MLR* 432; id., 'The judicial review caseload 1987–89', 1991 *Public Law* 490; H. Woolf, 'Judicial Review: A Possible Programme for Reform', 1992 *Public Law* 221; Law Commission, *Judicial Review and Statutory Appeals*, Law Com. No. 226 (London, 1994) paras. 212–13.

[169] See, e.g., Lord Browne-Wilkinson, 'The Independence of the Judiciary', 1988 *Public Law* 44, 45 ('there is . . . an interference with the enforcement of the rule of law if there is a failure to finance the appointment of sufficient judges or the provision of adequate courts and court staff to meet society's current demands for justice'); D. Pannick, 'Who is subject to judicial review and in respect of what?', 1992 *Public Law* 1, 7 ('If an expanding jurisdiction threatens further to increase waiting lists (already scandalously long), then the remedy is the appointment of more judges to the Crown Office list, not self-imposed fetters on what cases will be heard.')

[170] H. Woolf, 'Judicial Review: A Possible Programme for Reform', 1992 *Public Law* 221.

are rapidly transformed into problems is because of basic deficiencies in developing a coherent and comprehensive transport policy. So also with judicial review. The reason the reforms of the late 1970s have so quickly generated problems of a potentially intractable nature may well be because of our failure for so long to address certain fundamental issues concerning the character of our administrative law. Juridification without an appropriate institutional infrastructure provides no solutions to contemporary difficulties.

There has, nevertheless, been one important principle which has prevented the courts, through the exercise of judicial review, becoming drawn centrally into the management of public policy programmes. This is the principle that '[u]nder public law, it is not the role of the courts to find facts'.[171] The primary concern of the courts here has been to emphasize that it is no part of the judicial review function to review the merits of a public authority's decision,[172] since this would be to substitute its own opinion[173] and thus convert review into a form of appeal.[174] The judiciary have, as a consequence, imposed particular limitations on the use of judicial review for fact-finding purposes.

The main limitations concern the availability of discovery of documents and the ability to obtain cross-examination of deponents of affidavits. Although discovery and cross-examination are in principle now available 'whenever the justice of the case requires',[175] the judiciary do not regard these powers as part of their ordinary stock-in-trade. The public law jurisdiction is concerned with judicial supervision to ensure legality and it has been suggested that it is not appropriate in circumstances in which there is a challenge to the facts or a basic conflict of evidence.[176] Consequently, although there have been certain unusual circumstances in which councillors have been cross-examined,[177] it is virtually impossible through judicial review to obtain leave to cross-examine Ministers or departmental officials on their affidavits. Similarly, discovery will not be permitted 'as a fishing expedition in the hope of obtaining . . . something which might

---

[171] H. Woolf, 'Public Law–Private Law' (above, n. 142), 225. See, *O'Reilly* v. *Mackman* [1983] 2 AC 237, 282.

[172] See, e.g., *Council on Civil Service Unions* v. *Minister for the Civil Service* [1985] AC 374, 410 (*per* Lord Fraser): 'The issue here is not whether the minister's instruction was proper or fair or justifiable on its merits. These matters are not for the courts to determine.'

[173] See, e.g., *R* v. *Birmingham City Council, ex p. O* [1983] 1 AC 578, 594–5 (*per* Lord Brightman): 'The court has no jurisdiction to substitute its own opinion. The decision of the council is the final word, subject only to an application for judicial review . . . on *Wednesbury* principles.'

[174] See, e.g., *R* v. *Secretary of State for the Home Department, ex p. Brind* [1991] 1 AC 696, 762 (*per* Lord Ackner): 'to stray into the realms of appellate jurisdiction involves the courts in a wrongful usurpation of power'.

[175] *O'Reilly* v. *Mackman* [1983] 2 AC 237, 282.

[176] See, e.g., *R* v. *Inland Revenue Commissioners, ex p. Rossminster* [1980] AC 952, 1027; *R* v. *Derbyshire CC, ex p. Noble* [1990] ICR 808, 813; *Roy* v. *Kensington & Chelsea & Westminster Family Practitioner Committee* [1992] 1 AC 624, 647.

[177] See, e.g., *R* v. *Waltham Forest LBC, ex p. Baxter* [1988] QB 419, 422; *R* v. *Derbyshire CC, ex p. The Times Supplements Ltd* (1991) 3 Admin. LR 241, 248.

counter that which appears clearly from the affidavits'.[178] Consequently, in those circumstances in which local authorities are claiming an abuse of power against central government, the requirements for evidence are much greater and, without the capacity to probe beyond the official documentation, it is likely to be an uphill struggle.

These limitations on the judicial review function perform an important role in protecting the courts from becoming absorbed into a managerialist ethos and thereby becoming bureaucratized. But these procedural limitations also highlight the limited penetrative capacity of judicial review. Though the courts have in recent years boldly asserted their power to review governmental decision-making which constitutes an abuse of power,[179] their usefulness in so doing seems in practice to be significantly diminished if they are not prepared to probe behind the formal account of what has taken place.[180] In seeking to develop the public law jurisdiction along such lines and within a system of parliamentary government, however, the courts seem to face a basic dilemma: 'judicial restraint is unsatisfactory while judicial activism is ill-informed'.[181]

These general facets of the emerging public law jurisdiction of the High Court would appear to cast basic doubts on the question of whether the courts are able competently to perform the role of umpire in the resolution of central–local disputes. If this process of juridification is to continue, then the only way in which these issues could adequately be addressed is by strengthening the capacity of the entire structure of accountability within the system of central–local government relations.[182] This observation is, I believe, considerably reinforced by reflecting on two particular aspects of the recent experience: the balance between description and evaluation in court judgments and the general outcome of these disputes.

Many of these central–local disputes, especially those with a financial dimension, have involved a convoluted set of facts which unfold against the background of a statutory framework of great complexity. Consequently, the great bulk of the judgments handed down in such cases has been devoted to an

---

[178] *R* v. *Inland Revenue Commissioners, ex p. National Federation of Self-Employed and Small Businesses Ltd* [1982] AC 617, 664. See, e.g., *R* v. *Secretary of State for the Environment, ex p. Islington LBC, The Independent*, 6 September 1991, a case in which the Court of Appeal overturned Henry J's order to grant discovery relating to the Government's refusal to give consent to the disposal of premises held by the London Residuary Body to Islington LBC and which were being used as offices for the London Lesbian and Gay Centre.

[179] See, e.g., *R* v. *Secretary of State for the Home Department, ex p. Brind* [1991] 1 AC 696, 751 (*per* Lord Templeman): 'judicial review, a remedy invented by the judges to restrain the excess or abuse of power'.

[180] See, M. Purdue, 'The scope for fact-finding in judicial review' in G. Hand and J. MacBride (eds.), *Droit Sans Frontiers. Essays in Honour of L. Neville Brown* (Birmingham, 1991) 193, 201.

[181] J. Allison, 'The Procedural Reason for Judicial Restraint', 1994 *Public Law* 452, 466.

[182] For an elaboration of this argument see, M. Loughlin, *Administrative Accountability in Local Government* (York, 1992), esp. ch. 7.

exposition of the facts and an elaboration of the statutory procedures. The proportion of the judgment actually devoted to a critical evaluation on the basis of public law principles is often minuscule. In short, the lack of balance between the complexity of the facts and the simplicity of the applicable concepts is quite striking. This asymmetry, in conjunction with the court's unwillingness to investigate beyond the official version of the facts, seems in itself to suggest that the courts in the exercise of their public law jurisdiction may not be an appropriate institution for resolving such disputes.

The general tenor of this observation is strongly reinforced, especially from the local authority's perspective, when we analyse outcomes. Once we focus on the results in these recent disputes, a remarkable pattern emerges. It is so marked that it may even be expressed in the form of a law: the further up the court hierarchy the dispute progresses, the greater the likelihood of a principle restrictive of local authority action being enunciated. The existence of this law may most easily be demonstrated by examining the outcome of those cases which concern either the innovative use of local authority powers or disputes between local authorities and central departments – and which thus lie at the heart of this study – which have proceeded to the final tribunal. There are seven such cases which have been examined in some detail in the study: *Bromley*, in which the Divisional Court found for the GLC, the Court of Appeal was against and the House, especially because of the Diplock dictum, entrenched further on local authority action;[183] the *Westminster* forward funding case, where the Divisional Court again found for the GLC but were overturned by the Court of Appeal and that finding was upheld by the House;[184] the *Nottinghamshire* case, in which, though the local authorities lost at first instance, the Court of Appeal found in their favour, only to have that decision overturned in the Lords;[185] *Wheeler*, a case in which, notwithstanding findings for the local authority in each of the lower courts, the House of Lords struck down the decision;[186] the Liverpool and Lambeth audit case in which, although the councillors lost at all three levels, the House disagreed with lower court dicta suggesting that the auditor should have offered the councillors an oral hearing;[187] the community charge capping case in which the local authorities lost at all three levels and the House sought to emphasize the difficulties local authorities face when seeking to impugn the decisions of Ministers;[188] and the Hammersmith swaps case in which the purposive interpretation adopted by the Court of Appeal (and which could be used to justify swaps transactions for the purpose of debt management) was rejected by the

[183] *Bromley LBC* v. *Greater London Council* [1983] 1 AC 768. See, above, ch. 4, 231–7.
[184] *Re Westminster City Council* [1986] AC 668. See, ch. 3, 163–5.
[185] *Nottinghamshire CC* v. *Secretary of State for the Environment* [1986] 2 WLR 1. See, above, ch. 5, 282–9.
[186] *Wheeler* v. *Leicester City Council* [1985] 1 AC 1054. See, ch. 3, 173–4.
[187] *Lloyd* v. *McMahon* [1987] 2 WLR 821. See, above, ch. 3, 192–4.
[188] *Hammersmith & Fulham LBC* v. *Secretary of State for the Environment* [1990] 3 All ER 589. See, above, ch. 5, 309–13.

Lords which held that local authorities possessed no powers to use these financial instruments.[189]

This general pattern would signify little of interest to the study of central–local government relations if it is taken simply to reflect the fact that the senior judiciary, being more experienced, have a greater propensity to reach the correct decision in law. That explanation, however, is scarcely non-controversial. One major difficulty with this explanation is the fact that, in most of these cases, the majority views of the Lords have been highly contentious. In this study I have, for example, tried to show how the courts in such cases as *Nottinghamshire*, *Wheeler* and the *Hammersmith* swaps case failed fully to appreciate the issues at stake in these disputes. But this point has also been underscored by the fact that, in two of these cases, the majority approach has itself been subject to powerful criticism from the bench. Thus, the majority's interpretation of the meaning of the 1969 Act in the *Bromley* case was exposed to a forceful critique by Lord Diplock and in *Re Westminister City Council* the majority view was the subject of a cogent dissent from Lord Bridge. It is, I believe, difficult to explain this pattern of outcomes by reference to the clearer visionary powers of the senior judiciary.

Why, then, should the claims of local government systematically fare worse as the court hierarchy is scaled? It is relatively easy here to present an argument that the judiciary display political bias in such cases. Indeed, this argument comes into clearer focus when these cases are contrasted with pre-1979 opinions of the House of Lords on similar issues. Thus, so the argument runs, the expansive local authority claim succeeded in the *Manchester* case[190] but was the subject of restrictive refinement in *Re Westminster* precisely because the former concerned action by a Labour-controlled borough council seeking to prevent a county council from using its powers in an innovative way to facilitate the advancement of Conservative education policies whereas the latter involved action by a Conservative-controlled borough council seeking to restrict a county authority from using similar powers to facilitate the continuity of socialist community policies. Further, the decision in *Tameside*,[191] in which the interventionist powers of the (Labour) Education Secretary were restrictively interpreted when action was taken against a (Conservative) local education authority may be contrasted with the short shrift given to the (Labour-controlled GLC's) local electoral mandate in *Bromley* or the arguments of many Labour-controlled authorities – from *Norwich*[192] to *Hackney*,[193] *Nottinghamshire*[194] to *Hammersmith*[195]

---

[189] *Hazell* v. *Hammersmith & Fulham LBC* [1990] 2 WLR 1038. See, above, ch. 6, 344–54.

[190] *Manchester City Council* v. *Greater Manchester CC* (1980) 78 LGR 560. See, above, ch. 3, 162.

[191] *Secretary of State for Education* v. *Tameside MBC* [1977] AC 1014. See, above, ch. 1, 68.

[192] *R* v. *Secretary of State for the Environment, ex p. Norwich City Council* [1982] QB 808. See, above, ch. 7, 390–1.

[193] *R* v. *Secretary of State for the Environment, ex p. Hackney LBC* (1986) 84 LGR 32. See, above, ch. 5, 278–80.

[194] [1986] 2 WLR 1.   [195] [1990] 3 All ER 589.

– who presented a range of arguments for imposing restrictive interpretations on the powers of the Secretary of State.

These arguments seem to me to have a degree of credence.[196] However, these specifically political factors should not cause us to neglect a basic institutional issue which is of particular importance to the theme of juridification. As we ascend into the rarefied atmosphere of the higher courts, we find that the issues presented to the courts become more remote from the tangled complexity of the actual grievance. We thus find a greater propensity for the courts to remove themselves from the specificities of the dispute and to attempt to deal with the issue in terms of general legal principles. Consequently, we find Lord Diplock resolving *Bromley* through the assertion of fiduciary duty as a quasi-constitutional principle, Lord Scarman rejecting the *Nottinghamshire* claims apparently through the formulation of a general principle on the limits of judicial review of irrationality claims against Ministers, and Lord Templeman in *Wheeler* enunciating a general principle that local authorities may not use their powers to punish individuals who have not committed any wrong. This issue, of course, is directly connected to the general point about the balance between factual exposition and critical evaluation in this type of judgment. Having become marginal to the regulation of this field of governance throughout much of the century, the courts, on being dragged into the field in recent years, lack the institutional infrastructure to be competent properly to regulate this activity. We therefore find the courts seeking to apply a set of rather simple principles to this complex world of government. There may be nothing, as such, wrong with that. The difficulty has been that, in the process of applying these simple principles, the courts have also tended to construct their judgments by assuming a simple set of facts on which these principles bear. And this exercise in simplification may not, ultimately, be conducive to good government.

Public law jurisprudence

As we have seen, the compact which has been forged between central and local government over the last century or so, though it has been underpinned by a legal framework, has not directly been expressed in positive law. This basic fact highlights many of the difficulties which the courts have faced in recent years in being prevailed on to mediate the constitutional claims of these two institutions of government. At the turn of the century, Redlich recognized that the main reason why the formal plenary powers of the judiciary had not resulted in government by the bench lay in the fact that, unlike the continental judges 'who, from the outset of their career, have been removed by disciplinary rules from any free and open participation in the political life of the country', our judges

---

[196] For illustrations of this argument see: P. McAuslan, 'Administrative Law, Collective Consumption and Judicial Policy' (1983) 46 *Mod.L Rev.* 1; J. Griffith, *Judicial Politics since 1920: A Chronicle* (Oxford, 1993), esp. chs. 5, 6.

'are not drawn from the Civil Service, but from the ranks of practising barristers who have taken some part in public and parliamentary life'.[197] The judiciary not only knew what they could say, but when they should remain silent. Having been educated in the political traditions of the country, they could be relied on to provide a sound interpretation of the meaning of the facilitative framework of local government law.

Those legal disputes involving government thus required a sensitive appreciation of the relationship between jurist-law and folk-law. But could such an informal regime ensure the necessary degree of consistency in the judicial resolution of disputes? While the volume of such judicial business remained quite small, this quality was achieved primarily through the shared values of the small club of the higher judiciary. Since most public law business came to the courts through prerogative order applications, the Lord Chief Justice, as presiding judge over the Divisional Court, played a particularly important role in filtering cases and in giving particular meaning to the rather fluid principles on which this jurisdiction rested. With the increase in caseload, however, delays resulted, as the Lord Chief Justice struggled to maintain personal control over the work of the Divisional Court. After the Order 53 reforms, this ambition was abandoned and Divisional Court procedures were streamlined: cases could be heard by a single judge rather than the traditional bench of three and consistency was to be maintained by establishing a panel of 'nominated' judges to hear all cases on the Crown Office list.[198] With the tremendous growth in the judicial review caseload since the 1980s the original panel of four rapidly expanded to eighteen and, in Lord Woolf's words, '[w]ith this number of judges, it is impossible to maintain the consistency of approach which was originally intended'.[199] Nominated judges may be technically competent and have experience of the processes of government, but may not possess the necessary political nous to deal in this discretionary jurisdiction. More precise guidelines were required. Procedural rationalization has thus provided a major impetus for the formalization of the substantive principles of public law.

The reformulation of the principles of public law has therefore not simply been an exercise in re-labelling; it has been carried out in conjunction with a process of formalization and, through the gradual promotion of jurist-law over folk-law, is seeking ultimately to establish an autonomous set of public law principles. This transition raises major issues in public law. Many of the differences expressed in recent cases reflect judicial perceptions of the nature and significance of this process. Within this particular field of study, we find a classic example in *Wheeler*. Here, the Divisional Court and the majority in the Court

---

[197] J. Redlich and F.W. Hirst, *Local Government in England* (London, 1903), vol. II, 370. See, above, ch. 1, 27.

[198] See L. Blom-Cooper, 'The new face of judicial review: administrative changes in Order 53', 1982 *Public Law* 250.

[199] H. Woolf, 'Judicial Review: A Possible Programme for Reform', 1992 *Public Law* 221, 224.

of Appeal took the traditional approach and simply held that the council's decision was neither perverse nor unreasonable in the *Wednesbury* sense. In his
Court of Appeal dissenting judgment, Browne-Wilkinson LJ adopted a different
approach and examined the issue not from the perspective of public powers but
rather from that of individual rights. Though the Lords aligned themselves with
Browne-Wilkinson LJ's finding, however, they were not prepared to embrace
his reasoning. Essentially, the House recognized that the adoption of a rights-
based review marked a radical change and were not, at that stage, prepared to
lend their imprimatur to this shift in the basis of review. In finding against the
authority without embracing the rights-based reasoning, however, their Lordships' opinions read simply as attempts to second-guess the council's policy
decision.

Expressions of these underlying differences have been felt throughout public
law jurisprudence for some time. Since we remain within a period of rapid
change, we cannot be sure of the eventual form which rationalization will take.
The trajectory is nevertheless relatively clear; the thrust is to view the structure
of public law as a juridical network of rights and duties. What are the likely
consequences for local government of the adoption of this approach? This question can perhaps best be addressed by examining the recent judgment of Laws J
in *R* v. *Somerset CC, ex parte Fewings*.[200] The issue faced by the court was
whether the council's power to acquire land for the benefit of its area enabled
it to ban deer hunting on council-owned land. Laws J held that the council,
having imposed the ban on the ground that it was opposed to deer hunting on
ethical grounds, exceeded its powers. What is most interesting, however, is the
reasoning which led him to that conclusion. Laws J began with a classic statement of the view that public law is essentially concerned with the proper performance of public duties:

> A public body has no heritage of legal rights which it enjoys for its own sake; at every
> turn, all its dealings constitute the fulfilment of duties which it owes to others; indeed,
> it exists for no other purpose. I would assert that a public body enjoys no rights
> properly so called ... [W]here a public body asserts claims or defences in court, it
> does so ... only to vindicate the better performance of the duties for whose fulfilment
> it exists. It is in this sense that it has no rights of its own, no axe to grind beyond its
> public responsibility which defines its purpose and justifies its existence. Under our
> law, this is true of every public body.[201]

In one sense, this declaration is non-contentious. What is controversial is the
fact that Laws J, in the course of his judgment, makes no concession to the

---

[200] (1994) 92 LGR 674. Note that this decision was, by a majority, upheld on appeal though the
Court of Appeal did not fully endorse the reasoning of Laws J: [1995] 3 All ER 20. See, above, ch.
3, 174–5.
[201] (1994) 92 LGR 674, 688.

tradition which acknowledges that the judiciary may not be competent to define many of those public purposes in a precise legal form. This tradition may, in appropriate circumstances, require silence or deference on the part of the judiciary. It is an approach which was well-expressed by Lord Russell of Killowen CJ who in *Kruse* v. *Johnson* stated that 'in matters which directly and mainly concern the people of the county, who have the right to choose those whom they think best fitted to represent them in their local government bodies, such representatives may be trusted to understand their own requirements better than judges'.[202] It is precisely this type of deference which is missing in *Fewings*. Consequently, in reply to the council's argument that the whole point of the power to acquire land was so that the authority could then use the land 'for what it considered to be for the benefit of the area', Laws J stated that this 'is to assume what has to be demonstrated'.[203] That is, decisions of the council to use its resources for the benefit of the area must be capable of being rationally demonstrated to further that objective, and, ultimately, must be demonstrated to the satisfaction of a judge.

The council was therefore required to present a specific justification for its decision. Somerset CC sought to do so essentially by rooting its arguments in a set of assumptions which have underpinned our tradition of local government. The council contended that 'it is . . . integral to its function that it should represent the feelings, including the ethical perceptions, of its electorate', that it is part of the essence of local democracy that 'strongly held views on issues arising in the locality may find vigorous expression in the deliberations of the elected representatives' and that 'it is simply artificial to suppose that, in the vindication of their duties as representatives, councillors should disregard the moral dimension in any debate upon which they are engaged'.[204] This 'eloquent plea to the sturdy values of the representation of the people at the local level' was summarily dismissed by Laws J. '[H]owever much I may be moved by it', the learned judge continued, 'I do not sit here as a political philosopher; what I am concerned with is an altogether tighter question, namely whether the power delegated to the elected local authority by Parliament is wide enough to allow what was done in this case.'[205] Laws J then specifically rejected the argument that powers conferred on elected bodies ought, on that ground, to be interpreted more broadly or benevolently since this 'amounts to no more nor less than an invitation to adopt differential rules of statutory construction on the ground that democratic institutions ought to be encouraged' and 'I know of no principle of statutory construction upon which this argument could be supported'.[206] It followed that the statutory power of land acquisition for public benefit 'confers no entitlement on a local authority to impose its opinions about the morals of hunting on the neighbourhood'.[207]

---

[202] [1898] 2 QB 91, 100.   [203] (1994) 92 LGR 674, 691.
[204] Ibid., 692.   [205] Ibid., 692.   [206] Ibid., 694.   [207] Ibid., 695.

This judgment contains a number of contentious issues. The requirement of rational demonstration of public benefit would, if treated rigorously, effectively deny any value to local knowledge. The rejection of a differential approach to the statutory construction of local government powers flies in the face of the practices of the judiciary over the last 150 years.[208] The failure to give weight to the check provided by the political accountability of the local council seems to undermine a basic principle of local democracy.[209] Nor does Laws J always maintain discipline in his foray into legal metaphysics. Though avowedly not sitting as a political philosopher he suggests that 'whether hunting should be banned, or limited, seems to me to be pre-eminently a matter for the national legislature'.[210] Whilst perhaps understandable as an expression of his political philosophy, what is not apparent is the relevance of this opinion to the resolution of the legal issues in this case.

It is important to analyse the reasoning processes of such judgments as those of Browne-Wilkinson LJ in *Wheeler* and Laws J in *Fewings* because what they illuminate is the image of local government contained within the new public law jurisprudence which is gradually emerging. The hallmark of this new jurisprudence is the replacement of the concept of jurisdiction as the foundation of judicial supervision with that of a general principle of legality.[211] One particularly important consequence of this shift in the basis of review has been to alter the focus from the examination of powers towards an analysis of rights and duties. Whatever impact this may have had in public law generally (and there

---

[208] One specific illustration is provided by the developments leading to the enactment of what is now s. 111 of the Local Government Act 1972: see, above, ch. 1, 45 (n. 162).

[209] In *Kruse* v. *Johnson* it was held that though the court 'should jealously watch the exercise of these powers' to make bye-laws when, as in many cases, the power is vested in 'railway companies, dock companies, or other like companies, which carry on their business for their own profit . . . when the Court is called upon to consider the bye-laws of public representative bodies . . . [t]hey ought to be supported if possible. They ought to be . . . "benevolently" interpreted . . . This involves the introduction of no new canon of construction.' ([1898] 2 QB 91, 99). Laws J rejected the argument that *Kruse* stands for the general principle of benevolent construction for elected bodies on the ground that in that case the bye-law was subject to central approval. Though Lord Russell did indeed make reference to the 'checks and safeguards' on the exercise of the power he was referring not only to central approval but also 'to the character of the body legislating under the delegated authority of Parliament' (ibid.). Laws J seems to have given great weight to the procedure of central approval and none to local accountability.

[210] (1994) 92 LGR 674, 696.

[211] Elsewhere, Sir John Laws has been more open about the nature of this shift. Writing extra-judicially, he states: '"Ultra vires" is, in truth, a fig-leaf; it has enabled the courts to intervene in decisions without an assertion of judicial power which too nakedly confronts the established authority of the Executive or other bodies. . . . Intellectual fig-leaves surely have their part to play in the development of the common law, whose peculiar characteristic is the possession of a benign alchemy by which the recall of old principles is without offence to other interests turned into new law. That it is done, in the end, by something no more than legerdemain, should be a cause, not of purist disapproval, but of a recognition that our law, in this field at least, can meet and answer new challenges without disturbing the tranquillity of the state.' 'Illegality: the problem of jurisdiction' in M. Supperstone and J. Goudie (eds.), *Judicial Review* (London, 1992) 51, at 67–8.

certainly is evidence which indicates that this re-orientation has not been wholly deleterious) the consequences for local government must be a cause of some concern.

This shift in review focus has had a significant effect on the intensity of the scrutiny to which local authority action has been subjected. There is, of course, nothing especially novel about this point, since it has already been underscored in the general assessment which has been undertaken about the role of fiduciary duty in local government. The basic issue is highlighted by contrasting the approaches taken by the Court of Appeal (review of local authority powers) and the House of Lords (invocation of duty) in the Poplar wages case.[212] It might also be noted that Atkin LJ's observation in the Poplar case that the focus on duty could oblige the court to make an assessment of precise staffing levels for the purpose of adequately carrying out any particular task, applies with equal effect to Laws J's view that the council, when exercising its general powers to act for the benefit of the area, must be capable of demonstrating to the court's satisfaction that those benefits are realized. The critical point is that attempts by the judiciary to reconstruct principles of review of local authority action as a juridical network of individual rights and public duties have the effect of establishing a pincer movement which may significantly circumscribe the capacity for local democratic decision-making.

Why should this be so? The answer, I believe, can best be given by linking these judicial developments to the three themes which Taylor[213] identified as being key features of contemporary politics: individualism, instrumental reason and political freedom. Judicial benevolence in the review of local authority powers was indeed, *pace* Laws J, the manner in which the courts were best able to reflect the principle of local self-government within our system. The shift in review focus to rights and duties in effect symbolizes the growing importance of individualism and instrumental reason in the emerging principles of public law. Each theme undoubtedly reflects an important political value. My particular concern, however, is that, within the rarefied atmosphere of the higher courts and without extensive deliberation on countervailing considerations, these values can all too easily come to be articulated either in a strident tone or a simplistic form. Rights discourse, for example, often assumes an absolutist character, with the result that collective values tend to become marginalized.[214] And

---

[212] *R* v. *Roberts, ex p. Scurr* [1924] 2 KB 695; *Roberts* v. *Hopwood* [1925] AC 578. See, above, ch. 4, 210–12.

[213] See the discussion, above, at 371–4.

[214] The point may be illustrated by reference to the work of Ronald Dworkin. On the role which the right to liberty plays in political deliberation, for example, Dworkin states: 'If someone has a right to something, then it is wrong for the government to deny it to him even though it would be in the general interest to do so.' *Taking Rights Seriously* (London, 1977), 269. For a critique of contemporary rights discourse see: M.A. Glendon, *Rights Discourse. The Impoverishment of Political Discourse* (New York, 1991).

the focus on public duties can all too readily come to be gauged essentially in terms of the most economical application of means to a given end.[215] As Taylor suggests, the pre-eminence of these political values exacerbates the difficulties of maintaining an active culture of self-government. Similarly, the shift in the focus of judicial review towards a concern with performance of public duties and the protection of private rights gives priority to these values within the legal order and has a tendency to undermine the value of local self-government.

But must this be the case? Though this trend does not inevitably follow from the shift in review focus, the problem is that the courts seem consistently to have followed this line whenever they have undertaken strict scrutiny of local authority action. The judiciary have generally been reticent in acknowledging the political value of local self-government; notwithstanding occasional puffs,[216] the best that local government can hope for is a benevolent interpretation of statutory powers or an acknowledgement that a grievance raised, being concerned with policy, is best directed to Ministers. Local democracy is, however, never asserted as a positive legal value. Given the structure of constitutional law this is hardly surprising. What the courts have yet to recognize, however, is that active judicial review of governmental action of the type which is now emerging must, at some level or other, pay regard to the conception of democracy which is reflected in our constitutional arrangements. The basic problem is that, in seeking to shift the foundations of judicial review from jurisdiction to legality, the courts have not been prepared to develop a constitutional jurisprudence in which the sharing of governmental power which must in practice take place is also identified as a positive value. The concept of legality which is being forged through the explication of the principles of public law seems to place no positive value on the idea of locality.

Legality and Locality

In this study I have sought to identify not only our traditions of local government but also the manner in which those traditions are linked to a particular heritage of public law. Just as Maitland claimed that we cannot understand constitutional history without knowing a good deal about land law,[217] I would today suggest that we cannot appreciate the modern relationship between government and law without understanding our traditions of local government and the tensions between the centre and the localities which are manifest in our

---

[215] A good illustration of this point, and the dangers of its expression by the judiciary, is provided by Lord Diplock's application of the fiduciary principle to block grant allocation in *Bromley*: see, above, ch. 4, 231–7.

[216] See, e.g., *R* v. *Secretary of State for the Environment, ex p. Norwich City Council* [1982] QB 808, 824 (see, above, 391).

[217] F.W. Maitland, *The Constitutional History of England* (Cambridge, 1908), 538.

constitutional arrangements. Within these arrangements, Parliament, understood as the forum within which the grievances of people (incorporated in local communities) could be presented to Government, has played a pivotal role. It was mainly because of the work undertaken by Parliament that no formal hierarchical relationship between the central State and local authorities came to be forged, thereby enabling a tradition of local government to be maintained. And it is largely owing to this achievement that no special system of administrative law has evolved in this country. The consequent tensions between the practices of local government and the claims of the central State have largely been resolved through administrative networks whose status and importance, whilst occasionally being accommodated by the law, have not generally been entrenched in law.

This book has focused on various aspects of our recent experience. We have seen, in particular, that the central–local government relationship has been both politicized and juridified and that these related trends may be understood as reflections of an inexorable process of rationalization of social life. The emergence of ideological politics has imposed severe strains on our anti-Rationalist constitutional arrangements. The Conservative Government's agenda for local government since 1979 may be viewed as a specific illustration of this tendency. The Government's action has often failed to conform to traditional patterns of political behaviour and the administrative network, which has emerged this century as a regulatory mechanism in the conduct of central–local relations, has often been by-passed or subverted. The Government's programme for local government, being based on value-for-money criteria, has been rooted in an instrumental rationality which has occasionally been reinforced by vesting individual rights in consumers of local services. The overall impact of this programme has been to undermine the institution of local government. Further, because of the manner in which the Government has implemented the programme, the central–local relationship has been reconstructed in much more explicitly hierarchical terms.

These recent developments raise important political questions. Parliament has once again become actively involved in local government affairs, though as we have seen this has been mainly in the role of legitimating the Government's legislative programme. There certainly remains little sense of the importance of Parliament as an institution for airing local grievances. Furthermore, the basic thrust of the Government's programme seems to deny that local authorities should any longer be treated as institutions of governance; they seem now to be treated merely as agencies for delivering centrally-determined policies. And there has been little in the recent experience to suggest that toleration of political differences is any longer an accepted part of our governing arrangements. Locality no longer seems to be a significant touchstone within modern government. Some may, of course, argue to the contrary that the devolution of power from local councils to schools, housing estates and the like will lead to a reinvigoration of local politics. As Taylor points out, however, this trend also signifies a shift in the character of politics, with the politics of democratic will-formation in danger of being supplanted by the politics of the rights-bearing subject. One major problem is that this type of fragmented politics does not seem conducive to the maintenance of an active culture of self-government and, if this is lost at the level of the localities, the principle of elective dictatorship will become even more firmly entrenched.

The primary focus of this work, however, has been on the role of law in regulating the central–local relationship. Though local government has since the nineteenth century been placed on a statutory foundation, positive law has not been a primary determinant of this relationship. Statute law has established a facilitative framework through which conventional arrangements for regulating central–local relations could evolve and which, in effect, constituted a non-juridified structure of administrative law. One consequence of the Government's recent actions in subverting the administrative network has been to transform law into a primary instrument of regulation. This instrumentalization of law is most obviously evinced by the major legislative programme promoted by the Government since 1979. The manner in which the programme has been implemented has served mainly to demonstrate the ineffectiveness of parliamentary scrutiny of Government legislation and the basic difficulties involved in trying to prescribe in law the precise terms of the regulatory regime.

This instrumentalization of law has also had a major impact on the role of the courts in the system. As the authority of the adminstrative network dwindled, the parties turned to the courts for the authoritative resolution of their grievances. This has, in many respects, been an unsettling and somewhat perplexing experience. Juridification of the central–local relationship has brought about a basic shift in the function of much of the traditional legislation; from providing the visible means of support for the administrative norms, the legislation came to be looked upon as the source of those norms. Hardly surprisingly, the courts often experienced great difficulty in interpreting the legislation in such a manner as to provide a coherent regulatory framework. Some of the new legislation has also caused bewilderment as it gradually dawned that the hastily prepared measure had been drafted without any consideration having been given to the issue in dispute. Furthermore, this turn to the courts has rarely served to clarify the nature of the relationship. The disposal of many of the claims that local authorities or central departments had exceeded or abused their powers has tended only to confirm the impression that the courts are not ideally suited for the resolution of these disputes. A range of factors point to this conclusion including the complexity of the basic facts in many cases, the limited investigatory powers of the courts, the rudimentary nature of the public law principles to be applied, and the difficulties experienced by adversarial institutions in grasping the various dimensions of the policy questions at issue. Juridification should therefore be viewed mainly as a symptom of certain basic problems faced by our system of government as a result of the growing rationalization of social life. If juridification is to remain a permanent feature of the central–local relationship, the general message seems to be that the entire structure of administrative law will need to be reviewed; it is simply asking too much of a judiciary traditionally insulated from these issues to develop a set of sound principles for regulating the central–local relationship without an adequate institutional infrastructure being set in place.

INDEX

Learning Resources
Centre